The CHURCH ORDER COMMENTARY

BEING

A Brief Explanation of the Church Order of the Christian Reformed Church

By

IDZERD VAN DELLEN, MINISTER EMERITUS
First Chr. Ref. Church, Denver, Colo.

AND

MARTIN MONSMA, MINISTER
Grandville, Ave Chr. Ref. Church
Grand Rapids, Mich.

WIPF & STOCK · Eugene, Oregon

Wipf and Stock Publishers
199 W 8th Ave, Suite 3
Eugene, OR 97401

The Church Order Commentary, Third Edition
A Brief Explanation of the Church Order of the Christian Reformed Church
By Van Dellen, Idzerd and Monsma, Martin

ISBN 13: 978-1-60899-172-3
Publication date 11/2/2009
Previously published by Zondervan Publishing House, 1954

Introduction

The esteemed authors of this Commentary on the Church Order of the Christian Reformed Church have asked me to introduce their book to its readers by way of a foreword. In complying with their request I need not pause to acquaint you with the Church Order which they felt impelled to explain. The instrument is well known and its provisions are familiar to all the office-bearers and to many members of the church that operates under it.

It may not be superfluous, however, to observe that the document, familiar though its text may be, is not above the need of interpretation. Mere reading of the Church Order leaves that impression without fail; while its study is well calculated to raise the question: understandest thou what thou readest? And to say no more, the execution of its several provisions on the part of the officers of the church, particularly on the part of those whose duty it is to administer the affairs of the church in its graduated series of assemblies, does not fail to bring home to them the need of a competent commentator. The extreme brevity of the Church Order and its predominantly archaic editorial cast are not unrelated to this situation.

The authors of the present volume must have prepared it under a sense of constraint. Each of them is crowded with pastoral labors as the regular Minister of a church. Moreover, both are engaged in journalistic activities. The book which they produced collaboratively is conclusive evidence that they took a far from inconsiderable burden upon themselves when they undertook to write it. True, they leaned heavily upon certain Dutch canonists whom they accordingly give due credit for aid rendered. But even so, their own labors as embodied in the sizeable book before you constitutes ample proof of a fine measure of industry, perseverance and devotion.

I have not been so informed by the respected authors of this Commentary, but I feel wholly confident nevertheless that they would have all their readers constantly bear in mind at least two pertinent facts as they turn to this volume for light. The first is that this is not an official, that is, synodically approved, commentary on the Church Order. It carries no more weight than the intrinsic correctness of the positions taken in the book will bear. And the second is that not all the views propounded by the authors command the assent of all who are able to judge of matters canonical.

A rather careful reading of this comparatively lengthy Commentary has convinced me that it will prove to be a very useful manual indeed, and that it will not fail to meet with the generous appreciation that it deserves. I cherish the desire that this Commentary may have a wide sale and that it may be consulted diligently and studied critically in the interest of soundly Reformed canonical theory and practice in the church which the authors dearly love and devotedly serve.

Grand Rapids, Mich.

S. VOLBEDA.

REGARDING THE THIRD EDITION

This third edition of THE CHURCH ORDER COMMENTARY differs only from the second edition in that occasional typographical errors have been corrected, and two or three statements have been brought up-to-date. We are happy over the fact that a constant demand for this Commentary made a new edition necessary, and it is our hope and prayer that God may see fit to use also this issue for the coming of His Kingdom and the glory of His Name.

THE AUTHORS

August, 1954

Preface

In the following pages the authors have endeavored to give a brief exposition of the Church Order of Dort (1618-19) as amended by the Synod of the Christian Reformed Churches in the year 1914.

For the benefit of the uninformed it may be said that the Christian Reformed Church dates back to the year 1857. Some years previous, (1847), a new migration movement from the shores of the Netherlands to the United States began. Those who left the homeland in large numbers and colonized especially in the regions of present-day Holland, Michigan, and Pella, Iowa, were of Calvinistic stock theologically.

Ecclesiastically they were, in the main, members of the Secession Church of Holland; (Christelijke Afgescheiden Kerk). This Secession Church of Holland, dating back to 1834, was an off-shoot of the Established or State Church of Holland (Hervormde Kerk) which had become corrupt in doctrine and had set aside the historic form of government as last ratified by the great Synod of Dort, 1618-19.

As the re-organized and purified Churches of Holland had done in 1834, so the Christian Reformed Churches in 1857 restored the venerable Church Order of Dort as their rule and guide in matters of church government. In these church governmental rules of order, the founders of the Christian Reformed denomination found what they believed to be the correct Biblical system of government for the Church of Christ on earth. In the Church Order of Dort, these Churches found a faithful reflection of church governmental principles as developed in Reformation days under the influence of John Calvin and other leading Bible students and Reformers.

But circumstances had changed considerably since Reformation and post-Reformation days. The fundamental, basic principles of Reformed Church polity are drawn directly from Holy Writ. Even as the Bible is ever the unchanging Word of God for all times and lands, thus also—so the re-organized and purified Churches of the former century held—the basic principles for church government drawn from the Bible are the same for all times and all lands. But the application of these basic principles will vary as times and conditions vary. New conditions demand new approaches and adjustments.

The Secession Churches of Holland (1834) were greatly enriched and strengthened by a second exodus from the corrupt State Church toward the close of the former century (1886). This second secession movement was largely under the leadership of the great Dr. Abraham Kuyper. The Churches joining this secession were known as "de Doleerende Kerken" (Latin, "doleo," to be hurt; to be aggrieved). These "Doleerende Kerken" and the Secession Churches of 1834 united in 1892 and adopted the name, the Reformed Churches of the Netherlands (de Gereformeerde Kerken van Nederland). Now these united Churches in the year 1905 revised several articles of the Church Order and brought this treasured set of rules up-to-date. And the Christian Reformed Churches here in the United States of America, did the same in 1914 (Synod of 1914, Roseland, Chicago, Illinois). It is this Church Order of Dort, 1618-19, as amended in 1914, which we are seeking to explain in the present volume.

The name "Church Order" is of Dutch origin; it being a rendition of the expression, "Kerkenordening." The first regular Synod of the Reformed Churches of Holland was held in Emden, Germany, in 1571. Persecution and hostility made a gathering in the homeland inadvisable. Since the year 1571, Synod met at regular intervals. By 1581 the fundamental principles of church government had found expression and application in various synodical pronouncements. The Synod of Middelburg, 1581, gathered these into one document and called it in Latin, "Corpus Disciplinae," and in Dutch, "Kerckenordeninghe." The Synod of 's Gravenhage, 1586, called the document, "The Church Order of the Reformed Churches of the Netherlands" (Kerckenordeninghe der Nederlandtsche Gereformeerde Kercken). This, altho in simplified modern spelling, is still the official name of this body of church rules today. (Kerkenordening van de Gereformeerde Kerken in Nederland).

Note the plural "Kerken" in the name of this Church Order. This name, as just indicated, dates back to the post-Reformation era. This plural form of the word Church in this title, is therefore not the invention of the Doleantie leaders, Kuyper, Rutgers, and others, as some have thought; but it is found in the original name, altho the name was not used in toto for more than two and one-half centuries.

Realizing the foregoing may also help us to understand that the word "church" in "Church Order" is an adjective. It merely tells us that the document is an ecclesiastical order; not a political or a social order, for instance. That is, it is not a set of rules for a political organization nor for a social organization. The singular "church" in the name "Church Order" therefore does not indicate that we look upon our denomination as one large super-Church. The full name of our Church Order in its original languages, Latin and Dutch, clearly indicates that our denomination is a federation of local Churches holding a common confession and form of church government, firmly united by the confessional standards and Church Order adopted. The Christian Reformed Church is therefore not a body or union of individuals, but a union or federation of Churches, each one of which is a complete manifestation of the body of Christ. It may be said in this connection that if the Synod of 1914 had adopted the title "Church Order of the Christian Reformed Churches" in harmony with the historic name of our Church Order, this would have helped to ward off misunderstanding on this score.

One of the characteristics of our Church Order is its **brevity.** There are only 86 articles and these are in most instances very brief. Our fathers purposely steered in the direction of brevity. They believed that the best interests of the Churches and the cause of God would be served by a limited number of rules. They feared "rule upon rule and precept upon precept." They felt that multiple and detailed rules would bind the Churches needlessly. They loved their liberties, and believed that each Church group (Classis) or Church should retain as much of its inherent freedom as the true welfare of the Church of Christ would warrant. In this respect a different course has been pursued by many Reformed and Presbyterian Churches which have a large number of rules and regulations, going into great detail.

We are convinced that the brevity of our Church Order is one of its merits. More than once, for instance, numberless detailed and involved rules have been used by modernistic majorities at church assemblies, against loyal minorities. Rules needlessly detailed always have a tendency to impede and hinder free action and development.

As to its nature, the Church order is a body of rules for the maintenance of good order in the Churches. As such the Church Order should not be confused with synodical or with classical decisions. The Church Order and ecclesiastical decisions by no means stand on par. A Church Order is a group of ecclesiastical rules, mutually adopted, and binding for all the Churches having so adopted these rules, i.e., for all the Churches of the denomination concerned; whereas ecclesiastical decisions are merely distinct applications of one or more of the general and basic rules of the Church Order.

The authority of the Church Order is based upon the Biblical demand of subjection to duly appointed authorities. Children are instructed to obey their parents. (Eph. 6:1; Col. 3:20.) Romans 13 definitely enjoins obedience to lawful state authorities. Thus Holy Writ likewise attributes authority to office-bearers in the Church. "Jesus therefore said to them again, Peace be unto you; **as the Father hath sent me, even so send I you.** And when he had said this, he breathed on them, and saith unto them, **Receive ye the Holy Spirit; whose soever sins ye forgive, they are forgiven unto them; whose soever sins ye retain, they are retained."** (John 20:21-23.) Acts 15:27-29 also very clearly reflects ecclesiastical authority, for we read in this passage: **"For it seemed good to the Holy Spirit and to us, to lay upon you** no greater burden than these necessary things." Judas and Silas are delegated to convey the decision of the Jerusalem Assembly by letter and word of mouth to the various Churches. Furthermore, Heb. 13:17 bids us, **"Obey them that have the rule over you, and submit to them:** for they watch in behalf of your souls, as they that shall give account; that they may do this with joy, and not with grief: for this were unprofitable for you."

Ecclesiastical authority as exercised by the Churches, however, does not bind the conscience as is claimed by the Roman Church and by some of the Protestant Churches. The Word of God, however, does bind the conscience. And whenever the Church clearly reflects the Word of God, the decisions of the Church should also bind the conscience. But whether or not ecclesiastical rules repeat and apply the clear dictates of God's Word—judgment on this question must, in the last analysis, be left to every individual believer. Rules and decisions are binding and compelling only for those that are and remain under the authority of the Church. He who feels in conscience bound before God to refuse submission is free to do so. But such a believer cannot consistently remain under the authority of the Churches in question. That would make for disorder and confusion as well as for spiritual damage.

That church government is of very great import to the Church of Christ goes without saying. True, purity in doctrine, and therefore confessional purity, ranks first. But no Church being pure and true confessionally, will continue to be such except the Word of God is purely preached, and the sacraments are administered according to the Word of God. A Church that is not governed according to the Word of God cannot remain true to the Word of God. Impurity in church government fosters impurity in church doctrine. Form and content stand closely related also in this instant.

From what precedes it follows that the Church Order should not be considered to be a legalistic document, a book of laws in the civil sense. The Church Order consists of rules and regulations mutually agreed upon, and that by common consent. (cf. Art. 86.) It does not force and compel after the fashion of a civil law. It is not superimposed upon the Churches, demanding unreasoned and legalistic obedience. The Church Order guides and directs, in order that all things may be done "decently and in order," for the furtherance of the Church of Christ, even as the Bible enjoins. (I Cor. 14:40.) However, as will appear from the pages following, the authors firmly believe that every one of our Churches and every member of our Churches is in duty bound to respect the authority of the Church Order, and to show constant loyalty to its provisions.

As might be expected, we have sought to base the contents of this book exclusively on Scriptural principles and historic facts.

Special mention should be made in this preface of the fact that the authors owe much to the church governmental labors of Dr. F. L. Rutgers, (1836-1917) one time professor in church polity at the Free University of Amsterdam, Netherlands. Not only have they often consulted the published works of this authority, but the unpublished class lectures on church government of Dr. Rutgers were also in their possession. We would also gratefully acknowledge the work of Rev. Joh. Jansen, a student of Dr. Rutgers, whose "Korte Verklaring van de Kerkenordening" has been of great help to us in the preparation of this Commentary.

May the King of His Church abundantly bless our labors!

THE AUTHORS.

PREFACE TO THE SECOND EDITION

The authors of this Commentary are grateful to God for the favorable reception which the first edition of this work received. The first edition had been out of print for some years, and we were happy to learn that the publishers desired to put a second, somewhat revised, and up-to-date edition of our Commentary on the market at this time. May God's blessing also attend this second edition.

Our readers will appreciate the fact that the text of the Church Order appears consecutively and separately in this new edition. We have made it a point, in this reproduction of the Church Order, to give **only the official text**, amended to the year 1950.

The Authors.

June, 1949.

The Church Order Commentary

The complete, official text of the Church Order, article by article, may be found on pages 374-385 of this commentary.

The CHURCH ORDER COMMENTARY

ARTICLE 1

For the maintenance of good order in the Church of Christ it is necessary that there should be: offices, assemblies, supervision of doctrine, sacraments and ceremonies, and Christian discipline; of which matters the following articles treat in due order.

PURPOSE AND MAIN CONTENT OF CHURCH ORDER

1. Concerning the purpose of the Church Order.

No Christian can observe and study life and the world in which we live without seeing that God loves order. The seasons of the year, our own bodies, and all things created tell us, in spite of the mars and scars of sin, that the great Creator of all things is a God of order. The Bible, God's special revelation, tells us the same thing emphatically.

Now God is ever true to Himself. Sublime harmony and order mark His triune being. Consequently God can do nothing in a haphazard, slipshod fashion. That would militate against His very essence. That would be ruinous in its effect upon His creation.

For these reasons the Church at Corinth is also admonished: "But let all things be done decently and in order." (I Cor. 14:40.) And it is for the maintenance of good order in the Church of Christ, and for the promotion of its true welfare, that "offices, assemblies, supervision of doctrine, sacraments and ceremonies, and Christian discipline," have been instituted. For these same reasons our fathers of Reformation days accepted a limited set of rules regulating these several matters. These rules comprise our Church Order.

By maintaining well organized Churches with their, "offices, assemblies, etc." we vary definitely from certain mystical, inner-light groups who neglect all these important matters and even stand opposed to them. Our fathers definitely disagreed with the Anabaptists of the sixteenth century on this score, and felt persuaded by Holy Writ to sponsor well organized Churches.

At the same time it should be remembered that it is not the purpose of the Church Order to force the Churches to walk its beaten path with arbitrary, fettering and chafing compulsion. The Church Order means to be regulatory. It means to regulate ecclesiastical life reasonably and with full maintenance of the rights of every congregation and of the individual members of the Churches. The Church Order is moral in character, not judicial. It is a regulatory set of rules, not a legalistic set of laws.

Regarding the expression "Church of Christ" in Article 1, it should be remarked that the Church Order sometimes speaks of "Church" in the singular (Kerk). Now the word "Church" in the Church Order always refers to a local congregation viewed as a definite organization. The plural, "Churches", (Kerken) refers to a number of organized congregations. Usually it refers to all the Churches belonging to the denomination. The expression "Church of Christ", (Gemeente van Christus) is used to indicate the body of believers living in a certain region or country. It designates the body of Christ from its non-organizational aspect, and as scattered in various localities. And finally, the name "congregation" (de gemeente) is used to designate a definite group of believers living in one communion and organized into one particular church, altho the term "congregation" in the Church Order also refers to the Church from its non-organizational aspect.[1] Concisely the matter stands thus as to Church Order usage:

Kerk — Church — Organized or instituted Church.

Kerken — Churches — Denomination, or, Federation of organized Churches.

Gemeente van Christus — Church of Christ — Sum-total of believers living in various localities.

De gemeente — the congregation — definite group of believers living in one locality.

It is evident therefore that Article 1 thinks of the believers as found in various localities when it speaks of the Church of Christ, and more specifically of the believers belonging to our Christian Reformed denomination.

The Church Order considered from the aspect of its purpose may be said to fill a real necessity. To be sure a Church can exist without a Church Order but it cannot flourish and thrive properly without it. Furthermore, denominational harmony and co-operation require a definite set of rules, inasmuch as all co-operation requires an expressed basis. Besides, the Church Order is a constant guardian against wilfulness and abuse of power, which evils are ever ready to creep in to disturb the peace and progress of the Church.

2. Concerning the main content of the Church Order.

Article 1 declares that for the maintenance of good order in the Church of Christ it is necessary that there should be: offices; assemblies; supervision of doctrine, sacraments and ceremonies; and Christian discipline. The things here enumerated constitute the subject matter of the Church Order. Every article of the Church Order deals with matters which may be listed under one of the four heads indicated.

Concerning the first head, the offices, (Articles 2-28) it is noteworthy that the Dutch text speaks of "diensten", which as the Latin "functiones" in the original text, stresses the element of service to be rendered, rather than authority to be exercised. The word "ministrations" or "services" would be more exact translations for "diensten" than the present "offices." But there are objections to the suggested word also. "Ministrations" is rather cumbersome, and "services" is too vague and has too many other meanings in the English language. The term "offices" is wholly satisfactory, just so we bear in mind that the primary emphasis in this case falls on the element of service; altho the element of authority should not be ignored.

The Bible clearly stresses this element of service for office-bearers. II Cor. 8:4 speaks of "the fellowship **in the ministering** to the saints." Eph. 4:11, 12 tell us that God gave the various offices "for the perfecting of the saints, **unto the work of ministering**, unto the building up of the body of Christ."

Ecclesiastical offices are not merely beneficial to the Church of Christ, but they should be termed indispensable, inasmuch as they were instituted of God. Were not the Apostles sent forth by Christ, vested with His authority? (Matt. 28:18-20; John 20:21; II Cor. 5: 18-21). And does not the Bible offer abundant evidence for the con-

1. Cf. Jansen: **Korte Verklaring van de Kerkenordening**, 1923, pp. 3, 4.

tention that the offices in the Church, both special and regular offices, are ordained of God? I Cor. 12:28 tells us that **"God hath set some in the church;** first apostles, secondly prophets, ..." Rom. 10:15 asks, **"And how shall they preach, except they be sent?"** In I Thess. 5:12 the apostle says, "But we beseech you, brethren to know them that labor among you, **and are over you in the Lord . . . ."** Confer also Eph. 4:11-13; II Tim. 2:2; Titus 1:5.

Furthermore, subjection to such as minister as office-bearers is also urged in Matt. 10:40; **"He that receiveth you receiveth me,** and he that receiveth me receiveth Him that sent me."; and in Heb. 13:17, **"Obey them that have the rule over you, and submit to them."**

Secondly Article 1 mentions the assemblies. (Articles 29-52). Almost needless to say, the Church Order does not refer in this article to the "assembling together" (Heb. 10:25) of the believers on the Lord's Day for worship. Article 1, when speaking of assemblies has reference to ecclesiastical assemblies, i. e., consistory meetings, classical meetings and synodical meetings. (cf. Art. 29).

These assemblies have been instituted and these gatherings are being held for the purpose of governing the Church or Churches aright; to assist each other in difficult cases; to help each other in the maintenance of doctrinal purity; to maintain the offices ordained of God, and to promote order and congregational worship.

Next, supervision of doctrine, sacraments and ceremonies, are mentioned. (Articles 53-70.) Supervision of doctrine is very necessary inasmuch as purity of doctrine is to the Church of Christ what a good foundation is to a building. Without purity of doctrine the Church of Christ fails and falls. (cf. Acts 28:28-31; Gal. 1:8, 9; II John 10.)

Supervision regarding the sacraments is necessary because these are the signs of God's saving grace in Christ, and the sealing ordinances of His covenant to His people. Abuse and corruption regarding the sacraments is a very serious matter. Indeed, desecration of the sacraments merits the wrath of God over His congregation. (cf. I Cor. 11:17-34.)

The ceremonies mentioned in Article 1 include the installation of office-bearer, the solemnization of marriage before the Church of God, and other ecclesiastical solemnities. "Let all things be done decently and in order." (I Cor. 14:40) also pertains to these solemnities of congregational worship.

Finally, this first article mentions Christian discipline. Christian discipline concerns first of all the profession and conduct of all church members. Secondly it concerns in a special way the profession and conduct of office-bearers in their capacity as office-bearers. Discipline as it pertains to church members as such, consists of admonition and ultimately, if need be, of excommunication. Discipline regarding office-bearers in their capacity as office-bearers consists of admonition, and furthermore, if need be, of suspension and deposition. The right and the duty of the Churches to exercise discipline cannot be questioned by anyone who acknowledges the Bible as God's own Word. Matt. 16:19, "I will give unto thee the keys of the kingdom of Heaven . . . . ." Matt. 18:17, ". . . If he refuses to hear the church also, let him be unto thee as the Gentile and the publican." Titus 3:10, "A factious man after a first and second admonition refuse." (cf. also John 20:23; Rom. 16:17; I Cor. 5:3-5; II Thess. 3:6, 14, etc.)

ARTICLE 2

The offices are of four kinds: of the Ministers of the Word, of the Professors of Theology, of the Elders, and of the Deacons.

THE OFFICES

1. Ecclesiastic offices three in number.

All ecclesiastical offices find their origin in Christ, the Church's only Head and Supreme Ruler. No office-bearer in the Church has any authority in himself. All the authority which any ecclesiastical office-bearers possess is delegated authority, authority given to them by Christ and to be exercised by them for Christ. Christ is the Church's chief Prophet, only High Priest, and Eternal King. (Heidelberg Catechism Q.31.) Consequently, the offices as they have been ordained for the organized Church here on earth are nothing but extensions and continuations of Christ's three-fold office. Again, back of all authority, also all ecclesiastical authority, standeth God, the Triune, absolutely sovereign God. Through the second person of the Trinity, Christ Jesus, He governs and blesses His church. Our fall into sin is three-fold. We fell as prophets, priests, and kings. We lost true knowledge, holiness, and righteousness. As rational thinking creatures we lost true knowledge and fell from our prophetic office; we became prophets of falsehood, of the devil's lie. As moral creatures (capable of choice, desire, and devotion) we lost true holiness; i. e., love and consecration to God, and we fell from our priestly office; we became priests unto Satan and sin. As executive creatures (capable of rationally and morally conditional activity) we lost true righteousness, and fell from our royal office; we became kings of unrighteousness. We repeat therefore, our fall into sin was three-fold, in keeping with man's essential being as God's image-bearer. Consequently, we must be saved in a three-fold sense, and restored in a three-fold sense, i. e., as prophets, priests, and kings. From the foregoing it follows that the Saviour also holds a three-fold office. He is the second Adam and as such the Prophet, Priest, and King of His Church.

For this reason the Old Testament knew three primary offices; no more, no less: Prophets, Priests, and Kings. They were representatives of the Christ to come. For this same reason the New Testament period has three primary offices; no more, no less: Ministers, Deacons, and Elders, representing Christ respectively as Prophet, Priest, and King of His Church.

It should not be forgotten, however, that particularly during the transitional period of the Church of Christ on earth, for some time after Christ's ascension to Heaven, the three-fold office of Christ did not stand out clearly. Various temporary offices and circumstances somewhat obscured the facts set forth above. But as the formative period of the New Testament passes (and with it the special and inclusive apostolic office, the temporary prophetic offices, etc.) and conditions assume a more permanent aspect, the three-fold office of Christ in His Church also begins to stand out with greater clarity. The office of the Ministry of the Word is spoken of or alluded to in II Cor. 5:18-19; Eph. 4:11, 12; I Tim. 5:17; Titus 1:9; Heb. 13:7. The office of the diaconate or deaconship finds Scriptural expression especially in Acts 6:1-7; Phil. 1:1; I Tim. 3:8-12. Of the office of the eldership we read especially in Acts 14:23; Rom. 12:8; Eph. 4:11-13; I Thess. 5:12; I Tim. 3:1-7; Titus 1:5-9; Heb. 13:17-24.

2. Why Article 2 mentions four kinds of offices.

But if there is Scriptural warrant for but three permanent New Testament offices, why then does our Church Order mention four? There is a historical explanation for this fact. In Eph. 4:11 we read: "And He gave some to be apostles and some prophets; and some evangelists; and some pastors and teachers." Now the offices of apostles, prophets, and evangelists, it is generally agreed, were temporary offices which God did not mean to continue, and which passed away when the Churches were fully established. As to the latter expression of Eph. 4:11, "and some pastors and teachers," some of the Reformers believed that it referred to two distinct offices in the New Testament Church, namely that of the Ministers of the Word, and that of the Teachers of Theology. Calvin himself gave this interpretation of Eph. 4:11. (Cf. Calvin's Commentary on Ephesians.)

As a result of this interpretation the Church Order, already in its first redaction gave four permanent New Testament offices. Today it is generally realized that the expression "and some, pastors and teachers," of Eph. 4:11, refers to the single offices of the Ministry of the Word. If this were not the case, then in keeping with the whole passage the expression should and would read as follows: "and some pastors; and some, teachers;" note the difference in punctuation and its significance. It is true that the Bible clearly speaks of the duties of teachers of Theology (cf. f. i. II Tim. 2:2) but this task is but a specialized duty of the Gospel ministry. Professors of Theology as far as our Churches are concerned, are Ministers of the Gospel. (Cf. Form for the Installation of Professors of Theology.)

The separate mention of Professors of Theology in Article 2 is confusing, and rests upon a misunderstanding of former years. In fact, the original expression used in Latin was "Doctor," which simply means teacher or instructor. And this term "Doctor" was applied to all teachers of religion also in State universities, though these teachers held no ecclesiastical office whatsoever. Do not forget in this connection that there was a very close bond of union between the Government and the Churches in these early days. Our fathers sought the sponsorship and special, if not exclusive, favor of the Government. And the Government often insisted on a definite measure of control over the Churches. It is not unlikely that this situation, which time and a further removal from Rome would correct, influenced our fathers to view matters on this score as they did.

It is agreed by many that it would have been far better if in 1914 we had simply rendered Article 2 as follows: "The offices are of three kinds: of the Ministers of the Word, of the Elders, and of the Deacons." Now our redaction of 1914 still reads: "De diensten zijn vierderlei: der Dienaren des Woords, der Doctoren, der Ouderlingen, en der Diakenen." And in our English translation of 1920 we have conveniently substituted, "Professors of Theology," for the expression, "der Doctoren."

The Reformed Churches of Holland have to this day also retained the old redaction on this point. The Rev. Joh. Jansen, one of Holland's outstanding authorities in Church Order matters, attributes this fact to ecclesiastical conservatism in the evil sense of the word.

Almost needless to say, the fact that the actual offices in the Church of Christ are limited to the three indicated, does not mean that there is no room for various assistants. The Levites, for instance, were assistants to the Priests. Their work and authority belonged to the primary office of the priesthood. I Cor. 12:28 speaks specifically of "helps." Paul refers to assistants and helpers repeatedly. Student exhorters, Catechism teachers not holding office, organists, Sunday School teachers, Sick visitors, Gospel workers. Finance Committees, Collectors, Building and Ground Committees, Ushers, Janitors, etc., all these (when they are appointed and controlled by the consistories) may be considered to be "helps." They all fill a useful and necessary place in our churches.

ARTICLE 3

No one, though he be a Professor of Theology, Elder or Deacon, shall be permitted to enter upon the Ministry of the Word and the Sacraments without having been lawfully called thereunto. And when anyone acts contrary thereto, and after being frequently admonished does not desist, the Classis shall judge whether he is to be declared a schismatic or is to be punished in some other way.

NO MINISTRY OF WORD AND SACRAMENTS WITHOUT A LAWFUL CALL

1. What is the historical background of Article 3?

One of the many problems that the Churches of the Reformation period had to cope with was that of self-appointed preachers. Church life during the first few decades was not at all well ordered. It could not be. It was a period of new beginnings and of persecution. Many of the Ministers of that early day were former priests. Others were men without special theological training, though having in other respects more than ordinary ability. Some of those who aspired to the Ministry simply started to preach wherever they could get a hearing. Many of these men refused to submit to an examination and did not care to place themselves under the supervision of any Consistory. Men of questionable character and purposes, by eloquent and fair speech would create a following for themselves, to the disruption of Churches and ultimate spiritual damage to many. Very often they would travel from place to place. Our fathers had more than one designation for this class of self-seeking, self-appointed, religious freebooters, whose sensational methods often attracted many. They were called "tramps," "intruders," and "schismatics" (loopers, indringers, scheurmakers.)

As early as 1563 the Churches of Flanders decided: "That none shall be permitted to administer the Word of God without a lawful call, and such as boldly intrude themselves shall be punished." The Weselian Convention, 1568, decided that none should be admitted to the Ministry "without lawful calling, election, approbation, proper examination and observance of that lawful order." Subsequent Synods, Embden, 1571; Dordrecht, 1574; Dordrecht, 1578, took additional action against these wilful, self-seeking, office-less men. The Synod of Middelburg, 1581, gave us Article 3 of our Church Order as it now reads.

2. Who alone may administer the Word and Sacraments in our Churches?

Article 3 provides that none "shall be permitted to enter upon the Ministry of the Word and of the Sacraments without having been called thereunto." The Church Order stipulates in Article 4 that a lawful call includes election, examination, approbation, and ordination. Of these we shall speak in due order. Just now we consider not the call to the Ministry and its elements, but rather the ground upon which Article 3 rests. These grounds are Biblical, beyond doubt.

The Old Testament office-bearers were called and charged of God. The Apostles were called directly by Christ. False prophets and false apostles had no calling and charge of God. (cf. Jer. 23:21, 32; John 5:43.) Those who were called and sent of God came upon His authority. (cf. Isaiah 6:8; Jer. 1:1; Rom. 1:1; Eph. 1:1; etc.) The Apostles and their helpers were called "Ministers of Christ," Col. 1:7; "servants of Christ," II Cor. 5:20. And because the Apostles and their helpers did not come upon their own authority, nor upon the authority of men, but solely upon God's authority, the Churches had to obey them and respect them. "Obey them that have the rule over you, and submit to them." Heb. 13:17a; "Esteem them exceeding highly in love for their work's sake." I Thess. 5:13.

Clearly, the Bible stresses divine appointment for the Prophets and Apostles. But this is likewise true for those that were to succeed them. They also are sent of God and called of the Holy Spirit. "Pray ye therefore the Lord of the harvest, that he **send forth laborers** into his harvest." Matt. 9:38; "Take heed unto yourselves, and to all the flock, **in which the Holy Spirit hath made you bishops,** to feed the Church of the Lord which He purchased with His own blood." Acts 20:28. (cf. also I Cor. 12:28; Eph. 4:11, etc.) To preach, one must be sent. "And how shall they preach, except they be sent?" Rom. 10:15. No man may assume this task upon his own authority. "And **no man taketh the honor unto himself**, but when he is called of God, even as was Aaron." Heb. 5:4.

What would we think of a man who without an election, would nevertheless insist on doing the work of an Elder or of a Deacon?

Dr. H. Bavinck is thoroughly Biblical when he maintains that all believers have a calling to preach or to witness, but that only those who have a definite charge of God may do so with authority and in the name of the Lord, preaching the Gospel as a savor of life unto life, and as a savor of death unto death.[1] (cf. Isaiah 43:10, 12; Luke 10:16; Acts 8:4; II Cor. 2:14-17.)

This special call to the ministry and its charge is no longer given in direct and extraordinary fashion, as in the case of the Apostles. In their day the Church of Christ was in its infancy and conditions were extraordinary. When extraordinary circumstances cease to exist, God uses ordinary means. These ordinary means pertaining to the calling to the ministry include the internal and the external call.

What do we mean by the internal call? The internal call may be designated as a personal conviction of heart on the part of a brother in Christ that God would have him become a Minister of the Gospel. Dr. H. Bouwman, in his Gereformeerd Kerkrecht, enumerates and describes five elements essential to the internal call to the ministry.[2] Briefly stated, they are:

1. A persistent love for the gospel ministry, a strong desire to serve God and His Kingdom in the ministry, born of prayerful meditation.

2. A certain amount of ability. He who aspires to the ministry must not only have the necessary strength of body and character, but

---

1. H. Bavinck: **Gereformeerde Dogmatiek,** 1918, IV, pp. 410-415.
2. H. Bouwman: **Gereformeerd Kerkrecht,** 1928, Vol. I, pp. 368-70.

also certain indispensable talents, as for instance, pertaining to mind and speech.

3. Readiness to deny oneself utterly; readiness to serve the Lord wherever and however He may appoint.

4. Unselfish aims; a desire to see God glorified and His Kingdom extended. None should desire the ministry merely as a profession and as a livelihood.

5. An open road; the ways and means essential for the necessary preparation will be provided by God in His providence, if one is truly called of Him. If one feels called to the ministry but finds that the road leading to the ministry is providentially closed, all his prayers notwithstanding, then he may be sure that he is not actually called of God.

But the internal call must always receive its ratification of God through the external call. One may "feel" that he is called of God, but one's feelings are not infallible. One may be well prepared and well qualified as far as man can judge, and yet not be called of God. How can one know that his feelings and desires are actually tokens of a call of God? Of this he may rest assured if, in addition to what he sincerely believes, and feels in his heart to be a divine call to the ministry, God also calls him through the instrumentality of one of His Churches. This we term the external call.

That God calls His servants to the ministry of the Word and of the Sacraments, under normal New Testament conditions, through the Church, is beyond doubt. When an Apostle was needed to fill the vacancy created by Judas Iscariot, we read: "And they (the believers, the Church) put forward two, Joseph called Barsabas, who was surnamed Justus, and Matthias." Acts 1:23. And concerning Titus we read: "Who was also appointed of the churches to travel with us in the matter of this grace." II Cor. 8:19. No one may ignore this ecclesiastical appointment and just assume the ministry unto himself.

3. Why professors of theology, Elders and Deacons are specifically excluded from the ministry of the Word and the Sacraments.

Elders and Deacons receive special mention in Article 3 for no other reason than that some Elders and Deacons assumed unto themselves the duties and privileges of the ministry. Elders represent Christ as King. It is their specific duty and privilege to rule. Deacons represent Christ as Priest. It is their specific duty and privilege to show mercy. Ministers represent Christ as Prophet. It is their specific duty and privilege to make known the will of God; to speak His Word. And although it is true that Ministers as we know them, are at the same time Elders, and therefore help to rule the Church over and above their duty and privilege to instruct the people, yet it is not true that Elders have the right of the ministry of the Word and the Sacraments. (cf. I Tim 5:17, and the Form for the Ordination of Elders and Deacons.)

Regarding professors of theology, it should be recalled that years ago many men were professors of theology at state universities, who had never been ordained to the regular ministry. Some of these were tempted to preach nevertheless. Yet our fathers realized that such should not be done. No one, unless he has received a charge from God can act as His representative or as His messenger to His people. A man may be a doctor of law and have excellent qualifications to serve as judge, but unless he is appointed to serve as judge, he has no authority to act the part of a judge in our courts. Unordained intruders may not be admitted to our pulpits, but neither may unordained professors of theology. The founders of the Reformed Churches certainly held the office and divine appointment to office in very high esteem.

Inasmuch as our present theological professors are all ordained men, this article does not affect them. But they are permitted to preach by virtue of the fact that they are Ministers, and not because they are professors of theology. Our Form for the Installation of Professors of Theology even presupposes that all who are appointed as professors of theology are ordained men. It speaks of the brother to be installed as being "a brother in the holy ministry." On the other hand, Synod of 1930 decided: "The nominees (for professors of theology) shall preferably be ordained men that have had some experience in the Ministry of the Word." (Acts, Synod 1930, Art. 23.)

4. What is to be done when anyone administers the Word or the Sacraments without due ordination?

Anyone transgressing the good rule shall be admonished concerning the error of his way. By whom? By his consistory of course. For all discipline concerning church members in their non-office-bearing capacity, originates and centers in the local Churches. If the guilty one persists, Classis must judge whether he is to be declared a schismatic (one who creates factions or divisions in Churches) or whether he shall be punished in some other way. The first three Synods (1571, 1574, 1578) left no choice. He who persisted should be declared to other Classes to be schismatic. This implied, as it does today, that such an one should be disciplined as a schismatic. For he who is guilty of tearing apart the Church of God is unworthy of the Lord's Table, except he repent. (cf. Form for the Administration of the Lord's Supper.) The Synod of 1581 made milder treatment possible. It added the concluding phrase to Article 3: ". . . . or is to be punished in some other way." This clause permits for instance, mere admonition, without the giving of publicity of the transgressor's irregularity as a warning measure to all the Churches.

What is to be done when an unordained individual, not a member of one of our Churches, is permitted to preach the Word from any of our pulpits? Or what is to be done if a Minister of another denomination, concerning whose soundness there is a well-founded doubt, is admitted to one of our pulpits? In such cases it becomes the duty of Classis to warn its Churches and to admonish the guilty consistory. If this should not help, more drastic action would be in order.

Needless to say, cases of this kind often require a great deal of consideration, instruction, and patience, inasmuch as many church members are not clear on the issues at stake and the dangers involved. And many "intruders" seem to be very sincere and effective. Swayed by eloquence and emotionalism, and in the midst of controversy, very few people can judge objectively and soberly.

Nevertheless, let it also be said, that violations on this point also require determined opposition. Laxity on this score would ultimately open our pulpits to errors of all kinds.

ARTICLE 4

The lawful calling of those who have not been previously in office, consists:

First, in the ELECTION by the Consistory and the Deacons, after preceding prayers, with due observance of the regulations established by the Consistory for this purpose, and of the ecclesiastical ordinance, that only those can for the first time be called to the Ministry of the Word who have been declared eligible by the Churches, according to the rule in this matter; and furthermore with the advice of Classis or of the counselor appointed for this purpose by the Classis;

Secondly, in the EXAMINATION both of doctrine and life which shall be conducted by the Classis, to which the call must be submitted for approval, and which shall take place in the presence of three Delegates of Synod from the nearest Classes:

Thirdly, in the APPROBATION by the members of the calling church, when, the name of the Minister having been announced for two successive Sundays, no lawful objection arises; which approbation, however, is not required in case the election takes place with the co-operation of the congregation by choosing out of a nomination previously made.

Finally, in the public ORDINATION in the presence of the congregation, which shall take place with appropriate stipulations and interrogations, admonitions and prayers and imposition of hands by the officiating Minister (and by other Ministers who are present) agreeably to the Form for that purpose.

CALLING TO THE MINISTRY OF THE WORD AND SACRAMENTS

1. The Election.

a. Election takes place "after preceding prayers."

In Church Order redactions of the sixteenth century this phrase reads: "after preceding fastings and prayers." The task of securing a worthy Minister of the Gospel was much more difficult in former years than it is now. At first there was not a class or group of men known as candidates for the ministry. Our candidates must be well prepared and well qualified spiritually and only then are they declared candidates. In former days the Churches as a rule, had to find their own way. "Indringers" (intruders) and "loopers" (migratory, self-appointed preachers) were numerous. And then as now, people were apt to be swayed by some unworthy but eloquent stranger. And so the calling of a Minister was a very serious and difficult task. After matters were arranged so that unworthy persons could no longer creep in without much difficulty, days of fasting for this special purpose became less necessary. Finally, fasting in connection with the calling of a minister fell completely into disuse. Under these changed conditions the Synod of Utrecht, 1905 (Netherlands) and likewise our own Synod of 1914 altered the phrase in question so that we now have merely, "after preceding prayers." It is worthy of note that provisions for fasting were never made regarding the election of Elders and Deacons. Neither when it concerned the calling of a Minister already ordained and having served some other Church. Doubtless, the fact that the custom of fasting was abandoned for all other occasions, also helped to make this present provision obsolete. (We are not now answering the question whether or not this discontinuance of fasting in our Churches can be fully justified.)

From the foregoing it may also be inferred that it was the original intent of this article that the congregation should come together for a special prayer service before the work of securing a Minister was undertaken, particularly when a choice was to be made from brethren who had not previously served as Ministers. We now, as a rule, interpret it to mean that no election shall take place unless the meeting has been opened with prayer. If the Church Order meant no more the expression would be rather superfluous. Who would think of conducting a congregational gathering without due prayers? Should we not go back to the old custom? Is not the calling of a Minister amply worthy of a special prayer service? However, in this connection let us also remember that conditions have changed. Today **much prayerful labor** is being performed before applicants are declared candidates. When Article 4 was first written the Churches did not declare men to be candidates for the Ministry. They had to choose more or less at random from men whom they thought fit for the ministry. At any rate, upon the Sunday before the work of calling a Minister begins in Consistory, the sermon should be appropriate and the congregational prayers specific.

b. Election "by the Consistory and the Deacons."

Properly the Elders of a Church constitute its Consistory and the Deacons its Diaconate. The Elders represent Christ as the King of His Church. The Deacons represent Christ as the Priest of His Church. The Consistory rules the Church in the name of Christ. The Diaconate shows mercy in the name of Christ. Now the Church Order stipulates that in small Churches the Deacons may, and in certain cases must be added to the Consistory. (cf. Art. 37). In all such cases Elders are really Assistant-Deacons, and Deacons Assistant-Elders. They partake of each other's office in a very distinct fashion. In all Churches in which Article 37 is operating, the Elders and Deacons, (and the Ministers inasmuch as Ministers are members of the Consistory, in their capacity as Elders) naturally work together in nominating and electing men to the ministerial office.

But Article 4 stipulates that also in Churches where the normal situation obtains, i.e. where the two offices function each in their own sphere, that also in these Churches the Elders and the Deacons shall meet together whenever a brother is to be elected to the ministry. Why? It is the position of the Church Order that the duty of election to office (Minister, Deacon, Elder), does not belong to any one of the offices in particular, but to all the offices working in unison. Strictly speaking of course, appointment to office in the Church belongs to Christ only. Normally He designates through the Church and appoints through the offices. (For a fuller consideration of the matter of appointment to office through all three offices of the Church, see our discussion of Article 22.)

The Church Order neither here nor elsewhere prescribed direct appointment through the congregation. So-called "free elections" in Churches already organized, are contrary to our adopted rules. The Churches of the Reformation period ruled against these "free elections" for more than one reason. In the first place many were very ignorant in those early days. Large numbers of those who left the Roman Church, in the wake of the majority, lacked consecration and conviction. Others, feeling the sway of Independentism or Congregationalism—today we might speak of Undenominationalism—were too revolutionary. Then there was also the danger that men, not to be desired for the work of the ministry but with pleasing personalities and eloquent speech, might be elected, if the whole matter rested with the congregation.

But Bouwman judges: "Although Article 4 of the Church Order does not mean to limit the congregation in any of its rights, the formulation of this article does not give full expression to the prerogatives of the congregation."[1] And Jansen suggests that a future redaction of the Church Order of the Reformed Churches of the Netherlands should incorporate the phrase: "with the co-operation of the congregation" in Article 4.[2] We agree with him. Article 4 of our redaction would likewise be more complete if it read: ". . . . election by the Consistory and the Deacons, with the co-operation of the congregation. . . ." For to be sure, co-operation on the part of the congregation is in full harmony with Reformed Church polity. In the Church of Rome office-bearers appoint new office-bearers without consulting the congregation. The original Lutherans permitted the Government to elect its office-bearers. According to the Independent or Congregational systems, the congregation must appoint directly. But according to the Presbyterian or Reformed system Christ elects His office-bearers, by vote of the Church under the guidance and supervision of the office-bearers previously appointed. And this is doubtlessly Scriptural. For the Bible attributes a guiding control over elections and power of appointment to the office-bearers. Acts 6:3: "Look ye out therefore, brethren, from among you seven men of good report, full of the Spirit and wisdom, **whom we may appoint over this business.**" Acts 14:23: "And **when they had appointed for them elders** in every church . . . ." I Tim. 5:22: "**Lay hands hastily on no man.** . ." Titus 1:5: "For this cause I left thee in Crete, that thou shouldest set in order the things that are wanting, **and appoint elders in every city** as I gave thee charge." However it should never be forgotten that the duty of control and guidance, and the power of appointment which Consistories exercise, have come to them through the Churches. Christ authorizes in the first place His Church, and secondly, and in a derived sense the Consistories. The truth of this contention becomes plain when we remember that when congregations are organized, the body of believers appoints office-bearers directly. If this were no inherent right of the congregation, this could never be done.

But the Bible also exemplifies congregational co-operation. According to Acts 1:23 a group of one hundred twenty believers co-operated with the Apostles in the nomination of two men, one of whom was to be appointed Apostle in the place of Judas Iscariot. And before the Apostles appointed the first seven Deacons (Acts 6:1-6) the congregation chose them. And in II Cor. 8:19 Paul speaks of an Evangelist or Helper, "who was appointed by the Churches to travel with us in the matter of this grace. . ."

Consistories should therefore work for congregational co-operation, also in making nominations for the ministerial office. It is well to give all members an opportunity to commit themselves. Names of brethren which anyone desires to see nominated can be presented in writing to the Consistory and upon invitation of the Consistory prior to the making of nominations. If ever a large portion of a Church desires to see a brother nominated, but the Consistory judges that he should not be nominated, the Consistory may find it advisable and

---

1. Bouwman: **Gereformeerd Kerkrecht,** 1928, I, p. 385.
2. Jansen: **Korte Verklaring van de Kerkenordening,** 1923, p. 17.

necessary to explain its stand. In cases of serious conflict and differences of opinion, and as a measure of last resort, the major assemblies (Classis, in this case) may be consulted. This step, needless to say, should seldom be necessary.

The question whether or not women should take part in congregational elections we would answer negatively. Voetius, the great expert in Reformed Church government, excludes women from Church elections inasmuch as congregational elections are Church governmental in character.[1] And women, according to Holy Writ, are not to teach in the Churches nor to help govern the same. (I Cor. 14:34.) Bouwman judges likewise.[2] So does Jansen.[3] Those who have not yet made confession of faith have no right to vote inasmuch as they are, ecclesiastically speaking, minors. Members being disciplined have no right to vote inasmuch as censure implies that all rights of Church membership are held in abeyance, rendered non-active, temporarily at least.

c. Regulations adopted by Consistories for election of Ministers, to be observed.

The Church Order presupposes, here in Article 4, and again in the article governing the election of Elders and Deacons, that each Consistory has a set of rules according to which elections shall be conducted. Whenever the congregation is called together for the purpose of electing office-bearers, partiality and arbitrariness should be out of the question. To avoid these evils, a set of rules consistently followed, is very desirable.

Then again, certain questions should not merely be left to usage and custom. For instance: Proper announcement of nominations should be made prior to every election; elections should take place by ballot; a majority vote should elect; etc. These and like rules are not found in the Church Order. They should be incorporated in a short set of rules governing election. Furthermore, problems are apt to present themselves at any meeting. For example: In case more brethren receive a majority vote than the number of vacancies to be filled, what is to be done? When two candidates for one office receive an equal number of votes, what should be the procedure? Questions such as these cannot be decided by the congregation inasmuch as the Consistory is the ruling body and not the congregational gathering. Moreover, for the Consistory to decide on such problems at the time when they present themselves might open the door to partiality or at least to the semblance of partiality. Permanent rules should govern such cases.

d. Only those declared eligible by the Churches may be called.

The original Church Order (Dort 1618-19) did not contain the provision now under consideration. A "praeparatoir" examination, i.e., a preparatory examination was unknown. The Churches could call whomsoever they saw fit. However, preliminary examination soon proved to be very necessary. Without proper guidance in this respect many inferior and undesirable men entered the ministry. Later the evil of Arminianism urged and compelled the Church to establish greater safe-guards. The Synod of Dort 1578 already provided that none should be called unless they had first been tried or examined, so that the Churches might receive greater assurance that only "be-

---

1. cf. Bouwman: **Gereformeerd Kerkrecht**, 1928, I, p. 386.
2. **Idem.**
3. Jansen: **Korte Verklaring van Kerkenordening**, 1923, p. 18.

quaeme personen" (qualified persons) should be called. Various Provincial Synods, before and after the great Synod of Dort referred to above, made like decisions. But it found no expression in the general Church Order of Dort. The Secession Churches of Holland (1834) instituted a preliminary examination conducted by the curators of its Theological School. Successful applicants were declared Candidates by these curators. After the union with the Doleantie Churches (1892) this preliminary examination and right of declaring men Candidates was returned to the various Classes. Then in 1905 the Synod of Utrecht included the following provision in Article 4 of the Church Order: "Met onderhouding . . . . van de kerkelijke ordinantie dat alleen diegenen voor het eerst tot den dienst des Woords kunnen beroepen worden, die door de Classe, waarin zij wonen, praeparatoir geexamineerd zijn." This provision stipulates that a preliminary examination must be taken by men who desire to enter the ministry, which examination is to be conducted by the Classes in which they reside, and which body also declares successful applicants Candidates.

In our own Christian Reformed Churches the curators have up to the year 1937 examined and declared men Candidates. (Our body of curators are now known by the more common designation: Board of Trustees.) However Synod of 1937 decided that beginning with the year 1938, Synod itself will examine and declare men Candidates for the ministry, instead of doing so through a board of trustees. This decision was taken upon the following two grounds:

"1. The best interest of our Church requires that whatsoever our Church assemblies can reasonably do directly should not be delegated to committees, particularly not when it concerns very important Church work.

2. Under the present system (Board of Trustees of Calvin College and Seminary declaring Candidates) our Eldership has no part in this very essential work. If Synod would do this work itself, this undesirable situation would be rectified." (Acts 1937, Art. 53)

The Synod of 1939 declared that the synodical examination is preparatory in character and deals with the following matters: 1. Dogmatics; 2. Practica; 3. Specimen sermon. (cf. Acts, 1939, p. 74.)

e. Election not to take place without advice of Classis or Counselor.

Article 4 also provides that no election to the ministry shall take place without advice of Classis. Why this ruling? No Christian Reformed Church stands by itself. There is a very close bond between the various Churches. He who receives the right to administer the Word and Sacraments in one Church, is thereby given authority to do the same in all other Christian Reformed Churches, upon request of the Consistories concerned, of course. Furthermore, the Minister will be constantly delegated to the major assemblies, and he will thus help to govern other Christian Reformed Churches, particularly those of his own Classis. He also becomes eligible to the ministry in any other local Church in the denomination without reexamination by a Classis. For these reasons, the Classis, and through the Classis, all the Churches, have been given a certain measure of control in this important matter. However this provision is first of all meant to be a safe-guard for the Church calling. A whole Classis is sometimes in better position to judge concerning the desirability of a contemplated call than the one calling Church by itself. The phrase "or of the counselor appointed for this purpose by the Classis," was added for practical reasons. A Classis meets in regular session only intermittently and in regions where distances are great only twice a year. A Church in need of a Minister usually desires to call forthwith, rather than wait for Classes to meet. For a Church to wait with the calling of a Minister for a Classical gathering would mean a vacancy of many years in many instances, inasmuch as Churches are often compelled to call several times before securing a Minister. Moreover, the counselor as representative of Classis must assist the vacant Church with his help and advice regarding the work of calling a Minister whenever necessary. He is expected to do what Classis would do directly if it were in session, namely advise the Consistory as to a prospective Minister. He is also expected to be present if circumstances permit, at the election, in order that he preside at the meeting for the congregation, and he must sign the letter of call, to assure the brother elected that all things have proceeded according to ecclesiastical rules and that the call in so far is valid and carries Classical approval.

Strictly speaking, the work of a counselor requires that the Consistories of vacant calling Churches consult him before nominating men for the vacancy. This, however, is very seldom done. The counselor is usually asked for his approval after the nomination (usually a trio) has been made. And counselors almost uniformly approve of nominations without offering advice, inasmuch as advice is not asked. Sometimes this procedure is doubtlessly harmful. Good advice asked for and given at the proper time and place would be a real boon to many a vacant Church. But on the other hand, Consistories which do not need advice should not be made to feel that they must ask for advice. The liberty of each Church should be unhampered as far as denominational unity and agreement permit.

In practice the counselor does a great deal more than the Church Order really indicates. He often installs Elders and Deacons, administers the Sacraments, conducts funerals, etc. There is nothing against this, although no Church should feel that it is obliged to call on its counselor for all these matters. And no counselor should ever feel that the Church concerned is in duty bound to call on him for all these labors.

Often vacant Churches when they wish to call a Minister will request "hand-opening" which is usually termed "permission to call." This is unnecessary. Every Church has an inherent right to call a Minister, and should do so if at all possible. "Hand-opening" is an old Dutch term. Years ago, when the government of Holland had gained possession of Church properties and paid or helped to pay the salary of Ministers, Classes would ask "hand-opening" for certain Churches which desired to call. What then was the significance of all this? Simply that Classis was requesting the Government to promise to pay the salary of a Minister, which a certain Church desired to call. The Church concerned would receive as it were, permission to extend its open hand to the Government for a donation toward the Minister's salary. They who received "hand-opening" were thus placed in position to call. But all this is a thing of the past, and so the whole custom should be shelved.

This does not mean that Churches may not and should not ask their sister Churches for advice in regard to the desirability of calling a Minister. Circumstances may make this very desirable. Furthermore, a Church which finds itself unable to pay an adequate salary, will have to ask assistance from her sister Churches, and cannot well proceed with calling a Minister without advice from Classis. But no Church is in duty bound to ask "permission to call." It should not be done as it tends to obscure the fact that each local Church has the inherent right to call. At best a certain Church may find it necessary to take counsel with the other Churches, or to ask a promise of financial aid toward salaries to be paid. Rulings pertaining to minimum salaries to be paid, find no support in the Church Order either. A Classis may express itself and urge its Churches not to go beneath a certain stipulated minimum, but no resolution of this kind should be worded or interpreted in such a fashion that it exercises compelling force. The matter of salaries to be paid is ultimately a matter between the Church concerned and the Minister called. A Minister of some means, for instance, should be at full liberty to serve a Church for a very small salary, or no salary at all, if he so desired. Almost needless to say, if a Classis finds that one of its Churches is paying its Minister an insufficient salary, it may call the attention of such a Church to its neglect of duty and urge instant improvement, or if need be, help to improve the situation.

2. The Examination.

a. The "Peremptoir" or Decisive Examination.

The examination to which Article 4 refers in its second section is the **decisive examination**, the examination by which a brother is admitted to the ministry. The **preliminary examination**, which merely admits men to the candidacy, has already been considered in the previous sections. The peremptoir or decisive examination has been in use ever since the federal unity of Reformed Churches of Holland first began to function. At their very first general assembly, the Weselian Convention, 1568, it was instituted. Successive Synods maintained it. The praeparatoir or preliminary examination was added at a latter day, (1686, Synod of Den Haag; 1688, Synod of South Holland) to provide Churches, desiring to call such as had not previously served, with much needed guidance and safe-guards.

b. Subject matter of Decisive Examinations.

The decisive examination which admits to the ministry concerns itself with doctrine and practice, faith and conduct. Thus it was stipulated from the beginning. The subject matter for these classical examinations was regulated anew by our Synod of 1939. Regarding the nature of Classical examinations and the subject matter of these examinations, this Synod adopted the following:

"That the Classical examination is decisive, and deal with the following matters:

1. Dogmatics (including knowledge of Standards and Controvers);
2. Practica;
3. Specimen sermon;
4. Knowledge of the Scriptures;
5. Church History;
6. Church Polity;
7. Ethics." (Acts, 1939, P. 74.)

For a differentiation between the synodical examination and the Classical examination, i.e., between the preparatory or preliminary examination and the decisive and final examination, confer the report on "Synodical and Classical Examinations", Agenda, Synod 1939, Part I or a short excerpt of this report, Acts, Synod 1939, pages 250-2.

As will be understood, this report as such has no official standing. But Synod of 1939 did accept the conclusions of this report as quoted above. And Synod was motivated, we may believe, by the material contained in this report. Candidates as well as examiners will therefore do wise to take note of this report.

Concerning the sermon to be delivered at the time of the classical examination Synod of 1920 decided that the candidate should preach for the congregation in whose midst the Classis is being held, and that the classical delegates should attend this special congregational service. Synod of 1934 made this matter optional. Each Classis now arranges this matter as it judges best. The specimen sermon may be delivered before the entertaining Church, usually on the evening before the actual examination, or the specimen sermon may be delivered before the Classis at one of its regular sessions.

The present authors much prefer the former method. It is fairer to the candidate for it gives him a "real" audience and more time. And the Classical delegates can judge far better as to the candidate's ability on the pulpit.

c. By whom the decisive examination is to be conducted.

According to the inherent rights of every local Church, it would be up to the Consistory of the calling Church to take the final examinations of admittance, after a Candidate had accepted the call extended to him. But denominational unity requires approbation of the call by the Classis. Consequently, for very good and practical reasons, this examination has been assigned to the Classes. First of all, because Consistories as a rule are not qualified to conduct this examination as it should be done, nor are they always able to evaluate an examination aright. Consequently, the Classis lends its assistance. Secondly, this examination has been assigned to the Classes, inasmuch as the Classis is asked to approve of a call extended, and therefore in the matter of calling definitely exercises its right and duty of supervision. And furthermore, the decisive examination admits not only to the administration of the Word and the Sacraments in the one Church calling, but to all the Churches of the denomination, by dint of federal agreement.

It is even added that this examination "shall take place in the presence of three Delegates of Synod from the nearest Classes." This provision was included as an additional safeguard. In days of laxity and error sometimes a whole territory or Classes is more or less weak and unsound. Representative delegates from other Classes in such instances might prove to be a real blessing. Moreover, as noted above, the decisive examination of admittance is valid for all the Churches of the whole denomination. Consequently, so the conclusions ran, all the Churches should be represented, at least by a few able men.

In cases of differences of opinion between a Classis and the Synodical Delegates, mutual deliberations are in order. If these fail to remove the differences of opinion, the whole question of admittance or non-admittance goes to Synod.

The Synodical Delegates have no decisive votes. They serve the Classis with their advice, as a body, after the examination. As a matter of custom the Classes do extend the opportunity to these Delegates to question the Candidate.

d. Who are to be examined?

Article 4 replies in its opening clause: "those who have not been previously in office." In other words, those who are not as yet Ministers. The examination is not required of Ministers who, already serving one of our Churches, have accepted a call to another Church in another Classis. Because of denominational unity one Church or group of Churches fully acknowledges the examination conducted by another Church or group of Churches. Just as we honor each other's certificates of membership, so do we honor each other's examinations for the Ministry. However, in days of error or neglect, a certain Classis might require an additional statement or examination from all incoming Ministers. But only then should such a step be taken when there are just grounds to believe that the letters of testimony of incoming Ministers are no longer reliable and true to fact. Thus the Classis of Walcheren, Nov. 5, 1693, decreed that all incoming Ministers would have to sign the "Walcherse Artikelen," articles condemning certain prevalent errors of that day.

3. The Approbation.

The New Testament teaches us clearly that the early Churches cooperated in the appointment of men to office, though it is Christ who actually appoints and ordains to office. Consequently, our Church Order provides that the congregation be recognized in the important matter of elections. And no Consistory or major assembly may ignore the voice of the Church, or arbitrarily set aside just complaints. For direct congregational participation in the work of elections again consult Acts 6:3-5. The multitude, at the request of the Apostles looked out for seven men of good report from among their own number, whom the Apostles then proceeded to ordain as Deacons. Again, II Cor. 8:49 speaks of an evangelist who had been appointed "by the churches to travel" with Paul. And in II Cor. 8:25 the Apostle calls his helpers, "messengers of the Churches."

How may this approbation of the congregation spoken of in Article 4 be secured? First, the Consistory may announce to the congregation whom it intends to call, by which announcement the Consistory submits its choice for the approval of the whole Church. Those who might have valid objections should be invited to come to the next Consistory meeting to state their objections. If lawful or valid objections are registered with the Consistory, and if these are of such a nature that they cannot be removed, the contemplated call will be withheld. If no valid objections are registered, the Consistory can proceed with the call.

But the present article also permits a second possibility. The Consistory may nominate two or three or four men (as many as it sees fit) and then call together the congregation in order that the body of believers may elect one of the nominees. This latter method of approbation, as is well known, is now in general use in our Churches. Of the two, it is under all normal circumstances to be preferred, as it gives the congregation a very definite voice in the matter. Election by the congregation manifestly implies approbation, and therefore according to Article 4, approbation "is not required in case the election takes place with the co-operation of the congregation by choosing out of a nomination previously made." It should not be forgotten, however, that the nomination must be announced to the congregation for its approval. If anyone in the Church concerned has lawful objections against one or more of the nominees, he should report at a Consistory meeting, which meeting should always be held before the election takes place, in order that members may have opportunity to register objections. Some Consistories meet a few minutes before the congregational meeting at which the election is to take place. This cannot be called a very appropriate time for such a meeting, for what opportunity would a Consistory have to investigate charges or objections?

When a Candidate has been elected should his name be announced to the congregation for approval? Not before the call is actually sent by the Consistory, for the elected brother has the preliminary approval of the congregation by virtue of the procedure followed regarding his election. But if he accepts the call, then this fact is announced to the Church, stating that he will be installed as Minister unless valid objections should prevent. The "Form of Ordination of the Ministers of God's Word" clearly implies this final approbation by the whole congregation The opening sentence of this form reads as follows: "Beloved brethren, it is known unto you, that we have, at three different times, published the name of our brother N., here present, to learn whether any person has aught to offer concerning his doctrine and life, why he might not be ordained to the Ministry of the Word."

Article 4 provides that announcement to the congregation, when the first possible method of calling a Minister is followed, shall take place "for two successive Sundays." Our Dutch redaction of which this is a translation has "de naam des Dienaars den tijd van veertien dagen in de Kerk afgekondigd zijnde, ..." Which is: "the name of the Minister having been announced to the Church **for the period of two weeks.**" The original intent is therefore that the name or the names be announced at the services of the congregation for a period of two weeks. At the end of this two weeks' period the Consistory meets to receive possible objections. Very often a nomination is announced on two successive Sundays, the congregational meeting being held on the following Monday. This gives the congregation little more than one week for consideration and investigation and the Consistory no time at all prior to the election. Of course, the Consistory could call the meeting and election off at the last minute if necessary. But this surely would be unpleasant and disturbing. It would be far better, to avoid possible difficulties, to follow the original reading and intent of the Church Order. In harmony with this reading and intent the Form of Ordination even speaks of three announcements, referring to three announcements made on three successive Sundays, as all will grant.

Inasmuch as the office-bearers issue the call, may a Consistory overrule the choice of a congregation? No. If the second method of calling a Minister, provided for in this Article, is followed, then the Consistory is duty bound to send the call to the brother elected by the Church. The congregational vote is binding, it is not merely advisory. The voice of the congregation is a constituent element in the whole process of calling and may not be side-tracked. If the Consistory had valid objections against any of the nominees, their names should have been removed from the nomination, and should never have been submitted to the choice of the Church. Only if the Consistory should hear of very serious well-founded objections, after the election, would she be permitted to withhold the call. In such a case, the Consistory, if at all possible, should seek the approval of the congregation.

4. The Ordination.

a. Significance of the ordination.

The ordination may be described as the solemn acceptance of the ministerial office on the part of the Minister-elect, and the public uniting of the Minister-elect to the calling congregation. The essence of the call to the ministry, however, is to be sought in the election; not in the public acceptance of, and dedication to the office.

Under special circumstances men have entered upon their office without ordination or installation. During the Reformation era, persecution sometimes made public ordination or installation impossible. Then this public ceremony was simply omitted by our fathers. The great authority on Reformed Church polity of Holland, Gysbertus Voetius, was never formally installed as Minister of Heusden, due to government interference. However, when circumstances are normal, ordination or installation may not be omitted. One simply is not considered to be a Minister of a certain Church unless he has been duly installed. We do not look upon ordination or installation as a Sacrament as does the Roman Church. According to Reformed Church polity it is a ceremony through which a Minister-elect openly accepts his office in the presence of the whole congregation, and by which he is also openly, publicly inducted into his sacred office. All this is to take place, so this article provides, "with appropriate stipulation and interrogations, admonitions, and prayers and imposition of hands by the officiating Ministers (and by other Ministers who are present) agreeable to the Form for that purpose."

As the concluding phrase indicates, these matters have been regulated and provided for in our Form of Ordination of the Ministers of God's Word, found on appended page 99-102 of the Psalter Hymnal.

Years ago the matter of imposition or laying on of hands was not prescribed. It was left to the judgment of each local Church. Many of the Reformation Churches in Holland were opposed to the practice. In the Roman Church it was regarded as essential. By the imposition of hands, so this Church holds, brethren already ordained impart certain necessary gifts needed for the office. Now our fathers feared this error. But the Synod of 1581 ruled that those who were being installed in the ministerial office for the first time, should be ordained by imposition of hands. Five years later this ruling was permanently established. (Synod 1586.) By this time the people had learned to distinguish sufficiently between the wrong and the right conception of this solemn act.

What then is the significance of this solemnity? Dr. Bouwman, substantiating his position by a reference to Dr. Bavinck's teachings, gives us in effect the following circumscription: "The laying on of hands is therefore a symbolic act whereby it is signified that the brother concerned has received the necessary gifts of office (through the Holy Spirit) and that these gifts are now dedicated to the service of the Church." And further: "It is a solemn, public declaration on God's part, before the congregation, that the elected brother is lawfully called of God Himself, and is to be regarded by the congregation as His servant; whereas the office-bearer himself is urged by this solemn exercise, to develop the gifts allotted to him, and to use them for the glory of God, and the welfare of the congregation."[1]

All Ministers present at the solemn occasion, according to Article 4, should lay their hands on him who is being ordained. Why? In order to signify that they all, as special servants of God and in His name do testify alike that God has granted the special gifts of the Holy Spirit for the work of the ministry to the brother concerned, that he now dedicates these gifts for office to the ministry of the Word and to the Church calling him, and that the congregation is to

---

1. cf. Bouwman: **Gereformeerd Kerkrecht,** 1928, I, 410, and Bavinck: **Gereformeerde Dogmatiek,** 1918, IV, 418.

receive him as such; and furthermore that all Ministers by this solemn act may urge the brother to apply himself wholly to his glorious work.

Of course, as all symbols, so also this symbol of the imposition of hands is meaningless in itself. He on whom we lay hands must be sincere in his heart and really called of God, if the symbol is to mean anything to him and to the Church. And both he and the Church must understand this beautiful symbol in order to appreciate it.

ARTICLE 5

Ministers already in the Ministry of the Word, who are called to another congregation, shall likewise be called in the aforesaid manner by the Consistory and the Deacons, with observance of the regulations made for the purpose by the Consistory and of the general ecclesiastical ordinances for the eligibility of those who have served outside of the Christian Reformed Church and for the repeated calling of the same Minister during the same vacancy; further, with the advice of the Classis or of the counselor, appointed by the Classis, and with the approval of the Classis or of the Delegates appointed by the Classis, to whom the Ministers called show good ecclesiastical testimonials of doctrine and life, with the approval of the members of the calling congregation, as stated in Article 4; whereupon the Minister called shall be installed with appropriate stipulations and prayers agreeably to the Form for this purpose.

THE CALLING OF THOSE ALREADY IN THE MINISTRY

Article 4 and Article 5 are very much alike. They cover much the same territory and we shall therefore avoid much needless repetition. It will be noted that the matter of examination and the item concerning the imposition of hands provided for in Article 4 are omitted in Article 5. The examination conducted by one Classis is acknowledged by all the others, and therefore in the case of Ministers already in service, letters of testimony take the place of the examination of admission. And the ceremony of the imposition of hands is omitted when a Minister is installed in a new charge, inasmuch as this solemnity is for life, and should therefore not be repeated.

1. The Calling of a Minister to another Congregation.

When one is called and ordained as a Minister of a certain congregation, he is called and ordained for an unlimited period, or if you will, for life. This, however, does not mean that the tie between a Minister and a Church cannot be broken. Various circumstances, such as unfaithfulness in doctrine or life, may terminate the ministry of a Minister in and to a certain Church. Moreover, as the present Article specifies, the tie can also be severed by the acceptance of a call to another congregation. But no Church should call a Minister, united as a servant of God, to another congregation of Christ, rashly. And without weighty reasons no Minister should seek to break the tie, providentially existing between himself and his Church. Circumstances or conditions often enumerated and which may be of sufficient weight for a Minister to seek release from the Church he is serving in order to accept a call to another Church, are the following: When a younger Minister receives a call to a larger or more responsible field; when an older Minister receives a call to a smaller and less strenuous field; when a Minister of average or ordinary ability, after several years of labor in his present Church, receives a call to another field; when constant conflict between a Minister and other consistory members hampers the work of the ministry; when past trouble has left a restricting atmosphere in a congregation; when the salary paid a Minister of a certain Church does not meet the needs of his family, and improvement cannot be made.

Life is full of sin and its results. The evil one does not hesitate to enter the sacred domains of Christ's Church here on earth to exert his baneful influence. Therefore we should not be surprised that evils easily attach themselves to the important work of filling a ministerial vacancy. Some of the evils to be avoided are these: Underhanded, perhaps insincere solicitations of a call; prodding a Minister for some favorable remark about the church building, parsonage, etc.; promising to call without due warrant; calling without due consideration of the suitableness of the Minister; seeking merely a good public speaker, ignoring far more essential qualifications.

In certain denominations the practice of soliciting a call is considered proper. The Presbyterians, for instance, speak of "candidating." Both Candidates and Ministers already serving a certain Church will apply for the ministerial office of a vacant Church, if they so desire.

Amongst us this is not done. Any solicitation of a call would be condemned most severely. Candidates sometimes write to vacant Churches seeking to preach for such Churches one or more Sundays. The same is true for Ministers without a charge but ready to consider a call. (For instance Ministers who were compelled to become emeriti because of impaired health, but sufficiently restored to resume the regular duties of the ministry.) But outright applications for calls are unknown among us. The Reformed Churches have always held that the Church is a very special institution among men, and that its offices are therefore also very special. God calls to office, though through the Church, and none should solicit for its offices, as we do for ordinary secular positions. The Church and its offices should never be put on par with ordinary organizations. In Heb. 5:4 the Word of God tells us: "And no man taketh the honor unto himself, but when he is called of God, even as was Aaron." Some have quoted I Tim. 3:1 in defense of the practice of "candidating" or soliciting. This passage reads as follows: "Faithful is the saying, If a man seeketh the office of a bishop, he desireth a good work." But here the inner desire of the heart should be stressed. The passage does not speak of soliciting for office. One certainly may desire the holy office. One may hold himself in readiness and may prepare himself for service by diligent study of God's Word and the work of an office-bearer. One may certainly bring the matter in prayer before God. But the call must come freely, and in the providence of God, unsolicited.

The practice of solicitation of calls opens the door to a host of evils. If a Minister finds that a change is highly necessary, for example because of his health or that of a member of his family, or for any other reason which he judges to be urgent, then let his Consistory judge, and if the Consistory agrees, let this body seek the advice of Classis in order that the Classis, if it concurs, may announce the brother's predicament to all of our vacant Churches, either by letter directly, or through the Church papers.

Needless to say, great care should be exercised in the filling of a vacancy. There is a great variety of gifts and qualifications amongst those called to the ministry. And there is also a great variety as to the needs and conditions of the Churches. Not every cover fits every dish equally well. Only those should be called to the pulpits of vacant Churches of whom it may be expected that they somewhat fill the needs peculiar to the Church concerned. How should Churches and Consistories go about this all important work? In other words, how can vacant Churches know whom they should call? In many instances they will know of a number of men who can all fill the needs of their Church as well as may be expected in an imperfect world. In that case the Consistory should not begin to look for extraordinary men. So for instance, a Church might call a man of whom it knows next to nothing, but concerning whom it hopes that he may be a power of attraction as a pulpiteer.

If a Consistory is really at a loss, then what should it do? Let that Consistory (by means of a competent committee) inquire from trustworthy, well qualified men, concerning gifts and abilities of men under consideration. In cases of this kind the counselor certainly should not be ignored. Furthermore, if possible, a committee of men well qualified to judge sermons should listen to Ministers under consideration, in their own Churches and report their impressions to the Consistory. Should a Consistory invite men under consideration to preach for their Church? As a rule, not. The Minister preaching under these conditions cannot well be his natural self. He is bound to feel that he is "on the spot." He may well fall far below his natural self, but he may also far exceed his normal self. Let it also be remembered that a flashy, emotional speaker, who is really an inferior preacher of the Word and perchance a careless shepherd, may captivate the majority of a congregation and thus secure a call, to the exclusion of worthier and better qualified men. Moreover, the congregation under these circumstances listens with a very critical ear, detecting every flaw, failing to note the good and the excellent, perchance. The result may be that ultimately the choice of the Church falls on a comparatively unknown man, whose faults are not known, but who is actually inferior to those it has heard. And again neither Minister nor congregation can well worship the Lord as He ought to be worshipped at these "trial" services. The congregational services are sacred and no practice should be permitted which tends to degrade their sacredness.

We would therefore recommend, objective, impartial investigation and consideration of a Minister's past record as expounder of the Word, teacher, and shepherd. This will mean a great deal more than one or two sermons preached on trial.

2. Which "general ecclesiastical ordinances" does this article refer to?

First of all it refers to Synodical rulings regarding the eligibility of Ministers not belonging to the Christian Reformed Church. The latest ruling regarding this matter was made by the Synod of 1928, and confirmed in 1934. Synod ruled, "that henceforth a nomination of a Consistory containing the name or names of Minister (s) of another denomination than the Christian Reformed Church, such nominations must have the approbation not only of the Classis or of the counselor, but also of the nearest Delegates of Examination." (cf. Acts. 1928, Art. 132, and Acts. 1934, Art. 145.)

Those who are required to judge must assure themselves that the

Minister or Ministers concerned are desirable because of their training, doctrinal position, piety, and character. And in case a Minister from another denomination is called, and he accepts the call, then a **colloquium doctum** is held with him before the Classis to which the calling Church belongs. "Colloquium doctum" is a handy Latin phrase which signifies, "a doctrinal conference or conversation." A **colloquium doctum** is therefore not a classical examination. It is meant to be an informal conference to assure the Classis that the brother concerned is doctrinally sound and well-informed. At this conference the Synodical Delegates for Examination are also present as representatives of all the Churches.

As Churches we are not at all exclusive in the evil sense of the word. We bid a hearty welcome to **anyone** who is whole-heartedly in agreement with our position. But we are, as appears from the foregoing, cautious. And rightly so. If we have good reasons for our continual separate existence (and of this none who knows and appreciates the facts aright can doubt), then it is no more than good sense and clear duty to be very careful regarding the admittance of Ministers from other denominations. The more so when doctrinal laxity and lack of distinctive, Biblical Christianity is becoming more popular in many circles as the years go by. (Also see Appendix 1, page 363.)

There is another Synodical ruling which should be mentioned in this connection. It refers to the calling of the same Ministers for the same vacancy within a year. It reads as follows: "A second call to the same Minister during the same vacancy may not be extended within a year without the advice of Classis." (Acts 1906, Art. 35.) This is no doubt a good ruling.

When a Minister after prayerful, conscientious consideration has declined a call, such a decision should be regarded as final, and according to God's will. To repeat the call in less than a year's time would be out of keeping with the solemnity of the whole situation. Yet definite circumstances which compelled a Minister to decline a call may alter suddenly, so that the Minister would be ready to accept the call. If a Consistory hears of these altered circumstances and still desires the brother, then the way should be open for the extension of a second call. The Synodical ruling leaves room for this.

There are also other rulings which our Synods have adopted and which should be mentioned here. Thus Synod of 1916 ruled that "Consistories shall not nominate Ministers who have served their present Church for less than two years, unless special weighty reasons exist; and a counselor who approves of such a nominee must give account of his reasons to Classis." (Acts 1916, Art. 30.) Strictly speaking, there is no time requirement. Any Minister, including the theological professors at our seminary and other Ministers who have been appointed to special positions, any Minister in good standing, is eligible to a call. Theoretically everyone of our Ministers is eligible to a call at all times, even when he has just been installed in a new charge. This concerns the inherent right of every Church. But experience has taught us that it is good to have some general rule. Therefore Synod of 1916 ruled as it did. This is a good rule. Thus far all of our Consistories have taken due note of it. Generally speaking, very short pastorates are not to the welfare of the Churches. And yet there are exceptions. But the rule leaves ample room for these exceptions.

Another Synodical ruling passed in 1884, states: "If a Minister serves a Church only a year, and the moving expenses have exceeded fifty dollars, the calling Church shall refund to the Church he leaves, three-fourths of the expenses; if he serves only two years, one-half; if three years, one-fourth of the moving expenses. This decision shall be incorporated in the letter of call." (Acts 1884, Art. 52; Acts 1890, Art. 63.)

Synod of 1926 decided that when a Minister leaves one Church for another, his new Church becomes responsible for his salary from the day that he preached his farewell sermon in the Church he left, unless other arrangements are made. This is no doubt a fair arrangement. But it should not be necessary for a Synod to regulate all these details. We should avoid rule upon rule, and precept upon precept. Multiplicity of rules tends to exert an unwholesome hampering effect on our ecclesiastical life. And Synod as a rule should spend its valuable time considering major matters, matters touching the maintenance and development of spiritual life and should cultivate true appreciation for our Reformed principles.

3. Advice and approval of Classis.

The advice of Classis is prescribed in Article 5, just as in Article 4, and for the same reasons. (See our discussion under Art. 4, first section.) Article 4, concerning itself with the calling and induction into office of those who have not previously served, provides for classical examinations. Article 5 regulating the calling of men already in the ministry, omits the provision for examinations, but provides for "the approval of the Classis or of the Delegates appointed by the Classis." This Classical approbation is here demanded for reasons already considered. Who are the "Delegates appointed by the Classis"? Whenever possible Classis should give or withhold its approbation of a call accepted directly. Whatever the assemblies (Consistories, Classes, Synods) can do themselves they should never delegate to committees. To avoid abuse and assumption of power, that is, to safeguard true presbyterianism and sound church government. But sometimes a Minister accepts a call, just after Classis has met. It would entail hardships if the calling Church would have to wait for Classis to meet again. Therefore the Church Order permits approbation by means of delegates. In every Classis so-called "Classical Committees" have been charged to do this work. Classical committees are standing committees, usually consisting of three Ministers, who are charged to do certain labors, performed by Classis directly if in session. Classical Committees with vague and general charges find no support in our Church Order. It would be wiser and safer for Classes to appointed committees as occasion requires. These committees should receive special, well defined instructions. At any rate, every Classis should stipulate very clearly just what the duties and powers of its classical committees are. But it is noteworthy that originally Article 5 did not permit approbation of calls through a committee. Even today the Church Order redaction of the Reformed Churches of the Netherlands does not allow for approbation of calls through committees. The Synod of 1905 of these Churches, assigned this task to two neighboring Churches. These two neighboring Churches notify all the other Churches of Classis that the question of approving a certain call (accepted) will be decided upon at a certain place, day, and hour. All the Churches of the Classis are invited to be present. As a rule of course, no objections are entertained and the two Consistories merely approve of the call and the installation, etc., for the whole Classis. It cannot be denied that our way of working is much simpler. But neither can it be denied that the method of the Holland Churches is safer. Our fathers learned by experience that hierarchical dominance easily creeps in through standing committees and so-called Church Boards. And it is evident that whenever authority must be delegated it is more in harmony with Reformed Church polity, to delegate such authority to minor assemblies, (Consistories and Classes) than to boards or committees. And doubtless usurpation of power and unwarranted influence is thus rendered less probable.

Which documents must be present at a Classis which is asked to approve a call accepted? Jansen enumerates five, namely these:

a. The letter of call, with the original letter of acceptance, so that Classis may be sure that no undesirable or sinful restrictions have been made.
b. A testimony from the Consistory of the Church which the Minister has served declaring that said Consistory has agreed to the acceptance of the call, and has dismissed him as Minister. Without this official release and dismissal no other Church may receive him. (cf. Art. 10, Church Order.)
c. Membership certificate regarding doctrine and life (cf. Art. 5, Church Order) testifying that the departing Minister is sound in both doctrine and life.
d. Proof of regular dismissal from the Classis in which he served. No Church being permitted to receive him unless he has been dismissed also by his Classis. (cf. Art. 10, Church Order.)
e. A testimony from the Consistory of the calling Church that the call has been duly submitted for approbation to the whole congregation (cf. Art. 5, Church Order) and that no valid objections have been registered against the brother's ordination. (If objections were registered, but overruled by the Consistory the objector can of course always appeal to Classis, and if he so desires to Synod.)[1]

4. The installation.

The Church of Rome does transfer its officers from one congregation to another, but never re-installs them. The prerogatives and duties of an ecclesiastical officer according to Rome, are indestructible. But according to the Reformed conception the offices are all local in character. One is an Elder or Deacon of a local Church, of a certain congregation, never of Churches in general or of a whole denomination. Hence also Ministers are called by and ordained by local Churches. Consequently when a Minister assumes the ministerial office in another congregation, re-installation is in order. Only the ceremony of the imposition of hands, as we have noted previously, is not repeated.

ARTICLE 6

No Minister shall be at liberty to serve in institutions of mercy or otherwise, unless he be previously admitted in accordance with the preceding articles, and he shall, no less than others, be subject to the Church Order.

MINISTERS SERVING INSTITUTIONS OF MERCY, ETC.

1. The burden and intent of Article 6.

Article 6 provides that no Minister shall have the right to accept an appointment as spiritual worker in an institution of mercy, or a like institution, unless he has actually been called to this work, just

1. Jansen: **Korte Verklaring van de Kerkenordening**, 1923, p. 29.

as a Minister is called to the Ministry of a congregation. In other words, whether a Minister has an ordinary sphere of labor (Minister of a local Church), or an extraordinary sphere of labor (such as spiritual worker in a hospital) he must be called as stipulated in Articles 4 and 5 of the Church Order.

It is implied in Article 6 that he who accepts an appointment to do ministerial work in some Christian institution without a call according to Articles 4 and 5 of the Church Order, thereby forfeits his office. And no one can lay claim to the office of the ministry just because he does ministerial work, unless he has first been lawfully called and charged. Furthermore, it is specifically stipulated that Ministers who have extraordinary charges and fields of labor must submit themselves in all things to the Church Order. What holds for regular Ministers holds for them as well. In this connection it is to be noted that Synod of 1918 decided that: "Spiritual advisors for institutions shall be called by a neighboring Church in consultation with the respective Board." (cf. Acts 1918, Art. 37.)

A decade later the Synod ruled as follows: "Synod rules that the status of a Minister, who labors officially in non-ecclesiastical institutions of charity is covered by Article 6 of the Church Order; that all non-official work performed for such institutions, as for instance, the collection of funds or solicitation of membership, whether the Minister be in active service or retired, is covered by Article 12 of the Church Order and is in conflict with "being bound to the service of the Church for life," and not in harmony with Article 13 nor Article 14." (cf. Acts, 1928, Art. 37.)

2. General principles basic to Article 6.

In the first place, the Churches can recognize only one kind of Ministers of the Gospel. Not two kinds, one of which is charged and called by the Churches, and the other appointed by some organization or group of individuals. The Church can recognize only those as Ministers of the Gospel who have been lawfully called and charged by the Church of Jesus Christ, and who also live and work in agreement with, and submission to the Church Order. All this for the simple reason that the Bible knows only of one kind of Ministers; namely, those who have been lawfully called to office.

Secondly, even as one cannot be an Elder or Deacon without being Elder or Deacon of a particular local Church, so one cannot be a Minister without being such of a particular local Church, though one's charge as a Minister may be very special.

3. Ecclesiastical position of Ministers serving as hospital pastors, etc.

According to the present article, when an institution desires the full-time services of one of our Ministers that institution should go to a neighboring Church and ask the Consistory of that Church to call a Minister for the work they have in mind. If the Church asked is satisfied with the considerations and needs presented and the stipulations promised, it can proceed with the calling. And this procedure, should be more than a mere formality. The regular, most common way would, of course, be that the Consistory nominate and that the congregation elect. However, in most instances the management of an institution might prefer to select a Minister. In that case the Consistory, after due consideration, could approve of the institution's nominee and then announce to the congregation that the brother will be called unless valid objections are registered with the Consistory.

Even the decision to call a Minister for the extraordinary duties in question, should certainly be submitted to the congregation for its approval. It is the Church that calls, though through those already in office, and under their direction, and therefore the Church must also decide to call. The Consistory can call a congregational meeting for this matter, or in many instances it may be sufficient to announce to the congregation that in answer to a request received, the Consistory is minded to call an extra Minister to labor in the institution indicated, and that all members who have any valid objections to the proposed plan, are requested to report at the next Consistory meeting.

It should also be definitely understood that by requesting a Consistory to place a Minister in their institution, the authorities concerned are placing the work of the Minister under supervision of that Church. This does not mean that the Consistory would arrange the schedule of work to be done by the Minister, the hours, etc., for the institution. Adequate stipulations regarding formal matters should be made at the time when the agreement between the institution and the calling Church is made, and the institution should certainly be permitted at all times to manage its own affairs. But the Consistory very definitely stands responsible for the character and nature of the Minister's work, and should exercise supervision.

Furthermore, a Minister who accepts a call as now under discussion, should be considered a member of the calling Church and Consistory, though his charge would be very special and different from the charge of the regular congregational Minister. So, for instance, a hospital pastor is rightfully a member of the Consistory which called him. And as a member of the Consistory he should be allowed his full rights. For example: It is his right and duty to preside at Consistory meetings when his turn comes (Art. 17) and to go to Classis, either as delegate or as advisory member (Art. 42). And as far as his special task permits he is subject to Consistory work. For Article 6 clearly provides that "no less than others" he shall be "subject to the Church Order." In every case a definite understanding should be reached at the time a special call, according to Article 6, is about to be accepted. And, of course, every case should be considered and acted upon as circumstances require. We have simply indicated what the Church Order stipulates regarding extraordinary pastorates in general. But in writing up any agreement or schedule, the Church Order should not be ignored and arbitrarily suspended. Today we have a number of Ministers doing extraordinary ministerial work who have no close contacts with any Consistory and cannot even be delegated to our major assemblies. They form a class of Ministers shorn of certain rights and duties which are definitely theirs. We are convinced that this is contrary to the best interests of the Churches and the Ministers concerned. To mention no more, the work of these Ministers is not controlled as the work of other Ministers is.

4. Does this article also govern the ecclesiastical position of Ministers who are teachers of Reformed doctrine or Bible history in our high schools and colleges?

We believe that it does. Not that this matter was in the minds of our fathers when this article was first framed. But inasmuch as the teaching of the subjects referred to is very definitely ministerial work, just as much so as the pastoral work of a hospital pastor, and as this article plainly states: "No Minister shall be at liberty to serve in institutions of mercy **or otherwise** . . . . .", and inasmuch as the intent of the article is not to regulate the ecclesiastical position of one particular class of extraordinary Ministers, but rather the ecclesiastical position of extraordinary Ministers in general, therefore we believe that Article 6 should be applied to Ministers who act as Bible teachers.

ARTICLE 7

No one shall be called to the Ministry of the Word, without his being stationed in a particular place, except he be sent to do church extension work.

DEFINITE FIELDS OF LABOR.

1. The historical origin of this article.

Article 7 finds its origin in the fact that the Reformation Churches had to guard themselves against certain self-appointed itinerant preachers. Many of these refused to be connected ministerially with any local Church. They wanted to travel from place to place as they saw fit. They appealed the example of the Apostles and evangelists, forgetting and ignoring the fact, that the Apostles and their helpers, the evangelists, occupied a special temporary office being ordained of God for the establishment of the New Testament Church; forgetting and ignoring also that Acts 13:1-4 tells us very definitely that great men like Paul and Barnabas were sent forth by the Church of Antioch. The Synod of Dort, 1574, ruled that preachers without fixed charges should submit themselves to a Classis for examination. Then if they received a call they could be properly installed to labor in the Church calling them. And the Synod of 1578, (also Dort) definitely declared itself against all itinerant preaching as in vogue at that time. The Synod of Middelburg, 1581, decreed that none should be permitted to go from place to place, having no fixed charge, without the consent and authority of Synod or Classis. This Synod therefore judged that itinerant preaching might be necessary and advisable, but no one should decide this question for himself; not even a local Church should act for and by itself, but Synod or Classis should judge whether or not work of this type is necessary. And the Synod of 's Gravenhage, 1586, decided that work of this kind should be done amongst Churches which, due to persecution, had no Ministers, and perhaps even lost their Consistories, and often lived in "dispersion", away from home. "Gemeenten onder het kruis," they were called, i.e. Cross-bearing Churches. Furthermore this Synod specified that the work of gathering Churches in general required traveling Ministers. Doubtless our fathers were thinking in this connection of mission work amongst those still under the sway of Rome.

2. The significance of the Article.

The original of Article 7 was written in 1581 by the Synod of Middelburg. "No one shall be called to the Ministry of the Word, except he be stationed in a Church which he shall serve." Article 7 therefore clearly enunciates this principle that the call to the ministry always implies a definite connection with the calling Church. The local Church calls (Art. 4, 5) and that for labors within its own confines.

Article 7 thus placed the Churches in opposition, first of all, to the Roman Church which ordains men in general, without uniting them to a local Church. It also condemns the mode of procedure followed by the Churches of the province of Friesland in former years. The Friesian Churches ordained men at their Synodical or Classical gatherings, without a call from a local Church. The fallacy of this procedure was clearly seen by the other Churches and the Friesian Churches in due season conformed themselves to the true Reformed principles regarding this matter. The offices in the Church are specific, not general. Recall that one cannot be an Elder or Deacon except he be Elder or Deacon of a local Church. The same holds for the ministerial office. Without the locally instituted or organized Church the offices simply do not exist. Therefore Article 7 specifies "No one shall be called to the Ministry of the Word, without his being stationed in a particular place."

3. **The exception.**

But there is an exception. The assemblies at which our Church Order was written felt that itinerant preachers, i.e., Ministers who would devote all their time to home mission work or evangelization work, might be very necessary. And so the clause "except he be sent to gather Churches here and there" was added. This original reading of the exceptive clause of Article 7 is somewhat broader than our present reading. The present reading speaks only of Church extension work, which ordinarily refers only to "home missions;" i.e., the organization of new Churches amongst those already believers and in most instances members of some Christian Reformed Church, but living in communities where no Church of ours is found. The original reading of the clause makes it applicable to all types of mission work. The present reading should therefore be allowed a broad interpretation.

Note well that the exceptive clause does not alter the fact that a Minister is called by a Church, and not by Classis or Synod. The exceptive clause concerns itself only with the field or sphere of labor of Missionary Ministers, not with their calling or ordination. The calling and ordination to the ministry has been regulated in Article 4 and Article 5. What these articles contain stands. Article 7 does not alter these matters in the least. It is well to note the significance of the articles just preceding the present, in order to see the connection and train of thought. Article 3 specifies that none shall be permitted to preach unless he be lawfully called. (Even as no one can go as ambassador from our United States to a foreign land unless he be lawfully called or appointed.) Articles 4 and 5 specify that this calling to the ministry is exercised by the local Church, albeit with the guidance of the Consistory. Article 6 adds that this one and only mode of calling also holds for Ministers laboring in institutions of mercy, etc. And then Article 7 specifies still further that a call to the ministry is always for a definite field of labor, except when a Minister be called for mission work. Hence the exceptive clause in Article 7 does not imply that Missionary Ministers can be called and ordained and installed by Classes or Synods.

In this connection it may be well to warn against an erroneous approach to the Church Order. When you take a passage of God's Word and begin to explain it without any consideration for the rest of the chapter, you are almost sure to make the Bible say what it does not say. The Bible is a unit. When you explain a passage you must do so in the light of the chapter and the book in which it is found. In fact, nothing of what God has said may be ignored. Only when a particular passage is explained in the light of the whole Word can you expect a correct interpretation. So it is to a certain extent with our Church Order. The Church Order is a unit. It is not a systematic presentation of Reformed Church polity, but is expressive of fundamental principles pertaining to Church government. And these principles, fundamental to the various articles of the Church Order, may not be ignored when you begin to interpret individual articles. If you do, you will make the Church Order say what it does not mean to say. And you will even make it contradict itself again and again. The result will be mistaken notions and a sorry confusion, and in practice you will consequently blunder again and again.

From our interpretation of Article 7 it follows that we cannot agree with our Synod of 1930, which held that the "calling and sending, as also the regulation of the labors, of ordained Missionaries is the task and the right of the Consistory, Classis, or Synod engaging in that particular mission activity." (Acts 1930, p. 143.) We see no chance of substantiating this pronouncement with the Church Order. We are convinced that Articles 4, 5, and 7 gainsay this deliverance.

Does this mean that more than one Church cannot co-operate in calling and sending Missionaries? Not at all. Two or more Churches may enter into close and definitely stipulated co-operation for the selection and calling of a Missionary. But the provisions of Articles 4, 5, and 7 should not be brushed aside. One Church must always be designated as the executer for all the rest. To this Church, the brother called will stand officially responsible. And this Church also will initiate disciplinary action in case the Missionary Minister should become delinquent. When matters are arranged thus, in harmony with the rules of our Church Order, confusion and irregularity will be avoided.

So also a Classis cannot call and ordain, though it can carry on mission work as a Classis. But one of the Churches must again be appointed as executer for all the Churches of the Classis. And Synod of 1936 certainly did the right thing when it provided in the new home mission order, that although Synod (i.e., all the Churches of our denomination) may select Missionaries, the actual work of election, ordination or installation, shall be delegated to the local Churches appointed for this purpose. With these local Churches the Missionaries then stand in close and actual relationship as executers for all the Churches concerned. This method of procedure is in harmony with our Church Order, and the basic principles of our Reformed Church polity. In practice this method of procedure will work out too. For instance, if a Classis or Synod would actually call and ordain, who could act with real responsibility and authority if an emergency should arise while these assemblies are not in session?

ARTICLE 8

Persons who have not pursued the regular course of study in preparation for the Ministry of the Word, and have therefore not been declared eligible according to Article 4, shall not be admitted to the Ministry unless there is assurance of their exceptional gifts, godliness, humility, modesty, common sense and discretion, as also gifts of public address. When such persons present themselves for the Ministry, the Classis (if the [particular] Synod approve) shall first examine them, and further deal with them as it shall deem edifying, according to the general regulations of the Churches.

ADMITTANCE TO THE MINISTRY OF THOSE WHO LACK SPECIAL PREPARATION.

1. Why is it the position of our Churches that its Ministers shall be seminary graduates?

It is the rule of our Churches that only those who have prepared themselves adequately by completing a satisfactory seminary course, shall be admitted to its ministry. This rule is not embodied into a separate article but is implied in Article 8. Admittedly, a good training at a good theological school does not necessarily make a good Minister. There are certain qualifications for the sacred ministry which the best theological school can never give. Such are those enumerated in this article, namely: godliness, humility, modesty, common sense, and discretion. And even the gift of public address is not merely a matter of training. True it is, that training may foster and greatly develop these gifts of God, but in and by itself, a theological course will make no one godly, humble, modest, etc.

It is this latter truth which our fathers realized full well. They did not agree with certain mystical groups, such as Quakers, Dunkers, Darbyites, and many Anabaptists, who taught that all scholastic training for the Ministry of the Word was unnecessary and even cumbersome in many cases. Some said that the Holy Spirit did not need scholastic learning for the accomplishment of His purposes. (Who of us would care to deny this claim in the abstract? But is that the point?) Others even said that learning was trash which hindered the Spirit in His work.

But our fathers knew better. They realized that without the gifts of God and the calling of God mere school training is vain. But they also realized that a knowledge of the language which God used when He gave the Holy Scriptures by inspiration, was, to say the least, highly desirable. Furthermore, they knew that a thorough acquaintance with the Sacred Scriptures, and a broad knowledge of human history, ideals and tendencies, and a well disciplined intellect were all requisites for good ministerial work. They were not unmindful of the fact that Jesus virtually gave His disciples a three year training course before He sent them out as Apostles. And that in the providence of God, Paul sat at the feet of Gamaliel, and had a very thorough general training before God called him for his great task.

Neither did our forbears feel free to ignore Paul's injunction to Timothy: "And the things which thou hast heard from me among many witnesses, the same commit thou to faithful men, who shall be able to teach others also." (II Tim. 2:2.)

2. Why do our Churches have the ruling of Article 8?

When times are extraordinary for the Church of God, scarcity of fully prepared Ministers is apt to occur. So, for example, at the time of the Reformation there was a crying need for Ministers. Many congregations were without regular Ministers year after year. In many communities the Church remained unorganized for want of leadership. Thus also when the Reformed Churches of Holland left the corrupted State Church a half century ago, there was a great need for Ministers. At such times the Churches should be at liberty to ordain of their most worthy and able men, though they lack a thorough and systematic training. For as we have noted, scholastic training for the ministry is highly desirable, but not indispensable.

In the second place: In His sovereign good pleasure God sometimes endows some of His children with extraordinary gifts and qualifications for the ministry, though they have not followed a prescribed course and are therefore deficient in scholastic training. When God qualifies a man for the ministry by endowing him with excellent and extraordinary gifts for that office, then to be sure the Church of Christ is in duty bound to recognize this fact with appreciation. The rule is and should ever remain to be: Those that feel called to the ministry must follow the prescribed course of study. But at the same time the door must ever remain open for such as God graciously qualifies for service without special training.

3. The exceptional gifts of Article 8.

Article 8 speaks of "exceptional gifts, godliness, humility, modesty, common sense, and discretion." The present redaction of the Church Order of the Reformed Churches of Holland, corresponds to our reading. However, the original Latin text of the Synod of Dort, 1618-19, would require that we place a colon (:) after the expression "exceptional gifts." The correct interpretation of this Article therefore requires that we look upon the expression, "godliness, humility, modesty, common sense and discretion," as a specific enumeration of what is meant by "exceptional gifts." That is to say, he who would come under the rule of Article 8, must excel in godliness, humility, modesty, common sense and discretion. He must not only have all these characteristics, but he must be exceptionally gifted with respect to them.

Several authorities have called attention to the incorrect punctuation of our present day redactions of Article 8 on this score. Jansen, Bouwman, H. H. Kuyper and Heyns all agree with the interpretation as just indicated.

The first exceptional gift mentioned is **godliness.** The Latin expression is "pietas," i. e. one who is pious, godly, moved by a reverence for God, filled with consecration to God. This, to be sure, is the primary requisite. Next, **humility,** from the Latin original "humilitas," is mentioned. Godliness must be accompanied by humbleness of heart. One who is exceptionally gifted stands in danger of becoming proud in word and deed. He is also in danger of over-estimating his gifts and abilities. Lack of humility would disqualify one for the ministry, though he might be exceptionally gifted otherwise. Next **modesty** is enumerated. The Latin word is "modestia," which really indicates morality. Doubtless our Dutch translation "zedigheid," is to be preferred above our English "modesty." The concept "modesty" is closely akin to humility, the previous characteristic. However in the original modestia seems to refer to a well-balanced, well-controlled life, a life strictly moral. Then follows **common sense.** In Dutch we find "goed verstand," and in Latin "excellens ingenium." Just why our English translation has rendered these expressions "common sense' is not clear. The present Dutch, as well as the Latin original certainly refers to intellectual ability. Doubtless we should think in this connection of keenness of intellect which is so essential for the correct interpretation of Holy Writ. As our reading now stands, this very essential qualification for all Ministers is not mentioned in Article 8. Perhaps our translators, and Synod of 1920 which ratified this translation, felt that expression "exceptional gifts" did not refer to godliness, modesty, etc., but to other gifts not mentioned by name. And in that case one would, under the circumstances, think first of all of intellectual gifts. But as we have said, the original Latin text simply does not leave room for this interpretation. Furthermore, **discretion** is mentioned. The Latin here is "prudentia," and the Dutch "discretie."

This word refers to clarity and soundness of judgment, i. e. the ability to judge between true and false, right and wrong. Finally the enumeration closes with **"gifts of public address."** Latin: "eloquentia;" Dutch: "gaven van welsprekendheid." These original expressions do not signify that the applicant must be eloquent of speech as we now understand this term. But he must be able to express himself well in public address. He must be able to address people with ease, clarity, and in orderly fashion, without serious faults.

(Also see Appendix 2, page 365.)

4. The procedure to be followed for admittance to the Ministry according to Article 8.

The last sentence of Article 8 states in a general way how an aspirant to the ministry under this article should proceed. The "general regulations" of which the very last clause speaks were officially adopted by the Synod of 1922. These regulations specify in greater detail what the exact mode of procedure should be.

We reproduce these rulings as rendered by Stuart and Hoeksema. (Rules of Order, pp. 24, 25).

(1) If anyone desires to be admitted to the Ministry of the Word according to Article 8, he must apply to his Consistory and after that to his Classis. This Classis, in conjunction with the Delegates for Examination of three adjacent Classes, first examines the written credentials of the Consistory concerning the required qualifications stated in Article 8 and subsequently itself investigates in this respect. If the preliminary judgment is favorable, he shall be given the right to speak a word of edification for a limited time in the vacant churches of his Classis. He must also speak a few times in the non-vacant Churches in the presence of the respective Ministers of these churches. Classis shall regulate these appointments in conjunction with the Consistories of those churches. Classis determines the length of this period of probation.

(2) At the close of the period of probation the Classis, in conjunction with the said Delegates for Examination, takes a final decision regarding the presence of exceptional gifts. If the decision is in the affirmative, then the Classis shall take a peremptory examination in the following branches:
   a) Exegesis of Old and New Testaments;
   b) Bible History;
   c) Dogmatics;
   d) General and American Church History.

(3) In case of favorable issue, he is declared eligible to a call.

(4) The examination for ordination follows later according to existing rules, except the classical languages. Acts 1922, Art. 37, X. (Agendum 1920, pages 26, 27.)

It will be noted that one who would become a Minister according to Article 8 must have a knowledge of the facts far above the average, even though he has never attended high school, college, or seminary.

We should consider it a favor of God when He from time to time qualifies certain brethren for the ministry through the abundant indwelling and blessings of the Holy Spirit, without the ordinary course of study.

On the other hand, let us ever appreciate a sound and thorough theological training, and let us ever hold in high esteem scholastic attainment and a thorough preparation for the ministry.

And let us likewise remember that even for Ministers so exceptionally gifted that they were admitted to the ministry without having completed a theological course, a theological training would not have been an item of luxury. For they will always be somewhat handicapped for lack of it, and would be abler workers in God's vineyard, had they enjoyed its advantages.

ARTICLE 9

Preachers without fixed charge, or others who have left some sect, shall not be admitted to the Ministry in the Church until they have been declared eligible, after careful examination, by the Classis, with the approval of Synod.

ADMITTING CHURCH-LESS PREACHERS OR LEADERS OF SECTARIAN GROUPS

1. The historical background of this article.

In the unrevised Church Order of Dort Article 9 reads as follows: "Novices, priests, monks, and others that have left some sect, shall not be admitted to the service of the Church (as Ministers) except with great carefulness and due consideration (groote zorgvuldigheid en voorzichtigheid), and after they have been on probation for some time."

The word "novices" with which this reading of Article 9 opens is taken from I Tim. 3:6. The Apostle enumerating the required qualities for a bishop, says, "Not a novice, lest being puffed up he fall into condemnation of the devil." Our forebears apply this expression in this connection to such as recently turned their backs upon the Church of Rome, or upon the Anabaptist groups.

At the beginning of the Reformation it took real courage and conviction to leave the Church of Rome. But after the storm of persecution began to subside, and when the Reformed Churches of Holland received official recognition of the government, many insincere and unworthy individuals having served in the degenerate Church of Rome, sought the ministry in the Reformation Churches. Consequently, the Churches had to exercise the maximum of care regarding these numerous applicants. The Synod of Dort, 1574, already decided: "Die monniken ofte Papen geweest zijn, en zich tot de Kerkendienst begeeren te begeven, sal men niet toelaten dan van de Classe geexamineert zynde. . ." (Art. 20.) The element of classical examination is not specifically mentioned in the redaction of 1618-19, but has been re-incorporated in our reading of 1914.

The priests who sought admittance to the Reformed Churches as Ministers were as a rule "vagabond priests," priests who were indeed ordained to office but who had no fixed charge. They preached and baptized, etc., so Voetius informs us,[1] wherever opportunity offered itself. Their work fell largely amongst migratory groups such as fishermen, hunters, traveling small-tradesmen, inland boatsmen, etc. The Reformed Church acknowledged the baptism administered by these vagabond priests inasmuch as they held office in the Church of Rome. (Our fathers looked upon the Roman Church as being fearfully cor-

1. Voetius, Pol. Eccl. III, 660. cf. Bouwman: **Gereformeerd Kerkrecht, 1928, I, 441.**

rupt, deformed, teaching and practicing God-dishonoring and un-Biblical doctrine, but they did not deny that at heart it was a manifestation and representation of the body of Christ. Consequently, they acknowledged the baptism administered by those duly appointed by the Church of Rome.)

Monks belong neither to the clergy, nor to the laity with Rome. They form a class of men which are under certain strict vows, promoting sanctity and service, so they hold. Monks were therefore not ordained to office by Rome and consequently the Reformation Churches did not acknowledge Baptism administered by them.

Inasmuch as they were often men of theological learning, they could be admitted to the ministry as far as their knowledge was concerned. But the Churches had to exercise the utmost care with them. Many were insincere and unworthy. Those that left the Anabaptists also required a great deal of caution. The Anabaptists believed neither in regular office-bearers nor in special training for the work of the ministry. Leadership in their service was open to all. Some of their leaders could not even read or write. Consequently, the Anabaptists, leaders and followers, were extremely weak in Scriptural understanding; and erroneous, subjective conceptions were common. It stands to reason that the Churches had to use much discretion and care in the admittance of this class of applicants to the ministry.

But times and circumstances have changed. The applicants with which Article 9 in its original form concerned itself, are virtually nonexistent today. However our Churches in the United States of America did meet with problems regarding the admission to the ministry, kindred to those of former centuries and which were governed by Article 9. Consequently, our Synod of 1914 revised this article to cover the new situation.

2. To which classes of applicants our present redaction of Article 9 refers.

In the first place Article 9 speaks of "preachers without fixed charge." This phrase refers to Ministers, not of the Christian Reformed denomination, but of some other Reformed denomination, who for some reason are no longer serving their congregation and who seek to enter our pulpits and are desirous of obtaining a call from one of our Churches.

It has happened in the past that a Minister would make his appearance in our midst, uninvited and unlooked for, (as a rule hailing from the Netherlands) and would begin to work for a call. With fluency of speech and pleasant manners the favor of more than one vacant Church would be gained. Yet upon close investigation by counselors or Classes, it sometimes appeared that the man in question was not at all desirable. But not all vacant Churches would always believe the findings of those who investigated, and trouble, even permanent division would result. (cf. the Van der Valk episode of a few decades ago.)

The second type of applicants for the ministry in our Churches referred to in Article 9, are designated as "others who have left some sect." This clause refers to such as have left some group or sect, and claim that they have changed their views and have forsaken their errors and now wish to be admitted to the ministry of our Churches. In many cases, however, sad to say, these have proved to be insincere. The men concerned were only looking for a livelihood it seems.

And yet an occasional one of these two classes of applicants may be worthy. Now Article 9 points the way to worthy applicants of these types. And, above all, it constitutes a safe-guard for the Churches against unworthy individuals.

3. How can applicants referred to in Article 9 be admitted to the ministry in our Churches?

Such applicants must apply to a Classis of our Churches, and ask the Classis to declare him eligible for a call. This, however, no Classis may do unless it has first made a careful investigation. This careful investigation includes more than an examination of certain credentials which the applicant may carry with him, for these may be spurious, false, or not true to fact, or incomplete.

Furthermore, Classis must examine him, and may declare him eligible for a call, only after having gained the approval of Synod.

These are strict rules, but past experiences have taught the Churches to be very careful and strict.

ARTICLE 10

A Minister, once lawfully called, may not leave the congregation with which he is connected, to accept a call elsewhere, without the consent of the Consistory, together with the Deacons, and knowledge on the part of the Classis; likewise no other Church may receive him until he has presented a proper certificate of dismission from the Church and the Classis where he served.

Article 5 stipulates how a Minister serving one Church, may be called by another Church. Article 10 does not repeat the stipulations of Article 5, but the present article tells us how a Minister receiving a call from another congregation should proceed if he desires to accept the call. In post-Reformation days, as Jansen remarks, there were itinerant, self-appointed preachers who transgressed in the threefold way. First, they began to preach without an examination, and without a calling; against this evil Articles 3 and 4 were formulated. Secondly, these irregular preachers insisted on traveling from place to place and refused to become the Minister of a certain Church; with a view to this evil Article 7 was adopted. Thirdly, these men, if they did not accept a call to a certain Church, would leave their Church when they grew tired of it and when they saw fit, without consent of the Consistory or Classis; against this irregularity Article 10 was adopted.

1. Conditional and unconditional calls.

Originally Article 10 read as follows: "Een Dienaer, eens wettelycken beroepen zijnde, mach de Ghemeente, daarhij sonder conditie aanghenomen is, niet verlaten. . . ." That is, "A Minister once lawfully called, may not forsake the congregation which accepted him without conditions. . . . ." The words "without conditions" were left out of the Church Order as revised in 1905 by the Churches of Holland. In the early days of the Reformed Churches of Holland, calls were often issued conditionally. Some Ministers were forced to leave their regular congregations to save their lives. They would remove to another territory where the persecution was not pressed. Often this would be across the national borders. Some regularly organized Church or some refugee Church might desire the services of one of the refugee Ministers. In such a case the call letter would stipulate that the Minister was free to return to his own Church when conditions would permit. But there was a second reason why calls were often extended with a condition attached. Since there were no regular training schools for the ministry many Ministers were not very competent, and hence Ministers were often called to serve for a certain period on trial. If they proved to be undesirable because they lacked knowledge or did not study sufficiently, or did not show Christian consecration, no permanent call was issued.

When persecution ceased, and when only those were called to the Ministry who had previously been declared candidates, there was no longer need for the provision of conditional calls. Moreover, conditional calls, so it was judged, were not ideal. For emergency situations they are permissible. But for ordinary circumstances the best interests of the Church of Christ requires that calls be for a definite period. Unconditional calls are also in full harmony with Scripture since Prophets and Apostles were called of God for life. However, if ever the conditions become extraordinary once more, or if any Church finds itself in extraordinary circumstances, conditional calls would be permissible. Needless to say, no Classes should ever approve of conditional calls unless there are very extraordinary and weighty reasons.

2. The duty of a Minister toward the Church he is serving, when he desires to accept a call to another Church.

A Minister "may not leave the congregation with which he is connected" without consent of his fellow office-bearers in the Church which he is serving. In Dutch the expression "niet verlaten" is used. This does not simply mean "not to leave", but "not to forsake." It is the same word that Scripture employs when it tells us that husbands shall not forsake their wives. There is a bond of union between a Minister and his flock, which is, not identical with the bond of union between husband and wife, but which is akin to the marriage bond. Pastor and flock belong together. And not without prayerful weighty reasons should this bond be broken.

Neither is it up to the Minister alone to decide that he must sever his connections with his Church. Article 10 clearly and specifically states that no Minister shall accept a call to another congregation except his fellow office-bearers of the Church he is serving (Consistory and Deacons), give their consent. In other words, Article 10 prescribes that when a Minister comes to the conclusion that he should accept a certain call, such a Minister must inform the Consistory and the Deacons and seek their consent. It stands to reason that the Minister is required to state, in a general way at least, why he feels that he should accept the call in question. How else could the Consistory and the Diaconate reach a conscientious decision?

In their considerations the Elders and Deacons may not be governed by personal favor or antipathy, but only by the facts at hand. The glory of God through the coming of His Kingdom should control them also in this case.

If ever the Elders and Deacons feel that they should not give consent, and when a frank and mutual discussion fails to change the mind of a Minister as well as that of the Elders and Deacons, then the case goes to Classis for disposal.

It is rather remarkable that this very plain stipulation of our

Church Order is almost completely ignored in our Churches. To the best of our knowledge the great majority of our Ministers, when they wish to accept a call, simply notify the Church whose call they are accepting, and then give notice to the Church they are serving. Others accept and then ask consent of the Consistory by way of asking ministerial credentials, of which anon.

Yet the way prescribed in Article 10 is the only correct procedure. The tie that binds the Minister and his Church was not made, as far as human factors are concerned, merely by the Minister, but by him and the office-bearers for the congregation. It is no more than reasonable that both parties also co-operate when the tie is severed.

It stands to reason that it would seldom happen that a Minister, after prayerful consideration, would feel that he should accept a call, that then his fellow office-bearers would refuse to release him. But it is worthy of note that many years ago it often happened (namely in the Reformed Churches of the Netherlands), that a Minister desired to accept a call to another Church, but that the decisions of Consistory and Classis were contrary, so that he continued to labor in the Church which he thought he should leave.[1]

3. Approval on the part of the Classis also required.

Article 10 here prescribes that a Minister who desires to leave his charge in order to accept a call to another congregation, must also notify his Classis. This notification should precede the actual, official acceptance of a call. This is clear from the wording of Article 10, for it plainly states that a Minister shall not accept a call to another Church without the knowledge of Classis. This provision aims at more than a mere notification for information.

The fact that Article 10 requires more than a formal notification to Classis is also evident from the original Dutch wording. It uses the phrase "met voorweten van de Classe." Now the expression "met voorweten", fully rendered in English would read: "with prior knowledge of." The Minister who desires to accept a call to another Church must therefore seek consent from his Consistory not only, but also the approval of the Classis. And that before he notifies the calling Church that he has accepted their call.

Why should a Classis have this opportunity? Because the Classis has a very definite interest in the matter. There may be so many vacancies in the Classis or in the neighborhood of the Church which the Minister concerned is serving, that in the estimation of the Classis he cannot well be spared at that time. Classis may also judge that the continued labors of that particular Minister are very desirable in the Church which he is serving.

This acknowledgment of Classical rights would not prohibit a Minister from sending a provisional letter of acceptance to the Church concerned. He should notify the Consistory of the calling Church that he has determined to accept the call of their Church; that his present Consistory has given its consent; and that he is seeking classical approval. In our day a matter of this kind would go directly to Classis if a meeting of Classis is near at hand. If not, the matter would go to the Classical Committee, which in most Classes is charged by Classis to act for it in such matters between sessions of Classis.

---

1. For instances see Bouwman: **Gereformeerd Kerkrecht,** I, pp. 444, 5.

4. Certificates which a Minister must present to the Church having called him, before he can be installed.

Article 10 mentions two certificates which a Minister must present to the Church in which he is to be installed. One from the Church which he has just served, and one from the Classis to which this Church belongs. Certain official and important matters require official documents. This is for the safety of all concerned. Mere verbal assurances are sometimes unreliable.

What should these certificates certify? According to Article 5 these certificates must give testimony to the fact that the Minister concerned is sound as to doctrine, and worthy and desirable as to his conduct. Or as Article 5 literally states, he must show "good ecclesiastical testimonies of doctrine and life."

In the case of a Minister changing from one Church to another, when does his term of office officially cease in the Church he is leaving, and when does it begin in his new charge? Synod of 1926 ruled that, "When a Minister changes pastorates, the new Church becomes responsible for his salary, etc., from the day of his farewell in the former charge, unless some other terms were agreed upon between the Minister and the new Consistory (as, for example, in the matter of a vacation.)" Acts 1926, Art. 57, p. 7.

Should a Minister entertaining a call from another Church always confer with his Consistory, and ask the brethren whether in their opinion he should continue his labors with them or accept the call? If the Minister is fully persuaded that his Consistory is anxious to have him continue his labors with them, such a consultation is hardly necessary. But as a rule it is no doubt advisable that the Minister consult his fellow office-bearers. A frank discussion and a frank vote may be very beneficial for him. If a Consistory really feels that a change would be good for both Minister and congregation they should be fair and frank enough to say so. And it stands to reason that a Minister should not lightly ignore the opinion of his Consistory, although the decision rests with him and not with the Consistory. That is to say, if a Minister is persuaded in mind and heart that God would have him continue his labors in the Church he is serving, then he must decline the call under consideration, even though the Consistory should desire to see him go.

ARTICLE 11

On the other hand, the Consistory, as representing the congregation, shall also be bound to provide for the proper support of its Ministers, and shall not dismiss them from service without the knowledge and approbation of the Classis and of the Delegates of the (particular) Synod.

SUPPORT AND DISMISSAL.

This and the foregoing article are closely related. Article 10 stipulates what the obligations of a Minister toward his Church are. He may not forsake his Church. Departure for another field of labor must be in keeping with the rules adopted, including consent of the Consistory of the Church he desires to leave. Article 11, on the other hand, specifies the Church's duty toward its Ministers. It may not forsake him. He is entitled to proper support, etc.

1. Proper ministerial support.

Why do our Churches stipulate in the present article that our Ministers must be properly supported? In the first place from considerations of expediency. It is to the best interest of the Churches that their Ministers receive sufficient support. If our Ministers were not supported by the Churches which they serve they would have to support themselves. This would prevent them from giving all their time and attention to the all-important work of the ministry. Insufficient support would compel the Ministers concerned to seek other means of income with which to augment their insufficient salaries.

Now it is not below the dignity of any man to engage in some secular art or trade. Not at all. It was not below the dignity of the great Apostle Paul to do the work of a tent-maker at Corinth. (Paul, let us remember, plied his trade of tent-maker at Corinth because of a certain narrow, unwholesome, critical spirit which prevailed there. He supported himself so that none could say that Paul sought himself, and so that the Gospel might have its free course. (cf. I Cor. 9:12.) Neither would it be below the dignity of any one of our Ministers or theological professors to work in an office or factory; to run a farm, carpenter shop, or grocery store. But it is very emphatically inadvisable. Ministers should give all their time and thought and energy to the great and glorious calling which is theirs. If they do not, the Churches are bound to suffer spiritually. Therefore Churches must see to it, if at all possible, that Ministers do not have to forsake their calling in the least. Let the words of I Cor. 6:12, "All things are lawful for me, but all things are not expedient", also be remembered in this connection.

Secondly, Churches should properly provide for their Ministers because Scripture demands this very specifically. When Jesus sent forth His disciples to preach the Gospel of the Kingdom, He said that they needed not to make prior provisions for their needs, ". . . for the laborer is worthy of his food" (Matt. 10:10). And again, "the laborer is worthy of his hire." (Luke 10:7). In I Cor. 9 Paul tells us that proper support of those that labor in the Gospel is the natural and normal thing. He shows us that the principle which would dictate this support is operative in the natural realm, as it was also by God's decree in the spiritual service of the Old Testament dispensation. And then he concludes with the unmistakable dictum: "Even so did the Lord ordain that they that proclaim the Gospel should live of the gospel" (I Cor. 9:14).

Furthermore, the primary application of the much quoted passage, "Be not deceived, God is not mocked: for whatsoever a man soweth, that shall he also reap," (Gal. 6:7) pertains to the proper support of those that labor in the Gospel.

What does the Church Order mean when it speaks of proper support? He who receives a salary which permits him to work with undue worries, and with reasonable comfort, may be said to receive proper support.

It may also be said in this connection, that the term "proper support", from the nature of the case, includes more than the bare necessities of life. For example: a Minister certainly should be able to pay off his student debts. He should also be able to buy books constantly. And books as a rule are expensive. He should also be able to give liberally, as a good example to others. And for the sake of his calling he should be able to present a neat appearance.

Local and individual circumstances should also be considered by a Church when it seeks to determine which salary to pay. For instance, the prices for food and clothing are not the same for every section of the country. And some have small families, whereas others have large families. We have heard of one of our Churches which called its Minister for a certain stipulated sum, plus $100 for every dependent child in the family. This basic salary plan is also in operation in some of the Reformed Churches of the Netherlands. Missionaries of various denominations have for years been paid according to this plan. We certainly would endorse it, inasmuch as it appears altogether just and in strict harmony with the present article.

Would it be wise and just to work for uniform salaries? Some have contended that it would be. But there simply is too much variation as to living expenses between the various localities in which our Churches are found; between city and rural communities; and between small families and large families. And every Minister, according to Article 11, should receive enough to support himself and his family. The exact amount should be determined according to local and individual conditions.

Let us not fail to acknowledge, however, that there has been, and that there still is too much irregularity. Some Ministers receive much larger salaries than others; in some instances twice as much as others, although the needs and requirements are equal. In general it may be said that we should remedy this situation by urging all our Churches to do their utmost, and by giving substantial subsidies to weak Churches in order that these may bring the salaries of their Ministers to a proper level. Large and strong Churches should ever be ready to help their small and weak sister Churches. The words of Holy Writ: "Bear ye one another's burdens, and so fulfill the law of Christ." (Gal. 6:2), were not only written for individual Christians, but also for Churches.

Each Church is at liberty to gather the salary of its Minister as it sees fit. However, money raising schemes such as bazaars, baked-goods sales, etc., to which many Churches of our land have resorted, stand condemned. The giving should always be voluntary and from a motive of love and duty toward the Kingdom. Most of our Churches for some years past have employed the budget system for all their congregational expenses, including the salaries of Ministers. Weekly contributions are made by means of "budget envelopes." The budget contribution, it should be remembered, is also a gift, not a payment of an ecclesiastical tax. No Consistory may assume to tax the members of its Church. All our giving for the Church should be held on a high plane. Giving for the Church of God should also be an act of worship, gratitude, and joy. He who gives under compulsion misses a real blessing, and dishonors God and His Church. Consistories, on the other hand, may and must admonish those who fail to give according to the measure of prosperity which God has given them. But mere taxation should not be tolerated in God's Church. Consistories may and should inform the congregation as to the amount needed to cover the budget. But a member should not feel that he has done his full duty if he has given the average of what is required per family in order to "raise the budget." Some can and should give far more than the average for the sake of those that cannot nearly reach the average.

In former years, both in Europe and in America, the Minister's salary would be raised in part at least through the renting of pews. Some Churches still have this practice. The custom has met with increasing disfavor, however, and rightly so. It is not in harmony with the Lord's admonition as found in James 2:1-5. Some Churches maintain "family pews" although not charging pew-rent. Definite pews are assigned to each family. This practice has much in its favor. Parents and children belong together in God's providence. Why should they separate, as is often done in our Churches today, when they worship God in His house? Our present custom of free pews for all, has points in its favor, but it also has its defects. The assigned pew plan would at least keep parents and children together in worship. And that would also promote attentiveness and good order on the part of the growing youth.

If a Minister should be a man of means, then would his Church nevertheless be obligated to support him? I Cor. 9 leaves no room for doubt. It clearly teaches that such as labor in the Gospel are entitled to live by the Gospel. There is no intimation at all that such as have other means of subsistence, are not entitled to support. Also, during Old Testament times the Priests and Levites received tithes regardless of their personal circumstances. This was by command of God. Hence we take it, our Church Order makes no exception, but simply states what the Churches should do in all cases. The moneys to which their labors entitle Ministers of some means (to be sure a rather hypothetical class of Ministers as far as our Church is concerned) these moneys are theirs, to use or to give away as they see fit, and concerning which they shall have to render an account before God. Of course, if any Minister of means desires to labor for but a small salary, or for no salary at all, that would be entirely his business. And in case the Church concerned should happen to be a poor struggling Church, good-will of this type certainly would be very commendatory.

2. Dismissal from service.

Dismissal according to Article 11 is not suspension, and far less is it deposition. (cf. Art. 79 and 80.) A dismissed Minister is one who has been debarred from his ministerial rights and duties in the Church whose Minister he is. Or again, a dismissed Minister is one who is not allowed to exercise his ministerial duties in his own Church. As far as the active execution of his duties in his own Church is concerned, a dismissed Minister is a debarred Minister. He has been barred from his ministerial work in and for his Church. If any other Church asks him to preach for them or to work in their midst, he is fully at liberty to do so. He is also eligible for a call from another Church.

Troubles and difficulties may arise which make it impossible or undesirable that a Minister continue to serve his Church, even though these troubles and difficulties are not of such a nature that the Minister must be suspended (depriving him temporarily of his ministerial rights for the whole denomination), or that he must be deposed. (Again cf. Art. 79 and 80.) Now Article 11 provides that in such a case the Consistory can notify Classis of the sad state of affairs and seek the approval of Classis for its desire to debar their Minister from exercising his ministerial rights and duties in and for their congregation. If Classis, together with the three Synodical Delegates, deems debarment necessary or advisable, it so decides. Proper notice of this action is then made and notice is given to the Churches that the brother is permitted to preach the Word and to administer the

Sacraments elsewhere, and that he is eligible for a call from any Church which may desire his services. As a rule the dismissing Church agrees to pay the Minister part of his salary for a few months to come.

This article does therefore not apply when a Minister is doctrinally unsound or wanting in his Christian conduct. Dismissal may never be substituted for suspension or deposition. Neither may Article 11 be used when a congregation or Consistory desires to "get rid" of its Minister for insufficient and unworthy reasons. But this article does apply when the relationship between a Church and its Minister has become so strained that real co-operation seems impossible, or when the congregation refuses to support him (wrong though this may be in and by itself), or when it is evident that he cannot be a blessing unto the Church concerned because of past happenings. It may be that wide differences as to character constantly make for trouble, or that a certain Minister lacks native ability to labor successfully for many years. Situations may arise which do not call for suspension or deposition, but very definitely for dismissal.

During the first century after the Reformation, Ministers were sometimes transferred by the Classes from one Church to another. As Church life became better regulated and close supervision was exercised over those who sought the ministry and their admission to office, different situations regarding Ministers and their Churches began to decrease, and transference was less necessary. But, more important, it was also recognized that this latter procedure was really hierarchical, Roman Catholic in origin, and not Reformed. Consequently a concluding provision of Article 11, which permitted a Classis to transfer a Minister from one Church to another in case he was not supported properly, was dropped by the Reformed Churches of Holland in 1905 and also by our Churches in 1914. The provision, let it be said, had been obsolete and out of practice for many years.

Why may no Consistory discharge its Ministers from active service in its Church without the knowledge and approbation of the Classis and of the Synodical Delegates? To guard against abuse. When a congregation is in a disturbed condition and feelings run high, abuse so easily creeps in. Often the parties most intimately involved and concerned can not judge objectively. They may speak and act very unjustly, though hardly aware of it. And unjust debarment of Ministers from the execution of their God-given calling is, of course, always calamitous for both Ministers and congregations, and an evil against which we must safeguard ourselves.

Furthermore, the Minister concerned will object in every case well nigh. Also when there is just cause for debarment. Consequently Classis must decide as the logical and best qualified and authoritative third party.

And, not to be forgotten, no one is merely Minister of his own local Church. He has received the privilege to preach the Word and to administer the Sacraments in any Church of the denomination. (Only upon proper request, of course.) In fact, he has been placed in office with the approval of Classis. No local Church, as long as it lives under the Church Order, can ordain a man to the ministry in and by itself. Neither can it depose, suspend, or debar a Minister from his office without the approval of Classis.

What is the standing of a Minister who has been dismissed from his charge? He continues to be a Minister of the local Church which he was serving, but he has been barred from exercising the rights and duties of the ministerial office in his own congregation. He awaits a call from another congregation. When a call comes which he accepts his ministerial certificate will state the facts of his case objectively and briefly. With the acceptance of a call to another Church he ceases to be a Minister of the Church he is leaving.

The relation of a debarred Minister toward his Church is therefore akin to that of an emeritus Minister to his Church. The latter was **excused** from active execution of his ministerial duties, although he continues to be a Minister of the Church concerned. For instance: If an emeritus Minister should have to be deposed, this sad task would fall to the Consistory of the Church he served last and its Classis, would it not? So also the debarred Minister officially continues to be Minister of the Church that debarred him.

In case no call is forthcoming, the debarred Minister will ultimately lose all his ministerial rights. His abnormal position can, from the nature of the case, be only temporary. By force of circumstances he would sooner or later "enter upon a secular vocation" (Article 12), inasmuch as his Church cannot be expected to support him indefinitely, and because the position of a debarred Minister is from its very nature temporary.

ARTICLE 12

Inasmuch as a Minister of the Word, once lawfully called as described above, is bound to the service of the Church for life, he is not allowed to enter upon a secular vocation except for such weighty reasons as shall receive the approval of the Classis.

Article 12 in the first place posits the principle that a Minister is bound to the service of the Church for life. Next the article states a rule which follows from this principle of service for life; namely, that a Minister may not enter upon a secular vocation. Thirdly, the article allows for exceptions to the rule that Ministers may not leave the ministry to engage in a secular calling.

1. The principle of life-long service.

The Roman Church teaches that the nature of the ecclesiastical office is such that he who once receives the office can never lose it. The office and the office-bearer are inseparably united for life. Consequently, when an office-holder in the Roman Church makes himself unworthy of his office, that office is not taken from him, but he is merely prohibited from exercising it.

This is not our position. Yet we hold that a Minister "is bound to the service of the Church for life." Why? In the first place because this is Biblical. Even in Old Testament days Elijah, Isaiah, Jeremiah, and other Prophets were called to the Ministry for life. The disciples also and the apostles and evangelists were "separated" unto their ministry, not temporarily, but permanently, for life.

Scripture also indicates that the service of the Word demands our undivided love, (John 21:15-17; II Cor. 5:14) our full time, (John 9:4) our readiness of will, (I Cor. 9:16, 17) our unfailing perseverance (II Tim. 4:1-6) and our complete separation unto the work (Rom. 1:1).

In full harmony with this principle of life-long service it may be noted that the internal call to the ministry in the heart of the future Ministers, is always interpreted to be a call for life.

Let it also be remembered that the dignity of the office of the ministry of the Word is advanced by appointment for life. And it is also true that young men can hardly be expected to go through a course of training extended over many years unless they can look forward to the ministry as a life-long work. (Also see Appendix 3, page 365.)

2. What the term "secular vocation" signifies.

The word "secular" is here used in contrast with "spiritual," and is applied to things belonging to this world and man's life upon this earth from its material, temporal aspect.

By secular callings we therefore understand arts and trades which pertain primarily to the temporal things of life. Such are all occupations and positions which do not belong to the gospel ministry in its primary form, (the preaching of the Gospel in regularly organized Churches, or to people not yet believers), not to the gospel ministry in its secondary and derived forms, (such as held by professors of theology, teachers of Bible, Ministers at institutions of mercy, etc.). School teachers, farmers, lawyers, builders, etc., therefore perform secular vocations.

Needless to add, the Church Order does not mean to imply that secular vocations should not be performed spiritually. "Whether, therefore, ye eat, or drink, or whatever ye do, do all to the glory of God" (I Cor. 10:31).

3. Why does the Church Order allow for exceptions to Article 12?

As noted above, the ministerial office is not irrevocably united with the person of the Minister. Nowhere in Holy Writ do we find a rule which would uphold this view. The office-holder can lose his office. Ministers are called and ordained for life in harmony with Biblical example and the nature of their internal calling and for reasons of great desirability. But conditions may arise, in the providence of God, because of which a Minister is warranted to leave his office. For example: a Minister might be called to fill an important chair in a Christian college; or to occupy a very responsible position in the government of his country; or a Minister may be compelled to assume a secular position when upon debarment according to Article 11 he receives no new field of labor. Another may find that he lacks the necessary gifts and qualifications for the ministry, and thus feels himself bound in conscience to withdraw. Still another may be so disturbed and handicapped by doubts as to his divine calling to the ministry that ultimate withdrawal from office is permissible and advisable.

But withdrawal from office is a very serious matter. Our fathers felt that the matter was so all-important that it should not be left merely to the Minister's own judgment. And not even to that of the Minister and his Consistory. In all cases the judgment of Classis must be sought, and no withdrawal from the ministry is permitted to take effect without its approval. And to this the Reformed Churches of Holland have added in 1920: "Welk oordeel de Classis niet zal uitspreken zonder kennis en approbatie van de deputaten der Particuliere Synode." This means that in Holland today no Classis can sanction withdrawal from the ministry without prior approval of the delegates of the Particular Synod. This provision is altogether in harmony with the Reformed principle of denominational unity. It should also be added that the Churches of Holland by the addition of 1920 merely restored what the early Reformed Churches had written into Article 12, but which had been eliminated in later years. It might be well to incorporate this provision in this article by adding to it: "not without the approval of the Synodical Delegates." It affords additional safety against abuse, and even as the Churches in general were recognized through their Synodical Delegates when the Minister in question was admitted to the ministry, so also these Churches should be recognized when the Minister concerned wishes to leave his office.

We have already indicated some reasons for leaving the ministry which may be termed worthy and sufficient. But the motives of those who desire to enter upon a secular vocation are not always worthy and sufficient. As unworthy and insufficient reasons for leaving the ministry we note the following: Seeking to escape the burden of the work of the ministry; aggravated by troubles in the Consistory or Church, or both; desiring greater financial income and luxuries of life; craving for greater honor and social prestige; seeking to escape confession, etc., after one has fallen into sin and abuse of office.

4. Entering upon a secular vocation without consent.

What should a Church and Classis do when a Minister forsakes his office and engages in a secular vocation without proper sanction or contrary to the decision of his Church and Classis? They should admonish the brother concerned, and endeavor to show him the error of his way.

It may happen that a Minister resigns from office and that the Consistory and Classis really feel that he is unfit for the ministry. In such a case these bodies might be tempted to let matters run. This, however, would be against the Church Order. In such a case the brother concerned should be urged to seek release from office in the regular way. Respect for the high office of the ministry and for the good order of the Churches demands this. No one should ever be permitted to trifle with the office of the ministry.

Anyone who persists in resigning from office and refuses to seek release in the prescribed way, or who persists in resigning his ministerial office contrary to the decision of his Consistory and Classis, such a one should be suspended and if need be, deposed from office. (cf. Art. 80.)

Jansen[1] answers the question whether a Minister, who forsakes his office contrary to the mind of his Consistory and Classis, becomes subject to discipline or not, negatively. He states that one who deserts his office may have to be censured as an individual member, but that he cannot be disciplined as an office-bearer. With this latter judgment we disagree. Jansen finds that the phrases "faithless desertion of office or intrusion upon that of another" as found in Article 80 (which article indicates sins "worthy of being punished with suspension or deposition from office") do not require or permit discipline for those who leave the ministry unlawfully. In his judgment Article 80 refers only to Ministers who leave their own Churches and begin to preach and work elsewhere, without forsaking their ministerial office as such. But this interpretation of Article 80 is faulty. To be sure, he who leaves his own Church and begins to work and preach elsewhere is guilty of "faithless desertion of office". But so is he that enters upon a secular vocation without just cause and contrary to his Consistory and Classis. Article 80 as we now have it was essentially already adopted by the Weselian Convention, 1568, the very first general ecclesiastical assembly of the Church of Holland. In the Weselian rules our present "faithless desertion of office or intrusion upon that of another," reads: "oneerlijke onderkruijpinge van een

1. Joh. Jansen: **Korte Verklaring,** etc. 1923, p. 55.

anders plaatse, verlatinge zijnes Dienst en zijne Gemeynte sonder wettelijke toestemminge," (Wesel, Chap. VII, Art. 14). The matter of Article 80 is covered in Article 10 of the Church Order of 1578. The rule of 1568 was rewritten by the Synod of 1578, but no essential changes were made. In this Church Order the phrases in which we are at present interested, read as follows: "trouloose verlatinge sijnes Dienste en indringinge in eens anders dienst." Three years later, Synod of 1581, another very slight change was introduced in the expression under discussion. The connective particle "en" was changed to "ofte", resulting in the following reading: "trouloose verlatinge zijnes Dienst, ofte indringinge in eens anders Dienst." Synod of 1618-19 left the article unchanged on this point. And thus it stands today. We believe that the foregoing facts clearly indicate that Article 80 of our Church Order, refers not only to those who would leave their own Churches to begin preaching elsewhere, but also to those who leave their Churches without doing ministerial work elsewhere. Consequently we hold that according to Article 80, he who resigns or forsakes his office unlawfully becomes subject to discipline as an office-bearer.

It is worthy of note that the older readings of Article 80, including the redaction of 1618-19, divide the two members of the phrase just discussed by means of a comma. This comma is not found in our present Church Order editions. Perhaps the loss of the comma has helped to promote an unhistorical interpretation of the stipulation.

Dr. Rutgers [1] does not commit himself on the question, whether deserters from office are subject to discipline or not.

This having been said, we add that in real exceptional cases, when the situation is somewhat dubious, or when extenuating circumstances are clearly present, a Consistory and Classis may be at liberty to acquiesce (submit quietly) in the fact that a Minister has assumed a secular vocation. A dismissed Minister, for instance, not receiving a call from another Church, may feel himself compelled and in duty bound to assume a secular vocation. Circumstances may be such that a Consistory and Classis dare not find fault with the brother, nor demand of him that he seek release from office in the regular way. But at all events the responsibility for the brother's step should be left to him. The Consistory concerned should declare to the Churches that the party in question has entered upon a secular vocation entirely upon his own responsibility and that the Consistory and Classis have decided to acquiesce, and that the brother is therefore no longer a Minister of the Gospel.

Almost needless to say, those who leave the ministry for a secular vocation lose all pulpit rights. They may not serve in the Churches as exhorters, unless special permission is granted. And no Classis should extend this privilege unless the brother concerned left the ministry with full approval of the ecclesiastical bodies involved, and unless there are very weighty reasons for extending this privilege. And to be sure, the Churches must request this privilege. No one should receive permission to exhort as a personal favor.

---

1. cf. Rutgers: Kerkelijke Adviesen 1921, and College-voordrachten, Gereformeerd Kerkrecht, 1918.

ARTICLE 13

Ministers, who by reason of age, sickness, or otherwise, are rendered incapable of performing the duties of their Office, shall nevertheless retain the honor and title of a Minister, and the Church which they have served shall provide honorably for them in their need (likewise for the orphans and widows of Ministers) out of the common fund of the Churches, according to the general ecclesiastical ordinances in this matter.[1]

Article 11 regulates dismissal from service. Article 12 concerns entrance upon a secular vocation. The present article concerns emeritation. The word "emeritus" is Latin and was formerly used of a Roman soldier "who had served his time, a veteran." An emeritus Minister is therefore one who has served his time, one no longer in active service. Lately the terms **superannuated** and **emeritus** have been used among us.

A standard dictionary tells us that to superannuate signifies: "to incapacitate by age; retire on account of age." This same authority defines emeritus as follows: "retired from active service (as on account of age), but retained in an honorary position; as, pastor emeritus." From this it appears that we should persist in the use of the words emeritus and emeritation. For the specific meaning of these words harmonizes with our position regarding retired Ministers as expressed in Article 13.

1. Valid reasons for emeritation.

Two valid reasons for emeritation are specifically named in this article: age and sickness. When one becomes too old to perform his office properly, emeritation is in order. The Church Order does not designate a definite age. Some denominations permit their Ministers to retire at 65, others at 70. We are glad that our Churches have never named a definite figure. Some men are older at 60 than others at 75. Also here God is our sovereign disposer. And so every case should be judged on its own merits. We surely need earnest and experienced leaders. And a hard and fast rule would rob the Churches of some of their best qualified leaders. Would anyone think of barring men from our legislative, executive, and judicial halls at Washington, D.C., just because they reached a certain age? Of course not. For it is a fact that the real leaders in the affairs of our nation are as a rule elderly men. Even at 80 and older, some statesmen are still active and influential.

The tendency on the part of our Churches, and of other Churches as well, "to shelve" older Ministers, is partly due no doubt to the Ministers themselves. They should keep abreast of their time, and remain aggressive and persistently seek to apply the truth of God, not merely according to conditions as they were known during bygone decades, nor merely to needs which are common to every century of Christianity, but also to contemporary conditions and problems.

However, the tendency under consideration is due in no small measure to spiritual shallowness on the part of our Churches. A good speaker, though he be a poor pastor and lacks spiritual depth and earnestness, is to many a "good Minister." And a man with average

---

1. Synod of 1939 adopted a new reading of Article 13. See note appended to our discussion of this article, page 67.

speaking abilities but with exceptional pastoral qualifications, spiritual depth, judicious judgment, and a wide experience, is often referred to as "no good." The younger man who with oratorical flash and catch phrases preaching a topical sermon, is much preferred by many to an older man, who expounds and applies the Word of God to his flock, and who by means of thorough expository sermons brings to view the jewels of God's eternal truth and the treasures of heavenly comfort and direction.

Who would try to deny that this attitude reveals spiritual shallowness? Do not interpret these comments to be mere indictments of our people. For, as has been indicated, the responsibility for this spiritual shallowness must, to a large extent, be placed at the very doors of the Ministers themselves. For are not they the spiritual leaders and teachers of our people? Of course, we should not forget that there are extenuating circumstances. The spirit of the age is against our Ministers. We live in an age and land of shallowness. Again, many of our Ministers are too busy with all kinds of activities which lie at best on the periphery, and not at the center of the circle of their responsibilities as Ministers. Many of them lack time for the best pulpit work of which they are capable. But it is no less true that our Ministers have yielded too much to the spirit of the age, and they have digressed somewhat from thorough and fervent expository preaching. They have catered to the shallowness of some, perverting their tastes still more, and starting others in that direction constantly.

Now this whole situation has led us to depreciate to an unwarranted extent many of our abler older Ministers. But, for all that, we need them and they can be of very valuable service to us. For this reason a hard and fast rule as to age of retirement should not be made. Article 13 is specific enough. The remedy for undesirable situations does not lie in the direction of "shelving."

The second valid reason for emeritation specifically named is sickness. Little need be said in this connection. Continued illness as a rule naturally renders a Minister incapable of performing the duties of his office.

After mentioning age and sickness, the Church Order adds, "or otherwise." This refers to conditions pertaining to the person of the Minister, just as age and sickness do. For the expressions are clearly kindred. The word "otherwise" simply refers to conditions which can be justly classified with old age and sickness. For example: nervous break-downs, permanent bodily injury, etc. Let it also be said that aged Ministers should not serve too long. If the advancing years or the increasing weaknesses of old age hinder a Minister from doing justice to all the work that is required of him, he ought to seek emeritation. He may not sacrifice his church's welfare for his own benefit. And our Churches should never exact the utmost from our Ministers. To demand that a Minister continue to serve to the bitter end of his life, during his fast declining years, is neither charitable nor wise. Let us not forget in this connection that our retired Ministers can still serve the Churches in a variety of capacities. They are not doomed to fruitlessness and inactivity just because they have been relieved from strenuous duties.

2. The standing of emeritus Ministers.

The emeritus Minister, so the Church Order stipulates, retains the "honor and title of a Minister." In other words, he remains in office.

If the phrase meant anything less than that, no emeritus Minister could administer the Word and the Sacraments.

Furthermore, he continues to be the Minister of the local congregation which he last served. For no one according to Reformed Church polity and our own Church Order, can be an office-bearer, except he be such of a particular Church or congregation.

What, then, is the standing of an emeritus Minister? Simply this: He is a full-fledged Minister of the Gospel of the Church which he served when he became emeritus. But he has been excused from the active execution of his ministerial duties. He does not have to preach. But he may if requested to do so. He does not have to attend Consistory meetings. But he may, if he is asked to do so. His relation to his Church even permits of his delegation to Classis and Synod.

True, many emeritus Ministers leave their Church and become members of some other Church. But even so, he continues to be the Minister of the Church he served last. This is also plain from the fact that if ever deposition from office would become, necessary, this would be the task of said Church and the Classis to which it belongs. The emeritus Minister who removes from his congregation remains officially connected with this Church as a Minister. As an individual member he can join the Church to which he moves. He may even serve the Church to which he removes after emeritation, as Elder or Deacon. But as a Minister he remains with the Church he last served as Minister.

These opinions let it be said, are not at all new or original with us. They follow logically from the fact that the particular Churches are our ecclesiastical units, and that Reformed Church polity does not know a big super-Church of which one can be a member, and of which the particular Churches are but sub-divisions. Church membership attaches itself to the particular Churches and not to the denomination as such. The same principle holds for the offices recognized and maintained by us. And to be sure, these opinions have the full backing of men like Rutgers, Bouwman and Jansen.

3. Extent of support to which our emeritus Ministers are entitled.

Up to the year 1939 Art. 13 stipulated that "the Church which they served shall provide honorably for them in their need." From a comparison of this statement with the article as it now reads it will be noted that the words "in their need" were lifted out of the article in the year indicated above. For more than one reason we have allowed our comments on the phrase "in their need" to stand. The phrase and our comments have at least some historical value.

Here is what we wrote on this point before the deletion of 1939:

"What is the meaning of the phrase 'in their need' as it occurs in the present article? On this question there has been a difference of opinion for many years. Some say that the expression "in their need" stands on par with "proper support," as spoken of in Article 11, concerning the support allotted to Ministers in active service. According to these, Article 13 provides that our emeritus Ministers or their dependents are entitled to full support, whether they are in need of this support or not.

"Others hold that the expression 'in their need' refers to actual needs, needs which exist because the parties concerned have no other means of support.

"We are convinced that the latter group is right. We believe that the correct interpretation of our Church Order demands that we interpret the phrase "in their need" literally, i.e., the Churches concerned are in duty bound to see to it that emeritus Ministers and their dependents shall not suffer want, but can live honorably and comfortably.

"Three considerations favor this interpretation:

"(1) The adverb "honorably" in the phrase points to the fact that our fathers were anxious that their incapacitated Ministers should be able to live honorably. Not that they should be supported by the Churches concerned, even if the Minister in question had an income sufficient for him and his dependents;

"(2) The Synod of Dort, 1618-19, adopted in essence Article 13 as it now reads. But this great Synod merely approved of and restated what previous Synods had already agreed upon. For example: The Synod of Dort, 1578, decreed: '. . . dat sij den overighen tijd hares levens eerlick toebrenghen moghen.' That is to say, '. . . that they may be able to conclude their lives in an honorable way.' Synod of Middelburg, 1581: '. . . dat hem soo veel toegheleijt werde, daarop hij de reste zijns levens eerlick en bequamelick door comen moghe.' That is: '. . . so much shall be given him, that he may be able to finish his life honorably and satisfactorily.' Synod of 's Gravenhage, 1586, gave the following renderings: '. . . eerlijcken in haren nooddruft versorghet worden.' And this rendering was approved of or adopted by the great Synod 1618-19. And thus we have it today. '. . . provide honorably for them in their need.'[1]

"The renderings given above, basic to what we have today, prompt us to favor the literal reading of the term 'in their need.'

"(3) The expression is a translation of the original: 'in hunne nooddruft.' Admittedly this word is all-important for the present question. According to Van Dale's dictionary it means: 'dringende behoefte, datgene wat tot onderhoud van het leven noodig, is, levensbehoeften, levensmiddelen.'

"Furthermore, common usage of the words 'nooddruft' or 'nooddruftig' still refers to actual needs, and not to mere support or cost of living. (cf. Van Dale's Groot Woordenboek).

"Moreover, the etymology of the word 'nooddruft' demands that we favor the literal interpretation of the expression 'in their need.' What does the origin of the word 'nooddruft' reveal? Prof. J. Vercoullie in his **Beknopt Etymologisch Woordenboek der Nederlandsche Taal**, tells us concerning this word: 'het tweede lid is een afleiding van **durven;** het geheel—**dringende behoefte.**' And the word 'durven' stands related, so this same authority says, to 'derven,' which according to its primary meaning signifies, 'ontberen,' 'noodig hebben.'

"Does this interpretation of Article 13 imply that our emeritus Ministers receive gifts of charity? Not at all. They continue to be full-time ordained workers in God's Church, though either temporarily or permanently unable to perform their duties. And even as the Priests and Levites shared in the tithes and offerings of the people, though unable to perform their duties by reason of age or sickness, so our incapacitated Ministers receive their just dues, and not charity.

"And yet the Church Order makes a distinction. Article 11, concerning Ministers in active service, speaks of **proper support,** but Article 13 speaks of **provision of needs.** Virtually the position of the Church Order is this: If the amount allowed, during the period of active service, is sufficient to cover the period of inactivity also, good and well. But if the salary paid proved to be just enough for the needs of each year so that the Minister upon emeritation is still in need of support, then the Church is in duty bound to give this. How much? Enough to rule out want and distress and to make a decent living possible.

"And if any emeritus Minister should have another source of income sufficient to make a decent living possible, then the Churches are not in duty bound to pay such a Minister anything toward his support, inasmuch as he is no longer actually laboring in the Gospel, and has the means for an honorable living at his disposal.

"Upon which grounds does the Church Order stipulate that emeritus Ministers shall be honorably provided for in their needs? Ministers are required to give all their time and thought, and their whole life, to the Church and its task. The Churches do not allow them to provide for the future through some money-making side-line. This is as it should be. But then it also follows upon a principle of common justice and fairness, that the Churches assure them the necessities of life. Consequently the Churches have obligated themselves to see to it that their incapacitated Ministers receive their necessities of life, also then when their years and strength are spent. To this support he is also entitled for his dependents who may need this help after his demise.

"Furthermore, I Cor. 9:14, "Even so did the Lord ordain that they that proclaim the gospel should live by the gospel," and kindred passages noted when we discussed Article 11, certainly do not restrict support to those still healthy and active.

"Yet, the Church Order, according to our interpretation, does not say that the Churches must support their emeritus Ministers if the sufficiency of life and comfort is already theirs. Why not? It seems to us that the difference between that which the Scriptural principle warrants and what the Church Order prescribes is to be explained by the fact that our fathers did not care to demand their ultimate rights. In matters which did not violate a principle as such, they often were big-hearted, and would take a self-denying attitude. For this they deserve our admiration. Moreover, in keeping with this our Church Order often displays a remarkably well-balanced judgment. The provision of Article 13 we deem to be an example of this. They felt that a difference between active and inactive Ministers was in order. And so the first class the Church Order entitles to full support, whatever their personal circumstances, but the inactive by reason of old age or sickness, it entitles to that which constitutes their actual needs."

The words "in their need" were deleted from Article 13 by the Synod of 1939 inasmuch as this Synod approved a plan which divided the Emeritus Fund into two distinct funds, known as Pension Fund and Relief Fund.

According to the plan of 1939, as amended by the Synod of 1946, all Ministers in active service who desire to participate in the Pension Plan, contribute 3½ percent of their annual salary toward the Pension Fund, in return for which all Ministers upon their emeritation will receive an amount out of the Pension Fund equaling 50 percent of the current average salary of the Christian Reformed ministry, or their widows 40 percent. Those who need more than the amount allowed as pension money, are to receive additional support out of the Relief Fund.

(Also see Appendix 4, page 365.)

In case a Consistory finds that its Minister can no longer discharge his office properly by reason of age, sickness, etc., that body may take the initiative. The Consistory need not wait for the Minister to make the first move. The Reformed Churches of Holland adopted the following rule at their Synod held in 1893: "Emeritation, where necessary, takes place upon the request of the parties concerned, (either Minister or Consistory) by action of the Classis, supported by the Synodical Examiners of the Provincial Synod."

Neither is it necessary to wait until both parties, the Minister and the Consistory, can agree on the question of the Minister's emeritation. In case of disagreement they can simply let Classis decide.

To the common fund mentioned in this article, all the Churches are expected to contribute a proportionate amount annually. The exact sum needed is estimated by each Synod.

The maintenance of a general fund is no doubt fair and proper. The first responsibility rests upon the Church concerned. But co-operation of all the Churches is highly necessary. If no common fund existed many Churches would be overburdened and much handicapped in their work. Moreover, fairness dictates co-operation by all the Churches. A Minister may serve several Churches strong and able financially, but at the conclusion of his years of service may accept a call to a smaller Church. Yet, without co-operation, this smaller and weaker Church would have to shoulder the full burden of responsibility.

If no common fund were maintained, Churches would certainly be inclined to refrain from calling elderly Ministers, who could serve them acceptably, because of the excessive financial burdens, which might come after a few years.

However, originally our Church Order did not call for a common fund. This provision was added to Article 13 by our Synod of 1914. It would have been better if this revision had not been made. It creates a dualism in Article 13, inasmuch as the article clearly attributes responsibility to the Church whose Minister the incapacitated office-bearer is, and at the same time rules that he shall be paid out of a common fund. Was this revision perhaps made under the impression that the phrase, "the Church which they have served" refers to the sum-total of our Churches? Or was it made because the emeriti were paid out of a common fund, while the Church they served last was not considered at all? At any rate, the revision tends to create the impression that "the Church" referred to is the denomination. And yet this certainly is not the case.

We have no objection to a common fund properly organized and maintained as appears from what we have said above. Even our mother-Churches in the Netherlands have organized common funds. But we do believe that Synodical action toward the establishment of a common fund, without the incorporation of the clause under question in Article 13, would have been better. Thus the dualism referred to would have been avoided and the principle fundamental to Article 13 could have been fully maintained.

Synod of 1928 decided that when an emeritated Minister desires to re-enter active service he may not be called until the Consistory and the Classis that recommended him for emeritation deem that the reasons for his emeritation do no longer exist. (Art. 137, IX, 1928.) Is this a proper ruling? An emeritus Minister is a Minister in good and regular standing. Why should he not be permitted to consider and accept a call? Would it not be better to leave this whole matter to the brother concerned, the Church and Consistory calling and the

Classis of the Church? Sometimes Synods are tempted to make blanket rules, because of one or two irregular cases. But this is a dangerous policy, and not to the best interest of our Churches.

(After the major part of this commentary was completed the Synod of 1939 adopted the following reading of Article 13:

> "Ministers, who by reason of age, sickness or otherwise, are rendered incapable of performing the duties of their Office, shall nevertheless retain the honor and title of a Minister, and the Church which they have served shall provide honorably for them (likewise for the orphans and widows of Ministers) out of the common funds of the Churches according to the general ecclesiastical ordinance in the matter."

The important differences between this revision of Article 13 and its previous reading, is the fact that the words, "in their need" have been deleted.

This revision was made inasmuch as this same Synod approved of a plan which divided the Emeritus Fund into two distinct funds, known as Pension Fund and Relief Fund. According to the plan of 1939 all Ministers in active service are to contribute 3 percent of their salary annually toward the Pension Fund, in return for which all Ministers upon their emeritation, or their dependents, will receive an amount out of the Pension Fund equalling two-fifths of the current average salary of the Christian Reformed ministry. Those who need more than the amount allowed as pension are to receive additional support out of the Relief Fund.

Cf. Acts of Synod, 1939, pp. 21, 22, and Supplement XII-b, "Rules for the Pension and Relief Funds of the Christian Reformed Church," pp. 227-231.)

ARTICLE 14

If any Minister, for the aforesaid or any other reason, is compelled to discontinue his service for a time, which shall not take place without the advice of the Consistory, he shall nevertheless at all times be and remain subject to the call of the congregation.

TEMPORARY RELEASE

Article 14 concerns itself with what we usually call leave-of-absence. When a Minister seeks and receives temporary release from the duties of his office, he is said to be on leave-of-absence. This term is borrowed from secular life, and although passable it might be better to speak of temporary exemption from duty, or temporary release from service, inasmuch as one may be temporarily released from the execution of the duties of his office, though not at all absent from his field of labor. However, this objection is not serious, and we shall use the expression when convenient in the consideration of the article.

It may be noted also that Article 14 does not say that the granting of temporary release from service is permissible. The article presupposes the necessity of such leaves. For that reason we read: "If any Minister . . . . is compelled to discontinue his service for a time . . . ." The main burden of Article 14 is therefore found in its concluding sentence, which reads: ". . . he shall nevertheless at all times be and remain subject to the call of the congregation." From this it appears that the article would avoid irregularities as to the relationship between Ministers on leave-of-absence and their Churches.

1. Reasons for temporary release.

For which reasons is the taking and granting of leave-of-absence permissible? Article 14 answers: ". . . . for the aforesaid or any other reason. . . ." Doubtless the expression first of all refers back to Article 13 which speaks of old age, sickness, etc. Sickness, accidents, etc., may be of such a nature that an indefinite discharge from duty is called for. Then emeritation is in order. But these difficulties may also be of rather long duration, and yet according to all appearances, of a temporary and passing nature. In the latter case, leave-of-absence would be in order rather than emeritation.

There are good reasons to believe that the words "or any other reason," were also meant to cover the cases of Ministers who were compelled to leave their Churches to save their lives in the days of persecution. It should be noted that Article 14 was in principle already adopted in 1578, when the Roman persecutions had not yet spent their force in the Netherlands.

The words: "or any other reason," make room for any other weighty consideration of a compelling nature. For instance: in the past men have received leave-of-absence because they were appointed on Bible translation committees, or because they were appointed as delegates to foreign lands for the period of a few weeks or months.

Repeatedly Ministers have received leave-of-absence according to Article 14 for the purpose of taking post-graduate work at some theological school. It has been objected that such should not be done inasmuch as Article 14 speaks of compelling circumstances and that one who desires to continue his studies is certainly not compelled to do so. In arguing thus one has the letter of this article in his favor but no more, for as indicated above, the final sentence of the article constitutes its core. In other words: the burden of this article is not that Ministers may not receive leave-of-absence unless they are forced to do so by circumstances, but that a Minister on leave-of-absence, "shall nevertheless at all times be and remain subject to the call of the congregation." The significance of this provision we shall discuss forthwith.

Now, to be sure, if a Minister has the inclination and the means for qualifying himself still further for useful service, and consequently asks for a leave-of-absence, and if conditions in his congregation do not forbid his Consistory to grant him his desire, then neither he nor his Consistory is violating the intent of Article 14 when they proceed. As long as the motive is worthy, and the condition of the congregation permits, a leave-of-absence is altogether in order.

Does this article tolerate indefinite leave-of-absence? No. The article states specifically: "If any Minister is compelled to discontinue his services **for a time**. . ." Leave-of-absence should therefore cover a specific period of time. Indefinite leave-of-absence, not uncommon in our Churches a few years ago, violates the intent of this article. Synod of 1928 was doubtlessly correct when it ruled that leave-of-absence should be given for only a definite period. This does not mean that the exact length of the leave must always be indicated in weeks or months or years. This is advisable and should be done if at all possible. When this appears to be impossible the approximate length of time should be stipulated. If this approximate period proves to be too short, for instance in cases of broken health, extensions can be arranged. The purpose of the leave must always be valid and definitely stated, for our Churches must ever guard the uniqueness and sacred character of the office.

If circumstances are such that an indefinite release from active service is required, Article 13 applies and not Article 14.

2. Significance of advice of the Consistory.

What is the significance of the expression: "which shall not take place without the advice of the Consistory?" The term advice here stands on par with approval. If a Consistory advises against a contemplated leave the Minister is required to stay, unless, of course, he appeals to a major assembly and the major assembly should deem that the Consistory acted without sufficient grounds.

The tie which binds a Minister to his Church was established by both Minister and Church. Consequently no Minister can do as he sees fit and ignore the opinion of his Consistory. That would be a grievous violation of rights and would call for disciplinary action.

3. Subject to the call of the congregation.

Article 14 stipulates that a Minister who has received a temporary release "shall nevertheless at all times be and remain subject to the call of the congregation." What does this mean?

That the Minister to whom temporary release from active service is granted, continues to be Minister of the congregation which grants him such temporary release or leave-of-absence, and that he continues to be subject to the calling with which he was bound to that Church. The Dutch article speaks of, "de beroeping der gemeente." The significance of this calling or "beroeping" is clearly set forth in Article 4. It consists of election, examination, approbation, and ordination. The calling of a Minister into the sacred office places him under definite obligations. There is a definite relationship between him and his Church. He is ever subject to the calling with which he was called. His promises are ever binding. He has submitted himself to the jurisdiction of his Church, etc., etc. Now Article 14 stipulates that this calling, with all its implications, remains in force even though he has been temporarily excused from the active execution of the duties of his office.

From the foregoing it follows that at the end of his leave-of-absence the Minister concerned goes back to work in his Church. Unless it has been clearly stipulated that at the termination of his leave he will endeavor to secure a call from another Church and will await such a call. Usually this understanding exists. Then the Minister forfeits all rights to salary, parsonage, etc., in order that his Church can call another Minister. There is nothing in this article which forbids this arrangement. Its **advisability** depends on the circumstances involved. But as long as he has not accepted a call to another Church in the regular way, which includes permanent release from his present Church, he is and remains subject to the call of that Church whose inactive Minister he is. He stands under the supervision of the Consistory of that Church, etc.

The concluding sentence of Article 14 must be explained in the light of preceding articles and of the general principles of Reformed Church government. In our humble opinion, the article is not at all hard to understand when this is done. If it be remarked that some of the renderings of Article 14 in our old Dutch Church Orders speak of **congregations** ("subject to the call of the congregations") and that the use of the plural favors the interpretation which holds that Article 14 stipulates that a Minister on leave-of-absence may be called by any Church at any time while he is on leave, then we would reply with Dr. Bouwman that the plural is not used in these old

Church Orders. It is true that our Article 14 of today is essentially the same as what the Synod of 1578 already adopted, and that there is a direct connection between these older readings and our present readings. It is also true that the article of 1578 speaks of "gemeenten" (soo sullense nochtans haar tot allen tijden de beroepinge der Gemeenten onderwerpen), but it is not true that this word "gemeenten" is plural. According to old Dutch usage this word "gemeenten" in the phrase under consideration is a singular, possessive case.[1]

Besides, any Minister in good standing in the Christian Reformed Churches, whether he be on leave-of-absence or not, is always eligible to a call and must always give serious consideration to each call coming to him. This is such a self-evident fact that our Church Order does not even mention it specifically, neither here nor elsewhere.

ARTICLE 15

No one shall be permitted, neglecting the Ministry of his Church or being without a fixed charge, to preach indiscriminately without the consent and authority of Synod or Classis. Likewise, no one shall be permitted to preach or administer the Sacraments in another Church without the consent of the Consistory of that Church.

NO PREACHING ANYWHERE WITHOUT AUTHORITY

In Article 3 the Church Order specifies that none shall be permitted to administer the Word and the Sacraments unless he be lawfully called. Article 4 attributes the right of calling to the particular Churches. And Article 7 rules that none shall be called to the ministry unless they be stationed in a particular place. (Except they be sent to do Church extension work.)

At the basis of Article 7 and the whole Church Order lies the church governmental principle which acknowledges each particular Church to be an authoritative organization, and which holds that only they have a right to administer the Word and Sacraments who have been called to the ministry by a particular Church. Reformed Church polity does not look upon the denomination as being the real Church and the particular Churches, as being local subdivisions of the larger body. But Reformed Church polity holds that the particular Churches are the essential units, and that the denomination is a God-ordained federation of Churches. Now from these principles our Church Order in the present article deduces two additional principles. First, none shall be permitted to preach indiscriminately without the consent of Synod or Classis. Secondly, none shall be permitted to preach or administer the Sacraments in another Church without the consent of the Consistory of that Church.

1. None shall be permitted to preach indiscriminately.

This provision of Article 15 would prevent Ministers from leaving their pulpits and fields of labor, to preach and work in other fields,

---

1. cf. Dr. W. L. van Helten, **Middennederlandsche Spraakkunst**, p. 367; Dr. F. L. Rutgers, Acta, 492-95. Cited by Bouwman: **Gereformeerd Kerkrecht**, 1934, II, 480.

not assigned to them. Shortly after the Reformation, and also at a later date, some brethren would leave their own pulpits and fields, at certain intervals or permanently, and begin preaching in other localities. Perhaps they just wanted a change. Perhaps they cherished just or unjust grievances against the Churches which they were serving. Perhaps they were moved by the needs of the territories in which they began to preach. Whatever the motive, good or bad, the Churches found that this practice was harmful for more than one reason.

But the article was also and especially meant for men "without a fixed charge" who roamed from place to place and "preached" wherever they could. We have spoken of this class of workers under Article 9. Many of these roamers were unworthy because of limited ability or character. Many made a good impression but were nevertheless undesirable. Yet they forced themselves upon the Churches, or they began to preach in localities without an organized Church, entirely upon their own responsibility, instead of seeking a mandate in the regular way.

Today the phrase, "being without a fixed charge," refers particularly to Ministers that have been dismissed from their Churches according to Article 11, i. e., Ministers who have been barred from the active execution of their task in their Churches, due to trouble, etc. These brethren may not go about preaching in various unchurched communities without consent of Synod or Classis. Furthermore, there are stranded Ministers, Ministers whose congregations have dwindled away due to the removal of their members to other regions, because of constant crop failures or like reasons. These also should not take matters in their own hands and begin preaching where and when they see fit. It certainly is laudable when Ministers without fixed charges are anxious to work and are eager to bring the Gospel to the unchurched. But work of this type should be under the supervision of the Churches. The wisdom and rights of all the Churches concerned must be fully recognized by Ministers that desire to establish new Churches.

Some of these roaming preachers of former years defended their unauthorized practices by saying that their position corresponded with that of the Apostles and Evangelists of New Testament times.

But the Synod of Dort, 1578, Article 7, already refuted this statement by saying that the offices of the Apostles and Evangelists had ceased long ago.

The phrase, "to preach indiscriminately," we judge, is a rather unhappy translation of the Dutch "hier en daar te gaan prediken." To preach indiscriminately is to preach carelessly, without discrimination, without distinction. The article, of course, refers to preaching in various localities, particularly Churchless communities.

2. Consent and authority of Synod or Classis.

Why should the Church Order prescribe authority to Synod or Classis in this matter?

Because Church extension work, the organization of new Churches, is not merely the interest of one Church. Far less is it the interest and concern of some individual Minister. But it is the interest of all the Churches concerned. Consequently it is proper that when any Minister without a field desires to work as Missionary or Church organizer in any community, that he seek permission from all the Churches concerned (Classis or Synod) and not just from one Church.

Synod or Classis, the article reads. As a rule Classis can best regulate and supervise this Church organization work. However, if it appears to be more expedient that Synod give consent and authority, then such is altogether permissible and proper. Synod is even mentioned in Article 15.

Let it be noted that this article does not say that Ministers who are engaged in Church extension work, must do so under the direct charge and supervision of a major assembly. Every Minister labors first of all upon the charge of his particular Church and under supervision of its Consistory, (cf. Art. 4, 5) and secondarily and indirectly he stands under the authority of the major assemblies. Even Ministers who according to Article 11 are debarred from active service in their Churches continue to stand under the supervision of their Consistories as long as they have not accepted a call to another congregation or have not entered upon a secular field of labor. Article 15 only stipulates that home mission work is not to be undertaken by any Minister who lacks a field, without authorization by a major assembly.

Furthermore, Article 15 refers especially to men, "without a fixed charge." These individuals often held no official relationship to any particular Church. That is still the case with stranded Ministers, Ministers whose Churches have disbanded. In such a case the individual concerned may do some mission work under the direct supervision of a major assembly, but then only as a temporary emergency measure, which would cease to operate as soon as the regular relationships had been established. Only under special circumstances do the Churches in general begin to perform a task which essentially belongs to the particular Church. It is well to note in this connection that our new Home Mission Order, adopted by the Synod of 1936, and which put our Home Mission or Church Extension work under direct authority of Synod, very definitely demands that every Home Missionary be called and charged by a particular Church, with which Church he stands connected as Minister of the Gospel.

3. No administration of Word and Sacraments without Consistorial consent.

The primary purpose of the first part of Article 15 is to safeguard the cause of God against roaming, self-appointed preachers. It puts this class of men, often without any official ministerial connections with any particular Church, under the authority of the united Churches. The primary purpose of the second part of this article is to safeguard the integrity and rights of the particular Churches. Without the consent and authority of the Consistory of the particular Church, no one is allowed to administer the Word or the Sacraments in its domain or locality.

So for Churchless communities, lying outside of the territory of any particular Church, those who desire to do mission work must receive permission from the united Churches. But he who would preach within the bounds of one of our Churches must seek his consent from the Consistory of the Church concerned.

This provision and safeguard would not be found in our Church Order if we had the collegiate system of church government. For according to the collegialistic system the denomination is the Church, and the particular Churches are looked upon as mere sub-divisions of the Church. Ministers of collegialistic Churches are Ministers of the denomination, the super-church, stationed in various sections of the Church. They can be sent by those in authority within the bounds of one of their local Churches to preach and administer the Sacraments, without consulting the particular Church concerned. The Churches of a collegiate Church are ruled from the top down, not from the bottom up.

But we have the Reformed system of church government. Consequently our Church Order always maintains the integrity and authority of the particular Churches.

Now in keeping with the integrity and authority which our system attributes to the particular Churches, each Church has its own field or territory. In former years neighboring Churches set up definite boundary lines. Removal across the boundary line also meant removal from the Church to the Church of that neighborhood or community. Boundary lines are still held in honor in the Netherlands. The system of allotting certain territories to certain Churches and of maintaining ecclesiastical boundary lines doubtless has much in its favor. Without the maintenance of boundary lines the territory of one Church overlaps that of another. Think of our situation, for instance, in Grand Rapids, Michigan. There is an overlapping and crisscrossing of territories there which is confusing. And the same situation obtains for almost every other center with more than one of our Churches. This does not make for good order. One congregation often grows too fast for its own good and another sustains losses in membership which are uncalled for. Very often personal attachment to a building or a Minister impel our people to remain with a certain Church although logically they belong elsewhere. This is true not only for our urban Churches but also for our rural Churches. And this overcrowds some Churches and weakens others. It also makes for an unwholesome spirit of competition. Young people particularly are tempted to roam from Church to Church, especially for the evening service. Some seldom attend their own Church for the second service. The most popular Minister becomes the drawing card for the crowd.

But we Americans love our liberties, and it is doubtful, now that we have operated under the present system for so many years, whether any move to improve our situation would be well received by the bulk of our membership. However that may be, the system of well defined territories and certain boundary lines was certainly in the minds of our fathers when they wrote Article 15 and ruled that no one should be permitted to preach and to administer the Sacraments in another Church without the consent of the Consistory of that Church. This does not refer to the administration of Word and Sacraments in the church building of the congregation concerned. The fact that each Consistory has full control over its own pulpit, and that none can preach in the services of a certain congregation without consent of its Consistory, is so self-evident that it needs no expression in the Church Order. Article 15 goes much further. It recognizes the rights of a Church over its own territory, and makes it unlawful for one of our Ministers to preach within the limits of its territory without consent of the Consistory concerned.

Sometimes it happens that our Ministers preach in Churches of other denominations. Aside from all other questions as to the advisability of this practice, this preaching for other Churches should not take place by any of our men without consent of the Consistory of that place. In case the city or town has more than one of our Churches the nearest Church or Churches should be asked for this approval and permission. If at some future time we should get a new redaction of our Church Order this matter might well be specifically named in Article 15.

Our Synod of 1904 ruled that a Consistory should not admit to its pulpits a Minister not of our own denomination except when it is convinced that such a Minister is of sound Reformed confession. (Art. 125, 5.) And still stronger, Synod of 1882 ruled that Ministers who in doctrine and church government, and with respect to secret societies, take the position that is held by our Churches, may on occasion occupy our pulpits (Art. 58). These rulings are at present doubtless more timely than they were when they were made. They should not be forgotten or ignored. If they are we may feel ourselves obligated at some future day to accept even more drastic rules. The Reformed Churches of the Netherlands have found it advisable to appoint a Synodical Committee, without the approval of which no Minister belonging to another denomination is permitted to preach in said Churches.

Synod of 1904 also ruled that a Candidate as to his membership is under the supervision of the Consistory of the Church to which he belongs, but that with regard to his labors as a Candidate he is subject to the supervision of the Classis in whose district he labors. (Art. 126.) This really should be corrected to conclude as follows: ". . . . of the Classis in whose district he has his membership, whether he labors within the boundaries of this particular Classis or not." Of course, he is subject to the supervision of the local Church where he labors temporarily, and if that Church detects something wrong in doctrine or life, the Consistory of that Church should notify, as a last resort, his Classis, which Classis would then have the right to revoke his license to exhort, and his candidature for the Ministry.

ARTICLE 16

The office of the Minister is to continue in prayer and in the ministry of the Word, to dispense the Sacraments, to watch over his brethren, the Elders and Deacons, as well as the Congregation, and finally, with the Elders, to exercise church discipline and to see to it that everything is done decently and in good order.

THE DUTIES OF MINISTERS.

It should be noted that Article 16 speaks of the duty, work or task of the Minister, and not of the office of the ministry as such. The word office as used in our Church Order sometimes refers to the official, authoritative position of the office-bearers in the Church of Christ, and sometimes to the duties of the office, and not to the office itself. Article 35 even speaks of "the office of the president" of an ecclesiastical gathering, when it clearly refers to the work of the president. Now the content of Article 16 clearly indicates that it has reference to the work which a Minister should do and not to his official position.

1. The task of the Ministers as Ministers.

The work of the ministry as mentioned in this article is in the main three-fold. First: the service of the Word, consisting of preaching and teaching with appropriate prayers. Secondly: the service of the Sacraments, as seals upon the Word. Thirdly: the service of supervision. Strictly speaking the service of supervision does not belong to the task of the ministry, i.e., to the prophetic office in Christ's Church, but to the task of the Eldership, or the ruling office in Christ's Church. But the Ministers do not only represent Christ as to His prophetic office, but also as to His ruling or pastoral office (cf. Eph. 4:11). Consequently Article 16 speaks of supervision and discipline and the maintenance of good order, though these clearly belong to the domain of the Elders.

What does the phrase, "to continue in prayer and in the ministry of the Word" teach us? This phrase refers to congregational worship, of which two elements are mentioned, namely, prayer and preaching. It teaches us:

(1) That the Word of God, God's revelation of Himself as Creator and Saviour and all that it implies, must be preached. Mere lectures and discourses, though very good and altogether in place elsewhere, may never supplant the Word of God in the hour of Worship.

This point cannot be stressed too strongly in our day. Addresses on secular subjects may not take the place of sermons based on God's own Word. Neither should we be satisfied if the Ministers should deliver excellent religious addresses. Topical sermons are very often little more than religious discourses, in which the preacher's opinion looms up large. What we should demand without wavering, is exposition and application of God's own Word. Religious discourses are often much more popular with the crowd than regular sermons. But in the interest of the spiritual welfare of our members and the future of our Churches we should continue to present expository sermons. Of course this does not mean that our sermons should not be practical. A good sermon expounds and applies God's special revelation.

(2) That inasmuch as man is completely dependent upon God and owes Him full allegiance, prayer should constitute an important part in every service.

(3) That he who fills this office is a Minister. That is to say, he is a servant. But not of the people. Of the Word of God and of God standing back of His Word.

(4) That this service of the Word must continue without interruption. Ministers must preach the Word with due regularity.

It is worthy of note that this article does not mention the catechizing of children and young people, family visitation, sick-visiting, and the solemnization of marriages. None should infer from the fact that these matters are not specifically mentioned here, that they do not belong to the duties of the ministry. No one who might be inclined to defend this position could legitimately and successfully appeal to Article 16 of the Church Order. For this article does not mean to give an exhaustive enumeration of all ministerial duties; it merely indicates the essential responsibilities of the ministry. As both Jansen and Bouwman state, Article 16 is not limitative in character, but rather prescriptive.

As to catechism work, this certainly belongs to the Minister's field of operation. The teaching of a catechism class is essentially administration of the Word, just as preaching is. Only, catechism teaching is a specialized form of the administration of the Word, adapted to the needs of the youth. Its purpose is the indoctrination of covenant children so that they may, by the grace of God, confess Christ heartily, and serve Him loyally and correctly as well informed believers. This work belongs in the first place to those Elders who are called to labor in the Word, i.e., to the Ministers.

As to home visitation work and sick-visiting, in this work the Minister brings the Word of God, not publicly as at congregational worship, but privately. Not that only, for in the work of home visitation and sick calling the Minister goes also in his capacity as pastor, i.e., as Elder. It may be argued that the work under discussion is largely supervisory, and that therefore the overseers, that is the Elders, should do this work. With this we agree. But Ministers have a share in the Elders' work, and as such are certainly called upon to perform this work as much as their time will permit. Such is also for their own good as Ministers. It helps them to know the needs of their people.

Regarding the solemnization of marriages, the Ministers of our Churches really occupy a two-fold position at these ceremonies. According to the laws of our states any regularly ordained Minister has the right to unite in marriage those who have been properly licensed to marry. When a Minister performs a marriage ceremony he is acting for the state and insofar as a state official. But the Church of Christ also has a great interest in the marriages contracted by its young people. Consequently, our Churches have an official form for the solemnization of marriage, and Article 70 of the Church Order states that it is proper that the matrimonial state be confirmed in the presence of Christ's Church and stipulates that Consistories shall attend to this. Now when the marriage takes place in the presence of the congregation, at a service previously announced and under the supervision of the Consistory, then the Minister not only acts for the state, but also for the Church in his capacity as Minister of the Gospel. This is therefore also very definitely ministerial work.

Why may only lawfully ordained Ministers officiate at the service of the Word and of the Sacraments? Because the Scriptures so teach. To such as had been ordained to office Christ committed the charge of Matt. 28:19, "Go ye therefore and make disciples of all the nations, baptizing them into the name of the Father, and of the Son, and of the Holy Spirit."

In the Epistles those are constantly told to preach the Word, who had been previously ordained to office. We read of no baptisms but by such as were in the office of the ministry in some form or other.

Should men who are not in office and who in some instances do not belong to any Church anywhere, be permitted to preach the Word in our Churches? No, this would be decidedly against our rules of agreement, the Church Order.

Does it make any material difference whether such takes place by permission of the Consistory some week-day evening, or under the auspices of the Consistory during the hour of worship on Sunday? No, the one as well as the other is against the rule and against the best interest of our Churches.

2. The task of Ministers as overseers.

What precedes refers to the prophetic aspect of the ministerial office. As noted, the ministerial office also partakes of the task of the Pastors, Shepherds, Overseers, or Elders. All these names apply to the Elders' office. We now come to that work of Ministers which is theirs in their capacity as Elders. The work of Elders will come up for consideration in Article 23. Yet a few words regarding pastoral work as it applies particularly to the Ministers will not be amiss.

First of all then Ministers must watch over the confession and lives of their fellow office-bearers, the Elders and Deacons. They must encourage, instruct or admonish them faithfully. This same oversight must likewise be exercised over the whole flock. But pertaining to their fellow office-bearers it is specialized.

The pastoral work of a Minister is very difficult, but also very important. The Minister that fails to perform this phase of his pastoral work is inefficient at best. It requires true piety, love, patience, self-denial, tact, fearlessness, and certainly a thorough knowledge of Holy Writ and an understanding of human nature as affected by sin in both regenerate and unregenerate, in old as well as in young.

Secondly, the pastoral work of a Minister includes the exercise of church discipline. The expression here refers to church discipline in a narrower sense, i.e., excommunication and the official admonition which precedes it. Church discipline in the broader sense includes all protective and corrective pastoral work. Of discipline in this narrower sense, the Church Order speaks in detail in Articles 71-80.

Thirdly, the Minister must "see to it that everything is done decently and in good order." In this phrase the Church Order specifies particularly what is clearly implied in the general task of an overseer. It refers, no doubt, to the government of the Church in general, such as strict honesty, and the elimination of arbitrariness and partiality in the exercise of church discipline, and the promotion of good conduct at church gatherings.

If anywhere, then surely due order must be observed in the Church of God. And all things should be done decently, or honorably. That is, all things should be done in such a way that they will reflect creditably upon the Church, and will enhance the honor of Christ, the Head of the Church.

What are some of the things Ministers are expected to counteract and forbid? Harshness, wilfulness, partiality, impatience and insincerity in matters of discipline. Angry words, domineering, electioneering, clique-spirit, etc., at church gatherings.

3. The matter of assistants.

There are in our denomination those who perform work which is really ministerial in character. There are first of all those, though not ordained to the ministry, who nevertheless at times take the lead in congregational worship. We call them exhorters. The Dutch speak of "oefenaars." At times when the Church of Christ experienced a great dearth of regular preachers these exhorters have rendered invaluable services. Exhorters hold no office, though often they are or have been Elders. They are men who, in the providence of God, have special gifts for exhortation, a thorough knowledge of the Bible and our Reformed confession, and ability to compose and speak.

As will be realized the regular seminary students of the middler and senior years at our seminary at Grand Rapids form a very special class of exhorters for whom special rules have been adopted.

The Reformed Churches of the Netherlands adopted a few brief rules regarding the appointment of exhorters. They are in substance as follows:

"The request to examine a brother in order to grant him permission to exhort shall always proceed from the Church which desires his services as exhorter. Said request shall be addressed to the Classis to which this Church belongs. This Classis shall have the right to extend the privilege of exhorting to the brother for whom the request is made, not only for the Church making the request, but also, if it so desires, for all the Churches of the Classis, but not for the Churches outside of the Classis. If a Church belonging to another Classis should desire the services of the same brother, then the Classis of that Church shall judge if and how said brother shall be re-examined by it. But in no case shall he be permitted to exhort in any Church unless its Classis has first granted him permission" (Synod of 's Gravenhage, 1914, Art. 109). A bit more remains to be said regarding these ministerial helpers when we discuss Article 20.

A second class of assistants to the Ministers are the so-called "readers." Shortly after the Reformation many Churches had no regular Ministers. To assist needy Churches somewhat, men were appointed and sent to read sermons and to lead various groups of believers in public worship. As time progressed and Ministers became available these services became less necessary. Readers are seldom sent out by our Churches. Our Detroit Church, however, has often delegated one of its members, usually an Elder, to read a sermon for a group of believers in Windsor, Canada. Consistories still appoint readers, but as a rule only to read sermons at the regular Sunday services whilst the Minister is absent from his pulpit or the Church is vacant. Usually all Elders who have sufficient ability for this work are appointed to take their turn at "reading services." Churches within easy reach of emeritus Ministers, theological professors, theological students, etc., seldom have "reading services."

Readers need not necessarily be Consistory members. If none of the Elders or Deacons have a suitable voice for reading or ability to read well in public, some other brother in the Church may be appointed.

Readers are not allowed to bring their own message, nor to alter that which they read essentially. They act as assistants to the Minister, and as such, should read what the Minister himself has written, or what some other trustworthy Reformed Minister has written. The Consistory should know what is being read at reading services, and no book of sermons should be used which has not been approved of by the Consistory. It is well for the reader to announce the author of the sermon he is to read. Many readers will prefer to use one of the approved prayers for the services which they must lead, rather than using their own words. These prayers may be found in the Psalter Hymnal.

Another class of assistants to our Ministers are our non-ministerial Catechism teachers. During the sixteenth and seventeenth centuries the Churches in the Netherlands often appointed men not serving in the Consistory to act as sick-visitors and catechism teachers. This practice was common in the large city Churches. These catechism teachers and sick-visitors were not appointed before their knowledge, faithfulness, doctrinal purity and piety had been investigated. Only those who proved worthy were appointed. As a rule it is best to appoint Consistory members as catechism teachers. Then the Consistory may be sure that it is being served by consecrated trustworthy men. But in some Churches this may be impossible. Then let the Consistory appoint others well qualified for this work. But let great care be exercised in the appointment of these assistants in the ministerial work. No one should be appointed unless the Consistory is convinced that he is doctrinally well-informed and sound. All lesson books, etc., should be selected by the Consistory, and a definite system of supervision should be devised.

Another large group of members constantly doing ministerial work in our Churches are our Sunday School teachers. Sunday Schools are found in most of our Churches. The influence of our Sunday School should not be underestimated. It is therefore very advisable that the Consistories appoint teachers directly, and not from a list suggested by the Sunday School teachers' meetings. And far less should the teachers' meetings select and appoint provisionally, and then ask the Consistory for its approval. The Sunday School is an influential force and so it is very important who the teachers are. Only those who are well-informed, doctrinally sound, and in full unquestioned sympathy with our distinctive position as a Christian Reformed denomination, should be permitted to teach our youth the year around, and very often year after year. In the appointment of Sunday School teachers the Consistory should therefore be altogether free.

The superintendent and his assistant should both be Consistory members, preferably Elders, so that there may be a very close contact between the Consistory and the Sunday School. Let them be appointed annually. It might be a good plan to appoint the teachers annually, so that inferior and undesirable teachers might be eliminated the easier. Never should the Sunday School teachers meeting carry on its work independently. There should be close harmony between the Consistory and the men and women that have been appointed to instruct the youth of our Church. It goes without saying that the Consistory should always decide which lesson material the School is to follow, which ages are to be taught, etc.

ARTICLE 17

Among the Ministers of the Word equality shall be maintained with respect to the duties of their office and also in other matters as far as possible according to the judgment of the Consistory, and if necessary, of the Classis; which equality shall also be maintained in the case of the Elders and the Deacons.

EQUALITY OF OFFICE-BEARERS

Article 17 puts all hierarchical tendencies in our Churches under the ban. Hierarchical Churches are governed by various officers, varying in rank and authority. The most perfect hierarchical system has been developed by the Church of Rome with the Bishop of Rome, the Pope, at its head. The disciples of Jesus already showed hierarchical tendencies when they "disputed one with the other on the way, who was the greatest." But Jesus told them, "If any man would be first, he shall be last of all, and servant of all" (Mark 9:34, 35). At another occasion Jesus admonished them: "But be not ye called Rabbi; for one is your teacher, and all ye are brethren" (Matt. 23:8).

1. Equality of office-bearers as stipulated in Article 17.

Equality amongst Ministers is stipulated in Article 17, although the principle is applied with equal force to the Elders and Deacons, as the conclusion of the article also clearly states.

The article refers to the relationship and duties of office-bearers toward their fellow office-bearers within the congregation which they are serving. That is to say Article 17 does not say that equality must be maintained amongst the Ministers, Elders, and Deacons of various Churches, but of the local Church to which they happen to belong, and in which they are serving together.

The principle of equality also applies beyond the confines of the local Church, but Article 17 does not concern itself with this phase of the question. Article 41, for example, clearly posits the principle of equality of office-bearers beyond the limits of the local congregation.

The fact that the article speaks of Ministers (plural), might lead some to think that equality at denominational meetings and in denominational interests is meant. However, let us remember that in Holland, where our Church Order originated, many Churches have more than one Minister. In the larger cities of Holland the Reformed believers are organized into one large Church, having one Consistory, but several Ministers, and several church buildings perhaps. We have not followed this system but have consistently organized separate Churches as the need required. Consequently with us each Church has but one Minister and but one building. To this rule we have had an occasional exception. So, for instance, the Churches of Midland Park, New Jersey, and Denver, Colorado, each had two Ministers for a number of years. More recently, the Fourth Church of Chicago called a second Minister. (There are a few more Churches which really have more than one Minister. Most of our missionaries, for instance, are called by some local Church. They are officially connected with the calling Church, but in actuality we seldom regard them as such, and seldom are they accorded the privileges to which they have a right as Ministers of their Church.)

It is hardly necessary to say that Article 17 refers to **official** duties and privileges. When a Church has more than one Minister it can not be expected that they will be alike in all respects. One may be more able than the other. One may labor more zealously than another. One Minister may show greater sympathy and tactfulness than another. It is but natural that one is held in higher esteem than another, and that one is called to work of a greater responsibility and another not. Consequently this article stipulates that "equality shall be maintained **with respect to the duties of their offices.**" The bold-face words refer to preaching, administration of the Sacraments, catechizing, presiding at Consistory meetings, etc. In the performance of these duties equality shall be maintained. Thus the Church Order rules out the possibility of one Minister assuming the role of superintendent or dictator over others. Assistant Pastors, working as subordinates under other Ministers, are unknown in our Churches.

Which "other matters" does this article refer to? To such matters as maintenance, esteem for the office held, mode of address, etc. Regarding Ministers and their salaries, no personal favoritism should ever be tolerated. Each Minister of a given local Church must be honorably supported. This does not mean that equal amounts should be paid to all. The Minister with a large family will need more than one with a small family, etc. But all should be dealt with, with equal fairness.

2. Reasons for equality.

We have neither example nor commandment in Holy Writ which would support inequality. True, the Apostles did exercise a certain authority over the Ministers, Elders, and Deacons, and they did have privileges and duties wanting to the office-bearers in the local Churches. But nowhere do we read of Elders and Deacons being elevated in authority and honor above other Elders and Deacons. Nor of one Minister having the official preeminence above other Ministers.

Christ is the one head of His Church. All office-bearers are but prophets, priests, and kings under Him, acting with equal authority and equal rights, even as also all the Apostles stood on par as far as their duties and rights were concerned. It is true that Peter in many respects was the foremost of the disciples. But this preeminence of Peter was not preeminence of authority, as Rome holds, but merely a preeminence of ability and esteem.

The Synod of 1581, the very Synod which incorporated the article under discussion into our Church Order, received overtures from more than one quarter to appoint inspectors or superintendents. But the Synod decided not to do so inasmuch as this step would be "onnoodich ende zorghelick," i.e., "unnecessary and not without danger." Unnecessary inasmuch as the various Classes and Particular Synods were well able to supervise the Churches. And not without danger, inasmuch as it tended to elevate one office-bearer above another as to authority exercised. The Churches had suffered too much under a corrupt hierarchical Church to venture again in the direction of hierarchism. These overtures for superintendents may have occasioned the adoption of Article 17, which provides for equality amongst office-bearers.

It is generally admitted that there are other practical considerations which make it highly desirable that equality be maintained. Inequality easily produces wilfulness, "boss-ism", and abuse. And these are never more out of place and obnoxious than in the Church of Christ. Inequality also tends to promote jealousy and an unholy rivalry to the damage of the Church and the dishonor of God.

3. The conditional clause: as far as possible.

But it is also added, "as far as possible." Our Church Order is not a rigid book of law. It means to regulate church life according to God's Word and the best interest of the Churches. Now in certain matters ironclad rigidity might work severe damage and defeat the very purpose of the rule concerned, namely, the honor of God and the welfare of Christ's Church. And so we find the modifying phrase, "as far as possible," attached to this rule. This is altogether proper. For example: Supposing a certain Church has more than one Minister. Because of advanced age one of them finds it extremely hard to preach regularly and every Sunday, but pastoral work he is still able to perform with comparative ease. Why should not the Consistory in such a case release said Minister in part of his share in conducting congregational worship, and add to his task as sick-visitor? Or supposing a man has excellent qualification for the eldership, but reading a sermon in public is extremely hard for him, and the Church is not edified when he is forced to take his turn. Why should not the Consistory excuse him from this extra task?

And so there may be numerous conditions which demand that the division of labor be somewhat unequal, without an actual infringement upon the principle of equality of office-bearers in God's Church. As soon as we would begin to make unnecessary and arbitrary differences, the principle of equality would be violated. The exception does not do so.

Who decides as to each office-bearer's share in the common task? The Consistory, inasmuch as this is the governing body in each Church. This matter is therefore not left to individuals or groups of individuals, but the Consistory as a body judges and determines.

If in any case the Consistory cannot decide, or if the party or parties concerned are dissatisfied with the ruling of the Consistory, then as in all other cases, the matter can be brought for decision to Classis.

ARTICLE 18

The office of the Professors of Theology is to expound the Holy Scripture and to vindicate sound doctrine against heresies and errors.

THE TASK OF THEOLOGICAL PROFESSORS

The word office in Article 18 refers to work, task, duties. What we have said concerning the use of the word office under Article 16 is true also for the present article.

Our Dutch redaction of the Church Order (1914) reads as follows: "Het ambt der Doctoren of Professoren in de Theologie is, de Heilige Schriftuur uit te leggen, en de zuivere leer tegen de ketterijen en dolingen voor te staan." It will be noted that our English translation of this official Dutch text has dropped the term "Doctoren," i.e., Doctors. This translation was approved by Synod of 1920 so that we now have a slight variation between the official Dutch and the official English text of Article 18. Happily, the matter is not at all serious. Practically it makes very little difference whether or not this historical reading was maintained. On the other hand, variations in two official texts of the Church Order should not occur.

1. The historical background of Article 18.

Article 18 clearly refers to our Professors of Theology. It states very briefly what the brethren who teach at our Seminary must do. In other words, this article does not seek to control and regulate the work of teachers of theology in general, but it means to indicate the task of those who have been appointed for this work by our own churches.

Historically this article really goes back as far as Calvin. Calvin held that it was the duty of those that had been appointed to teach theology to expound the Bible and to defend the true interpretation and doctrine of the Bible over against those that are in error. He even favored the thought that teachers of theology should constitute a separate office, though it should also be said that Calvin saw a very close relation between "Pastors and Teachers." Says he: "But all these are embraced in the pastoral office" (cf. **Institutes**, Book IV, Chapter III. 4).

The Convention of Wesel 1568, a preparatory church gathering, followed Calvin. Its description of the task of "Doctors," (the term then used from the Latin doctor meaning teacher), agrees with that of Calvin. This Convention, like him, regarded these Doctors as ecclesiastical office-bearers next to the Ministers. However, as Jansen points out, the next three Synods of Holland, 1571, 1574, 1578, are all silent as to the office of the Doctors of Theology. This the author named explains from the fact that by this time the protestant State had organized schools at which theology was taught and at which Ministers were trained. The Synods of 1581, 1586, 1618-'19 again include the office in their Church Orders, but clearly refer not to an ecclesiastical office in its strict sense, but rather to teachers of theology at the various public universities whose work the Churches were thus endeavoring to control. In the Church Order of Dort (1618-'19), the original of our own Church Order (1914), the expression, "Doctor or Teacher of Theology", is therefore at best a semi-ecclesiastical one. The professors to which it refers were not even ordained, unless those appointed happened to be Ministers previous to their appointment (cf. in this connection what we find even in our own Church Order, Art. 4).

Now, in our redaction of the Church Order (1914), due to radically different conditions, Article 18 was made to apply to the professors of theology at our own seminary.

2. The office of our professors of theology a specialized form of the ministerial office.

Is the office of our professors of theology a specialized form of the ministerial office? Yes, for note: Christ was annointed to a three-fold office, namely, prophet, priest, and king. In harmony with this fact Christ's representatives for the O. T. Church were three in kind: prophets, priests, and kings. Likewise, in harmony with Christ's three-fold office the N. T. Church offices are three in number: Ministers, Deacons, and Elders, representing Christ respectively as our great Prophet, our merciful High Priest, and our eternal King.

This divine plan simply leaves no room for a fourth office. Neither, indeed, does the work of professors of theology demand that we consider theirs a separate office. In fact, the work of professors of theology is identical with the work of all Ministers, only, the work of the professor is specialized. But this does not alter the fact that our seminary professors are actually Ministers of the Gospel.

3. Why the expounding of the Scriptures is stressed in this article.

Theology is based on Scripture. It is the one source of knowledge and the one standard of truth for the science of theology. Neither man's experience and contemplation, nor general revelation can constitute the true source for our theological knowledge. Only through the Bible do we learn to know God correctly. It is God's special infallible revelation of Himself. And he who makes this universe, God's general revelation, or man's experience, his object for the study of God is sure to err, for sin has marred God's general revelation, and the natural man is spiritually dead so that his understanding of spiritual things is blurred at best, and he cannot know God as He is. And even after regenerating grace is ours, then yet it can not be said that the true knowledge of paradise has been fully restored to us. And so special revelation, the Holy Scriptures, is indispensable to us.

But these Holy Scriptures must be expounded, explained. The deep things of God are revealed to us in human language. Moreover, they are revealed to us in the language of the day in which the various parts of the Bible were written, a language belonging to a people differing radically from us in habits and ways of living.

Moreover, many profound truths are revealed to us repeatedly in Holy Writ, both in Old and New Testaments. Not that we find meaningless repetition in Holy Writ. Far from it, for the profound truths of God, the cardinal truths of Christianity revealed to us in the Bible, are not simple in their significance, but very often complex. They are somewhat like a beautiful valley landscape which may be viewed from many points, and which at each new point reveals new beauty. The sum total of the beauty of that valley simply cannot be seen from one hilltop. So, for instance, the significance of the truth of God's absolute sovereignty is not exhausted in one verse or even one chapter of Holy Writ. The significance of that great truth for God Himself is spoken of in one place; as to its significance for the world of sin, in another; as to its significance for God's children in still another; and as to its cosmic, universal significance, in still another, etc.

Now, our professors are called to expound God's Word. They must endeavor to translate correctly; to establish the historical and psychological setting; to determine the logical thought process; to bring together all that the Scriptures reveal concerning a particular truth, so that the true significance of the several parts may be understood, and so that the full significance of the sum total may appear.

What qualifications then are required in a good expounder of Holy Writ? Several. He should have at least a good working knowledge of Hebrew and Greek. He should know the history, customs, institutions, literary modes of expression, bent of mind or psychological make-up of Bible peoples. He should have ability to think logically. He should, of course, have a thorough knowledge of the whole Bible. And above all, he should have a sanctified heart and mind. For unless one believes in the supernatural character of Holy Writ, unless one has the indwelling light of the Holy Spirit, unless one has faith, love, and devotion, one will never sense the true significance of Holy Writ, no matter how bright one's intellect or how thorough one's factual knowledge may be.

4. To which heresies and errors does the Church Order here refer?

By heresies we mean false religions. And under the heading of false religions we place first of all Judaism, Mohammedanism, and all pagan religions. But under this heading we also place Neo-paganism (Unitarianism, Modernism, Liberalism), Russellism, Christian Science, Theosophism, Lodgeism, etc. These are all perversions of true Christianity and constitute a constant and very dangerous anti-Christian force.

By errors the Church Order means to indicate digressive movements and doctrines within the pale of the Christian Church. Errors in this sense are impure and wrong conceptions of the truth of God, which weaken the Church and dishonor God, but which do not deny the essence of the central truth of Christianity, namely, sin and redemption through Christ. Under this heading we find Roman Catholicism, Anabaptism, Methodism, etc. Or, to put it differently, all tenets which deny: Infant Baptism, the Covenant of Grace, Total Depravity, Election, Perseverance of Saints, etc., etc.

When and where should our professors vindicate sound doctrine against heresies and errors? First of all in the class-room and before their students. This is so self-evident that we shall not stop to discuss. But Art. 18 also implies that our professors must contend for the faith and against heresy and error outside of the classroom, i.e., in the Churches from the pulpits; through lectures, church papers, books, pamphlets, etc. There is a crying need for leadership of this kind. The very future of our churches and the maintenance of true Christianity and of our Calvinistic conceptions amongst us make it imperative!

Regarding the appointment of theological professors the decisions of Synod, 1930 are of note. They are as follows:

"1. When a theological professor is to be appointed, Curatorium shall present a nomination to Synod. The nominees shall preferably be ordained men that have had some experience in the ministry of the Word. The nomination shall not be made until a conference has been held with the Theological Faculty. It must be made in time so that it may appear in our church papers at least twice before Synod meets. To this end the Executive Committee of the Curatorium shall prepare a proposal in time for the meeting of the full Curatorium in May. When Curatorium convenes, the first duty shall be the making of the nomination and its publication. In order to lengthen the time for possible objections to reach Synod, the election shall take place at Synod as late as possible, and certainly not before the twentieth of June.

2. As in the past, a professor will be appointed for a term of two years; in case of reappointment, this will be for a term of six years; if again reappointed at the completion of his second term, he will be appointed indefinitely." (Synod, 1930, Art. 23, pp. 20, 21)

Previous to this the Synod of 1924 had already decided as follows: "It shall be the rule to appoint only men who have prepared themselves in a special way for the branch which they will have to teach. In case one or more years of special preparation are necessary, Synod shall appoint such a person with the understanding that he will resume his duties after one or two years." (Synod, 1924, Art. 26, p. 21)

It should not be forgotten that Synodical decisions of this kind are no laws of the Medes and Persians. It is well to have some general understanding as to the mode of procedure to be followed in matters of this kind. However, time and circumstances do not always permit rigid adherence to general decisions. If necessary the rules just quoted may be suspended. Each Synod must in the last analysis use its own judgment.

ARTICLE 19

The Churches shall exert themselves, as far as necessary, that there may be students supported by them to be trained for the Ministry of the Word.

SUPPORTING STUDENTS FOR THE MINISTRY

The material of Article 19 follows logically upon that of Article 18. The previous article has indicated the task of professors of theology, the present article makes provision for an adequate number of students.

1. The purpose of Article 19.

Without the regular ministry of the Word our Churches cannot be expected to flourish. Shepherdless Churches are Churches abnormally situated. God has so constituted our spiritual life for the Church militant, that constant care and nourishment are necessary. Consequently Ministers of the Gospel must ever be available.

Now, the first requirement for the ministry is no doubt that one have true piety and whole-hearted consecration. Next we would mention certain natural qualifications and abilities without which one cannot labor effectively in this sacred work. But besides all this one must have acquired a generous knowledge of God's Word and of theology in general before he can work effectively as a Minister.

But to go to school year after year takes a great deal of money. And so it has often happened that but few young men studied for the ministry, inasmuch as but few could afford to go to school. At the same time many young men of good ability and splendid qualifications and with an earnest desire to serve God in the Ministry, were anxious and ready to go. All of which simply means that many Churches would be without ministerial pastors year after year, while some of the best qualified young men were not available to the Churches because they could not afford to go to school to prepare themselves.

And so to assure the Churches of an adequate supply of well-qualified Ministers, the Church Order provides that "The Churches shall exert themselves, as far as necessary, that there may be students supported by them to be trained for the Ministry of the Word."

The first regular Synod of the Churches of Holland (Emden, 1571) already provided that several students should be supported for the ministry just as soon as the Churches, then yet dispersed in England and Germany by reason of the persecution, should have been restored in the homeland. Already the year before Marnix van St. Aldegonde had written to the refugee Churches in England concerning this matter. He wrote concerning a "crying need for students," and urges the Churches to begin the support of needy students as soon as possible.

At first Holland had no theological schools of its own. Those that studied for the ministry would go to Wittenburg, Geneva, Heidelberg, Zurich, or Basel. Others received some training from well-qualified Ministers. Eventually, however, the University of Leyden was organized, and this became the seat of learning which trained many men for the ministry. As conditions became more settled other schools were added. More than one Synod of that period dealt with the matter of securing suitable and sufficient candidates for the ministry. But Article 19, as it read in those days, did not stipulate that the Churches had to support an adequate number of students for the ministry, but merely that the Churches should see to it that there would be a sufficient number of students for the ministry, which students were to receive aid from the government upon recommendation of the Churches. When Protestantism in the Netherlands became victorious many Roman Church lands and funds fell to the government. Out of this fund of Roman Church properties the government would pay aged Ministers, needy students, etc. (Let us remember that there was a very close connection between Church and State in these early days.) Until very recently our Student Funds were commonly known as E. P. B. Funds. This designation goes back to this period. Needy students were said to receive support **ex bonis publicis**, a Latin phrase meaning "out of the public goods," the public goods being the former Roman Church properties referred to above.

2. How our Christian Reformed Churches have carried out the provision of Article 19.

At first there was one common fund under the administration and control of Synod. This was when our Christian Reformed Churches were less numerous than now. But already in 1888 Synod decided that each Classis should have its own Student Fund. Thus it has been ever since. Every Classis has its own Student Fund and has full control over it.

The first responsibility, let it be noted, regarding this matter, the Church Order clearly places at the door of the individual Churches. When this article was first formulated and adopted individual Churches would sometimes actually send desirable young men from their own midst to school with the understanding that they serve such sending Churches upon completion of their course. But our Churches for practical reasons deemed it better to co-operate and to carry out the provisions of this article through their classical organizations.

3. Why the phrase "as far as necessary" is included in this article.

The purpose of Article 19 is not to help needy students, but rather to help the Churches. Article 19 is a provision against a dangerous and detrimental dearth of Ministers. If, therefore, at any given time there is no scarcity of Ministers, the Churches need not exert themselves in this respect.

This is, no doubt, a wise inclusion. And yet we should be careful not to interpret this proviso too mechanically. For should we merely aim to supply the existing demand for Ministers in Churches already established? We should have a larger outlook and, if financial conditions at all permit, we should always look for young men whom God has given the natural qualifications for the ministry and who at the same time excel in consecration and loyalty, and who have a desire to serve the Lord in the ministry, in order that new Churches may be established and the work of God's Kingdom may move forward constantly.

During recent years several of our Classes decided not to accept additional students for the time being, inasmuch as funds were low and in view of the fact that several candidates were still available. If funds are low, as they naturally will be in years of economic depressions, and if the Churches are contributing to the best of their ability to these funds, then under the circumstances we can certainly justify the classical decisions referred to.

But, on the other hand, inasmuch as circumstances change constantly, so that the causes for temporary so-called over-supplies may no longer be operative a few years later; and inasmuch as there is ever a crying need for able and consecrated preachers of the Gospel in every nook and corner of our great land; and inasmuch as the world at large in these days of doubt and darkness is desperately in need of Christ's Gospel, therefore we should continue to encourage able and pious young men to study for the ministry, and we should assist them financially if need be.

Besides all the foregoing, if God pleases to give us young men who are able and consecrated and who have an ardent and unselfish desire for the Ministry, then should we not look upon that fact as a great favor of God and as a grave responsibility toward Him? And should we not make it possible for such young men to prepare themselves if this is at all within the range of possibilities?

We should judge with great care, but if God calls, then let us be sure to answer. But, of course, while helping young men to prepare themselves for the ministry, let us by all means open fields of labor as far as conditions permit.

4. How should Churches proceed in securing worthy applicants for support from their Student Funds?

Many young men begin to study for the ministry entirely upon their own initiative. Elders and Deacons are nominated by the Consistory and chosen by the Church, and no man amongst us thinks of suggesting himself as a fit candidate for these offices. But when it comes to the ministerial office, men—and very young men and inexperienced men at that—are very often expected to take the first steps toward the office independently. We expect them to suggest themselves. We know that there are reasons for this. And yet we believe that the Churches from the very outset should play a larger part in the calling of a man to the ministry than has been the case in the past. This, we believe, will save many a man and many a Church from bitter experiences.

Consistories should be on the alert constantly. They should most certainly encourage worthy and able young men. Ministers especially should use their good influence, urging eminent young men of their flock to consider prayerfully the question whether perhaps God is calling them to the ministry, and encouraging and directing them if this desire and conviction is present. Such as are financially handicapped should be encouraged to apply to the Classis for aid.

On the other hand ministers and Consistories should not hesitate to advise against any young men whom they deem to be lacking in any essential qualification. Our Classis should be very careful in their choice. They should not hesitate to turn down any and all applicants for aid. They should not merely go by a simple examination upon the floor of Classis and a formal recommendation of the young man's Consistory. Perhaps trustworthy brethren who know the young man should be quizzed a great deal more than the young man himself.

Intellectual ability and knowledge should be stressed. **But character and piety not a whit less.**

5. Should those who receive support from the Churches according to this article be required to repay?

Some of our Classes do not require repayment, but others do. Again others require partial repayment.

Article 19 certainly favors those Classes which do not require repayment. The article does not provide for a loan fund, but it stipulates that the Churches shall try hard to secure worthy young men to study for the ministry, which young men are to be supported by the Churches during their years of study. Thus the article has been interpreted from the beginning, and so it is interpreted today. As is agreed by all, the article refers to worthy young men, **who lack the necessary money** to go to school.

The fact that as a rule a Minister does not receive more money than he really needs for his family, car, books, etc., no doubt caused the Churches to provide for simple support of poor students and no more.

Synod of 1928 went on record as favoring non-repavment. It suggested that the various Classes work in this direction.

It is very true that some of our Ministers with good salaries and small families, during pre-depression years, received more salary than they actually needed for current expenses. But these were exceptional years for most of our people. And these years were exceptional for some Ministers also.

We seriously question the propriety of the establishment of a semi-loan fund for needy students **on the basis of Article 19.**

6. Who should receive aid from our Student Funds?

Should only those receive aid who are ready to attend our own Calvin College or Calvin Seminary, or should we also extend sunport to those who must still do high school work? The latter as well as the former. A very able and promising young man may not have finished his high school work by reason of circumstances. He may find it impossible to finish his high school work without aid. Then why should any Classis exclude him from aid on that account? Of course, he should be expected to attend one of our Christian High Schools.

Should our Classes ever extend financial aid to students who have finished the prescribed course at our own school, and who desire to do some post-graduate work elsewhere? Every case of this kind should be judged on its own merits. But if there be no urgent need for

Ministers, i.e. if there are not a large number of vacant Churches anxiously waiting for candidates, and if the student can offer good reasons for his desire to do post-graduate work, then, generally speaking, his request should be granted. We should encourage our young men to prepare themselves for the Gospel ministry as adequately as possible.

Of course, the Classis which supports him has a right to judge about the nature of his post-graduate studies and may decide at what school he is going to study.

7. The problem of those who fail to enter the ministry and refuse to repay.

Sometimes it happens that a man receives aid from a Student Fund but never finishes his course and never enters the ministry, and yet refuses to repay the moneys allowed. All Classes now require a written promise that they will repay the full amount received in case they do not enter the ministry. Does refusal to repay under these circumstances constitute a censurable sin? Beyond a doubt, it does. If need be a Classis would even be justified in seeking the aid of the civil laws to collect these Kingdom moneys. No one, who is in the position to restore money of this kind and under the circumstances noted, has any right to retain these moneys.

ARTICLE 20

Students who have received permission according to the rule in this matter, and persons who have according to Article 8 been judged competent to be prepared for the Ministry of the Word, shall, for their own training, and for the sake of becoming known to the Congregations, be allowed to speak a word of edification in the meetings for public worship.

CONCERNING EXHORTERS

1. The historical antecedents of Article 20.

Originally, shortly after the Reformation, regularly organized theological schools did not exist. Hence training for the ministry was a personal enterprise and irregular at best.

The Wezelian Convention (1568) decided that Churches which had Ministers with exceptional ability should institute "propositiën," i.e., classes for men with gifts and desires for the ministry, which men should be trained in preaching, not publicly but privately.

Synod of 1586 ruled that after having passed an examination "at the university or Classis," students for the ministry at one of these training centers, were permitted to teach in the public assemblies of the Churches. The examination "at the university" referred no doubt to the theological faculties of the universities, which faculties were at first Reformed and reliable. The great Synod of Dort in its Church Order, however, went back to the Wezelian stipulation, ruling out the practice of what is sometimes called "student preaching." Practice preaching was again limited to the confines of the private class rooms. Authorities explain this move in the light of the Arminian difficulties. Synod, for good reasons, no longer trusted the faculties at the universities, and yet did not wish to stir up more trouble by limiting the examination for "license to preach" to the Churches themselves through their Classes, and so discontinued the whole practice of "student preaching."

The Churches of the Secession in Holland, 1834, again permitted the practice. The Churches of the Doleantie, 1886, (the second secession movement under leadership of Kuyper and others) did not favor the practice. In the united Churches, the Gereformeerde Kerken, the practice varied from time to time, but in 1908 they definitely decided against "student preaching." Thus it has been in these Churches ever since.

Our revision (1914) of the Church Order of Dort, as far as Article 20 is concerned, is quite radical. In the Church Order of Dort Article 20 provides for training centers or "propositiën" in Churches with gifted Ministers. In our Church Order Article 20 governs the speaking of "a word of edification" in public worship.

2. The two classes of unordained men included in the provision of Article 20.

In the first place the article concerns regular students for the ministry. That is to say, men who are looking forward to the ministry and are taking a course of study at our seminary. Art. 20 does not state specifically that it refers to students at our own seminary, but inasmuch as we would not think of licensing students regardless of the schools which they might be attending, and inasmuch as the "rule in this matter" to which the article makes reference is a rule which pertains to students of our own Calvin Seminary in Grand Rapids, this inference is altogether valid. The latest rulings of Synod regarding these matters were made in 1936. They read as follows:

"1. The Board of Trustees of Calvin College and Seminary may grant licensure to conduct religious services in our Churches only to such as:

a. Are enrolled as regular students in our Seminary.
b. Have successfully passed the final examinations of the Junior year in the Seminary.

2. The Board shall not grant licensure to such students until it has made sure of the following with respect to each applicant:

a. That he is a member in good standing in our Churches.
b. That he has the spiritual qualification necessary for the ministry, and that he considers himself called of God to prepare himself for the office of ministering the Gospel of Jesus Christ.
c. That he intends to enter the ministry of the Christian Reformed Church.
d. That he has sufficient knowledge of the Bible, and especially of our Reformed principles to act as a guide to others.
e. That he can speak acceptably and to the edification of the churches. It is left to the discretion of the Board, however, whether it will obtain this information by consulting the Seminary Faculty or by examining the applicants.

3. The Board has the right to extend the licensure of those who want to take post-graduate work, but with the understanding:

a. That this privilege is to be granted only to such as are taking post-graduate work in theology, and declare that it is their definite intention to enter the ministry in the Christian Reformed Church.
b. That this extension is valid for no more than one year.
c. That further extension may be given at the end of the first year in case the applicant makes his request in writing, and at the end of the second year if he appears in person and is willing to submit to another examination. (The latter part of Rule 3c does not apply to those who are taking post-graduate work in theology outside of the United States or Canada.)

4. The Board is obliged to revoke the licensure:
   a. Of those who have completed their theological studies and have failed to take steps to enter into the sacred ministry of the Word.
   b. Of those undergraduate students who either discontinue their studies or fail to enroll again at the Seminary."

By saying that Art. 20 refers to students of our own seminary, we do not mean to say that Classes have not the right to license young men belonging to one of our Churches, but studying at some other seminary, in the abstract. They have this right. Synod of 1924 even specifically stated that the various Classes most assuredly had the right to license students of other schools to exhort in their respective confines, but urged the Classes not to make use of this right in behalf of our own school and as a measure of safety.

In the second place Article 20 specifies that "persons who have according to Article 8 been judged competent to be prepared for the Ministry of the Word," may be given the right to preach in the Churches. This right to be given by the Classes, of course, inasmuch as this is strictly a classical matter and not a matter falling under the charge of Curatorium, i.e. the Board of Trustees of Calvin College and Seminary.

3. The designation "a word of edification."

Why is the phrase "a word of edification" used? No doubt to distinguish between the leadership and work of the ordained and the unordained in public worship.

To preach really signifies to proclaim upon the authority of and as legal appointee by one in authority. He who preaches, according to the meaning of the concept, comes upon special authority of God and His Christ to speak as representative of God. Now it can only be said of those who have been regularly called by God (through the Church), and ordained by Him to this prophetic office, that they are His legal ambassadors proclaiming the Word and will of God. The unordained man can speak to the edification of his fellow-believers, but he cannot speak with that special authority with which the ordained Minister may and must come.

Externally, as far as form and words are concerned, the messages of the ordained and the unordained will often differ very little. But this does not alter the fact that there is a difference. The selfsame words may be spoken by a private citizen and a legally appointed judge sitting in judgment. And yet there is a difference. And so again and again we are dealing with essential differences in life, when formal differences are negligible.

Our Methodist friends speak of exhortation. This term has also been used in our circles. It is to be preferred above edification. The verb to exhort is at least more telling and distinctive than the verb to edify.

What can be said in favor of the practice of exhorting? It is helpful to the student. What the student receives at school is predominately theory. But as an exhorter in the Churches he receives practical training. Theory is fundamental and indispensable. But if a good theoretical training can be reenforced and capped off with some practical training, then that certainly should be appreciated. Compare the method of training medical doctors.

In the second place, it is also helpful to the Churches. They not only profit by the exhortation of the student exhorter, but also learn to know the future candidates and Ministers somewhat, so that they can call more intelligently during future months or years.

Which are some of the objections raised against the practice of permitting students to exhort? It is said to be detrimental to the student, inasmuch as it robs him of much valuable time which he should spend on his studies at school, and to some extent lessens his desire for thorough work at school, centering his thought and endeavors on the practical work in the Churches when he should be mastering his theological studies.

In the second place it is claimed to be detrimental to the Churches, inasmuch as young men who have not yet finished their course of training are not in position to lead and teach in public worship. Inferior material will often be presented to the Church, so it is said, and in some cases erroneous doctrines or presentations may be held forth from the pulpits, due to lack of sufficient training on the part of the students.

These objections are surely not without weight. But we feel that there is more to be said in favor of the practice than against it. We believe that the valuable practical training which exhorting affords our students can be secured without permitting the theoretical basis of our ministerial training to suffer. Theory and practice cannot and need not and should not always be separated by a high and straight fence. Educational psychology also tells us this. And through proper supervision and regulation the evils which are apt to attend this usage can surely be held down to a minimum.

Let us remember in this connection that there is no difference in principle here. The case is not thus, that one favors the practice of permitting unordained men to lead in public worship upon special occasion, but that the other considers this practice to be unbiblical. For those who are opposed to the practice of permitting students to exhort, heartily favor the practice of permitting candidates to exhort, whereas candidates are unordained as well as students.

4. Why does Art. 20 only concern the speaking of "a word of edification."

Because this is the only activity that exhorters may engage in. Only the ordained official representatives of God may administer the sacraments. This is also true as far as the preaching of the Word is concerned. But for the official proclamation of God's Word and will, the exhortation of an exhorter, as brother amongst brethren, can be substituted by way of exception. But we have no substitute for the sealing ordinances of God's covenant, i.e., the sacraments.

ARTICLE 21

The Consistories shall see to it that there are good Christian Schools in which the parents have their children instructed according to the demands of the covenant.

CONSISTORIES AND CHRISTIAN SCHOOLS.

1. The main difference between our present reading of Art. 21 and the original reading in the Church Order of Dort, 1618-19.

Article 21 in our venerable and historic Church Order (Dort, 1618-19) reads as follows: De Kerkeraden zullen alomme toezien, dat er goede schoolmeesters zijn, die niet alleen de kinderen leeren lezen, schrijven, spraken en vrije kunsten, maar ook dezelve in godzaligheid en in den Catechismus onderwijzen. That is to say: "Everywhere Consistories shall see to it, that there are good schoolmasters who shall not only instruct the children in reading, writing, languages and the liberal arts, but likewise in godliness and in the Catechism."

As will be noted, the ruling of Dort charges the Consistories to see to it that there shall be good teachers, whereas our present reading of the article charges the Consistories to see to it that there are good Christian Schools.

Why this difference? At the time when the original Church Order was adopted (this particular article was already adopted by the Synod of 1586) free, parental Christian Schools were unknown. Holland was leading the world in popular education, but its schools were controlled and supported by the government.

Conditions were altogether different from what they are today. The governments of Europe all stood officially committed to either the Roman Church or to the Protestants and their Churches. Separation between Church and State was virtually unknown. Secondly, by common consent the governments officially promoted and sponsored both religion and education.

Now the government of Holland, (that of the Republic) stood definitely committed to the Reformed faith, though Roman and humanistic forces were not silent. Consequently the schools which the government sponsored and supported were Reformed. They were Christian Day Schools, distinctly Reformed.

But it should be noted further that the government used the Reformed Churches to establish, promote, and supervise its schools. As might be expected, not all saw the need of a general schooling for all children, and not all realized the import of thorough Christian education. In some places the people failed to organize and to open schools. In other places inferior teachers were in charge, some of whom were not Reformed in confession and life. Consequently, at various times the Churches gathered in Synod charged the Consistories to be loyal and vigilant. And whereas the true welfare of the Churches depended to a large extent upon the schools, the promotion and control of which the government committed to the Churches, Article 21 of the Church Order of Dort charges the Consistories as it does.

Various measures were adopted during these years by the Churches and approved of by the government, which point to a very close cooperation between the Churches and the government in the establishment and maintenance of Christian Schools. For instance, the law required that schoolmasters be professors of the Reformed faith, and hold membership in one of the Reformed Churches; they had to be Godly in all their conduct; they were required to subscribe to the Reformed confessions; they had to give proof of knowing the Catechism and of ability to teach it in the school rooms; they were under special supervision of the Consistories and accountable to them.

Today circumstances are altogether different. Separation between Church and State is duly recognized, especially in our country. Consequently the government cannot favor one above another through its schools, but must aim at strict neutrality.

Furthermore, progress of Protestantism and a better understanding of the distinctive and special task of the State and of the Church, and of the rights and duties of fathers and mothers, has caused us to see that the ideal, according to God's ordinances, should ever be schools owned and controlled by the parents concerned.

Consider in this connection that the Bible persistently charges the parents with the training of their children, (cf. Deut. 6:7; 11:19; Eph. 6:4). Children are constantly referred to as belonging to their parents and not as belonging to the Church or the State. Responsibility is therefore always fixed on the fathers and mothers.

Moreover, regarding the State, the Word of God teaches that governments have been instituted to maintain good order in civil affairs, which includes armed defense against men and forces which disturb the peace and which trample upon justice, as well as the punishment of all law-breakers, (cf. Rom. 13:1-7). Nowhere does the Word of God charge the State to rear children.

And regarding the Church, in keeping with the three-fold office of Christ its glorious Head, the Church must preach the Word; must show mercy in His name; and must govern the Church under Him. To be sure, by reason of its prophetic task the Church is charged to teach. But the subject matter which the Church is required to teach pertains to the Gospel of the Kingdom and is limited to the domain of special grace. Only by exception is the Church permitted to teach so-called secular subjects, such as reading, arithmetic, chemistry, psychology, etc. Why? Because these and kindred subjects are of secondary importance to the welfare of the Church. Flourishing Church life requires that these subjects be taught, but they do not concern the heart and core of the Church and its task. They are not absolutely indispensable to the Church. And so the Church should concentrate on its own specific task, and teach only that which pertains to the Gospel and the doctrine of the Kingdom.

However, all of life is related, and all of life stands related therefore to the Kingdom. And the so-called secular subjects have a definite import also for the Church. If, therefore, the proper parties neglect to instruct the youth in these subjects, or neglect to instruct the youth in keeping with the Word of God, then the Church may step in and do that which strictly speaking does not belong to her specific charge. Whenever her true welfare requires such, the Church may take to hand things which lie at the outside of the circle of her interests and not at the center. (For instance, to state the case extremely: A Church may not go into the business of laying sidewalks or of graveling roads. But a Church would not hesitate to lay a sidewalk along the public highway or to gravel a road miles in length if the proper authorities failed to do so, and if the true welfare of the Church required said sidewalk or graveling.)

But clearly, the Church is not charged to run grade schools, high schools, or colleges. No more than the State.

Now it was out of consideration of the foregoing reasons that Art. 21 was made to read as it does today, when our Synod of Roseland, 1914, revised our time-honored Church Order.

2. The significance of Article 21.

The wording of this article might lead one who is not fully informed to think that our Church Order stipulates that Consistories, (1) must organize and maintain good Christian Schools, (2) must see to it that parents send their children to these Church schools. This, however, is not the meaning of Article 21. The wording of the Article may be explained from a desire to adhere as closely as possible to the wording of Article 21 in its historic form. Church schools have never been advocated by the Reformed Churches. All that know the history of our Churches and the history of Article 21, realize that the article as it reads today means to say that our Consistories must promote the organization and proper maintenance of good Christian Day Schools by believing parents, and must urge the members of our Churches to use these schools for the education of their God entrusted children, if at all possible.

But why does the Church Order stipulate that Consistories must promote Christian Day Schools, whereas the general schooling of the child is admittedly not the task of the Church?

In part this question has already been answered in the foregoing. Consequently we can be brief at this time. Let us remember then that life is a unit. There is not a subject on the schedule of any school that does not bear some relation to God and our faith in Him and our life for Him.

To be specific, we preach and teach in our Churches that the sovereign hand of God guides all of life, that we must acknowledge and obey God at all times and everywhere. But if our children go to a school in which this fact is ignored or gainsaid, directly or by implication, we must not be surprised if the teachings of the Church taken from God's Word are cast to the winds. This needs no further argument.

The school should teach in full harmony with the Word of God, as well as the Church. That will make, by God's grace, for strong and well informed Christians. The Church cannot afford, and before God cannot tolerate, to see much of her precious teachings contradicted and silenced five days a week, year after year, before our children, and that while they are in their formative years. Godless and Christless instruction clearly runs counter to the best interests of the Church, the Kingdom of God in general, the welfare of the child, and the solemn obligation of Christian parents.

Consequently it becomes the plain duty of the Church to promote good Christian Schools, and to urge parents to use these schools if at all possible.

3. What is the significance of the phrase, "according to the covenant of grace"?

The covenant of grace may be designated as a league of friendship between God and His people in Christ Jesus. Not all men are included in this covenant, but only the believers and their seed. The covenant of grace draws a line of separation between men and men; some are God's children; others are the children of the world. And only by the irresistible operation of God's grace can one who is a child of Satan become a child of God and a member of the covenant of grace. Consequently, he who is a believer in Christ as Saviour is in league with God. He is God's child; God's friend. All that he is and has he would dedicate to God. All of life he relates to God.

Now the privileges and prerogatives of the covenant pertain not only to believers, but also to the children of believers, (cf. Gen. 17:7; I Cor. 7:14).

It is not that every child born of believing parents shall surely share in the full blessings of the covenant. There are exceptions to this rule also. Some will reject and break God's covenant. But God's special claim on them, in common with those to whom all the gracious implications of the covenant shall be realized, cannot be denied. And therefore, as far as God's claim is concerned, and as far as special advantages are concerned, all children born of believing parents are covenant children. Moreover, all children born of believing parents should be regarded as covenant members to whom the full and blessed significance of the covenant pertains, until their failure to profess Christ in word and deed forces us to infer that the full and actual significance of the covenant is not theirs.

And so all covenant children must be treated and trained as children of God. Most assuredly then, if at all possible, we should establish schools which train the child to recognize the wisdom and glory of God in all things, as well as the dire effects of sin, and the glorious redemption through Christ; the constant conflict in life between God and the devil; God's special claim on him and his life, etc. This type of training is clearly demanded by the covenant of grace.

4. Good Christian schools.

Why does the Church Order speak of **Good** Christian schools? Because not all schools which are Christian day schools are necessarily good. The ideals after which our Christian schools must strive lie very high, so high, indeed, that we shall never reach them. And yet we must bring our schools as near to those ideals as we possibly can.

Not that only. There is always the danger of retrogression. Eternal vigilance is also the price of genuine Christian instruction. Good buildings, and good educational facilities and thoroughly-trained teachers who profess the Christian religion, do not necessarily make good Christian schools. Good equipment, etc., are very desirable. But love for, and a grasp on the implications of the covenant, and ability to teach these implications are indispensable for good Christian schools, worthy of that name and designation. Therefore, Article 21 stipulates that Consistories shall promote "good" Christian schools.

5. How can Consistories best carry out the charge of Article 21?

As to the establishment of Christian day schools, the Consistories may urge parents to do their utmost in this respect at the occasion of family visitation. Furthermore, Consistories can arrange for parents' meetings at which the need and possibilities of Christian instruction is discussed. They can faithfully distribute Christian school literature, such as published by the Union of Christian Schools. They can urge the Minister and all members of the Consistory to promote the cause in their personal contacts with parents. But Consistories should especially urge their Ministers to remember this cause in their sermons. The Word of God certainly demands Christian instruction. These demands should be preached wisely, timely, but also persistently in places where parents are neglectful.

Article 21 also includes the element of supervision over Christian day schools. It stands to reason that no Consistory should attempt to act as a super-board over the lawfully appointed school board. The rightful authority of the parents who constitute the school society, and of the school board, should never be ignored.

Briefly stated, to carry out this phase of the charge, Consistory members may visit the school, or schools, more or less regularly but voluntarily. They may also make it a point to establish repeated contacts with the teachers as individual Christians. Through these means a most natural supervision would result. But Consistory members might fail to visit the schools with sufficient frequency unless appointed to do so. Consequently the appointment of a committee charged to visit the school or schools repeatedly, and reporting its impressions to the Consistory, works better. In case one or more Consistory members also serve on the school board, that in itself would constitute a constant medium of contact between the school and the Consistory.

In case Consistories have good reasons to fear that erroneous doctrines or tendencies are fostered in the school, or that the school is remiss in its task as a distinctively Christian school, the matter should be brought to the attention of the teacher, the principal, the school board, or to all, depending on circumstances and the gravity of the case.

Some hold that in matters of doctrine the Consistory should have powers beyond the authority of the school board, so that the Consistory would virtually have the right to discharge a teacher over the decision of a school board. This is by no means the stand of Dr. F. Rutgers, with whom we concur entirely on this point. He holds that cases of irreconcilable conflict between a school board and a Consistory, as to the orthodoxy of teachers will be very, very rare. But if they do occur, the final step for the Consistory would be to warn parents against said school, and to sponsor the organization of a sound school. Of course, individuals involved in the case might have to be disciplined.

We fail to see how a Consistory can ever step into an extra congregational association and make authoritative decisions for it, no matter how just its cause may be, unless that association has voluntarily placed itself under the final word of a certain Consistory. (The question whether or not a Consistory should ever accept such final power is, of course, another matter.) Nothing in the Church Order, as we see it, would warrant interference as above referred to, and the whole genius of Reformed church polity is against it.

6. Article 21 and our public schools.

Can the charge of this article in any case be applied to our public schools? We would answer in the negative inasmuch as all states, to the best of our knowledge, have laws prohibiting sectarian instruction in the public schools. The Christian religion, and its approach to life and the world in general, by court decisions falls under this term "sectarian." Bible reading without comment is permitted in most states, provided that no parent of the district concerned objects. Real Christian instruction as we conceive of it, is practically out of the question in a public school. The state must aim at strict neutrality as long as the laws governing education stand as they are today.

However, in communities in which a parental Christian school is out of the question, and in which Christian citizens have a free hand, they should by all means engage teachers who are Christians, so that the Bible may be read with reverence, and the general atmosphere of the school room may not be antagonistic to Christianity, but may rather be congenial to Christianity. (Let us remember in this connection that strict neutrality is really out of the question. We are either for Christ or against Him in all things. Also in the realm of education.) These parents could even do more. They could also petition their legislators to revise the law in such a way, that positive Christian instruction may be given in public schools, if all the parents of a certain district give consent.

We do not make much of this point inasmuch as legislators would be unwilling to enact laws as designated. And if they did, very few school districts would be without some objector which would make Christian instruction in the public school impossible once more.

But supposing all parents of a given district desire Christian instruction for their children, would it be wrong to introduce it in view of what the state statutes say? If all parents of certain school districts desire positive Christian instruction for their children through the medium of the public school, they should not begin to introduce said instruction without the knowledge of all the authorities concerned. These should be notified previously so that the giving of Christian instruction may be altogether open and above board, and that the instruction may be given with at least the tacit approval of the rightful authorities. We do not believe that the giving of Christian instruction in any of our public schools **under these circumstances** can be called unChristian or unethical inasmuch as the statutes which prescribe neutral instruction were adopted generally speaking not from Godless and unChristian motives, but rather to safeguard the rights of parents who might object to "sectarian instruction". If in any of our states the statutes were made to provide for "non-sectarian instruction" in public schools, from the clear and expressed motive of desiring to bar any and all religious instruction from all their public schools, and to see to it that no school tax money is in any way spent for so-called "sectarian instruction", then in such states and as long as such laws are on the statute books our people should not undertake to introduce Christian instruction in their public schools.

By all means, let our Consistories faithfully sponsor Christian day schools as conceived of in Article 21. Even in communities where a Christian school is out of the question for the time being, the ideal should be held before Christian parents constantly.

7. Parental neglect and discipline.

Should Consistories discipline parents who fail to give their children Christian day school instruction though it be within their power to do so?

There may be cases in which parents refrain from sending their children to a Christian school for reasons which they consider valid before God, although others question or deny the validity of their position. In all such cases the matter must be left to the consciences of the parents concerned, although the Consistory should urge prayerful reconsideration repeatedly.

There may be other parents who simply do not feel the need of Christian day school instruction. Their confession may be blameless as well as their consecration of life. And their Christian conduct regarding other matters may be altogether proper and unoffensive. But there is something present or lacking in their make-up and outlook which causes them to prefer the public school for their children. The position of such parents is grossly inconsistent to put it mildly. Now, all such people may and must be disciplined in the sense of admonishment, but cannot be disciplined in the sense of ecclesiastical censure, which ultimately might culminate in excommunication. Why not? None can be disciplined in the latter sense unless he has given serious doubt as to his Christianity, through impenitence regarding a special sin, or sin in general. And none can be excommunicated except a Church is compelled to believe that the party in question is not a Christian. (Cf. Form for Excommunication.)

They who can, but do not use the Christian school for their children are making a big mistake, and are chargeable before God. But they may be serious-minded Christians for all that. The training of those parents may have much to do with their conception.

Parents who fail to send their children to a Christian school because they assume a careless attitude toward their Christian obligation and make light of their baptismal vows, should be admonished, censured, and perhaps excommunicated because of their unChristian attitude toward God and His commands in general. In other words, mere failure to send children to a Christian school may never constitute a basis for censure and excommunication, but persistent indifference toward Christian duty, including proper child training, may. For by such indifference we clearly testify that we are either temporarily wandering away from God, or that our Christianity is only a sham, without reality, and that we are Godless at heart.

8. Consistory members out of sympathy with Christian schools.

Can one who is opposed to Christian schools serve as Consistory member? Not very well. Those who serve in Consistory pledge themselves to uphold the doctrine and government of our Churches. (Cf. Form of Subscription.) Now, the Church Order, according to which they help to govern the Church, requires that they promote and sponsor Christian schools. Therefore one who is opposed to these schools cannot serve in the Consistory. He cannot do what is expected of him. Even those who assume a lukewarm attitude toward the Christian school movement are not desirable candidates for the Consistory.

We should, of course, remember that every case must be judged on its own merits. A general rule in this matter should never be made.

Furthermore, some men who feel the need of Christian schools, are sadly weak and wanting in other respects. Consequently a Consistory may be compelled to nominate one who is not a promoter and lover of Christian schools, for the simple reason that other brethren have still more serious faults.

9. Catechetical instruction.

In addition to what has been remarked regarding catechetical instruction under Art. 16 we here note that the Synod of Dort (1618-19) spoke of three kinds of catechetical instruction; namely that given in the home, in the school, and in the Church. Parents were expected to instruct their children and their whole household in the Word of God and the catechism which had been adopted. This parental instruction has not always received its just due. We of today can stand a good reminder on this point. How important that children shall learn to know the true teachings of God's Holy Word from their parents. What a noble work and beneficial exercise it would be for the parents themselves. And would not this work faithfully performed draw parents and children closer together, and make them more confidential regarding matters spiritual?

Regarding the catechetical work in the schools the Synod of Dort decided: (1) That the government should open schools everywhere, and that the children of the poor should receive free instruction in these schools. (2) That the schoolmasters had to be members of a Reformed Church, pious in their conduct and well versed in the catechism. (3) That three booklets should be used for catechetical instruction, one for the smaller children, one for the more advanced scholars, and then the regular Heidelberg Catechism. (4) That supervision over the schools should repose with the Ministers, who together with an Elder or one of the magistrates should visit the schools, and encourage both teachers and pupils. (5) That the schoolmasters, in case they were delinquent, should be admonished by the Consistories, and if this did not help, the authorities should be asked to act.

From all this it certainly appears that the governmental schools of this period were certainly Reformed governmental schools. Where at first such was not the case, but where the schools were under the influence and dominance of Rome, the reformatory work of the Churches was soon extended to the schools.

Regarding Church instruction it was deemed desirable that Ministers in rural districts should personally teach the catechism in the schools, and that they should instruct the older scholars at his home or in the Consistory room and that weekly. Those that desired to receive permission to come to the Lord's Table he should instruct diligently for three or four weeks.

Our Synod of 1928 urged and encouraged Consistories to continue catechetical instruction for a nine-month term each year. (Art. 46.) And Synod of 1918 already held that as a Reformed group and in regard to the training of our children we should place all emphasis upon catechetical instruction in the home and by the Church, as well as upon Christian school instruction. If these are held in honor amongst us as they should be, so Synod declared, then there will be but small need for Sunday schools in our midst for our own children.

Furthermore Synod held that the Sunday school could only be accorded a place of its own in our Churches if it were used as a means of evangelization. Synod urged the Churches in this direction. (Cf. Acts, 1918, pp. 53, 150.)

And Synod of 1888 ruled that parents who neglect to send their children to catechism, though they can do so, become subject to discipline. And young people who have come to years of discretion and refuse to attend catechetical instruction classes subject themselves to discipline also.

Regarding our Sunday schools, their place, management, etc., we refer to what we have said under Article 16.

ARTICLE 22

The Elders shall be chosen by the judgment of the Consistory and the Deacons according to the regulations for that purpose established by the Consistory. In pursuance of these regulations, every church shall be at liberty, according to its circumstances, to give the members an opportunity to direct attention to suitable persons, in order that the Consistory may thereupon either present to the congregation for election as many Elders as are needed, that they may, after they are approved by it, unless any obstacle arise, be installed with public prayers and stipulations; or present a double number to the congregation and thereupon install the one-half chosen by it, in the aforesaid manner, agreeably to the Form for this purpose.

THE APPOINTMENT OF ELDERS

John Calvin restored, by the grace and in the providence of God, the Elders to their rightful position in the Church. The Roman Church was much deformed in its conception of the various offices in God's Church. The Ministers were changed into bishops who not only had the right to administer the sacraments but also the right to ordain or appoint priests. The Elder's office was deformed into the priest's office, and they were charged to administer the sacraments.

The Deacons no longer cared for the poor, the work of mercy having been largely delegated to the various orders, but they were made to be assistants to the priests in the celebration of the mass, as the Levites of old assisted the priests in the temple.

The Lutheran Church in Germany failed to restore the Elder's office, the government of the Church being left to the civil authorities. Even Zwingli, as Jansen points out,* permitted the civil government to rule the Church. But Calvin sponsored the appointment of Elders as the Reformed Churches have known them ever since. He did this inasmuch as he saw that this was Biblical, and because he considered it very necessary in view of the dangers of hierarchism, i.e., the abuse of power on the part of one or a few.

1. The calling of Elders: Its constituent elements.

Article 22 provides for three distinct elements which together constitute the process by which men are inducted into the Elder's office. They are: Election, Approbation, and Installation. These same three are also provided for in Article 4, which governs the calling of Ministers into office. But in addition to these three Article 4 also provides for a fourth step. Namely: Examination. No one can be ordained to the ministry without being examined. For the Eldership however, our Churches do not require an examination. The matter has been mentioned and suggested repeatedly. Those who favored an examination for Elders would point to I Tim. 3:10, which even demands that Deacons "first be proved" before they begin to serve. Moreover, the import of the work of an Elder, so it was said, demands that he be well versed in the Bible and the Confessions, and that he prove his qualifications for Church governmental and pastoral work.

But the Churches have never taken steps to introduce examinations for Elders. The practical objections against the suggestion are in the main the following:

(1) The "proving" required in I Tim. 3:10 can be conveniently carried out informally by due consideration of the brethren to be nominated for Elder at the Consistory meeting. (2) A regular course of instruction for the Eldership cannot be called necessary. The general training which the catechism classes, the societies and general reading afford our wide awake members is sufficient. The most desirable men might even be too modest to take a course designed to fit one for the Elder's office, and the bold but less desirable might be anxious to take such a course. (3) Courses of study for the eldership would at best be introduced in only a few Churches and that would make for irregularity and inequality. Consequently Article 22 requires only: election, approbation, and installation.

2. The election of Elders.

Who may be elected to the Elder's office? Those that answer to the descriptions given in I Tim. 3:1-7 and Titus 1:5-9. These two passages give a fuller description of qualities desirable and necessary in an Elder than any other in Holy Writ. They are therefore very important and should be borne in mind constantly.

As a general rule it may be said that the following are some of the chief requisites for a good Elder in our Churches: A thorough knowledge of God's Word; unquestioned sincerity of heart as a professing Christian; whole-hearted loyalty to the Church as to its doctrinal position; exemplary conduct in everyday life; ability to instruct

---

* Jansen: **Korte Verklaring**, etc., page 93.

others; forbearance; good judgment; self-denying devotion. All these as will be noted are virtually implied in the passages of Scripture referred to above.

Are they who have close relatives, such as father or a brother in the Consistory, eligible to election? They certainly are. When there are a number of men available in a certain Church it may not be the part of wisdom to nominate sons or brothers of those already holding office, but it would not be against the Bible and our Church Order. It is well to remember in this connection that Jesus chose more than one set of brothers to serve as Apostles, (cf. Peter and Andrew, James and John.) But again we say, if others are available, it may be better not to nominate close relatives of those already in office. But to exclude them systematically and regardless of circumstances would be wrong. It would often work injury to the Church and be an injustice toward many excellent brethren.

The question is sometimes asked whether brethren otherwise well qualified and desirable, but whose wife or children manifest some very disagreeable characteristics or even unChristian attitudes, are eligible to office. It is certainly advisable to take note of all the characteristics enumerated in Holy Writ in the passages already referred to, but if a Consistory is convinced that a certain brother is not responsible for undesirable conditions in his home, then these undesirable conditions need not bar him from office. However, if a large number of brethren are available, then it is best to select those whose families are also exemplary.

By whom are the Elders to be elected to office? According to the wording of Article 22 Elders are chosen to office "by the judgment of the Consistory and Deacons." The term "Consistory," when used in distinction from "Deacons" in the Church Order, has reference to Ministers and Elders. (cf. our interpretation of Article 4.) Article 22 therefore stipulates that in the election of Elders, all three offices shall co-operate. Just as we find it in Articles 4, 5, and 24.

This does not mean that the body of believers as such has no right and voice in the matter. In the last analysis Christ is the only ruler in the Church. He is its government. For He is the Church's great Prophet, only High Priest and eternal King. This three-fold authority of Christ is delegated by Him to our Ministers, Deacons and Elders. But clearly, no man would assume to himself this delegated authority of Christ. He must be appointed by Christ. Through whom? Through the Church, the organized body of believers, acting as agents of Christ, either directly, as is the case when a Church is newly organized and when the office-bearers are appointed for the first time, or more indirectly, as is the case when the office-bearers previously appointed in consultation with the Congregation, make new appointments for the Church concerned.

Consequently our Confession of Faith begins as follows: "We believe that the Ministers of God's Word, the elders, and the deacons ought to be chosen by a lawful election by the Church, ..." And for this reason the first question to which Elders and Deacons must respond at the time of their installation reads as follows: "Do you, both elders and deacons, feel in your hearts that you are lawfully called of God's church, and consequently of God Himself, to these your respective holy offices?"

Article 22 does not mean to say that inherently the office-bearers, and they only, have the right to appoint to office. It is well to remember in this connection that in our Three Forms of Unity we have a statement of doctrine and Biblical principles, but that the

Church Order is a set of rules accepted by the Churches for the promotion of good order and due regularity in Church affairs. The Church Order is not even in the first place a summary of Church governmental principles, gleaned from Holy Writ, but rather a compilation of rules according to which the Churches are to be ruled and according to which the task and interests of the Churches are to be promoted. Of course, nothing in the Church Order runs counter to Holy Writ and the principles set forth in our doctrinal standards. But this is the point: the various stipulations of the Church Order cannot always be given that dogmatical interpretation which their mere words might seem to demand. Very often a given stipulation is but a rule of good order which all the Churches have agreed to follow, and hence must follow under all normal circumstances, for reasons of expediency, i.e., for the promotion of the true welfare of the Churches.

Now Reformed Church governmental principles on this score, together with what the Bible presents to us regarding appointment to office, f.i. Acts 1 and Acts 6, and the statement from our Confession, and the first questions from the Form of installation, all lead us to hold that Article 22 does not read as it does, because office-bearers have in and by themselves inherent authority to appoint to office. This interpretation would, moreover, agree with the Roman conception of the offices and its teaching concerning the minority of the believers. But it would run counter to the Reformed conception concerning the rights and duties of the congregation and the three-fold office of all believers.

Briefly stated, this article of our Church Order provides that the office-bearers, upon the authority vested in them by Christ, shall exercise the right of guidance and definite control in the matter of appointment to office by the Congregation. This article acknowledges the authority and the responsibility of the office-bearers entrusted to them by Christ, and at the same time does justice to the rights of the body of believers forming a local Church. It is also a very wise arrangement. A smaller group of select men, vested with special authority in the Church and in position to know the needs of the Church and its membership, is better qualified to make wise decisions than the body of believers acting directly and without guidance and safeguards.

Which modes of procedure does Article 22 permit the Consistories to follow in the matter of calling men to the office of Elder? **In the first place** the Consistory may give the congregation an opportunity to suggest various brethren for candidacy. The Consistory is, of course, at liberty to supplement this list. With the complete list before it, the Consistory now selects as many names as there are vacancies to be filled. Their choice is next made known to the Congregation and unless valid objections are presented to the Consistory, the brethren concerned are inducted into office in the regular manner. **The second mode** of procedure which Consistories may employ is as follows: The Consistories nominate for office twice as many brethren as there are vacancies to be filled. In due time the congregation chooses one-half of these nominees, who, unless valid objections should be presented, are properly installed at the time appointed. We know of no Church in our whole denomination which does not follow the second mode of procedure. This method is also in general use in the Reformed Churches in the Netherlands.

It may be said that when this second and common mode of appointing brethren to office is followed, Consistories are at liberty to give the congregation an opportunity to suggest possible nominees. This element of the first mode of procedure in calling men to office, may certainly be used when the second mode is followed. It may be less necessary to do so in our smaller Churches inasmuch as the Consistories of these smaller Churches will know the membership of their Churches sufficiently well to nominate without this activity on the part of the Church, but in larger Churches it is doubtless very desirable.

What is the significance of the phrase "according to the regulations for that purpose established by the Consistory"? The Church Order presupposes that each Consistory has a set of rules according to which elections shall be conducted. In Article 4, which concerns the election of Ministers, this same phrase occurs. Whenever the congregation is called together for the purpose of electing office-bearers, partiality and arbitrariness should be out of the question. To avoid these a set of rules consistently followed is very desirable.

Then again, certain questions should not merely be left to usage and custom. For instance: Proper announcement of nominations should be made prior to every election; elections should take place by ballot; a majority vote should elect; etc. These and like rules are not found in the Church Order. They should be incorporated in a short set of rules governing elections. Furthermore, problems are apt to present themselves at any meeting. For example: In case more brethren receive a majority vote than the number of vacancies to be filled, what is to be done? When two candidates for one office receive an equal number of votes, what should be the procedure? Questions such as these cannot be decided by the congregation inasmuch as the Consistory is the ruling body and not the congregational gathering. Moreover, for the Consistory to decide on such problems at the time when they present themselves might open the door to partiality or at least the semblance of partiality. Permanent rules should govern all such cases.

To the best of our knowledge, very few of our Churches have a set of regulations such as the Church Order here prescribes. This is not as it should be. Various Church Order manuals published in the Netherlands offer model sets of rules for this purpose. For completeness' sake, and to give our Churches an example in the English language, we here add a model of our own.

Suggested Set of Rules Governing the Election of Elders and Deacons

Art. 1. Elders and Deacons for this Church shall be chosen according to the stipulations of Articles 22 and 24 of our Church Order, and with the observance of the rules contained in the following articles of this set of rules.

Art. 2. During the autumn of each year the Consistory with the Deacons shall meet to nominate candidates for Elders and Deacons. Twice as many brethren are to be nominated as the number of vacancies occurring. The nominations are announced at least for the space of two weeks. Before election takes place at least one Consistory meeting must occur in order that possible objections may be duly considered.

Art. 3. During the latter part of November the Consistory calls a Congregational meeting together to which all male members in good and regular standing are invited. All such and only such are entitled to a vote. The number of those eligible to vote shall be recorded.

The President will announce the nominees once more and give instructions if need be. Voting shall always be by ballot.

Art. 4. A majority of those voting elects. Blank ballots are to be deducted from the total. One half of the valid votes plus one shall constitute a majority when the number of votes is an even figure. When the number of valid votes is uneven, one-half of such votes plus a half a vote shall constitute the majority. (Thus 8 would be the majority of 15.)

In case more brethren received a majority of votes than are needed those having received 4/5 or more of the votes cast shall be considered elected. A new vote shall be taken on all the others that received a majority. When a tie vote occurs between brethren, only one of whom can be chosen, another vote is taken between these two. If the result is again a tie, the lot is to be cast.

Art. 5. The results of the elections are announced at least two weeks after which a Consistory meeting must be held for the receiving and consideration of possible objections. If a re-election must be held for one or more of the vacancies, the same general rules are to be observed.

Art. 6. Installation into office takes place on Jan. 1 or the first Sunday of the New Year. The term of service of a newly elected office-bearer begins with his installation and ceases as soon as a successor has been installed in his place at the end of his term of service.

Art. 7. Vacancies which occur during the course of the year shall be filled in keeping with the foregoing rules. If the end of the year is near, the Consistory may decide to wait until the regular elections.

Art. 8. Objections against methods of procedure should be offered at the same meeting at which they occur. Those who fail to reveal such objections at the same meeting at which they take place forfeit their right of protest.

3. The approbation of elected Elders.

The approbation, or approval of the congregation takes place after the election and before the installation. When the second mode of procedure permitted by our Church Order is followed then there is also a preliminary approval on the part of the congregation. For the nominations are announced to the Church and those who have objections can register these. But the actual and final approbation on the part of the Church takes place after election. Some have contended that the approbation prior to election is sufficient. But the Form for Installation clearly addresses the congregation thus:

"Beloved Christians, having previously made known unto you the names of our brethren who were chosen to the office of Elders and Deacons in this church, and no one having appeared to allege anything lawful against them, we shall therefore in the name of the Lord, proceed to their ordination."

This is as might be expected. Surely if one has serious objections against his own nomination or the nomination of another he ought not to wait, but make known his difficulty prior to the election. But if the Consistory maintains the nomination and the brother concerned is elected, the complaining party must certainly receive opportunity to voice his objections once more. And those elected may lack the liberty of conscience to accept the office. They must be able to say that being duly elected of God's Church, they feel themselves called of God to their office. If they have serious objections on this score they must make these known to the Consistory. Moreover, certain valid objections against one of the elected brethren may arise after the election. To use an extreme illustration: An elected brother might drink himself drunk after an election and thus make himself undesirable for the time being at least, although his conduct on this score was above reproach previously.

If objections are entered against any elected brother, but the Consistory finds that the objections are not valid and insufficient then the party concerned is installed as usual. But if the complaining member gives notice of appeal to Classis, then the installation should wait until after the Classis has considered the matter. However, if the Consistory is fully persuaded that the objector is merely motivated by jealousy or ill-will then the Consistory has the right to proceed with the installation in spite of the appeal to Classis. But it stands to reason that a Consistory will await the verdict of its Classis unless the circumstances are very extraordinary. And when a Consistory is minded to install a brother in spite of an appeal to Classis, it should first consult a neighboring Consistory or its Church visitors as a matter of good order and Christian consideration toward the aggrieved party. If a Consistory has awaited the verdict of its Classis, and if the Classis advises to install, then the Consistory should install without delay, even though the protesting brother should appeal to Synod. No one duly elected should be barred from office for months by a series of protests. That would be unjust toward the elected brother, and toward the Church.

If the Consistory sustains any objections raised against an elected brother, and if the objections cannot be removed, then the Consistory should declare the election of the brother concerned void, and should let the congregation make a new choice.

4. The Installation.

What is the significance of the installation of office-bearers? Installation of office-bearers is not to be identified with appointment to office. Appointment to office takes place through the process of election by the Church. Under special circumstances men have assumed office without formal installation. For instance, in days of persecution no one ever questioned the legality of their position as office-bearers. Why then does the Church Order provide for proper installation? So that the appointees may publicly accept their appointment to office, and publicly assume their responsibilities, openly promising before God and His Church loyalty and devotion, and openly testify that they accept the appointment as coming from God Himself. Also, in order that the congregation may receive its new office-bearers in the right attitude of heart and mind. Furthermore, in order that the congregation may appropriately implore God's blessing upon the newly elected office-bearers.

In small congregations it sometimes is necessary to nominate those for office whose term is expiring. In case of re-election such men therefore continue to serve without intermission. In this connection the question has often been asked: Should those who are re-elected also be reinstalled? Synod of 1928 declared that installation in such cases was not only desirable, but also proper. (Art. 85.) Synod had good reasons for assuming this position. When our Elders and Deacons are elected they are chosen and appointed for a definite period of years, in most Churches for two or three years. When office-bearers so elected are installed they are installed for a definite number of years; they assume the duties of office by solemn promises for that same definite number of years. Consequently, reinstallation is in place.

ARTICLE 23

The office of the Elders, in addition to what was said in Article 16 to be their duty in common with the Minister of the Word, is to take heed that the Ministers, together with their fellow-Elders and the Deacons, faithfully discharge their office, and both before and after the Lord's Supper, as time and circumstances may demand, for the edification of the Churches to visit the families of the Congregation, in order particularly to comfort and instruct the members, and also to exhort others in respect to the Christian Religion.

THE DUTIES OF ELDERS

This article gives us a brief statement of the work of the Elders. The Wezelian Convention (1568, pre-cursor of the regular Synods) already gave a rather lengthy description of the Elder's tasks. But seemingly the Synod of Gravenhage, 1586, considers this description too detailed for Church Order purposes. This Synod at least gave us the brief redaction of Article 23 as we have it today.

1. Government and discipline.

Article 16 indicates the duties included in the office of the ministry. The last of these duties enumerated in Article 16 is also ascribed to Elders. It reads as follows: ". . . . and finally, with the Elders, to exercise church discipline and to see to it that everything is done decently and in good order." We considered the significance of this provision when Article 16 was under consideration, and shall, therefore, not repeat what has already been said. And the matter of discipline as such will be considered at length as we discuss Articles 71 to 80.

Does the administration of finances, building and grounds, etc., belong to the domain of the Elders? Yes, inasmuch as the government of the Church is the task of the Elders and administrative duties are indeed governmental duties. This however, does not mean that the Consistory may not appoint a finance committee or helpers from amongst able and worthy members of the Church. The appointment of committees for various duties which concern the temporal interests of the Churches should be encouraged. It will give the Elders more time for the all important spiritual phase of their charge and will bring the work of the Churches somewhat closer to our membership. The practice here suggested is in wide usage in the larger Reformed Churches of Holland.

However, all such helpers and committees should be appointed directly by the Consistories for the term of one year only and they should know themselves strictly accountable to the Consistories.

Should the Elders have a specific charge for every task or bit of work which they do in the congregation? As far as the work of discipline is concerned, each Elder may and should admonish erring sheep of the flock as time and occasion may demand, but no Elder may bar a member from the use of the sacraments upon his own authority and initiative. Membership rights may be withdrawn either as a temporary measure or decisively only upon concerted, united action of the whole body of Elders. But without a doubt the individual Elders may and must do a great deal of pastoral work upon their own initiative just as the Ministers do a great deal of pastoral work without awaiting a specific charge from the Consistory. By all means let our Elders diligently call on the sick, the erring, the unfaithful, the mourning, etc.

2. Supervision over fellow-office-bearers.

Supervision over office-bearers in Episcopal Churches (Roman Catholic, Methodist, etc.) is exercised in the first place by superior officers, Bishops, Cardinals, etc. With us all officers stand on par as to their official authority. Consequently, inasmuch as supervision in this imperfect and partial dispensation of the Church is highly necessary, all supervision amongst office-bearers must be mutual. Each must oversee, supervise the other. (cf. Acts 20:28.) "Take heed unto yourselves, and to all the flock, in which the Holy Spirit hath made you bishops (overseers) . . ."

This supervision covers, in the first place, doctrine and life, as well as the discharge of one's office. In doctrine one must be sound, in conduct exemplary and beyond reproach, and as an office-bearer faithful and diligent withal.

The Elders should give particular heed to the Ministers of the Gospel. It is of prime importance that these preach and teach correctly and effectively, and that their labors are performed in all faithfulness. But the other officers in the Church must also be true and faithful if the cause of God is to flourish. Error, disloyalty and neglect may not be tolerated in any office-bearer. That would be contrary to God's Word and would undermine the very foundations of the Churches.

What mode of procedure must an Elder follow when he finds that one of his fellow office-bearers does not faithfully discharge his office? He should confer with him personally and in a brotherly spirit. A personal conference may accomplish the end sought, or perchance prove that the fear entertained or the objection cherished rested upon a misunderstanding. The promotion of good will and common sense itself prescribes this first step. Moreover, this procedure, though not prescribed by Christ in Matt. 18:14 (for this passage does not speak of mutual supervision amongst office-bearers), nevertheless finds its analogy in this passage.

If after a personal conference the objections remain, the aggrieved Elder should bring the matter to the Consistory for its consideration. If the matter be urgent and weighty such should be done at first opportunity. If less urgent, the matter should be mentioned at the time of "censura morum," i.e., mutual censure pertaining to morals, or Christian censure as it is termed in Article 81. This mutual censure, according to Article 81, is to be held before each celebration of the Lord's Supper. Consequently at least four times a year.

As stands to reason a flagrant and public sin, making the guilty one worthy of suspension or deposition from office, may require immediate action by the Consistory.

3. Home-visitation work.

In the third place Article 23 charges Elders with home-visitation work. The Churches of the Reformation did not favor the Roman practice of auricular and sacramental confession, i.e., the acknowledgment of sin to a priest in order to obtain forgiveness through him. They found no Scriptural warrant for the practice, and knew its many evil attendants. But our fathers did believe in personal supervision by the overseers and personal consultation by the overseers in order to instruct, correct and comfort each one according to his individual need. Christ Himself spoke not only to large groups of listeners, but also engaged in personal work. Confer the instance of Nicodemus, the Samaritan woman, Peter at the time of his restoration, etc. And the Apostles enjoin personal work by word and example. Psychologically also personal work, conducted by the duly appointed office-bearers, is altogether desirable and necessary. Now our fathers believed that this work could best be carried on through periodic visits on the part of the office-bearers at the homes of the parishioners. To this day our Churches have maintained this practice, although most Protestant Churches have discontinued it, no doubt to their loss. We may safely regard the practice of holding periodic supervisory visits with all our members at their own homes, gathered in family groups, as one of our denominational strongholds. Needless to say, this institution will utterly fail us, if and in as far as it should deteriorate into a bare and formal custom. But conducted in the spirit and with the intent of the institution, it will continue to be a source of great good.

Why does Article 23 provide that home visitation work must be carried on "both before and after the Lord's Supper"? Our fathers were no doubt convinced that a personal conference by the Elders with the members of their Church concerning the significance of the Lord's Table, and the attitude of the heart in which they should come to communion, would be highly beneficial. Likewise that a personal conference on the benefits derived from attendance at the Lord's Table and the duties involved in the privilege, would also be of great value. They had seen the ruinous effects of mere formalism in the corrupt Church which they had left behind. They were anxious to promote true spirituality in the Reformed, liberated Churches.

But in the second place it must be remembered that home-visitation as established by the Reformed Churches took the place of the Roman confession before the priest. None are permitted to go to mass unless they have been to confession just previous to the celebration of the mass. It may be that our fathers stipulated visits before and after the celebration of the Lord's Supper because of this Roman Catholic usage. We merely suggest the connection, inasmuch as we are not able to verify it at this time. This much is sure, inasmuch as a good many Church members had recently left the Roman Church, and were not well founded in the truth, repeated instruction and constant conferences would be very necessary. It should also be noted that the very first "major assembly" of the Reformed Churches of the Netherlands, the Wezelian Convention, 1568, ruled that home-visitation should be conducted by the Elders **every week**. Today as we know, loyal Roman Catholics still go to confession **every week.**

The visits under consideration must be made furthermore "as time and circumstances may demand." Today home-visitation calls are made annually in all of our Churches. The same condition prevails in the Reformed Churches of the Netherlands.

What is the specific purpose of home-visitation according to Article 23? In the first place "the edification of the Churches" is mentioned. The Churches must be edified, that is builded, strengthened, increased. To edify simply means to build up. The cause of God represented by our Churches must grow and increase. His Kingdom must come. This end may be accomplished, under God's blessing, through the preaching of the Word, the teaching of the youth, but also through periodic visits on the part of the office-bearers with the Church members in their homes.

Secondly Article 23 stipulates under this point "in order particularly to comfort and instruct the members." Comfort and instruction were greatly needed during the youth period of the Reformed Churches. But we still need comfort and instruction. But this comfort and instruction which God's Word offers so abundantly for every need and circumstance of life must be individualized through personal contact and conversation.

The present reading of this article is the redaction of 1586 and constitutes an abbreviation or summary of what the Wezelian Convention had formulated on this score, and which in part reads as follows: "They (the Elders) shall faithfully investigate whether they (the Church members) manifest themselves uprightly in walk and conduct, in the duties of godliness, in the faithful instruction of their households in the matter of family prayers, (morning and evening prayers) and such like matters; they shall admonish them to these duties with consideration, but also in all seriousness and according to conditions and circumstances; they shall admonish them to steadfastness, or strengthen them to patience, or spur them on to a serious minded fear of God; such as need comfort and admonition they shall comfort and admonish, and if need be they shall report a matter to their fellow Elders, who together with them are appointed to exercise discipline; and besides these matters they shall correct that which can be corrected according to the gravity of the sin committed; nor shall they neglect, each one in his own district, to encourage them to send their children to catechism."

This designation is too long, as was soon felt, (1586), but who would care to deny that it contains a wealth of valuable suggestive material even for this day and age?

Does home-visitation also belong to the task of the Ministers? Not in the first place. In the first place it belongs to the office of those that are called to be overseers, the Elders. Consequently it is not even mentioned in Article 16, which indicates the task of Ministers. But in as far as Ministers are teaching-elders, (cf. Form of Installation), and in so far Elders, the work of Elders, (government, discipline, etc.), also falls to them, though not primarily.

As much as their primary duties allow, Ministers should do personal work through home-visitation, visiting of the sick, the afflicted, and the aged, calling on delinquents, etc. All this may be included under what Article 16 terms "to watch over the Congregation." Moreover, effective ministerial work also requires close contact with the Congregation through personal work. But again, primarily, Ministers must preach and teach. And that, if they are to do it correctly and effectively, will require nearly all their time. And primarily home-visitation, etc., is the work of the regular Elders.

4. The exhortation of others.

This provision was incorporated in this article when the Reformed Churches were the official Churches of the Netherlands. The Reformed Churches, and these only, had official recognition of the government. Consequently all people inhabiting a certain district were considered to fall under the jurisdiction of the Reformed Church of that district. The office-bearers had duties toward all, though not all held membership with the Church. And although this conception and situation changed in course of time, yet the Churches in the Netherlands, and also our own (1914), have maintained this provision.

To be sure the Church has a duty toward those that are without. The gospel should reach the de-Christianized masses round about the Church. The Church must seek to win back that which was lost. God's covenant claims they must hear and God's saving love must be presented to them.

Now Article 23 stipulates that especially the Elders shall exhort the outsiders and ungodly to the Christian religion. This is significant indeed and often entirely overlooked. Every Church should expect its overseers, as far as possible, to oversee in the name of Christ, also those who as yet do not recognize their jurisdiction, and who as wandering sheep will not heed the voice of the shepherd but must be won back to the fold. Or, inasfar as these ungodly and perishing souls are direct descendants of pagan ancestors, (of which there are strictly speaking but very few in our country) they also must be exhorted to seek after God in Christ Jesus.

All this is in full harmony with a declaration of Synod 1932, which reads as follows: "The rampant neopaganism of our day and land requires that every one of our churches, whether alone or in collaboration with a neighboring church or churches, enter upon evangelistic activities. It also requires that, if possible, in addition to the regular pastor, the church or churches engage an ordained minister especially for this evangelistic work." Acts 1932, Art. 25. And the fact that nearly all of our Synods have dealt with the subject of evangelization and home mission proves that our Churches are alive to the great need of this all important and challenging phase of Kingdom work.

ARTICLE 24

The Deacons shall be chosen, approved and installed in the same manner as was stated concerning the Elders.

THE APPOINTMENT OF DEACONS

This brief article makes a general reference to the stipulations of Article 22. Article 22 regulates the election of Elders. Three elements are included in this election: election proper, approbation, and installation. These same elements are also mentioned in the present article. Inasmuch as these matters received consideration under Article 22, we shall not repeat now what has already been said. But we shall briefly note three matters which deserve consideration, namely: The essential character of the Deacon's office; the qualification for this office; the matter of deaconesses.

1. Essential character of the Deacon's office.

What is the essential character of the Deacon's office? In answer to this question the origin of the names "Deacon" and "Diaconate" may be considered first of all. These words are derived from the Greek word **Diakonos**, and this word signifies one who serves or ministers. In general it may be said that in Scripture the word **Diakonos** refers either to the ministry of the Word or the ministry of mercy. Confer Matt. 25:44; Mark 1:13; Luke 8:3; Acts 1:27; Acts 6:4; II Cor. 4:1; Col. 4:17. In all these passages the word **Diakonos** or a word derived from it is used.

To-day we still speak of the servants of the Word as Ministers of the Gospel. As a rule they are simply called Ministers. These office-bearers, on the other hand, who in a special way are required to show mercy, are never called by this name, although the word Deacon (**Diakonos**) signifies a minister. The name Deacon, therefore, tells us that he is a minister, a minister of mercy.

The establishment of the Diaconate should also be considered when one inquires after the essential character of the Deacon's office. The institution or origin of the Deacon's office we find recorded in Acts 6:1-6. From this passage it is clear that the work of mercy was somewhat neglected in Jerusalem's Church because the time of the Apostles was wholly taken up by the ministry of the Word and the government of the Church. By the guidance of the Holy Spirit seven men were elected and appointed as Deacons or ministers of mercy. This distinct office was also introduced in the other Churches, as frequent mention of the office in the epistles indicates. See, for instance, Phil 1:1.

But most important for the determination of the true nature of this office, is the question: In what special way does the Deacon represent Christ, the Head of His Church?

Christ, let us remember, is our chief Prophet, our only High Priest, and our eternal King (cf. H. Catechism, Lord's Day XII).

Now this three-fold office of our representative before God was typified in the O. T. Church in its prophets, priests, and kings. When the real Prophet, Priest, and King came these types ceased. Nevertheless, Christ did ordain through His Spirit three permanent offices for His N. T. Church namely, Ministers of the Word, Deacons, and Elders, representing Christ respectively as Prophet, Priest, and King.

Deacons are, therefore, representatives of Christ as the merciful High Priest. They are ministers of God's mercy and love in Christ Jesus. There is not a single passage in the N. T. which aims to give us a complete characterization of the office of Deacon. Neither Acts 6 nor I Tim. 3:8-10 does this. But the fact that the Deacons are Christ's special representatives in His work of mercy in fundamental and all-important, and should govern us when we seek to determine the essential character of the Deacon's office.

Already in the second century after Christ the character of the Diaconate was severely corrupted and changed. Originally the Churches were ruled by bodies of Elders or Presbyteries. But during the century mentioned above a few of the Elders assumed the position of Bishops, and the other Elder as well as the Deacons became subservient to them. Eventually the Bishops occupied a place comparable to the positions of High Priests during the O. T. dispensation and the Elders were regarded to be ordinary priests, whereas the Deacons were looked upon as Levites, who were expected to assist the priests. At first the Deacons still assisted in the work of mercy but when, in course of time, the work of mercy was absorbed by the various orders of monks, the Deacons' office was wholly robbed of its rightful and precious heritage. The Deacon now assisted at the ministration of the Word and of the Sacraments. The serving of the table mentioned in Acts 6:2, so the Roman Church ruled, referred to the serving of the sacramental tables in spite of the fact that the reference is clearly to the work of charity and mercy as practiced in the early Church at Jerusalem.

Luther did not restore the Deacon to his rightful and God-given position. The Lutheran Church left the work of mercy to the civil government, and the name Deacon was later applied to those who acted as assistant pastors in large cities. But John Calvin restored the work of Christian mercy to the Deacon, and the Deacon to this work of mercy. Calvin even distinguished between two types of Deacons. To some he assigned the work of caring for the poor and to others the care of the sick, i.e. nursing the sick and infirm.

Eventually only the former type was perpetuated in the Reformed Churches of Germany, France, Scotland, and Holland. Not as if the

Reformed Churches ever felt that the sick and the aged, and mentally deficient might be neglected, but their care, though often sponsored directly by the Churches through their Deacons was often left to private Christian initiative, supported and encouraged by the Churches.

2. Qualifications for this office.

The qualifications for the Deacon's office may be gleaned particularly from the passages of Holy Writ already referred to, namely, Acts 6:1-7 and I Tim. 3:8-12.

Acts 6:3 reads as follows: "Look ye out therefore, brethren, from among you seven men of good report, full of the Spirit and of wisdom, whom we may appoint over this business." This text mentions three essential qualifications which must be present in those holding the Deacon's office. They must be: **of good report,** i.e., men held in esteem, especially by their Christian associates, because of their exemplary Christian conduct; **full of the** Spirit, i.e., men full of the Spirit's consecration and love, so essential to one dispensing the mercy of Christ; **full of wisdom,** i.e. men having a large amount of good judgment, so that they may help and sustain the right parties in the right way.

And in I Tim. 3:8-12 we read: "Deacons in like manner must be grave, not double-tongued, not given to much wine, not greedy of filthy lucre; holding the mystery of the faith in a pure conscience. And let these also first be proved; then let them serve as deacons if they be blameless. Women in like manner must be grave, not slanderers, temperate, faithful in all things. Let deacons be husbands of one wife, ruling their children and their own houses well." Briefly stated we may summarize the requirements contained in this passage as follows: Deacons must not be shallow and insincere, but serious minded; they must not be undependable and two-faced, but steadfast and honest; they must be temperate, even shunning the use of much wine; not stingy nor apt to accept bribes; they must live according to the life of faith, graciously revealed unto them, in such a way that their conscience need not accuse them constantly; they must be men not suddenly and prematurely called to office, but tried and observed and found worthy; they must be men free from polygamy (Calvin's interpretation: Men having more than one wife, while converted were seemingly not forced to forsake their additional wives, but for the sake of the example and because of their abnormal situations such could not serve as office-bearers); they must be men governing their own households according to God's Word.

Sometimes it has been claimed that one who is hard-pressed financially and who may be in need of assistance on the part of the Church is really disqualified to serve as Deacon. But this is merely a conception of man, for which we find no support in the Bible. It might even be contended that, other things being equal, one who is himself hard-pressed is by that very fact better able to sympathize with a needy brother, than he who has never felt the pinch of poverty.

3. The matter of deaconesses.

It cannot be proven from Holy Writ that so-called deaconesses were actually called and ordained to office, just as the Deacons were. I Tim. 3:11, quoted above, does indicate that women had a share in the work of mercy practiced by the early Churches. But in the absence of any indication that women were ever inducted into office we conclude that these deaconesses were appointed to assist the Deacons in an unofficial capacity.

The Wezelian Convention, 1568, judged that it might be well to appoint worthy women to the office under discussion. Evidently, the Convention did not mean that women should be ordained as Deaconesses, but that they should be appointed to assist the Deacons. For in 1581 the Classis of Wezel asked the Synod of Middelburg, 1581, whether it would not be "advisable to re-institute the office of deaconesses." But this Synod answered in the negative, "because of various inconveniences which might follow." It did however declare that in times of wide-spread epidemics or much sickness, which called for nurse duties which the Deacons could not perform with propriety, the Deacons should call in the assistance of their wives, or other suitable women.

And thus the Reformed Churches never ordained deaconesses. Nevertheless women can do excellent and indispensable work as assistants to the Deacons. Neither the O.T. nor the N.T. knows of offices peculiar to women or open to men and women alike. God's plan as revealed in Holy Writ, knows of no women as officials in God's Church. Nevertheless also in this respect the woman is often a helpmeet for man. Women assisted Jesus, and also the Apostles, even in the prophetic work of the Church. So also our women can do wonderful service through our various Church organizations and if need be, in our Catechism classes, as well as in our Sunday schools. Thus also she can definitely assist the Deacons in the discharge of their duties. In our evangelization work at home or abroad she can take an active and useful part. And, as stands to reason, in non-ecclesiastical spheres she can occupy a place of Christian leadership, particularly through and for agencies definitely Christian, such as our Christian day schools.

ARTICLE 25

The office peculiar to the Deacons is diligently to collect alms and other contributions of charity, and after mutual counsel, faithfully and diligently to distribute the same to the poor as their needs may require it; to visit and comfort the distressed and to exercise care that the alms are not misused; of which they shall render an account in Consistory, and also (if anyone desires to be present) to the Congregation, at such a time as the Consistory may see fit.

THE DUTIES OF DEACONS

Article 25 speaks of "the office peculiar to the Deacons." Here again the Church Order does not refer to the essence of the Deacon's office, but rather to the labors which Scripture attributes to Deacons. Five matters are mentioned in this article. They are: the diligent collection of alms and other contributions of charity; the faithful and diligent distribution of alms and other contributions of charity; the visiting and comforting of those that are in distress; the exercise of care against the misuse of alms; the rendering of periodic reports to the Consistory and Congregation concerning collections and distributions made. We shall consider each of these.

1. Collection of alms and other contributions of charity.

First of all a word regarding the difference between "alms" and "other contributions of charity." Strictly speaking, there is no difference. Alms, as the Dutch "aalmoezen," are gifts of charity. The word has a general meaning. The English word as well as its Dutch equivalent stands related to a Greek word signifying, "to be merciful." Up to the year 1581 the Church Order spoke only of alms, and did not refer to "other contributions of charity." The Synod of Middelburg, 1581, speaks of "de aalmoessen, en andere armengoederen." Now it should not be overlooked that "other contributions of charity" is not a literal translation of "andere armengoederen." The Dutch expression armengoederen is used to indicate legacies and other gifts in the form of real estate property given to the Diaconates for the benefit of the poor. Our translation, however, rather makes us think of gifts in the form of food, clothing, etc.

It may also be noted that the expression "contributions of charity," is a rather general one, also employed by the world at large. However, in Article 25 it has a restricted significance. It does not merely signify "good-will contributions," but rather contributions made in the first place for God's sake, motivated by Christian love.

Deacons then must collect and solicit these moneys and gifts for the poor. In times of special stress gifts in the form of food, clothing, etc., are very valuable. These are most conveniently solicited and collected on week-days. Gifts in the form of money should be collected in the first place at the regular Sunday services, of which services gifts of gratitude are an integral part. When these gifts are inadequate the Deacons should ask the Consistories to make the situation known to the Church. The preaching of the Word should also help make the congregation faithful in its contribution toward the needy poor. At times the Deacons may find it necessary to collect gifts of money from members in the Church who are blessed above the average.

Years ago the benevolence offering for the poor was taken at the doors as the congregation was being dismissed. Our present method is doubtlessly more appropriate. Bringing our gifts of love and gratitude to the Lord should be more than an appendix to the service. It is an actual part of the service.

Our gifts must be given from the right motive and conscientiously, not to be seen and praised of men. Christ said: "But when thou doest alms, let not thy left hand know what they right hand doeth: that thine alms may be in secret: and thy Father which seeth in secret shall recompense thee," Matt. 6:3, 4. From these considerations some have preferred not to use open collection plates as are quite generally in use in our Churches today, but rather pocket-like receptacles, a convenient type of which are still on the market today. We fail to see, however, that our open collection plates greatly promote the sins against which Christ warns in Matthew 6. The possibilities at least are very limited, and can never be ruled out entirely, no matter what type of receptacle may be used.

It is altogether proper for our Diaconates to urge able relatives of needy poor to do their Christian duty first of all. Parents that are able to do so are in duty bound to help needy children though these have long since left the parental fireside. And children likewise should be anxious to help their needy parents. This all is so obvious that argument is unnecessary. And Deacons should not permit delinquency on this score to go unheeded and unreported.

Neither would it be out of place for Deacons to solicit employment for their needy poor, if it appears that assistance to secure work is needed. Not that our Diaconates must stand ready to answer everyone's beck and call in this respect. But in exceptional cases an official request from one of our Church Diaconates might do what mere individual effort failed to accomplish. In such a case Deacons ought to act. Prevention is better than a cure we say. So also in this case, termination is better than continuation.

Money-raising schemes, such as bazaars, suppers, etc., should never be resorted to by our representatives of Christ as merciful High Priest.

In extreme circumstances it may be necessary to seek government aid. Conditions, for instance, during recent years may have forced our Deacons to advise needy brethren to apply for county aid, or these conditions may have caused some of our Diaconates to accept government aid offered them by government agencies in the form of food and clothing. But these situations are never ideal. The Lord's poor should be relieved by the Lord's own people, from love and gratitude toward Him. To help relieve Churches in great need, also during days of economic depressions, all of our Churches should maintain a goodly surplus in their poor funds, so that the strong and the favored can come to the assistance of those that are in distress. In our care for the poor we are often too individualistic. We should feel the tie that binds us together in Christ and help each other, rather than permit poverty stricken Churches to appeal to the government for aid. It is true that as tax-payers we are helping to create the funds with which the government supports its indigent subjects. But this is merely our duty as citizens. Over and above this, if at all possible, we should support our own needy, so that they need not depend upon the world or upon the government.

2. The distribution.

Why does the Church Order stipulate that distribution must be made "faithfully and diligently"?

For more than one reason. In the first place, the Deacon's work is very much the Lord's work. And in the Lord's work we should always be faithful—true and loyal—to the charge committed, and diligent—zealous and prompt—as well. Moreover, the work to which our Deacons are called is the Lord's work of mercy. Unfaithfulness and laxity are altogether out of place where mercy is needed. Suffering and want must be relieved faithfully and promptly. Furthermore, again and again the Deacons will find that the need which calls for help is rather urgent inasmuch as many do not call for aid until dire want compels them. Consequently "God's Ministers of Mercy" must be on the look-out constantly and be ready to act with promptness.

The Deacons should bring their gifts to those in need as friends of Christ to friends of Christ, standing on par with them. Attitudes of superiority on the part of the Deacons would be altogether out of place. And therefore, under ordinary circumstances the gifts of Christian charity to the Lord's needy should be given directly to the parties concerned in their own homes. Ordinarily they should not be required to call for them at stipulated hours, as was sometimes done in former years.

According to which standard must distribution be made? The Church Order says that distribution must be made to the poor "as their needs may require it." The daily needs of the indigent in the midst of the Church must be supplied. That which ordinary comfort requires must be given. This is according to Biblical example: "And distribution was made unto each, according as anyone had need," Acts 4:35. None of the needy should suffer lack where such can be avoided, though it is also true that the Church should not give for needless luxuries. If times are hard and consequently the needy poor numerous, the Deacons must do all they can to meet each one's need, but they may be forced to reduce their distribution below the bare minimum proportionately. But never should this be done until the Church has done its utmost to meet its responsibility toward the Lord's poor fully. And needless to say. in the spirit of Christian mercy, none should ever begrudge a needy brother or sister a little more than he or she actually needs. Liberality toward our poor should never be frowned upon, but always encouraged.

What is the significance of the phrase "after mutual consent"? Our Deacons are not allowed to act independently, as individuals in the collection and distribution of gifts. The needs of those that require support, temporarily or more permanently, should be discussed at a Deacons' Meeting, so that they together, upon due investigation or trustworthy information may decide what is to be done. "After mutual counsel" the Deacons shall thus make distribution. This does not mean that in special emergencies one or two Deacons may never act independently and instantly. For instance, sickness or accidents may call emergency situations into existence and may require instant relief. But such cases will be the exceptions, and should always be reported in full at the very next Deacons' Meeting for the approval, or else disapproval, of the whole body. And let us not forget, the exception does not alter the rule. Some Churches have an emergency committee to which emergency cases are referred. Much can be said in favor of such committees.

Mutual counsel is necessary also because our Deacons administer mercy in name of the whole congregation. Now a number of officebearers acting in unison give better expression to this principle than individual and independent action could do. Moreover, mutual counsel greatly reduces the possibilities of arbitrariness and faulty decisions. In the multitude of counselors there is wisdom.

3. Visiting and comforting those in distress.

Why does the Church Order specify that Deacons shall "visit and comfort the distressed"? Because our Deacons represent, as has been said before, Christ in the dispensation of His mercy. Our Diaconates are therefore far more than committees for relief work. They must relieve want and distress, but not in a mere functional way, as the county or state would do, but with a heart of sympathy and love. And they must give not merely with a humanitarian sympathy and love, but with the sympathy and love of Christ Himself. This requires interest and a personal, warm touch which only a personal visit can convey. Moreover, sometimes the distressed may not need money, food, or clothing nearly as much as assistance in some other form, such as sick care, or words of comfort from Holy Writ. Our Form for the installations of Elders and Deacons very appropriately states that one of the tasks of our Deacons is to relieve "the distressed both with kindly deeds and words of consolation and cheer from Scripture." This phase of the Deacon's work is very important and very beautiful. But to a large extent this all-important work of Christ as merciful High-Priest is forgotten and neglected. Some Churches seem to prefer young men as Deacons, especially if they have some business ability. Spiritual qualifications and Christian experience, which are certainly very essential for one who shall have to "visit and comfort the distressed," are forgotten all too generally.

4. Care against misuse of alms.

Regarding this rather difficult and delicate matter it is impossible to lay down a general rule which our Deacons can just apply in a uniform and press-the-button fashion. We live in a world of sin and we deal with imperfect men and women,—also in the Church. Now, nearly all who draw from congregational poor funds do so only under stress of circumstances. They will, of course, exercise great care not to misuse that which comes to them by way of Christian charity from the Church of God. But some that are in want and distress are, to say the least, poor managers, if not wilfully careless. Now the Church may not condone the appropriation of the Lord's benevolence money for unnecessary luxuries or wasteful expenditures. And so if there is **just cause** for suspicion on the part of the Deacons on this score, they should confer with the parties concerned, and sympathetically but firmly tell them that the practice in question can not continue. If it does continue, support should be given in kind, that is, in the form of food, clothing, etc. However, our Deacons must never play the part of "inquisitors." The God-given responsibilities and liberties of brothers and sisters in Christ should ever be respected by them. They must, in the spirit of Christian charity, avoid all suspicious questioning and needless wounding. Only when necessity compels them should they go beyond an ordinary investigation.

5. Rendering periodic reports.

Our Diaconates are, under normal circumstances, separate bodies, but never independent bodies. In many of our Churches however they always meet with the Elders as a Consistory, and at these meetings all the diaconal affairs are discussed and decided upon. But normally, according to the set-up of our Church Order, our Deacons have their separate meetings, at which they deliberate and also decide and act. But all their decisions and actions must be reported to the Consistory for approval. Reformed church polity knows only one ruling body in the Church and that is the Consistory, ideally consisting of the ruling and teaching Elders, or, putting it in our present terminology, consisting of Ministers and Elders. The government of the Church has been entrusted by Christ to the bishops, shepherds, or Elders. Consequently they also, according to Biblical precept and example, have supervision over the service of the Word and Sacraments by the Ministers and over the service of mercy by the Deacons. The Church Order accords our Diaconates a certain amount of independent activity, which should not be ignored, neglected, and infringed upon. But the unity of the Church and of the various offices in Christ as head of the Church requires that they should submit regular reports of their work to the Consistory for approval.

But the concluding provision of Article 25 also provides that a report shall be rendered to the congregation. Why so? Not that the congregation may give official approval or disapproval, for the Consistory is the only ruling body in and for the congregation. However the work of the Deacons is, after all, not the work of the personnel of the Diaconate, nor of the Consistory, but it is the work of the whole congregation. When our Deacons perform deeds of mercy or give gifts of Christian charity then the Church as a whole does this through them in the name of Christ. Consequently, the congregation should be informed. And the Deacons should stand in close touch with the membership of the Church. Therefore they should report to the congregation periodically under the direction of the Consistory. Of course, these reports should be general. Names and amounts should be reported to the Consistory but not to the congregation. That would be out of keeping with the spirit of Christian love. Moreover, the congregation is not interested in names and individual amounts, but rather in the fact that its work of mercy is properly carried on; that the needy poor, and the widows and orphans, and the sick and distressed are properly supplied, provided for and visited.

Beyond a doubt this provision of our Church Order is a very excellent one. But as many of its excellent and wise provisions have fallen into disuse to a large extent, so also this one. To our hurt and the hurt of our ecclesiastical work of mercy no doubt.

ARTICLE 26

In places where others are devoting themselves to the care of the poor, the Deacons shall seek a mutual understanding with them to the end that the alms may all the better be distributed among those who have greatest need. Moreover, they shall make it possible for the poor to make use of institutions of mercy, and to that end they shall request the Board of Directors of such institutions to keep in close touch with them. It is also desirable that the Deaconates assist and consult one another, especially in caring for the poor in such institutions.

DIACONAL CO-OPERATION

In this article the Church Order provides first of all for contacts between our diaconates and other agencies caring for those in want; secondly for contacts between our diaconates and Christian institutions of mercy; lastly, for mutual co-operation and assistance on the part of various diaconates.

1. The historical background of Article 26.

When our Synod of 1914 adopted the present reading of our Church Order it merely accepted an up-to-date rendering of the Church Order of the great Synod of Dort, 1618-19. The Church Order was garbed in present day Dutch, (largely modeled after the rendering accepted by the Reformed Churches of the Netherlands in 1905) and obsolete provisions applicable to conditions no longer extant were replaced by rulings which time and circumstances now require.

Article 26 as it had stood since 1618-19 was one of the articles that was well-nigh entirely out of date, especially as to the terminology employed. The original article reads as follows: "De Diakenen zullen ter plaatse waar huiszittenmeesters of andere aalmoezeniers zijn, van dezen begeeren goede correspondentie met hen te willen houden, teneinde de almoezen te beter uitgedeeld mogen worden onder degenen die meest gebrek hebben."

Amongst many other things the Reformation of the 16th Century also restored the Diaconate as a divine and Biblical institution. In the Roman Church, Deacons were and are still subservient helpers to the priests. In the Reformed Churches the Deacons again became ministers of mercy, representatives of Christ as merciful High-Priest.

Now the Reformed Churches of the Netherlands very logically claimed that the possessions and moneys which were originally given to the Churches in their deformed condition for the alleviation of poverty and suffering, should go to them and their Deacons and not to the government agencies for relief work. But not in every case did the government agree. In many instances the government wanted to administer all poor relief work. Not so much as a matter of Christian mercy, but more as a matter of state business. The Churches, however, notwithstanding the close connection between Church and State at this time, everywhere instituted the office of the Deacons and insisted on maintaining their own poor relief work, and that not merely in the secular or humanitarian sense, but in the Biblical sense of showing mercy to Christ's own in His stead.

But the government also appointed its poor relief agencies. It was soon discovered that certain parties would receive aid through the Church of their locality and also from the local government agency, whereas others suffered from insufficient support. To avoid needless duplication and to conserve funds for necessary relief, the Churches decided that the Deacons should request "goede correspondentie" (literally translated, "good correspondence") from the government agencies for poor relief. No doubt they meant by "good correspondence" that each should report to the other to whom aid was extended. Let us remember in this connection that the tie between the government and the Churches was a very close one in former years. The Reformed Churches of the Netherlands were at that time the only church organization officially recognized as such, and even to a certain extent sponsored by the government. Especially the Church Orders prior to the great Synod of Dort exemplify this close connection abundantly.

2. Contacts with other agencies.

What is the significance of the first provision of Article 20 as it now reads? Today we still find that poor relief is extended through government agencies. Moreover, we have our Red Cross and a host of more local charitable organizations as a rule. These agencies regularly or in times of special stress extend the helping hand to those in want, regardless of Church affiliations. Now to avoid needless extension of help Article 26 provides that our Diaconates are to request "good correspondence" (Dutch rendering, 1914) with these agencies. The official English translation speaks of a "mutual understanding." This term is no doubt stronger than its Dutch equivalent. The Dutch rendering, also in the light of history, merely acknowledges the fact that some of our needy Church members at times receive aid from agencies outside of the Church. It does not commit itself in favor of this situation, not even by implication. From our English redaction it might be inferred that it is the position of our Churches that secular support of our Church members is perfectly proper and normal. However, it is the position of all loyal Reformed Churches that the Church of Christ must fully take care of its own needy. Needy and afflicted children of God should never be compelled to seek aid from the world, but should be assisted by their own brothers and sisters in Christ. That is the Biblical rule. That is the ideal. And only when dire necessity forces us should we deviate from this rule and ideal. Consequently we would prefer "adequate correspondence," "necessary contacts" or some kindred term to the present "mutual understanding."

Or better still, we would prefer to eliminate this whole provision. In its original form it dates back to a semi-State Church condition regulating somewhat an irregular state of affairs. For our condition and situation the present provision is either not necessary, or impossible of adequate execution, in view of the numerous agencies which are engaged in relief work. And as the provision stands it obscures a principle, namely that the Church is fully responsible for its own needy. If in times of special stress some of our people must seek and accept aid from other agencies, then common sense will tell our Deacons that they must avoid duplication by all legitimate means. We really need no Church Order provision for this.

3. Contacts with institutions of mercy.

The second provision of Article 26, stipulating that the Deacons "shall make it possible for the poor to make use of institutions of mercy," etc., as well as the balance of this article, is an addition of our Christian Reformed Churches. The original article contains nothing of this. The Reformed Churches of Holland, which accepted a revision of the Church Order in 1905, left Article 26 unchanged. Consequently this second provision of Article 26 and what follows it, is not found in the Church Order of Holland.

The significance of this ruling is obvious to all who know our people and their activities somewhat. During the last few decades our people have had a very prominent part in establishing certain institutions of mercy, especially for the care of the mentally abnormal. Besides, at various centers there are Holland Homes, or Homes for the Aged, which are also in part at least, institutions of mercy.

A large number of afflicted could not be placed in the first-named institutions for lack of funds. Diaconates began to aid the afflicted or their relatives financially, so that this very necessary Christian care could be shared by such as would otherwise have to forego this privilege. To assure the continuance of this practice the second provision of Article 26 was added to this Article.

It is well that our leaders of 1914 exercised this wise forethought and added this timely ruling to Article 26. It is altogether proper that the Deacons extend their helping hand to members who need institutional care. This is self-evident to us. But future generations might grow lax in this respect. This provision may help to avoid neglect, or to recall delinquents to duty.

". . . they shall request the Board of Directors of such institutions to keep in close touch with them." This part of the ruling most likely refers to individual cases. If there be a member of one of our Churches who receives care at an institution of Christian mercy, but who is unable to pay the required sum, then the authorities of the institution concerned should notify the Diaconate concerned. This would also hold when application is made for admittance and the necessary amount cannot be paid by the party or parties involved.

But this latter provision might also be interpreted to mean that any and all Diaconates ought to ask all institutions of mercy in which our group is particularly interested, to keep in close touch with them, so that they may be well-informed as to the work and needs of these institutions and be ready to extend aid in any particular case that may occur.

To the best of our knowledge, the former interpretation is the generally accepted one.

4. The matter of ecclesiastical institutions of mercy.

There have been those that would prefer to see the Churches build and maintain institutions of Christian mercy, instead of leaving this to other organizations. Others have contended that it is not the business of the Church to take this matter to hand. The Church, so they say, must preach the Gospel, and leave the building and managing of institutions of mercy to groups of believers organized into societies for this purpose. Secondly, those that do not favor ecclesiastical institutions of mercy state that this would require a separate and powerful ecclesiastical organization of Diaconates, whereas Reformed Church polity knows but one type of ruling or governing bodies, viz.: Consistories, Classes, Synods. Church-owned and Church-managed institutions of mercy would require the organization of a second type of ruling bodies, which would run counter to the divine plan, and create confusion and dualism. There are other considerations of a more practical nature, but these two are the main objections.

The first of these arguments we do not care to support. Jesus indeed charged His Church to preach the Gospel, but He also charged it to heal the sick. And the Church represents Him as merciful High Priest as well as great Prophet and eternal King. Of course, the plan would involve the Church in business transactions. But what of this? It may be practical wisdom to reduce the Church's business transactions to a minimum, but speaking from the aspect of principles, this is not a requirement. The construction and care of church buildings is business, too.

Regarding the second objection we quote our late Prof. Heyns rather at length: "On almost every Diaconal Conference, as Prof. Biesterveld relates (**Het Diaconaat**, p. 386), the question was brought forward whether it was not possible to come to representative diaconal meetings with power to act. In 1888 a treatise was published by Prof. W. Vanden Bergh of the Free University,[1] in which the creation of such an organization of the Diaconates of Classes and Provinces was advocated. In the same year the Diaconal Congress adopted the following proposition: 'Especially with a view to social problems, to the providing and maintenance of institutions of mercy for the care of the blind, the deaf-mute, the orphans, the insane, etc., it is desirable that there be joint meetings of the Diaconates of Classes and Provinces, charged and authorized; a) to discuss social problems and miseries, their causes and cure; b) to establish or maintain institutions for the care of the blind, etc.; c) to tend to the matter of well-to-do Diaconates rendering assistance to the poorly provided ones. In 1899, however, the question was brought before the General Synod of Groningen, and its decision was, 'that the organization of separate major Assemblies for diaconal matters was not in agreement with the mutual relation and co-operation of Church Assemblies as these are presented by the Confession and the Church Order.'

"In the meantime a different way of bringing about contact and the possibility of co-operation of the local Diaconates had been proposed by Dr. Bavinck (Dogmatiek, IV, 2nd ed., p. 469). It was that Deacons, together with Ministers and Elders, should be delegated to major Assemblies, and should have in these major Assemblies a decisive vote in all matters pertaining to the service of mercy."[2]

This suggestion of Bavinck, vigorously seconded by Heyns, would evidently meet the well-founded second objection against Church-owned and Church-managed institutions of mercy. Incidentally, it would give the Diaconates of our Churches the consideration and development to which they are entitled. Nevertheless we fear that for various reasons this suggestion would prove to be impractical. How-

---

1. This should read: "Dr. Mr. W. VandenBergh, Minister at Voorthuizen," Vanden Bergh never having been professor at any school.

2. Prof. Wm. Heyns: **Handbook for Elders and Deacons**, pp. 350-1.

ever as far as the principle involved in this question is concerned, we would ask: Why should the Church as an institution be required to delegate a very important branch of its work of mercy to certain groups of believers? There are, no doubt, a number of practical objections against diaconal institutions of mercy. For instance: Diaconal institutions of mercy would make co-operation with believers of other denominations more difficult. But on the score of principles we failed to locate a valid one. And there are also practical considerations which favor diaconal institutions of mercy.

Dr. F. L. Rutgers (Kerkelijke Adviezen, I, p. 210) cites instances which show that diaconal institutions of mercy, managed by large Diaconates under supervision of the Consistories, were not entirely unknown in the past. In fact some of the Reformed Churches in Holland still maintain their own institutions of mercy.

5. Mutual consultation and assistance.

Article 26 finally suggests mutual consultation and assistance. Co-operation between our various diaconates, particularly neighboring diaconates, is certainlv proper. There are practical considerations which make co-operation advisable. For instance: One Church may have many needy in the providence of God and but little ability to help. Another Church may have but few needy and numerous well-to-do members who can help those in need. Moreover, the inherent unity of all the Churches, and denominational unity, would suggest co-operation also. "Bear ye one another's burden," holds here as well as elsewhere.

Note well that Article 26 does not say that our Diaconates should hold combined gatherings, such as classical and synodical gatherings are. The Church Order merely urges consultation and assistance.

Regarding the spelling of the word Deaconates in Article 26 see our comments on page 167.

ARTICLE 27

The Elders and Deacons shall serve two or more years according to local regulations, and a proportionate number shall retire each year. The retiring officers shall be succeeded by others unless the circumstances and the profit of any Church, in the execution of Articles 22 and 24, render a re-election advisable.

TENURE OF OFFICE FOR ELDERS AND DEACONS

Article 27 first of all speaks of the length of time for which Elders and Deacons are to be chosen and appointed. Secondly this article provides for definite retirement of these office-bearers, though it permits exceptions to this rule.

1. Limited tenure of office for Elders and Deacons.

The Presbyterian Church in the U. S. A. differentiates between Term or Rotary Eldership, and Permanent Eldership. Doctrinally the Presbyterian Churches hold that all the offices of the Church are permanent. He who is once inducted into office, whether as Minister, Elder, or Deacon, remains in office as long as he remains a member in good standing of the Presbyterian Church. Removal from the particular Church which inducted him into office, or old age, does terminate the active execution of office, but he does not lose the office as such.

When referring to this conception and practice consistent with it the Presbyterians speak of Permanent Eldership.

However, certain practical difficulties obstructed the practice of Permanent Eldership. After much discussion the General Assembly of 1875 authorized Term or Rotary Eldership. That is to say, Elders might be elected for a definite term of years as far as the actual execution of their office is concerned. But the principle underlying Permanent Eldership was maintained. Elders may either be elected for life or for a term of three years. Term Elders may retire from active service at the end of their term, but they continue to be office-bearers. It was even decided, consistently so, that: "Elders, once ordained, shall not be divested of the office when they are not re-elected." Such Elders, in common with all retired Elders, have no vote in their Session (Consistory), but may be asked for advice and may also be sent as delegates to the meetings of Presbyteries, Synods, and General Assemblies. At a later period "Term Deaconship" was also made permissible.

Our Church Order in this present article stipulates a limited tenure of office for Elders and Deacons. How do we account for this fact? Historically this provision of Article 27 dates back to none other than John Calvin himself. Calvin and his co-workers re-instituted the Elders' and Deacons' office in the Reformed Churches. Now Calvin found no definite stipulation in the Bible which compelled him to look upon these offices as permanent in their very essence. Nowhere does the Bible even say—thus Calvin—that appointment to these offices in the days of the Apostles was for life, although it must be granted forthwith that term appointment is not mentioned either. Scripture, in the absence of definite stipulations, so the Reformers concluded, leaves this matter free, so that the Churches may regulate this matter according to their own best interests and welfare.

Now, to avoid a repetition of Roman misuse of power through its hierarchical system from which the Churches had suffered so much, and because very few brethren could afford to give much of their time to church work continuously, Calvin thought it wise to appoint Elders and Deacons, not for life, but for a limited period of time. In Geneva they were appointed for one-year terms only. The Reformed Churches in Holland followed Calvin's example. The Wezelian Convention still spoke of one-year terms. Those who were able and competent might be continued. Why such extremely short terms, and that in a day when everything moved much slower? To avoid misuse of power. But especially because the demands were very heavy on the time of the Elders especially. All the Churches were young. Many church members had been reared in the Roman Church. Consequently they were very ignorant as to the true faith and they were constantly surrounded and confronted with all kinds of problems and dangers to their spiritual life. For a while, as we had occasion to mention heretofore, the Elders were expected to conduct home-visitation with every family of the Church every week, each Elder having his own district for this purpose.

Soon, however, already in 1571, the normal period of service for Elders and Deacons became two years. Continuation in office, by decision of the Consistory with the approbation of the congregation, or immediate re-election by the congregation, were made permissible, if the welfare of a particular Church seemed to demand this. But definite retirement for the ensuing year became the rule.

Gradually the period of service was lengthened in many Churches. Yet, inasmuch as there were no Synodical gatherings for the 17th to the 19th century, Article 27 remained unaltered. However, in 1905 the Churches of Holland revised the Article as we now have it, their redaction having been adopted by us in 1914.

We appreciate the element of flexibility which we find in this article also. Why make hard and fast rules when such is not necessary and often contrary to the true welfare of the Churches? "Two or more years." Two years may be advisable in exceptional cases, but as a rule a two-year term is too brief. A Consistory, to do consistent and thorough work, needs a certain amount of stability and continuity. Short terms do not make for these desirable qualities. In Churches where the two-year term is in force, every twelfth month one-half of the Consistory is unacquainted with matters that may be pending. Continuity is promoted by less frequent and less complete changes. In the Netherlands many Churches today elect their Elders and Deacons for four or five or even six-year terms. Most of our Churches seem to maintain three-year terms.

Why does the Church Order stipulate that a **proportionate** number **of Elders and Deacons shall retire each year?** Obviously to rule out all arbitrariness. All things pertaining to God's Church should be conducted with due order and impartial regularity. If the retirement of office-bearers and their induction into office were not definitely regulated thus, misuse of power on the part of Consistories might occur with greater ease. Suppose, for an example, a certain Consistory should become unfaithful and disloyal as to the majority of its members. Then, if the common Church Order did not oblige them to do otherwise, they might so manipulate the retirement of office-bearers as to hold the balance of power.

This provision makes for good order and regularity. It shields Consistories against suspicion on the score of what we mentioned, and safeguards the Churches against evil practices which might otherwise creep in with greater ease.

2. Definite retirement.

Article 27 provides for definite retirement from office. That is to say, when one's term of office expires he is not immediately eligible to re-election to that office.

Against the practice of definite retirement the following considerations have been urged:

—The Church of Christ is worthy of the best talents at all times. The Church should not be compelled to pass by efficient men, not even for one year.

—Those that have served well should continue to serve without interruption, for the Churches need experienced men.

—The number of brethren well qualified in every way to serve is limited as it is. Their numbers should not be limited needlessly still further.

—Definite retirement reduces the prestige of the office which it sorely needs. Former respect for Elders, for instance, is fast waning.

—Definite retirement does not make for continuity, an element highly desirable for good Consistory work.

—Definite retirement promotes laxness as to studious application on the part of Consistory members, inasmuch as their service is only temporary.

—Definite retirement breaks the connecting link between office-bearers and the work of the major assemblies, to the hurt of both.

In favor of definite retirement the following considerations are the most weighty:

—Continuous service in Consistory would constitute a real hardship for many busy and burdened men. Many would feel compelled to withhold themselves altogether.

—Long continued periods of service in Consistory tends to promote hierarchical tendencies. Experience has taught that when men have served for a long period of years continuously, they are inclined to feel indispensable, and are inclined to become wilful.

—Definite retirement helps to ward off conservatism. Elderly men naturally tend to become overly conservative and immediate eligibility for re-election as a rule tends to keep the same men in office continuously, until they are too old to serve, and sometimes beyond that period.

—Definite retirement brings to the fore and puts into the harness new talents, while the others, if they have served well, enjoy a well-earned rest, ready to serve again in due season.

—Retired office-bearers are a good influence in the midst of the congregation.

—Inferior men (inferior as far as their work and ability as office-bearers is concerned, though they may be very good in doctrine and life), are thus retired from service in the least offensive way.

Although it must be admitted that there are good arguments on both sides of this question, yet those favoring definite retirement doubtlessly outweigh the arguments against the practice. We do believe, however, that the term of service could be lengthened in many of our Churches beyond the present-day two- and three-year limit, to very good advantage. This would somewhat meet the altogether valid objections against definite retirement.

3. Definite retirement not always required.

Definite retirement has been the rule in the Reformed Churches of our fathers ever since the Reformation, although at certain periods and at times it fell into disuse. But our fathers never held that it was the only possible way. Nor that it was for all Churches and under all circumstances the best policy.

In small Churches definite retirement would very often work real harm and hardship. In other Churches, though larger, it may be impossible to secure a sufficient number of worthy men for the nominations without including the names of retiring Consistory-members. For all such exceptional cases we have the provision that immediate renomination is permissible. The true welfare of the Churches is of far greater importance than adherence to a general rule adopted to promote the welfare of the Churches, but application of which in some cases would be to the detriment of the Churches.

Wherever conditions make immediate eligibility advisable, Consistories should not hesitate to make use of this exceptive provision.

A few practical questions, related to the material of Art. 27 still await our reply.

Should the number of Elders and Deacons always be equal? Not necessarily. In the majority of our Churches it may be perfectly proper to appoint an equal number of each. But in many Churches today there is much more work for the Elders than for the Deacons, and consequently a larger number of Elders should be appointed, if at least suitable men are available.

Supposing a Consistory desires to nominate a retiring Deacon for Elder or vice versa, would this be permissible in view of Art. 27? Yes. This article provides that no Elder shall immediately succeed himself as Elder, and no Deacon shall immediately succeed himself as Deacon. But one who retires from one office could be chosen to another office without any lapse of time. If someone has served as Deacon, and the Consistory finds that he has gifts for the Elder's office, then such a Consistory may instantly nominate him. It stands to reason, however, that it is better to wait if a sufficient number of men are available. But if the Consistory nominates such a one immediately, no rule is violated. In fact, one whose term as Elder or Deacon has not yet expired, may, even if circumstances render the step advisable, be nominated for the other office. If such a nominee is elected, the Church immediately elects his successor to the office which is thus vacated, from among the candidates nominated for the office concerned.

Some find fault with their Consistories when they nominate as office-bearers men who have retired the previous year. They would favor a rule which would discourage early renomination. Would such a rule be advisable? We answer in the negative. The Churches should be served by the best and most experienced of its members. Why systematically eliminate previous office-bearers longer than one year? If said former office-bearers are unworthy of the office, or if better qualified brethren are available, these brethren in the providence of God will eventually be chosen. The Churches, after all, elect. Ex-office-bearers that are inferior and undesirable are naturally passed by, either at the Consistory meeting or at the congregational meeting.

Suppose the newly elected office-bearers cannot be inducted into office at the appointed time, do they begin to function without installation? Synod of 1912 decided that in case the installation of newly-elected Elders and Deacons must be postponed for weighty reasons, the tenure of the retiring Elders and Deacons is extended, and they remain legal trustees of the Church.

ARTICLE 28

The Consistory shall take care, that the Churches for the possession of their property, and the peace and order of their meetings can claim the protection of the Authorities; it should be well understood, however, that for the sake of peace and material possession they may never suffer the royal government of Christ over His Church to be in the least infringed upon.

GOVERNMENTAL PROTECTION

The present article has but a brief history. It first saw the light of day as recently as 1914, having been adopted by our Synod of that year. Nearly all the articles of our Church Order wear the honorable crown of old age, and come to us with the prestige of antiquity, having been written and adopted by Reformed Synods before the year 1600, and having been reviewed and approbated by the great Synod of Dort, 1618-19. And so Article 28 is as a youthful child standing in the midst of men of mature years.

1. The original 28th article.

Of course, there was an Article 28 also before 1914. But its content and provision seemed out of date and out of position to our Synod of 1914, especially for our Churches in the United States of America. The Reformed Churches of Holland, in their revision of 1905, have left Article 28 unchanged. The following is our own rendering in English of the original 28th Article: "As it is the duty of the Christian governments to promote the sacred services of the Churches as much as possible, and to recommend their activity to all their subjects by personal example, and to assist the Ministers, Elders and Deacons in all cases of need or emergency, and to protect them in the execution of their tasks as governors of the Churches, so also the Ministers, Elders and Deacons are in duty bound zealously and in sincerity to urge obedience, love and respect toward the magistrates upon the whole congregation; they shall, moreover, make themselves good examples to the Church in this matter, and through the manifestation of due respect and the establishment of correspondence with the civil authorities they shall endeavor to secure and hold the good-will of the government toward the Churches; to the end that, each doing his duty in the fear of the Lord, all suspicion and distrust may be avoided and that thus due co-operation may be maintained for the welfare of the Churches."

Jansen says it is not clear why the Synod of Dort added this article. He suggests two possibilities, viz., (1) In order to secure civil approbation of the Church Order. This our post-Reformation fathers were very eager to secure. For that would mean that the Church Order would virtually have the force of civil law. And that in turn would promote the cause of Reformed Churches and unity. (2) To indicate clearly the duties and authority of both Government and Church, thus also committing themselves against the Arminian conception, which would virtually place the Government in authority over the Churches, and against the Roman conception which would subject the State to the Church.

Historically the original reading of Article 28 is not without significance. It tells us in plain words what the Fathers of Dort thought as to the proper relation between Church and State. A question ever up-to-date to be sure. And one which may become very urgent at any time also in our own country. Confer government interference with Church affairs during the World War, and think of the situation in certain European countries.

If Jansen is correct when he surmises that our Fathers adopted the original 28th Article because they desired to elevate the Church Order to the level of state laws through civil approbation, then in so far we would not concur. Neither do we today agree with all that the original article contains. But neither do we throw overboard every sentiment embodied in this article of 1618-19.

We question the wisdom of our Synod of 1914 when it eliminated the original article altogether. True, however, that the loss is not as great as it might be, inasmuch as we have an official commitment and expression regarding the relation between Church and State on the part of our Churches today in Article 36 of the Confession and the decision of the Synod of 1910 appended.

2. The chief provision of the present 28th article.

What is the chief provision of Article 28? That Consistories are in duty bound to secure proper recognition on the part of the Government for their respective Churches. Not that our Churches hold that the secular government, local, state, or national, have authority over the ecclesiastical affairs of its subjects. Not that we would attribute any supervisory authority to the State in regard to matters ecclesiastical. Churches are inherently, by dint of their very nature, free from State domination and State regulation. But each congregation, as an institution among men, has certain rights and privileges. Our Churches have the right to buy and build; to serve God unmolested; to retain their properties, etc. The Government is the God-ordained institution among men which, amongst other things, must also secure to the Churches their liberties and rights. Now, to assure the Churches the maximum of protection, also if need be through the courts, they must have legal recognition on the part of the Government. The obtainment of this legal standing or legal recognition Article 28 provides for.

The article states that **Consistories** shall see to it that the Churches can claim the protection of the authorities. The responsibility regarding this matter is therefore placed with the Consistories. They are the governing bodies in our Reformed system and so this is perfectly proper. In the Congregational system (Congregational and Baptist Churches, etc.), a matter of this kind would be referred to the congregation as a whole. Not so with us. This, however, does not mean that the congregation takes no action in this matter, and that the Consistory is the legal body which is incorporated. For the individual believers act also here. But under the direction and control of the office-bearers appointed.

We stated above that Article 28 does not mean to attribute supervisory authority to the Government, and that the Churches of Jesus Christ are inherently free from State domination. This is certainly correct. The Churches know no King but Jesus. Under Him they are sovereign within their own sphere. However, we do not mean to deny that the State has certain regulatory rights, which also touch the domain of the Churches. Civil authorities, for instance, may insist, for the safety of all concerned, that the general rules of fire prevention be observed as we erect our church buildings. For the protection of the health of the church-members, as well as for the community, they have a right to insist on proper sanitation. In matters as these the State authorities have a certain God-given responsibility, also regarding Churches. But as to matters of faith and confession; the internal arrangement of congregational activities; the government of the Church in spiritual matters, etc., these matters are strictly ecclesiastical, and not political. And concerning these matters the Church may and must say to the State: Hands off!

How should this provision be carried out? Through incorporation. This is evidently the intent of Article 28. It is true that also unincorporate groups are entitled to the protection of civil authorities, but the phrase, "for the possession of their property," clearly refers to incorporation. This was so self-evident to the Synod of 1914 that it did not even deem it necessary to use this term in formulating this article. The list of questions for Church Visitation approbated by Synod of 1922 does contain a specific query regarding proper incorporation.

Every State in our Union has provided for the incorporation of Church groups. After incorporation papers have been filed with the

Secretary of State, usually through the County Clerk, and after these have been properly approved and registered, the congregation has legal standing. As a corporate body it may transact its material affairs and claim the protection of the courts in case of necessity. Always within the terms of the incorporation document, of course. Without incorporation a Church may organize itself in our country and also transact its material business, but in cases of emergency it could never claim the protection of the courts. Ordinary police protection, etc., could be secured under normal circumstances, also by unincorporated Churches.

The main purpose for which incorporation is urged upon the Churches is no doubt to assure the Churches against unfair infringement upon their property rights, both on the part of individuals and groups—the latter especially. Sad to say, divergent doctrines are apt to be preached and advocated from our pulpits from time to time. Sometimes these culminate in sharp differences and separations. Almost invariably these divergent groups feel that they are not divergent or that they have not received a square deal, or both, and insist on holding the properties in their possession. Without proper incorporation the faithful groups and sections would in most cases lose all their possessions. Through incorporation legal claims and vindication becomes possible.

Too bad that these serious disputes occur. But let us appreciate the fact that our Churches have life enough left for these disputes when they are necessary.

3. The condition attached to this article.

The condition which concludes Article 28 reads as follows: It should be well understood, however, that for the sake of peace and material possession they may never suffer the royal government of Christ over His Church to be in the least infringed upon.

Our Synod of 1914 was thoroughly convinced that State domination over the Church may never be tolerated. It prized very highly the liberties which is the just right of each Church. State domination ever stands condemned inasmuch as Christ is the Church's absolute monarch. Never may the Church give unto Caesar that which is God's. Never may she detract from the authority and honor which is Christ's and give it to the State. Church history is replete with blunders and sins belonging to this category, blunders and sins committed to the dishonor of Christ and to the damage of the Churches concerned. Every time!

And so Synod of 1914 ruled, that, rather than detract in the least from Christ's authority over us, our Churches should remain unincorporated. Rather suffer loss of property and incur injustice than bring the Churches in bondage to the State. Whenever incorporation should entail this evil, so the article rules, Churches must refrain from incorporating.

Too bad that our civil governments incorporate our Churches as if they are ordinary societies or corporations. This is not as it should be. The Churches of Jesus Christ are not man-made corporations in the sense that secular organizations are. This evil should be rectified as soon as possible. But inasmuch as this feature has never entailed practices which we must condemn, incorporation is permissible even so.

CONCERNING ECCLESIASTICAL ASSEMBLIES

ARTICLE 29

Four kinds of ecclesiastical assemblies shall be maintained: the Consistory, the Classis (the particular Synod), and the General Synod.

FOUR KINDS OF ASSEMBLIES

Article 29 introduces us to a new division of our Church Order. Thus far we have considered matters pertaining to the officers in our Churches. Art. 29-52 concern the ecclesiastical assemblies. Art. 29-36 embody a number of general rules concerning our assemblies. Art. 37-40 deal particularly with matters consistorial. Art. 41-45 regulate classical matters. Art. 46-49 concern Particular Synods. And Art. 50-52 stipulate what is to be observed regarding our General Synods.

1. The historical origin of the ecclesiastical assemblies.

Consistory meetings, as stands to reason, were held from the very beginning of the Reformation movement. As soon as groups of believers had organized themselves, or were organized, into Reformed Churches, the ruling office-bearers met more or less regularly. But Major Assemblies were not held until several years later. Persecution, war, and lack of ecclesiastical understanding and development in many cases, account for this fact. The first few decades of the Reformation era were naturally formative to a high degree.

In France, where the Calvinistic Reformation had acquired a strong foothold, there were over 2,000 Reformed congregations by the year 1561. Three years prior, in 1558, there had been a gathering of a number of Reformed Ministers at the Church of Poitiers, where also a representative of the Church of Paris was in attendance. Here the advisability and need of Synodical gatherings was discussed. The Church of Paris was asked to call all the Reformed Churches of France in Synodical gathering. This Synod was held in Paris the following year, in 1559.

At this first Synod of Reformed Churches of France a Church Order was adopted to which the integrity of the several congregations is basic, but which also provides for provincial and national Synods, at which the common interests of the Churches might be discussed and acted upon. Classical meetings were not introduced in France until 1572.

The Reformed Churches of the southern Netherlands (now largely Belgium), met repeatedly since 1563, regulating their affairs largely according to the Orders in force in France and Geneva under Calvin.

The refugee Churches in England and Germany at this time also held their meetings.

The Wezelian Convention, 1568, though not a Synod inasmuch as the various delegates were not authorized to act for the various Churches, was the most representative gathering of Holland Churches held up to that year. Tentative regulations for definite federation were adopted.

The first Synod of the Reformed Churches of the Low Countries was held in 1571, at Emden, Germany. Conditions in the Netherlands were as yet too hostile and irregular for a Synodical gathering. The Emden Church Order provided for Consistories, Classes, Provincial Synods, and National Synods. At this time, according to Prof. H. Bouwman, the Churches of our forefathers yielded some of their individual rights regarding government and discipline for the sake of the general welfare of the Churches.* All delegates to this first Synod had been summoned and delegated with authority to act in this direction. At the same time rules were agreed upon which protected the rights of the individual members of the Churches, and which would counteract all wilfulness and arbitrariness. The Churches also agreed to admit candidates to the ministry only after consultation with the other neighboring Churches, and that Ministers would henceforth not be called or disciplined without such consultation.

A common Confession and a Church Order were adopted. In substance, as to its fundamental principles, we are still governed by this first Church Order, although it was revised according to need several times.

2. The significance of names given to these assemblies.

The word Consistory is derived from the Latin "consistorium," meaning, place of meeting. It indicates the body of men chosen to govern the affairs of a local Church. The Dutch speak of "Kerkeraad," i.e., Church Council. The Presbyterians refer to the body of their pastors and ruling Elders as the Session.

The word Classis (plural: Classes) is also Latin and indicates a division or class of people or of other objects.

And the word Synod is derived from the Greek "sunodos," indicating, "a coming together, assembly, meeting." The term "Particular Synod" indicates the gathering of a number of Classes. The Dutch original of our Article 29 speaks of "Provinciale Synoden," inasmuch as the borders of the various provinces of the Netherlands were made to serve as borders for the territory of Particular Synods also.

And finally, the term General Synod is used to indicate the gathering of all the federated Churches. The expression is used synonymous in the Netherlands with National Synod.

Art. 46-49, which pertain to Particular Synods, have no present and immediate value for us, inasmuch as our Churches do not hold Particular Synods. These articles were left in the Church Order for completeness sake. They, as will have been noted, are printed between parentheses.

3. The character of ecclesiastical assemblies.

Regarding the nature of ecclesiastical assemblies, note first of all that according to Reformed church polity, only such Churches as are confessionally like-minded can have part in these gatherings. For Churches to be federally united, these must have a common conception of Holy Writ, and thus a common working platform. Co-operation and promotion of each other's welfare would be impossible without confessional unity. Ecclesiastical federation without confessional unity would make for shallowness and fruitlessness, or else for trouble and constant conflict.

---

*Bouwman: **Ger. Kerkrecht,** 1934, II, pp. 2, 3.

Secondly, Churches ecclesiastically federated are and remain complete in themselves. The various local Churches do not dissolve themselves into a large classical Church, or into a national, synodical Church. The local congregation is a complete manifestation of the body of Christ, a unit in itself, and is not to be looked upon as a sub-division of a large super-Church ruling with superior power.

Furthermore, the nature of ecclesiastical federation ("kerkverband" is the Dutch term) is nevertheless such that the major assemblies exercise a binding authority regarding all matters which concern the Churches in general and which have not been specifically left to the individual Churches or congregations. At major assemblies the individual Churches act in unison by common consent. Decisions must therefore be respected unless proven contrary to the Bible or the Church Order previously agreed upon.

Reformed Church polity therefore upholds the integrity of the local Church, but at the same time does full justice to all the Churches federally united and the spiritual unity underlying the federation. Also because of this spiritual unity in Christ and confessional unity doctrinally, by God's providence, federation is not left merely to the judgment of each Church. There is a very definite spiritual obligation flowering forth from a real spiritual union and agreement which makes ecclesiastical federation and its implications mandatory upon the Churches.

4. The character and purpose of congregational meetings.

Our Churches know of four types of governing assemblies and only four; those mentioned in the present article. The congregational meeting is not amongst them. In the Congregational system (Congregational Churches, Baptist Churches, etc.) the congregational meeting is really the one and only authoritative Church assembly. Office-bearers are to execute the decision of the congregational meeting. In the Reformed system, however, it is held that Christ governs His Church through the offices instituted for that purpose. Is there no room, then, in the Reformed system for congregational meeting? Indeed there is. Repeatedly, for instance, the Church Order prescribes that matters must be submitted to the congregation for approbation. (Cf. Articles 4, 5, 22, etc.) Now, this may be done by announcing decisions which the Consistory is minded to take, so that the members can express themselves at a given consistory meeting, in case they desire to do so. Or the Consistory may call together all members in good and regular standing and submit the matter at hand to the Church as a body, for consideration and decision.

It has been held by many that our congregational meetings really have only advisory power, and no governmental, decisive authority. The present authors also once committed themselves in this direction. But careful consideration does not warrant this position.

Note, first of all, that Acts 1 and 6 clearly indicate that the office-bearers mentioned in these chapters, were elected to office **by the church**, and not by the Apostles, although the latter directed the appointment to office.

Note also that Article 22 of the Church Order speaks of the office-bearers as having been chosen by the Church, ". . . **chosen by it.**" And Article 31 of our Confession of Faith speaks of office-bearers by a lawful election "**by the Church.**" Question 85 of the Heidelberg Catechism also speaks of them as having been "**appointed by the Church.**" And at the time of their installation the Elders and Deacons are asked to declare that they feel in their hearts that they have been lawfully called of God's Church. And, finally, the suggested Articles of Incorporation, approved by the Synod of 1926, provide that no Consistory can sell or buy properties, mortgage or lease, or fix salaries "unless the affirmative vote of a majority of the members of this church organization . . . . shall first be obtained . . . ."

Indeed, the office-bearers guide and direct matters at congregational meetings. But the voice of the congregation is more than advice. The Consistory may not lay decisions of congregational meetings aside. They stand. If a Consistory finds that an error has been made, and if the matter is weighty, then it may resubmit the matter to the congregation. But it may not simply invalidate the Church's choice and then follow its own desires.

The correctness of this position is also evident from the fact that a group of believers which desires to organize itself into a Church may and does elect its office-bearers without previously made nominations. Believers therefore have the inherent right to elect office-bearers. For this reason also new office-bearers may be elected by a Church, a body of believers, if at any time their present office-bearers become unfaithful and untrue.

To say that a congregational meeting has only advisory power and that it is really just another Consistory meeting to which the members have been invited to state their opinions, is untenable.

5. **The matter of universal Synods of Reformed Churches.**

The Reformed Churches of the Netherlands of the Sixteenth Century certainly favored ecumenical or international Synods. But their plan and hopes concerning such Synods never materialized. The government frowned upon these plans fearing interference by foreign powers in matters national. The difference in languages was also a formidable barrier. And the heavy expenditures involved furthermore kept the cherished ideals from being realized. And until very recent years the great Synod of Dort was really the only major assembly of the Reformed Churches which was ecumenical or international in character. However, in 1946, during the month of August, duly elected or appointed delegates from the Reformed Churches of the Netherlands, the Reformed Churches of South Africa, and from the Christian Reformed Churches of North America, met in Grand Rapids, Michigan. This First Reformed Ecumenical Synod did a great deal of preparatory work with a view to subsequent and more inclusive Ecumenical Synods. The Second Reformed Ecumenical Synod is scheduled to meet in Amsterdam, the month of August, 1949.

We are very happy with this beginning. We need each other. And in this day of internationalism, when many organizations meet internationally to promote their aims, the Church of God should not come trailing on behind. If even Communists, and other Godless organizations. can meet internationally, why cannot the Church of God?

(Also see Appendix 5, page 365.)

ARTICLE 30

In these assemblies ecclesiastical matters only shall be transacted and that in an ecclesiastical manner. In major assemblies only such matters shall be dealt with as could not be finished in minor assemblies, or such as pertain to the Churches of the major assembly in common.

THE AUTHORITY OF ECCLESIASTICAL ASSEMBLIES

Beyond dispute, this 30th article of our Church Order is very significant. The article concerns, in the main, three matters, viz.; (1) That the authority of ecclesiastical assemblies is limited to ecclesiastical matters; (2) The manner in which ecclesiastical gatherings must transact their affairs; (3) The limited authority of major assemblies. For practical reasons, in the interest of clarity we have, however, divided the consideration of Art. 30 into seven points.

1. The authority of ecclesiastical assemblies limited to ecclesiastical matters.

The assemblies to which this article has reference are those enumerated in Article 29, namely: Consistory, Classis, Particular Synod, and General Synod. At all these ecclesiastical meetings, none but ecclesiastical matters shall be transacted. Why this provision? In the first place because the domain over which the instituted Church of Christ has authority is not general, but limited. It is limited to that which concerns the preaching of the Gospel, the administration of the Sacraments, the calling and ordination to office, the exercise of discipline, the promotion of a consecrated scriptural Church communion, and kindred matters. The former of these, as will be evident, require the latter.

The Reformation Churches of Holland soon realized that although the Church of Christ—conceived of as the body of true believers, living in various lands and belonging to various Church organizations —is the salt of the earth, and has a very definite task in all domains of life, that the organized or instituted Church as such has authority only in matters ecclesiastical. Individual believers and groups of believers have rights and obligations extending over all domains of life, but the organized Church, though it stands related to all of life, cannot act authoritatively beyond its own domain. Nowhere do we find that Holy Writ attributes extra-ecclesiastical authority to the instituted Church. The prophets and Apostles do have a message again and again pertaining to social, political, or economic life. But at no time do we find the prophets or Apostles and Elders actually transacting affairs belonging to these domains.

In this respect also our fathers took a position quite different from the Roman Catholic Church which seeks to control all domains of life, and regards the bishop of Rome (the Pope) as supreme ruler of the Church not only, but also over all temporal affairs. The Reformation was definitely a "back-to-the-Bible" movement also in this respect.

In the very first redaction of our Church Order we consequently already find the provision before us, i.e., "In ecclesiastical assemblies none but ecclesiastical matters shall be transacted." Even when William the Silent, who so nobly fought the cause of Protestant Holland against oppressive, domineering Roman Spain, solicited the direct support of the Reformed Churches of Holland convened in their first Synod (Emden, 1571), through Marnix van St. Aldegonde, these Churches refrained from taking such action.

Moreover, if the Churches should busy themselves with secular matters, they would in all likelihood neglect their real task. The right management of the Churches and the promotion of things spiritual would suffer if the Churches should spend their time and efforts on non-ecclesiastical territory, even as a farmer cannot do justice to his farm, if he is constantly employed in town.

Furthermore, the transaction of non-ecclesiastical affairs would most naturally lead to undesirable entanglements. It would lead the Churches concerned into conflict and trouble repeatedly.

2. Matters not to be considered and acted upon at ecclesiastical assemblies.

Which matters should not be considered and acted upon at ecclesiastical assemblies? Matters which do not concern the Churches in the administration of the Word and the Sacraments, or in their exercise of discipline, or in their regulation of divine worship, and the promotion of sound doctrine and vital spiritual living and ecclesiastical activity. Thus, e.g., political issues and the question regarding the government of State and nation are non-ecclesiastical and cannot be acted upon in our assemblies. Furthermore, matters social and economic are also non-ecclesiastical. Discussion and action pertaining to these spheres cannot take place at our Consistory meetings, Classes, or Synods.

Let it be clear, however, that this restriction of our Church Order does not imply that Christianity has no interest and message for the various spheres of life, political, social, etc. It most certainly has. The sovereignty of God, denied and contested by sin, must be recognized in every domain of life. Christ is not only King of the Church, but also King of kings and Lord of lords, to whom all power is given in heaven and on earth. As His loyal subjects we Christians must proclaim and insist on His royal rights.

Neither does it mean that the instituted Church as such has no message for and interest in things governmental, social, economic, educational, etc. It assuredly has. Through the preaching of the Word, f.i., the instituted Churches must proclaim the will of God for all of life, and condemn sin and evil in all spheres of life. But though the Churches have a directive and enlightening task, they have no legislative and executive task regarding the secular affairs and departments of life. Consequently questions pertaining to a certain war, our political parties, unemployment, taxation, old age pension, etc., are not to be discussed at our assemblies, unless it be indirectly, in as far as many matters political, economic, social, and educational stand very closely related to things ecclesiastical. But even so the Churches should go no further than is required for the correct government and the best interests of the Churches. So, f.i., a Consistory may not take action for or against a week-day half-holiday grocery store closing movement, or the question of retail sales taxes.

Today there is a strong tendency in many Churches all around us to busy themselves at their assemblies with social and economic problems. This our Church Order condemns. And rightly so. The Church which engages itself with all kinds of questions (questions urgent and very vital in themselves, even crying for consideration and solution on the part of Christian leaders and Christian organizations), will do so at the expense of its true spiritual welfare and its real calling. The best service which the instituted Churches of Christ can render our country, also economically and socially, is that they mind their own specific business, and thus constitute themselves a saving salt in this world of sin, and a beacon light of safety for the storm-tossed sailors of life's dark and stormy waters.

3. Are Consistories ever obligated to settle disputes concerning things material?

No. Sometimes brethren entertain claims against each other. Mr. A may contend that Mr. B owes him a certain amount of money which he refuses to pay. May A bring this matter to the Consistory and ask the Consistory to take matters in hand? No, he may not. However, if A is convinced that B is defrauding him, that would involve a sin against the eighth commandment. Concerning this alleged sin he may and must admonish Mr. B. according to the rule of Matt. 18. If unsuccessful he may have to bring the matter to the attention of the Consistory in that form. But the Consistory may never permit itself to be used as a collecting agency.

Again, Mr. C may claim that Mr. D has moved a certain line fence to the latter's advantage. D may deny the charge. C may take the matter to the Consistory. Should the Consistory, if asked to do so, endeavor to determine who is right? No.

For all such cases our Lord's "Man, who made me a judge or a divider over you?" (Luke 12:14) is altogether applicable. Let the parties concerned in all such cases appoint an impartial committee of arbitration of Christian brethren, and let these settle the matter, the parties at variance first promising to abide by the findings of the committee. Or else, if this way is not wanted (which attitude would certainly not be to the credit of the parties involved), let the divinely-appointed courts decide. However, the admonition of I Cor. 6 should weigh heavy on us of this day also, inasmuch as the courts of our day are largely presided over by unbelievers and are under the control of unbelievers.

4. Significance of the phrase: "and that in an ecclesiastical manner".

Only ecclesiastical matters are to be considered at our ecclesiastical assemblies. And the manner of their consideration must also be ecclesiastical. What does this mean? The Church Order here contrasts the Church assemblies particularly with our State and federal assemblies. Congress and Senate, as well as any other civil government body, decides and legislates according to parliamentary rules. Often the majority is fully satisfied when a bill is passed, though large numbers are bitterly opposed and disappointed. But in our ecclesiastical assemblies we should by all means seek to convince and persuade each other from the Word of God. We should not seek to force our opinions and convictions onto others. Our assemblies should far rather guide and direct. By mutual consultation and consideration of God's Word we should endeavor to come to a mutual conclusion.

Furthermore, all business should be transacted according to the adopted Church Order. Complicated parliamentary rules are out of place in ecclesiastical assemblies. Our Church gatherings are not courts of law, nor bodies for civil legislation, nor commercial gatherings. To be sure, all things should be done "decently and in good order," but neither **Roberts' Rules of Order** nor complicated and technical synodically approved sets of detailed rules of procedure should be permitted to hinder and hurt our ecclesiastical assemblies in their work. Rules are necessary, but too many rules are a hindrance. A hindrance to unhampered deliberation and mutual consideration. To deliberate and decide upon ecclesiastical matters in an unecclesiastical way brings spiritual damage. Freedom should be maintained and fostered. All members at our Church gatherings should feel free to express themselves without too much fear of transgressing some parliamentary rule and of being called to order by the president. We should appreciate the fact that our Church Order is a non-technical, simple document. Let us value and maintain these features.

5. What should be noted regarding the terms "major assemblies" and "minor assemblies"?

This latter provision of Article 30 is also very important. It is typically Reformed. It is fundamental for Reformed Church government.

Reformed church polity does not know a system of lower and higher courts in the usual sense of the word. It does not, as is done particularly by the Roman Catholic Church and to a certain extent by some Protestant bodies, attribute a small and limited measure of authority to the governing body of the local Congregation, a somewhat greater and more extensive measure of authority to groups of neighboring Churches convening together, and a still greater and still more extensive measure of authority to assemblies next in order, and finally the greatest and most extensive measure of authority to the gathering representing all the Churches. If this were the case the Church Order might speak of lower and higher assemblies. For in that case Consistories would have only a limited and smaller degree of authority, and Synod a very wide and high degree of authority, while our Classes would exercise an intermediate measure of authority. But Reformed Church polity does not hold that Consistories have a lower and more limited degree of authority, and Classes and Synods a higher and more extensive degree. Consequently our Church Order speaks of major and minor assemblies, and not of higher and lower assemblies.

The Latin word minor, signifies "less," and the Latin word major "more." If our fathers had desired to indicate that our Classes and Synods are invested with higher authority than the Consistories, higher in the sense of having inherent powers not vested in the ruling bodies of the local Churches, then they would have used the comparative of some other Latin word, f.i., altus, signifying "high." But they used major, inasmuch as the authority of our major assemblies (Classes and Synods) is the same in essence as the authority vested in the local Church.

In fact, Reformed Church polity knows of only one type and degree of authority: that vested in the local congregation or its ruling body, the Consistory. The authority exercised by the major assemblies is no higher and greater essentially, but merely the sum-total of the authority exercised by the individual Consistories meeting as Classis or Synod. The authority of our major assemblies may therefore be looked upon as an accumulation or combination of consistorial authority.

Furthermore, the authority of our Consistories is not less extensive than that of our Classes and Synods, but more extensive than that of Classes and Synods. That is to say, the domain over which our Consistories have authority is much more extensive than that of Classes and Synods.

Many denominations, Roman Catholicism especially, regard their denomination as being a large super-Church, and the local Churches as mere subdivisions of the one large Church. Consequently, the highest authority they find inherently in the high courts or judicial bodies of their Church. And to these superior institutions they also attribute the widest scope of authority. The Reformed system, however, maintains that each local congregation is a complete Church, a complete manifestation of the body of Christ. In that sense and in so far each Church or congregation is independent in essence (zelfstandig). Local Churches can even exist without denominational federation, but a denomination cannot exist without local Churches. The real unit is therefore the individual Church. And the local Churches do not exist for the sake of the denomination, but denominations exist for the sake of the local and individual Churches.

The terms "major" and "minor", in Art. 30, do not, therefore, refer to a system of lower and higher ecclesiastical courts, exercising various inherent degrees of authority, but they designate, in the first place, that at major assemblies a **number of Churches** are **gathered** together, and that consequently, in the second place, at major assemblies **a larger measure of authority is present** than at minor assemblies, even as ten men have more strength than one alone.

It is interesting to note that the Synod of Dordrecht (1578) used the phrase, "grooter en minderen versamelinghen," i.e., larger and smaller assemblies. In this sense our Dutch Church Order still speaks of, "meerdere en mindere vergaderingen."

Bearing the foregoing in mind it is not difficult to see why Article 30 limits the scope of authority of major assemblies, and safeguards the rights of all the Churches.

How does this article further maintain the integrity of our congregations? Article 30 specifies very clearly that only such matters shall be considered and acted upon at major assemblies as could not be finished by the minor assemblies.

No Classis or Synod may therefore assume to do that which rightfully belongs to the domain of the local Church, and which can be acted upon by its Consistory. No major assembly may therefore needlessly interfere with the management of congregational affairs. There are a good many matters and instances concerning which a Consistory would have the right to say, if need should require, to major assemblies: Hands off!

The authority of major assemblies is very clearly limited in this article, thus maintaining the integrity and autonomy of each Church.

At the same time the article wards off the danger of an oligarchical rule by a few men, vested with superior authority.

Furthermore, the provision also rules out the danger of flooding the tables of major assemblies with overmuch work, which makes for hasty superficiality and blunderous decisions. No individual or assembly may expect a major assembly to act regarding matters which could be finished at minor assemblies.

6. Matters that "could not be finished in minor assemblies."

Sometimes matters, which as to their essence belong to the domain of the minor assemblies cannot well be finished by them. Now the Church Order provides that such cases shall be acted upon by the major assemblies. For example, a matter may be so complicated and difficult that a Consistory feels itself incompetent to deal with the matter. It may then ask the Classis with its greater numbers and superior wisdom and experience, to extend its helping hand. Or again the absence from home or the long continued illness of some Consistory members may so weaken a small Consistory that it is for the time being unable to finish a matter in itself not so overly difficult.

Furthermore, when a member or a body desires to make an appeal concerning any action of a minor assembly, such an appeal as a matter of course goes to the major assembly to which the appeal is rightfully made. No minor assembly can in such cases sit in judgment over its own actions, although reconsideration of previous decisions is, of course, always permissible. If an appeal is made to Classis or Synod, the appellant must always notify the minor assembly concerned and thus give opportunity to the minor assembly to present the case from its point of view at the major assembly.

7. Which matters pertain to "the Churches in common"?

In general, as Bouwman states,* this phrase concerns matters mutually agreed upon by the Churches, and which concern continued denominational fellowship and the maintenance of principles set forth in the Bible, and (consequently) in the Confessional Standards and Church Order.

The Church Order specifies in Article 2 what is to be observed by all the Churches regarding the offices in Christ's Church; in Article 3, that none shall assume to preach in the Churches without a lawful call; how one may be called, in Articles 4 and 5; support and emeritation of Ministers is regulated in Articles 11 and 13; matters to be observed regarding Elders and Deacons are covered by Articles 22 to 27; when Deacons may be and when they must be added to the Consistory, Article 37; missionary work, Article 51; subscription to the Forms of Unity by all office-bearers, Article 53 and 54; matters pertaining to Baptism and the Lord's Supper, Articles 56 to 64; songs to be sung in the Churches, Article 69; solemnization of marriages, Article 70; disciplinary matters, Articles 70 to 81; certification of membership, Article 82. (This enumeration is not exhaustive.) All matters thus regulated in the Church Order pertain to the Churches in general, and the major assemblies may take action regarding them directly as far as their general aspect is concerned. But no Classis or Synod may take to hand a matter which is clearly the affair of a certain Consistory, though it should concern a matter regulated for all the Churches in the Church Order.

And thus matters which are of a general interest for all the Churches of a Classis or Synod may be taken directly before these bodies, and these bodies may also take action upon such matters upon their own initiative. So, f.i., our Synod may decide to initiate a consideration concerning the proper mode of observing the Lord's Supper, whenever it so desires, for this is a matter which concerns all the Churches, and not just one or a few. For this same reason individual members even have the right of requesting classical or synodical action, through petitions addressed directly to said assemblies, when it concerns matters which pertain to the Churches in common.

ARTICLE 31

If any one complains that he has been wronged by the decision of a minor assembly, he shall have the right to appeal to a major ecclesiastical assembly, and whatever may be agreed upon by a majority vote shall be considered settled and binding, unless it be proved to conflict with the Word of God or with the Articles of the Church Order, as long as they are not changed by a General Synod.

RIGHT OF APPEAL AND VALIDITY OF ECCLESIASTICAL DECISIONS

Article 31 concerns itself with two principles of Reformed Church government, namely **the right of appeal,** and **the validity of ecclesias-**

*Bouwman: **Gereformeerd Kerkrecht,** 1934, II, 37.

tical decisions. Both of these principles are very important and merit full consideration.

1. Why does the Church Order provide for right of appeal?

In the first place because our assemblies (Consistories, Classes, and Synods) are not infallible. We have the promise of the Christ that the Holy Spirit will guide us into all the truth (John 16:13). But nowhere does the Bible say that the Spirit will guide us inerrantly. As individual Christians, and as office-bearers at ecclesiastical assemblies, we can and do err. The Word of God is inerrant. But the Church is not. Consequently, if any one feels convinced that a minor assembly has made a mistake through an error of judgment or from neglect of duty, such a one should have the right of appeal to the assembly next in order. A major assembly being composed of a larger number of brethren, and often further removed from the personal elements which so easily enter its cases on home territory, may sustain an aggrieved brother, or it may serve to convince the party concerned regarding the correctness of the minor assemblies' stand.

Right of appeal also follows from the fact that all believers partake of Christ's threefold office. Each believer as prophet, priest, and king under Christ has a right to be heard and to receive full consideration. Moreover, denial of the right of appeal would often work havoc practically. Many a man, who now appeals, would otherwise nurse his griefs and create unrest and division perhaps.

2. To which cases does this right of appeal apply?

To cases in which one "complains that he has been wronged by the decision of a minor assembly." Not every adverse decision can therefore constitute a just cause for appeal. Only then may one appeal to a major assembly, when he is convinced that he has been wronged; that is, when according to his conception an injustice has been committed. The very word appeal would also signify this. Only he who is in pressing circumstances makes an appeal for help. So only he who feels that he has been wronged is justified to make an appeal. Jansen (**Korte Verklaring, etc.**) uses a very apt illustration. Says he in effect: suppose a Consistory decides that the morning service is to begin at 10 instead of at 9 o'clock. One of the members may not like this change, but that in itself does not give him just reasons for an appeal to Classis. But if the new hour makes worship for him, and perhaps others, impossible, whereas all can worship at the old hour, then he and these others are being wronged, and this injustice would constitute a just basis for complaint and appeal.

No one should conclude from the foregoing that it is our opinion that Article 31 limits appeals to cases of personal injury. He who feels that a minor assembly has come to an incorrect and dangerous conclusion, contrary to the Bible, the confessional writings, the Church Order, or the welfare of the Churches, may and should indeed appeal to Classis or Synod.

3. To which body must the appeal be made?

To major assemblies. Consistorial decisions may be appealed to Classis. Classical decisions may be appealed to Synod. In exceptional cases one may appeal from one assembly to the next. That is from one classical gathering to the next classical gathering, or from one synodical gathering to the following synodical gathering. But, as a rule, this is both needless and out of place.

The Reformed system of church government knows of no appeal to the congregation. The independent systems (Congregationalists, Baptists, etc.) do. In these systems decisions of the ruling body of the local Church may be challenged and brought before the congregation. However, we find no warrant for this in Scripture. Christ vested the power of government over His Church in the office-bearers. When the question of circumcision disturbed the apostolic Church, the matter was not placed before the congregation as such, but before a meeting of Apostles and Elders at Jerusalem (Acts 15).

4. Proper time limits and methods for appeals.

The article says nothing as to proper time limits to be observed in cases of appeal. Neither have we any classical or synodical decision seeking to control this matter. There has been a time when some Reformed Churches stipulated that appeals to be valid had to be registered inside of three weeks. Others allowed a six weeks' limit. But such limitations proved to be rather arbitrary and harmful. Some matters are exceedingly complicated, and a time limit of a few days or weeks for the registration of appeals may cause damage. Moreover, there was always the danger that proper appeals would be ruled out of order for the simple reason that they came a day or more late.

However, appeals should be made as soon as possible and not beyond a reasonable length of time after the decision by which the appellant claims to have been wronged has been taken. The Churches of Holland (Gereformeerde Kerken) adopted the following rule in 1893: "Appeals concerning any decision of an ecclesiastical assembly must be made before the following major assembly to which the appeal is directed meets, the clerk of the assembly by whose decision the appellant feels aggrieved, having been notified. The parties concerned shall be notified regarding every decision made." This is no doubt a good general rule. But even so there must remain room for exceptions. One might, f.i., be hindered by sickness from complying with this rule.

Multiplication of rules and stipulations in ecclesiastical matters often works for more harm than good. We should be very careful on this score. Let each assembly judge with good-will and Christian forbearance as to the propriety of each appeal directed to it. This is the unwritten rule which we have followed thus far and it seems to have worked well.

What should we answer as to the proper method of appeal? Concerning this Jansen recommends that an appeal should include the following points: (1) Presentation of the matter at issue in the appellant's own words. (2) Quotation of the official decision concerning which the appeal is being made. (3) Enumeration of the reasons because of which the appellant feels himself aggrieved and upon which his appeal rests. (4) Petition that the major assembly declare for reasons adduced, that the minor assembly's decision was erroneous and unfounded.

It should also be noted here that the Reformed Churches of former years have always permitted an appellant to explain and defend his position by means of another, called "een mond," i.e., a mouth. Such an advocate, however, had to be a member of one of the Reformed Churches in good and regular standing, and he was of course expected to respect the rule of the assembly and to deport himself in a worthy manner. From recent Presbyterian trials it will have been noted that this same custom is honored by these Churches. This usage and privilege is altogether defensible and praise-worthy. One may have a just ground of complaint and yet not have the ability to make a desirable presentation. It is to the Churches' own welfare that the appellant receive every legitimate opportunity to defend his position or to clarify the matter at hand.

5. If a member appeals to a major assembly, should the minor assembly involved suspend action regarding the matter concerned until the appeal has been acted upon?

The question is often asked: Should decisions of minor assemblies await execution pending an appeal? We would answer in the affirmative. If at all possible no assembly must begin to execute a decision the correctness of which is to be judged by a major assembly. To illustrate, supposing some one objects to the installation of a certain brother as Elder, and that his objection is overruled, and that he appeals to Classis; then if the Consistory would proceed with the installation, and after a few weeks Classis should sustain the appellant, such a Consistory would find itself in a very difficult position.

If and when possible, action on appeals should be awaited. Sometimes, however, this is not possible, or not advisable. Thus in the illustration at hand, if the appellant were not sustained by Classis he might appeal to Synod. This would mean a long extended delay as to the brother's installation (if synodical decision were awaited), which would be unfair to both the Church concerned and the Elder-elect concerned. The rule should be one appeal. And during that appeal, in all possible cases, action on the appeal should be awaited. If an appellant feels burdened to such an extent that he cannot submit after the first appeal, then let him proceed. But as a rule he should not ask or expect the minor assembly to suspend action.

6. Can a major assembly invalidate a decision of a minor assembly?

No. In the Church of Rome this would most assuredly be the case. Also with Churches which regard the denomination to be the real Church or Church unit, and the local congregations and the minor assemblies of the Churches as divisions of the one real Church. But according to the Reformed conception and set-up, Biblically formed and historically conditioned, the local congregation is the unit, a complete Church of Christ. Major assemblies most certainly can deliberate and decide. But if their decisions are contrary to decisions taken by minor assemblies, these minor assemblies must conform themselves to the conclusions of the major assemblies. Either by actual reconsideration of the question, or by silent acquiescense. As a rule the latter method is followed. Practically it does not make much difference whether one looks upon an adverse decision of a major assembly as an invalidation or nullification of the minor assembly's decision, or as being essentially an advice, and no decision to nullify the minor assembly's conclusion. The minor assembly as a rule follows the advise of the major assembly. And it must do so, inasmuch as all the Churches have agreed to submit themselves to the opinion of the majority and to abide by decisions mutually taken. Only when the Word of God forbids may any Church or group of Churches refrain from abiding by the decision of major assemblies. But for all this, major assemblies do not dictate, and they do not have the inherent right to invalidate decisions of minor assemblies. The local Church or groups of Churches do not receive superior orders which they must obey without further question, but they receive conclusions reached by common consent, and as such they will respect these conclusions. And as such they will accept them as their own, either formally, or by silent acquiescence.

7. All decisions made by majority vote.

Article 31 further stipulates that "... whatever may be agreed upon by a majority vote shall be considered settled and binding." Whatever, therefore, the majority of those entitled to vote decide, becomes binding for all. And bv a majority vote we simply mean more than one half of the total number of votes cast. Sometimes the majority may be large; sometimes very small, one vote being sufficient to constitute a majority.

Sometimes certain organizations decide by plurality vote. The largest number of votes, though less than one half of the actual votes decides. This method, however, is out of place at our ecclesiastical meetings. It might foster the evil of permitting minorities to rule over majorities, which is least of all desirable in church affairs. (However, when the matter at hand concerns no principle or policy, but the appointment to minor functions, the assembly may decide that he who receives the largest number of votes shall be considered elected, provided all agree to this method. This method of procedure should always be exceptional.)

No ecclesiastical gathering should be satisfied when decisions are made by bare or small majorities, for this is never ideal. At our Consistory meetings as well as at our major assemblies we should seek to convince each other from the Word of God, and we should seek to persuade each other with arguments in harmony with our confessional writings and our Church Order. Decisions should be arrived at with as much unanimity as possible. That will make for unity of purpose and endeavor. That was also the clear conception of things as held by our post-reformation fathers. For instance, the Synod of 1571 decided: "All matters shall be presented by the President specifically and orderly; he shall also gain the opinion of the whole assembly concerning the matter at hand, and take the vote of those eligible to vote, after which he will announce in the main the opinion of the majority; the Clerk will record the results and read the same to the assembly, in order that the decision may be established by common consent."[1]

Jansen informs us that the earlier assemblies in the Reformed Churches of the Netherlands would vote twice on every issue. The first vote was taken to determine the opinion of the majority. Then a second vote followed for the purpose of making the expressed opinion of the majority the unanimous decision of the whole gathering. Thus matters would literally be agreed upon by common consent.[2]

An example of this common consent method of procedure is also illustrated in the final article of the Church Order, Article 86, which states that the articles of the Church Order have been adopted by common consent. And this article and its declaration date back to the very first regular Synod of the Reformed Churches of Holland, the Synod of Emden, 1571. (Cf. Acts, 1571, Article 53.)

Today we ballot or vote only once on each issue. Does this mean that minorities are ignored and silenced by majorities, sometimes by bare majorities? Does it mean that minorities are forced to accept the opinions of the majorities? No. Whatever is decided by majority vote becomes settled and binding for all, not against the will of minorities, but by their own consent. Minorities conform themselves voluntarily to the officially expressed opinion of the majority, for the sake of good order and the welfare of the Churches concerned. In other

1. Bouwman: **Gereformeerd Kerkrecht**, 1934, II, 54.
2. Jansen: **Korte Verklaring**, etc., 1923, pp. 164 and 363.

words, minorities now silently submit themselves to the opinion expressed by their brethren of the majority. And, let it be said, the minorities at our ecclesiastical assemblies are in duty bound to do so. For note that every Church has voluntarily joined itself to the federation of Churches forming one denomination. Together they have agreed to coöperate, upon the basis of the Church Order, which Church Order presupposes and even expresses cooperation on the part of all the Churches regarding all decisions which agree with the Word of God and the Church Order in force. Read again the present article: ". . . and whatever may be agreed upon by a majority vote shall be considered settled and binding. . "

Furthermore, Biblical example also prescribes submission to decisions mutually taken. (Confer, Acts 15:22-29, especially verse 28.) The Assembly at Jerusalem made authoritative and binding decisions for all the Churches.

8. All decisions settled and binding.

Doubtlessly this double expression is used purposefully. Anything that is settled should not continue to be the subject of discussion at ecclesiastical gatherings. That would raise discord and require much time needed for other matters. The second word, "binding," indicates that all the Churches are obligated to live up to the decisions of the assemblies concerned.

This provision is indeed a jewel of great value. It is as indispensable for Reformed church government as the connecting-rod is for your car.

However, inasmuch as this principle is important and indispensable it should never be abused. Let decisions be taken upon due consideration, and only after the majority has endeavored to prove the necessity, permissability and desirability of the matter proposed. And let us avoid needless multiplication of rules and decisions. And when conclusions have been reached, let us not begin to advocate a reversal unless we are fully persuaded that the Churches have erred when they decided on a certain issue as they did. At times brethren and Consistories begin to advocate for the reversal of decisions almost as soon as these decisions have been passed, and often seemingly largely from personal inclination or opinion, and not so much from the urge of soul-born convictions and genuine concern for the Churches.

That which has been mutually decided upon at our assemblies, should be considered **settled,** and should be considered **binding.** And to this rule the article appends only two general, but all-important exceptions.

9. Two exceptions to the foregoing rule.

Which are the two exceptions to the foregoing rule? They are embodied in the concluding statement of Art. 31, and reads as follows: ". . . unless it be proved to conflict with the Word of God or with the Articles of the Church Order, as long as they are not changed by a General Synod."

This exception embodies the great Reformation principle regarding the supremacy of the Word of God, first of all. The Reformation recognized no authority above or beside the Bible. The Church of Rome had virtually elevated the Church through its councils above the Bible. The Church's interpretation of God's Word became binding for the conscience of all believers. In case of conflict between the Bible and Rome, the believer was to follow Rome. The Reformation again made the Bible the final court of appeal, not only for the Churches, but also for the individual believers. The Word of God became once more the only rule for faith and life. Consequently, when our forebears agreed that all conclusions properly reached at ecclesiastical assemblies should be considered settled and binding they did not neglect to add: ". . . unless it be proved to conflict with the Word of God." If a conclusion proves to be contrary to the Bible the matter is not to be considered settled and binding. Then the matter may again be discussed and then the decision need not be adhered to. For that which is contrary to God's Word should be altered as soon as possible and does not bind the believer.

The question is sometimes asked: To whom must it be proved that a certain decision is in conflict with the Bible, before a Church or an individual may count that a matter is not settled and binding? Must the ecclesiastical assembly which made the decision first declare that the unBiblical nature of the decision has been proven, before any one may withhold submission? Or may a Church or an individual withhold submission when that Church or individual is fully convinced that the conclusion reached is unBiblical, even before the assembly concerned has reversed its conclusion? The latter by all means. The Church or the Churches cannot bind the conscience. The Bible only, as God's infallible and authoritative Word, can do this. If one is convinced that the Churches bid him to do one thing, and the Bible another, he must follow what he believes to be Scriptural. Of course, he should study the matter carefully and prayerfully before refusing submission. Rashness would be altogether out of place. And of course he must do all he can to show the assembly concerned what he believes to be the error of its way.

If after due consideration the assembly concerned decides that its decision is unBiblical, then instant reversal is naturally in order. If, however, the appellant cannot persuade the assembly, and the assembly fails to persuade the appellant, and the appellant does not feel free before God to submit and conform himself, then the Churches must bear with the aggrieved brother, if at all possible. If, however, the matter be of far-reaching import, then the aggrieved brother should be asked to conform and submit as long as he remains to be a member of the Church concerned. If his conscience will not at all permit this, he should ultimately affiliate with a Church not so binding his conscience.

There is a second exception. If any decision is contrary to the Church Order in force, the matter need not be considered settled and binding. Denominational unity and co-operation rests upon a set of definite rules, mutually agreed upon. The 86 articles of our Church Order are these rules for us. No decision should ever be made which runs counter to these agreements of federation. If such decisions are made these need not be considered settled or binding. The aggrieved Church or individual should make its or his mind known to the assembly concerned and ask for a revision or nullification. In the meantime the Church or party appealing or petitioning should conform itself or himself to the decision in question if at all possible. But no one should be urged to do so against his conscience. If the assembly, after due consideration, finds that the decision in question does not run counter to the Church Order, then the party or parties concerned should submit and conform, as long as he remains a member of one of the Churches concerned. But again, in minor matters Consistories and other assemblies may exercise a great deal of tolerance, bearing the weaker brother according to Paul's instruction to the Church at Rome

(Romans 14), meanwhile instructing him with patience and kindness in Christ.

The concluding words of Article 31 indicate that the Church Order may be revised, as also Article 86 clearly states, but only by the General Synod. But as long as it is not changed it should be respected. To ignore it, as is sometimes done, or to decide things out of harmony with the Church Order, constitute an essential undermining of our whole denominational or ecclesiastical life, and is dangerous to the purity of the Church of Christ as we represent it.

ARTICLE 32

The proceedings of all assemblies shall begin by calling upon the Name of God and be closed with thanksgiving.

BEGINNING AND ENDING ALL ASSEMBLIES WITH PRAYER

1. The history and value of this ruling.

The incorporation of this provision in our Church Order goes back to the first regular Synod of our mother Churches, i. e., the Synod of Emden, 1571, which ruled: "When thus assembled, the Minister of the Church where the meeting is held, or if the Church is vacant, the president of the former meeting, shall lead in prayer with a view to the election of a president, an assistant and a clerk. . . . The president, having been appointed, shall then lead in prayer with a view to all the work before the gathering."*

But in 1581, at the Synod of Middelburg, the provision for two distinct prayers was altered. The provision, namely, for a separate prayer regarding the election of directors for the meeting, was dropped, and the wording of a ruling pertaining to the second prayer was retained so that we now read: "The proceedings of all assemblies shall begin by calling upon the Name of God. . ." Dutch: "De handelingen aller samenkomsten. . ." Originally the word "proceedings" in this article therefore referred to the actual questions requiring action on the part of the assembly. Later the term was taken to refer to all work performed, including the opening and closing of the meetings. And thus matters stand today.

The provision of Article 32 might be considered unnecessary. Why should our Church Order stipulate that ecclesiastical meetings should begin and end with prayer? Would any serious-minded group of men think of doing otherwise?

We may be happy that the ruling is actually unnecessary for us at present. May it ever remain to be such! But what could be more important than prayer and thanksgiving at our ecclesiastical gatherings? All our work would be fruitless without the Lord's blessing. And problem upon problem remains unsolved except the Father of lights (James 1:17) enlightens us. Then surely no Church Order would be complete without recognition of these facts and without definite mention of these important numbers on the program of every ecclesiastical gathering. Besides, in days of spiritual decline, the good custom provided for in this article sometimes tends to fall into

*Bouwman: **Geref. Kerkrecht,** 1934, II, p. 93.

disuse. Think of the gross neglect regarding family prayers in many Christian circles. And so it is not altogether unnecessary that Article 32 should occupy the place of a constant guardian against neglect of prayer at our ecclesiastical assemblies.

2. The matter of free and liturgical prayers.

Should those who lead in prayer at our assemblies use words of their own choice, or should they use one of our liturgical prayers written for ecclesiastical assemblies? The use of one of our form prayers for ecclesiastical gatherings is sometimes advisable. But no one is bound to these. And when there is more than one session, perhaps several sessions, the constant repetition of the same prayer would not be conducive to the spirit of prayer. As a rule a free prayer is to be preferred to a form prayer.

However, if one is called upon to lead whose talents are very much limited, then let such a one use one of our form prayers, written and approved for these gatherings. Furthermore, when sharp differences arise, particularly when a brother's name or standing is involved, it may be well to use a liturgical prayer in preference to a free prayer, to avoid offense. We so much need God's special guidance and the control of His Spirit when the atmosphere is tense and the situation perhaps critical. And yet, under special circumstances, it is hard to pray objectively, so that all the members of the meeting can say amen in their hearts to the prayer uttered. But when a form prayer is used, no one can be offended, and all should be able to pray fervently.

But again, as a rule, a free prayer is to be preferred above a form prayer, especially when there are several sessions. For although the article, strictly speaking, only calls for prayer at the beginning of the assembly and at its close, certainly our custom of beginning and ending each session with prayer is altogether proper. And furthermore, when one chooses his own words and thoughts in prayer, his prayer can be made appropriate to the special problems and conditions which obtain.

Our Churches have one approved "Opening Prayer for Ecclesiastical Assemblies," and one "Closing Prayer for Ecclesiastical Assemblies." (Cf. Psalter Hymnal, appended pp. 80, 81.) There is also an "Opening Prayer for the Meeting of the Deacons" (Idem, pp. 81, 82.) This prayer does not date back to Reformation days as do the others, but to the beginning of the 18th century. It was never officially approved at the time of its incorporation into the liturgy, as were the two first mentioned prayers. But for more than 200 years it has been acknowledged as one of our official prayers. And by its publication along with the other prayers upon decision of our Synod of 1934, it really stands fully approved.

3. Pre-service prayer by Consistories.

Does Article 32 require pre-service prayers by the Consistory? No, it does not. The Church Order does not regulate congregational worship. And this article refers only to consistorial, classical, and synodical gatherings, the official assemblies of the Churches.

Seemingly the good custom of a pre-service meeting for prayer by the Consistory was born from the pressure of circumstances. During the days of the Secession in Holland (Afscheiding, 1834, and following years) congregational worship was often disturbed by the interference of the government, or antagonistic citizens. The office-bearers in charge of a service therefore felt the need of first asking for God's protection and blessing, praying in particular that God might qualify

His servant to bring His Word without fear and hindrance, and with His indispensable blessing. The spirit of a revived faith in God and His Christ as our only Redeemer and of man's absolute dependence on God's Spirit in the work of grace, no doubt also urged them to seek God's blessing before each service.

The Churches of the second exodus from the corrupt Hervormde Kerk, the movement known as the Doleantie, 1886, quickly adopted this good usage from the Secession Churches.

Moreover, pre-service prayers by the Consistories are also required by the fact that every service is in charge of the Consistory. Well may the office-bearers therefore pray for God's benediction upon the Minister and the people of God who are about to serve Him.

4. Sermons or devotional addresses, etc., at our assemblies.

Does Article 32 require the preaching of sermons, or the inclusion of devotional addresses at our assemblies? It does not. Article 32 clearly stipulates that prayer and thanksgiving shall be offered with a view to the matters which must be transacted. The ecclesiastical assemblies are not meant to be meetings for worship or instruction. Consistory meetings as well as classical and synodical gatherings are assemblies of the Church or the Churches at which the business of the Church or Churches is acted upon. They are not inspirational conventions or Bible Institutes. The Churches must be governed according to God's Word and according to the varying conditions as they arise from time to time. This is the business of the assemblies. Inspiration we need. Increased knowledge we need. Worship and praise we must. But all this is not the business of ecclesiastical assemblies.

Does this mean that we should not be devotional at our Church gatherings? Not at all. Let the meetings begin with prayer and praise and song. And if a gathering feels that a brief address by one of the brethren upon a passage of God's Word is desirable, there can be no objections. Only let those who so address our assemblies preferably choose passages which stand directly related to the government of God's Church. But never should our assemblies make a specialty of addresses and devotionals. The correct government of our Churches is so all-important and urgent that we cannot afford to change the character of our ecclesiastical assemblies. We may not do so! Neither, of course, should we permit them to become mere "business meetings," that is, meetings at which the financial affairs and the external management of our ecclesiastical life is discussed and acted upon. That would be far worse. Let us keep balance and spend the major part of our precious time and efforts for the promotion of the spiritual welfare of our people and their Churches.

Which songs should we sing at our ecclesiastical assemblies? Only those that have been officially approved by Synod for worship in our Churches. In the past it has happened that even our Synod would use books not synodically approved. Why should we do this? The very excellent content of our Psalter and of our Psalter Hymnal makes the use of other books at our assemblies wholly unnecessary. To do so encourages irregularity. If our office-bearers, at official gatherings of the Churches use unapproved books, what then will we say if local Churches introduce such books for worship?

Is it necessary that the Bible be read at the opening of our ecclesiastical assemblies? In consideration of what has already been said we would answer negatively. It is not necessary. However, it is a good custom. The Word of God should occupy a central and controlling place in our lives. Therefore, it is altogether appropriate to read a fitting portion of God's Word as we begin to deliberate in the affairs of God's people and His Church.

Should we encourage the giving of all kinds of addresses at our classical and synodical gatherings by men representing various good causes? At our ecclesiastical gatherings we come together to transact the business of the Churches, and to promote their spiritual welfare, and not to listen to various addresses and inspirational speeches. Consequently, addresses by representatives of various agencies should be few. Those f.i. that wish to address our Synods should receive permission from Synod itself. And the privilege of addressing Synod should only be extended to applicants, if Synod is convinced that the brother's cause and message should be heard by Synod; never as a matter of mere good-will and courtesy.

ARTICLE 33

Those who are delegated to the assemblies shall bring with them their credentials and instructions, signed by those sending them, and they shall have a vote in all matters, except such as particularly concern their persons or Churches.

CREDENTIALS AND INSTRUCTIONS; RIGHT OF VOTE AT MAJOR ASSEMBLIES

1. Credentials.

The main content of this article goes back to the first regular Synod of the Reformed Churches of Holland (Emden, 1571). Proper certificates, testifying that those who claimed to be delegates from a certain Church or group of Churches, (Classis or Particular Synod), were actually delegated, were necessary especially then.

The Churches were just beginning to reach a period of stability, having gone through a long struggle of reformation. Moreover, they often knew but little of each other, distances being much greater than now, inasmuch as modern means of travel were still unknown. And the bloody persecutions of Reformation days had prevented them from establishing regular contacts with their fellow-believers. So the Churches felt that all who claimed to be the legal representatives of a Reformed Church or group of Churches should carry with them proper certificates, verifying their delegation. Thus fraudulent impostors and enemies of the Churches would be excluded.

Moreover, our fathers no doubt felt that at official gatherings of the Churches only those should be received who came with official credentials. And so it is still for us today. The danger of fraud is now very small. But certain affairs simply require official action. It would be improper to organize an ecclesiastical assembly merely upon the testimony of those who claim to be delegates. All such should be able to produce a black-on-white letter of appointment and delegation. This is too self-evident to require further discussion.

2. Instructions.

Those delegated to our assemblies must come with authority to act. It must be very clear that the representatives of the various Churches are more than visiting delegates. Thus the assembly concerned will know that all its members are there as real representatives of the Churches which sent them. And decisions made will thus have binding effect for all the Churches assembled.

And even as a written certificate of delegation should be produced and presented at the assembly meeting, so also a written copy of the instructions given; that is the authority delegated should be presented.

What is included under the term instructions, as used in the present article?

First of all a charge on the part of the sending body to its representatives **to help decide on all matters which are brought before the meeting in due order.** It being understood and expressed, however, that they shall take no part in, nor assume responsibility for matters which are contrary to the Bible as interpreted in the doctrinal standards of the Churches, or which are contrary to the rules of government agreed upon. Our Synod of 1888 ruled that all delegates to our major assemblies should be charged and authorized to help transact all matters brought before the assemblies in due order, according to the Word of God, as interpreted in the Forms of Unity, and the accepted Church Order. This ruling was made to assure the Churches that all the delegates would come properly authorized. And this charge includes the right and duty to consider all legitimately presented grievances and protests.

In the second place the instructions which delegates to major assemblies must bring with them according to Article 33 would concern **matters which the sending body itself brings to the meeting.** In other words, if the Church or Classis has any overtures or questions for the assembly, these should be written out on the credential letter. Instructions written on separate sheets of paper should be properly signed as well as the credential letter. The signing is, of course, done by the president and clerk of the sending and authorizing body.

3. Should the charge and authorization to delegates be specific or general?

The instructions to delegates should, as a rule, always be general. To illustrate, no Consistory should endeavor to instruct its delegates to Classis how to vote on any particular issue. Each delegate must use his own best judgment, and then vote as his conscience before God bids him vote. Abstractly and inherently the Churches would have a right to give their delegates a definite mandate, telling them how to vote. But the true welfare of the Churches requires that all delegates have their hands free and unbound. For our assemblies are not merely meetings at which the votes of the various Churches are recorded. But they are gatherings at which the problems and the affairs of the Churches are mutually considered and decided upon. Our gatherings are and should remain deliberative assemblies. And our delegates should not be reduced to the role of voting machines.

It is a very good practice for the sending bodies to consider the major issues which will require action at the assemblies to be held. That promotes general interest and counteracts hurtful ignorance. And that will help those that go as delegates to the major gatherings to know the mind of their brethren at home. But the delegates should not be bound. After a good discussion at the major assembly they may feel compelled to vote exactly opposite from their first contemplations.

Only when the circumstances are very extraordinary, as when a sending body knows all the issues involved in a specific case, would it be justified to instruct its delegates how to vote. So, for example, at the great Synod of Dort, 1618-19, some Particular Synods had instructed their delegates previously to vote so as to maintain the purity of doctrine, i.e., against the Arminians. Or as Jansen states, sending bodies can only give definite instruction as to how delegates should vote regarding matters which are clearly expressed in Holy Writ, and concerning which therefore further deliberation is unnecessary, and change of opinion out of place.

What else should credential letters contain in order to be complete? An assurance on the part of the sending body that it will abide by all the decisions of the assembly taken in conformity with Holy Writ as interpreted in the Three Forms of Unity (the Confession, the Heidelberg Catechism, and the Five Articles of Dort). The sending body ought to state in its credentials that it will regard such decisions as settled and binding, and that it will faithfully help to put them into practice.

Really an assurance as here referred to is implied and understood in the instruction already discussed. It is also essential to all denominational unity and cooperation. But it is well to give deliberate expression to this obligation and intent, inasmuch as some Churches and individuals at times forget these matters. The spirit of independentism sometimes asserts itself, when cooperation should hold sway.

The credential letter, almost needless to say, is properly concluded with Christian greetings and a committal to the grace of God and the guidance of His Spirit.

4. The Signature.

Why is it added: "signed by those sending them"? Years ago, in the land of our forefathers, when the relationship between State and Church was very close, the town or city officials would sometimes sign the credentials of ecclesiastical delegates. Our fathers, however, feared State dominance and so they soon objected to this practice and insisted that the ecclesiastical body sending should also write and sign the credentials and instructions. Moreover, every official document must be properly signed.

The phrase, "signed by those sending them," therefore originally provided for the signing of all credentials, and for the signing by the proper authorities. For us today it merely means that no letter of delegation is valid except it be properly signed.

5. Why does the Church Order provide that delegates shall not vote when a matter particularly concerns their persons or Churches?

As a matter of common sense and fairness. It is very hard for us to judge calmly and objectively when we ourselves are concerned. Yet every decision should be objective. And so the Churches have wisely agreed in the interest of the Kingdom, that those who are directly involved in a matter before an ecclesiastical gathering shall not vote. Let the other delegates decide and then let all abide by the opinion of the majority.

Abstractly it might be reasoned, that all lawful delegates have a right to vote in all matters coming before the gathering. But as a matter of expedience we have agreed to forego our rights when we ourselves are directly involved.

It is also true that in certain cases it would be manifestly unfair to have a delegate sit in judgment over himself. Particularly if he should stand accused on any score by such as are not delegated and who therefore would have no right to vote.

6. Advisory votes.

There is one class of brethren to whom the Church Order accords advisory votes at classical gatherings. Art. 42, n. l. provides that if a Church have more than one Minister, the Minister or Ministers not delegated to a certain classical meeting shall also have the right to attend Classis "with advisory vote." Such Ministers are therefore privileged to go not only to Classis, but are permitted to speak their mind on any matter up for consideration. They help Classis in all its deliberations, but they do not have a decisive vote. The membership of a Classis does not consist of Ministers and Elders, but of Churches. Each Church is entitled to two votes and no more.

Visiting Ministers, i.e., Ministers of Christian Reformed Churches belonging to another Classis who happen to visit a Classical gathering, are often accorded the privilege of the floor, i.e., advisory vote. There is nothing against this practice as long as such visitors do not abuse the privilege extended to them by asking the floor too often.

Our seminary professors are expected to be present at Synod in order to serve Synod in an advisory capacity. They have an advisory vote on all matters and serve as advisors and on the various Advisory Committees of Synod.

Is it proper and in harmony with our Church Order to extend the right of vote to Ministers not delegated? No it is not. It has happened that Home Missionaries, f.i., would be given the right to vote by a Classis in spite of the fact that they were not authorized and delegated by any Church. Should our Home Missionaries then be excluded from an active part in our Classical gatherings? Not at all. They should be delegated by their Consistories when their turn comes, just as regular Ministers are. At all other Classical gatherings they receive an advisory vote, as Art. 42 stipulates. In many instances our Home Missionaries will be the Ministers of some small Churches having no other Ministers. In such cases they naturally go to Classis regularly as full-fledged delegates.

ARTICLE 34

In all assemblies there shall be not only a president, but also a clerk to keep a faithful record of all important matters.

ASSEMBLY OFFICERS

1. The officers specified in Article 34.

In Dutch the officers of an ecclesiastical gathering are known as moderators. The officers as a body are designated as "het moderamen." The word "moderamen" is Latin, and signifies that by which anything is governed and managed. Rendered in English this term would therefore read, "the management" or "the body of directors." But the expression has no direct English equivalent. We do speak of moderators. A moderator is (1) "one who restrains or regulates," or (2) "The presiding officer of a meeting, especially in the Presbyterian and Congregational Churches." *

We use the expression "assembly officers" although the word "officer" is really too official, too authoritative for the present purpose.

*Funk and Wagnall's Dictionary.

Compare our "office" with the Dutch "ambt," and our "office-bearer" with the Dutch "ambtsdrager." They who are called upon to lead an ecclesiastical assembly do not occupy an authoritative position, as f.i. our Ministers, Elders, and Deacons do in their respective offices. They who lead our ecclesiastical assemblies merely guide and direct the assemblies as self-governing gatherings. When using the term "assembly officers", these facts should be borne in mind.

Which officers does Article 34 specify? Only two: a president and a clerk. The very oldest redactions of our Church Order, dating back to 1571 and 1578, also provided for the appointment of an "assessor," that is, an assistant to the president. But in 1581 this provision for this third officer for ecclesiastical assemblies was dropped, seemingly because it was judged that ecclesiastical gatherings do not always require an assistant president, as f. i. our Consistory meetings. Yet today all our Consistories have a vice-president, an assistant Clerk, a treasurer, and often other minor functionaries. Our Synods also invariably elect not only a president and a clerk, but also a vice-president and an assistant clerk. Yet our classical gatherings as a rule have no assistant president.

It is certainly advisable for our classical gatherings to choose an assistant president as well as a president. The assistant president relieves the president whenever necessary; he is asked to preside by the president when the latter wishes to address the gathering or when the matter at hand concerns the person of the president; he reminds the president of any item or point of procedure which the latter may overlook, etc. The appointment of an assistant president by a Classis is certainly not against the Church Order, though the Church Order does not require it. (Classis Pella has a rule that the Minister next in order to preside according to Article 41, acts as assistant president.) However, it would not be amiss, when a new redaction of the Church Order is prepared, to restore the old provision of 1571 and 1578 to Article 34.

2. What should be remarked regarding the nature of the position of assembly officers?

First of all, as has been indicated, that they do not occupy positions of superior authority above their brethren. Theirs is merely a position of leadership. They do not hold an office investing them with inherent superior authority. They are "directors" charged to direct the affairs of the assembly concerned. The original Latin term "moderamen" was doubtless chosen by our fathers to stress this fact.

In the second place, their work and charge is temporary. They are appointed for the length of the assembly only. Their charge ends when the assembly ends. Consequently they do not occupy a position different from other office-bearers, the assembly having disbanded. Presbyterian denominations seem to regard their assembly presidents as holding their offices until a successor has been elected at the next assembly. Our Classes and Synods, however, know of no permanent officers. It is true that our minor assemblies, i.e., our Consistories, are organized on a permanent basis. But Consistories are the governing bodies of our ecclesiastical units, the individual Churches. Consistories are therefore permanent bodies. But even so the Church Order provides that if a Church have more than one Minister, these shall preside in turn.

Anything which might lead to the errors and faults of hierarchical dominance has been avoided in our Church Order.

3. The work of clerks.

It is the duty of the clerks of our various assemblies to keep a record of all important matters transacted. Accurate record should be kept: (1) so that the Church or Churches may know with precision what has been decided in any given instance. At Consistory meetings, f.i., the minutes are referred to again and again to determine what has been decided at some previous meeting. Without an accurate record, confusion and misunderstanding and ill-will would be multiplied. (2) To avoid needless duplication of work accurate records are also necessary. A matter thoroughly discussed and acted upon and properly recorded as a rule need not be reconsidered, unless circumstances have altered themselves considerably, or if it be proven that an error has been made. Yet without a good record the same straw would be thrashed repeatedly. Even now, though we have good records, this sometimes happens. (3) And furthermore, we should preserve our decisions and deliverances for the benefit of posterity. Later generations may profit by our work, even as we are profiting by means of the records kept by our forefathers. The lessons of history are ever so extremely valuable, also in the field of church government.

What should our clerks record? Not the discussions and opinions put forward and offered for consideration at our assemblies, but only the conclusions reached together with the reasons or grounds for such conclusions, if the matter is of any import at all. It is not wise to enter upon the official and permanent records of our assemblies the discussions and opinions offered, especially not if the names of the brethren are mentioned, as f.i. was done in the early records of our Christian Reformed major assemblies.* Discussions and opinions offered are only scaffolding which is used to rear the building, not the building itself. It is preparatory work. To record this preliminary material may hamper the work in that it may exercise a restraining influence upon discussion. Our assemblies must continue to be deliberative gatherings. The true welfare of our Churches demands this. Moreover, no one could give an accurate reproduction of a discussion unless he be a court stenographer. Our records should not become too bulky and too expensive.

4. Sundry matters.

What other matters are worthy of note in this connection? First of all that the person of the clerk should be a member of the Consistory, preferably an Elder. Treasurers, Building and Ground Committees, etc., can under certain circumstances be well chosen from those not holding office. To do so may save the Elders much valuable time which they should use for the spiritual upbuilding of the Church. But the record of Consistory meetings contain many matters which, for the good of all, the Consistory only should know.

What name should we give to our assembly records? The records of our Consistories and Classes we usually call minutes; those of our Synods, Acts.

Minutes, as the Dutch "notulen" (from the Latin **notula,** derived from **nota,** meaning mark or sign) indicates a minute or detailed account of transactions. Acts, from **acta,** meaning deeds, decrees, or resolutions, indicates a record limited to actual resolutions or decisions passed. Consequently the term "acts" would be the more appropriate to use for all the records of all our assemblies, Consistories, Classes, and Synods. However, it is understood by all that in naming the

*Compiled Acts of Synod from 1857-80.

records of our Consistories and Classes "minutes" we do not mean to say that these records should be detailed, recording the discussions as well as the decisions.

Must our assemblies permit any member of our Churches the privilege of reading the minutes for himself? No. They may if they see fit, but they need not. Particularly the minutes of a Consistory may contain matters of discipline, which only the Consistory members should know. But parties involved in any case are entitled to a certified copy of any and all decisions which touch their case.

When should the records of our assemblies be approved? Consistory minutes can conveniently be approved at the next meeting to be held, but the acts of Classes and Synods should be approved of while these assemblies are still in session, inasmuch as the membership of these gatherings change constantly, and no one would recall accurately all the rulings of a Classis or Synod taken at a previous gathering. Moreover, these gatherings in themselves are non-continuous. Each assembly must therefore pass on the correctness of its own records.

What positions do our stated clerks occupy? Synod of 1904 (Art. 132, 7) stipulated that the stated clerks of our Classes and Synod should not be looked upon as permanent clerks, a position unknown to our Churches, but that a stated clerk is a regular delegate whose duties are threefold: he inscribes the minutes; he attends to all official correspondence; and he prepares the agendum. It is well that the work of the stated clerks be clearly defined. Jansen does not favor the appointment of stated clerks. He would rather appoint a Church for this work so that the Consistory concerned may have the responsibility. And then he would appoint a different Church for every next classical or synodical gathering to be held. These Churches could then also be expected to call the next classical or synodical gathering to be held. All this, of course, to avoid the danger of assumption of authority. But in the interest of regularity and good order the custom of appointing stated clerks is no doubt to be preferred. But let every stated clerk hold himself strictly to the limitations of his charge!

Should classical reports to our church papers be approved by the Classes before they are published? Preferably, yes. The Classes should at least indicate what should be included in these reports. The matter should have some measure of control. Consistories, when in position to do so, through church bulletins, etc., should also publish their activities in so far as these are of general interest to the congregation. This will help to create a sympathetic atmosphere, so highly desirable.

ARTICLE 35

The office of the president is to state and explain the business to be transacted, to see to it that everyone observe due order in speaking, to silence the captious and those who are vehement in speaking; and to properly discipline them if they refuse to listen. Furthermore his office shall cease when the assembly arises.

THE OFFICE OF PRESIDENTS

1. The duty of presidents.

Article 35 is indeed venerable with age. It was formulated in the year 1571. It was drafted and accepted by the first regular Synod of our Churches in Holland meeting in Emden, Germany, during that year. But it only referred to Particular and General Synods, not to Consistories and Classes. However, the Synod of Middelburg, 1581, placed this article before those which regulate the activities of all our assemblies, Consistories, Classes, and Synods (Articles 37 to 52). Consequently, from the year 1581 on, Article 35 applies to presidents of our Synods. However, from the nature of the case it follows that this article is of primary import for classical and synodical presidents.

The first duty of our ecclesiastical presidents is **"to state and explain the business to be transacted."** For those of our gatherings which mail printed or typewritten agenda to the delegates or the delegating bodies, prior to the meeting of the assembly, this task of our presidents is much simplified, inasmuch as these agenda or programs give every delegate a rather complete knowledge of all the business coming before the assembly. However, certain matters may require explanation from time to time as they are presented for consideration and decision. As often as necessary a president should give elucidations.

It should be noted that the Church Order requires that the president "state and explain" the business to be transacted. It does not say that he must constantly advise the assembly. If he feels that advice on his part is required he may certainly speak his mind, but then he should first give the gavel to the assistant president so that he may speak on the matter at hand in the capacity of an ordinary delegate. The president should also avoid the danger of using his position to swing a meeting his way. He should be as objective as possible in his capacity as president, and he should not forget that it is his task as president **to direct** the gathering in its free deliberation of all its affairs. It is his privilege and duty to guide and direct, not his right to pull and compel. Though he stands at the controls of the meeting, he may not be partial and wilful in the handling of these controls.

Secondly the president must **"see to it that everyone observes due order in speaking."** This provision sums up the main task of presidents of our major assemblies. At Consistory meetings the president may find it necessary to take part in the discussion again and again. But at classical and synodical gatherings the task of our presidents will be largely that of directing the deliberations.

By observance of due order the Church Order refers to an orderly transaction of business. Delegates, f.i., must "stick to the point" in their discussions. If any one begins to talk about things not related to the matter up for consideration the president must stop him and call his attention to his mistake. If the same delegate should desire to speak repeatedly on the same matter while others are waiting for the floor, the president should refuse him the privilege of speaking. As a rule the same delegate should not speak oftener than twice or thrice on any one matter. Hard and fast rules in this respect should not be passed, for under certain circumstances a delegate might have to speak very often. Neither should we by arbitrary, parliamentary rules, make it impossible for a brother to give an assembly all the light that he may have. Nor should we make it impossible for any delegate to unburden his Christian conscience. An ecclesiastical assembly is not to be put on par with an ordinary business meeting of some board. But no delegate to Classis or Synod should abuse his privileges and hold the floor repeatedly. The presidents must use a great deal of discretion also on this score.

It stands to reason that all delegates should use good manners in addressing the president or the assembly. If any should fail to do so, the president must call him to order.

When a matter has been considered for some time and no new light is being shed on the issues involved, and the gathering seems ready for a conclusion, the president ought to summarize the main sentiments expressed, and then if necessary suggest that a motion be offered. Endless discussions, take up a great deal of time; they promote a nervous tension which is harmful; and they are often nearly fruitless. But premature motions and motions prematurely passed for a vote are also to be condemned. After a calm and careful discussion on the matter at hand, a motion should be formulated, and then after a reasonable consideration of the merits and demerits of the motion, it should be voted upon.

There has been a tendency during recent years to multiply rules and regulations for our classical and synodical gatherings (cf. Acts of Synod, 1934, pp. 306-312). It is doubtful whether the majority of delegates to our assemblies will and can bear all these detailed rules in mind. This is true for our Elders, but also for our Ministers. Moreover, discussion should be free and not hampered by a large number of technical rules. We fear the rules approved in 1934 are too detailed and rigid. It is doubtful whether any Synod can really observe all these rules. Our Synods should continue to be deliberative gatherings. Strict enforcement of the rules adopted would keep many a delegate from speaking his opinion for fear that he would be transgressing some rule and should be called out of order. We should have a few fundamental rules perchance, over and above what the Church Order gives us. But let us ever avoid sets of detailed, legalistic, parliamentary rules. Our ecclesiastical gatherings are not political gatherings. Even in political gatherings and gatherings akin to these, rule upon rule and precept upon precept often work their harm and are grossly abused.

In the third place, Article 35 stipulates that it is the president's duty **"to silence the captious and those that are vehement in speaking; and to properly discipline them if they refuse to listen."** Captious persons are such as are fault-finders and overly critical. The original Latin term is "acriores," and designates those who irritate by their sharp and cutting remarks. In the Dutch we have "knibbelachtigen." This term applies to those that are small and petty in their criticism; real fault-finders.

The use of sarcasm should seldom be used, especially at our ecclesiastical gatherings. Cutting remarks should likewise be ruled out. Any unChristian word, attitude, or assumption should be contraband at our ecclesiastical meetings.

Those that are too vehement must also be silenced by the president. The Latin word here is "contentiose," and the Dutch "heftig." The term vehement, therefore, refers to those that are too violent in their words. Vehemence in speech is usually provoked by anger and is easily carried too far. Even if a speaker is motivated in his vehemence by righteous indignation he should watch his words. Anyone who loses control of himself in this respect should be called back to his normal self by the chair.

Usually a word from the president will be enough. But if a mere reminder or admonition is not enough, then the president must forbid him in the name of the meeting to continue. This is what the Church Order means when it speaks of disciplining those that refuse to listen. Sometimes the president may find it necessary to call for a motion of disapproval on the part of the assembly. In extreme cases the president should ask the offending brother to leave the meeting in order that the assembly may decide in his absence what is to be done in his case. The first Synod (Emden, 1571) already advised that this latter procedure might be followed in some cases.

If the president himself should offend on any of these points it would become the duty of the assistant president to call him to order. And if need be the assembly should be called upon to censure him by a vote of disapproval.

From all the foregoing it follows that the task of presidents at our assemblies is far from easy. Not all are equally well qualified for this important function. Says Bouwman, "A president must be a man possessing calmness of character, clearness of insight, and determination of will".* Self-control, the ability to give definite leadership, and the ability of expressing one's self clearly and fluently may also be mentioned as desirable qualities for presidents of our major assemblies. He should be a man of ability and conviction; and who, because of these qualities, has the confidence of the assembly over which he is to preside.

2. The duration of their office.

The Church Order stipulates: "His office shall cease when the assembly arises." Which simply means that when the meetings of the assembly have ended the president's term as president has also ended. He is not appointed for a definite period of time, but only for the duration of the assembly concerned, whether that assembly meet for just one session or for several sessions, for one day or for several days.

This provision is very natural. The president's office is not an office in its ordinary sense, but only a function. Yet this provision has been included in the Church Order for a good purpose, namely, to make it very clear that the presidents of our assemblies are not to be considered superior officers. We have no bishops as Churches with the hierarchical form of government have. (The Roman Catholic Church is hierarchical in the extreme. The Methodist and other Churches are also essentially hierarchical in Church government, although in a very mild form.) Our Churches are ruled neither by priests nor bishops, but they govern themselves through duly organized assemblies.

In many Presbyterian denominations, as also in the (Dutch) Reformed Church of America, the president (called Moderator) of major gatherings is considered to be chosen for the term of one year. The Moderator chosen one year is recognized as such until his "successor" is chosen at the next general assembly. Several authorities, however, realize that this custom does not agree with Presbyterian Church government and that it finds no support in the Constitution of said Churches. It is well that our Church Order definitely rules a conception as just alluded to out of court.

It is worthy of note that our Reformed fathers were very much afraid of the evils and dangers of hierarchism. To avoid hierarchical evils and tendencies, Article 37 even provides that in our Consistories, if a Church have more than one Minister, these Ministers shall preside in turn. And again, to avoid hierarchical evils and tendencies, Article 41 provides that the same brother shall not preside at two successive classical meetings.

But if the directors of our assemblies serve only while these bodies

*__Gereformeerd Kerkrecht__, II, p. 87.

are in session, then who takes care of matters that require the attention of these assemblies while they are not in session? For urgent matters every Classis has a Classical Committee, consisting of three of its office-bearers. So also Synod has a Synodical Committee. These committees act upon matters which cannot wait until the assembly meets. Their task is limited to matters which require immediate action and yet are not of such a nature that a special session of the assembly is warranted. These committees must submit a report of all their activities to the next assembly concerned, for the approval or disapproval of these bodies. Men who serve on these committees should have a thorough knowledge and a seasoned judgment. They should know the Church Order and its underlying principles. Elders are just as eligible, as far as their office is concerned, for these committees as Ministers are. Needless to say, members of Classical or Synodical Committees should carefully avoid the assumption of authority not entrusted to them.

Those who wish to address letters or reports to our assemblies while they are not in session can write to the Stated Clerks, of whom we have already spoken. (Cf. comments under Article 34). Our minor assemblies, i.e., our Consistories, all have regular clerks.

ARTICLE 36

The Classis has the same jurisdiction over the Consistory as the Particular Synod has over the Classis and the General Synod over the Particular.

AUTHORITY OF MAJOR ASSEMBLIES OVER MINOR ASSEMBLIES

1. Major assemblies have authority over minor assemblies.

Our English redaction of Article 36 speaks of jurisdiction. We believe the word authority would have been a better term to use. The word jurisdiction has a distinct legal bias. It is derived from the Latin "jurisdictio" (**jus** - law, **dico** - to say) which in the first place refers to the administration of justice in civil matters. Now the original Latin Church Order did not use the word "jurisdictio," but "auctoritas," from the word "auctor" which signifies an author, founder, originator, etc., or an advisor, counselor, promoter, pattern. "Auctoritas" as used in the Latin original of the Church Order indicates the right to act, order, rule, advise, or exhort. Our English word authority indicates the right to act officially. Consequently we would rather speak of authority than of jurisdiction. Perhaps the simplest and safest reading would be, "The classis has **the same rights** over the Consistory . . ." The word authority is often used in a legalistic, compelling sense whereas the Church Order refers to a moral and spiritual authority.

The practical import of this brief consideration is illustrated by the decision of the Synod of 1926, which ruled that major assemblies had the right to depose a Consistory inasmuch as Article 36 attributed jurisdiction to Classes over Consistories. Now aside from the question whether or not a Classis has the right to depose a Consistory, Synod should not have based its decision on the use of the word jurisdiction in Article 36, inasmuch as the use of this term is really a mistake, out of keeping with the fundamental principles of the Church Order.

Is the exercise of ecclesiastical authority as provided for in Article 36 based on Biblical example? Yes. We read in Acts 15 that the Church in Antioch sent delegates to the Church at Jerusalem to consider with it certain vexing questions regarding the keeping of the Mosaic ordinances. The Apostles and Elders were gathered to consider this matter. After due deliberation certain decisions were reached. These decisions were laid upon the Churches as necessary things (vs. 28). The Churches had to respect the decisions of this assembly. The authoritative character of this gathering should not be explained by saying that this meeting was primarily a gathering of Apostles, men who were infallibly led in their official work by the Spirit of God. The Elders at Jerusalem took part in the work of this assembly, and even the whole body of believers seems to have been involved at least indirectly (cf. vs. 22). And the representatives from Antioch took an active part in the deliberations and decisions (vs. 12).

This meeting at Jerusalem therefore clearly partakes of the character of major assemblies. It may be regarded as a forerunner of what became well-organized and regular later on. True, we do not read of regularly-instituted major gatherings. But in the first place, since the Apostles were still alive and active, there was no urgent need for major assemblies. And furthermore, the Church of Christ was just beginning to manifest itself in well-organized groups locally. In other words, time did not yet permit and demand the regular organization of major assemblies. Even so we do read of other instances where Churches take united action (Rom. 15:26; II Cor. 8:19).

The exercise of authority on the part of major assemblies over minor assemblies is also wholly reasonable. For indeed, groups of Churches have a larger sphere of influence and domain of authority than just one Church. Each particular Church has a certain authority received of Christ and vested in its Consistory. Now when a Church, through its Consistory, sends delegates to a major assembly, that Church thereby brings a measure of its authority to this assembly, at the same time submitting itself to the accumulated authority of all the Churches convened. Indeed, the very fact that a particular Church is affiliated with other Churches in one denomination implies transfer of and submission to authority.

All the Churches of a Classis have submitted themselves to the just guidance and rule of the Classis. And all the Classes have submitted themselves to the just guidance and rule of the Synods. Let us not forget that denominational co-operation would be out of the question if classical and synodical gatherings were not vested with the authority attributed to them in Article 36. Ecclesiastical federation according to the Reformed conception simply implies authoritative rights on the part of major assemblies over minor assemblies.

2. The nature of the authority which major assemblies have over minor assemblies.

The authority which the government exercises over its subjects is juridical authority. The authority which the Reformed Churches have attributed to their major assemblies in relation to their minor assemblies is not juridical, but moral and spiritual. In Dutch we distinguish in like manner between "rechterlijk gezag" and "zedelijk, geestelijk gezag."

According to Reformed church polity the authority of major assemblies is:

1. **Derived,** and not original. Consistories receive their authority directly from Christ the King of His Church. Classes and Synods receive their authority only by delegation. Consistories therefore exercise original authority, but major assemblies have no other than derived authority;

2. **Limited,** and not general. A Consistory exercises a general authority. It has authority to act on all matters pertaining to its congregation. But a Classis and Synod has authority to act only concerning matters that could not be finished at minor assemblies, or that pertain to the Churches in general (Art. 30). The authority of major assemblies does not extend beyond the provisions of the Church Order and the instructions given it by the minor assemblies;

3. **Smaller in measure,** and not higher in degree. One who is delegated will naturally have less authority than the delegating body. And essentially there is no ecclesiastical authority other than the authority vested in the office-bearers of the particular Churches;

4. **Ministering,** and not compelling. A major assembly cannot force a minor assembly to accept and execute its decisions. A minor assembly, if it feels that a decision of a major assembly is unBiblical, should appeal to the next gathering of the assembly, or to the assembly next in order. In the meantime the appealing body should submit, unless it cannot do so because of great conscientious objections before God. If the objections are not removed, and if the decision stands, then the brethren concerned should, if at all possible, submit if need be under continued protest and always with the clear understanding that the burdened parties have a full right to retain their own convictions. But if the brethren concerned feel fully persuaded that they may not submit, even under conditions as just indicated, then the only other course open to them is withdrawal from the denomination. Needless to say, this is a very serious and extreme step, and should only be taken in case the matter is very urgent.

5. **Conditional,** and not unconditional. The Word of God only is independent. Its deliverances and commandments are, from their very nature, unconditional. But all decisions of ecclesiastical gatherings are valid only if they agree with the Bible.

These fundamental principles should never be lost out of sight. If the Church of Christ ever does lose sight of these all-important principles, she will suffer for it. And sometimes very severely. Consider the trials of Dr. J. G. Machen and others by the Presbyterian Church of the U. S. A. What a loss for that denomination!

It is also well to remember what Dr. Bouwman tells us in his previously quoted and very valuable work. Says he: "All ecclesiastical authority, given unto His Church by Christ, resides in the particular Church. The keys of the Kingdom of Heaven, given to the Apostles by Christ, and in them to the congregation were, when the Apostles passed from the scenes of life, exercised by the office-bearers who had been chosen under their guidance in the particular Churches. This ecclesiastical authority consists of three things: Authority to administer the Word and the Sacraments; authority to elect ecclesiastical office-bearers; and authority to exercise ecclesiastical discipline. There is no other authority in the ecclesiastical sphere. And this three-fold authority does not pertain to the Major Assemblies, but to the office-bearers of the particular Churches."[1] From the principle here enunciated it follows that major assemblies have no more au-

1. Bouwman: **Geref. Kerkrecht,** 1934, II, 21.

thority than that which the Churches have attributed to them by mutual agreement.

3. The authority of major assemblies over minor assemblies differentiated from the authority of Consistories over congregations.

There is a distinct difference between the authority of Major assemblies over minor assemblies, and the authority of Consistories over congregations. For this reason Article 36 does not speak of this authority of Consistories over congregations.

Voetius, Bouwman, and Jansen[1] all enumerate certain differences between consistorial authority and the authority of our major assemblies. There is a difference (1) **as to origin.** Major assemblies have no other authority than that which they have derived from the Consistories. Consistories, however, exercise an authority given unto them directly by Christ. There is a difference (2) **as to necessity.** Major assemblies are necessary for the welfare or well-being of the Churches. Consistories are necessary for the being, the very existence of the Churches. There is a difference (3) **as to essence.** The authority of Classes and Synods is derived and accidental. The particular Church possesses original and essential authority. (Heat is essential to fire, but accidental to water heated by fire.—Jansen.) There is a difference (4) **as to duration.** The authority of Classes and Synods, from the nature of the case, would cease if the particular Churches constituting the denomination would cease. But though Classes and Synod should cease to function, yet the Churches could continue to exist. There is furthermore a difference (5) **as to purpose.** Consistories have an independent existence and do not exist for the sake of the major assemblies. But the major assemblies do exist for the sake of the particular Churches, namely, to minister to their welfare with good advice and wise guidance.

ARTICLE 37

In all Churches there shall be a Consistory composed of the Ministers of the Word and the Elders, who at least in larger congregations, shall, as a rule, meet once a week. The Minister of the Word (or the Ministers, if there be more than one, in turn) shall preside and regulate the proceedings. Wherever the number of Elders is small, the Deacons may be added to the Consistory by local regulation; this shall invariably be the rule where the number is less than three.

CONSISTORIES

Articles 37 to 40 concern our Consistories. Article 29 enumerates four kinds of ecclesiastical assemblies. Of these four the Consistory is mentioned first of all, namely, in Article 37. Article 38 regulates the constitution of Consistories for the first time, i.e., in other words, the organization of new Churches. Article 39 tells us what is to be done for localities where there are believers, but where organization cannot as yet take place. And Article 40 regulates the matter of diaconal gatherings.

1. Bouwman: **Geref. Kerkrecht**, 1934, II. 22; Voetius: **Pol. Eccl.**, I, 122; IV, 166, 226 (Cf. Bouwman, II, 22); Jansen, **Korte Verklaring**, etc., 1923, 165, 166.

1. A Consistory in every Church.

Reformed Church polity holds that every Church must have its own Consistory. There are good reasons for this position. In the first place note that every Church is a complete unit in itself. Holy Writ, f.i., speaks concerning the Churches at Antioch, at Corinth, etc., as local and particular Churches, and acknowledges them to be complete units of the general Church of Christ (cf. Acts 13:1; 1 Cor. 1:2). We also find that every Church has its own office-bearers (cf. Acts. 14:23; Titus 1:5). These office-bearers are charged with the service of the Word and the Sacraments, with the maintenance of purity in doctrine and the exercise of discipline (cf. Acts 20:28; I Peter 5:2,3). Moreover, the office-bearers form a body taking united action whenever necessary (Acts 15:6; 20:17; 21:17, 18). Thus also I Tim. 4:14 speaks of "the presbytery," definitely referring to a body of Elders it would seem.

Denominational unity and confederation is certainly Biblical, and is based upon our essential unity in Christ and under Christ our great Prophet, only High Priest, and eternal King. And confederation of Churches certainly supports and promotes the welfare of the particular Churches. But it should not be forgotten that even without this God-ordained confederacy a particular Church has all that is essential to a Church (offices, right and duty to preach the Word, administration of the Sacraments, exercise of discipline).

Calvin held that ultimately the government of the Church was vested in the congregation.[1] To the congregation of believers it is said: "But as ye are an elect race, a royal priesthood, a holy nation, a people for God's own possession, that ye may show forth the excellencies of him who called you out of darkness into his marvelous light" (I Peter 2:9). This passage marks the believers as prophets, priests, and kings. Related to this principle stands the fact that in our Churches the congregation of believers always takes part in the appointment of men to office and in the exercise of discipline. The Consistories must always, according to the general rules of the Church Order, acknowledge and consult the congregation. But, as Dr. Bouwman points out,[2] the members of the visible manifestation of the body of Christ, i.e., the members of each particular Church, exercise their rights and duties as an organism organically, through the offices. When a Church is to be organized the believers appoint certain brethren to office, under guidance of neighboring Churches if possible. However, as soon as the offices have been instituted, these offices begin to govern and guide the affairs of the Church. But this original authority, common to all believers, again begins to function directly and without the guidance and authority of these office-bearers, in case these office-bearers become unfaithful to their charge and refuse to amend their neglect and errors. Then, again with the assistance of neighboring Churches if possible, the believers as such are called upon to exercise their prerogatives under Christ their absolute Sovereign.

As Voetius states, the Consistory is the organ through which the Church functions, even as the eye is the organ through which the body sees.[3]

---

1. cf. Calvin, **Institutes**, IV, 1.

2. Bouwman, **Gereformeerde Kerkrecht**, 1934, II, 102.

3. Voetius, **Pol. Eccl.** 4:893, quoted by Bouwman, **Geref. Kerkrecht**, 1934, II, 102.

2. Members of the Consistory.

Article 37 clearly specifies that Consistories shall be composed of Ministers and Elders. This is as might be expected. In I Tim. 4:14, for instance, the term presbytery refers to a body of Elders. In the following chapter (I Tim. 5:17) these officers are spoken of in a twofold sense. They are referred to as teaching Elders and ruling Elders. It should also be noted that the term Consistory, as used in the Church Order, uniformly signifies the body of Ministers and Elders. This is especially clear from Articles 4, 5, 10, etc., in which articles the Consistory is distinguished from the body of Deacons.

The first regular Synod of the Reformed Churches of Holland, Emden 1571, declared that in each Church there should be "gatherings or Consistories of Ministers of the Word, Elders, and Deacons" (Emden 1571, Art. 6). There seems to have been some difference of opinion regarding this 6th article of Emden. The question seemingly arose whether the Synod had meant that all these three offices must meet in one gathering, or whether the Deacons might, or perhaps should, constitute a separate gathering. In most of the Churches the Elders and Deacons met separately.* In some Churches the Deacons were definitely not admitted to the Consistory. In still other Churches the Deacons refused to meet with the Consistory. So three years later the Synod of Dort, 1574, being questioned in regard to this matter, declared: "In explanation of Article 6 of Emden, providing that in every Church there shall be gatherings of Ministers of the Word, Elders, and Deacons the brethren understand: That the Ministers and Elders shall meet by themselves, and the Deacons by themselves, so that each may transact their own affairs. But in places where there are few Elders, the Deacons shall be permitted to be a part of the Consistory, and having been called into the Consistory, they shall be obliged to come" (Art. 4, Dort, 1574).

This explanatory decision of 1574 has been maintained ever since and finds its reflection in Article 37 of our Church Order and in other articles as well. But our mother Churches in the Netherlands decided in 1905 that Deacons must be reckoned with the Consistory if the number of Elders is less than three. This slight revision, a measure of wisdom and safety, was also incorporated in our redaction of the Church Order in 1914.

Our Church Order therefore clearly stipulates that regularly the Ministers and Elders constitute the Consistory, but that in small Churches the Deacons may be added to the Consistory, and that these must be added in case there are less than three Elders.

Now, in Article 30 of the Confession our Churches declare that: ". . . there must be Ministers or pastors to preach the Word of God and to administer the Sacraments; also Elders and Deacons who, together with the pastors, form the council of the Church. . ." Some have concluded that there is a conflict between our Confession and our Church Order on this score. But let it be noted that in Article 30 of the Confession we declare by whom the Churches ought to be governed, and that in the Church Order we stipulate how the work of the office-bearers is to be executed. Or again: In the Confession we have the declaration of a fundamental principle. In the Church Order the statement regarding a method of work. The Confession, as might be expected, commits itself regarding a fundamental principle, and the Church Order, without denying this fundamental principle,

* Cf. Bouwman, **Geref. Kerkrecht,** 1934, II, 113, 114.

provides for a limited measure of division of labor in keeping with the peculiar duties of the offices.

Inasmuch as this is a point of importance, and inasmuch as there has been a measure of confusion and misunderstanding in our circles regarding these matters, it may be well for us to state the whole situation in a summary way. First of all then, the three offices of the N. T. Church are derived from Christ's threefold office and correspond to these. The threefold office of Christ was vested in the Apostles temporarily. In due time Ministers, Elders, and Deacons continued the work of the Apostles, that is to say, the abiding elements of their office. The Ministers of the Gospel (or teaching Elders) represent Christ as Prophet of truth; the Elders (or ruling Elders) represent Christ as King of righteousness; and the Deacons represent Christ as Priest of mercy. Each office has its distinct task, though the offices are more or less inter-related and they have their unity in Christ.

Whenever necessary these three types of office-bearers may work together in governing the Churches and in caring for the poor. Elders then act as assistant Deacons and Deacons as assistant Elders. Thus it must be done in very small congregations, numbering less than three Elders.

This special arrangement of full cooperation of all the offices is altogether permissible in view of the essential unity of the office in Christ. Ordinarily, however, for reasons of expediency and in keeping with their own special work, the Ministers and Elders meet to govern the Church as its Consistory, and the Deacons meet as its Diaconate for the work of mercy. However, in matters of appointment to office (Articles 4, 5, 22) or release from office (Article 10) and the exercise of supervision over each other as office-bearers (Art. 81), all three offices must cooperate and work as one body, even in the largest Churches.

The division of labor provisions of the Church Order, i.e., the provision that the Elders hold their separate meetings and the Deacons theirs, this provision is therefore both restricted and conditional.

From the foregoing it will be clear that when the Deacons are part of the Consistory they should be considered to be full-fledged Consistory members. They have a voice and vote in all matters which pertain to the government of the Church, even as the Elders under these circumstances have a voice and vote in all matters regarding the Church's work of mercy. To deny the Deacons a right to vote in cases of discipline, for instance, would be contrary to the Church Order and the duties which have been imposed on them by local arrangement. However, when matters pertaining to the government of the Church are being considered the Deacons should certainly bear in mind that governmental matters belong first of all to the domain of the Elders. Thus it might happen regarding a disciplinary matter that a Consistory consisting of four Elders and four Deacons would vote to bar a certain member from the Sacraments with a vote of five to three, four Deacons and one Elder favoring the step, but all the Elders except one being against it. A situation like this certainly would be very abnormal, though technically in order. In cases akin to the hypothetical illustration the Consistory would do best to postpone action until a greater measure of agreement could be reached, or until at least the majority of the Elders feel that the step mentioned is necessary. So also the Elders should be very slow to outvote the Deacons in diaconal affairs. The Deacons should also give first opportunity to the Elders to speak on governmental questions and the Elders should, as a matter of common sense and courtesy, allow the Deacons to voice their opinions before committing themselves regarding any matter which concerns the administration of Christian mercy.

In this connection we would refer to a report drafted by a committee which reported to the Synod of 1938, on the position of our Deacons in the Consistory. (Cf. Agenda, 1938, II, pp. 91-99.) We also quote the decision of Synod in regard to this question:

"In view of the fact that the basic problem in regard to the status of Deacons in the Consistory hinges on the interpretation of the phrase, 'added to the Consistory' in Art. 37 of the Church Order, Synod declares that:

1. The phrase, 'added to the Consistory,' can mean only that the Deacons become members of the Consistory, and as such they are warranted in performing presbyterial functions including the right to vote in matters of Church government.

2. This concession by our Church Order, namely, that Deacons may function as Elders, is made to avoid the unReformed practice of oligarchic rule which would be the only alternative.

3. It ought, however, to be added that such deacons, in matters of Church government, should naturally give due consideration to the judgment of the elders. **Adopted.**" (Cf. Acts of Synod, 1938, Art. 96, p. 81.)

3. When separate meetings for Elders and Deacons are held, how should the work be divided?

Churches which maintain separate meetings for Elders and Deacons have, as is to be understood, three types of gatherings. First of all there will be regular Consistory meetings consisting of Ministers and Elders. Then, they will also have regular Deacons' meetings. And in the third place, according to the requirement of the Church Order for all Churches, there will be meetings of all office-bearers together —Ministers, Elders, and Deacons.

In the Netherlands our brethren in the faith often speak of the "breede kerkeraad," which term indicates the general meeting of all the office-bearers. The "smalle kerkeraad" indicates the gathering of Ministers and Elders. And the "diaconale vergadering" is the term used to designate the gathering of the Deacons. With us these various gatherings are sometimes designated as Council Meetings, Consistory Meetings, and Deacons' Meetings. Other possible designations would be: the General Consistory, the Restricted Consistory, and the Diaconate. The term "Deaconate," in spite of the fact that it is less cumbersome and that many in our circles use it regularly, is not good English. Diaconate is. Deaconry would also be good English.

Jansen enumerates rather fully the matters which are usually acted upon at the meetings of General Consistories in the Netherlands.*

They are as follows:

1. All matters pertaining to the election of office-bearers: Nominations; final decision whether or not one chosen shall be called; consideration of objections registered; releasing one from his call to office, etc. (Cf. Ch. O., Art. 4, 5, 22, 24, etc.)
2. The issuing and receiving of certificates of Ministers arriving or departing. (Ch. O. Art. 5 and 10.)
3. Provisional consideration of and decision regarding emeritation. (Ch. O., Art. 13.)
4. Mutual Censure. (Ch. O., Art. 81.)

---

* Jansen, **Korte Verklaring, etc.**, 1923, pp. 170, 171.

5. Church Visitation. (Ch. O., Art. 44.)
6. Administration of finances (Ch. O., Art. 11); appointing and instructing Building and Grounds Committees; regulating the various collections and distribution of funds collected; determining the amount of salaries to be paid.
7. The general administration of benevolence matters; Regulating the matter of poor fund collections; extension of advice to the Deacons; approval of diaconal activities regarding help extended, etc. (Ch. O., Art. 25, 26.)
8. General business administration of the material interests of the Church, including the erection of buildings for congregational purposes, for the poor, etc.
9. Consideration of general correspondence. (Correspondence regarding more spiritual matters concerns the Restricted Consistory, and that regarding the care for the poor concerns the Diaconate.)

The same author attributes the following activities to the Restricted Consistory meetings:

1. Regulating the services of the Word and catechism instruction.
2. The exercise of discipline.
3. The matter of home-visitation work.
4. Admission to the sacraments.
5. Consideration of all correspondence which concerns the Elders particularly.

Bouwman rightly adds to these: Delegation of representatives to major assemblies.

Regarding the activities which Jansen assigns to the General Consistories, Bouwman is not nearly as elaborate but both authorities are in substantial agreement.[1]

How large should Consistories be before division of labor can be introduced with profit? No one should attempt to lay down an absolute rule regarding this matter. Separate meetings should not be introduced too early, but neither should they be postponed unduly. There are reasons to believe that a number of our Churches which have failed to do so until now, could do so with profit. Division of labor, where it is possible, makes for specialization and concentration. Dr. F. L. Rutgers suggests that Consistories of six Elders and more should consider the desirability of introducing separate gatherings.[2]

4. How often should Consistories meet, and who should act as president?

Originally the Consistories would meet once a week. This was in accord with the stipulations made in the first Synod (Emden, 1571). However, it soon became apparent that especially in smaller Churches it was not necessary that Consistories should meet every week. The Netherland Churches, in their redaction of 1905, made this provision less binding by providing that Consistories in "larger Churches" should "as a rule" meet once a week. We followed this example in 1914. In practice Consistories meet monthly or bi-weekly, depending upon the size of the Church and the amount of work constantly requiring attention.

In those of our Churches which maintain division of labor for their office-bearers it will doubtlessly be found expedient in most cases to have the General Consistory meet once a month and the Restricted Consistory likewise. The Deacons should meet bi-weekly or monthly, or as often as their work may demand.

Who calls the Consistory meetings together? The next president. In Churches with only one Minister it will always be the same brother,

---

1. Bouwman, **Gereformeerd Kerkrecht**, II, 1934, pp. 117, 118.
2. Rutgers, **Kerkelijke Adviezen** I, 1921, p. 282.

but in Churches with more than one Minister these serve in turn. Art. 37 provides that the Ministers preside in turn in order to counteract the danger of inequality and hierarchism in those Churches which have more than one Minister. The presidency at Consistory meetings the Church Order attributes to the Ministers and not to the Elders. This is done not because the office of Elders is inferior, but because as a rule the Ministers are better qualified by reason of their special training and more extended experience.

The presidents are to regulate the proceedings. The gatherings consider and act. The president merely presides and regulates as a brother amongst brethren.

The next president also has the right to call a special meeting of the Consistory. But no special meeting can take valid action, as stands to reason, unless all the members have been properly notified.

How many members must be present in order to render consistorial action valid? At least a majority. If a majority is not present it is better to postpone the meeting. If again a majority fails to come, though all have been notified, and the meeting has not been called at an hour or place at which the majority could not possibly come, (say 9 a. m., when nearly all must be at work) then the meeting should proceed, and can do so validly.

5. The Consistory meetings and the congregation.

First of all, Consistory meetings are, as is proper, private. Some have contended that the members of the Church should be admitted. An appeal has been made to the case of Acts 15. But it should be remembered that the gathering of Acts 15 partakes far more of the nature of a major gathering than of a Consistory meeting. Furthermore the matter up for consideration at this meeting was not of local interest but very definitely of general interest, i.e., the question of circumcision for converts from paganism.

It certainly is to the best interest of the Churches that Consistory meetings are private. On the other hand, it should not be forgotten that every member has a full right to present himself at the Consistory meetings to give or to gain information, or to present a request, grievance, appeal, or protest.

Furthermore our Consistories should do their utmost to keep the congregation well informed as to those activities which it is entitled to know. Consistories should avoid giving the impression that they are independent bodies, ruling and acting with superior power. Since Consistories are the God ordained organs of the Church there should be a close contact between Consistory and congregation.

What is the nature of congregational meetings? Our Church Order knows of only three types of ecclesiastical gatherings, namely, Consistories, Classes, and Synods. Our so-called congregational meetings are really Consistory meetings to which all male members in full and regular standing have been invited, in order that certain definite matters may be considered under the direction of the Consistories. They are really deliberative gatherings, called together by the Consistory, at which the Consistory seeks to gain the opinion of the congregation. At these meetings office-bearers are also designated. But all action taken at these meetings becomes valid only after the Consistory as such has given its decision or approval. Usually this approval is assumed. That is to say, if no objections are raised against the opinions voiced at the congregational meetings, the Consistory acts forthwith in accord with the expression of opinion registered on the part of the congregation.

When we say that consistorial action is needed to make decisions made at congregational meetings valid we do not mean to say that Consistories may act arbitrarily. Not in the least. Consistories are bound to abide by certain expressions of opinion made at these congregational gatherings, unless they are prevented by the Word of God or circumstances. But this is the point, the Consistories are the responsible agencies of God to rule the Churches aright. If the office-bearers therefore clearly see that a congregation has made a mistake in its expression of opinion then they must refrain from acting in harmony with such an opinion expressed, and if need be, consult the Church anew, explaining the difficulties.

Should all Consistory meetings be announced to the Church? Yes, all regular meetings of office-bearers, whether of the General Consistory, the Restricted Consistory, or of the Diaconate, should be announced, in order that those who wish to appear before the gathering may know when the meeting is to be held. Special meetings called for the consideration of special or unfinished business as a rule do not need to be announced.

ARTICLE 38

In places where the Consistory is to be constituted for the first time or anew, this shall not take place except with the advice of the Classis.

NEW CHURCHES AND ADVICE OF CLASSIS

1. Significance of the term used to indicate the organization of new Churches.

This article clearly refers to the matter of Church organization. Yet the expression, "organization of new Churches," does not occur. How is this to be explained? To the institute or organized Churches the administration of Word and Sacraments has been entrusted. This significant task has not been committed by God to unorganized groups of believers. Nor has it been left to the initiative of individual believers. Not as if the believers have no rights and duties regarding the Gospel of salvation. We should all be witnesses and spokesmen of God. We should all permit the light of God, graciously given unto us, to shine. But the administration of the Word in its official sense and the administration of the Sacraments pertain only to the organized and authorized Church of God. This authorized Church has the charge to go with divine authority proclaiming the Word and Will of God, and to signify and to seal the same by means of the Sacraments. And the Church must discharge itself of this beautiful and important task through the duly appointed office-bearers. Likewise, the Churches govern themselves, under Christ, through the offices, and engage in the work of Christian mercy through the offices.

Consequently the organized Church functions through the offices and does not even exist without the offices. Hence it follows that only when the offices have been instituted can it be said that the Church of Christ has acquired a definite and authoritative form. Wherever the offices have been instituted there the Church has been organized.

The organization of Churches is therefore indicated in Article 38 according to its essential and indispensable characteristic. And the terminology used in Article 38 stresses this important and essential character of the offices for the organized Church of Christ on earth.

2. Why the phrase, "for the first time or anew"?

At the time when this article was originally drafted the Churches of Holland were still suffering by reason of the Spanish persecution. Sometimes Churches were badly shattered, inasmuch as their members had to flee for their lives. Many sought temporary refuge in England and Germany. Consequently many Churches were nearly or entirely disorganized. Now as the persecutor was driven from certain localities before the armies of William of Orange or his associates, the refugees of these sections would return to their homes. As stands to reason, these returned refugees soon sought to restore their broken Churches. But now it was agreed that these former Churches should not be reorganized unless Classis had first declared itself in favor of this move. Without the advice of Classis the offices should not be reinstituted.

Why this provision? Seemingly the Churches deemed it unwise and harmful to act prematurely in the matter of reorganizing a Church. Organizing a Church is always an important step. For a Church is far more than an ordinary man-made society. Consequently, the numbers of those desiring a Church should be sufficient, and there must be a reasonable assurance that the proposed Church will continue to exist.

But the provision also covers localities which had never yet had a Church. This element of the phrase under consideration was added in Holland in 1905, and by us in 1914. Perhaps it should be assumed that it was always understood that if the organization of a Church was desired in a locality which had never yet had one of our Churches, then the same rule would hold which had been agreed upon for the reestablishment of a Church. For surely if no Church ought to be reestablished without the advice of all the neighboring Churches, through Classis, then it stands to reason that no new Church ought to be established by a group of believers without such approval and advice.

But in 1914 this stipulation has been included in our Church Order as we have just noted. Because of entirely changed circumstances a Church once disbanded, perhaps by reason of group removals to other sections, is seldom reorganized. On the other hand, Churches are organized repeatedly in new localities. Therefore the renderings of 1905 and 1914 are entirely to the point.

3. Significance of the advice of Classis.

Essentially any group of believers has a right to organize itself into a Church. For instance, if a group of believers, by extraordinary circumstances, should find itself isolated from the rest of the world, say on a distant island, would not this group have the God-given right to organize itself into a Church through the election of officebearers, etc.? Would anyone care to maintain that the resultant Church was really non-existent simply because no major ecclesiastical assembly had sponsored, effected, or advised its organization? Only he who belongs to a strict hierarchical Church organization would care to champion the suggested contention. By this admission we grant that believers have an essential right to organize themselves into a Church if they so desire.

The Classical decisions regarding the organization of particular

Churches are therefore not necessary for the very existence of our Churches. Why then does the Church Order prescribe classical advice? As a matter of good policy; as a matter of common consent and wisdom, and not as a matter of superior authority without which no Church can be organized. The advice of Classis for the institution of the offices in a new locality, so it has been expressed by more than one authority in Reformed Church government in Holland, is necessary, not for the "being" of the Church, but for its "well-being."

The advice referred to in the present phrase has the significance of judgment, counsel, or help. If Classis decides against the organization in question, then the matter must wait. The petitioning group cannot proceed without, i.e., against, the advice of Classis. If they should proceed, they would simply not be recognized as one of our Churches but as an independent and perhaps schismatic Church.

It may be said in this connection that Article 38 does not mean to imply that our Classes should sit and wait until petitioners come to ask the advice and assistance of Classis for organization. Every Classis should be active and eager to organize new Churches wherever groups of believers belonging to our Churches, or desiring to join us, are found to be in need of a Church of their own.

A Classis can never decide to organize a Church without a request to do so from the brothers and sisters concerned. Reformed church polity seeks to do full justice to the rights of every believer under Christ. But a Classis should encourage the individual believers in a certain locality to take the necessary steps for church organization. Church extension and home mission work is very necessary and of great blessing to many.

If a Church cannot be regularly and validly organized without the advice of Classis, then it follows that no Church ought to be disbanded without the advice of Classis. If ever a Church dwindles away until but a few members are left so that the Church cannot well continue to exist, then this remnant should become a branch of a neighboring Christian Reformed Church. And the Consistory of this neighboring Church should govern the affairs of this group as well as it may. In case all members leave the community, the property which the Church concerned may have attained should fall to Classis for disposal. Minute books etc., should be turned over to Classis also.

4. Sundry matters.

How many members are required for the organization of a new Church? Our Church Order does not stipulate this. In Holland the mission deputies have a rule that no new Church shall be organized in Java unless there are at least twelve brethren which desire the Church. Jansen feels that a new Church should begin with at least 20 or 25 families. But neither with us, nor in the Netherlands, have the Churches ever set a definite figure. And wisely so. Circumstances alter cases. When prospects for growth and continuance are favorable a very small number of families and individuals are warranted to organize themselves into a separate Church. Some of our biggest and most flourishing Churches began with ten families or less. But let every Classis judge soberly and with caution before it advises a petitioning group to organize.

What is the minimum number of Consistory-members for small Churches? It is generally judged that three should be the minimum; for example, two Elders and one Deacon; or one Minister, one Elder, and one Deacon.

What is the mode of procedure which should be followed in the organization of a new Church? All professing Christians of Reformed persuasion who desire a Christian Reformed Church in a new locality and intend to join this proposed new Church, sign a petition addressed to Classis requesting the approval and assistance of Classis. If the Classis, upon due consideration, acts favorably upon the request, it appoints a neighboring Consistory to help the brethren and sisters in the organization. Classis should consider whether the interested group is large enough to be organized, whether there is a sufficient number of brethren able to serve in the Consistory, and kindred questions.

The Consistory appointed by Classis arranges for a service of worship, after which the committee of the Consistory appointed requests those who desire to join the new Church to present their certificates of membership. All acceptable certificates are acknowledged as such by the meeting, upon recommendation of the committee of the Consistory in charge of the organization. All confessing male members are given the right to vote. Those that have never yet made confession of faith may submit themselves for examination and may be received instantly if the results of the examination be satisfactory, and if their testimonials, in as far as these are available, are satisfactory. Then the number of Elders and Deacons to be chosen is determined. Balloting follows. Those chosen are instantly installed. If possible, the matter of legal incorporation should be attended to at this meeting also.

Sometimes Classes merely appoint committees which are charged to effect the organization in name of Classis. It is better to do through Consistories whatever can conveniently be done through these governing bodies than through committees. Furthermore, it is well to note that the task of a Consistory designated by a Classis to help in the organization of a Church is merely to act as an authorized advisor and guide. The group organizes itself into a Church.

What do we understand by combined Churches? Sometimes two or more neighboring Churches find that they are too small and too weak to support a Minister. If then such neighboring Churches make an agreement providing that they are to call a Minister together, these Churches so co-operating are often termed combined Churches. They remain independent one of another, but at times the Churches may meet as one Congregation for the consideration of their mutual affairs. And sometimes two or more Consistories of combined Churches may meet as one Consistory for the same purpose. Whenever Churches thus combine their strength and efforts they should be careful to draw up a good set of rules by which all parties concerned will be guided. If this should be neglected disharmony and friction easily result.

ARTICLE 39

Places where as yet no Consistory can be constituted shall be placed under the care of a neighboring Consistory.

PLACES WITHOUT ORGANIZED CHURCHES

This article, as nearly all the rulings and agreements of our Church Order, dates back to the 16th century, the time of the great Reformation. The question constantly confronting the Churches already organized in those days was this: What should we do for those localities which have no Reformed Churches as yet? Calvin had urged not to institute the administration of Word and Sacraments without the institution of the offices. He was persuaded that in order to maintain the purity of the preaching of the Word and the administration of the Sacraments, proper supervision and control was necessary. For this reason the institution of the offices or the organization of Churches should not be neglected. Believers having been converted from the errors of Rome and having broken with Rome certainly might gather for mutual edification, but they should not initiate the administration of Word and Sacraments unless they had first instituted the offices.

1. How did the Churches formerly proceed regarding localities without organized Churches?

The very first Synod of the Reformed Churches of Holland which met in Emden, Germany, in 1571, already considered the need of localities without organized Churches. In the 42nd article of its decisions this Synod stipulated that Ministers and Elders of Classes "bearing the cross," i.e., being persecuted, should diligently ascertain whether or not there were any in their near-by cities or villages who were favorably inclined toward the Reformation, and urge such to do their duty. To this end the Minister and Elders of these Classes should attempt to organize Churches, or at least the beginnings of Churches. In order to carry on this work the Classes were to divide the various cities and villages amongst themselves so that no localities might be neglected. And the dispersed Churches, Churches consisting of believers who had fled to distant parts for their safety, should also be active in their new localities it was urged. Dispersed believers should further the work of the Consistories active in the gathering of Churches by cautiously supplying the Church officers with names of persons who had in the past manifested their interest in the true religion in their home community from which they had been driven, or in the place to which they had fled.

Again we read in the Acts of Synod, 1578, Art. 11, that to localities in which a Church should be gathered and organized a Minister should be sent who should use some of the most God-fearing men of such localities to help him in the government of the Church and the care of the poor; further, he should urge his listeners to confess their faith and come to Holy Communion. And when the Congregation had increased somewhat, Elders and Deacons should be selected according to the accepted Order out of those who had come to communion. This method of procedure was confirmed in 1581. In response to the 10th question considered by this Synod it was decided that a Minister sent out to gather Churches should, beginning the work of organization provisionally, appoint some of the most God-fearing brethren as Elders and Deacons by whose help he should administer the Lord's Supper.

By 1586 the work of reformation and Church organization had progressed greatly. The Synod of that year decided that in localities which had no Consistories as yet the Classis should do that which the Church Order assigned under normal circumstances to the Consistories. Neighboring Churches, through their classical organization, were therefore to minister to the spiritual needs of those living in communities not yet having a Church. They were to do this particularly, we may assume, by sending a Minister who could sponsor the organization of Churches, even as former Synods had urged and decided.

The great Synod of Dort, 1618-19, confirmed this decision of 1586 and it became the 39th article of the Church Order. And thus the article remained until it was slightly altered in 1905 in the Netherlands and by us in 1914. Our redaction of 1914 is identical to that of the Netherlands of 1905, except that the Holland article retained the words "door de Classe." Their 39th article therefore reads: "Localities, where as yet no Consistory can be constituted shall by Classis be placed under the care of a neighboring Consistory." In our redaction the fact that Classis places localities in need of a Church under the care of a Consistory is understood, though not specifically mentioned.

It is better for a Classis to assign work of this type to a Consistory than to a committee. Whatever can be done through the regular assemblies (Consistories, Classes, Synods), in the interest of good order and safety, should not be assigned to boards and committees. Our method of appointing a committee when a Consistory could be appointed just as well tends to place too much power in the hands of individuals, while the regular offices are neglected. It also tends to sponsor what has been termed "dominocracy" (rule by Ministers, to the exclusion of Elders) inasmuch as committees are as a rule largely composed of Ministers.

The revision of 1905 and 1914, it may be noted, are in full harmony with what the earliest Synods decided on this score. It is also true that Ministers, Elders, and Deacons are always such of particular Churches, never in the abstract or of the Churches in general. And in harmony with this the administration of Word and Sacraments are prerogatives of the particular Churches and not of the major assemblies. These principles of Reformed church polity find expression in several articles of our Church Order.

2. What is the significance of Article 39?

Article 39 stipulates that localities not having a Church shall be placed under the care of a neighboring Consistory. By whom? As has been noted, by the Classis. Classis regulates this all-important work. This is as it should be. Without proper organization certain fields may be neglected, and others might be worked by more than one Consistory. But by cooperative action through Classis groups of neighboring Churches divide the various fields amongst themselves. At times it may also be expedient for all the Churches of a Classis to sponsor home mission or Church extension work in unison. Of course, we should not forget in this connection that Classical Missionaries, as well as all other Ministers, must be called according to the principle embodied in the Church Order, particularly in Articles 4 and 5. The calling Church in such cases acts as the authorized agent of all the Churches concerned, under certain definite stipulations.

It may be noted in this connection that the Home Mission Order, accepted by our Synod of 1936, which makes Home Missions and Church Extension work synodical, also provides that missionaries shall be called, charged by and officially connected with a particular Church.

It should not be inferred from this article that Classes may begin the work of Church organization or evangelization within the territorial bounds of one of our Churches without the approval of the Church concerned. Major assemblies may never infringe upon the rights of the particular Churches.

What is included under the care which a neighboring Consistory is to exercise over localities referred to in Article 39? It includes the fullest spiritual care which circumstances permit a Consistory to give. If possible, gatherings should be sponsored at which the Word is preached and the Sacraments administered to those who are entitled to this privilege. As a rule believers who live under the care of a neighboring Church will become members of that Church, and the Consistory will keep a separate record of these members. It may be necessary that the Consistory institute "reading services," i.e., that the Consistory appoint one of its Elders or members, or one of the group concerned, to read a sermon at stated hours on the Lord's Day. Catechism and Sunday School classes may have to be organized and suitable teachers appointed. Home Visitation work should be conducted periodically and faithfully. For those that are not in any way connected with our Churches and not connected with another orthodox Church in the community, special canvasses should be conducted, especially if the field is not under the care of a regular Home Missionary. As soon as the proper time has come the Consistory should urge all the believers concerned to petition Classis to aid them in organizing themselves into a Church.

Very often we sit and wait until our help is requested by a district without one of our Churches. This, however, is not as it should be. Our Classes particularly should constantly be on the look-out for new openings and for needy fields.

The matter of evangelization is certainly very urgent. Thousands upon thousands have wandered away from the truth of God through shallow preaching and the preaching of man's conceptions. Modernism is slaying its thousands annually. Worldly-mindedness, godless instruction, Sabbath desecration, and other forces are fast increasing the de-Christianized masses. In view of this there are fields a plenty for our Churches. Let us appreciate the measure of loyalty and activity which is ours, but let us also press on to greater accomplishments. There is a crying need for true, Biblical, Reformed preaching and teaching. Let all our Churches be active and eager to work.

(Also see Appendix 6, page 366.)

ARTICLE 40

The Deacons shall meet, wherever necessary, every week to transact the business pertaining to their office, calling upon the Name of God; whereunto the Ministers shall take good heed and, if necessary, they shall be present.

MEETINGS OF THE DEACONS

The three previous articles concern our Consistories. Article 37 regulates matters directly consistorial. Article 38 concerns the formation of new Consistories. And Article 39 makes provision for localities which as yet have no Consistories. And now Article 40, as a matter closely related to the foregoing, provides for diaconal meetings.

Diaconal meetings are not mentioned in Article 29, which article stipulates which four ecclesiastical gatherings shall be maintained. The Synod of Emden, 1571, had ruled that the Deacons were Consistory members. But the Synod of Dort, 1574, declared that the Deacons should meet weekly in order to consider the affairs of their office fully. The Synod of 1586 added to the stipulation of 1574 that at these meetings they should call "upon the Name of God", and the Ministers should exercise due supervision over these meetings, and if necessary be present at these gatherings. The Synod of 1905, Holland, as well as our Synod of 1914 revised the article so that the Deacons must meet weekly "wherever necessary." Heretofore the article prescribed weekly meetings without exception.

1. In which Churches and how often Diaconal meetings should be held.

Should the Deacons hold separate meetings even in Churches in which the Deacons constantly meet with the Consistory? No. In Churches which have not yet introduced separate meetings for the Elders and for the Deacons the latter need not hold special meetings for Deacons alone. In these Churches, which are not operating according to the division of labor plan of the Church Order, see especially Art. 37, the work of mercy is regularly acted upon at the general Consistory meetings. Article 40 is intended for the larger Churches which have their general Consistory meetings and their Restricted Consistory meetings and consequently also need their Diaconal meetings.

The article stipulates that the Deacons should hold meetings. They should not merely confer informally as occasion may demand, say after the service on Sunday, but at regular hours, previously determined and announced to the Church. And at least in our larger Churches the Deacons should conduct their affairs according to an adopted order. Rules for Diaconal meetings should stipulate matters as follow: Time and place of meeting; Order of business; Election and duties of president, secretary, etc.; Duties and authority of committees; How funds are to be collected, etc. Needless to say a set of rules as here suggested should be approved by the General Consistory.

How often should the Deacons meet? As noted above, the old Orders specified "every week". Our present reading, however, says that the Deacons shall meet every week "whenever necessary." In our larger Churches Deacons may certainly find it necessary to meet every week regularly. In smaller Churches bi-weekly or monthly meetings may be sufficient. But haphazardness should not prevail. Meetings should be held at set times. If the practical work of the Deacon's office does not seem to require a Deacons' meeting at any time, then let the brethren devote some time to the consideration of the spiritual side of the work. Special meetings should be called when emergencies arise.

2. Matters to be acted upon at these meetings.

The article clearly states that the Deacons are to meet in order "to transact the business pertaining to their office." They should not discuss doctrinal questions pertaining to all the offices, or to consider Church governmental matters. They should also be very careful not to assume an attitude of parity with the Consistory, and far less should the Deacons at their meetings plan or plot against the Consistory. Things belonging to the domain of the General Consistory should not be discussed and considered at the meetings of the Elders (Restricted Consistory), nor at the meetings of the Deacons (Diaconal meetings). Nor should the Deacons attempt to solve the problems of our social ills at their meetings, though they should permit the light of God's Word to shine upon these problems. It is the duty and glorious privilege of our Deacons to dispense mercy in the Name of Christ. First of all to Christ's own and then also toward those that are without. This is "the business that pertains to their office." And to this their work at Diaconal meetings should be limited.

From the foregoing it also follows that the Deacons should not transact the financial affairs of the Church. In some of our Churches the Deacons have been made to function as a financial committee and little more. If one of the Deacons happens to be a good bookkeeper whom the Consistory would like to make budget treasurer, there can be nothing against his appointment, but he cannot be charged with this extra work in his capacity of Deacon. In many Churches the Consistories might well appoint financial committees from the membership of the Church, preferably choosing such men as are not burdened with other important duties. In some instances financial committees should be appointed so as to consist in part of office-bearers and in part of non-office-bearers. Circumstances also alter cases in this matter. But never should the Deacons of a Church be compelled to do mere committee work for the Elders. This should certainly not be done if the Deacons have much work of their own to be done.

Why does the article state specifically that the Deacons shall call upon the Name of God at their meetings? This provision was added in 1586. Some Diaconates were used by the civil authorities for the disbursement of moneys for the poor. Jansen thinks that due to this practice there were some who were beginning to look upon the Deacons' meetings as being civil and secular in nature. The Churches, however, desired to maintain the Deacon's office as an ecclesiastical institution, and to emphasize the ecclesiastical and spiritual nature of the Deacons' meeting they now stipulated that the Deacons should call upon God's Name in prayer at their meetings. Aside from this consideration, which may be true, there would be ample reasons for this provision in the fact that all our work must be done in deep dependency upon God. Intercession for the poor and the afflicted is certainly in place at the gatherings of those who have been charged to alleviate the burdens of the suffering.

As Article 32 provides that the other ecclesiastical meetings shall be opened with prayer and closed with prayer, so Article 40 rules the same for Deacons' meetings. The prayers which are found in our book of liturgy (Psalter Hymnal, appended pages) have largely fallen into disuse. This is to be regretted inasmuch as these prayers are very beautiful and meaningful in content.

3. Supervision by the Ministers over these meetings.

The clause "whereunto the Ministers shall take good heed and if necessary they shall be present," was added to this article in 1586. Article 25 already stipulated then, as it does now, that the Deacons are to render a report of their work to the Consistories, but seemingly some Diaconates considered themselves on equal footing with the Consistory or had a tendency to place themselves under the authority of the civil government. Consequently the Synod of 1586 added the clause under consideration. Thus the ecclesiastical character of the Deacon's office is emphasized and the rightful place of our Diaconates in relation to the Consistories as well.

The supervision here prescribed is unconditional. The Ministers must give good heed to the Deacons in their work. But the clause does not stipulate that they must always and regularly attend the Deacons' meetings. But if they deem it advisable to attend they may do so. They have a full right to go at any time and need not wait for an invitation. If any specific difficulties require the presence of the Ministers they should go. And if the Deacons request their opinion on any matter of principle they should also attend the meeting.

When Ministers attend Deacons' meetings they really do so in their capacity as Elders, for to these the government and supervision over the Church has been entrusted. It might be asked, then why does Article 40 not specify that the Elders shall "take good heed" to this matter? The fact that the Ministers are here charged to take good heed and if necessary be present at the meetings of the Deacons harmonizes with the stipulation of Article 16 regarding the Minister's duties. Article 16 among other matters states that the Minister is "to watch over his brethren, the Elders and Deacons." Furthermore, doubtless the Church Order assigns this work of supervision over the Deacons' activity to the ministerial Elders since they have received special training for their task and as a rule are also men of greater experience and prestige.

Should a Minister, if he attends a Deacons' meeting preside over it? He may, but he need not. Ordinarily, it is better that he does not. Let him simply act the part of a visitor and advisor.

In some of our Churches the Elders visit the Deacons' meetings in turn. This is doubtless a good custom. It establishes a close contact between the Consistory and the Diaconate and gives every Elder an opportunity to keep in touch with the work. The work of supervision is thus at least well regulated.

It should always be understood that Diaconates are subject to the judgment of the Consistories, Classes, and Synods.

4. The Deacons and the major assemblies.

During recent years the question has often been asked whether our Diaconates should not have their major assemblies. The question is not whether a Deacon under special circumstances may not take the place of an Elder, and go as a delegate to our major assemblies, for example, to Classis. That has often been done in former years and also more recently. Although it should be remembered that when a Deacon goes to Classis in the place of an Elder, that then he goes, not so much as a Deacon, but rather as an assistant Elder, just as all Deacons are assistant Elders in our smaller Churches, and all Elders assistant Deacons, according to the permissive clause of Article 37.

The question is therefore not: May Deacons be sent to major assemblies?, but rather: Should they be sent? Now some have suggested a special class of major gatherings for our Diaconates. But to this suggestion it may be objected that our present major assemblies, Classes and Synods, are representative of all the Churches and all the work of these Churches. There is therefore no room for specialized major assemblies. These would make for duplication and conflict. The Synod of the Reformed Churches of Holland, 1899, decided, in harmony with this opinion just expressed, that: "The organization of separate major assemblies for diaconal affairs certainly cannot be harmonized with the connection and cooperation of the offices and of the ecclesiastical assemblies, as these are indicated in the Confession and the Church Order."

Others have suggested that our Deacons should be delegated to Classis together with the Ministers and Elders, either with full rights, or with advisory vote only. But our Church Order has always ruled that only by way of exception should Deacons be added to the Consistory for all matters that require action. In very few of our larger Churches, if any, do the Deacons function in all matters which strictly speaking concern the Elders. Yet if Deacons should be delegated they would be placed on par with the Elders at the Classes. They would have to help settle discipline cases, etc., though never doing so at home in the government of their own Church. This certainly would be inconsistent and impractical. Furthermore, to send the Deacons in advisory capacity would hardly do. It would increase the expenses of the meetings. The actual instances of diaconal matters coming before the Classes are so few that this extra trouble and expense would hardly be warranted. Those diaconal affairs that do require attention at times can easily be acted upon by the Classes as now constituted, inasmuch as Ministers and Elders are required to know and approve or disapprove of all diaconal affairs as it is.

A third suggestion, in harmony with our last remark, would have all diaconal matters presented to Classes as these bodies are now constituted and through avenues now existing. Thus we already have: Question three of Article 41, "Are the poor cared for?"; the constant opportunity for overtures and petitions; Church Visitation; appointment of committees for special tasks and decisions. When committees are needed for matters diaconal Classis should not fail to appoint one or several Deacons on these committees, or perchance a whole Diaconate.

This latter suggestion has our full approval. It seems to be the best solution in as far as a solution is needed. Indeed it cannot be said that the problem on this point is pressing.

ARTICLE 41

The classical meetings shall consist of neighboring Churches that respectively delegate, with proper credentials, a Minister and an Elder to meet at such time and place as was determined by the previous classical meeting. Such meetings shall be held at least once in three months, unless great distances render this inadvisable. In these meetings the Ministers shall preside in rotation, or one shall be chosen to preside; however, the same Minister shall not be chosen twice in succession.

Furthermore, at the beginning of the meeting, the president shall, among other things, present the following questions to the delegates of each Church:

(1) Are the consistory meetings regularly held in your Church; and are they held according to the needs of the congregation?
(2) Is church discipline faithfully exercised?
(3) Are the poor adequately cared for?
(4) Does the consistory diligently promote the cause of Christian day schools?
(5) Have you submitted to the stated clerk of Classis the names and addresses of all baptized and communicant members who have, since the last meeting of Classis, moved to where no Christian Reformed Churches are found?

And finally, at one but the last meeting and, if necessary, at the last meeting before the (Particular) Synod, delegates shall be chosen to attend said Synod.

CONCERNING CLASSICAL MEETINGS

This article and the five which follow it concern in the main our Classical organization. The present article concerns the Classical meeting as such; Art. 42, the matter of Churches with more than one Minister and Delegation to Classis; Art. 43, Mutual Censure at Major Assemblies; Art. 44, Church Visitation; Art. 45, Acts of Previous Gatherings at Major Assemblies; Art. 46, Overtures to Major Assemblies.

1. Origin and nature of Classes.

While the Reformation was in its infancy ecclesiastical life was not at all well organized. However, the Reformed Churches of the Southern Netherlands (Belgium today), and the Calvinistic refugee Churches in England, as well as the Churches in France, soon began to form Classes and to meet classically. (Classis is a word derived from the Greek verb *kalein*, signifying: to call. A Classis is therefore ecclesiastically speaking a summoned gathering of Churches, or a group of Churches called together for a meeting, and secondarily, a group of Churches meeting together at regular intervals in major assembly.) Before the Wezelian Convention had met, 1568, the Reformed Churches had not yet been organized into Classes. However this convention declared that Classes should be organized as soon as the conditions of war and persecution permitted. Dr. Bouwman enumerates four reasons which demand Classical co-operation and organization. Classes are required, says this authority, (a) because of the unity of the Churches in Christ; (b) because the Churches need each other for their continuance, extension, and purity in faith and conduct; (c) because the liberty of the congregation must be maintained, and classical organization will be a safeguard against domineering and arbitrary office-bearers; (d) in order that all things may be regulated in the Church according to the Word of God, and order and discipline may be maintained in the congregation.[1]

The first Synod, Emden, 1571, drew up nine articles which provided for Classical organization. This Synod also called three Particular Synods into being; one for the Reformed Churches of Germany and Ostfriesland, one for the Reformed Churches in the Netherlands, and one for the Reformed refugee Churches in England.

Moreover, a number of Classes were called into existence. For Holland alone four Classes were formed. But the Reformation grew very fast at this time so that three years later, 1574, Holland alone numbered fourteen Classes. And in 1578 still others were added. Doubtless many refugees returned from England and Germany during these years, inasmuch as the persecution subsided. And this influx of returning refugees naturally stimulated church growth in the homeland. The Synod of Middelburg, 1581, summarized and combined a number of previous regulations for Classical gatherings and gave us Art. 41 as we have it in substance today. Seemingly some Churches did not immediately co-operate in forming a denomination. At least the provincial Synod of Gelderland, 1582, found it necessary to declare that, "it is neither advisable nor edifying, that a few Churches should continue to exist by themselves, but each Church is bound to join itself to a Classis." Bouwman holds that the Churches are indeed free to join the confederation of Churches (het kerkverband), but they are at the same time obliged to do so, though this obligation is a moral one and can never be forced. When a Church has accepted the unity of federation, then it is not at liberty to break away, except the Churches with which she was living in confederation have forsaken the basis of federation, the common confession according to the Word of God [2]

The article stipulates that classical meetings shall consist of neighboring Churches. A Classis is therefore not a body of men who, as a board of directors, occupy a position of superiority over and above the Churches.

---

1. Bouwman: **Ger. Kerkrecht,** II, 1934, 126-7.
2. Bouwman: **Ger. Kerkrecht,** II, 1934, 127.

A Classis is a gathering of Churches meeting for mutual counsel and support and for united action concerning certain matters common to the interest of all the Churches.

As a Consistory is a gathering of office-bearers authorized to govern the affairs of their Church, so a Classis is a gathering of men representing the various Churches belonging to the Classes, and charged and authorized by their respective Churches to take part in all the legitimate labors of Classes.

The Churches are to delegate their representatives "with proper credentials." A credential is a valid, black on white, proof of delegation. These consistorial credentials verify that they who claim to be delegates are actually such. —But that not only. The credentials, when properly written, also give Classis the assurance that the delegates are authorized representatives and have been given power to act and charged to take part in all the work of Classis in name of the Church which they represent. Without credentials no one can be seated with a decisive vote. If however through an error or through unavoidable circumstances certain delegates cannot present the prescribed credentials then Classis may hear their testimony and declaration of delegation and seat them, especially in our day when the Churches and the various delegates know each other well enough so that fraud is almost out of the question. The incentive to fraud by impostors does not exist in our day. Nevertheless, the rule stands and should be maintained. See also Art. 33 on these matters.

How many Churches are required to form a Classis? There is no rule regulating this matter. Classis Hackensack until 1937 numbered only six Churches while Classis Orange City consisted of 31 Churches. Due to the re-alignment of certain Classes and the creation of new Classes by the Synod of 1937, a greater measure of equality now exists. This is altogether proper. In 1603 the Synod of Harderwyk declared that no Classis should consist of less than 10 Churches. But a definite rule does not exist to this day. And this is well.

What is a Classis Contracta? When a number of nearby Churches of a certain Classis hold a meeting in order to consider and act on matters which can not well wait for the next regular session of Classis, this gathering is called a Classis Contracta. Literally it means a Contracted or Reduced Classis. All the Churches are notified and Churches at some distance from the meeting simply do not send delegates. They tacitly or silently approve of the action taken at the Classis Contracta. In Holland the approval of Ministerial credentials, etc., requiring action between the gatherings of Classis, is left to a Classis Contracta. We have a Classical Committee to take action in regard to matters of this kind which can not well wait. Consequently we seldom hold Classes Contractae. When they do occur they are usually previously agreed upon at a regular classical gathering in order that certain affairs which will require classical action in the near future, but not yet ready for consideration and action, may be properly attended to. All the Churches are notified, but it is understood that only the nearby Churches will respond, although all the Churches of Classis are free to send delegates.

2. Membership of classical meetings.

Who are to be delegated? Art. 41 stipulates: "a Minister and an Elder". The Synod of Dort, 1578, also ruled that each Church should be represented by a Minister and an Elder. But Ministers and Elders, serving Churches of Classis, but not delegated, were accorded an advisory vote by this Synod. The Synod of Middelburg, 1581, however, stipulated that these visiting Ministers and Elders should not begin to give advice unless asked to do so. Perhaps the visiting Ministers and Elders abused the courtesy and privilege somewhat. Perhaps they talked too often or too long. At least the Synod of 's Gravenhage, 1586, dropped the provision concerning advisory members altogether and simply stipulated that each Church should be represented by one Minister and one Elder.

Should Consistories delegate by rotation or by vote? Regarding delegation to Classis all authorities are agreed that the rotary system is to be preferred, even as these same authorities favor the method of choice by ballot for delegation to Synod. If a Church has only one Minister, the rule of Art. 41 requires that he be delegated constantly. If a Church has more than one Minister the rotary system would require that the Ministers are delegated in turn. Inasmuch as every Church has more than one Elder, it means that Churches which follow the rotary system of appointment will delegate the Elders in turn. Some Elders seldom go to Classes, whereas others go repeatedly. But this is due to circumstances. Some Elders simply can not leave their work one, two, or more days. Furthermore, Elders of smaller Churches will be delegated much more frequently than the Elders from larger Churches, as stands to reason.

It is true that not all office-bearers are equally well qualified for delegation to Classis. Some Elders excel in pastoral work, i. e., sick calling, home-visitation work, etc. Others excel in church governmental matters. In spite of this fact it is best to delegate Elders by rotation. All Elders should qualify themselves for service, and each delegation to Classis adds to the experience of the delegates. Furthermore, if delegation should be limited to certain Ministers or Elders, this might foster a spirit of superiority on the part of some. There are arguments in favor of delegation by ballot and according to ability. But for our classical meetings we do not believe that these arguments outweigh the reasons for delegation by rotation. This does not mean that Consistories should never set the rotary system of delegation aside, and appoint their delegates by deliberate choice. When certain matters must be presented to Classis with which one of the Elders is especially well acquainted for instance, the Consistory will do wise to appoint that Elder.

For each delegate the delegating Consistory should also designate an alternate. Inasmuch as very few of our Churches ever have more than one active Minister an Elder is usually appointed as alternate to the Minister. When a Church is vacant and has no Minister at all two Elders are appointed.

According to the provision of the present article the smaller Churches have just as many delegates at Classis as the larger Churches have. Every Church, regardless of size, sends two delegates. This is proper and fair since each individual Church, whether large or small, is complete in itself and a manifestation of the body of Christ. Our various Churches are not subdivisions of the real super-Church, i.e., the denomination. Each Church is an integrity by itself and not just a section of the actual Church, and laboring under a superior ruling body to which each section sends delegates in proportion to the number of its members. This conception would fit in with Churches that maintain the episcopal system of Church government, as for instance, the Methodist Churches have, but this conception is not according to our Reformed system of church government. The Reformed system is a system by which the Churches rule themselves either directly (Consistories) or indirectly through delegated authority (Classes and Synods). Our Churches are governed from the bottom up, not from the top down.

In as far as the varying sizes of our Churches cause a certain measure of disproportion, the Churches which are overly large should be divided into two or more Churches. That would also be to the spiritual welfare of these large Churches because individual work becomes very difficult in some of our larger Churches.

Those delegated should attend the sessions of Classis as faithfully as possible. None may absent himself without weighty reason. Pastoral duties should as a rule not keep a Minister from going to Classis. Those delegates who find themselves compelled to leave the gatherings before the close of the sessions, should before leaving obtain the approval of the assembly.

3. Frequency and place of meeting.

As to the place of meeting the Wezelian Convention, 1568, decided that the classical meetings should be held in all the Churches of a Classis in rotation. This was perhaps decided in order to treat all the Churches alike. Our fathers were always on the look-out for the dangers of hierarchism. But furthermore, they also had in mind that the Churches should thus exercise supervision over each other. Means of travel were primitive. The delegates would begin to arrive at the meeting place of Classis the day before, and thus they naturally and conveniently learned much concerning the affairs of the entertaining Church. The affairs of this Church were purposefully investigated. However, when at a later date it was decided that the Churches should exercise their supervision over each other especially by means of a classical committee of Church Visitors (see Art. 44) there was no need of holding Classis in every Church of Classis. Synod of 's Gravenhage, 1587, decided that classical gatherings should be held at the time fixed by previous gatherings and at the place determined by the previous gathering. From then on one Classis decided when and where the next would meet. This was, without question, a wise arrangement. Not every Church is situated so that it can be conveniently reached by all the delegates. Moreover, not every Church is able to entertain a large number of delegates conveniently. However, it is true that our Classes should meet in as many of its Churches as possible to give the members of our various Churches opportunity to attend the sessions of Classis and to stress the fact that all Churches are, as to their essence, equal.

As to the frequency of classical meetings, the Wezelian Convention, 1568, recommended that meetings be held every two or three months. The first Synod (Emden, 1571) because of the difficulties of the times, war and persecution, recommended that the Classes meet every three or six months. The Synod of Middelburg, 1581, stipulated that the Classis should meet at least every three months. Thus Art. 41 still stipulates for the Reformed Churches in Holland. Our redaction reads: "Such meetings shall be held at least once in three months, unless great distances render this inadvisable." For our situation in the U. S. A., particularly for our western Classes covering in some instances several states, meetings cannot well be held more than twice a year. For these reasons we have added the clause which permits Classes to meet less than four times a year. But the ideal is at least four times a year. If conditions permit four times a year is not any too often, for our Churches should remain in close touch with each other and consult each other frequently.

In the Netherlands each classical meeting designates one of its

Churches to call the next meeting of Classis together, to provide it with a copy of the minutes of the previous gathering, etc. We do have "calling Churches" for our Synods, Churches which summon our Synods. But we do not appoint a summoning or classical Church for calling together or convening the next Classis. We leave this matter to the stated clerk of Classis. Perhaps ours is the more efficient method, but it cannot be denied that whatever can conveniently be done through Churches should not be charged to individuals or committees. This is in harmony with Reformed church polity, and safer, too. However, as long as our stated clerks know the limits of their charge and watch their step, there is no danger.

4. Presidency at classical meetings.

The article assigns the presidency of classical meetings to the Ministers and not to the Elders. Ministers preside at these gatherings, not because they are better or higher in themselves, but simply because they as a rule are better qualified for this task, having had more experience in leading meetings and often more tact and ability inasmuch as all their time and talents are devoted to Church work. As far as the Elder's office is concerned he certainly would be permitted to preside. It is no question of office at all. It is only a question of practical wisdom.

Up to the year 1581 the Church Orders provided that the presidents at classical meetings should be elected. There were good reasons for this provision. Conditions were irregular and all kinds of matters would call for solution, for the Churches were still in the formative period. The most capable men should therefore preside over these gatherings. But as conditions became more settled and classical meetings had been held for a number of years, it was not so essential that only best qualified men should preside. And so the Synod of 1581 made this matter optional. That is to say, it decided that Classes could let their ministerial delegates preside in rotation, or they could elect one of them to preside. Presidency by rotation was made possible at this time, we may believe, in part to avoid also in this respect hierarchical tendencies and to stress the fact that all office-bearers are essentially equal. But Synod of 1581 did not say that the rotary system must be followed. It left the whole matter optional. If a certain Classis would prefer to elect its president at the beginning of each meeting, as had been the rule heretofore, it would be at full liberty to do so. And thus the matter stands today, in the Netherlands as with us. Even when a Classis regularly lets its ministerial delegates preside in turn, then yet it may decide to elect its president at any given meeting. When difficult cases are to come up for consideration and he whose turn it would be to preside is inexperienced, then for such and like reasons, the Classis should excuse the Minister concerned from the difficult task and elect a president.

But the Church Order adds a condition. It reads as follows: "however, the same Minister shall not be chosen twice in succession." This proviso was doubtlessly added to ward off hierarchical tendencies. Once again our Reformed fathers shunned whatever might restore the evils of a rule by bishops. They wanted the Churches to be truly presbyterian as to their self-government. The Churches should be ruled by the presbyters, not by superior and inferior bishops.

Supposing a certain Minister has just presided at a classical gathering according to his turn, would the following Classis be permitted to elect him as its president if it should so desire? Yes, for Art. 42 does not say that the same Minister shall not preside twice in succession, but that the same Minister shall not be chosen twice in succession. However, unless the circumstances are very pressing and extraordinary a Classis should not elect as its president a Minister who has just presided over the previous gatherings of Classis.

5. The business of classical meetings.

In the early days of our Reformed Churches one of the first activities on every classical program was the preaching of a sermon by the Ministers in turn. This was not done for purposes of worship. It was not a devotional number, but in those early days many Ministers were very poorly trained for their tasks as preachers of the Gospel. Some of them previously were monks and priests who had left the errors of Rome, having experienced the reviving and correcting grace which God sent so abundantly through the Reformation. Some of them had very little schooling and had formerly been tradesmen and workers at various occupations. They had been admitted to the ministry according to the rule of Article 8, Church Order. It stands to reason that many of these early Ministers could well afford some training. To supply this training these sermons were primarily held. After the sermon had been delivered it would be discussed and criticized, both as to content and form. That this was the nature and purpose of these classical sermons may be plain from the provision accepted by the Synod of Middelburg, 1581, Article 30. This article reads in part as follows: "The Minister, who has been charged to do so by the previous Classis, shall deliver a short sermon from the Word of God, concerning which the others shall judge, and if they find it lacking in some respect, they shall point this out." Eventually, however, nearly all Ministers were thoroughly trained in theology and also in the art of sermonizing so that there was no great need for the maintenance of classical sermons. The Holland Synod of 1905 therefore eliminated the classical sermon clause in the Church Order. Our own Synod of 1914 followed suit. The provision had long since fallen into disuse. Except for a rare exception classical sermons were no longer preached and had not been required since the early days of our denominational existence in the former century.

Our Classes are often required to give careful consideration to overtures, protests and appeals. Reports rendered by certain standing committees, such as the Classical Committee, the Home Mission Committee, etc., always require time and attention. Furthermore the reports rendered by delegates to Synod, or of those appointed to serve on the Board of Trustees of Calvin College and Seminary and the Board of Missions, must be received and considered.

An important work of our Classes recurring again and again is the examination and admittance of men to the ministry.

6. Questions for mutual supervision.

The matter of mutual supervision occupied a prominent place on the classical schedule of former days. With us the asking of the prescribed questions has become a mere detail on the classical menu card, usually performed in a rather mechanical fashion, and very often in great haste. Now the situation was quite different in years of yore. Formerly the supervisory questions were asked at the beginning of the meetings, and with variation as the president saw fit. He also added questions which he might consider pertinent. At least such were his rights. Synod of Dort, 1578, Art. 29 (14) decided: "The President having offered prayer, shall ask each delegation in particular, whether the ordinary discipline is being maintained in their congregations; whether they are being attacked by heresies; whether they doubt the correctness of any part of the accepted doctrine; whether they are giving good heed to the poor and the schools; whether they need the advice or help of the brethren regarding the government of their Church; and other like matters." Synod of Middelburg, 1581, revised this article somewhat and gave us the questions as we find them substantially in our present Article 41.

With what purpose then were these questions formulated? To give the Churches a brief guide in their supervision over each other. The Church of Rome exercises supervision through its superior officers. This system the reformation Churches rejected. But they did maintain the element of supervision. Only they believed that all Churches and office-bearers were essentially equal, so they decided that supervision should be exercised in a mutual fashion. The Churches should supervise each other. And this work of mutual supervision was made to be an important and prominent item in the bill of fare for each Classis. At a later date it was decided that this work of supervision at Classis should be supplemented by means of Church Visitors. (See Article 44.) From then on the supervisory work at Classis did not occupy quite such a prominent place on the schedule of each Classis, we may believe. But the Churches certainly did not intend that the exercise of mutual supervision at Classis should become a mere perfunctory, last-minute formality. This mutual supervision at the classical meeting bears a unique character since it is done in the presence of all the Churches represented there. Hence there is a place for such examination during the session of Classis though Classis also appoints special Church Visitors.

During recent years our Synods have altered the number and the reading of the supervisory questions of Article 41 once and again. Up to the year 1930—for more than 300 years therefore—these questions read as follows: "1. Are the Consistory meetings held in your Church? 2. Is church discipline exercised? 3. Are the poor and the Christian schools cared for? 4. Do you need the judgment and help of the Classis for the proper government of your Church?" The Synod of 1930 made question 3 to read: "Are the poor cared for?" Question 4 now reads: "Does the Consistory support the cause of the Christian schools?" The original fourth question became question 5.

Then the Synod of 1942 adopted a revision and an increase of these questions. Their number now totaled no less than eleven! (See Acts, 1942, p. 111.) It soon became evident that this alteration and increase was no improvement. The Churches felt that there was too much needless duplication of detailed questions asked at the time of Church Visitation (see Church Order, Article 44) and that the multiplicity of questions did not help to make the supervisory phase of our classical gatherings more valuable, but that the large number of these questions rather helped to render this Classical work even more fruitless than it already was.

And so the Synod of 1947—after more than one Synodical Committee had made a special study of these matters—once more reduced the number of questions to five. But in place of the very significant, original fifth question—"Do you need the judgment and help of the Classis for the proper government of your Church?"—Synod, dropping this question in toto, placed the far more secretarial question: "Have you submitted to the Stated Clerk of Classis the names and addresses of all baptized and communicant members who have, since the last meeting of Classis, moved to where no Christian Reformed Churches are found?"

We consider the omitting of what was once question 5 a serious loss and error. It was through this question that consistories could very conveniently confer with the sister Churches of their respective Classes regarding problems and difficulties arising in their Churches. Our Classes should offer the opportunity for careful, brotherly, mutual consultation. They should not reduce their activities to the hearing of reports and the making of official decrees and decisions. True, the Consistories can still approach Classis for advice by addressing Classis through letter or official credential, but this is always a bit more cumbersome and official. And the natural occasion and standing invitation for mutual conference on problems concerning Church government has at least been removed and canceled. We hope that this matter may some day be rectified.

The Synod of 1942 (see Acts, 1942, p. 110) made the significant declaration that the work of mutual supervision at our Classical meetings was of central and prime importance, and that consequently the questions of Article 41 should not be asked at the end of the Classical gathering, but rather at the beginning. Besides, this Synod also declared that the questions should never be asked and answered in a perfunctory manner, but they should serve as a basis for additional investigation and consideration.

With all this the authors are in hearty accord.

It is noteworthy that Article 41 now specifies that these questions shall be asked **at the beginning of our Classical sessions**, for the article reads: "Further, **at the beginning of the meeting**, the president shall . . . present the following questions . . ." It would be well if all our Classical Stated Clerks, as they draw up the program for our Classical gatherings, would take note of this provision.

It is noteworthy that the Synod of 1942 approved of the addition and provision "which questions may be answered either orally or in written form," but that this provision was deleted by the Synod of 1947. For this deletion we are grateful. No Classis can perform its supervisory task adequately by means of a printed questionnaire. This should be done orally, and as a distinct number on the Classical program, while all the delegates listen and profit.

It should be remarked that the Acts of 1947, p. 39, do contain the suggestion—a suggestion of the Advisory Committee—"That Synod **leave the method of asking questions optional**, provided official action is taken by the Consistory." But the Acts do not say that Synod adopted this suggestion, and the official text adopted by this Synod specifically deletes this provision of 1942. And so this provision is no longer in our Church Order.

To be sure, the reading of 1942 was contradictory. How can the president of Classis "put the . . . questions" if they are already answered on blanks previously filled in and placed on the Classical table? And how can the president of Classis ask additional questions—see our comments regarding the phrase "among other things"—if the questions are answered by merely filling in blanks, which blanks are briefly reviewed during intermission by a committee of two or three?

And now a few words regarding the prescribed questions:

Are the Consistory meetings regularly held in your Church; and are they held according to the needs of the congregation? If any Consistory fails to meet regularly, which even for the smallest Churches should mean at least once a month, then such a Consistory must be admonished by the president of Classis, then and there. Good order in the Church of Christ, and its spiritual welfare, require that our Consistories meet regularly and according to the needs of each Church.

Is Church discipline faithfully exercised? One of the great reasons for the complete breakdown of many Churches is that they have failed to exercise Church discipline. The chaff will ever mix itself with the wheat. Satan will always seek to harm the cause of God from within. If members who prove to be unfaithful in doctrine and conduct are tolerated in the Church the evil one has more than won half the battle. For the reclamation of the unfaithful, and for the preservation of the Church, constant vigilance on the score of discipline is absolutely necessary. Discipline is so easily neglected, especially when men become shallow and lukewarm, and when erroneous, false doctrines begin to creep in.

Are the poor adequately cared for? The significance of this question is whether the Church concerned provides for its poor. The poor may not be neglected. The love and mercy of Christ, our merciful High Priest, must constrain us to be faithful in relieving want and distress. And particular Churches which have no poor should be ready and eager to help those Churches which may have more poor than they can care for adequately.

Does the Consistory diligently promote the cause of Christian day schools? Not all of our people and Churches are fully aware of the dangers of humanistic, man-centered, Godless, Christless schools. Some Churches and Consistories are apt to be lukewarm and unfaithful. Consequently this supervisory question is asked at every Classical gathering. It is wholly in keeping with the provisions of Article 21. See our comments on this article.

Have you submitted to the Stated Clerk of Classis the names and addresses of all baptized and communicant members who have, since the last meeting of Classis, moved to where no Christian Reformed Churches are found? This question certainly has its practical value, but it is more a secretarial question than a supervisory question regarding the government of the Church or its purity of doctrine and life. As indicated above we would much prefer the former question regarding need for advice or help.

ARTICLE 42

Where in a Church there are more Ministers than one, also those not delegated according to the foregoing article shall have the right to attend Classis with advisory vote.

MINISTERS NOT DELEGATED TO CLASSIS ADVISORY MEMBERS

The present reading of this article dates back to 1914 when our Churches revised it following the example of the Reformed Churches in the Netherlands (1905).

1. Equality of representation at classical meetings.

Article 41, as we have noted, provides that every Church shall be represented at Classis by two delegates, a Minister and an Elder. Whether the Church is large or small, it is represented at Classis by two delegates. A Church which consists of 25 families sends two delegates just as well as a Church of 200 or 400 families. The question has often been asked: Is this method of delegation just and fair to the larger Churches? In the Netherlands this seeming inequality is still more prominent since many city Churches have a membership of thousands of families, each city having but one Church or congregation, although several church buildings and sometimes more Ministers than buildings.

In the consideration of this matter the principle involved should not escape us. Which principle? That our Classes are composed of Churches and not of individuals. The membership of our Classes does not consist of Ministers and Elders but of Churches. The individual Churches are the units of our classical organizations.

In this respect there is some difference between our conception and that of the Presbyterian Churches of our land. According to Presbyterian practice a Minister becomes a member of his Presbytery, or as we would say, Classis. He presides over the Session (Consistory) of the Church with which he is connected and is called Moderator of Session, but he is not a member of the Church which he serves. He is a member of the Presbytery. According to Reformed church polity, however, no individual is, strictly speaking, a member of Classis. A Minister or Elder can only be said to be a member of Classis in the sense that his Church has delegated him to represent it at a certain classical gathering.

Now this principle, as will be granted, demands two things. First of all, that all who receive and exercise a decisive vote at our Classes shall actually represent one of the Churches of Classis through official delegation. And secondly this principle demands that each Church be represented by an equal number of delegates. For practical reasons it has been agreed that each Church shall be represented by two brethren, a Minister and an Elder, or, in case the Church is vacant, by two Elders.

But so it has been asked, is not this arrangement after all unfair to the larger Churches? We answer: Overly large Churches should be divided into two or more smaller Churches. In overly large Churches the individual members do not receive the pastoral care which they require. By dividing the larger Churches individual spiritual care can be exercised much easier. Thus also the "inequality" at Classical gatherings will be corrected to some extent. But the main point is that every Church unit is a self-governing manifestation of the body of Christ standing on par as to rights and authority with every other Church.

Yet it is true that the larger Churches represent a much larger number of believers than do the smaller Churches. So it has been decided that those Churches which have more than one Minister may send all their Ministers to Classis, with the clear understanding however that only one shall have a decisive vote and all the rest merely an advisory vote. In this way the principle of equality is maintained for all the Churches have the same number of votes, but at the same time Classes is being served by the advice of all the Ministers laboring in its domain and all the larger Churches thus receive ample opportunity to voice their sentiments, problems and convictions.

2. The history of this article.

The Synod of Dort, 1578, ruled that every Church should be represented at Classis by a Minister and an Elder. Ministers not delegated received an advisory vote. The Elders of the places where Classis met also received an advisory vote.

It soon became customary to send all the Ministers which a Church had to Classis. The presence of all the Ministers was appreciated, particularly since some of the best informed men were Ministers of city Churches and many of the smaller Churches with but one Minister were served by men with but a meager training and little knowledge of Church government. Besides, the problems which the Churches had to solve were far from easy. Many felt that these Ministers who served the Classes in an advisory capacity should be seated with a decisive vote. Synod of 1581 was overtured so to decide but this Synod ruled against the petitioners. Matters remained as they were. Synod of South Holland, 1597, again considered the matter and referred the question to the next General Synod. But this General Synod was not held until the years 1618-19. During the intervening years the Classes used their own judgment. Many of them gave all the Ministers a decisive vote. And the great Synod of Dort, 1618-19, decided that all the Ministers of Churches having more than one Minister should have a decisive vote at Classes, except in matters which concerned their own Churches or their own persons. Synod of Dort, 1618-19, therefore adapted itself to the practice that had sprung up, but attached one condition, a condition which was meant to safeguard the Churches against unfairness and domination.

However, Article 42, as it was accepted by the Synod of 1618-19 was really in conflict with Article 41 as adopted by this same Synod. And Article 42 also violated the principles explained above. For these reasons the Churches of Holland returned to the reading of 1578, as has already been noticed. And we did the same in 1914 at our Synod in Roseland, Chicago.

ARTICLE 43

At the close of the Classical and other major assemblies, Censure shall be exercised over those, who in the meeting have done something worthy of punishment, or who have scorned the admonition of the minor assemblies.

MUTUAL CENSURE AT CLASSES AND SYNODS

1. Censure according to Article 43 differentiated from censure according to Article 35 and Article 81.

Article 35 provides that the presidents of our assemblies are "to see to it that everyone observe due order in speaking, to silence the captious and those who are vehement in speaking, and to properly discipline them if they refuse to listen." From this it is plain that Article 35 and Article 43 have much akin. However, the censure provided for in Article 35 is to be exercised by the person of the president in his capacity as assembly leader. He is to perform this duty while the meeting is in process. As soon as someone commits an offense the president must call him to order and rebuke him if need be.

The censure provided for in Article 43, however, is to be exercised "at the close" of major assemblies. Furthermore, this censure is to be exercised, not by the president, but by the assembly itself. The article does not specify who is to exercise the censure which it prescribes. It is not assigned to anyone in particular and therefore it follows that this censure is to be mutual. The gathering as such exercises this censure.

Censure according to Article 43 also differs from the mutual censure prescribed in Article 81. The 81st article of the Church Order provides that "The Ministers of the Word, Elders, and Deacons, shall before the celebration of the Lord's Supper exercise Christian censure among themselves and in a friendly spirit admonish one another with regard to the discharge of their office."

This censure is still often indicated by the Latin term "censura morum", i.e., censure of conduct. This censure is also mutual. The various members of the gathering are required to admonish or criticize each other. But Article 81 refers to Consistories and not to major assemblies. Furthermore, Article 81 concerns itself not so much with the conduct of the office-bearers at their meetings, as with "the discharge of their office." Mutual censure as exercised at Consistory meetings before the celebration of the Lord's Supper concerns itself with this question: Is there anything in the work of any of the Ministers, Elders or Deacons of the Consistory which should be criticised? But, Article 43, as stated above, refers to the conduct of office-bearers at Classis or Synods.

2. Why Article 43 was included in the Church Order.

During the Reformation era many entered the service of the Churches who knew little concerning good behavior and orderly conduct at ecclesiastical assemblies. Seemingly disorder would disturb classical and synodical gatherings. Men would speak out of turn or give way to angry words, etc. To curb this evil it was decided that mutual censure should be exercised at the conclusion of each meeting in order that the guilty ones might be admonished and rebuked. That this 43rd article was not included in the Church Order without good reason may be inferred from the concluding minute of the Particular Synod of Alkmaar, 1593, which reads as follows: "And furthermore, with this the Synod was concluded; and the censure being held, nothing was found (God be praised!) to be worthy of punishment, but all things took place with edification and peace, and thus the actions were concluded with thanksgiving to God." *

Seemingly some were also slow to submit themselves to the judgment of the assemblies, for the present article also provides that such as had "scorned the admonition of the minor assemblies" should be censured at the conclusion of classical or synodical gatherings.

By this provision our Churches do not say in the least that we must always submit to the judgment and declaration of ecclesiastical gatherings. Article 31, as has been noted, clearly specifies, "If anyone complains that he has been wronged by the decision of a minor assembly, he shall have the right to appeal to a major ecclesiastical assembly. . ." But, as Article 31 also specifies, ". . . and whatever may be agreed upon by a majority vote shall be considered settled and binding, unless it be proved to conflict with the Word of God or with the Articles of the Church Order, as long as they are not changed by a General Synod."

Now this latter ruling of Article 31 is altogether reasonable. Therefore Article 43 here declares that also they who have "scorned the admonition of the minor assemblies" shall be censured at the conclusion of major assemblies.

We may note with gratitude that we have really outgrown the need of Article 43, at least as far as its first provision is concerned. Yet the article does no harm in our Church Order and for the cur-

---

* cf. Jansen: **Korte Verklaring**, etc., p. 196.

tailment of any evil habits at our ecclesiastical gatherings it would be well for the presidents to ask before the gatherings disband whether any member of Classis or Synod desires to admonish or correct any of his fellow members regarding their conduct at the meetings of the assembly. And to be sure, in the interest of good order and denominational unity according to the Word of God, it is well that all who scorn the admonition of minor assemblies, be called to order by major assemblies as Article 43 demands.

ARTICLE 44

The Classis shall authorize at least two of her oldest, most experienced and competent Ministers to visit all the Churches once a year and to take heed whether the Minister and the Consistory faithfully perform the duties of their office, adhere to sound doctrine, observe in all things the adopted order, and properly promote as much as lies in them, through word and deed, the upbuilding of the congregation, in particular of the youth, to the end that they may in time fraternally admonish those who have in anything been negligent, and may by their advice and assistance help direct all things unto the peace, upbuilding, and greatest profit of the Churches. And each Classis may continue these visitors in service as long as it sees fit, except where the visitors themselves request to be released for reasons of which the Classis shall judge.

CHURCH VISITATION

The Synod of 's Gravenhage, 1586, drafted and accepted the first reading of this article. It was enlarged by the Synod of Dort, 1618-19, and was but slightly altered by our Synod of 1914. The original reading provided that the Church Visitors should by their advice and assistance "help direct all things unto the peace, up-building, and greatest profit of the churches and schools." In our redaction of 1914 the reference to schools was left out. The schools of Holland at the time were government owned but the management and control was left to the Churches. Inasmuch as our public schools are of an entirely different character and are not at all controlled by the Churches, and since our Christian Schools are owned and managed by Christian School Societies, the reference to schools was left out of Article 44 in 1914.

1. The origin of Church Visitation.

Church Visitation was not instantly introduced. It is some time after the Reformation that we hear of it. In fact, many leaders at first opposed its introduction. Some claimed that it was dangerous to introduce it inasmuch as it might lead to hierarchism, an evil of which the Churches were much afraid.

At first the need for Church Visitation was less urgent since the Classes met much oftener, in some instances every month. These classical meetings, as we have noted before (cf., Art. 41), were held in the various Churches of the Classes in turn. This was done to counteract hierarchism. Our fathers wanted to stress the fact that all Churches are equal in authority. But the classical gatherings were also held in all the Churches in rotation, so that the affairs of the Church with which the Classis met could be observed and investigated at close range. Mutual supervision was in this way exercised at Classis. But it was difficult to meet in rotation and to meet so frequently. Ultimately the Classes met four times a year and only in those Churches which could best entertain a number of delegates. Thus the need for Church Visitation became greater. The Churches of the province of Zeeland instituted Church Visitation in the year 1581. These Churches also asked the General Synod of that year to introduce it for all the Churches. But this Synod answered that it deemed a rule by General Synod in part unnecessary and in part dangerous: unnecessary, inasmuch as the Classes and Particular Synods could introduce Church Visitation wherever necessary; and dangerous, because the Visitors might begin to act as if they were superintendents. But demand for a general introduction of the custom continued, especially in the province of South Holland. Those who advocated the introduction of Church Visitation said that many of the Churches in their provinces showed little regard for denominational unity and that many of the Ministers lacked the necessary training, and therefore needed some supervision and control.

And so we find that the Synod of 's Gravenhage, 1586, recommended the introduction of Church Visitation to the Classes. Soon the practice was maintained in all the provinces except North Holland. The Churches of this province desired to keep the custom optional. But the great Synod of Dort, 1618-19, made the practice general and imperative. Perhaps the turmoil and harm caused by the Arminian errors had convinced this Synod that mutual censure, properly conducted, is highly necessary.

2. The task of Church Visitors.

The committee of Church Visitors, so Article 44 specifies first of all, are to take heed "whether the Minister and the Consistory faithfully perform the duties of their office." All the office-bearers should diligently perform their duties.

The welfare of the Churches demands loyalty and devotion to duty on the part of the office-bearers. The spiritual life of God's people cannot develop normally unless the office-bearers are true and diligent. All too many Protestant Churches have indeed offices and office-bearers, but little more. And the condition of these Churches show the clear results of this neglect.

In the second place the Visitors shall give particular heed to the doctrinal position of the office-bearers. Impure and false doctrine on the part of office-bearers is very dangerous. Office-bearers who cherish wrong conceptions will not only tolerate error in the Church, but they will also sponsor the spreading of wrong conceptions. False doctrine destroys both Churches and souls, and is always a dishonor to God.

In the third place the Visitors must determine whether or not the "adopted order" is observed in all things. This refers to the Church Order. The Church Order has been adopted by all the Churches and for all the Churches. Its fundamental rulings are gleaned from God's own Word or based upon the principles expressed in that Word. Others are rules for good order mutually agreed upon. The former should be maintained because they carry direct divine authority and the latter because good order demands it. Our Church Order is very brief. All of its rulings have been approved and adopted to promote the true spiritual welfare of God's people. Churches and office-bearers who ignore the "adopted order" promote disharmony and conflict. All wilfulness and arbitrariness should be barred from the Churches. The Church Order allows for much liberty and freedom of action. It does not rule out all differences of opinion and of methods. But regarding certain fundamental principles it is positive. Now the Visitors must note, in the interest of God's Church and His people, whether the rules agreed upon are adhered to.

In the fourth place the Church Visitors are to note whether the office-bearers are "properly promoting as much as lies in them, through word and deed, the upbuilding of the congregation, in particular of the youth." The forces of sin are constantly undermining the Church of God. Decay must ever be warded off. Forces within and without are ever threatening the welfare of God's heritage. Consequently God's special servants must always work for "the upbuilding of the congregation." They must do this by word and deed. Words are necessary, but words must be accompanied with deeds. Every Consistory must do its utmost. Vigorous application to duty is always necessary. Without constant vigilance and loyal activity the spiritual life of any Church will recede. It is especially gratifying that the young people and children receive special consideration in this connection. Unless the lambs of the flock are properly tended and fed how can the cause of God flourish? Church Visitors are therefore charged to bear the youth of the Churches in mind particularly as they confer with the various Consistories.

3. The appointment of Church Visitors.

Church Visitation is mutual in character. By means of this institution the Churches watch for each other's welfare and advise and admonish each other when necessary. Church Visitation is not an institution of supervision, exercised by superior officers over inferior officers. Neither is it supervision exercised by an authoritative superior body over inferior bodies. The various Churches comprising a Classis, being all equal in authority, supervise each other. Consequently the Visitors are also appointed by these Churches themselves as their representatives for this work. These appointments take place at classical gatherings of the Churches.

Are Elders also eligible for this work? Article 44 speaks only of Ministers. Yet this supervisory and advisory work is first of all the task of overseers or Elders and not that of its Ministers or preachers. Ministers who act as Visitors do so in their capacity of ruling Elders and not in their capacity as teaching Elders. Consequently as far as the office of our Elders is concerned they are altogether eligible for Church Visitation work. Yet Article 44 stipulates that Ministers shall be appointed for this work. Doubtless because Ministers as a rule have more time and better qualifications for this important work. But no Classis would violate a principle of Reformed church polity if it should appoint an Elder for this work. Years ago some of the provincial Synods of Holland, so Jansen informs us,* had rules which definitely permitted the appointment of Elders as Church Visitors.

How many Visitors should each Classis have? The article stipulates "at least two." The appointment of two Visitors for each Classis or group of Churches is common practice in all our Classes. Article 44, however, permits the appointment of more than two. If at any time a Classis deems it advisable, it may appoint three, four, or more Visitors to visit a Church or group of Churches. If ever more than

* Jansen: **Korte Verklaring**, etc., p. 198.

two Visitors are appointed, it may be well to include one or more Elders in order that the semblance and danger of ministerial dominance may be avoided.

Which Ministers should be appointed as Visitors? The article stipulates the "oldest, most experienced and competent." Church Visitors are often confronted with vexing problems. If they are to extend real help in the solution of such problems, it stands to reason that they must be men well versed in the principles and practices of Reformed Church government; they must have a good doctrinal understanding and must have a great deal of practical wisdom and experience. As a rule these qualifications are found in a greater measure with the older Ministers than with the younger ones. Consequently we read: "The Classis shall authorize at least two of her oldest, most experienced and competent Ministers. . ." Our fathers did not mean to say however, that the oldest men are always the most experienced and competent. The original Latin reads: "Minimum binos, aetate, experientia, et prudentia maxime conspicuos." The meaning, therefore, is clearly that the Classes shall choose at least two of its Ministers who, by reason of their age, experience and wisdom, are most outstanding. Now as a rule the older Ministers have more experience and wisdom than the younger Ministers. But not always. Classes may have to pass by an older man for a younger man inasmuch as the younger man is providentially better qualified for the work of Church Visitation than the older man. But as a rule the older men are best qualified for this service. In the past many of our Classes have appointed men almost at random. Young men just in the ministry would sometimes be appointed, even when they had no outstanding qualifications for this work and when much better qualified men were available. Doubtless these careless appointments were due to the fact that the real significance of Church Visitation according to Article 44 was lost sight of. The work was performed by many visitors in a routine, mechanical fashion. The list of questions approved by Synod of 1922 were asked in such a mechanical fashion that some suggested that this work be done by means of mailed questionnaires. That would save time, money, and trouble. Synod of 1936 urged all Classes: "to perform this work (the work of Church Visitation) in a way most conducive to the (welfare) of the Churches, in full accord with the spirit of Article 44 which militates against all mechanization and requires a thorough discussion on all matters pertaining to the welfare of the Church, particularly of the youth." *

This was no doubt a necessary and timely warning. It would not have been out of place if in this connection Synod had urged the Classes specifically not to choose the Visitors at random, but only from among those Ministers who by reason of their age, experience and wisdom, are most outstanding.

How are the Visitors to be appointed? Not by rotation, but only by deliberate choice as is plain from the foregoing, and also from the very words of Article 44. These Visitors should preferably be appointed for the term of one year with the understanding that the Church Order permits immediate reappointment. To appoint men for a long period of time might foster hierarchical tendencies. Voetius in his day urged that at least one of the two or three Visitors be reelected so as to secure a measure of continuity, a quality both desirable and necessary for Church Visitation work.**

---

* Acts of Synod, 1936, p. 123.

** Janen: **Korte Verklaring**, etc., 1923, p. 199.

4. Time and method of Visitation.

The Church Visitors are to visit all the Churches once a year. If special conditions require that the visit be repeated, the Visitors repeat their call. These special visits may be made at the request of the Consistory concerned, or upon the initiative of the Church Visitors. The Churches have a right to call upon the Church Visitors whenever their help or counsel is needed. And the Visitors have a right to come even when not requested to do so. Of course, the Visitors must give an account of all their work to Classis. Consistories or Consistory members who feel that the Visitors have neglected their duty, or have gone beyond their authorization, or have misdirected matters, may appeal to Classis.

Must the regular visits of Church Visitors be announced to the congregation? Yes, to give the members an opportunity to appear before the Consistory in the presence of the Visitors to voice their disagreement with the Consistory on a pending issue.

Must the Visitors consider possible complaints against a Consistory on the part of members? Yes, although as stands to reason, the Visitors must first assure themselves of the fact that the parties concerned have previously sought to secure satisfaction. New cases may not be brought before the Church Visitors. These must first be presented to the Consistory. Then if no settlement is reached and if the complaint remains, the Church Visitors are required to consider the case. In this connection it should be remembered, however, that Church Visitors can only advise a Consistory as representatives of all the Churches of a Classis. They can not make decisions which are binding for a Consistory.

Are the meetings at which the Visitors are present private or open? Private, inasmuch as personal matters are constantly touched upon. The true welfare of the Churches demands a certain measure of secrecy.

Who presides at Consistory meetings at which the Church Visitors are present? The president of the Consistory. Very often the Visitors take complete charge of the meeting, one of the Visitors acting as president and the other as secretary. In fact the "Rules for Church Visitation" approved by Synod of 1922 state, "At the meeting one of the Visitors shall function as president, and the other as clerk." This rule, however, should be altered in such a fashion that the Visitors merely act as president and clerk of the committee which meets with the Consistory. For Visitors to take over a Consistory meeting without being asked to do so specifically fits in well with Churches holding the Episcopal form of government, but not with those holding the Reformed system. When trouble disturbs, a Consistory will do wise to ask one of the Visitors to preside over the Consistory meeting.

Article 44 stipulates that all the Churches shall be visited once a year. This does not mean that the Visitors may not visit a Church more than once a year. The very fact that Church Visitors are not merely charged to visit each Church once, but for a period of one or two years, indicates that their work is not finished when the prescribed annual visit has been completed. At any time, as has been noted, they may be called in by one of the Churches. And whenever they feel in duty bound to do so they may repeat their visit. Due to great distances and the proportionate expense involved some Classes conduct regular Church Visitation only every other year. As soon as conditions permit the annual visits prescribed should be carried out.

Visitors should not dwell overly long on matters which are of minor import. They should conserve their time for matters of greater import. Certain matters require a very brief annual check-up, as a matter of safety. But the greatest amount of good proceeds from the work of Church Visitors if they will reduce the routine aspect of their labors to a minimum and individualize their work in each Church, stressing those matters which require special attention. They should by all means so arrange their work that ample time will be left for the consideration of questions which the Consistory may desire to present.

Should individual Consistory members also be permitted to bring up for discussion questions of their own choosing? If time permits, there can be no objections against this. Informal discussions on matters of Church government or matters which concern the spiritual welfare of our Churches may help to make the work of the Visitors more interesting and more fruitful.

According to the Rules for Church Visitation as approved by the Synod of 1922 certain matters were to be discussed in the presence of all the Consistory members, Ministers, Elders, and Deacons. But questions which concerned the work and the conduct of Ministers in particular were to be discussed in their absence. The same rule held for Elders and Deacons. In favor of this provision of the rules of 1922 it may be argued that if the work of mutual supervision carried on through Church Visitation is to have real significance, then thoroughness and frankness must mark this work. Faults and shortcomings, worthy of mention, will come to the attention of the visitors much more readily if the various groups of office-bearers will absent themselves for a little while than when they remain in the gathering. But it is also true that if a matter to be mentioned is worth mentioning that then the responding brother should be willing to broach the matter in the presence of the party or parties concerned.

Doubtlessly, there are arguments pro and con regarding this matter, but on the whole it is perhaps well that the Synod of 1942 altered the rule so that now all questions are asked in the presence of all.

It should not be forgotten in this connection that Consistory members should not lodge complaints against each other at the time of Church Visitation, unless the matter has first been discussed privately with the brother concerned, or has been mentioned at the time of "censura morum", i.e., mutual censure, held four times a year in each Consistory. (See Art. 81.) Only if Church Visitors in their discussion with the brethren discover a condition which requires correction do they have a right to mention the matter forthwith, and shall do so, unless they feel that another approach, i.e., action by the Consistory or private consultation, promises to be more fruitful.

Should the Church Visitors themselves record their visit in the minute book of each Consistory? Preferably this should be left to the Clerk of the Consistory. The custom referred to seems to have originated in the Hervormde Kerk van Nederland when the Reformed conception of Church government began to fade and wane. Church Visitors began to function more and more as superintendents. They examined the external affairs of the Churches rather closely. They inspected the Church buildings and grounds, the record books, etc. The spiritual emphasis was lost. The real task of the Visitors was largely or wholly neglected. Then the Visitors, at the conclusion of their visit as "inspectors", would declare over their signatures in the minute book not only that Church Visitation was conducted by them but also that all things were found to be in good order, or else the contrary if such were the case. Of course if a certain Consistory desires that the Church Visitors shall make a record in the minute book of the Consistory of the fact that they have visited with the Consistory that is harmless and needless. The clerk of the Consistory can just as well do this himself. And as far as the books are concerned, a committee of Church Visitors is not called upon to make a close inspection of all the books and records. A casual glance at the books or a paging of the Church records with a view to order and neatness, for instance, does not warrant the Visitors to declare over their signature that all things were found to be in good order.

(For Rules for Church Visitation see Appendix 7, page 367.)

ARTICLE 45

It shall be the duty of the Church in which the Classis and likewise the (Particular) or General Synod meets to furnish the following meeting with the minutes of the preceding.

ACTS OF PREVIOUS GATHERINGS AT MAJOR ASSEMBLIES

1. The reason for this ruling.

In Article 34 our Church Order stipulates, "In all assemblies there shall be not only a president, but also a clerk to keep a faithful record of all important matters." Now the present article rules that the Church, in which the Classis or the Synod meets, shall see to it that a copy of these previous minutes or Acts are present: not a copy of the Acts of all previous assemblies, but a copy of the Acts of the preceding gathering only. The provision of this article was first adopted by the Synod of Dort, 1578. As adopted by this Synod the article stipulated that the Acts of the previous Synod should be present at the next Synod. The convening Church, with which also the Synod would meet, was charged to see to it that said Minutes or Acts were present. The Synod of Middelburg, 1581, revised the article so that from this year on, the rule also applied to Classes.

In our day and age the provision of this article is less urgent. We have printed copies of our synodical Acts, a copy of which is sent to every Consistory member in the whole denomination. Moreover, each Consistory receives a copy for its files or archives. Individuals who desire a copy can secure one at a nominal charge. But in former days, when printing was much more costly, there was no such widespread circulation of Synodical decisions. Consequently the provision of Article 45 was wholly in place. To conduct a synodical meeting without the Acts of the previous gathering being on hand would be very unwise to say the least.

2. This responsibility attached to the convening Church.

We of today also see to it that the Acts or minutes of previous assemblies are present at the next one. As a rule the Acts or minutes of assemblies for several years back are on hand in order that these may be consulted if necessary. But we expect our stated clerks to see to it that these Acts or minutes are on hand. In former days, and this is still true for the Reformed Churches of the Netherlands today, the Churches preferred to leave such matters to particular Churches, rather than to individuals. Stated clerks might assume too much authority. Our fathers had seen and suffered much in the Roman

Church at the hands of individuals who were wrongfully entrusted with superior authority and who abused their authority fearfully. Our forebears always avoided that which was or might lead to the centralization of authority in individuals. They avoided this not only from practical considerations but also because they believed that the Churches should be governed by the Churches, through the office-bearers acting, not as individuals, but as organized groups, i.e., the Consistories. As we have said before, in the interest of efficiency, we have appointed stated clerks. But let these brethren watch their step and do no more than has been assigned to them. Let them shun all assumption of authority. Let us also remember that Article 45 continues to be in force. The convening and entertaining Church may rely on the stated clerk for the execution of this provision but the Church continues to be responsible.

3. The matter of ecclesiastical archives.

In connection with the foregoing we call attention to the subject of our ecclesiastical archives. Each Church should preserve all papers, documents and books or booklets which have bearing on its origin and history. This would include first of all the consistorial minute books and all legal documents, as well as membership records, reports, etc. But any booklets, articles, or papers which have or may have historical significance should be included. Many Churches have been negligent on this score so that the historical origin of some Churches is hardly known. Some Churches do not even have all their old minute books. Through neglect they have been lost. It is a good thing that the Rules for Church Visitors also contain a question regarding the archives of the Churches visited. Every Church should have a fire-proof repository where all valuable books and papers can be safely kept. All of our Churches, especially our larger ones, should appoint one of the Consistory members to act as archivist, whose duty it is to keep the archive in good order and up-to-date.

The classical archives should contain all valuable papers, reports, historical data, minute books, synodical Acts, etc. Each Classis should ask one of its Churches to keep the classical archive. And when the Church Visitors call they should make it a point to inquire after the management and state of this classical archive. They should report their findings to Classis.

Synod should likewise request a competent Church to keep the synodical archive. This synodical archive should again not only include all official documents and Acts, but also books, booklets, papers of a historical nature and dealing more or less directly with the origin and history of our denomination. To a certain extent the matter here referred to is covered by the Historical Committee which Synod of 1934 appointed and which it charged "to gather and preserve books and documents of historical value pertaining to the history of our Church and the Church from which we originated and to religion in general, and to provide a room and facilities in the College or Seminary building where they can be properly preserved and displayed." *

But this decision does not provide for the safekeeping of official documents, Acts of Synod, etc. Nor will that which is gathered by the Historical Committee be kept in a fire-proof vault. It would not be needless duplication if some Church were asked and authorized to secure a fire-proof vault in which the Consistory of that Church would

---

* Acts of Synod, 1934, p. 81.

keep the archives of Synod. The large, cosmopolitan Church of Amsterdam has acted as Archivist for the Reformed Churches of the Netherlands for many years. The Synod Zwolle, 1911, authorized this Church to build a special fire-proof vault, as we suggest above.

ARTICLE 46

Instructions concerning matters to be considered in major assemblies shall not be written until the decision of previous Synods touching these matters have been read, in order that what was once decided be not again proposed, unless a revision be deemed necessary.

READING OF PREVIOUS DECISIONS

1. Historical origin of this article.

Just as Article 45, so also this article finds its origin in the fact that formerly printing was far less common than it is now. Printing was indeed discovered during the early part of the 15th century, but it was at first a very expensive enterprise. The Reformation Churches could not afford to print the Acts of their major assemblies for wide distribution. They had to do the next best thing. The clerks of the assemblies, so we are told, would read the decisions of the meeting, and then the delegates would copy them. Consequently, only a few men or Churches would be in possession of a complete set of Acts of Synod. The result was that many Churches would come with questions and matters at their Classes to be presented to Synod which had already been acted upon. The Classes were not always aware of this fact and so duplication and reduplication resulted. To avoid this evil the Synod of Emden, 1571, decided that the decisions of previous Synods should be read (at classical gatherings) before any matters were sent on to Synod.

The Acts of the first few Synods were not so elaborate and bulky that the provision of Article 46 could not be carried out. Even the great Synod of Dort, 1618-19, maintained this article as to its original intent. The decisions of previous Synods had to be read at classical gatherings at which matters for the synodical assemblies were considered. As time progressed the instruction of Article 46 became well nigh impossible of execution and also less necessary, for printing became more common and synodical decisions became very numerous. And so the Reformed Churches of Holland in their redaction of Article 46, approved in 1905, changed the article so that it requires only the reading of those previous synodical decisions which have a direct bearing on the matter which is being considered for the synodical agenda. And the reading of these previous synodical decisions is now generally left to the individuals or Churches which bring matter to Classis for Synod.

2. Present significance of Article 46.

In the first place Article 46 stresses the fact for us that we should be well informed regarding synodical decisions in order that we may help to avoid needless repetition. **In the second place,** matters once decided upon must not be raised again unless there is a good reason for doing so. The time of our major assemblies is too precious to be spent needlessly. Furthermore, the Churches lose confidence in their major assemblies if these constantly change their decisions. Constant reconsideration and constant change reveals a certain ignorance regarding principles and issues involved and it undermines the stability of our church life. Decisions are not taken seriously when changes are constantly made. **In the third place,** Article 46 clearly indicates that matter previously acted upon may be resubmitted if this is deemed necessary. Our assemblies are not infallible. Errors are sometimes made. And erroneous decisions should be changed as soon as possible. Let us remember, however, that we should proceed with wisdom and care. As much as in us lies, we should avoid disturbance and confusion. The truth of God must always prevail, come what may. But changes in methods and plans not directly drawn from and dictated by the Word should be made cautiously and upon due consideration.

3. Various ways in which matters may be brought before major assemblies.

The present article speaks of instructions to be considered in major assemblies. **One way in which matter can be presented** to major assemblies is therefore by means of instructions. Delegates to our major assemblies (Classes or Synods) can take an active part in the gatherings because they have been instructed to do so. Their Consistories or Classes have sent them. These bodies do not instruct their delegates specifically, telling them just what to say and just how to vote. That would even be impossible for the delegating Churches do not know beforehand all the matters that will be presented. Besides, it would be harmful to instruct delegates just what to say and how to vote even if this were possible as we have indicated in our consideration of Article 33. But each delegating body does have the right to instruct its delegates to present certain information, suggestions or overtures to the assembly. These matters should be written on the letters of credence or accompany the letter of credence in written form, properly signed. By means of these instructions matters may therefore be presented to major assemblies.

In the second place, matters may come up for consideration at our classical gatherings through the avenue of Article 41. This article provides for what the Dutch call "de rondvraag." According to Article 41 the president of Classis must put the questions indicated in this article to all the delegates. By means of this general inquiry, matters may therefore be brought before Classis, particularly in response to the question: "Do you need the judgment and help of the Classis for the proper government of your Church?

In the third place, matters may be presented to our major assemblies by way of appeal. (Cf. Art. 31.) Reformed Church polity authorities do not make a sharp distinction between a protest and an appeal, nor between a grievance and a complaint. Neither are these distinguished in the Church Order. In civil courts technical terms and technical interpretation of terms means a great deal. But in the Church of God we are first of all interested in the matter as such. We stress spirit and content, not terms and technicalities. In general it may be said that **an appeal** is made regarding the decision of a minor assembly to a major assembly. The term **protest** would most naturally apply first of all to a verbal or written notice of vigorous disagreement with a decision of any assembly, which notice is delivered as soon as possible after the decision has been made and while the assembly is still in session. But the terms appeal and protest are also used interchangeably. A **grievance** or **complaint** is a written expression of dissatisfaction with the decision of a Consistory, Classis, or Synod, with the request that the assumed wrong be righted. The word grievance seems to imply that the conscience of the aggrieved person or body is burdened. The word complaint seems to imply that an injustice has been committed from which the complainant seeks relief. The Dutch speak of "bezwaar-schrift" and "aanklacht."

In the fourth place, matters may come up for consideration lawfully at our assemblies through motions formulated and presented right on the floor of the assembly and suggested by the need of the hour and growing out of discussions of matters presented to the gathering. It stands to reason that no Classis or Synod should act rashly in its consideration of matters which have not appeared upon the previously published agenda. Weighty matters, especially, should not be acted upon with overly much haste, but rather held in abeyance so that there may be time for study and consideration.

In this connection we would remark in the first place, that all questions and matters brought to major assemblies should concern definite problems. If there is no specific instance—sometimes called "concrete case" from the Dutch "concreet geval"—no question or problem should be presented to Classis or Synod. One major gathering can not begin to consider abstract and theoretical problems. Time would fail them utterly and the consideration of abstract problems, though very good in itself, is not the task of our ecclesiastical assemblies as such. A Classes or Synod is no question box. And it should also be remembered that specific instances should be presented as such. That is to say, no one should come to a Classis or Synod with questions or problems, phrased in general terms, expecting a general ruling of the major assembly, even though there be a specific instance which occasions the presentation of the question. Specific instances should be presented as specific instances and acted upon as specific instances.

Secondly it should be noted that ordinarily matters come to our major assemblies through and from our minor assemblies, either Consistories or Classes. However, individual members may go directly to Classis or Synod. Of course, if the matter be an appeal, protest, grievance, or complaint, the assemblies concerned should be previously informed a reasonable length of time previous to the gathering to which the appeal is made. The body concerned should receive an exact copy of the document going to the major gathering in order that it may still have opportunity to settle matters or to prepare an explanation and defense. Furthermore, every individual member, man or woman, of our Churches may address a request to Classis or Synod, petitioning certain actions or decisions if the matter concerns "the Churches of the major assembly in common." (Cf. Art. 30.)

In the third place, major assemblies may refer matters which come up for consideration, to the minor assemblies for their deliberation and reaction. But they need not do this. Often it is a wise policy to follow. But sometimes this method is unnecessary. Sometimes there is danger in delay and safety in immediate action.

Formerly it was not customary to send the agenda for major assemblies to minor assemblies. Only committees appointed at a former meeting to study difficult matters and to suggest a solution would send their findings and their advice to the minor assemblies previous to the gathering of major assemblies. As far as possible we now send the complete agenda to all Consistories. In fact, one copy of the synodical agenda, as well as a copy of the later Acts, is sent for each Consistory member. This is a commendable custom. It promotes a thorough knowledge of, and a lively interest in the affairs of the Churches. Let all Consistory members diligently read these documents! And let the minor assemblies take time to discuss the agenda.

Reports of standing committees, usually called boards, should also be presented to the minor assemblies. When this is not done it is far more difficult to follow and to control the work of these bodies.

ARTICLE 47

(Every year [or if need be oftener] four or five or more neighboring Classes shall meet as a Particular Synod, to which each Classis shall delegate two Ministers and two Elders. At the close of both the Particular and the General Synod, some Church shall be empowered to determine with advice of Classis, the time and place of the next Synod.)

PARTICULAR SYNODS

Article 47, as well as Article 48 and Article 49, is found between parentheses in the Church Order. This was done because we do not yet have Particular Synods, and all of these articles refer, in the first place, to Particular Synods. And yet, sooner or later, we may find that we should begin to meet as Particular Synods. Particular Synods will be held as soon as conditions warrant and require their institution. Consequently these articles have been retained in our redaction of the Church Order of Dort, but we have placed them between parentheses for the time being.

1. The origin of Particular Synods.

The Convention of Wezel, 1568, already advised the institution of Particular Synods. And the first Synod of the Reformed Churches of Holland, Emden, 1571, decided that three such Particular Synods should be organized. At this time the Churches were still badly persecuted. Many of the Reformed believers had taken refuge to Germany and England. So the Synod of Emden decided that three Particular Synods should be organized: one in Germany, one in England, and one in the Netherlands itself.

However,.from 1572 on the cause of the Reformation was carried forward by long strides, and greater measures of liberty were acquired so that large numbers of refugees soon returned to the home-land. Consequently the Synod of Dort, 1578, finding that the Churches were already gathering together in Particular Synods, regulated matters as follows: Each Particular Synod was to consist of four or five Classes. Two Ministers and two Elders were to be delegated from each Classis. Ministers and Elders not delegated were permitted to be present at the gatherings of the Particular Synods as guests, but they did not receive a decisive vote. Each Particular Synod should designate one of the Churches of its group to summon the next meeting of the Particular Synod, but this summoning was not to take place without advice of the Classis to which this summoning Church belonged. Each Particular Synod was to meet annually unless circumstances required the Synod to meet oftener.

These stipulations of the Synod of 1578 were subsequently gathered into one article and remained unchanged for the Reformed

Churches of Holland until 1905, when it was stipulated that the confines of the Particular Synods should, with minor exceptions, coincide with the confines of the various geographical provinces. Our redaction of 1914, however, left the 47th article as it has been for more than three centuries. Our situation did not require a change.

2. Character of Particular Synods.

Article 47 makes it plain that Synods are gatherings of Classes and not gatherings of persons. From this follows that every Synod is a gathering of Churches and not a gathering of men who constitute a ruling body in or over the Churches. True, Synods are further removed from the particular Churches than the Classes are. But they are nevertheless definitely gatherings of Churches. At Consistories all the Ministers and Elders (and Deacons) meet. At Classis only two Consistory members for each Church meet, but every Church is nevertheless represented directly. At Particular Synods all the Churches of every Classes are represented, but the majority of the Churches will be represented indirectly, through a limited number of Ministers and Elders chosen by the Churches at the various Classes. Synods are therefore further removed from the particular Churches than Classes are. The representation at Synods is less direct, and their task is more limited.

3. Delegation to Particular Synods.

Each Classis delegates an equal number of delegates. The larger Classes have no more representatives than do the smaller Classes. The same principle which operates in the matter of delegating to Classes operates here also, although in this instance it is more a matter of orderly procedure than of principle. For the particular Church is the unit of denominational federation and unity. This fact certainly demands that each Church be represented at Classes by an equal number of delegates, but it cannot be said that this fact also demands that every Classis, large or small, shall be represented by an equal number of delegates at our Synods. But for reasons of good order and regularity it is very desirable that all Classes or Particular Synods delegate the same number of men. Overly large Classes should be subdivided into smaller Classes. This makes for better work and at the same time assures the Churches of these Classes of an equitable representation at major assemblies.

Article 47 stipulates that two Ministers and two Elders shall be delegated by each Classes to the Particular Synods. If ever our Churches decide to establish Particular Synods these articles which pertain to such Synod will doubtlessly be carefully reviewed. In all likelihood some changes will have to be made, particularly as to the number of delegates which each Classis would send. Some Particular Synod would consist of but three Classes perhaps. Such Synods would then number but 12 delegates. This number would be needlessly and undesirably small. The Reformed Churches of Holland have revised the article in 1905 so that small Particular Synods numbering only three or four Classes may send three Ministers and three Elders each.

Delegates to Particular and General Synods should be chosen by ballot. They should never be sent according to some mechanical plan, for example, alphabetical order. Rotational delegation of Elders to Classes has very much in its favor, but synodical meetings are of such importance that those who are providentially most able and experienced should be sent.

4. Frequency of Particular Synods.

From the beginning the Reformed Churches maintained annual Particular Synods and they would meet more than once a year if such appeared to be necessary. However, in a few instances prior to the great Synod of Dort, 1618-19, the government interfered with the regular summoning of Synods so that the Particular Synods did not meet for a number of years in some sections of Holland. In fact for a number of years the Churches were prevented from holding General Synods. This prevention was due to political conditions and to the Arminian sympathies and convictions of some governmental authorities who had to give consent at that time.

Ordinarily annual meetings of Particular Synods should be enough. But extraordinary circumstances may demand extraordinary sessions. For this reason the article states: "or if need be oftener."

5. The summoning of Particular Synods, and their order of procedure.

Regarding the calling together of Synods Article 47 says: "At the close of both the Particular and the General Synod, some church shall be empowered to determine with advice of Classis, the time and place of the next Synod." The precise time and place of our Synods is therefore to be determined, according to this article, by the calling or summoning Church in consultation with its sister Churches through Classis.

As to the method of procedure, the president of the former Synod—Particular or General, whichever the case may be—calls the meeting together at the appointed place and hour, or the Minister (one of the Ministers appointed by the Consistory for this work) of the summoning Church does this. It is more in keeping with the principles governing Reformed church polity that the summoning Church open the sessions of a Synod than that the president of a former Synod should do this.

How are synodical gatherings to be opened? Usually the leader calls upon the assembly to sing an appropriate psalm or hymn; then he reads a passage from the Bible after which he leads in prayer, asking for God's guidance for the election of directors and for all the activities of the Synod. The temporary president then calls for the credentials. These being examined and found satisfactory the delegates are acknowledged as such and he declares the meeting legally constituted. Then the assembly proceeds to elect a president, clerk, etc. The appointment of directors for our Synod always takes place by ballot. Nominations and nominating addresses are unknown in these gatherings. Nominations are not necessary inasmuch as the leaders are sufficiently known to those delegated so that they can vote intelligently from them. Free balloting safeguards us from certain dangers which are apt to attend nominations and nominating speeches.

When the directors have been chosen and seated, so Jansen advises*, the president should first of all present doctrinal matters; then matters which concern government and discipline; and then various other matters that may require action. No doubt this is the logical order, the order of importance.

* **Jansen: Korte Verklaring,** etc., p. 212.

ARTICLE 48

(Each Synod shall be at liberty to solicit and hold correspondence with its neighboring Synod or Synods in such manner as they shall judge most conducive to general edification.)

INTER-SYNODICAL CONTACTS

This article, like the preceding and the following article of our Church Order, apply to Particular Synods. At this writing we have as yet not organized Particular Synods. They may not be organized for a long time to come. However, with a view to the possible future organization of Particular Synods, these articles 47 to 49, as has been pointed out previously, have been left in our Church Order. And for the sake of completeness we consider their significance in this commentary.

1. The historical origin and significance of this article.

The Churches of Holland did not feel the need of correspondence between neighboring Synods as long as the General Synod would meet regularly. But after the year 1586, for a long period of time, the General Synod did not meet regularly. This, as has been explained before, was due to interference of the government. Certain government officials were afraid that the Church would exert and develop too much power and influence and so they refused to authorize the gatherings of General Synods. The Churches being closely allied to the government at that time were helpless. This situation prevented the Churches from conferring with each other on various questions and from taking united action. To meet this condition somewhat the Particular Synods, usually called Provincial Synods in the Netherlands, began to send representatives to each other's meetings. The first step to initiate what the Church Order in this article calls "correspondence," was taken in 1593 by the Particular Synod of South Holland. This Synod sent two of its Ministers to the Particular Synod of North Holland.

Within a few years the custom became well-nigh general. All the Particular Synods of the Netherlands were sending representatives to each other's meetings except those of Drenthe and Zeeland. The civil authorities of the latter province prevented the Churches of Zeeland from establishing these contacts with neighboring Particular Synods.

Now the General Synod of 1618-19—finally permitted and called together by the civil government because of the Arminian troubles—regulated this custom of "correspondence" between Particular Synods, and read Article 48 into the Church Order.

The purpose of this correspondence, as may be noted from what has just been said, is to promote the necessary unity and cooperation between the various Churches. Thus the Churches made important agreements and took united action even while no General Synods were held. By means of these inter-synodical contacts, for example, the Churches agreed that students should not be admitted to the Ministry until after they had finished their course and passed their examinations. Thus the Churches also promoted the translation of the Bible. Furthermore, they took steps through this method of "correspondence" to stop the printing of undesirable books, and by means of this inter-synodical "correspondence" a new metrical version of the Psalms was introduced in 1775.

2. The manner of maintaining inter-synodical contacts.

Article 48 states that: "Each Synod shall be at liberty to solicit and hold correspondence with its neighboring Synod or Synods." The term "hold correspondence" is a literal translation of the Dutch "correspondentie te houden." But our English word "correspondence" as used in Article 48 instantly makes us think of communication by letter or written statements sent by mail. However, the "correspondence" referred to was always carried out by means of representatives who were charged to attend the meetings of neighboring Particular Synods in person.

Clearly it was not the intention of our church fathers of 1618-19 that this correspondence should be carried on by means of letters sent. The term should therefore be given a broad interpretation.

Inter-synodical contacts and conference may be established and maintained by letters, for the article states very clearly that this correspondence shall be maintained "in such manner as they shall judge most conducive to general edification." But from the very beginning representatives were sent and delegated. Doubtlessly this is by far the most effective and satisfactory method.

3. Present significance of this article.

The Churches in the Netherlands find that there is no great need for the maintenance of this correspondence between their various Particular Synods. Regarding some matters, such as boundary line questions and united mission activity, the provision of Article 48 is useful. For the rest, so it is claimed, now that General Synod again meets regularly all matters of general concern can be duly acted upon at the General Synods.

Some of our neighboring Classes send representatives or "fraternal delegates," as they are called, to each other's meetings. This is doubtlessly a good and beneficial custom and finds justification in this ruling of the Church Order pertaining to Particular Synods. Perhaps there should be more correspondence between our various Classes since we have no Particular Synods and since there is danger that we drift away from each other. We need to strengthen each other's hands and to cooperate in common interests.

In this connection it is well to call to mind that some of our Classes have their own particular background and history. For example, Classis Ostfriesland has a German background and for years used the German language at its meetings. Classis Hackensack, while part of our denomination, has always spoken the English language and has an altogether different historical background from the rest of our denomination which is almost exclusively Dutch in origin. These differences make for difference of viewpoint and emphasis.

Then it should also be remembered that our Churches are found in various localities and surroundings. Some of our Classes are composed of coastal Churches; others of inland Churches. Some are found in the East; others in the West. Some are largely urban in spirit and viewpoint others largely rural. Now our surroundings and particular circumstances of life have a tendency to incline us in certain directions and mould us in our thinking. Correspondence between our various Classes would help to maintain our unity and to promote a greater measure of unity. And by means of correspondence we could constantly learn from one another.

ARTICLE 49

(Each Synod shall delegate some to execute everything ordained by Synod both as to what pertains to the Government and to the respective Classes, resorting under it, and likewise to supervise together or in smaller number all examinations of future Ministers. And, moreover, in all other ventual difficulties they shall extend help to the Classes in ord · that proper unity, order, and soundness of doctrine may be r intained and established. Also they shall keep proper recor . of all their actions to report thereof to Synod, and if it be demanded, give reasons. They shall also not be discharged from their service before and until Synod itself discharges them.)

SYNODICAL COMMITTEES

Article 49, as well as the two preceding articles, is found in parentheses in our Church Order. As has been explained, Articles 47, 48, and 49 have reference to Particular Synods. Our Churches have up to this time refrained from organizing Particular Synods and consequently these three articles are not fully in force among us. We say that these articles are not fully in force among us. For these rulings are expressive of certain principles and policies which are in force as far as our Classes and Synods are concerned. This is particularly true for Article 49.

1. The nature of synodical committees.

Synodical committees consist of two or more men which have been delegated by a synod "to execute everything ordained by Synod," or to perform a special task which Synod could not itself perform. Synodical committee-men are therefore deputies of Synod, brethren that have been delegated to perform a special task in the name of all the Churches represented by the Synod concerned. They are men, as the word itself would indicate, to whom a special charge has been committed. The expression, synodical delegates, would have much in its favor, but we speak invariably of those who represent the Churches at Synod as delegates. Consequently to apply the term "Synodical Delegates" to those who are deputized by a Synod for the performance of a specific task would make for confusion. The Reformed Churches in Holland use the term "Synodale Deputaten," Synodical Deputies. This term would be unobjectionable in itself, but the word deputy or deputies is never used for ecclesiastical committees in our land. On the other hand the term "committee" is often used. And whereas this word is appropriate, in its implied meaning, we prefer to use the term Synodical Committees.

The very first regular Synod, Emden, 1571, already decided to appoint two Synodical Committees. One, consisting of two members, to represent the Churches of Holland at the Synod of the Reformed Churches in France; another, consisting of 16 members, to assist Marnix of St. Aldegonde in the gathering of historical data relative to the Reformation.

But Synodical Committees were not mentioned in the Church Order, by way of special article, until the Synod of Dort, 1618-19, met. Article 49 was incorporated into the Church Order by this Synod. Doubtless this Synod did so in order to help regulate an institution which was filling a real need and a worthy place in the various Particular Synods, but which was not altogether without dangers. Hugo Grotius for one charged that the "Synodical Deputies" were taking the place of the Synods while these were not in session and that these Committees were invested with power to rule. At any rate the Synod of Dort clearly regulated the matter of Synodical Committees, indicating their task and in so doing also limiting their rights and powers. As the article was originally drafted it applied only to Particular Synods. The Churches seemingly did not find it necessary at first to appoint Synodical Committees for the General Synods. But eventually the article was also applied to General Synods in Holland. In the year 1905 the Churches of Holland so revised the article that it applies to the General Synods as well as to the Particular Synods. In the Church Order of the Reformed Churches of the Netherlands Article 49 now reads as follows:

"Each Synod shall deputize some to execute everything ordained by Synod and to offer their assistance to the Classes in eventual difficulties; as much as possible separate groups of delegates shall be appointed for the various interests. At least two or three deputies shall supervise the peremptoir (decisive or final) examinations of future Ministers. All these deputies shall keep a good record of all their activities in order to report to Synod and in order to give reasons for their actions, if such be demanded. They shall also not be discharged from their service before and until Synod itself discharges them."

This revision of Article 49 differs in some respect from Article 49 in our Church Order. In our Church Order Article 49 refers in form only to Particular Synods. In the Holland Church Order the article applies to both Particular and General Synods. In our Church Order Article 49 speaks of one committee charged to do many and various things. The Holland Church Order now specifies that a separate Synodical Committee shall be appointed for each matter requiring attention. No doubt the Holland rendering of 1905 is an improvement over the old rule. Increased labors demand more than one committee. Moreover, one committee charged to do all that requires attention and action might assume power and thus foster the evils of hierarchism.

2. The specific charge and limited authority of synodical committees.

Synodical Committees, likewise Classical Committees, should be selected with due consideration. Those who are best qualified in the providence of God should be appointed. Appointment should be by ballot or by selection of the synodical officers or upon nomination by a nominating committee.

Those who are appointed to serve on a Synodical Committee (or Classical Committee) need not be delegates to the body making the appointment, although sometimes this may be advisable. Neither need appointees always be officer-bearers. Sometimes the matter at hand may require the knowledge and experience of experts such as physicians, lawyers, etc. Then these experts should be appointed though they may not be office-bearers. Needless to say however, only those who are in hearty accord with our Reformed conceptions should ever be appointed to serve on committees. Only in exceptional cases and when need requires would a Synod ask one outside of our own Christian Reformed Churches to serve on a Synodical Committee.

As far as permanent or standing Synodical Committees are concerned, some of which are called boards, periodic retirements may be encouraged to counteract the danger of hierarchism, provided the cause at hand would not be required to suffer. Certain causes need a large measure of permanency for efficient and thorough work. So, for example, a constant shift in the membership of our committees for the mission work of our Churches and for Calvin College and Seminary, (Christian Reformed Boards of Missions and Board of Trustees of Calvin College and Seminary) would be to the detriment of these causes.

Article 49 as we find it in our Church Order specifies that the one Synodical Committee which it calls for shall "execute everything ordained by Synod both as to what pertains to the government and to the respective Classes, resorting under it . . ." The 1905 revision of this article by the Reformed Churches of Holland, as may be noted from our translation of this revision just given, merely reads: "Each Synod shall deputize some to execute everything ordained by Synod." This is a good change. Why single out matters which concern the civil government and the Classes? Our reading, dating back to 1618-19, is too specific and exclusive.

Regarding the provision, "And, moreover, in all other eventual difficulties they shall extend help to the Classes...", it may be remarked our Synods do not appoint a committee to assist a Classes in the settlement of any difficulty unless Synod is asked to do so by the Classis concerned, except it be in answer to an appeal by an individual member or Church.

Matters which require the presence and advice of Synodical Committees are such as are mentioned in Article 11 (Dismissal from active service), and Article 79 (Deposition from office). The revision of Holland, 1905, eliminated the motivating phrase, "in order that proper unity, order, and soundness of doctrine may be maintained and established . . ." No doubt these words were dropped in the interest of brevity and because they are in part a duplication of what we find in Article 1 of the Church Order. But some matters can bear repetition, even in a brief Church Order. Moreover these words definitely indicate the purpose for the appointment of synodical committee-men, and at the same time this phrase stresses matters which are very vital to the Churches. For these reasons we favor the retention of these words.

The examinations of future Ministers which Synodical Delegates must supervise according to this article are the decisive, final, or classical examinations. In Holland these decisive examinations are spoken of as "peremptoire examens", in distinction from the "praeparatoire examens," by which latter term the preliminary examinations which merely admit one to candidacy for the ministry, are indicated.

Article 49 states that the Synodical Delegates, often indicated by the term "deputaten ad examina," shall supervise these final examinations "together or in smaller number." Article 4 requires that three delegates shall be present. A possible future revision of Article 49 should be changed to harmonize with Article 4. According to the present reading of Article 49 the presence of one Synodical Delegate would satisfy the letter of the article. Yet Article 4 calls for three, which number, if the usage is filling a necessary place, is none too large. (For further details regarding Synodical Delegates see our comments on Article 4.)

As to the authority of Synodical Committees, it should be stressed that they are not superintendents ruling with superior power. Not at all. They are the servants of the Synod which appointed them; they have no authority in themselves at all. Their authority is limited to that which the Synod has extended to them. Sometimes they are indeed charged to act with Synodical authority, but then only in specific cases, clearly definable. Sometimes the Committees are appointed "with power to act" as circumstances may demand, but as stands to reason, never upon their own authority, but ever upon the authority of the Synod which appointed the committee. Instances in which a Synod or Classis gives a Committee "power to act" should be exceptional. As much as possible our assemblies must rule directly and not indirectly.

What should a Synodical Committee do when facing an emergency situation? Should the committee act and take important steps and then ask the next Synod to approve of its actions? No. Now that we have annual Synods situations which are so acute that they cannot wait until Synod meets will be very few and far between. But if a serious situation arises which cannot be settled by Classis, and which cannot wait until Synod, then let the committee advise a special or earlier Synod. The following article, Article 50, as revised by the Synod of 1936, specifies: "If at least a majority of the Classes deem it necessary that the Synod meet either earlier or later than the regular time, the local Church charged with convening the Synod shall in due season determine when and where it is to meet." (cf. Acts 1936, p. 39)

Our standing or permanent Committees (Boards) should be very careful also not to take any important decisions without synodical authorization previously gained. To make important decisions, though pressure of circumstances does not require such, and then to ask for Synodical approval is to be condemned. Synodical Committees must ever remember that they are but delegates, deputies, committees of Synod, servants of Synod charged to do that which Synod has delegated or committed to them.

If Synod cannot meet at the appointed time, because of an epidemic, a war, etc., then the Committees continue to function. They are not discharged from service before and until Synod discharges them.

If a Synodical Committee member finds that he cannot serve, for instance because of long continued sickness, then he should not resign. This he cannot do since the body which appointed him is no longer in session. Only the next Synod can discharge him. He should notify the other Committee members that he finds it impossible to take an active part in the work of the Committee. Furthermore he reports his circumstances and actions to the next Synod, which body will approve or disapprove of his withdrawal. If a Synod finds that it must disapprove the withdrawal of any Committee-man the seriousness and clearness of the case will determine whether and in how far the party concerned is to be reproved or censured.

ARTICLE 50

The General Synod shall ordinarily meet annually. Each Classis shall delegate two Ministers and two Elders to this Synod. If at least a majority of the Classes deem it necessary that the Synod meet either earlier or later than the regular time, the local Church charged with convening the Synod shall in due season determine when and where it is to meet.

CONCERNING SYNOD

Article 50 as it now reads is the product of Synod 1936. At this Synod it was decided to hold annual Synods instead of bi-annual

Synods, and that two Ministers and two Elders should be delegated from each Classis instead of three Ministers and three Elders from each Classis, as it had been before 1936.

1. Frequency of synodical gatherings.

Article 50 speaks of "General" Synod. This term is used in view of the fact that the Church Order recognizes two types of Synods: Particular and General. As has been noted before, our Churches have not yet introduced Particular Synods inasmuch as our denomination is too small to warrant their introduction. But the articles which refer to Particular Synods have been retained in the revised Church Order because Particular Synods are a part of every normal Reformed church organization, and the time may come that we will feel called upon to introduce them. Thus, in distinction from Particular Synods covered by Articles 47-49, Article 50 uses the expression "General Synod." But inasmuch as we have no Particular Synods we never refer to our Synods as General Synods, but merely speak of them as Synods.

As noted, Synod of 1936 decided that thenceforth Synod should meet annually. Synod made this change from bi-annual to annual meetings in response to an overture from Classis Sioux Center, and upon the following considerations:

a. This is in accordance with the spirit of the Church Order, which favors frequent meetings, Articles 37, 41, 47.
b. This will make for shorter meetings of Synod. Our Synods at present are too long. Delegates complain that it is difficult for them to be away from their work for so long a time.
c. This will expedite matters in cases of protests and appeals.
d. This will open the way for a reduction in the membership of our Boards.
e. This will promote contact between the various parts of our Church, which is in harmony with the spirit of the Church Order."

The Reformed Churches in Holland, our mother Churches, originally desired an Annual General Synod, so Jansen informs us.* But disturbed civil conditions and government interferences prevented the realization of this ideal. Today the Reformed Churches of the lowlands meet annually through their several Particular Synods but only tri-annually in General Synod.

Nevertheless, some of the leading authorities in Holland advocate annual General Synods. Their motives for favoring annual General Synods harmonize pretty well with the consideration which moved our Synod of 1936 to introduce Annual Synods.**

It is also worthy of note that the Presbyterian Churches of Scotland and in our own U. S. A. all meet in General Assembly each year. The Reformed Churches of Hungary and France likewise have annual General Synods.***

At the Synod of 1936, and again in 1938, overtures to return to bi-annual Synods were rejected. It is still too early to say at this time how many actual gains will be harvested by the change from bi-annual to annual Synods. But this is sure, there is not enough contact between the various sections of our denomination. The fact that

---

* Jansen: **Korte Verklaring**, etc., p. 223; cf. also Bouwman, **Ger. Kerkrecht**, Vol. II, p. 199.

** cf. Jansen: **Korte Verklaring**, etc., p. 223; Bouwman: **Ger. Kerkr.**, Vol. II, p. 200, 201; Voetius and Dr. A. Kuiper favored annual Synods. Cf. Idem—more recently, 1938, Dr. H. H. Kuiper championed the cause of annual Synods in **De Heraut.**

*** Bouwman: **Ger. Kerkr.**, Vol. II, p. 199.

our Churches are scattered over a large geographical area makes it very difficult for us to know and to help each other properly. Yet we are one and we need each other. And perhaps for a while to come Particular Synods will be out of the question. It may therefore be expected, considering all angles involved, that the test of years will reveal that the merits of Annual Synods far outweighs their demerits.

2. Delegates to Synod.

Synod of 1936 also decided that two Ministers and two Elders should from then on represent each Classis at Synod. This decision was taken in view of the fact that Synod was to meet annually. This reduction in the number of delegates would help to reduce the increased expenses, which the change from bi-annual to annual Synods would occasion, considerably. Moreover, Synod of 1936 was fully aware of the fact that some Classes were far too large for their own good and that there was a growing demand for a redistricting of the Classes. This Synod took steps to adjust that which required adjusting. In 1937 three additional Classes were called into existence. This imminent increase in the number of Classes, also helped Synod of 1936 to decide that from thenceforth each Classis should send four delegates instead of six.

How should delegates to Synod be appointed? By ballot. Some Classes have introduced the so-called rotary system, appointing the ministerial delegates in alphabetical order. But this is out of harmony with Article 41 which specifies that "delegates shall be **chosen** to attend said Synod." Classes should send their best qualified men. Consequently the Classes should not be hampered by any written or unwritten rule in their selection of delegates to Synod, and far less should delegates be sent in rotation.

The spring session of Classis Pella (March 22, 1938) overtured the Synod of 1938 to adopt the following resolution:

"Synod of 1938, having taken note of the fact that more than one Classis has adopted the practice of delegating its ministerial delegates to Synod according to the rotation plan, hereby issues a word of serious warning against the dangers involved in this method of delegation to Synod, and declares that this method of delegation is not in accord with the genius and letter of our Church Order (cf. Art. 41), and furthermore resolves to urge all the Classes to send its delegates to Synod only by choice of ballot."

Synod did not adopt this suggested resolution, but accepted the following recommendation of its Advisory Committee instead: "Synod declares that there is no warrant in Articles 41 and 50 of the Church Order for Synod to enjoin upon the Classes a definite method of selecting its delegates to Synod but, with a view to the welfare of the Churches, it advises against the rotary method of selecting synodical delegates."

We believe that the proposed resolution of Classis Pella should have been adopted rather than the weaker resolution of the Advisory Committee. We agree with the sentiment expressed in a report to Classis Pella March, 1938. We quote:

"In the first place we should remember that our synodical gatherings are of vital import. The problems which confront our Synods are very crucial: If the decisions made at our Synods are faulty or lacking, the very future of our Churches as true Reformed Churches will suffer. Everything in the last analysis revolves around and depends on our Synods: our Mission work, our Theological School and College, our discipline, and our doctrinal soundness. Consequently we are agreed, Synod should be composed of the most capable and the best qualified men of every Classis. If the work of our Synods consisted in the main of listening to reports and of approving the same, it would be different. But our Synods are deliberative gatherings at which all the major questions of the Churches are considered and acted upon. This is as it should be. But this also requires our best talents.

. . . .

"We do not even believe that we should urge constant change of delegates to Synod. The ideal would be continuity with change. We should not have exactly the same set of delegates constantly—of course not. That might make for hierarchism, and a rule by a few. But neither should we aim at constant change. Every Synod should really have a large number of men who have been to previous Synods, and who know by experience how matters should be handled, and what the dangers are against which should be guarded. If our Synods are largely composed of those who have not attended the previous Synod or previous Synods perhaps, then our synodical committees, such as the Board of Missions, and the Board of Trustees of Calvin College and Seminary will be much stronger than Synod itself. For the members of these committees are appointed for two years and four years and are often re-elected repeatedly. And it is well. This makes for strength and efficiency. But then we should not aim at appointing new man as delegates to Synod constantly, purposefully passing by well qualified men perchance, simply because they have been to the previous Synod. To follow such a policy would weaken Synod. Comparatively speaking our boards would be much stronger than the body appointing them. And thus by a faulty method of delegation we would be fostering the evil of "boardism."

We also quote the following from the report referred to above:

"It is also well to note what leading men in our mother Churches in Holland have said regarding the matter of synodical delegation. The late Prof. Bouwman of Kampen declared, (**Gereformeerd Kerkrecht**, Vol. II, page 155.) 'It is not desirable to designate these delegates by rotation instead of by balloting. For indeed, not all Ministers and Elders are qualified to consider weighty questions of Church government. This becomes very evident when very involved problems regarding the Confession are to be considered, as was the case at the Synod of Dort. For these reasons it is advisable that the best qualified and most experienced brethren be delegated.'

"And Ds. J. Jansen, another outstanding authority in Church governmental matters has the following to say in regard to this matter: 'Should delegation take place **by balloting** or **by rotation?** From the very outset, free election by ballot was the rule. As a result very often the same individuals were delegated, because they were the most capable. Complaints were sometimes made concerning this fact, for example, at the Synod of 1581, Middelburg, at which Synod the question was asked, whether it would not be well that the same Minister should not be delegated twice in succession, in order that the others might also learn. But the Synod replied that the Consistories, Classes, and Synods should be free to send ' "those whom they deem to be qualified, . . . " ' Ecclesiastical assemblies are no schools of learning and practice but assemblies for government and discipline, at which the strongest, men (beste krachten) are needed. And the danger of hierarchism is not so great that the advantages of a free election should be sacrificed.' " (**Korte Verklaring**, etc., p. 225-6.)

God's Word tells us very clearly that not all office-bearers are talented alike. Cf. Rom. 12:6-8 and I Cor. 12:4-11. The various gifts and qualifications should not be ignored by us as we choose men to represent our Churches at Synod. We must be willing to use the special qualifications which the Spirit has given for special work.

3. Convening of Synod.

Article 50 provides for a convening Church. Each previous Synod designates a Church which is charged to call together the next Synod. This call to Synod is made by the Consistory of the convening Church through the official Church papers, three months before the date Synod is to meet. This Church is also expected to provide all facilities needed for the synodical meetings, to make arrangements for the lodging of delegates, etc. Expenses incurred by the convening Church are paid by Synod.

When special circumstances arise it may be advisable for Synod to meet before the ordinary time, which is the second Wednesday in the month of June. Or it is also possible that circumstances make it advisable for Synod to meet at a later time. General economic distress, pestilence, or war, for instance, may make it advisable for Synod not to meet at the regular time. Under these special circumstances, Article 50, as revised by Synod 1936, provides that Synod may be convened earlier or later than the regular time "if at least a majority of Classes deem it necessary." When at least one half of the total number of Classes desire an earlier meeting of Synod the convening Church, according to the present article, determines in due season when and where Synod is to meet.

4. Procedure at Synod.

Each Synod is called together by the convening Church, the particular Church designated and appointed by the previous Synod, to call the next Synod together and to make all the necessary preparations for it. The regular time for the opening of the sessions of each Synod is 9:30 a.m., on the second Wednesday of June, each year. The minister of the convening Church (its counselor when vacant) acts as president pro-tem until the directors have been chosen. On the evening before Synod begins to meet a Prayer Service is held under the auspices of the Consistory of the convening Church. At this service all the delegates are expected to be present and the president or vice-president of the previous Synod administers the Word and leads in prayer.

Synod of 1934 adopted a revised and elaborated set of "Rules for Synodical Procedure for the Christian Reformed Church." As stands to reason, some rules of procedure are necessary for the orderly and efficient operation of our synodical gatherings. But we do believe that rules of procedure which go into great detail are apt to work harm as as well as good. We feel, for instance, that part VI (Rules of Order) of the Rules for Synodical Procedure is in many instances too involved and too technical. To multiply rules and stipulations for our ecclesiastical gatherings we deem not only needless but also dangerous. At our ecclesiastical gatherings we should by all means conduct our business according to the essentials of Reformed church polity, most of all as these essentials of Reformed church polity are expressed in our Church Order. But for the rest spontaneity and freedom of action should be promoted. Multiplication of detailed rules and regulations for ecclesiastical assemblies have a binding tendency and are apt to turn our gatherings into the direction of mere business meetings, whereas we should far rather promote the larger consideration of the spiritual interests of the Churches. And for the due consideration of the spiritual interests of our Churches we need a certain amount of liberty. Rule upon rule and precept upon precept will have a binding and checking effect upon our Synods or Classes as deliberative gatherings and upon the majority of the delegates to these assemblies. When rules are multiplied, delegates in many instances will hesitate to take the floor for fear of being called to order for transgressing some rule. And let us always remember that there is a distinct difference in character and aim between a meeting of business directors or a gathering of civil legislators and a gathering of Churches. Parliamentary rules in large numbers may be in place in the former, but at our ecclesiastical gatherings they are out of place.

(Synod of 1952 adopted a simplified set of Rules for Synodical Procedure. See the Acts of 1952.)

ARTICLE 51

The Missionary Work of the Church is regulated by the General Synod in a Mission Order.

REGULATION OF MISSION WORK

Originally Article 51 did not concern the work of missions but stipulated that inasmuch as the Churches of the Netherlands—comprising both Belgium and the Netherlands of today—used two different languages, namely French and Dutch; therefore two groups of ecclesiastical gatherings should be maintained. The Dutch speaking Churches held their own Consistory meetings, classical gatherings, and Particular Synod. The French speaking Churches of the Southern Netherlands did likewise. The original Article 51 of the Church Order of Dort was out of date by the space of centuries when in 1914 our Synod accepted a new redaction of the Church Order. Consequently it was eliminated, and in its place the present article regarding mission work was written.

1. The scope and meaning of the phrase: the missionary work of the Church.

This article does not refer to all types of mission work undertaken by our Churches. Our Church Order, true to a fundamental principle of Reformed church polity, leaves as much liberty to the particular Churches as is consistent with the welfare of all the Churches. Thus evangelization work undertaken by any particular Church does not fall under the regulating authority of the major assemblies. Any Church that wishes to carry on gospel work in its own community or nearby communities is at full liberty to do so. The particular Churches have not agreed to carry on this type of mission work in cooperation with the other Churches of the denomination.

Neither does Article 51 refer to Home Missions or Church Extension work. At the time this article was written and adopted, 1914, Home Mission activity was under the care of the various Classes, and Synod of 1914 did not intimate that this arrangement should be changed in view of the adoption of Article 51. Neither has this been contended later on. For practical reasons Synod of 1936 adopted a new Home Mission Order which placed the home mission and church extension work of our Churches under the care and authority of our annual

Synods, but this action was not based upon the provision of Article 51, adopted in 1914.

The term "Missionary Work" in the present article only refers to mission work among pagan peoples, such as the American Indians, the Chinese, etc. The correctness of this contention becomes clear to all when we bear in mind that the article before us is an English translation, approved of by Synod 1920, of the original Dutch article adopted in 1914. The original article reads: "De arbeid der kerkelijke Zending onder de heidenen en Joden wordt door de Generale Synode in eene Zendings orde geregeld." The English translation of this article is not as specific as it should have been. But the Dutch original clearly tells us what type of Mission work is to be regulated by Synod according to this article.

The expression "of the Church" in this article is singular in form but plural in significance. For, as all will grant, the term does not refer to any particular or local Church. Neither does it refer to the Church of Christ as that term is used in Article 1 of this Church Order. It refers to all the Churches of the denomination, thought of as one united whole.

2. The significance of synodical regulation.

Reformed church polity is a well-balanced system of church government. It seeks to do full justice to the inherent rights of the individual Churches, but it also recognizes the need of co-operation and it acknowledges the authority of all the Churches working together through major assemblies.

Essentially every particular Church has the right to carry on mission work among pagan peoples. But pagan peoples are as a rule at a great distance from the Churches and one Church alone simply cannot carry on this all important and beautiful work. The obstacles and requirements are so many that individual Churches must cooperate in order to do anything at all as it ought to be done. Consequently our Churches have agreed that their mission work should be regulated by the synodical gatherings of the Churches. Article 51, let it be clear does not say that only the denomination as such has the inherent right to carry on mission work. For practical reasons Article 51 stipulates that the Churches in general through their Synods will regulate the mission work of the Churches. The Churches together can buy and sell, manage and supervise as no Church alone can do. For the progressive advancement of the work, the systematic occupation of a field, and the sound, Biblical establishment of Churches, denominational regulation is absolutely necessary.

But Article 51 does not nullify the rights and duties of particular Churches. Neither does it nullify what has been clearly stated and regulated in other articles of the Church Order. Thus, for example, Article 4 and 5 clearly state that the calling to the ministry pertains to the particular or local Churches. The right to call and ordain men to the ministry is nowhere attributed to the major assemblies by the Church Order. Consequently, no major assembly should call a man to the ministry. And if, by common agreement, a Classis or Synod designates a Candidate or Minister for any particular work of the Gospel ministry, then the actual call should proceed from a particular Church. And the relationship between the calling Church and the Minister concerned, in case he accepts the call, should be more than merely "official." We should not merely seek to satisfy "the letter of the law." The relationship between congregation and Minister should ever be real, vital, and active. Sham and mere form in matters spiritual and ecclesiastical are killing.

This latter principle, which we have merely used by way of illustration, received expression repeatedly. So f.i. Synod of 1912 decided that the calling and sending of missionary Ministers is the task of a local Church. If, however the circumstances demand it, the calling and sending is to be done by a combination of Churches in a manner to be determined by these Churches themselves and in compliance with synodical and classical decisions.* Thus also Home Missionaries, under the Home Mission Order of 1936, are selected by Synod, but called by particular Churches.

The revised Mission Order in which the mission work of our Churches is regulated was adopted by the Synod of 1939, and is known as: "**Mission Order** for the **Indian and China Missions** of the Christian Reformed Church."

ARTICLE 52

Inasmuch as different languages are spoken in the Churches, the necessary translations shall be made in the ecclesiastical assemblies, and in the publication of recommendations, instructions and decisions.

DIFFERENT LANGUAGES AND OUR ASSEMBLIES

1. The Dutch original of this article.

In our original Church Order (1618-19) Articles 51 and 52 regulated a situation which arose from the fact that two languages were used in the Churches. Some Churches, especially in what is now S. E. Belgium used the French or Walloon language. The rest, located in present day Netherlands and large sections of northern Belgium, used the Dutch language. These two groups of Churches, one in faith and hope and doctrine and one as to the bloody persecutions experienced in many instances, it was agreed, would meet in separate Consistories, Classes, and Particular Synods. This matter was regulated in Article 51 by the Synod of Dort. But the Walloon Churches requested that close contacts should be maintained and that Ministers and Elders of both groups of Churches, when found in one and the same city, should meet together once a month to help and advise each other. The Synod of Dort made provision for these combined Consistory meetings in Article 52 of the Church Order.

But eventually contact between these two groups of Reformed Churches was lost. Many of the Belgian Churches were utterly destroyed by the fearful persecutions. Articles 51 and 52 were long since obsolete. The Reformed Churches in Holland, in their redaction of the Church Order of 1905, substituted an article regulating the relationship between the Churches of the Netherlands and the Churches consisting of Europeans on the Dutch-East Indies for the antiquated 51st article of the original Church Order. And for the 52nd article these Churches substituted one providing for synodical regulation of the mission work of the Churches among the pagans of the Dutch East Indies.

---

* Schaver's rendering. Cf. Schaver: Chr. Ref. Church Order, 1937, p. 105.

Our Synod of 1914, however, found that a situation corresponding somewhat to the bi-lingual situation of the Dutch and Walloon Churches of former centuries obtained among us. We used both the Dutch and the English languages. Consequently, Article 52 was made to read: "Inasmuch as different languages are spoken in the Churches, the necessary translations shall be made in the ecclesiastical assemblies, and in the publication of recommendations, instructions and decisions."

2. The significance of this present article.

Sooner than the brethren of 1914 could have surmised, this new Article 51 is also fast becoming obsolete. The World War accentuated the use of the English language among us and brought immigration from Holland almost to a complete standstill. Consequently, although many of our people still prefer the Dutch and have real difficulty in understanding the English language when it concerns ecclesiastical and spiritual matters, the numbers of these are fast decreasing. Wherever and whenever it may still be necessary Dutch should be rendered in English or English in Dutch. That is what the Church Order demands. Our people are entitled to this courtesy. And the true welfare of our Churches calls for it.

DOCTRINES, SACRAMENTS AND OTHER CEREMONIES

ARTICLE 53

The Ministers of the Word of God and likewise the Professors of Theology (which also behooves the other Professors and School Teachers) shall subscribe to the Three Formulas of Unity, namely, the Belgic Confession of Faith, the Heidelberg Catechism, and the Cannons of Dordrecht, 1618-'19, and the Ministers of the Word who refuse to do so shall de facto be suspended from their office by the Consistory or Classis until they shall have given a full statement, and if they obstinately persist in refusing, they shall be deposed from their office.

ARTICLE 54

Likewise the Elders and Deacons shall subscribe to the aforesaid Formulas of Unity.

SIGNING OF FORM OF SUBSCRIPTION BY MINISTERS, PROFESSORS, ELDERS, AND DEACONS

With the consideration of these two articles we have reached the third major division of our Church order. Article 1 is introductory. It briefly indicates the purpose and content of the Church Order. Articles 2 to 28 concern the offices. Articles 29 to 52 cover matters regarding ecclesiastical assemblies. Articles 53 to 70 pertain to certain ceremonies; and Articles 71 to 86 concern censure and admonition.

Instead of considering Articles 53 and 54 successively we take them together. The subject matter of these two articles is one and the same. To avoid needless repetition, and in the interest of an orderly consideration of the subject matter, we follow this procedure.

It should not escape our attention that this present section of our Church Order places doctrines before Sacraments and ceremonies. This is logical. No ecclesiastical confederacy, denomination (the Dutch use the descriptive expression "kerkverband") can function properly without agreement regarding doctrines, Sacraments, and liturgical activities and ceremonies. And again, unless there be doctrinal unity first of all, there can be no unity regarding the Sacraments and ceremonies, for these are ordered and maintained by each Church or denomination according to doctrinal conception; that is to say, each Church or denomination maintains the Sacraments and orders its liturgy and ceremonies according to what it believes to be the teachings of the Bible regarding these matters. Consequently our Church Order follows the correct and logical order when in this present division it places the matter of doctrines first.

In connection with this it may be said that doctrinal unity forms the foundation for denominational unity. The confessional writings of our Churches are the very cornerstones of their existence. When Calvin began the work of reformation in Geneva, Switzerland, one of the first things that he did was to draft a Confession of Faith. When the Reformed Churches of France met in Synod for the first time (1559) they forthwith accepted a common Confession of Faith. When the Reformed Churches of the Southern Netherlands (present day Belgium) met in Synod for the first time (Armentieres, 1563) they likewise instantly accepted a Confession of Faith, namely the one written by Guido De Bres. And when the Churches of the northern provinces met in their first Synod (Emden, 1571), they forthwith made agreement with the Confession adopted obligatory. The Reformed Churches have felt the need and import of doctrinal purity and unity from the very beginning of their existence.

1. Historical origin of these articles.

During the first few decades the Reformed Churches of Holland did not have Forms of Subscription. The Churches simply did not require any one to sign his name in testimony of the fact that he was in full agreement with the Confession of the Churches. But as time progressed some Classes decided that conditions called for a definite declaration of agreement on the part of the office-bearers. It was especially in view of the errors of Arminianism which arose long before these errors were fully considered at the great Synod of Dort that several Classes and Particular Synods decreed that all Ministers and Professors should sign their name to the Catechism and the Confession, in token of their agreement with the same. But as early as 1608 one of the Classes (Alkmaar) judged that the mere signing of one's name to Catechism and Confession was insufficient. This Classis drafted a Form which contained a declaration of full agreement with the Catechism and the Confession and a promise that the subscriber would maintain the doctrines therein contained and that he openly rejected all doctrines opposed to the Catechism and the Confession. Other Classes and Particular Synods modeled Forms of Subscription after this original one of Classis Alkmaar. Finally, the Synod of Dort, 1618-19, wrote the Form as it has come down to us almost unchanged. This Synod, as might be expected, required agreement now not only with the Catechism and Confession but also with the doctrinal interpretation and pronouncements as contained in the Five Articles against the Arminians, known as the Canons of Dort.

2. Fourfold significance of the Form of Subscription.

The Form of Subscription as it came to us from the Synod of Dort, 1618-19, and which was not substantially changed by any of our Synods, consists, in the main, of (1) a declaration of agreement; (2) a promise to teach and to defend; (3) a promise to reject and refute all errors; (4) a promise to report doubts or changes of mind, and of subjection to examination for just cause.

First of all the Form of Subscription contains a **declaration of agreement.** "We, the undersigned," so we read ". . . do hereby, sincerely and in good conscience before the Lord, declare by this our subscription that we heartily believe and are persuaded that all the articles and points of doctrine, contained in the Confession and Catechism of the Reformed Churches, together with the explanation of some points of the aforesaid doctrine, made by the National Synod of Dordrecht, 1618-'19, do fully agree with the Word of God."

The Confession here referred to is the Belgic Confession of Faith, written in the main by Guido De Bres in the year 1561. The Catechism is the Heidelberg Catechism, published in the year 1563 by Zacharias Ursinus and Caspar Olevianus. It was written at the request of the Elector, Frederick III of the Palatinate. The latter reference is to the Five Articles or Canons of Dort. This declaration speaks of the "Confession and Catechism of the Reformed Churches." The reference is really to the Reformed Churches of the Netherlands. With these mother Churches of our Churches, this Form originated. To be technically correct the reading here should be "Confession and Catechism of the Christian Reformed Churches." But we are not advocating a change. The significance of this declaration is clear as it reads.

In the next place we read: "We promise therefore diligently to teach and faithfully to defend the aforesaid doctrine, without either directly or indirectly contradicting the same, by our public preaching or writing." The significance of this promise is clear and we pass it by without further comment.

Then follows another promise in the form of a declaration. We read: "We declare, moreover, that we not only reject all errors that militate against this doctrine and particularly those which were condemned by the above mentioned Synod, but that we are disposed to refute and contradict these, and to exert ourselves in keeping the Church free from such errors. And if hereafter any difficulties or different sentiments respecting the aforesaid doctrines should arise in our minds, we promise that we will neither publicly nor privately propose, teach, or defend the same, either by preaching or writing, until we have first revealed such sentiments to the Consistory, Classis or Synod, that the same may be there examined, being ready always cheerfully to submit to the judgment of the Consistory, Classis, or Synod, under the penalty in case of refusal to be, by that very fact, suspended from our office."

Note that the subscriber here promises not only to reject all errors militating against the doctrine of Holy Writ as confessed by the Churches but that he also promises active opposition. One who would merely confess the truth and deny error would not be doing his full duty. Only he does his full duty and is true to his promise who actively opposes erroneous conceptions. Our Form of Subscription expects us to be militant in our Christianity. By signing our names to it we promise to carry on a defensive and an offensive fight for the true doctrine of the Church and the Kingdom.

The phrase, "and to exert ourselves in keeping the Church free from such errors," is our English rendering for the Dutch original, "en helpen weren." In this simple expression the Church is not mentioned. The phrase as we have translated it would seem to refer most naturally to the organized Church or the denomination to which we belong. But in view of the Dutch expression, which covers much more than the limited domain of the organized Church and Churches, it is best to think in this connection of the Church of Christ on earth, the spiritual body of Christ manifesting itself in confession and conduct wherever believers are found. The interpretation would at least harmonize with the wording of the Dutch original of our Form of Subscription.

Note also that one who entertains serious doubts or who experiences a change of mind in regard to any points of doctrine here promises not to advocate these conceptions which are contrary to the accepted confession, but that he will reveal his sentiments to one of our ecclesiastical assemblies. Our Churches do not put their confessional standards on par with the Bible. Our standards are not infallible and unchangeable. But they should be accepted as the truth of God by all office-bearers especially until they have been proven to be in error. They have been found to be a summary of divine revelation by the Churches, under the direction of the Holy Spirit, and no one should set them aside when he entertains serious doubts as to their correctness, but rather in the interest of harmony and unity, and for the sake of the truth of God involved, reveal his doubts to the Churches in order that the Churches may together look into the matter, revising the creeds if need be, or else attempt to convince the erring brother concerning his misinterpretation of God's Word.

Doubts as to the scripturalness of our doctrinal summaries, or convictions as to their unscriptural character on any score may be reported to "the Consistory, Classis, or Synod." One burdened may, therefore, go to his Consistory with his difficulties. Or if he so desires he may go to the Classis to which his Church belongs. Or he may even go directly to Synod to reveal his difficulties. The method of procedure is left to the subscriber. Ordinarily the burdened brother will go to his own Consistory first. But if he so desires he may go directly to the major assemblies.

Furthermore the subscriber promises in this particular declaration that he will cheerfully submit himself to the conclusions of the Consistory, Classis, or Synod. And if he refuses to submit himself to the judgment of these bodies he is by that very fact suspended from office. Formal suspension would have to take place, but by his refusal to submit himself to the judgment of the Churches the brother concerned has virtually suspended himself. Whether or not deposition would follow suspension would depend on the question whether or not the brother concerned persisted in his error or errors.

In the fourth place subscribers to this Form promise: "and further, if at any time the Consistory, Classis, or Synod, upon sufficient grounds of suspicion and to preserve the uniformity and purity of doctrine, may deem it proper to require of us a further explanation of our sentiments respecting any particular article of the Confession of Faith, the Catechism, or the explanation of the National Synod, we do hereby promise to be always willing and ready to comply with such requisition, under the penalty above mentioned, reserving for ourselves, however, the right of appeal in case we should believe ourselves aggrieved by the sentence of the Consistory or the Classis; and until a decision is made upon such an appeal, we will acquiesce in the determination and judgment already passed."

As a burdened subscriber can go with his problem to Consistory, Classis, or Synod, so also a Consistory, a Classis, or a Synod may decide to require of a brother falling under their authority a further explanation concerning his sentiments regarding any article of our standards. Action of this kind may be taken by a Classis or a Synod as well as by a Consistory. The major assemblies need not wait for minor assemblies. As intimated above and as stands to reason, however, a Consistory can only require a further explanation of this kind from those office-bearers which are members of its body. And a Classis can only take action of this kind regarding office-bearers who belong to one of the Churches of Classis.

Requisitions of this kind may be made only "upon sufficient grounds of suspicion." Whether "sufficient grounds of suspicion" are present or not is decided upon by the assembly in question, not by the brother whose views are being questioned.

The explanation which any assembly may require must concern his interpretation or sentiment regarding any article or articles of our confessional writings. In other words, no assembly has the right to call a brother "on the carpet" and to require of him that he answer questions addressed to him at random. The doctrinal standards adopted are our confessions. Matters not included in these writings are left to the judgment of every believer. The basis for any examination of this kind is therefore always our confessional writings. And these not merely in general. The examination must concern itself with definite articles of our standards. This provision is altogether just and constitutes a safeguard against heresy hunting and abuse.

But in this fourth section of the Form of Subscription the subscriber also promises to comply with the requisition of his Consistory, Classis, or Synod. If not withstanding this solemn promise any subscriber at any time refuses to answer a summons, he thereby suspends himself from office, and the assembly concerned will so declare.

If the brother in question feels himself aggrieved by the sentence of his Consistory or Classis, he has the right of appeal, but he promises to abide by the decision of the assembly concerned in the meantime. That is to say, for example, a suspended Minister must recognize the fact of his suspension and not continue to preach, etc. A suspended party must await the outcome of his appeal and he may not ignore his suspension. All the privileges of office are held in abeyance as long as an office-bearer is under suspension. Whether deposition will follow depends on the question whether or not the suspension in question is upheld by the body appealed to, or whether or not this guilty brother clings to his errors in spite of the admonitions extended.

According to the Form before us, an aggrieved party may appeal from Consistory to Classis, or from Classis to Synod. Might he also appeal from one Synod to the next? Yes, although indefinite appeal from Synod to Synod is out of order. An appeal from the sentencing Synod to the next should be enough.

3. Scope of the Form of Subscription.

From the introductory statement of our Form of Subscription it becomes clear that professors, Ministers, Elders, and Deacons are required to sign this Form. We read: "We, the undersigned, Professors of the Christian Reformed Church, Ministers of the Gospel, Elders and Deacons of the Christian Reformed congregation of . . . ." Articles 53 and 54, now under consideration, mention the same office-bearers. The Form merely mentions professors, but Article 53 specifies: "Professors of Theology." The professors of our Calvin College are not covered by the phrase, "Professors of the Christian Reformed Church," of the Form of Subscription. Article 53 of the Church Order makes this clear. Moreover, the Form of Subscription presupposes throughout that those who subscribe to it are office-bearers. It speaks of suspension from office. But our college professors are not office-bearers, at least not by virtue of their professorship, although they may happen to be Ministers, Elders or Deacons of the Church to which they belong.

The Reformed Churches of Holland have three different forms of subscription. They all date back to years prior to the great Synod of Dort, although they were all revised and approved by this Synod. The first of these forms is for Ministers of the Gospel; the second for Professors of Theology; the third for Rectors and Schoolmasters. The Holland Churches do not have a general Form for Elders and Deacons, although Article 54 of the present Dutch Church Order requires that these office-bearers subscribe to the three Forms of Unity, just as our 54th Article requires such. This matter is left to the Classes in Holland. The Classes can use the Forms adopted for Ministers of the Gospel with some minor adaptations, or they may draw up a special form of subscription as has been done by some

Classes in years of yore. (Cf. Acts, Particular Synod of Zeeland, 1610, and Acts, Particular Synod of South Holland, 1622.) Our Form of Subscription has been written in such a way that all the office-bearers mentioned in Articles 53 and 54 of the Church Order can sign it. This unification makes for simplicity and convenience, but it does not in every instance make for clarity and co-ordination. For example, from a mere reading of our Form of Subscription one not fully informed might be led to think that our Elders and Deacons are permitted to preach, for Elders and Deacons, as well as Ministers and professors of theology, promise in our Form not to preach things contrary to the three Forms of Unity.

Article 54 of the Church Order of the Reformed Churches of Holland also provides that those who are declared Candidates by the Classes, shall sign their names to the Standards of the Churches. This is no doubt a good rule. As a matter of safety it might be well that we would require of all those who are licensed to exhort in our Churches that they first sign an appropriate form of subscription.

Candidates for the ministry who have accepted a call and have passed their final or decisive examination, their classical examination of admittance to the ministry, should sign the Form of Subscription at the time of their examination before receiving their document of admittance.

It is very necessary that we take this signing of the Form of Subscription very seriously. It should never become a mere form, a traditional performance. And the subscriber should know what he is signing. Those, for example, who are chosen to office for the first time should be notified ahead of time that they will be expected to sign this document in due season, informing them that if they have any scruples, after carefully reading the Form, that then it is their duty to notify the Consistory of their difficulty before their ordination or installation takes place.

In times of laxity and doctrinal indifference or in days when undercurrents of error seem to be present, the Churches should be very careful not to revise their Form of Subscription to their own hurt. A classic example of the need of vigilance on this score is the change which was introduced into the Form of Subscription by the Churches of Holland in 1816. A slight change was introduced into the old form of subscription drafted by the great Synod of Dort (1618-19). According to the old form prospective Ministers by signing declared that they believed that the Three Forms of Unity agreed altogether with the Word of God. According to the new reading of 1816, these prospective Ministers declared that they accepted the doctrines contained in the Three Forms of Unity, which agreed with the holy Word of God. The phrase in question was made to read: ". . . de leer, welke **overeenkomstig** Gods heilig Woord in de aangenomen Formulieren van Eenigheid is vervat, ter goeder trouw aan te nemen en hartelyk te gelooven."

This sounds good enough but it left a loop-hole. The question soon arose whether the "overeenkomstig" had the significance of **omdat**, (quia) "because," or **voor zoover** (quatenus) "in as far." Those who wanted to be loyal to the Word of God and Reformed faith held that the latter interpretation was possible and also intended by the leaders of the revision group. Some denied this charge vigorously. But in 1835 one of their leaders admitted that the change had been sponsored and made so that a candidate could sign the Form of Subscription even if he did not fully agree with the Standards of the

Churches.* He who signs this document in Holland today merely declares that he will be loyal to the Three Forms of Unity in as far as these agree with the Word of God. The result is that even Unitarians and Communists can become Ministers of the Hervormde Kerk in the Netherlands. The Gereformeerde Kerken van Nederland, the purified and reorganized Reformed Churches of Holland, as might be expected, immediately readopted the unequivocal Form of Subscription of Dort, 1618-19. Heretics cannot consistently sign this Form.

Article 53 contains the following parenthetic statements: "(which also behooves the other Professors and School Teachers)."

Originally this statement referred to non-theological professors teaching in various schools and universities in the Netherlands, and to all school masters, teaching and training the children in various local schools throughout the land. These schools were owned by the government, but managed and supervised by the Churches. (See our discussion of Article 21.)

This parenthetic statement was purposely retained in our Church Order. Our Churches by this statement commit themselves in favor of requiring all those that teach in our schools, Christian Day Schools, Christian High Schools, and our colleges or college, to sign a Form of Subscription. We do not know in how far this provision of the Church Order is practiced, but none will deny that all those that receive the privilege of teaching the youth of our Churches should be in hearty accord with the doctrine of our Churches and that this practice should be revived in as far as it has not been maintained.

ARTICLE 55

To ward off false doctrines and errors that multiply exceedingly through heretical writings, the Ministers and Elders shall use the means of teaching, of refutation, or warning, and of admonition, as well as in the Ministry of the Word as in Christian teaching and family-visiting.

HERETICAL WRITINGS

Originally this 55th article concerned the censure of books. The article provided that no one, being of the Reformed religion, should undertake to publish a book or a pamphlet dealing with a religious matter unless he had first received permission and approval of the Ministers of his Classes, or of the Ministers of his Particular Synod, or of the theological professors. These professors could not give approval without the foreknowledge of the Classis in which they resided. First of all we shall therefore say a few words regarding the censure of books as originally provided for in this article. Next we shall consider the article as it now reads.

1. The censure of books.

The censuring of writings and books and particularly the prohibition of the distribution of certain writings, is of old standing. The Roman government forbade the distribution of certain writings which it had deemed harmful. And when Constantine the Great became an

---

* **Christlyke Encyclopaedia** IV, p. 653.

adherent and defender of Christianity he promulgated strong edicts against anti-Christian writings. Other Emperors did the same.* Throughout the middle ages the Church of Rome maintained an authoritative position regarding this matter. Thus in 1415 Johannes Huss, the Bohemian forerunner to the Reformation and martyr for the cause of Christ, was condemned to die and his books were forbidden and ordered to be burned. Especially when the discovery of the printing press made the multiplication of books so much easier, did Rome seek to exercise jurisdiction on this point.

When the Reformers began to write and when printing presses everywhere began to publish the writings of the Reformation leaders and their translations of the Bible into the language of the people, Rome became very active in its censuring of these productions. It soon published its "Index", a list of forbidden books. It martyred and persecuted those who helped to publish and to distribute this forbidden literature.

When the Reformation gained headway and power the Churches naturally faced the problem regarding erroneous and heretical writings. They faced the question of a free or fully-controlled press. The Reformed Churches of Holland, true to the ancient example and the age-old practice of Rome and the general conceptions of their day, decided that no one of the Reformed Churches should write and publish merely upon his own initiative and according to his own mind. They decided that none should publish a book or writing without the approval of the Ministers of his Classis or Particular Synod or the professors of theology. In fact, the first Synod (Emden, 1571) ruled that no one regardless of the fact whether he belonged to one of the Reformed Churches or not, should be permitted to publish a book without proper authorization. Other Synods confirmed this same general ruling. The Churches seemingly hoped that the government would become wholly Reformed and would eventually take the same stand. This hope was never fully realized, and in 1586 the restriction of Article 55 was limited to those who professed to be Reformed and over whom the Churches therefore had supervision and control. The great Synod of Dort wrote the 55th article as we have indicated it in the introductory statement to our comments on this article.

But in actual practice Article 55 had little significance. It was soon found that the censuring of books, in the sense of permitting none but approved books to be printed and circulated, was impracticable. In the first place, the government did not cooperate sufficiently. In fact, in December, 1618, the government made a law of its own which was less drastic than what the Churches desired. Furthermore, the major assemblies are not always in session and could not possibly pass on all the writings submitted directly. They would have to appoint committees and thus foster hierarchism. Again, non-Reformed writers were not bound, whereas Reformed writers were bound. They could not publish without proper approval. This worked as an undesirable check upon the initiative of Reformed writers. And again, the rigid maintenance of Article 55 was after all no guarantee that no objectionable books would ever be published. Thus Fred. Van Leenhof published his **Heaven on Earth** in 1703 with proper approval, while the Churches had to depose him in 1708 because of heresies advocated in said book. On the other hand, worthy books were sometimes rejected and kept off the press, because they did not meet with the approval of the men examining them. Moreover, as both Bouw-

---

* Bouwman: **Ger. Kerkrecht,** II, 1934, p. 587.

man and Jansen say, "Stolen waters are sweet, and bread eaten in secret is pleasant." (Prov. 9:17.) Official disapproval of books often aroused curiosity and whetted the appetite of the public so that refusal of approval often made good advertisement and promoted the reading of such publications if they were published in spite of the opinion of those who reviewed the book.*

In view of the situation briefly indicated above the Synod of Utrecht, Netherlands, 1905, re-wrote Article 55 and rendered it as it now reads. Our Synod of 1914 adopted this reading.

2. The present reading and provisions of Article 55.

Article 55 of our Church Order as it now reads, clearly indicates that we believe that erroneous doctrines and presentations advocated in undesirable books and writings should be counteracted, not by prohibitions, but by teachings, refutations, warnings and admonitions. Moral and spiritual persuasions we now prefer above legalistic suppressions.

The first means of counteracting the influence exerted by dangerous reading material, mentioned in the article is the Ministry of the Word. Jansen says: "By elken tekst moet de waarheid zuiver **verkondigd**, de dwaling **weerlegd**, voor ketterijen **gewaarschuwd** en tot getrouwheid **vermaand** worden." With each text the truth must be **proclaimed** in its purity, errors must be **refuted**, heresies must be **warned** against, and there must be an **admonition** to loyalty. No doubt there is room and call for these four elements in the preaching of the Word, again and again. Our day and age calls for positive instruction in the truth of God. But our people should also have their attention called to erroneous conceptions which run counter to God's truth and which undermine God's truth, and very often in a very subtle fashion. Error must be unmasked and clearly indicated. Positive exposition of God's Word comes first and it should ever occupy the chief places in our sermons. But opposition to error and misconception may not be lacking. This will include serious warning and earnest admonition. Especially do our young people need all these elements mentioned in Article 55. They are entitled to definite, clear-cut messages which will help them against numberless dangers by which they are constantly surrounded.

The Christian teaching mentioned in this article refers to the Catechism class, inasmuch as the Catechism class is the regular means of instruction in our Churches. But our Sunday Schools and our Christian Schools and Colleges also have a very definite task here. Our schools have wonderful opportunities to render a noble service to our youth on this score.

And when the Consistory calls on the families of its Church year by year to consider the spiritual condition and welfare of the family, then the office-bearers also have a very choice opportunity to carry out the provisions of this article. Let the visitors not forget their charge on this point. Let them faithfully warn against the pernicious influence of undesirable literature and let them urge the reading of wholesome material, the Church papers, and other Reformed periodicals, as well as trustworthy books.

If a member of one of our Churches would write and distribute a heretical book, would he become justly subject to discipline? He certainly would. And although it is hard to lay down iron-bound

---

* For a fuller discussion of this matter cf. Bouwman, "De Boekencensuur," **Ger. Kerkr.**, II, pp. 584-593.

rules, if a member of our Churches should print and sell literature which is heretical and anti-Biblical he would also become the object of discipline. No one may wilfully and consciously help to break down the Kingdom of God. No one may help to poison the minds of our youth. He who does, though it be to him merely a business proposition, is sinning and should be admonished and dealt with accordingly.

The book reviews which our trustworthy papers supply can also render a great service in this field.

ARTICLE 56

The Covenant of God shall be sealed unto the children of Christians by Baptism, as soon as the administration thereof is feasible, in the public assembly when the Word of God is preached.

BAPTISM OF CHILDREN

The following nine articles concern the administration of the Sacraments.* Articles 56 to 60 regulate the administration of Baptism, and Articles 61 to 64 the administration of the Lord's Supper. The following matters regarding Baptism are covered in the next five articles: Article 56: Baptism of Children; Article 57: Baptismal Sponsors; Article 58: Form of Baptism; Article 59: Baptism of Adults; Article 60: Baptismal Records. The present article therefore regulates the matter of infant baptism.

1. Which children are to be baptized?

Article 56 stipulates that children of Christians shall be baptized. Originally the Wezelian Convention (1568) merely spoke of baptism that should be administered "to the children." This wording was also adopted by the Particular Synod of Dort, 1574. But these gatherings did not mean to say that all children should be baptized regardless of their parentage and the faith of their parents. The Synod of Dort, 1578, made this clear by adopting the following wording: "to the children of Christians." The Synod of Middelburg further amended the designation by rendering the phrase: "to the children of baptized Christians." But the Synod of 's Gravenhage, 1586, again dropped the adjective "baptized", perhaps because all who were Christians were naturally also baptized. Today we still have the indication, "unto the children of Christians," as it was already accepted in 1578.**

The expression, "unto the children of Christians" is indeed rather broad. But the Church Order should not go into all kinds of details. A Church Order should indicate leading principles. Moreover, the brevity of the stipulation also harmonizes with the brevity of the heading of our **Form for the Baptism of Infants.**

Children of Christians are children of the covenant and as such

---

* We are capitalizing the words Sacrament, Baptism and the Lord's Supper, for the following reasons: 1. The Church Order does so. 2. Usage favors the capitalization of the term, Lord's Supper. Consistancy requires that Baptism and Sacrament be capitalized likewise. 3. The great significance of the Sacraments warrants their capitalization.

** cf. Jansen: **Korte Verklaring**, etc., 1923, p. 247; or **Kerkelijk Handboekje**, Zalsman, 1882.

are included in the Church of God. (Gen. 3:15; 17:7; Acts 2:39; Eph. 6:1; I Cor. 7:14b; Mark 10:14b; I Joh. 2:13c.)

The general principle having been established a number of practical questions soon presented themselves. From the very outset it became the rule to baptize only children of parents who belonged to the Reformed Churches. But some parents, who were in sympathy with the Reformation and at heart at odds with the Roman Church, nevertheless failed to make a final break with Rome because they lacked the courage of faith and clarity of conviction. Officially they were still Roman Catholics. Sometimes such parents requested a Reformed Church to baptize their child. The first Synod (Emden, 1571) replied to a question regarding such cases by referring to the opinion of the theologians of Geneva, Ministers and professors. The rule should be, so Beza had written, that only children of Church members should receive baptism. But in abnormal times, as when the Church was in process of being reorganized, or when severe persecutions were raging, exceptions to this rule might be made. Children of weak and fearful parents might be baptized under these circumstances, though not without certain stipulations and promises. But as will be realized, that ruling was by way of concession for the period of transition.

Should children of parents who are under discipline be baptized? Such children are entitled to baptism because such parents are still within the Church. However, such parents, since their very Christianity is in question, are not in position to promise before God and the Church that they will train their children in harmony with the doctrine of God's Word. In other words, such parents under censure are not in position to take upon themselves the baptismal vows. They cannot pledge to give their child a training which harmonizes with the significance of baptism. Consequently the baptism of children of such parents is postponed until the censure can be lifted. Unless said parents should secure the grandparents or other close relatives or friends to act as sponsors. The child of censured parents is assumed to be a child of the covenant and therefore entitled to Baptism. But Baptism without being interpreted and understood becomes an empty form. Yet this Sacrament is too sacred to be reduced to an empty form. Consequently the Church and its office-bearers demand that the parents shall be qualified to explain to the child, as it grows up, the meaning of its Baptism, and that these parents shall also promise to do so. Now if for any reason parents of a child entitled to Baptism are disqualified to take upon themselves these solemn promises, then, if the child is to be baptized, witnesses must be found who promise to take the place of the parents to the best of their ability. If such sponsors cannot be secured the child should not be baptized until he is old enough to judge for himself, and to request Baptism upon profession of faith. If in any cases the parents are opposed to the Baptism of their child, and if it becomes clear that the proposed sponsors will in all likelihood not be able to instruct the child properly because of the ill-will of the parents, then again matters should not be forced or urged but Baptism should wait. It goes without saying that if only one of the parents is under censure the other may proceed with the Baptism of the child. Children born to excommunicated parents are not entitled to Baptism. Such parents can not be regarded as members of God's covenant and of the Church of Christ. This does not mean that their children may not be in the covenant. God often restores children or children's children of covenant-breakers unto Himself. But inasmuch as we have no definite assurance in God's Word regarding children of such unfaithful and unbelieving parents, and inasmuch as the instruction of such children by competent sponsors would be much hampered at best, it is better not to baptize children born to excommunicated parents. However, if children of unfaithful, unbelieving or ex-communicated parents make their permanent homes, say with their God-fearing grandparents who shall be able to explain the meaning of Baptism to them and who shall be in position to give them a good Christian training, then such children need not be barred from Baptism; the parties concerned being willing to serve as sponsors, taking upon them the baptismal vows.

Children of ex-communicated parents who have received Baptism before their parents' ex-communication are to be instructed by Christian relatives and by the Church, and their Baptism, given to them in God's providence, is not to be held null and void until such children, when come to years of discretion, show by word and deed that they have no part in the covenant of God and His Church. If only one of the parents is excommunicated the other has the right to have children baptized. This is sufficiently clear from I Cor. 7:14. "For the unbelieving husband is sanctified in the wife, and the unbelieving wife is sanctified in the brother: else were your children unclean; but now are they holy."

Another question which often arose is this: May illegitimate children, children born out of wedlock, be baptized? Supposing an unmarried woman gives birth to a child whose father is a non-Christian, may the mother of said child have it baptized? If she, being a professing member of the Church, repents sincerely of her sin, then she may have her child baptized. The child is a covenant child and the mother is competent to assume the baptismal promises. If the mother is a member-by-Baptism only, then she should first make profession of faith and confession of her specific sin. If she reveals true repentance concerning her special transgression, but if her faith be not yet clear enough for her to make profession of faith, then her repentance regarding her sin against the Seventh Commandment should be announced to the Church, and competent sponsors, say the grandparents, should assume the baptismal promises for her. If an illegitimate parent reveals no repentance of the sin committed and should even live a life of indifference and Godlessness, but place the child under the control of God-fearing relatives, then these relatives may apply for Baptism and act as sponsors at the time of Baptism.* The child belongs to the seed of the covenant and the relatives are competent to assume the baptismal vows.

May adopted children be baptized? If adopted children are of believing parentage the answer is yes. And the Reformed Churches have always been lenient regarding this question. If it can be established that the child concerned is of covenant lineage, though this lineage goes back three or more generations, then, as a rule, Baptism has been permitted. But regarding the Baptism of children legally adopted by believing parents but born of pagans or unbelievers, there has been a difference of opinion. The great Synod of Dort already faced this question. Specifically the question faced was this: Whether children born of pagan parents (in East India, the Dutch possessions) but adopted to be members of the household of believers, might receive Christian Baptism. The Synod judged that these children should not be baptized until they in due season should make profession of faith. Prof. Wm. Heyns, in his **Handbook for Elders**

---

* This position is also that of Voetius **(Pol. Eccl., 1:653)** cf. Jansen: **Korte Verklaring**, etc., p. 250.

and Deacons judges that those who do not favor the Baptism of adopted children of non-Christian birth cannot appeal to the Synod of Dort. Says he: "It (the question) came from East India and concerned such children of heathen natives as had been received usually after they had reached a certain age, in Christian families, but, as was expressly stated, received in such a manner that they were not legally adopted, that they were members of the family as slaves, not as children, and that occasionally they were removed again from these families and fell back among the heathen." * Prof. Heyns bases this statement upon information given to the Synod of Dort by the delegates from North Holland in the 18th session of Synod. But seemingly Prof. Heyns has overlooked the exact wording of the decision of the Synod regarding this matter, taken in the 19th session. First the Synod decided unanimously that those who were old enough to receive some instruction should not be baptized until they had made profession of their faith. Then we read: "Concerning children of pagans which, because of their youth, or because they cannot understand the language (of the Dutch in East Indian homes), have not been able to receive instruction from the Christians, **although they may have been incorporated into the homes of Christians by adoption,** it was also judged by majority vote that these should not be baptized before they have come to such years that they can be instructed in the first principles of the Christian Religion according to the measure of their understanding, and after such has also actually taken place." ** (Translation and bold face ours. Authors.) To be sure, the Synod of Dort declared itself against the Baptism of **adopted children** of non-Christian origin.

In the year 1910 our own Synod left the matter of Baptism or non-Baptism of adopted children of non-Christian parentage to the judgment of each Consistory. ***

The Synod 1930 answered the question, "whether children who were not born of believing parents, but who were adopted by believers, may be baptized," in the affirmative.

Against decisions of 1930 a number of protests appeared at the Synod of 1932. This Synod appointed a strong Committee to reconsider this whole matter thoroughly. This Committee reported four years later, in 1936. The report of this Committee was not by any means unanimous. It was three-fold. Four members delivered a majority report. Three members a minority report. And two members offered a third report. These reports which discuss the problems involved very thoroughly may all be found in the Agenda for Synod 1936, Part I. After some consideration Synod of 1936 decided: "That there is not sufficient ground to reverse the decision of the Synod of 1930 upholding the permissibility of the baptism of children born outside of the covenant circle and adopted by believing parents."

Furthermore this Synod decided: "That this 1930 decision in no way justifies the molestation of anyone who, whether as church member or in the specific capacity of office-bearer, may have conscientious scruples against the administration of the Sacrament of baptism to such children."***

It appears to us that one's position on this question regarding the permissibility or non-permissibility of the Baptism of adopted children

* Heyns: Idem, p. 194.

** Acta, ofte Handelingen des Nationalen Synodi tot Dordrecht, Anno 1618, ende 1619. 1621, p. 61.

*** cf. Acts, 1910, Art. 67.

**** Acts, 1930, pp. 54, 55.

of non-Christian birth, is largely determined by one's covenant view. If one holds that the covenant of grace is essentially only a covenantal form for the promise of salvation for those that believe, then in all likelihood he will favor the Baptism of all adopted children. If, on the other hand, one believes that the covenant of grace is an actual bond or league of life-relationship between God and His people in Christ Jesus as their federal head, then one will in all likelihood judge against the Baptism of adopted children of non-Christian birth.

We may also add that it is our conviction that the language of Article 34 of our Confession, and of Lord's Days 26 and 27 of our Heidelberg Catechism, as well as the language employed in our Form of Baptism, is against the practice of baptizing children of non-Christian birth. These writings all assume that the subject of Baptism is "in Christ", as His people's redeemer and second Adam. We find no warrant in Scripture for assuming that children born of unbelieving, Godless parents are "in Christ", simply because they are legally adopted by believing parents. According to our standards and our Form of Baptism, Baptism is not merely a sign and a seal upon a conditional promise of God, **but a sign and a seal of saving grace in Christ.** Those who are baptized, to say no more, are assumed to be federally, legally in Christ our second Adam. (Note well, our standards and Forms do not contend that every child born of believing parents is **actually** federally in Christ for there are exceptions to every rule, and far less that every child is actually, **subjectively** in possession of all the benefits of Christ's obedience and death; regeneration, etc.)

Upon what basis does the meaningful assumption referred to above rest? Upon the assurances of God regarding the (natural) children of believers. It cannot be assumed that children of pagans and non-Christians are (federally, representatively, covenantally) in Christ until they by their confession and walk of life manifest themselves as Christians. Consequently the present writers believe it is better to postpone the Baptism of adopted children in question until they manifest themselves as Christians. But we would urge all office-bearers to study the reports delivered at the Synod of 1936 and then let each come to a conscientious decision as to what he believes to be proper. The injunction of God to Abraham (Gen. 17) to circumcise also the children of his slaves, is a strong argument in favor of the administration of Baptism to the children in question. But those who do not favor the Baptism of these children reply and assume with the Synod of Dort that Abraham did not circumcise all children of pagans, but only those whose parents had been circumcised and taught to believe on the true God.

It may also be said that the recent or present day leaders of the Reformed Churches of the Netherlands are, as far as we know, all opposed to the practice of baptizing children of non-Christian parentage, though adopted into Christian homes.* This is most likely due to the fact that the question concerning the Baptism of adopted children, born of Godless parents, is at heart a question regarding the covenant. The stricter covenant conception, which holds that the covenant is in essence a bond of life-relationship between God and His people in Christ Jesus, is the prevalent conception in the Netherland Churches of our forebears.

Finally the question presents itself whether or not children of

---

* cf. Bouwman: **Ger. Kerkrecht,** II, 1934, pp. 284-300. In these pages the author gives lengthy consideration to our decision of 1930.

members-by-Baptism may be baptized. Children of such parents are entitled to Baptism but their own parents are not in position to take upon themselves the baptismal vows. Consequently the only way in which these children can be baptized is through the acceptance of competent sponsors of whom we have already spoken in the discussion of this article, and of whom we shall speak again in the consideration of Article 57.

2. By whom Baptism is to be administered.

In the final analysis, Christ Himself is the administrator of baptism. John said to Him, "I have need to be baptized of Thee." (Matt. 3:14.) We also read that Jesus tarried in the land of Judea and baptized. (John 3:22.) And, "Jesus was making and baptizing more disciples than John." (John 4:1.) But the next verse tells us plainly that Jesus delegated the actual administration of Baptism to His disciples, for we read: "although Jesus himself baptized not, but His disciples." (John 4:2.) Later on the Apostles were charged with this task (Matt. 28:19; Mark 16:15, 16; Acts 2:38).

The preaching of the Word and the administration of the Sacraments logically belong together. The Sacraments are seals upon the testimony of the Word. For this reason Scripture unites the two, and from the very beginning of Christian Church history they have been administered by the same class of office-bearers. The Apostles preached and baptized. Their logical and God-ordained successors as preachers are the Ministers of the Gospel. Consequently the Ministers of the Gospel and they only are the rightful administrators of Baptism today. For this reason Article 3 of this Church Order reads: "No one, though he be a Professor of Theology, Elder or Deacon, shall be permitted to enter upon the Ministry of the Word and the Sacraments without having been lawfully called thereunto." And Article 30 of our Confession declares that, "there must be Ministers or pastors to preach the Word of God and to administer the Sacraments."

Baptism administered by private parties has never been held valid, even though such parties should have acted upon instructions given by a Consistory, inasmuch as private parties are not called and ordained for this task. Neither was Baptism administered during the early years of the Reformation by assistants to the Ministers, such as catechetical instructors, sick-visitors, etc., held valid. However, the Synod of Dort, 1578, held that if an Elder, upon the authority of a Consistory or Church, had administered Baptism, that then such a Baptism was not to be repeated, inasmuch as such an Elder in a way had a call for this administration. But the Synod also decided that this practice should not be followed by other Churches or Consistories.

For reasons already indicated, students and Candidates are not permitted to Baptize, nor such as have entered upon a secular vocation and who are therefore no longer in the ministry.

The Reformation Churches soon faced the question of the validity of Baptism administered in the Roman Church. Synod of Emden, 1571, held that those who had been regularly baptized in the Roman Church did not have to be baptized once again, fearing that the Roman Baptism was of no value. But our fathers doubtlessly felt that although the Roman Church was filled with error, that yet it was a Church of Christ in essence, and that therefore its Baptisms were valid. If therefore Baptism was administered by an authorized priest, with water and in the name of the Triune God, then re-Baptism did not take place. Even the Baptism of "vagabond priests," constantly traveling from place to place, was held to be valid (Synod of

Middelburg, 1581) inasmuch as these were officially called. But the Baptism of monks was considered to be invalid for they have no charge to Baptize. Even "emergency Baptisms" administered by midwives, doctors, etc., were usually held to be valid because the Roman Church charges individuals to Baptize a child which is about to die. Whether the Reformation Churches were justified in acknowledging even these latter classes of Baptisms is indeed a question.

The Baptism of anabaptists was recognized, if Baptism had taken place in the name of the Triune God. This was not always the case, because some anabaptists entertained erroneous conceptions regarding the doctrine of the trinity. However, Baptism administered by the Socinians was rejected because they had broken with the essence of Christianity. We assume the same attitude toward the Baptism administered by Unitarians, Mormons, etc., inasmuch as these have broken with the Christian religion.

The early Reformed Churches also faced the question, what should be done by parents living in parts where there was no Reformed Church? Some had to flee to Germany during the days of persecution and lived for a time among the Lutherans. What of children born to these people? Should they remain unbaptized? The Reformed people residing at Frankfort also faced this question because the government of Frankfort forbade the Reformed religion in 1562. Many Reformed theologians held that none of these parents should turn to the Roman Church for Baptism but that the Lutheran Church should be asked to baptize their children, provided the Ministers were willing to omit certain Lutheran ceremonies such as exorcisms (banishing of evil spirits), etc. Calvin also judged that if Reformed parents found it impossible to move within the pale of a Reformed Church that then they should ask the Lutheran Church to baptize, with the understanding, however, that the Roman remnants of a superstitious character would be omitted, and that the parents retain their Reformed convictions and that the child would be reared in the Reformed faith.*

In general it may be said that the Reformed Churches have always recognized the validity of Baptisms administered by other groups if Baptism was administered 1) according to the institution of Christ (the rightful element, water, not wanting), 2) in a community or association of believers confessing the Trinity, which association is therefore in principle a Church of Christ, 3) by one duly authorized to administer this Sacrament by a Church or Christian association.

3. When Baptism should be administered.

When, or, how soon after birth should a child be baptized? Our Church Order, in the present article, answers: "as soon as the administration thereof is feasible." Baptism should take place as soon as possible. Individuals and families, concerning whose baptism Holy Writ makes mention, received this Sacrament as soon as possible, right after their confession of faith in Christ. (Acts 2:41; 16:14, 15; 16:33.)

Respect for and appreciation of the significance of Baptism should also tell us that this blessed Sacrament should be administered to our children as soon as possible. Baptism is a sign and seal of the washing away of the sins of our children. It is indeed a token of great value and honor. Now if the President of the United States wanted to give your child a token of great value and honor, you would not

* Jansen: **Korte Verklaring**, etc., 1923, p. 254.

let days and weeks pass by needlessly before claiming said token. You would call for the token at the appointed place at your earliest convenience.

The Roman Catholic Church maintains what the Dutch call "vroeg-doop," early Baptism. That is to say, in the Roman Church children were baptized as soon as possible in the literal sense, before the mother's restoration, the child being in some cases but one or two days old. This practice of Rome rests on her belief that Baptism imparts regeneration, and that if an infant dies unbaptized it cannot be saved. Its soul, if it dies prior to Baptism, goes neither to heaven nor hell, but to a special place indicated by the Latin term "limbus infantum." In this abode of infants the souls of these children are ever doomed to continue in an intermediate state, experiencing neither joy nor sorrow without ever being able to escape. Small wonder that Rome maintains the custom of baptizing without delay and has also invented emergency Baptisms, sometimes even administered to the child before its birth.

The Reformation Churches also maintained the practice of baptizing their children without delay. At the first service to be held after the birth of the child Baptism would take place. As a rule many Baptisms would take place at the regular week-day services as well as on Sunday. Guido de Bres, chief author of our Confession, so we read, had his first-born baptized the day after its birth. And this practice was not limited to Holland. In the colonial period of our own country, our God-fearing pioneers had the same custom. Benj. Franklin, for example, was baptized on the very first Sunday after his birth.

Needless to say the Reformation Churches practiced baptism without delay for entirely different reasons than did the Roman Church. The Reformed Churches in Holland today to a large extent favor and practice "vroeg-doop." The arguments in favor of this practice are, in the main, the following: Children of believers are born in the covenant, and should, therefore, receive the token of the covenant as soon as possible. Furthermore, the children of Israel had to wait until the 8th day before they might receive the sign and seal of the covenant for their children. Seven days, pointing to sin and impurity, had to be fulfilled before circumcision could take place. But for New Testament believers this barricade has been removed. Christ has died and fulfilled also this ceremonial injunction. We need not wait and it would be ingratitude if we should wait. Again it is said, New Testament examples of Baptisms teach us in every case that those who were entitled to Baptism were baptized without delay.

In our Christian Reformed Churches it has become the general custom to wait with Baptism until the mother is restored so that she together with the father may present the child for Baptism. Arguments used to defend this custom are as follows: The covenant is not established by Baptism, and therefore its administration need not be rushed; the child is a covenant child, apart from Baptism. Furthermore, the mother has a most vital part in bringing the child into being and therefore she should not be excluded from the great privilege of presenting the child for which she suffered and sacrified so much for Baptism together with the father. It is true that the father is the head of the family and that he represents the mother at the time of the child's Baptism, whether the mother be present or absent, yet it should not be overlooked that the mother has a personal interest and responsibility as well as a communal responsibility as wife. Moreover, it is said, the mother will have a very vital part in rearing the child, and therefore if possible, she should personally pledge to train the child in the aforesaid doctrine, before God and His Church. It is also agreed that inasmuch as the Bible gives us no injunction on this score, the Churches are not bound to any definite time and parents are therefore free to wait.

Personally we feel that it is well for both husband and wife, father and mother, to present their child for Baptism. We do not believe that a Scriptural principle is being violated when a father determines to wait for the mother's restoration. But we would warn against undue delay. Churches all around us have fallen into the evil habit of postponing the Baptism of infants for weeks and months. Many wait for Easter day. This is unBiblical. This is a custom born of shallowness, externalism, and ingratitude. Let us baptize "as soon as feasible." Let us not wait for better clothes, relatives, the home Minister, other fathers and mothers, etc. But let us baptize just as soon as the mother can be present in God's house. And if special circumstances compel her to remain at home beyond the ordinary number of days, then let the father proceed to have the child baptized without delay. If the blessed significance of Baptism may stand out prominently in our minds and hearts we shall be kept from evils and errors which threaten us also on this score.

The Sacraments are signs and seals of the Word. Logically, therefore, the preaching of the Word should precede the administration of Baptism. For practical reasons, however, we as a rule baptize during the first part of the service and not after the sermon. There is no objection to this since the **Form for the Baptism of Infants** gives a doctrinal exposition of the significance of Baptism.

4. Baptism to be administered "in the public assembly when the Word of God is preached."

Originally some parents were still affected by the erroneous conceptions of Rome regarding Baptism. If a young infant of such parents fell sick soon after birth, before Baptism in the Church service could take place, they might urgently ask to have the child baptized at home. The Wezelian Convention, 1568, advised to grant such requests for the time being, but held that such infants should be baptized in the presence of some believers who could be present. The Particular Synod of Dort 1574, however, already decided that henceforth children should be baptized only in a regular Church service.

The Synod of Dort, 1618-19, ruled that Baptism might be administered at home to children and adults who were sick and still unbaptized if circumstances were very urgent, and then only with the knowledge and in the presence of the Consistory; this Synod also permitted the baptizing of condemned criminals awaiting execution in jails, but only upon advice of the delegates of Classis. But the Synod may have feared ill effects of these concessions. At least it was decided not to publish these decisions, if the Acts were to be published. It wanted to maintain Article 56 of its Church Order.*

The article specifies not merely that the administration of Baptism shall take place in the public assembly, condemning private Baptisms as Rome practiced them in keeping with its erroneous baptismal doctrines, but the article also requires that Baptism shall be administered "when the Word of God is preached." Baptism in and by itself is meaningless. The form as such brings no benefit.

* cf. Synod of Dort, 1618-19, Post-Acta, Session 163:1 and Jansen: **Korte Verklaring**, p. 258.

It is a sign and seal of Christ's saving grace, of the washing away of the recipient's sin in the blood of Christ.

Superstition must be avoided. Ignorance must be fought. Consequently, our fathers ordained through their assemblies that henceforth the Word and the seal upon the Word should not be separated.

ARTICLE 57

The Ministers shall do their utmost to the end that the father present his child for Baptism.

PRESENTATION FOR BAPTISM BY FATHERS

1. The original reading and significance of this article.

Our Synod of 1914 abbreviated the original reading of this article considerably. We merely retained the first part of Article 57 as it was found in the Church Order of Dort and we erased the latter part. The full article used to read as follows:

> The Ministers shall do their utmost and work to the end that the father present his child for Baptism. And in those Congregations in which besides the fathers, sponsors or witnesses are taken at Baptism, (which custom, being in itself permissible, shall not be changed lightly) it is required that such sponsors or witnesses be taken who hold that pure doctrine and who are pious in their conduct.

The Church of Rome held that the natural parents were really unfit to present their child for Baptism inasmuch as children are born in a sinful state by reason of the sinfulness of the parents. Consequently God-fathers and God-mothers, sponsors, should be found who could act as spiritual fathers and mothers for the children. Rome contrasted nature and grace. The men and Churches of the Reformation said: The antithesis is not between nature and grace, but between sin and grace. Nature is of God and there is no essential conflict between nature and grace. Marriage and procreation are perfectly normal institutions and are not to be classified as things of a lower order and as necessary evils. And though every parent must confess all his sins committed in every relationship of life, parents should not be set aside and ruled out of court at the Baptism of their God-given offspring. Theirs is the privilege and duty to present their children for Baptism.

But for years and centuries children had been presented for Baptism by sponsors. And many who joined the Reformation movement and left the Church of Rome did not instantly see through all the errors of Rome. In some Churches the office-bearers still permitted sponsors. The father would remain in the background and the sponsors would occupy the foreground. Now Article 57 ruled that Ministers everywhere endeavor to remedy this wrong state of affairs. The father should himself have his child baptized, not the sponsors. But it was added: In those Churches in which sponsors were still employed, these should occupy a place next to the father. In other words, the father had to occupy his God-ordained place as father. And sponsors were only permitted to occupy a secondary place at baptismal services.

The Churches should see to it that only worthy sponsors were chosen. That is to say, only sponsors who were sound in doctrine and God-fearing in their conduct were to be chosen.

As will be noted the original article also stipulated that inasmuch as there were no serious objections against sponsors who would occupy a secondary place at a child's Baptism, the custom should not be changed lightly. The Churches did not care to cause needless disturbance over this question. The matter was one of minor import. As long as parents were not crowded out of their rightful place and wrongfully relieved of solemn duties and obligations toward their children, the Churches would not interfere with this custom. They doubtless saw some good in the custom. Well qualified sponsors who promised to help the parents to instruct their children in the right doctrine could do a great deal of good.

2. The significance of the article as it now reads.

From the foregoing it has become plain that our Article 57 is essentially an article which provides for parental presentation of children for Baptism over against the presentation of children for Baptism by sponsors or witnesses.

The article does not mean to say that the fathers shall hold the children in their arms at the moment of Baptism rather than the mothers. The fathers are mentioned in this article because they are in the first place the responsible parties, being heads of the family by God's own appointment. Furthermore, the Reformed Churches generally, as our discussion of Article 56 has revealed, baptized their children early, without delay, before the mother had fully recovered. (See comments on former article.) Consequently, the mothers, as a general rule, were not present at the Baptism of their children. In keeping with this situation Article 57 does not mention the mothers. Article 57 does not ignore the mothers. They are included in the fathers here mentioned, but as a matter of principle and practice took no direct part in the Baptism of their little ones.

Although Article 57 does not mean to say that the fathers, rather than the mothers, should hold their children at the moment of Baptism, it is generally agreed that there is some symbolism in the presentation of the child at the baptismal font by the father. He is the God-appointed head, bearing first responsibility for the child's training and education. But for the rest it is immaterial, whether the father or the mother presents the child at Baptism. Under special circumstances a relative or the baby's nurse will most likely hold the baby at the time of Baptism. This does not decrease one whit from the real significance of the Sacrament.

Inasmuch as the custom of employing sponsors next to the parents had not been practiced for many decades, our redaction of the Church Order (1914) left this whole clause regarding sponsors out of the article. The Reformed Churches of the Netherlands in their redaction of 1905 maintained this clause. In view of the fact that sponsors are sometimes necessary, as when both parents have died, or when neither the father nor the mother is competent to assume the baptismal vows, (see comments, Act 56) it might have been well that we also had retained the stricken provision concerning sponsors. At any rate, the provision found in Article 57 prior to 1914, that sponsors should be sound in doctrine and pious in their conduct, is a very essential one. And whenever Consistories make provisions for baptismal sponsors this rule should still be their standard.

ARTICLE 58

In the ceremony of Baptism, both of children and of adults, the Minister shall use the respective forms drawn up for the administration of this Sacrament.

FORMS FOR THE ADMINISTRATION OF BAPTISM

We come now to a consideration of Article 58 which specifies that the Forms for Baptism shall be used at every baptismal service. These forms are two in number, the first pertaining to children to be baptized, and the second pertaining to adults to be baptized.

1. The purpose of sacramental forms.

As has been said before, the Sacraments have no significance in and by themselves. They convey no grace apart from the Spirit and should be understood in order to be fruitful of much good. The Sacraments possess no magical power. They are dependent upon the Word and the Spirit. Consequently the correct understanding of the significance of the Sacraments is very important. For this reason the meaning of Baptism should be briefly explained at each administration of Baptism. The explanation should not be left to the Minister administering the Sacrament. Errors might thus creep in. One-sidedness would surely result in many instances. For the safety of the Churches it is well to have Forms which are brief and to the point and well balanced, approved and accepted by all the Churches through their official assemblies. Our fathers instantly felt the need of Forms for the administration of the Sacraments, the more so since Rome had erred grievously on the score of the Sacraments. All kinds of misconceptions and superstitious notions had found a harboring place in the Churches through erroneous conceptions and usages regarding the Sacraments.

2. The origin of the baptismal Forms.

Concerning our **Form for the Baptism of Infants** it may be noted that it was already in use before the first Synod of Reformed Churches of the Netherlands could meet. At the Wezelian Convention, 1568, the Churches were admonished to use the questions found in the baptismal Form verbally. This convention had reference to the Form written by Petrus Datheen in conjunction with Van der Heyden. Datheen had translated the Heidelberg Catechism from German into Dutch, 1563. He also prepared a new metrical version of the psalms and wrote certain liturgical documents for the Churches. In the year 1566 these were published. But when Datheen and Van der Heyden wrote their baptismal Form they modeled their draft after other baptismal forms already existing. Forms used in the preparation of our Form are those of Calvin, a Lasco, Micron, and Olevianus.

The Particular Synod of Dort, 1574, found that many Churches were not using the Forms of Datheen inasmuch as they were too lengthy. Many Ministers were using statements, explanations, and suggestions of their own. Synod deemed this a very dangerous procedure, and abbreviated the existing form. All Ministers were now expected to use the Form.

Several other Synods concerned themselves with the wording of the Form but no Synod adopted its own official text. The edition of 1611, published in Middelburg by Schilders, was reviewed by the Synod of Dort, but the revisions of this Synod were never published.

Not until Dr. F. L. Rutgers and his assistants, Dr. H. Bavinck and Dr. A. Kuyper, in the year 1897 published the 1611 edition, amended in accordance with the decisions taken at the great Synod of Dort, 1618-19, were the improvements of this Synod incorporated into the Form. At the Synod of Arnhem, 1902, the Reformed Churches of the Netherlands recommended this 1897 edition of the Form for the time being.

Regarding our synodically approved edition of the Form for Baptism we read as follows in the Psalter Hymnal of the Christian Reformed Church, appended pages, p. 72: "Until now our Church has availed itself of a translation of these forms (forms for the administration of Baptism and of the Lord's Supper) which was originally prepared in the Netherlands for the use of Churches composed of English and Scottish refugees, and later revised and adopted by the Reformed Church in America. This translation, slightly revised and corrected, was adopted by our Synod of 1912 for the use of our English speaking churches. A more thorough revision of these forms is now published for the first time in this volume. . . . The committee for the preparation of this Psalter Hymnal took upon itself the revision of the translation of the other forms mentioned above, (forms for Baptism and the Lord's Supper) and the Synod of 1934 adopted this revision, which offers a more faithful translation of the original in more idiomatic English."

The Reformed Churches of the Netherlands have revised their liturgical forms, including the **Form for the Baptism of Infants,** at their Synod of 1930. A comparison of the revised text of our baptismal Form with the revised text of the Holland Churches reveals the fact that our Committee has taken close note of revisions made by the Holland Synod of 1930. This is as it should be. Reformed Churches very closely related in background, doctrine and liturgy should benefit freely from each other's findings and actions. But it would have been well for us to have recognized the work of the Holland Churches adopted in 1930, if only by the mere mention of this revision in the report of the committee.

The **Form of Baptism for Adults** dates back to the Synod of Dort, 1618-19. This Synod drafted this form after the **Form for the Baptism of Infants.** The doctrinal exposition of Baptism in this Form therefore harmonizes with that of the other Form. And to this a special section concerning Baptism for adults with appropriate questions has been added. At the time when the Synod of Dort met there were already two Forms for adult Baptism in existence. In 1603 the Churches of North and South Holland had drafted and accepted a form at their Particular Synods. The Churches of Friesland and Gelderland also used this form. And in the year 1610 the Particular Synod of Vere ordered a Form for the Baptism of adults to be drafted. These two forms differed in this respect that the former, after the expository section taken from the **Form for the Baptism of Infants** immediately proceeds with the prayer and questions, whereas the Form of Zeeland incorporates a brief exposition of the significance of adult Baptism, between the explanatory section taken from the Form for Infants, and the prayer and questions. Synod of Dort in the main accepted the redaction of the Churches of Zeeland, but the Synod of Dort modeled the five questions of our Form for adult Baptism after the questions of North and South Holland.

The Holland Synod of Arnhem, 1930, made some necessary changes in this Form just as it had done in the Form for infant Baptism. Our Synod of 1934 did the same. However, the Holland redaction now requires the candidate for Baptism to respond to the five questions with but one affirmative reply. We have retained the five-fold response, the applicant for Baptism being required to respond with a solemn "I do" to every question individually. Because of the solemnity and import of the occasion we prefer the old five-fold response. Although it must be granted that if we require a separate response to each question asked of an adult about to be baptized, there can be no good reason for not asking parents or sponsors to answer each question asked of them separately. Consistency would require such. And the necessary need for emphasis would seem to plead for a separated response to all three questions of the Form for infant Baptism.

This is not the place for an exposition of our Form for Baptism, although it will be agreed by all who are able to judge that there is a real and urgent need for an exposition of these and other forms. Those who are able to read Dutch will find a very thorough and helpful commentary of these forms in Dr. B. Wielenga's **Ons Doopsfomulier.** Dr. Bouwman in his **Ger. Kerkrecht,** Vol II, pp. 244-264 gives explanatory notes that merit much appreciation.

ARTICLE 59

Adults are through Baptism incorporated into the Christian Church, and are accepted as members of the Church, and are therefore obliged also to partake of the Lord's Supper, which they shall promise to do at their Baptism.

ADULT BAPTISM AND THE LORD'S SUPPER

In the Reformed Churches infant Baptism is the rule and adult Baptism the exception. The vast majority of members of a Reformed Church will have been incorporated into the Church organization through infant Baptism. Nevertheless, many are also added to the Churches by adult Baptism. The present article concerns the Baptism of adults.

1. The age limit for infant Baptism.

Again and again the question occurs: What is the age limit for infant Baptism? From the very days of the Reformation the age of 14 years was regarded as the limit for infant or child Baptism. In other words if a boy or girl were 15 years or older, Baptism was not administered except upon personal profession of faith. However, no general and binding rule has ever been accepted. Some individuals mature much earlier than others. Some youths at the age of 12 or 13 have a greater measure of maturity than others at 14 or 15. Each case must therefore be judged by itself. The general principle which should guide is this: Only such children should be received into the Church through infant Baptism who have not yet come to years of discretion, years of understanding. Thus, for example, if a youth of 13 or 14 years appears to be developed beyond the average child of that age, able to grasp the fundamentals of Christianity, able to choose for himself and actually taking a stand of his own regarding the questions of sin and grace and related matters, then such a child should not be baptized upon application of its parents or sponsors, but only upon his own request and confession. At no time, seemingly, have the Reformed Churches baptized youths older than 14 years with infant Baptism, although children younger than 15 have been received through adult Baptism.

This practice harmonizes well with the fact that, as Jansen points out,* the years of youth leading to full manhood or womanhood are generally agreed to divide themselves into three equal periods of seven years. The age of childhood comprising the years 1 to 7, the years of youth (boys and girls), ages 8 to 14, and the years of young manhood and young womanhood, the years 15 to 21. Regarding those belonging to the first group, 1-7, all agreed that these were as far as their years were concerned, rightful subjects of infant Baptism. Those of the last period, 15-21, were by common consent, admitted to the Church only through adult Baptism. But regarding those belonging to the second class, 8-14, there was some difference of opinion. Especially regarding youth of 12, 13, and 14 who were advanced beyond the average of their age. But the practice of the Churches has been that these cases were dealt with according to providential circumstances, as has been indicated above. However, it should be added that such older children were often questioned before their parents were permitted to present them for Baptism. Questions regarding the Ten Commandments, the Twelve Articles of Faith, and the Lord's Prayer would be asked. Also questions touching the child's attitude toward God and religion. If an older youth appeared to be unbelieving, immoral, or hateful toward Christianity, infant Baptism would not be administered, even though the child was only 14 years or younger.**

2. Significance of the statement: "Adults are through Baptism incorporated into the Christian Church, and are accepted as members of the Church."

The significance of this statement is that those who have come to years of discretion and comparative independence can only be admitted to Church membership by profession of faith and Baptism administered upon this profession. The term "Christian Church" as used in Article 59, does not stand on par with the expression "Church of Christ" as used in Article 1. The expression "Church of Christ" is used to indicate the body of believers living in a certain region or country.* It does not as a rule refer to these believers as they are organized into a Church or Churches. (See comments, Article 1) The term "Christian Church" in the present article, however, refers to a specific congregation or organized Church. The opening provisions of Article 59 therefore simply specifies that adults who stand outside of the organized Churches can only be incorporated into a local or particular Church upon confession and Baptism, and that thus they are admitted to full membership rights in the Church which so receives them. A literal translation of Article 59 on this score would make this interpretation very evident. Literally we read: "Adults are to be incorporated into the Christian congregation by Baptism, and are thus to be accepted as members of the congregations." He who has been granted adult Baptism thereby receives all the privileges of Church membership. He stands on par with those who were baptized in infancy and who in later years made profession of their faith.

---

* Jansen: **Korte Verklaring**, etc., 1923, p. 26.

** Dr. F. L. Rutgers: **Kerkelyke Adviesen**, II, 1921, p. 69.

3. The obligation of those that are baptized as adults to partake of the Lord's Supper.

Prior to the Synod of Dort, 1618-19, there seems to have been some uncertainty on this score. Some unbaptized individuals applied for Baptism perhaps because Church-membership was required to hold certain positions in civil government. For a time there was a very close relationship between Church and State and not to be a member of a Reformed Church would often spell disadvantage. Others requested Baptism because they desired to marry a young man or woman of the Reformed Churches and no ecclesiastical confirmation of marriage would be granted if one of the parties was outside of the Church. Then again, some youths were admitted to baptism at an early age and these sometimes hesitated to go to the Lord's table forthwith.

Some Churches had been too easy and slack regarding this matter. The question reached the Synod of Dort from more than one Particular Synod, and the Synod of Dort answered by writing Article 59 as we still have it today, into the Church Order. Henceforth, therefore, only those who were competent to celebrate the Lord's death at His table would be admitted to Baptism. The confession and walk of those who requested Baptism should be such that the Consistories could admit them to the Lord's table. And those requesting and receiving Baptism should realize that they were expected to come to the Lord's Table. If they would not promise to partake of the Lord's Supper regularly, they were not to be admitted to Baptism.

This provision is sound. The two Sacraments signify and seal the same thing. They belong together. An adult who is not competent to celebrate the Lord's Supper is also incompetent to receive Baptism. And one who is competent to receive Baptism is also competent to celebrate Holy Communion.

In some of our Christian Reformed Churches a number of years ago individuals would be admitted to full membership privileges by making "profession of the truth." The Dutch phrases used were: "Belydenis der leer," or, "Belydenis der waarheid." This was considered to be profession of faith, made with the distinct understanding that the person making the profession, simply made an objective profession. He declared that he believed the Bible according to the Reformed conception but he made no appropriation of Christianity for himself. He did not profess to be a child of God, one saved from sin. And it was therefore distinctly understood that he would not be expected to come to Holy Communion. Many of these, we may believe, were at heart sincere children of God, although they did not dare to say so themselves. These were the victims of an unscriptural and unreformed emphasis upon subjective "experiences." These "experiences" of others were raised as standards and tests for true Christianity, although in many instances these experiences were of a very doubtful character and often contrary to God's Word. But many of these who made "professions of the truth" were not God-fearing at heart. They were external and indifferent.

The result of this practice of permitting people to make "profession of the truth" was that many in our Churches who had made profession of faith never went to the Lord's Table. There are still a few of this class left in some of our Churches. Needless to say that this whole type of profession of faith is contrary to the stipulation of Article 59. If those who are admitted to adult Baptism are expected to come to the Lord's Table, then surely those likewise who make profession of faith should celebrate our Lord's death regularly.

In some Churches of the Reformed faith, both here and in Europe, large numbers of those who make profession of faith never go to the Lord's Supper. This is a sickly, unbiblical situation and should be counteracted with tender regard for the convictions of sincere believers, but also with persistency and firmness.

To be sure, we should keep balance and judge discriminately here. We should not merely urge all who have made profession of faith to celebrate the Lord's Supper. Some members of the Church may be victimized by rationalism and unbelief to such an extent that they are not fit to approach the Lord's Table. They should first, by God's grace, overcome their unbelief regarding the very fundamentals of Christianity. And if one lives in spiritual indifference, he should likewise overcome this spiritual indifference before partaking of the Lord's Supper. And if one be remiss in his Christian conduct he should first repent of his sin and forsake his sin before coming to Holy Communion. One who would continue in his rationalistic indifference or unchristian conduct would soon become an object of discipline. Persistency in sin requires that all membership rights be temporarily withdrawn from the guilty one, and ultimately these sins would require excommunication. Article 59 in no way means to say that God's children are always fit to go to the Lord's Table and that they must promise never to absent themselves. We must warn against a light and vain and unworthy approach unto the Lord's Table. And we must urge believers who are worthy, to come with joy and gratitude, warning them against the evil of unwarranted abstinence.

In keeping with the provisions of Article 59, the adult who is about to be baptized promises, in answer to the fourth question of the Form for the Baptism of Adults, that he will persevere "not only in the hearing of the divine Word, but also in the use of the Holy Supper."

ARTICLE 60

The names of those baptized, together with those of the parents, and likewise the date of birth and baptism, shall be recorded.

RECORD OF BAPTISMS

Article 60 provides for the registration of all baptized children. We shall first endeavor to answer the question why records should be kept, and secondly we shall note what specifically should be included in this registration.

1. Why records should be kept.

The Wezelian Convention already judged that proper registration of those baptized was necessary, in the first place for the sake of the Church and in the second place for the civil community. At present the civil governments all require that the birth of infants be properly recorded. Years ago this was not the case. So, for instance, in the Netherlands civil registration of births, names of parents, etc., began in 1811.* Previous to this time the government depended on the Church

* Jansen: **Korte Verklaring**, etc., 1923, p. 269.

records if and when verification of year of birth or parentage was necessary. The relationship between Church and State being very close in post-Reformation days, the Churches adopted Article 60, not only for their own sake, but also for the sake of the government.

In answer to the question why we keep baptismal records the obvious reply is simply: In order that each Church may know who have been baptized. Or, to state it differently: In order that each Church may know which children and young people belong to it by virtue of their Baptism and so that each Consistory may know which children and young people fall under its special care and jurisdiction. And in case Baptism has taken place upon presentation of witnesses or sponsors that the Church and Consistory may know who the individuals are that promised to instruct the children in matters regarding the doctrine and significance of Baptism.

Furthermore record is also kept in order that the Church may know when Baptism was administered. Those that come to years of discretion and do not repent of sin and do not seek to come to a hearty appreciation of salvation by grace and all its implications should be admonished. And in this connection, office-bearers should know the age of non-professing members.

Again, it often happens that children leave one congregation for another, together with their parents. The Baptism of such children together with the time of Baptism should be certified to the Church with which this removing family desires to affiliate. The same is true for young people who remove to other communities and come under the care and jurisdiction of another Church. Their Baptism, and the time of their Baptism, should be certified to their new Church. Unless a good record is kept proper certification cannot take place.

2. That which should be recorded.

In the first place as the article clearly requires and as stands to reason, "the names of those baptized" must be recorded. In the second place the names of the parents are to be recorded. Proper identification requires that the names of parents be recorded as well as the names of the children baptized. But this is not the only reason. Parents at the time of Baptism assumed some very solemn and meaningful vows. They make important promises before God and His Church regarding the training of their children. They assume certain weighty and definite obligations. The names of the parents are therefore also recorded in token of the fact that these parents have assumed these obligations. This secondary significance of the recording of the names of the parents becomes evident from the fact that the article used to read: "The names of those baptized, together with those of the parents and sponsors . . . shall be recorded." The names of these sponsors had to be recorded inasmuch as they had assumed solemn obligations toward the children concerned and not because of relationship or for reasons of identification. In our redaction of the Church Order (1914) we dropped the words "en getuigen" (and sponsors). The Churches of Holland have retained them. Most likely our Synod of 1914 deemed this provision antiquated and needless inasmuch as in our day only the parents assume the baptismal obligations and the whole institution of sponsorships in connection with infant Baptism is out of date and out of use. But, as we have noted in our consideration of Article 57, there still is room for baptismal sponsors in our Churches. Whenever children are of the "seed of the Church" and of God's covenant and therefore entitled to Baptism but the parents are dead or incompetent to assume the baptismal vows, sponsors must take the place of these parents. Consequently it might have been better if our Synod of 1914 had also retained the words "and sponsors," or at least had given the following reading to this article: "The names of those baptized together with those of the parents or sponsors . . . shall be recorded." But even though sponsors are no longer mentioned in our 60th article, whenever sponsors present a child for Baptism their names must be recorded in the baptismal book next to those which indicate the child's parentage.

The date of Baptism is to be recorded also. This is done for reasons already indicated above and for reasons of completeness. The article also requires that the date of birth be recorded. This part of the provision is new. It was not found in the article prior to 1914, and is not yet found in the redaction of the Netherland Churches. It is well to know the exact age of a baptized child or youth, and this slight addition of 1914 is therefore a good one. Perhaps we incorporated it also because for secular affairs our members are often required to certify their exact age, and the civil records of birth are very incomplete. Consequently the Church officials are asked again and again to furnish a testimony as to some one's date of birth.

The records should be kept with accuracy and neatness. To facilitate both accuracy and neatness every Church should have a good record book to begin with. There are loose-leaf binders on the market which are durable and neat and which help the recorder to keep the record up-to-date and accurate. Some prefer the card index system and much can doubtless be said in favor of this system. The main point however is not this or that particular system, although it counts, but punctuality and care.

Are parents free to select from all kinds of names as they select a given name for their child? And must the Church baptize a child by whatever name parents may have selected? The naming of a child has rightly always been left to the parents. It is their privilege to name their children and not that of the state or the Church or any other agency. But this does not mean that Christian parents are not prevented by the very Christianity which they profess from giving certain names to their children. For example, no child should be called by the names of God. In the past some parents have used names as follows: Divine, Jesus, Immanuel. No one should consent to baptize a child by one of these names. Parents should also be discouraged from naming their children after angels inasmuch as these names are borrowed from a sinless domain, the sacredness of which would not be enhanced in our estimation and thought if its names were given to sinful beings. Nor would a Christian parent think of calling his child Cain, Judas, Jezebel, etc.

Years ago, particularly among the Puritans of New England, many parents named their children after Bible characters such as Abraham, Daniel, Jeremiah, Ezekiel, Paul, etc., or after certain Christian virtues as Charity, Love, Grace, Temperance, Hope. Some of these names are still very common. Selecting names from the Bible is certainly a great deal better than the choosing of names from present day novels or even from among movie stars as many are inclined to do in our day. It is also far better to name our children after Bible characters than to name them after outstanding men of unbelief such as Darwin, Marx, etc. For the rest the Bible permits parents to choose names as they see fit. Many N. T. believers had pagan names but the Bible nowhere urges these converts to adopt new names. We should never become overly scrupulous on this score.

Why is only the given name mentioned at the time of baptism and not the family name? Doubtless the primary explanation for this fact is a historical one. Years ago people had no family names but only their own personal given names. These were mentioned at baptism, and this custom continued also after family names were introduced. But the usage also has this significance, that the given name is the strictly personal name of the individual, whereas he holds the family name in common with many others. By mentioning only the given name or names the personal significance of the baptismal assurances stand out all the more. But even so we know of no serious argument by reason of which the complete name should not be pronounced at the time of Baptism. To do so would help larger Churches to know who the parents are which are having their children baptized. The congregation should know this. The parents at the time of Baptism assume certain vows, not only before God, but also before the Church. Consequently the Church should know who they are that have assumed solemn obligations. One way in which this object can be attained still more satisfactorily, however, is to have the Minister announce the names of the parents who are presenting their children for Baptism, just before the Form is being read, and in the order in which the children are to be baptized. In smaller Churches such measures are not out of place, but less necessary.

Nearly every Church, if not every Church, keeps not only a record of Baptisms, but a complete membership record. These membership records will, as a rule, give the full names of parents and children together with a record of the Baptisms, professions of faith, date of birth, removal through death, departure to another congregation, etc. Many of these matters are not required in Article 60 of the Church Order, but are nevertheless things that ought to be recorded and kept. We would commend our Churches for keeping these complete records.

ARTICLE 61

None shall be admitted to the Lord's Supper except those who, according to the usage of the Church with which they unite themselves, have made a confession of the Reformed Religion, besides being reputed to be of a godly walk, without which those who come from other Churches shall not be admitted.

ADMISSION TO THE LORD'S SUPPER

The next four articles concern the celebration of the Lord's Supper. Article 61 concerns admission to the Lord's Table; Article 62 refers to the manner in which the Lord's Supper is to be celebrated; Article 63 concerns the frequency of administering the Lord's Supper; and Article 64 stipulates a condition for the administration of Holy Communion.

In these four articles not nearly all questions of a church governmental nature pertaining to the Lord's Supper are covered. The Church Order merely indicates the fundamental principles which should guide us. It is, as has been said before, not a book of detailed rules and regulations to which one can merely turn when an emergency arises and find the solution in ready made form. The Church Order does not aim to dictate as to all manner of details, which may be very unessential. Thus the Church Order safe-guards our liberties, although it at the same time safeguards us against dangerous and un-Biblical policies. This it does by clearly and briefly putting down for us the governing principles which must be applied with discrimiation and care in every case.

Article 61 regulates two matters: The admission to the Lord's Table by profession of faith of those who are members by Baptism, and the admission to the Lord's Table of those who come from other Churches of the denomination.

1. Admission to the Lord's Supper of members by Baptism.

Article 61 makes it very plain that not all are welcome at the Lord's Table in our Churches. The Sacraments are signs and seals of the remission of our sins by the blood and Spirit of Jesus Christ. Now only those who are true believers have their sins forgiven. Consequently, the signs and seals of this forgiveness should be given only to those concerning whom we have reasons to believe that they are true believers.

Already at the Convention of Wezel, 1568, the question arose; who are to be admitted to Holy Communion? The Convention answered: No one shall be admitted to the Lord's Table unless he first shall have made profession of faith and shall have submitted himself to the discipline of the Church. This ruling was re-affirmed by the Synod of 1578 (Dordrecht) in slightly different words, and rewritten by the Middelburg Synod of 1581 in the wording as we still have it in Article 61 today.

From the foregoing it becomes evident that the Reformed Churches from the Reformation era on have held that attendance at the Lord's Table is not free to all. It is not a matter which is to be left to the judgment of individuals. The office-bearers are guardians over the Lord's Table. They must only admit those whom they believe to be worthy. Erastus and the Remonstrants—those defending the tenets of Arminianism—held that attendance or non-attendance at the Lord's Table should be left to the individual conscience. Many Christians all over the world still defend this theory. Some adhering to the Reformed faith seem to hold to this theory. For example, in many Reformed Churches of southern Holland large numbers of confessing members seldom come to the Lord's Table. The same is true for the Gereformeerde Gemeenten, "Oud-Gereformeerden," or Netherland-Reformed Churches. Members of these and other groups go to the Lord's Table if they have certain subjective experiences, and abstain if these are lacking at the time the Lord's Supper is observed. If they are spiritually at high-tide they partake. If they are spiritually depressed and at low-tide they abstain. But this practice does not harmonize with the position which our Reformed leaders took from the very outset. The attitude and policy referred to arose when spiritual life began to decline in the Reformed Churches, and was born in part from the reaction to worldly-mindedness and shallow-mindedness. But is it not typical of the historical Reformed position. In our own Churches there are still a few who, though they have made confession of faith, seldom or never come to the Lord's Table. In 1904 our Synod decided that Consistories should not receive into full membership those who did not intend to partake of the Lord's Table regularly. (Acts, Synod, Art. 125)

Yet not all baptized members of the Church were permitted to go to the Lord's Table. If all baptized children would be true to their baptism and manifest true faith in Christ and loyalty to His Word in conduct, then as soon as children would come to years of understanding they might approach unto the Lord's Supper without first securing permission to do so. But conditions are never ideal. There is always some chaff mixed with the wheat. There are Esaus among covenant-keeping young people in every Church. And so Voetius, in answer to the question whether not all baptized individuals should be considered as entitled to partake of the Lord's Table, answered, "No." Said he in substance: Faith may be present potentially without having as yet developed into actual faith. And actual faith is necessary for the proper celebration of the Lord's Supper. The essence of faith may be present by regeneration, but the fruit of regeneration, conversion, must also be present.*

Ordinarily we speak of confession or profession of faith, whereas Article 61 speaks of "confession of the Reformed Religion." There is no conflict here. He who makes "confession of the Reformed Religion," acknowledges all the essentials of the gospel of salvation with application to himself. So does he who makes confession or profession of faith." But the phrase "confession of the Reformed Religion" does include a little more than the expression "confession or profession of faith." The phrase of our Church Order implies that he who makes confession of faith in our Churches must not only assent with self-appropriation to the general truths of Christianity but he must be able to declare that he believes the Reformed interpretation to be correct, Biblical. Some Church groups do not require assent to their particular creed as a condition for membership. Thus the Presbyterian Churches generally do require of office-bearers that they agree with the specific doctrines of the Church, but the ordinary members need not declare agreement. Though they should question and reject some Reformed positions, yet they would be entitled to membership.

It should be plain however that a Church, if its members are admitted without confessing the Reformed fundamentals, cannot remain Reformed. After all the individual members, and not the clergy and the eldership, constitute the Church. And the confessional standards of a Church can only be Forms of Unity when the membership confesses these standards. If the members of a Church do not confess its standards to be Biblical the Church loses its power and also its **raison d'etre.** A Church which does not require of its members that they agree with its doctrinal tenets opens the doors to those who advocate false doctrines; heresy is bound to enter in, and eventually modernism may even predominate.

We may therefore thank God that our Churches still expect our young people—and all others that desire membership in our Churches—as they make confession of faith, to agree with the specific doctrines of our Churches. Not as if there is no room for difference of opinion within the walls of our ecclesiastical city. There certainly is and should be. But regarding the great doctrine of the Church of Christ as these find a clear expression in our doctrinal Standards, all those that seek and receive full membership rights in our Churches should be agreed. The peace and purity of the Churches require that all members be fully agreed on all vital, major, questions of doctrine. No Church can reasonably expect to remain pure and loyal which admits to membership such as are at odds with the Church on one or more vital doctrines. And this consistent position of our Churches does not spell injustice toward any child of God. They who do not

* Jansen: **Korte Verklaring,** etc., 1923, p. 271.

agree with us should simply seek and join a Church with which they are agreed. Let one who is methodistic in doctrine join a Methodist Church. Let one who is baptistic in doctrine affiliate with a Baptist Church, etc. Our Churches have always taken the stand expressed in Article 61, although we believe with all our hearts that there is a holy Catholic Church and that the Christian Church is by no means limited to the Christian Reformed denomination together with some other loyal Reformed organizations. Prof. Bouwman claims that for this very reason the first question of the Form for Confession of Faith speaks of the articles of the Christian faith, taught in this Christian Church, and not of the Reformed faith and the Reformed Church.* We thus give expression to our unity with the entire Christian Church, especially in regard to the Sacraments. We do not desire to separate ourselves from the general Christian Church, although we take a decided stand when testing those who ask to be admitted to the Lord's Supper.

Not only must those who receive admittance to the Lord's Table make confession of the Reformed religion, but they must also be "reputed to be of a godly walk." They who make confession of faith and thereby receive admission to the Lord's Table, must not merely profess to be Christians but their past conduct must be an evidence of this fact. They must be known as Christians. One who says that he believes but fails to manifest his faith is to be rejected. Although one should make a beautiful confession but should fail to live in keeping with the confession, he is to be rejected until his life, his conduct, sets the seal of genuineness upon his confession. Doctrine and life should therefore both receive proper attention.

It is well for our Consistories to be very careful on this score. God judges the hearts, it is true. But we should avoid all that may encourage externalism. We should question young people and all that come to make confession of faith personally. In larger Churches it may be necessary that an able Committee of the Consistory be appointed to confer with all applicants personally. When a number of applicants are questioned at the same time it is very difficult to say whether their replies regarding personal piety and faith are really their own. And no Consistory should be satisfied if applicants are only able to recite the Compendium. Doctrinal knowledge and purity is important. But personal piety is no less important. Neither should questions regarding personal piety be couched in such words that applicants can merely reply by a very evident "yes" or "no." Let the questions be formulated in such a way that the applicants must speak for themselves and so that they are required to formulate their replies. Of course, every Consistory or committee must exercise discretion. Some applicants will have very little to say. Their natural ability for self-expression may be very limited. They may be extremely nervous. In such cases, if the Consistory is convinced that the applicant is sincere, and if his past conduct reveals the fear of the Lord, the Consistory will be lenient and exercise charity and goodwill. But at the other hand, if an applicant gives just reasons for doubt he should not be admitted presently. The Minister or a committee should instruct him further, and prayerfully labor with him, until such a time that he can be admitted without hesitation.

We do not mean to say that youthful applicants and babes in Christ must be judged by standards which apply to Christians which are fully matured. Not at all. But the Consistories must have good

---

* Bouwman: *Ger. Kerkrecht*, II, pp. 382, 3.

reasons to believe that applicants are children of God, and that they have such a measure of knowledge and understanding of biblical doctrine as may reasonably be expected.

There is a synodical ruling which requires that Consistories shall ask every person making confession of faith whether or not the applicant is a member of any secret, oath-bound society. (Acts, Synod 1867, Art. 15 and Acts, Synod 1900, Article 84.) Those who are lodge members are not to be admitted. One main reason for withholding the Lord's Supper and membership rights from lodge-members is that the lodge is representative of a false, anti-Christian religion. The lodges teach that if a man is a good lodge-member, even though he fails to believe in Jesus Christ as the only Savior, he will be saved. Consequently lodge-membership and Church-membership cannot go together.

The Synod of 1928, faced with the fact that worldly-mindedness was very clearly on the increase in our Churches, made the following resolution: "Consistories are instructed to inquire of those who ask to be examined previous to making public confession of their faith and partaking of the Lord's Supper as to their stand and conduct in the matter of worldly amusements, and, if it appears that they are not minded to lead the life of Christian separation and consecration, not to permit their public confession." (Acts, Synod 1928, Article 96) This resolution should not be interpreted legalistically. Synod of 1928 did not try to write a catalogue of sinful practices. The resolution quoted is the sixth adopted regarding the problem of worldliness. Already in the third resolution Synod of 1928 spoke as follows: "Synod urges all our leaders and all our people to pray and labor for the awakening and deepening of spiritual life in general, and to be keenly aware of the absolute indispensability of keeping our religious life vital and powerful, through daily prayer, the earnest searching of the Scriptures, and through engaging in practical Christian works, which are the best antidote against worldliness."

Synod of 1928 took these and other praiseworthy resolutions **with a view to worldly-mindedness and worldly amusements in general,** although it mentioned in particular the familiar trio of theater-attendance, dancing, and card-playing.

None of us would care to maintain that all amusements are in themselves evil. There are many forms of amusements which are wholesome and good. Neither would we care to claim that all amusements which are contaminated with sin, and which are used by the devil to further his cause, are in themselves altogether evil. But we do maintain that all amusements which clearly hurt our spiritual life and tend to stem normal, Biblical, spiritual devotion, and which break down the God-built barriers of spiritual separation between the Church and the world, should be left alone by all Christians. (Cf. I Cor. 8:9; James 4:4; Col. 3:1, 2; Matt. 16:24; 18:8, 9; etc.)

Anyone who desires to indulge in practices which have constituted a damaging, down-breaking force to spiritual living, and who is not ready to forsake these things after the sinfulness of these amusements and their evil influence has been clearly demonstrated to him, **by that very attitude gives just reasons to doubt the sincerity of his heart, and just reasons to question his spiritual fitness for admission to the Lord's Table.** Consequently, our Churches are right in not permitting to the Lord's Table those who do not intend to lead a life of Christian separation.

The "Report on Worldly Amusements" found in the Agenda for the

Synod of 1928 should be read and prayerfully studied by all who question the correctness of our stand on this score.*

Confession before the Consistory or a committee of the Consistory is only preliminary to the real confession of faith, which takes place before the whole Church. For this reason the names of those who have made confession before the Consistory are announced to the Church in order that those who may have objections against their admission may register these with the Consistory. For admission to the Lord's Table and full membership rights must take place with the approval of the whole Church. The names of applicants are usually announced on two successive Sundays. This is no requirement of the Church Order. One announcement may be enough, especially in smaller Churches. But the general custom of announcing the names on two different Sundays is a good usage.

Formerly part of the actual questioning would also take place before the whole congregation, but this public examination was found to be impracticable. Young people with timid dispositions and nervously inclined dreaded this public questioning. Synod of Dordrecht, 1574, therefore introduced our present procedure. The actual examination takes place before the Consistory or a committee of the Consistory, and before the congregation the applicants merely answer affirmatively to a number of formulated questions.

We have a **Form for the Public Profession of Faith.** This form is of recent origin, having been approved by our Synod of 1932. It may be found on page 86 of the Psalter Hymnal, appended section. Our Churches formulated or modeled this beautiful and meaningful form after one adopted by the Reformed Churches of Holland in 1923.

The expression "with which they unite themselves," as this occurs in Article 61, might lead some to think that making confession of faith is really "joining the Church." It is sometimes said among us that those who make profession of faith and receive permission to go to the Lords' Table are "joining the Church." This expression has been rightly condemned. It comes to us from Churches who do not have the Reformed covenant conception regarding children of believing parents. Not only are those who have made confession of faith members of the Church organization to which they belong, but baptized children and young people are also Church members. The full membership rights are not theirs. But there is a definite tie that binds them to the Church organization in whose midst they live. They are not like strangers and outsiders. They are in the Church by virtue of their Baptism. Consequently they cannot join themselves to the Church by confession of faith. If I am already a citizen of the United States while still a mere child, I cannot **become** a citizen of the United States when I am of age. I can acknowledge my citizenship and I can receive my full citizenship rights, but I cannot become what I already am. Thus they who make confession of faith do not join the Church, although they do receive full membership rights and openly acknowledge their membership obligations.

The expression "with which they unite themselves" as found in this article was perhaps incorporated here inasmuch as many in the early years of the Reformation came from the Roman Church and actually united themselves with the Church in question when confession of faith was made. Article 61, let us remember, was formulated long before the Synod of Dort, 1618-19. If ever Article 61 should be re-

* This Report has been separately published by the Rev. John De Haan, Jr., of Grand Rapids, Michigan.

vised it might be well to make it read somewhat as follows: "None shall be admitted to the Lord's Supper except those who, according to the usage of the Church with which they stand connected by reason of their Baptism, shall have made confession . . ."

To what does the phrase, "... according to the usage of the Church," refer? The methods of receiving young people and other non-confessing members into full membership of the Churches differed on some points in various Churches. Some examined by means of a committee of the Consistory; some Consistories interrogated applicants before the whole body of the Consistory; still others examined their applicants in the presence of all the Church members. Also in regard to the announcement made and time intervening between private and public confession there was some variation. As in numerous other matters, the Churches wanted to leave as many liberties to the individual Churches as they possibly could. Each Church established its own rule. Today we have more uniformity. But we have no forced uniformity. Every Church still has the right to arrange various details regarding confession of faith as it sees fit.

Article 61 definitely commits our Churches against the practice of "open communion." Those who practice or advocate "open communion" often defend their stand by claiming that Holy Communion is the Lord's Supper, and not the supper of the Christian Reformed Churches, and that we may therefore not exclude those who belong to other Churches. This argument is, it seems to us, rather childlike. Of course, Holy Communion is an institution of our Lord. But every Church and every body of office-bearers has a solemn duty to guard the sacredness of this Supper of our Lord, and to restrain unworthy persons from increasing their guilt of sin by partaking of this holy institution. Essentially we bar no one, except unbelievers, from the Lord's Table. The greatest of sinners are welcome, if only they will confess their sins and manifest faith and sincerity. Let those who desire to celebrate Holy Communion take the proper steps to gain permission to share this great blessing. Let no one desire to set aside the offices which Christ has placed as guardians over His Table. And if one be a sincere believer but not in agreement with the doctrinal or practical position of our Churches, we have neither the desire nor the power to restrain him from going to the Lord's Table. Only let him celebrate the Lord's Supper with those with whom he agrees and according to the dictates of his own conscience. Thus he will promote good order and peace.

Fundamentally the difference between those who advocate "open communion" and those who maintain "close communion," is a question of recognition and non-recognition of the authority of Christ vested in the office-bearers. We and other Churches which maintain close communion say that Christ placed the office-bearers in charge of the Sacraments. The sanctity of the Sacraments must be zealously guarded by the servants of Christ. Whether or not one shall approach unto the Lord's Table is not simply up to the individual. He must recognize the officers appointed for this work by Christ. Neither may any Consistory delegate this charge to the individuals by announcing that all who are members of some other Church in good and regular standing and desirous of observing the Lord's Supper are invited to partake. This is not as bad as an unconditional invitation, but it is a form of open communion, for the question of attendance or non-attendance at the Lord's Table is after all left solely to the judgment of the individuals concerned. One altogether unworthy may thus be given permission to partake. This would be a desecration of the

Lord's Table which might have been avoided, and an opening of an avenue of sin by the office-bearers to the unworthy participant.

Is there any room for "visitors" at the Lord's Table in our Churches? Yes, there is. We should not become sentimental in the unwholesome sense of the word and think that it would be terrible if a believer of another Church, who partakes regularly in his own Church, should not partake at a Church which he happens to visit while Communion is being celebrated. But if a visitor has a desire to celebrate the Lord's death with the congregation with which he is to worship, then let him speak to the office-bearers before and, if possible during the week, or, if need be, just prior to the service. Unless one or more Consistory members know him personally, he should if he is able, bring someone with him who can give testimony regarding his faith and life. No Consistory will turn down a request of this kind, but gladly grant it. If this procedure is too much trouble to the individual concerned his desire is not very strong. Let him in that case merely worship sympathetically and prayerfully, without seeking permission to partake.

If young people are to make confession of faith intelligently and sincerely they must be well-informed. For the sake of our Churches and for the sake of our members our Churches have ever worked for thorough indoctrination. The catechism class has been the main means of indoctrination in the past. Catechetical instruction is indispensable to the welfare of our Churches as Reformed Churches. Synod of 1912 (Art. 57) appealed most earnestly and urgently to all Classes and Consistories to guard against the danger of relegating to the background, or of wholly neglecting catechetical instruction. And Synod of 1928 recommended a nine-month catechism season. And while our Churches were still in their early youth they already ruled that parents who wilfully neglected to send their children to catechism made themselves worthy of discipline, even to the extent of excommunication. And young people who refused to attend catechism although they had not yet made confession of faith were likewise to be disciplined.* (Also see Appendix 8, page 369.)

2. Admittance to the Lord's Supper to members of other affiliated Churches.

The concluding statement of Article 61 merely reads: "without which those who come from other Churches shall not be admitted." Those who have already made profession of faith before another Church and have therefore been admitted to the Lord's Table in this other Church, shall not be permitted to go to the Lord's Table in a Church of which they are not members except they be reputed to be of a godly walk. That is the sense of this concluding provision of Article 61. The reference is to such as remove from one locality to another. If someone had moved to another town or city, he was not to be accepted as a member of the Reformed Church of his new home and to receive permission to go to the Lord's Table unless he could give witness regarding his godliness. This witness was to be delivered by means of a certificate of membership, an attestation, or Church letter. Of these Article 82 speaks specifically and consequently we shall not go into details here.

Note that grammatically Article 61 only requires that those that come to us from another of our Churches be "reputed to be of a godly walk". Soundness in doctrine is not included. However, the context

* Cf. Algemeene Bepalingen, 62 and 62a, 1881.

speaks of both, soundness in doctrine and godliness of life. Both should be certified. This is the evident significance of the article. For both are required of members by Baptism applying for admission to the Lord's Supper. Then why should not both be required of those coming from elsewhere? Article 82 also makes this very plain.

At first members from elsewhere would be accepted upon their own testimony. But a number of unworthy persons who were looking for money and support would move from place to place and with pious talk gain the confidence of the believers. To check this abuse the rule of Article 61 was adopted. At first the Churches had to be lenient in this respect, for if fugitives from Roman civil authorities were found with membership attestations on their person, escape was impossible. Some had to flee for their lives and could not be expected to carry a certificate of membership. Consequently the Churches were very lenient and often gave applicants the benefit of the doubt. But as the persecution subsided the rule of Article 61 was generally enforced.

The article speaks simply of "other Churches." The reference is not to any other Churches in general, but to other affiliated Churches, other particular Reformed Churches. The denomination consisted of various individual Churches which all agreed in doctrine and church government. These Churches therefore formed a logical unit, and consequently lived and labored together. They agreed to honor each other's letters of testimony concerning members moving from one locality to another. Article 61 in no way means to say that our forefathers accepted such as belonged to a Lutheran Church or an Anabaptistic group upon the mere testimony of a letter from one of these Churches. And thus the matter stands today. We receive each other's members as Christian Reformed Churches upon letters of testimony to each other. And without such letters of testimony no Church is to receive a member from one of our other Churches. That is the point here.

It may be remarked here that our fathers found a precedent for letters of testimony in the Bible itself. (Cf. Acts 18:27 and Rom. 16:1.)

Some practical considerations which concern the matter of Church letters will come up for consideration when we discuss Article 82.

3. Admittance to the Lord's Supper of those who come from Churches of other denominations.

A letter of testimony presented by a member of one of the Reformed Churches of the Netherlands (Gereformeerde Kerken van Nederland) is accepted by us just as certificates from one of our own Churches. All letters coming to us from Churches of other related denominations are not accepted forthwith. Applicants for membership presenting letters of testimony from a Church belonging neither to our own denomination nor to the Gereformeerde Kerken van Nederland, are first to be examined as to their doctrinal soundness and their fitness to celebrate the Lord's Supper. The form of their admission is left to the Consistory, but the congregation must be given an opportunity to present possible objections. (Acts, Synod 1904, Article 125.) Schaver in his "Christian Reformed Church Order" (Zondervan's, Grand Rapids, Mich., 1937) gives us a list of related denominations with which at one time or another, our Synods have decided to establish correspondence. We quote:

"(1) The Reformed Churches of the Netherlands (Acts 1879, Art. 18); (2) The Old Reformed Churches of East Frisia and Bentheim (now united with the Reformed Churches of the Netherlands, J.L.S.), and the Evangelical Church in Silesia (Acts 1879, Art. 18a); (3) The Reformed Churches of South Africa (Acts 1879, Art. 18); (4) The Reformed Church in America (Acts 1893, p. 53); (5) The United Presbyterian Church (Acts 1898, p. 53); (6) Synod and General Synod, Reformed Presbyterian Churches (Acts 1900, p. 52); (7) Associate Presbyterian Church (Acts 1900, p. 52); (8) The Christian Reformed Church in the Netherlands (Acts 1910, p. 60; Acts 1936, p. 97)."

In regard to the newly organized Presbyterian Church of America (1936), now the Orthodox Presbyterian Church of America, our Synod of 1936 decided: "Inasmuch as the Presbyterian Church of America has not finally adopted its Constitution, Synod decides to postpone the question of correspondence with said body. This does not exclude, however, the sending of greetings and the sending of delegates to each other's major assemblies." (Acts of Synod, 1936, Article 143.)

Sad to say, many of these related denominations are far from being Reformed. There is much doctrinal laxness and consequent impurity among many of them. Consequently though we acknowledge all the good which may be found in many of these Churches, and though we appreciate the love and loyalty to our Reformed conceptions still present in these groups, yet laxness in doctrine and life prevents us from honoring membership certificates coming from these Churches at face value.

As a rule members from any of these Churches who apply for membership with one of our Churches will be visited by a competent committee of the Consistory. This committee reports its findings to the Consistory, and if the Consistory finds no objections to accept the applicant announcement is made to the Church, stating that unless valid objections are presented to the Consistory, applicants will be admitted at the next meeting of that body. However, if a Consistory deems it necessary and so desires the applicants are requested to appear before the whole Consistory, there to be questioned and conferred with.

Those who apply for membership in one of our Churches, and previously members of a non-related and unreformed Church, are first to be instructed. For instance those who were formerly Methodists, Baptists, etc., should be carefully and faithfully labored with. Age and circumstances should be considered. But those who are able should be thoroughly instructed in the doctrine of our Churches, either by means of a catechism class or privately. All those that come to us from non-reformed Churches should signify assent to the doctrines of our Churches publicly. Whether in every instance the **Form for Public Profession of Faith** should be used we would not determine, although it will be found appropriate in most instances. But acceptance should be in the meeting of all the believers, so that all may hear that the applicant professes the true faith. Many who come from related and nominally Reformed Churches should likewise be received publicly. This will be, we believe, to the welfare of both applicant and Church.

In every case those coming from other denominations should be carefully asked regarding their attitude toward the lodge, and many other practical attitudes and conceptions of life, such as Sabbath observance, worldly amusements, etc.

ARTICLE 62

Every Church shall administer the Lord's Supper in such a manner as it shall judge most conducive to edification; provided, however, that the outward ceremonies as prescribed in God's Word be not changed and all superstition avoided, and that at the conclusion of the sermon and the usual prayers, the Form for the Administration of the Lord's Supper, together with the prayer for that purpose, shall be read.

METHOD OF ADMINISTERING THE LORD'S SUPPER

Regarding the essence of the Lord's Supper the Reformed Churches differed radically from the Roman Churches. Concerning the communion table the issues were very pronounced and clear-cut. It stands to reason that this difference regarding the essence of the Lord's Table should reflect itself in the method of administration of this Sacrament.

1. Matters left to the judgment of the particular Churches.

One of the first practical questions which confronted the Reformation Churches was this: Should communicants stand, sit, kneel, or walk as they receive the bread and wine? Out of respect for the Lord's Table some believers desired to kneel while they partook of the elements. The Synod of Dort, 1578, raised its voice against this practice and ruled against it because of the danger of superstition. In the Roman Church communicants knelt and venerated the elements, which really meant that they prayed to the bread and wine which they believed to have been changed into the true body and blood of Christ. This idolatrous practice and conception our fathers naturally condemned, and they wanted nothing of the kind in the purified Churches. Therefore kneeling at the Lord's Table was ruled out.

Whether the communicants should sit or stand while the Minister gave them, each individually, the bread and the wine, or whether the communicants should walk past the Minister to receive the elements from his hand, these questions were left to the particular Churches to answer as they saw fit. Seemingly the custom of walking past the Minister to receive the bread and wine was soon discarded. At least the first regular Synod, Emden 1571, spoke only of standing or sitting, and left the choice between these two to the particular Churches. It also appears that the usage of sitting soon became common, for the Synod of Dort, 1574, judged that the standing posture was the most appropriate at the Lord's Table, but cautioned not to introduce standing at the Lord's Table abruptly, inasmuch as the sitting posture was already in common practice, but to bring about the change in this respect whenever such could be done conveniently. But the following Synod judged that it made no difference whether communicants sat or stood as they received the elements. Eventually the custom of sitting became common.

Another matter regarding which there is some difference, and which has been left to the judgment of each individual Church, is the question whether all the communicants shall partake at one and the same time, or whether they shall communicate in groups. In some of our Churches separate groups of believers come forward and take their place at or near the communion table and thus celebrate the Lord's Supper as a group. After the first distinct administration, a second follows for a second group; then a third, and so on, until all communicants have participated. These distinct servings or administrations in the one communion service are designated as "tafels," i.e., tables, in the Dutch language. In certain large Churches even a few years ago as many as twelve or more distinct tables or administrations occurred in one communion service. These long drawn-out services were not as edifying as the occasion demanded. At present many Churches have but one administration for every communion service. All communicants seat themselves toward the front of the church, within the limits of a designated area, and are thus served as one body. In some instances there are no designated pews for the communicants. The bread and the wine is merely passed through every pew, and communicants are seated all over the church building intermingling with non-communicants.

We deem it a good thing that the old method of maintaining several distinct administrations in one and the same communion service has been discontinued. But there was something in this old way which had real merit. Separate, small group administrations required the believers to arise and to go forward to take their place at the Lord's Table as a distinct act, before the whole congregation. There was a confession in that act. He who arose and walked forward thereby virtually declared: "As a poor sinner, guilty and doomed, I take refuge in Christ. I need Jesus. I believe on Him as my Saviour and Lord." The old way, moreover, introduced an element of self-expression into the service which is worthy of appreciation and which was favorable in its reaction on the communicants. Consequently we think that those Churches which have maintained the two or three distinct administrations for each celebration have done wisely. They have ruled out the un-edifying objections against numerous "tables", but have conserved and saved the good points of this method. This method is easily followed by simply setting aside a small number of pews, near the communion table, as "communion pews." The rule should be that communicants who wish to partake of the second or third administration do not come forward until those who communicated just before them are back in their seats.

If a Church maintains only one administration for every communion service, then yet the communicants should occupy a designated area. To pass the bread and wine through the whole church auditorium makes it well nigh impossible for a Consistory to control communion attendance. And parties not entitled to the Sacrament may do so with little or no difficulty if the elements are passed along every pew.

Of old it has been the custom in our Churches that the communicants bring an offering of gratitude for the special blessing given by God through the Lord's Supper. This is, beyond doubt, a noble practice and should be maintained. Many Churches set this offering aside for the needy poor. And it is well that we should remember the needy members of Christ's body as we sit at His Table. This is a laudable and appropriate way of exercising communion of saints. Some place these communion gifts in the budget fund. This practice we would condemn. A thank offering for the work of missions is far more appropriate.

Another matter which, according to our Synod of 1920, should be left to the judgment of the particular Churches, is the use of common or of individual cups. Some have questioned the claim that Christ at the institution of the Lord's Supper used a common cup. It seems to us that the words of Matt. 26:27 and Mark 14:23 leave no room for doubt. Concerning the cup which Christ took we read, "He gave to them: and they all drank of it." Concerning these words

Edersheim (speaking of the Passover) says: "I have often expressed my conviction that, in the ancient Services there was considerable elasticity and liberty left to the individual. At present a cup is filled for each individual but Christ seems to have passed the one cup round among the Disciples. Whether such was sometimes done, or the alteration was designedly, and as we readily see, significantly, made by Christ, cannot now be determined." (Edersheim: **The Life and Times of Jesus, the Messiah,** Vol. II, page 496, footnote 3).

We believe that it ought to be granted that the common cup at the Lord's Table is expressive of Christian unity even though one should desire to question whether Christ actually used the common cup with the deliberate purpose of giving expression to this Christian unity. Some say that Christ used the common cup merely because it was the custom of the day. Perhaps these are right, although it is only an opinion. It is worthy of note that men like Edersheim, (see above) and Godet (see his commentary on Luke, Chap. 22:17) seem to question whether the common cup was in vogue in Jesus' day and at the Passover feasts.

At the other hand we believe that it should be granted that the introduction of individual cups at the Lord's Table does not concern the essence of the Sacrament. We do lose a bit of symbolism but we lose nothing regarding the essence of the Lord's Table. And the symbolism which we lose is very likely only incidental. Let it also be remembered that over against the loss of symbolism which we suffer when we discard the common cup, we should note that which we gain by using the individual cups. In this day of widespread and more thorough knowledge concerning disease germs, of individual drinking cups in the home, of individual paper cups and drinking fountains in public places, it is very natural that the common cup at the Lord's Table, going from mouth to mouth, constitutes a detraction and a hindrance for at least some communicants. By using individual cups this source of detraction and hindrance is removed. And that is a gain.

The Reformed Churches of the Netherlands use the common cup exclusively. The individual cup has not met with favor thus far. Yet the Synod of 1920 of these Churches decided that when the use of the common cup at health institutions, by those who have contagious diseases, presents the danger of communicating these diseases, then the Consistory concerned, after having heard the advice of the physicians, may take measures regarding the celebration of the Lord's Supper which are designed to counteract the danger of infection. This permissive ruling of the Holland Churches indicates that the Reformed Churches of the Netherlands virtually agreed that the question of common or individual cups does not touch the real essence of the Sacrament. For surely these Churches would not adopt a ruling which would cripple the celebration of the Lord's Supper regarding an essential feature.

But we repeat, there are certainly arguments in favor of the common cup. Sometimes Ministers seek to cleanse the common cups somewhat with a napkin before they are circulated a second or third time. This measure of sanitation is well meant, but also serves to draw the attention of the new communicants to the fact that the cups are no longer fresh. Consistories could better buy so many common cups, that new groups of communicants would receive a fresh cup and so that only a limited number would use one and the same cup.

Another matter which is not considered to be essential is whether the administering office-bearer shall read from the Bible while the guests partake of the bread and wine or whether the congregation shall sing appropriately. In nearly all our Churches, as well as those of the Netherlands, the officiating Minister reads such passages as the Form suggests while the elements are being passed, and the congregation sings while the guests approach unto the table, or depart. The custom, still practiced a few years ago by many of our Ministers, to discourse on some subject while the communicants partake is fast becoming obsolete. Rightly so, we deem. These discourses often distracted the attention of the communicants from the silent language of the symbols, and perhaps even hindered some in their quiet meditations. Some Ministers preserve a reverential silence while the bread is passed and only break this silence with the reading of God's own Word as the cup is passed.

2. Things to be observed and things to be avoided.

The present article provides that "every Church shall administer the Lord's Supper in such a manner as it shall judge most conducive to edification." But a proviso or condition is added, the first part of which reads as follows: "provided, however, that the outward ceremonies as prescribed in God's Word be not changed and all superstition avoided . . . ."

The Wezelian Convention ruled that the breaking of the bread should be considered to be a necessary element in the administration of the Lord's Supper, inasmuch as Christ clearly included this feature in the institution of the Sacrament.

For generations back the Reformed Churches have been in the habit of cutting the bread to be used into long strips, which strips are to be broken into small fragments in the presence and sight of the communicants. In some of our Churches only a small part of the bread is broken at the time of the actual service. This is doubtlessly done to save time. We cannot approve of this new usage. The breaking of the bread has definite symbolic significance. It points to the breaking of Christ's body for us, and was by Him included in the ceremony. It is better to abbreviate the sermon so that there will be sufficient time for the proper celebration of the Lord's Supper, than to lengthen the sermon to almost normal duration at the expense of the Sacrament. Let us by all means so arrange the communion service and the program of the day that ample time will be found for the celebration of Holy Communion. The commemorative ordinance of the Lord's Supper should be a very meaningful and solemn event in the experience of believers. At the Communion Table if anywhere we should take our time and avoid rushing and crowding.

Inasmuch as Christ used Passover bread, some have contended that we should use unleavened bread at the Lord's Table. The Roman Church does. The Reformed Churches from the days of the Reformation have advocated the use of ordinary bread.* In some Churches at the beginning the unleavened wafers of the Roman Church were used, but it was only a question of time before these were everywhere supplanted by regular bread.

The wine which is to be used is real wine, inasmuch as Christ used wine and not merely grape juice. Without good reasons we should not introduce substitutes for the elements used by Christ. Not that our Reformed fathers were fanatic on this score. They allowed substitutes if ordinary bread and wine were not to be gotten. So, for instance, rice-bread was permitted if need required, and water was even substi-

* Bouwman: **Gereformeerd Kerkrecht,** IV, 1934, p. 415.

tuted for wine if the latter could not be secured, or if certain communicants were ordered not to use any wine by a physician.

Should teetotalers be permitted grape juice or water for wine? No, Christ used wine and unless necessity compels us we should use the element used by Christ.

Those in charge should provide enough bread for the Lord's Table so that each communicant may receive a fragment not overly small. And when individual cups are used some way should be found which permits the Minister to pour the wine in the sight of the communicants.

3. The Form for the Administration of the Lord's Supper to be read.

In our Forms our Churches have a clear, Biblical expression regarding the ceremonies and Sacraments. To avoid unbiblical conceptions it is required that these be constantly read as they are. We may thank God for the wealth which is ours through our various Forms. Without these Forms constantly read in the Churches it would be much harder to maintain the correct conceptions regarding the offices in the Church, its Sacraments, etc.

In some of our Churches the first part of the Form for the Lord's Supper has been read on the Sunday previous to the celebration of Holy Communion, and the concluding half just before the celebration. This is not according to Article 62. It says very clearly, "at the conclusion of the sermon and the usual prayers, the Form for the Administration of the Lord's Supper, . . . shall be read." The Form is not meant to be split in two. It constitutes a unit. The arguments in favor of the usage alluded to are not of sufficient weight. And the practice does not seem to give very good satisfaction where it has been tried.

When the Lord's Supper is served at two distinct services on Communion Sunday, say morning and afternoon or morning and evening, the Form should be read at both services. If this is not done, some communicants may constantly partake of the Lord's Supper without hearing the Form. This is not as it should be. All communicants need to hear its rich and meaningful content before approaching to the Lord's Table.

The formula which the officiating Minister should use before passing the bread and wine is not definitely prescribed by Holy Writ. We have it recorded in varying words. (Cf. Matt. 26:26:28; Mark 14:22-24; Luke 22:19, 20; I Cor. 11:23-25.) The early Reformation Churches in Holland used either of two formulae, that of Datheen or that of á Lasco. The latter was Minister to the Dutch refugee Church in London. He used the following formulae: "The bread which we break is a communion of the body of Christ. Take, eat, remember, and believe that the body of our Lord Jesus Christ was broken unto a complete remission of all our sins." And: "The cup of blessing which we bless is a communion of the blood of Christ. Take, drink ye all of it, remember, and believe that the precious blood of our Lord Jesus Christ was shed unto a complete remission of all our sins." The first parts of these formulae are based upon the wording of I Cor. 1:16. The additional words are explanatory exhortations.

Datheen in his Liturgy used only the first parts of these formulae, the words namely as they are found almost literally in I Cor. 16:10. As remarked above, both of these formulations were in use in the early Reformed Churches. However, the formulation of á Lasco was officially approved by the Synod of Dort, 1618-19, inasmuch as this Synod adopted the liturgy as published by Schilders in 1611, and this edition of the liturgy uses the fuller formula of á Lasco and not that of Datheen. Consequently, our Churches today also follow the á Lasco formulation. (Cf. **Form for the Lord's Supper.**) This formulation is indeed simple, clear and yet beautiful. We may appreciate the fact that its use has again become general both in the Netherlands and with us.

ARTICLE 63

The Lord's Supper shall be administered at least every two or three months.

FREQUENCY OF OBSERVING THE LORD'S SUPPER

In the consideration of this article we shall first consider its specific contents and then append a few words regarding the preparatory and applicatory sermons.

1. Frequency of administering the Lord's Supper.

Some contend that in the early apostolic Church, the Lord's Supper was celebrated every day or at least every day of rest. This is also Jansen's position.* The contention is based on Acts 2:46; 20:7. We do not believe that these passages prove this contention. Calvin himself, though he favored a weekly celebration of the Lord's Supper according to his **Institutes of the Christian Religion** (Book IV, Chap. XVII, 44), did not believe that the texts noted could be used to prove that the Apostolic Church celebrated Communion every day or every week. (Cf. Calvin's Commentary on Acts.)

The Synod of Dort, 1574, held that the observation should take place every two months. Following Synods endorsed this position. But the Synod of Dort, 1578, added that the "Kruiskerken," Churches beneath the cross of persecution, which often had to meet secretly, should celebrate the Lord's Supper whenever it was convenient. This was, of course, only a temporary ruling. As soon as persecution ceased the general rule went into effect. The Synod of 's Gravenhage, 1586, decided that if circumstances were favorable the Churches should also celebrate the Lord's Supper on Easter Sunday, the day of Pentecost and on Christmas. Until the year 1905 the Church Order provided: "The Lord's Supper shall be observed, as much as possible, once every two months. It will also tend to edification to have it on Easter, Pentecost, and Christmas, where the conditions of the Churches permit such."

The Netherlands Churches altered this reading in 1905, and our Synod of 1914 adopted this new redaction, so that Article 63 now simply reads: "The Lord's Supper shall be administered at least every two or three months."

In the Roman Church the people were used to frequent masses. According to Rome the Sacraments are vehicles of grace, in and by themselves. We should therefore not be surprised that frequent observations of Holy Communion were expected by the people, and that even leaders as Calvin, at first at least, advocated weekly Communion Services.

---

* cf. Jansen: **Korte Verklaring**, etc., 1923, p. 282.

In our Christian Reformed Churches, as is the case in the Reformed Churches of Holland, the Lord's Supper is celebrated four times a year, or every three months. In our opinion this is a well-timed arrangement. To celebrate the Lord's Supper very frequently might detract somewhat from its sacredness and effectiveness. To celebrate it less frequently, say once or twice a year, would rob the Churches needlessly of a much needed blessing.

2. Preparatory and applicatory sermons.

The Church Order is silent regarding the preparatory and applicatory services. At the Wezelian Convention, however, it was already stipulated that the Lord's Supper should be announced two weeks before the celebration, in order that the members might prepare themselves aright, and in order that the Elders might call on the communicants living in their respective districts or wards. The Synod of Dort ruled that the preparatory sermon should deal with matters such as follow: Conversion, self-examination, reconciliation with God and one's neighbors, and kindred subjects. Furthermore, this Synod held that just previous to the celebration the advantages and significance of the Lord's Supper should be explained. Since the Synod of 's Gravenhage, 1586, these stipulations have been left out of the Church Order, for the sake of brevity perhaps. But the preaching of a preparatory sermon is nevertheless a fixed custom in our Churches.

In regard to the post-communion applicatory sermon no specific stipulations were ever incorporated into the Church Order.

Whether a Minister would preach on the Lord's Day division in order, or on a selected passage of God's Word appropriate to the occasion, was left to the discretion of each Consistory. More than one Synod ruled in this vein. Many Churches and Ministers desired to preach through the whole catechism once a year, according to its 52 Lord's Day divisions. A special applicatory sermon four times a year interferred with this schedule. Many Ministers adapted the Lord's Day material to the occasion, however. Others preferred to preach a regular applicatory sermon. As stated above, the matter was left to the wisdom of each Church.

Our Synod of 1912 decided that the celebration of the Lord's Supper must always be preceded by a preparatory sermon and followed by an applicatory sermon. (Cf. Acts of Synod, 1912, Art. 72, 9. See also our directory for Church Visitation.)

ARTICLE 64

The administration of the Lord's Supper shall take place only where there is supervision of Elders, according to the ecclesiastical order and in a public gathering of the Congregation.

CHURCH ORGANIZATION REQUIRED FOR THE ADMINISTRATION OF THE LORD'S SUPPER

In the consideration of this article we first devote some attention to the original reading and content of Article 64, and then to the ruling as it now reads.

1. The original reading of Article 64 and its significance.

Originally the present article read as follows: "Inasmuch as the Evening-Prayers are found to be very fruitful in many places, each Church in maintaining these will conduct them as is most edifying. When there is a desire to discontinue them, this shall not be done without the judgment of Classis."

The Evening-Prayers were daily gatherings of the congregation in the church building for Prayer. They might be called vesper prayer meetings, held daily during the latter part of the afternoon, toward evening. During the 16th century they were quite common in Reformed Churches in the Netherlands. The Roman Church observed these Evening Prayers, and the Reformation did not set them aside immediately. He who was in charge of the meeting would explain a passage from the Bible and then lead in prayer.

Eventually objections were raised against the maintenance of these daily services in the Churches. Synod of Dort, 1574, ruled that the Evening-Prayers should not be introduced in Churches which until then had not observed these daily gatherings; and in places in which they were in use, they should be discontinued as soon as possible, and that for three specific reasons: 1. In order that the regular Sunday services might be attended more diligently; 2. In order that family worship might be maintained more diligently; 3. In order that the common prayers held on days of fasting might be used more diligently and zealously.

Seemingly the people in many places relied on these vesper services for their daily devotions to such an extent that it was difficult to discontinue the practice. At least the Synod of Middelburg, 1581, ruled that Evening-Prayers should not be introduced in places where they were not observed, but that they should be discontinued in Churches which maintained these daily meetings, without the advice of Classis. These daily vesper services, inherited from the Roman Church, did not disappear from the domain of the Reformation Churches of Holland until the 17th century. The fact that it was impossible to gather the whole Church together for prayer daily, aside from other considerations, made their discontinuance advisable.

During late years many Protestants in our own land have urged that our church buildings should be open at all times for quiet meditation and prayer. This idea has found many advocates, especially in our larger cities with their constant rush and restlessness. In itself this new practice is harmless, although it may strengthen the tendency to regard our Churches as places of superior holiness. It is to be understood that the sacred, consecrated atmosphere of our Church auditoriums appeals to sensitive souls in this age of rush and sin and materialism. "Spiritual retreats" are apt to promote prayer and devotion. But we do believe that it is far better to stress individual devotion to God in one's own home and the promotion and improvement of family worship. Furthermore, let us stress consecrated, consistent Christian living in the midst of the world and upon its busy marts. And let us continue to stress loyal attendance of the whole congregation, as far as possible, at the regular Sabbath services.

As all will realize, Article 64 as it read originally, was thoroughly out of date when the Netherland Churches adopted a new redaction of the Church Order in 1905. These Churches therefore substituted the present 64th article. We copied their reading in 1914, and consequently Article 64 now reads as it does.

2. Why the Lord's Supper is to be administered only where supervision is exercised.

Article 64 provides that the Lord's Supper shall be administered only there where there is supervision of Elders. In general this means that believers must first be organized into a Church before Holy Communion can be celebrated. This has been the position of our Churches ever since the Reformation. In certain localities the number of believers breaking with the Roman Church and joining the Reformation movement was so small initially that Elders and Deacons could not be appointed. This meant that regular organization was as yet impossible, and that supervision and discipline could not be exercised. Regarding such places Calvin judged, so Jansen informs us,* that the services should be limited to the reading and explaining of God's Word. The Sacrament should not be administered there inasmuch as a definite Church organization was lacking, and supervision and discipline could not be exercised. The Synod of Dort, 1574, ruled in harmony with this opinion of Calvin. Synod of 's Gravenhage, 1586, provided that in places where the number of believers was too small for regular organization, provisional, temporary Elders and Deacons should be designated, before the Lord's Supper was celebrated, in order that supervision and control might not be lacking. In harmony with these sentiments and decisions the present 64th article was written into the Church Order.

There are indeed good reasons for this ruling. Christ dispenses the Sacraments as signs and seals of the forgiveness of sin through His Church, duly organized, and through the office-bearers appointed and charged for this work. Unworthy participation is against His Will and Word. The office-bearers bear responsibility regarding this matter. The Lord's Supper should not be celebrated where control and discipline is not exercised.

This does not mean that the Lord's Supper can never be administered in a place where the Church has not yet been organized. Small groups of believers should be incorporated into neighboring Churches as "branches" of these neighboring Churches. From time to time the Consistories of such Churches can administer the Sacraments to such groups. If at all possible one or more Elders or Deacons should be chosen from among the members of such distant groups who are in position to exercise supervision and who meet with the Consistory of the neighboring Church regularly if possible, or, upon special request of the Consistory, if the distance be too great for regular attendance. Every Lord's Day the group should meet for worship. If no office-bearers can be appointed from among the unorganized group of believers, then one or two Elders should, if possible, accompany the Minister when he goes to the distant group to administer the Sacraments. However, if the Sacraments are administered upon decision of the Consistory, the Minister may conduct the service without the presence of any Elders. When circumstances permit the presence of one or more Elders then their attendance is certainly desirable to assist the Minister and to help supervise the whole service.

The same rule holds for groups of members of our Churches confined in our institutions or hospitals and not well able to attend the regular gatherings of the local congregation; for example, members of our Churches who are patients at Bethesda Sanatorium at Denver.

The Synod of the Reformed Churches of the Netherlands, Leeuwarden, 1920, Art. 25, decided regarding the administration of the

---

* Jansen: **Korte Verklaring**, etc., 1923, p. 286.

Lord's Supper in institutions located within the domain of one of their Churches to permit such a Church to administer the Lord's Supper to members of the Reformed Churches who are patients at such institutions or who belong to their personnel and who cannot very well attend the meeting of the congregation. The Consistory must be represented at such services. Members of Churches, other than the Reformed Churches, may be admitted to these special communion services provided they cannot partake of the Lord's Supper in their own Churches. Such non-member guests must request the privilege of participating from the Consistory in charge in due time, and the Consistory must be assured that such guests are admitted to the Lord's Table in their own Churches and that they agree with the Reformed Churches as to the fundamentals of the Christian religion, that they are without reproach in their conduct, and that they submit themselves to the supervision of the Consistory concerned as long as they partake of the Lord's Supper as non-member guests.

The Synod of Middelburg, 1933, Article 131, decided that it was undesirable to introduce communion for the sick in their homes. Our own Churches, Synod 1914, Article 19, deemed that the administration of the Lord's Supper to those who have not been able to come to Church for years because of sickness, was permissible, provided that the congregation be represented.

If ever a Consistory should receive a request for the privilege of celebrating the Lord's Supper in the home of sick or handicapped and bound to his home for years, how should this Consistory proceed? Let announcement be made to the Church when such a special communion service is to take place and let those living nearest the residence of the sick party be invited to be present. Let the Consistory make sure that at least part of its number can and will be present.

ARTICLE 65

Funerals are not ecclesiastical, but family affairs, and should be conducted accordingly.

FUNERALS NON-ECCLESIASTICAL

1. The nature of funeral sermons and funeral services prior to the Reformation.

The Church of Rome had ecclesiastical burials, funeral services conducted by the Church in an official way. For those who died in good standing with the Church, a Church service would be held. The priest would speak over the body of the deceased; he would offer a prayer in behalf of the dead person, the parishioners would sing a farewell hymn, etc. The tolling or ringing of the church bell was part of the ceremony. According to Jansen it served a two-fold purpose in the Roman conception of things: It drove away the evil spirits; it reminded people that they should pray for the dead person.

It stands to reason that the Reformed Churches disapproved of all this. Official, ecclesiastical burials are unnecessary and uncalled for. The Church as such has no functions to fulfill at a funeral. The Church labors with and for the living. The living God has given His Church a very definite charge, not at all for the dead. In the first place because one's death decides one's eternal state. They who die in the Lord need no further labors by the Church; they are not in purgatory, but in heaven. And those who have died out of the Lord are forever lost, and beyond the reach of the Church. In the second place the Church has no charge of God regarding the burial of the dead because this is a matter which can well be taken care of by the relatives and friends of the deceased, and belongs to their domain and responsibility.

Moreover, the Reformed Churches frowned on Church funerals and sermons because of all the abuses that went with these burials. A whole body of superstitious notions and practices had sprung up around these Roman funerals and many people were attached to these customs, relying on them rather than on the only saving grace of God in Christ.

Now to be sure, no Reformed Church taking official charge of a burial during the first days of the Reformation attached unbiblical value to the address or sermon, and to the prayers offered at a funeral. Nor did the ringing of the church bells have the pagan, superstitious significance which it did have for the Church of Rome. But the people in many instances did attach superstitious value to these activities. Thus it is to be understood that one of the first Synods, Dort, 1574, ruled that funeral sermons should be discontinued as soon as possible, and that localities which had not yet introduced them should not do so, in order to avoid the danger of superstition. Synod of Dort, 1578, judged likewise, and added that in places where these funeral sermons could not be discontinued as yet they should not be regular sermons but merely extemporaneous words of admonition. This Synod did not even favor prayer at these funeral "services", doubtless because many people would attach superstitious value to such prayers in behalf of the dead person. The Synod of Middelburg, 1581, decided that funeral sermons should not be introduced in places where such had not as yet been done, and that they should be discontinued in the most suitable way in those places in which they had already been introduced. This decision became Article 65 of the old Church Order. Thus the ruling stood until 1905, when the Holland Churches accepted the simple reading as we also adopted it in 1914: "Funeral sermons and funeral services shall not be introduced."

2. **Our present customs appraised.**

Before the year 1940 Article 65 read: "Funeral sermons or funeral services shall not be introduced." The Synod of 1940 adopted our present reading. The sense is the same. We did not and we do not maintain official, ecclesiastical funerals. But our present reading expresses the thought a bit more clearly.

The solemnities which we ordinarily observe regarding the burial of our dead are not Church funerals in the technical sense. The Consistories are not in charge of these funerals but the relatives are. If our homes were large enough, or if funeral homes were large enough, we would not, and should not, resort to the Church building at all. At our funerals, moreover, the Minister does not preach a sermon; he does not administer the Word of God officially and to the congregation of God. He only addresses the mourning relatives and their friends appropriately. As we bury our dead we pause for reflection, instruction, and comfort. Many Ministers give their remarks the form of a sermon. This should not be done.

Article 65 as it once read was not an obsolete, antiquated ruling. It is true that the superstitious customs and notions of Rome are hardly known to us anymore. But the article constantly and officially commits our Churches against ecclesiastical burials and their evils. Furthermore, Article 65 should be a constant warning to us against usages and dangers which might easily creep into our circles regarding the burial of our dead. And let it not be overlooked that though we have no funeral services officially, yet unofficially we have introduced something of the kind. Confer what was said regarding the funeral addresses by many Ministers. They are as to form very often actually "sermons." Now this surely is not serious, but neither is it advisable and practical. It also happens that people insist on a "church funeral," when their home can adequately accommodate the relatives and friends. Why? Is there perhaps a lingering bit of superstition in this demand?

It should be noted that although we have no funeral services in the real and official sense of the word, that yet, inasmuch as our church buildings are often used for funeral addresses, the Consistories do have a voice in matters. That is to say, when our Churches permit their buildings to be used for "funeral services" they have a right to stipulate certain conditions if they so desire. Our Consistories need not permit innovations which they might deem out of place. When the use of our church auditoriums is requested for funeral addresses, we have a right to grant the request upon condition, for instance, that unconverted, modernistic singers shall not take part in the "service," or that excessive floral displays be omitted, etc. A wreath, or a spray or two of flowers on the casket does not offend. But should we carry large numbers of floral offerings into our church buildings when used for funeral addresses? Why?

Doubtless it would be better if we would cease using the expression "funeral sermons" when referring to our funeral addresses. Likewise it would be better if we would speak of burials rather than of "funeral services" inasmuch as we have neither funeral sermons nor funeral services in the ordinary sense of these expressions. Many denominations have both funeral services and funeral sermons in the real sense of the word. So do the lodges of our land.

Our Synod of 1888 held that when our church buildings are used for burials it is a matter of indifference whether or not the corpse is brought into the building. Each Consistory can decide this matter as it sees fit.

The tolling of the church bell at burials is entirely unobjectionable for our day and age. It is a solemn usage reminding us of the reality and solemnity of death.

What should be our attitude toward cremation? The Bible does not forbid the burning of dead bodies, but honorable burial was the rule in both Old Testament and New Testament times. The patriarchs were buried. God Himself buried Moses. Lazarus rested in a grave. Our Lord Himself underwent burial, not burning. In the ancient apostolic Church burial was the common custom. On the other hand, many pagan peoples burned the bodies of their dead. And the only instances in which burning is prescribed by God for Israel is in the case of great sinners, as a special condemnation of such sinners on God's part. (Cf. Lev. 20:14; 21:9; Joshua 7:15.) Many people today favor cremation from materialistic unbelieving considerations. Death to these ends all. Christian burial, at the other hand, is expressive of the hope and expectation of the resurrection. The body is sown in corruption, as a seed is sown, but it will be raised incorruptible. (I Cor. 15.)

ARTICLE 66

In time of war, pestilence, national calamities, and other great afflictions, the pressure of which is felt throughout the Churches, it is fitting that the Classes proclaim a Day of Prayer.

DAYS OF PRAYER

1. Former rulings and usages.

Originally Article 66 read as follows: "In times of war, pestilence, depression, persecution of Churches, and other general calamities, the Ministers of the Churches shall request the government that upon its authority and order public fast and prayer days be appointed and hallowed."

As is well known, the Roman Church made much of days of fasting and prayer. There was much externalism in the observance of these days in the Roman Church. This the Reformation Churches condemned. But they saw much good in special days of fasting and prayer. They believed that when circumstances and times were trying believers should humble themselves before God and pray for relief. The Churches therefore maintained days of fasting and prayer. But by reason of persecution united action was difficult at first. The individual Churches would hold their own days of fasting and prayer whenever the Consistories felt that such days should be observed. Jansen informs us that at first these days would be observed when a new Minister had to be called, but later the usage was applied to emergency conditions as referred to above.* This same authority informs us also that when a fast and prayer day was proclaimed the congregation would come to the church upon the week-day appointed and would sometimes remain in church all day at the same time refraining from eating and drinking. Two sermons would be preached and between the sermons passages from the Bible would be read to the gathering.

It will be noted that the Churches initiated the observances of these days apart from the government. But when the Reformation had gained considerable head-way, and when the government was sympathetic toward the Reformed Churches, the government would be requested to proclaim these days of fasting and prayer. Consequently the original 65th article reads as it does.

It therefore appears that our Church Order originally provided for days of fasting and prayer, and not merely for days of prayer as it does now.

According to the "Christelyke Encyclopaedie," the 16th century Reformation broke with the meritorious fasts of the Roman Churches and returned to Scriptural fasting, which aims to repress and curb the flesh and constitutes a spiritual exercise. Calvin especially, so this same source tells us, warned against the Roman practice of fasting. Fasting should be practiced to repress the flesh and to prepare for prayer and humiliation before God. But during the 17th and 18th centuries the custom of fasting fell completely into disuse. It was revived for a brief period during the days of the Secession of 1834 and following years, because of persecutions experienced, but soon fell into disuse once more.**

The Synod of the Reformed Churches of the Netherlands 1905 re-

---

* Jansen: **Korte Verklaring,** etc., 1923, p. 289.

** **Christelyk Encyclopaedie:** Article "Vasten".

vised Article 66 and among other changes left the provision for fasting out. In 1914 our Synod did likewise.

Whether the discontinuance of fasting in our circles can be defended from every aspect is a question which is certainly open for debate, but which we are not now considering. But it is a question worthy of serious consideration.

2. Conditions which warrant special Days of Prayer.

We have our annual Day of Prayer for Crops. This Day of Prayer is observed every second Wednesday in the month of March. But besides this regular Day of Prayer the present article provides for special Days of Prayer. In days of great affliction such as brought about by war, pestilence, and other national calamities, it is fitting, Article 66 declares, that Days of Prayer be proclaimed. The article refers to afflictions, "the presence of which is felt throughout the Churches." This does not refer to all the Churches of our denomination, scattered as they are from the Atlantic to the Pacific, but rather to the Churches of certain Classes. For the Churches of one sector may be visited by calamities which are not felt at all by Churches of another region. Yet this fact should not keep the Churches affected from holding special prayer services. Moreover the article authorizes the Classes to proclaim these special Days of Prayer. Doubtless Synod of 1914 adopted this reading with a purpose. For thus each group of Churches can act for itself. This method of procedure is altogether proper for a denomination the Churches of which are widely scattered over a large territory. This does not mean that Synod cannot prescribe a general Day of Prayer for all the Churches in case of calamities which are general. Nor does the article mean to say that individual Churches may not set aside special Days of Prayer when they see fit to do so.

The conclusion of the present article as maintained by us differs somewhat from the conclusion of the Holland Churches. We say: "In time of war, . . . , it is fitting that the Classes proclaim a Day of Prayer." The Reformed Churches of the Netherlands say, "In time of war, . . . , a Day of Prayer shall be appointed by the Classis appointed for this purpose by the last general Synod." In Holland therefore a Classis is designated by each general Synod, which is charged to appoint special Days of Prayer for all the Churches of the denomination whenever this Classis may deem such a step advisable. Synod of 's Gravenhage, 1914, favored holding such special Days of Prayer on Sabbath days rather than on week days. But this question was left to the Classis charged with this matter. We, by our reading of Article 66, have made the matter of appointing special Days of Prayer a classical matter. Doubtless this was done because our Churches cover a wide extent of territory, and consequently our Classes often represent various needs.

It is worthy of note, that the Churches of Holland delegate this matter, not to a committee as we would be apt to do, but to a Classis. This is in harmony with the principle that Church governmental matters which can be acted upon directly through the governing bodies themselves should not be delegated to committees.

ARTICLE 67

The Churches shall observe, in addition to the Sunday, also Christmas, Good Friday, Easter, Ascension Day, Pentecost, the Day of Prayer, the National Thanksgiving Day, and Old and New Year's Day.

SPECIAL DAYS TO BE OBSERVED

1. The original position of the Reformed Churches regarding special days.

During the early days of the Reformation some Reformed localities observed only Sunday. All special days sanctioned and revered by Rome were set aside. Zwingli and Calvin both encouraged the rejection of all ecclesiastical festive days. In Geneva all special days were discontinued as soon as the Reformation took a firm hold in that city. Already before the arrival of Calvin in Geneva this had been accomplished under the leadership of Farel and Viret. But Calvin agreed heartily. And Knox, the Reformer of Scotland, shared these same convictions, he being a disciple of Calvin in Geneva. Consequently the Scottish Churches also banned the Roman sacred days.

These eminent Reformers took this stand for the following reasons: The festival days are not ordained of God but are a human invention; they minimize Sunday, the God-ordained weekly day of rest; they lead to paganistic celebrations and promote licentiousness.* In view of present day celebrations of days as Christmas and Easter by the general public and many believers it must be said that the contentions of the Reformers as to this last point were certainly correct. Present day celebration of these days is more pagan than Christian. Neither can it be denied that the observance of these days is but an invention of man, and that many people hold these festivals in higher esteem than Sunday.

Considering the position of the Reformers, we are not surprised that the Synod of Dort, 1574, held that the weekly Sabbath alone should be observed, and that the observance of all other days should be discouraged. This same Synod, however, also decided that the Ministers should preach about the birth of Christ on the Sunday preceding Christmas day, and Ministers were also permitted to preach on the resurrection of Jesus on Easter Sunday and on the outpouring of the Spirit on Pentecost Sunday.** The "tweede feestdagen," i.e., second festival days, still observed in Holland on December 26 and on the days following Easter and Pentecost, were set aside and ignored completely by this Synod.

2. Why the provisions of this article were included in the Church Order

Consulting the present article we find that it prescribes the observation of several special or festival days. How is this to be explained? The government of Holland was loath to set all the Christian festivals aside inasmuch as many of the people delighted in these days for the sake of their pleasures and because the government officials and employees hated to part with a number of holidays which afforded them rest and recreation. Rather than see these days given over to the danger of abuse and frivolity, the Churches accommodated themselves

---

* Bouwman: **Ger. Kerkrecht,** Vol. II, 1934, p. 486.

** Rutgers, Acta der Nat. Syn., p. 142, quoted by Bouwman, **Ger. Kerkrecht,** Vol. II, 1934, p. 487.

to circumstances and began to celebrate these days after a fashion. Thus the Synod of Dort, 1578, Article 75, declared in substance that it would be desirable to celebrate Sunday only according to God's ordinance. But, inasmuch as Christmas Day and the day following upon Christmas, as well as the days following upon Easter and Pentecost and in some places also New Year's Day, and Ascension Day were legal holidays by authority of the governments, the Ministers should preach appropriately on these days in order to turn a fruitless and harmful idleness (lediggang) into a holy and profitable exercise. Furthermore, Ministers of cities which observed other festivals by authority of local governments, should hold services on these days also. At the same time this Synod urged that the Churches should work toward the setting aside of all festive-days, except Christmas, Easter, and Pentecost.*

Subsequent Synods made like decisions and concessions. The great Synod of Dort, 1618-19, adopted the following reading of Article 67: "The Churches shall keep, besides Sunday, also Christmas, Easter and Pentecost, with the days following upon these days. And whereas most cities and provinces of the Netherlands also keep the day of (Christ's) Circumcision, and the Ascension of Christ, the Ministers shall in all places in which such is not yet being done, advocate the matter (zullen arbeiden) so that these localities may conform themselves to the others."

We note that the early Reformed Synods yielded increasingly to pressure from without regarding the observation of "Christian festivals." The government of the Netherlands made something like legal holidays out of these festivals, and so the Churches, although not favoring the observation of these days, for practical reasons ruled as they did. To prevent people from spending these days in worldiness they introduced Church services for these festive occasions.

The Synod of the Reformed Churches of the Netherlands, 1905, adopted the following redaction of Article 67: "The congregations shall keep, besides Sunday, also Christmas, Easter, Pentecost and Ascension Day. The observation of the second festival days is left to the freedom of the Churches."

It will be noted that our redaction of 1914 includes several more special days, namely, Good Friday, the Day of Prayer (for Crops, second Wednesday in March) the National Thanksgiving Day, and Old and New Year's Day. These days had all received a semi-official standing in our Churches. There is much to be said for their observation. And so it was only logical that we should include them in Article 67.

Regarding Good Friday, the Holland Churches have not included it with its festive days mentioned in Article 67. This was seemingly done because Good Friday is celebrated superstitiously by the various Churches. It is often elevated above Sunday, especially by the Roman Church. The Lord's Supper is celebrated on Good Friday instead of on the Lord's Day as was done by the Apostolic Churches. Hence the Reformed Churches hesitated to mention the day officially, although many of these Churches hold an evening service on Good Friday. We keep the day officially. It is indeed a very meaningful day on the Christian Church calendar. But we should also guard ourselves against an unwholesome, unscriptural overemphasis here. We should guard against Roman and Lutheran practices which border on

---

* Acta, Synode Dordrecht, 1578, Act. 75. Kerkelyk Handboekje, G. Ph. Zalsman, Kampen, 1882.

things superstitious. And let us not overestimate celebrations which are often superficial and external by men and women who ordinarily manifest very little knowledge of and appreciation for the atoning death of our Lord and Savior. We would appreciate all Scriptural and sincere commemoration of Christ's death and suffering. But we would also note that leading modernists are often foremost in the celebration of Good Friday, whereas modernists deny the heart and core of Christ's suffering and death.

Our Churches, and also some of us as individuals, have at various times petitioned our government to proclaim a Day of Prayer annually. Thus far this has not brought results. Nevertheless, we as Churches observe the day. However, it is to be regretted that we do not keep **a day of prayer** to invoke God's blessings on our agricultural endeavors. At most we keep an **hour of prayer.** The day of prayer has indeed shrunk to small proportions.

It is doubtless advisable that we continue to follow the method of introducing our petitional prayers and our prayers of thanksgiving at these special services by an appropriate sermon and that the Minister then leads the Church in prayer. We do not believe that the introduction of prayer meeting methods for these special services would be an advancement. Needless to say, as individuals, as families and as groups of believers, we should not neglect prayer and praise for these special needs on these special days.

Watch hour services for New Year's eve and sunrise services on Easter morning are indeed harmless in themselves, although they may foster reliance on external things. It is a fact well known to Church historians that as spiritual life begins to wane, formalistic and extraordinary observances begin to increase. He who serves God in Spirit and with devotion will have little need for the unusual, and for constant innovations. And not to be forgotten, the regular services of the Church, held at the regular hours, which all, old and young can attend, should never be crowded upon the background.

3. The position of our Churches as to the weekly Lord's Day.

Our Churches observe first and foremost, as the present article also indicates, the Lord's Day or Sunday. We believe that the Sabbath (Day of Rest) should be kept, not as a matter of good policy merely, as Roman Catholics, Lutherans, and the majority of present day Protestants seem to hold, but by commandment of God.

We hold that the whole decalogue, that all the Ten Commandments are still in force. The Ten Commandments are God's summary of His universal laws. They hold for the New Testament period as well as for the Old Testament period. The fourth commandment is no exception to this rule. Of course, the Israelitish, ancient cloak in which the fourth commandment in common with the other commandments is dressed is not essential to the heart of the commandment. We maintain that one day out of every seven, according to a definite cycle of days, must be set aside for service of and devotion to God. That is the abiding principle. And this abiding principle is not Jewish but universal. God hallowed the Sabbath day unto Himself even before sin entered the world.

We hold that it is the Christian's privilege and duty on "the day of rest (to) diligently attend the Church of God, to learn in God's Word, to use the Sacraments, to call publicly upon the Lord and to give Christian alms." (Heidelberg Catechism, qu. 103.) At the same time we believe it to be our duty to refrain from all unnecessary activities which divert our attentions and which tend to make the day common.

The great Synod of Dort, 1618-19, adopted six points regarding the Sabbath which, translated almost verbatim, read as follows:

1. In the fourth commandment of God's Law there is a ceremonial and a moral element.

2. The rest on the seventh day after the creation, and the strict observance of this day with which the Jewish people were charged particularly, was ceremonial.

3. That a definite and appointed day has been set aside to the service of God, and that for this purpose as much rest is required as is necessary for the service of God and for hallowed contemplation, this element is moral.

4. The Sabbath of the Jews having been set aside, Christians are in duty bound to hallow the Day of the Lord solemnly.

5. This day has always been kept in the early Church since the time of the Apostles.

6. This day must be so consecrated unto the service of God that upon it men rest from all servile labors, except those required by charity and present necessities, and likewise from all such recreations as prevent the service of God.*

These six points were adopted by our own Synod of 1881. And according to our Synod of 1926 (Art. 136, pp. 191, 192) they must be considered doctrinal in their nature and hence binding and also in full accord with the fundamental principles expressed in Lord's Day 38 of the Catechism, to the effect that the fourth commandment also applies to the New Testament Church in its observance of the day of rest and worship. Synod also declared that these six points are an official interpretation of our confession and not an addition to our Forms of Unity. (Also see Appendix 9, page 370.)

ARTICLE 68

The Ministers shall on Sunday explain briefly the sum of Christian Doctrine comprehended in the Heidelberg Catechism so that as much as possible the explanation shall be annually completed, according to the division of the Catechism itself, for that purpose.

CATECHISM PREACHING

1. The purpose and value of catechism preaching.

The Heidelberg Catechism is a brief, practical summary of the way of salvation as revealed in the Bible. It covers the whole field of doctrine, from beginning to end, systematically. The Catechism is not something which the Churches have added to the Bible, but it is a short, systematic, practical summary of the doctrine of salvation as revealed in the Bible. The contents of the Catechism are gleaned from the Bible and are based on the Bible. Our Churches hold that believers should have a clear understanding of the way in which God saves His people. The teachings concerning man's fall into sin, the degree of his sinfulness, the hopelessness of his condition in and by himself, the sovereignty of God's redeeming grace in Christ, the Deity of Christ and its necessity, the origin, nature and purpose of the

---

* Cf. Post-Acta, 164th Session, Synod 1618-19.

Church, concerning these and many other things God has something very definite to say in His Word. Consequently God's people should take close note of all that God teaches them. Let them remember that: "Every scripture inspired of God is also profitable for teaching, for reproof, for correction, for instruction which is in righteousness: that the Man of God may be complete, furnished completely unto every good work." (II Tim. 3:16, 17.) Now by preaching the truth of God constantly and systematically according to the summary of the Heidelberg Catechism the congregation of God receives regular instruction in all the fundamentals of the Christian faith as revealed in the Bible. It is true that apart from Catechism preaching a Minister might indoctrinate his congregation according to God's revelations. But Catechism preaching assures us that **all Ministers will preach the whole truth of God**, and that not according to their personal conceptions, but according to the common conception of all the Churches. We are safe in saying that if it were not for Catechism preaching, certain truths of God's Word would be seldom touched upon in our sermons. All Ministers are but men, and all men are apt to be one-sided and forgetful. The preaching of God's Word according to the summary of that Word found in the Catechism safeguards the Churches against the danger of partial and one-sided preaching. And at the same time it offers the Churches some security against unbiblical, erroneous presentations. Every Minister must be loyal in his interpretations to the Word of God as reproduced in the Catechism.

Catechism preaching, to be sure, is doctrinal preaching. We need doctrinal preaching. Every believer should be a well informed Christian. One who is not well informed as to the main teachings of Holy Writ cannot be a strong Christian. And especially in our day and age of shallow Christianity and self-conceived, self-constructed conceptions, a thorough understanding of God's truth is very necessary. Besides, every doctrine of Holy Writ, rightly understood, is full of comfort for the believer. We need this comfort in this world of disappointments and conflicts.

Sometimes it has been objected that Catechism preaching is the setting aside of the Word of God. It is claimed to be preaching of man's Word. This presentation is utterly false for every Lord's Day division of the Catechism is the summary of several Bible passages. Virtually therefore, the Minister who preaches on a certain Lord's Day division of the Catechism is preaching on several passages of God's Word. It may be said in this connection that Catechism sermons should be so constructed that the congregation sees very clearly that the truths embodied in the Catechism are indeed but reproductions of God's own Word. When we preach a Catechism sermon, we are preaching the Word of God just as well as if we preach on a certain text or passage taken directly from the Bible. Only, in case of catechism preaching, one expounds and applies the Word of God according to a summary of that Word **adopted by all the Churches and agreed to by all the members of our Churches.**

2. The origin of catechism preaching.

The custom of preaching God's Word at one of the Sunday services, according to the summary of the Heidelberg Catechism is of old standing. The Holland Churches adopted the usage from Reformed Churches of other countries. We hear of the practice as early as 1566. In 1574 a question reached the Synod of Dort, asking whether it would not be advisable to make some good sermons on the Catechism. These were doubtlessly desired for the people to read and perhaps to serve the Ministers as guides in constructing catechism sermons. And in 1578 the Synod of Dort decided that after the Lord's Supper had been served on Sunday afternoons the Minister should proceed to preach on the Catechism as usual. However, the first binding decision for all the Churches we find in the Church Order of the Synod of 1586, 's Gravenhage, Article 61. "The Ministers shall everywhere on Sunday, ordinarily in the afternoon sermon, explain briefly the summary of Christian doctrine contained in the Catechism, which at this time has been accepted in the Netherland Churches, in such a way that this explanation may be finished annually, following the division of the Catechism itself as made for this purpose."

Our present reading of Article 68 is a redaction of this original. The only change which was made in this article by the Churches of Holland in 1905 was the provision that the explanation should be finished annually, "as much as possible" (zooveel mogelijk). Jansen is slightly in error when he states that the Synod of Dort, 1618-19, inserted the phrase, "which at this time has been accepted in the Netherland Churches" (die tegenwoordig in de Nederlandsche Kerken aangenomen is). This phrase was in the article from the day of its first adoption. (1586.)

Our redaction of 1914 omits this phrase as being unnecessary and out of place in a Church Order for our Churches here in America. Our 1914 revision also omitted the provision that these catechism sermons should ordinarily be preached on Sunday afternoon. This matter is left to the judgment of each Church. Many of our Churches now have evening services instead of afternoon services, and find it more suitable to preach according to the Catechism in the morning service, when minds are fresh and heavier material seems more in place. Others doubtlessly favor preaching the Catechism sermon at the second service no matter when it is held. Each Church is free in this matter.

To make clear which Catechism is meant our redaction of 1914 also added the word: "Heidelberg." Moreover, we also decided that the Catechism should be covered in one year's time, "as much as possible."

At first the people did not take to catechism preaching. However, as appears from certain decisions taken by Synods in regard to this matter, perhaps many refrained from attending the service at which the catechism was preached because they did not care to go to Church twice a day. The Catechism was always preached in the afternoon service as the original article stipulated. Many had joined the Reformation, but not sincerely. They went along with the crowd. Others were not as spiritually minded as they should have been. The Roman Church was very lax and legalistic. This spirit many maintained after they had officially broken with Rome. These felt that one service a day was enough. And they were adverse to doctrinal studies perhaps. Let it also be remembered that the Reformed Churches were really the official, state-recognized, Churches of Holland. This gave them special favor and protection, but also handicapped them in the exercise of discipline and it opened the doors of the Churches to many evils. A "volkskerk", a Church seeking to include all the people within its walls, is making a mistake, for all are not God's people, and it is bound to suffer for its error.

Some of the complaints which reached the Synod of Dort, 1618-19, regarding non-attendance at Catechism preaching and its causes are the following: failure of Ministers to hold afternoon services at which the Catechism sermon could be preached; many people insisted on working or playing on Sunday afternoon; some Ministers had two or more Churches to serve and could not attend to their flocks properly; the Remonstrants (Arminians) were opposed to Catechism preaching; the government failed to maintain Sunday as a day of rest and permitted field labor.

Briefly stated the Synod took the following decisions to curb the evil and to improve the situation:

1. It reiterated the decision of the Synod of 1586 regarding Catechism preaching. Ministers who should fail to do their duty in this respect would be censured. Catechism sermons should be brief and understandable to the common people.
2. No Minister should neglect to maintain this service because the attendance is small. Though only the Minister's own family should be in attendance, he should proceed. This would be a good example.
3. The government was to be asked to forbid all unnecessary Sunday labor, and especially sports, drinking parties, etc., so that people might learn to hallow the Sabbath day and come to Church regularly.
4. Every Church should have its own Minister as much as possible and unnecessary combinations of two or more Churches should be severed, or else the Catechism sermons should be maintained at least every other Sunday afternoon.
5. Church Visitors were charged to take close note of this matter regarding every Church. Negligent, unwilling Ministers had to be reported to Classis for censure. Confessing members who refused to attend the catechism sermons seemingly had to be censured also.*

3. Dangers to be avoided.

Catechism preaching is beyond a doubt one of our strongholds. Consequently we must guard it against any and all dangers which threaten its continuance or which may help to bring the custom into disfavor.

Ministers should always see to it that their catechism sermons are really sermons. They should not be class room lectures on some theological question, however important. A catechism sermon should be an exposition and application of God's Word just as every other sermon.

Furthermore Ministers should avoid abstract Catechism preaching which goes over the heads and beside the hearts of the congregation. Let our catechism sermons be vital and understandable even to the simplest minds.

Again, sermons that go into great detail, so that two, three or more sermons are required for one Lord's Day division should be avoided. Let the rule of Article 68 be observed. If our fathers, having more time and moving much slower than we, found it best to cover the Catechism in one year's time, then in all likelihood it is best for us also.

Should a text from the Bible be chosen and quoted together with the Lord's Day division of the Catechism as text for the sermon? No. This practice may lead some people to think that a catechism sermon is really not a sermon on the Word of God. This erroneous conception should not be encouraged in the least. Furthermore, no Lord's Day division of the Catechism is based on a single Bible passage. If a Minister desires to quote the Biblical foundation for any given Lord's Day division, then he shall have to quote a good many passages.

---

* Cf. H. Kaajan, De Pro-Acta der Dordsche Synode, pp. 154-167, quoted by Jansen, **Korte Verklaring**, etc., 1923, p. 295-6.

And in some instances the doctrine deduced is not found in so many words in any Bible passage, but is rather the legitimate conclusion based on certain facts clearly revealed.

We deem that it is better, far better, for the Minister to quote and interpret Scripture in the body of the sermon so that the congregation feels instinctively that the Minister is really bringing them God's own Word.

At the beginning of the catechism sermon, as he announces his sermon, let the Minister use some statement as follows: "The Word of God, congregation, as I expound and apply it for you at this time, is summarized for us in Lord's Day division . . . . of our Catechism." Then let him read the Lord's Day division.

We have heard of instances in which the Minister would read a text taken directly from the Bible, but he would omit announcing and reading the Lord's Day division. This is of course all wrong. We suppose that this was done to satisfy some who objected to catechism preaching. But we gain nothing in the long run by yielding to mistaken notions. Rather let us labor to remove such mistaken conceptions. This cannot be done effectively and fairly by preaching camouflaged catechism sermons. In such a case as this it is better to face the issue squarely than to dilly-dally.

We should also be careful not to omit the catechism sermon in favor of a free-choice-text sermon without due cause. Some have permitted the Catechism to rest during the pre-Christmas season or perhaps during Lent. This is unnecessary and contrary to the present article of the Church Order. Let the exceptions which we make to the adopted rule be few and well founded.

Already in 1902 our Synod found it necessary to admonish the Churches as follows: "With a view to dangers from without that threaten sound doctrine, and in consideration of the great need of, and the very meager interest in the regular development of dogmatical truths, Synod emphasizes the time-honored custom of catechism preaching, and the Classes are urged to give proper attention to this matter, that the regular consideration of the catechism may be observed." *

ARTICLE 69

In the Churches only the 150 Psalms of David and the collection of hymns for Church use, approved and adopted by Synod, shall be sung. However, while the singing of the Psalms in divine worship is a requirement, the use of the approved hymns is left to the freedom of the Churches.

PSALMS AND HYMNS FOR PUBLIC WORSHIP

In the consideration of this article we first of all speak briefly concerning its historical background. Then we shall indicate the specific significance of the article as it now reads. Finally, the matter of choir singing and the use of instrumental music for congregational worship will be taken up.

* Acts, 1902, Art. 103 and 110, translation by Stuart and Hoeksema: Church Order, under Art. 68.

1. Historical background of this article.

In the ancient Church the singing of psalms was undoubtedly common. Psalm singing was well known to the Jews as they worshipped in their synagogues and so we are not surprised to find this practice back in the early Christian Churches. It cannot be said with certainty that the early Churches also used hymns in congregational worship, although there are many things which seem to point in this direction. However, Augustine tells us that in his time the North African Churches sang only the psalms. And the counsel of Bracatara, 563, decided that no hymns should be used in the Churches besides the psalms and hymns taken directly from the Old Testament and New Testament. Eventually, however, psalm singing diminished. Gregory the Great, bishop of Rome from 590 to 604, substituted choir singing for congregational singing. This move relegated the psalms still farther upon the background, as stands to reason.

Zwingli did not approve of singing in Church services. Perhaps Roman ritualism and its externalism drove him to this extreme and unwarranted position. We may be thankful that the other leader of the Reformed Churches did not share this view. In the Roman Church the choir sang and the congregation listened. The people did not sing. This met with disapproval on Calvin's part. He restored congregational singing and silenced the choir. He believed that all the believers should praise God in song. A number of psalms, versified by Clement Marot and Beza were introduced by him. The melodies were written by Louis Bourgeois and Maitre Pierre at Calvin's request. Not only were the children taught to sing these psalms in the schools, but some of the older folks also received instruction in the singing of psalms.

The example of the Genevan Reformer found a ready following in all Reformed Churches, although the Zwinglian Churches did not introduce congregational singing until the close of the century.

The Reformed Churches of Holland first sang the "Souterliedekens" of Willem van Zuylen van Nijevelt. These were versifications of the psalms collected and in all likelihood also written by the author. (Souter-salter-psalter.)

In 1566 the Rev. Petrus Datheen published his book of psalms. These psalms by Datheen became very popular. They appealed to the heart of the believer. This versification was modeled after the French edition of Marot and Beza. The Convention of Wezel recommended the Dathenian Psalms for Church services.

In 1580 a new rendering by Marnix van St. Aldegonde made its appearance. The psalms by Marnix were original versifications. In many respects they were superior to those written by Datheen, but they were less popular. Datheen's rendering, though less accurate, spoke to the hearts of God's people. Synod of Middelburg, 1581, stipulated that the Psalms of David should be sung in the Churches but no longer specified that the Psalms of Datheen should be used.

The Synods favored the Marnix psalms. When the Synod of Dort, 1618-19, met it did specify psalm singing as previous Synods had done, but it did not choose between Datheen and Marnix. Seemingly it did not care to stir up discord over this matter. The people in general still much preferred Datheen's work. The psalms of Marnix were consequently never put into general use. It was not until the year 1775 that the Dathenian psalms were finally set aside. In that year the present Psalter was introduced by order of the States General.— Almost needless to say, the fact that this body introduced the present Psalter in Holland, points to a state domination in ecclesiastical affairs which deserves condemnation. — The committee which compiled the present Dutch psalter drew from three sources: from a versification by Hendrik Ghijsen of Amsterdam; from another by an association named "Laus Deo, Salus populo"; and from a versification by J. E. Voet, M. D., of 's Gravenhage. There are serious faults attached to this Dutch psalter. Doctrinal, exegetical, and aesthetical objections have rightfully been raised against this versification. It is well that an improved versification is being introduced.

Our own Churches here in America have made changes more frequently during recent years, not as to the psalter used in our Dutch services, however. For these services we have constantly used the present Dutch Psalter. But as to the psalms sung in our English services changes have been made. The True Reformed Protestant Dutch Church in 1886 adopted as its book of praise, the **Metrical Version of the Psalter used by the United Presbyterian Church of North America.** This Church united with the Christian Reformed Church in 1890 and became known as Classis Hackensack. The Psalter referred to became the book of praise for our Churches. This book also contained fifty-two hymns arranged and numbered agreeably to the fifty-two Lord's Day sections of the Heidelberg Catechism; the Songs of Mary, Zacharias. At the time of the union of 1890 it was understood and stipulated that the Churches of Classes Hackensack were permitted to use these hymns. This Psalter was the official book of praise for our Churches until 1914, when Synod decided to adopt the new U. P. Psalter. This Psalter had been composed by a joint committee of nine American and Canadian denominations. Our Churches were represented first by Rev. J. Groen and later by Dr. H. Beets. This Psalter served our Churches in many ways very acceptably for 20 years. In 1934 it was succeeded by the Psalter Hymnal. The best of the former Psalter was incorporated into this book. Moreover, many of the choice numbers of the venerable Dutch Psalter were translated or re-versified by some of our own men with poetic ability and set to the much appreciated chorales of Reformation times as found in the Dutch Psalter. Consequently today we are once more singing some of the beautiful and highly spiritual chorales of Bourgeois (1551), Pierre (1562), and others. Moreover, this Psalter Hymnal adopted as the official book of praise for all of our Churches, contains a large number of hymns, 140, the overwhelming majority of which were not to be sung in our Churches prior to the revision of Article 69 by the Synod of 1934, and its approval of the Psalter Hymnal.

2. The article as it now reads.

Before the year 1932, the 69th article read as follows: "In the Churches only the 150 Psalms of David, the Ten Commandments, the Lord's Prayer, the Twelve Articles of Faith, the Songs of Mary, Zacharias and Simeon, the Morning and Evening Hymns, and the Hymn of Prayer before the service shall be sung." Synod of 1932 revised this article and rendered it as it now reads and as it is found at the head of this present discussion.

The revision of 1932 took place, as will be realized, to make the adoption of a large number of select hymns possible.

The Reformed Churches have sung a few hymns from the very beginning. Datheen's Psalter contained versifications of the Ten Commandments, the Lord's Prayer, the Twelve Articles, the Songs of Zacharias, Mary, and Simeon, and a Prayer to be sung before the

Sermon. In some sections, such as Overijsel, a number of other hymns of German origin were permitted for the time being.

Yet it is also a fact that various early Synods refused to introduce and permit more hymns than had been introduced through the Psalter of Datheen. Synod of Dort, 1574, decided that the Churches "should be satisfied" with the Psalter of Datheen until the General Synod should judge otherwise. Synod of Dort, 1578, decided that hymns which were not direct reproductions of parts of Holy Writ, should not be sung in the Churches. Other hymns, though very good but merely reflecting Christian experience and aspirations, were therefore ruled out. (Idem, Middelburg, 1581.) The great Synod of Dort, 1618-19, permitted the very limited number of hymns introduced through Datheen's Psalter, but this Synod definitely added the following clause to Article 69: "All other Hymns shall be barred from the Churches, and where some have already been introduced, these shall be set aside by means found to be most appropriate."

For nearly two centuries the Churches of Holland abided by this decision of Dort. But in 1807 a committee composed of delegates from various Provincial Synods introduced 192 hymns, which it recommended to the Churches. Later on the singing of these hymns, some of which were doctrinally objectionable, was made compulsory. This factor became a source of much trouble. It helped to call into life the Secession of 1834, under De Cock, Scholte, e.a.

The chief objections which the Reformed believers have constantly entertained against hymn singing in the Churches are as follows: 1. God gave us the psalms by inspiration to be used in worship. We should not add uninspired songs to these inspired, Biblical songs. 2. The psalms are deeply spiritual. Many hymns are shallow and do not require as much spiritual understanding and experience as the psalms do. Consequently they are apt to crowd the psalms into disuse more and more. Hymns tend to become out of date. Consequently there will be a periodic demand for new hymns. And thus misconceptions and false doctrines may readily enter the Church through the practice of hymn singing. Many erroneous conceptions have entered the hearts and minds of God's people in the past through repeated singing of appealing, but faulty hymns.

None should deny that these arguments carry weight. They should call us to constant vigilance. They might even justifiably move a Church or a denomination not to permit the singing of hymns in worship. But we do not believe that the Word of God is violated when hymn singing is introduced. Essentially the singing of hymns in worship is not wrong. The New Testament Church may well sing in New Testament language. Moved by these convictions our Synod of 1932 altered Article 69 so as to permit the introduction of a large number of hymns. And moved by these same convictions the Reformed Churches of the Netherlands altered the article likewise, at the Synod of Middelburg, 1933. These latter Churches introduced a much smaller number of additional hymns than did our Churches, no doubt to assure the psalms of their rightful place in worship. For although it was well for our Synod of 1930 to warn our Churches against the danger of neglecting the psalms, and for this Synod to state that our Churches should continue to be psalm singing Churches in the main, yet by accepting a large number of hymns subsequently (1934), the danger of neglecting the psalms was much increased.

At the other hand it should not be forgotten that if only a small number of hymns had been accepted, a call for additional hymns would soon be heard. We may believe that with a large number of hymns selected our Churches will be at rest on this question for a long time to come. And the ever-present danger of introducing inferior and unsound hymns will not harass us for a good number of years.

It should be noted that Article 69 requires the singing of psalms. No Church may set them aside and sing only the hymns. But a Church need not use the approved hymns. If any Church desires to sing only the psalms it is at full liberty to do so. The psalms should predominate in every service unless the subject matter be very special, for instance, on Christmas day.

For our Dutch services Synod of 1934 decided that the Churches were at liberty to use, besides the psalms, the selections of hymns approved by the Holland Synod of 1933.

It may be added here that some Reformed leaders do not favor the singing of ordinary hymns in the services of the Church, but they do not object to the singing of New Testament passages which have been versified. In other words, they do not object to the singing of hymns which are renderings of specific parts of the Bible.

In order to help safeguard the singing of the Psalms in public worship, Synod of 1932 decided to urge all our Consistories to see to it that the memorization of psalter verses is emphasized in the Catechism and Sunday School classes. (Acts, 1932, p. 136.)

3. Choir singing and instrumental music.

The Synod of 1926 (Art. 57, p. 70) left the matter of choir singing to the discretion of the Consistories, but at the same time Synod discouraged the practice. Synod feared that choir singing in Church services would tend to discourage singing by the whole congregation. In the Roman Church, prior to the Reformation, as we have noted, choir singing was the chief factor in silencing the congregation. Today many Churches all around us have excellent choirs and soloists, but congregational singing in these very Churches is often extremely weak. Secondly, Synod of 1926 discouraged the introduction of choir singing because it would be very hard to hold choirs to Article 69 of the Church Order. Choirs easily sing songs which are inferior or unsound doctrinally, because the music or sentiment of certain songs appeal. Neither should it be forgotten that good solo and choir singing easily becomes an attraction at Church services. Some singers are tempted to exhibit. And some church-goers go not so much to worship and to listen to the message of God's Word, but to hear good singing. The singing by experts occupies the center of their interest. Furthermore, Churches in their attempt to secure good choirs are often tempted to let unworthy persons sing in their choir. Many employ paid singers. But even if the commercial element is avoided the primary requisite with many is not true spirituality, but rather a good voice, ability to sing well. Church choirs have often been a source of trouble and grief. Petty jealousies and unworthy ambitions are factors which have made for ill-will again and again. Those of us that feel much for the introduction of choirs in our services should talk with some unbiased and experienced Church choir leaders regarding these matters. A great preacher like Spurgeon never introduced choir singing. He wanted the people to sing for themselves, the whole congregation. And he wanted to keep the Word of God at the center of his services. Good singing is a marvelous art and a precious gift of God. But in the Church services we believe it is best for the whole Church to sing. Strangers who may happen to visit our services often express their appreciation of the fact that we have splendid congregational singing, that all, young and old, sing at our church services. We may be sure that with the introduction of choirs our congregational singing would suffer and wane. Such at best has been the general experience of other Churches. And this is but natural. When the inferior or average singer hears experts sing he naturally becomes timid. He prefers to let the good singers sing for him.

All this does not mean that we should not bring our congregational singing to higher levels. We should improve our singing wherever possible. The organization of Choral Societies should be encouraged. Good singing should be promoted. But let us continue to emphasize and to improve congregational singing. And let our good singers help to improve our congregational singing.

The Synod of 1930 decided that in Churches that have choirs, only the psalms and hymns approved according to Article 69, Church Order, shall be sung. Except anthems be sung which contain only the exact words of portions of Holy Writ (Acts 1930, p. 10). To this provision the Synod of 1944 added: "Or such anthems or hymns which have previous Consistorial approval as to their Scriptural soundness" (Acts, 1944. p. 28).

The Synod of 1928 admonished the Consistories of Churches which have choirs to exercise close supervision over the membership of the choir (Acts, 1928, Article 67).

Some of our Churches maintain "song services." That is to say, by arrangement of the Consistory, the congregation sings a number of songs for a brief period, just before the service begins. This is no doubt a commendatory practice. But why not make this song service a part of the regular service? Even when it precedes the service, only the approved and adopted psalms and hymns should be sung, as stands to reason. We definitely favor the incorporation of these song services into the regular service. Praise is an important part of every service.

Originally the Reformed leaders, led by Calvin were firmly opposed to organ accompaniment of congregational singing. As noted, he discontinued the choirs which in the Roman Churches sang with the accompaniment of organs. He preferred to have the congregation sing without the aid of these organs. He maintained that musical instruments in divine worship belonged to the period of shadows, i.e., to the Old Testament period.

No doubt Calvin went too far on this score. The evils of Rome urged him on. Voetius, long after Calvin, also felt that organ playing in church services did not edify, and it might easily detract attention from the sermon and become an object of abuse. It should not be forgotten in this connection that at first the Church just met in homes and barns and other places so that they had to sing without the organs. But even when the Reformation was an accomplished fact in Holland so that the Roman Churches with their beautiful organs became the possessions of the Reformed Churches, even then for a long time these organs were not used in worship. Week-day concerts were permitted, but on Sunday the instruments were at first not used for accompaniment of the singing, but the organ in many instances did play before and after the sermon.

The Synod of Dort, 1574, decided that all organ playing at the services should cease. This decision was based especially on I Cor. 14:19, where Paul says that he would rather speak five words with his understanding than ten thousand words in a tongue.

No doubt these fathers went to this extreme in reaction to the abuse as experienced and seen in the Roman Church. In the year 1637 at Leyden the Church organ was used for the first time for congregational singing. Other Churches soon followed the example.

Needless to say, our organists should never aim to give anything like a concert during divine worship. And the organ should not be predominant during the singing but should merely guide and sustain the singing of the congregation.

It may be noted that some old Scotch-Presbyterian Churches still condemn the use of organs, as well as the singing of hymns in public worship. This is, for instance, the position of the Reformed Presbyterian (Covenanter) Church of our own land.

There should be understanding and cooperation between the Minister and the organist. Ideally, the organist should know the text on which the Minister is to preach and the main thrust of the sermon, so that he may reckon with this in his playing. The organist should by all means study the words of the songs to be sung so that he may play in keeping with the meaning of the words.

ARTICLE 70

Since it is proper that the matrimonial state be confirmed in the presence of Christ's Church, according to the Form for that purpose, the Consistories shall attend to it.

CHURCH WEDDINGS

1. Past and present usage in the Netherlands.

The Roman Church holds that marriage is a Sacrament. Prior to the Reformation the Church had full control over marriages. The government did not concern itself with this important institution. After the Reformation the solemnization of marriages continued as a function of the Ministers and the Churches. But it was soon felt that the government should have something to say regarding this all important matter. The first Synod (Emden, 1571) already declared that marriage is in part an ecclesiastical interest and in part a civil interest. The Churches urged the adoption of uniform, Scriptural marriage laws. But the government seemed loath to do its part. For a long time the state held itself aloof and left the matter of marriages almost entirely to the Churches. Even those who held no connection with any Church sought marriage by Ministers. For this reason the Synod of Dort, 1618-19, decided that marriages of those who stood outside of the Church should not be solemnized publicly and with the solemn blessing in the Church.* The Ministers were permitted to unite such parties in marriage privately. Jews and others were married by government appointees from the close of the 16th century on.

Not until after the French Revolution of 1789 did the governments solemnize all marriages, taking this right away from the Churches. And not until 1848 did the Dutch government annex this right to itself. From then on the Church could and did "confirm" the mar-

* Post-Acta, 162nd Session, III.

riages of its members, but the actual solemnization, valid before the law, was performed by government officials.

In one of the oldest editions of our Church Order, 1586, we therefore find that the Churches are urged to abide by usages regarding marriage ceremonies then prevalent, until the government should have taken action. The Synod of Dort, 1618-19, virtually adopted the same reading, and stressed that uniformity was highly desirable and that the government should be asked as soon as possible to take action. In 1905 the Churches of Holland rewrote this antiquated 70th article of the Church Order, as it is also found in our Church Order since 1914.

At present the marriage proper takes place before a civil magistrate. The Church no longer has the right to solemnize marriages. Consequently Christian marriages are confirmed in the Church, upon authorization of the Consistory concerned, immediately after the marriage as a civil institution has been consummated at the courthouse. For this reason the Holland Form speaks of confirmation of marriages and not of their solemnization. We copied the Dutch wording in 1914, but this is a mistake, since our weddings are the actual solemnization of marriages. Our new Form has reckoned with these facts and it is very correctly called: **Form for the Solemnization of Marriage.** With us solemnization for the state and confirmation by the Church coincide. In private weddings the Minister only solemnizes the marriage for the state. In Church weddings he solemnizes the marriage for the state, and confirms the same for the Church.

2. Why is it "proper that the matrimonial state be confirmed in the presence of Christ's Church"?

Because the Church has a very vital interest in marriage. Confirmation of the matrimonial state by the Church implies, first of all, that the Church and the domain of the covenant of grace which it occupies officially sanction the marriage in question; and secondly, that the Church in its special prayers specifically pleads for God's blessing upon the marriage. The interest of the Church in the marriages its members contract is just as real and vital as the interest of the relatives and of the state in these marriages. The Church should therefore be recognized. The marriages of its members means much to the Church because God builds His Church covenantally through the seed of the Church. From children to be born God continues and expands His Church, and without thorough Christian homes the Church is bound to wane and fail.

In many of our American Churches all around us couples will be married in the church building, although the marriages are private in character. For reasons of sentiment and style perhaps some of our own people who do not care for a Church wedding in the real sense of that term, nevertheless desire to be "married in church." Such private marriages performed in the church building are of course not Church weddings. Our Ministers and Consistories should discourage the use of our church auditoriums for private weddings. Regular Church weddings should become common. Private marriages performed in the church building will only retard the general introduction of Church weddings.

3. Proper procedure regarding Church weddings.

The privilege of having their marriage solemnized before the congregation of God should be requested by the parties concerned at a regular Consistory meeting, or the request should be presented to a committee of the Consistory appointed for this purpose. As the Form stipulates the contemplated Church marriage is announced to the Church and thus takes place with the approval of the congregation. If anyone knows of reasons why the marriage should not take place —such as unbelief and godlessness in one or both parties concerned, or immoral conduct in one of the parties which would render the contemplated marriage illegal before the state, or contrary to Scriptures —, he is duty bound to notify the Consistory without delay.

As to the day of the week for Church weddings, it is perfectly proper that marriages be solemnized in one of the regular Sunday services. This is to be preferred to week-day Church weddings. When the marriage takes place on Sunday the Minister can preach an appropriate sermon. And sermons on the significance of Christian marriage, and our duty before God in the marriage state are certainly very necessary in this day and age of divorces, elopements, carnal-mindedness, etc. True, when marriage takes place during a week-day the Minister will also preach a short sermon, but in a brief sermonette he can say very little. And what he says will perhaps be less effective because of the wedding reception and distracting activities of various kinds. Besides, as a rule, only a small part of the congregation can be expected at week-day Church marriages, especially if these become the rule rather than the exception. We also feel that marriages solemnized at Sunday services are as a rule more solemn than those which take place at a special week-day service. But week-day Church weddings are not to be condemned.

Week-day services held for the purpose of uniting a couple in marriage are to be considered and ordered as services of the Word in the ordinary sense. They are services held under supervision of the Consistory as all regular services. The salutation and benediction are pronounced as usual. The Word is also preached, though briefly.

Marriages before Christ's Church should be well arranged, but also sober in the good sense of that word. Frats and frills should be avoided. Overly much "style" tends to detract. Our Church weddings should never become "big attractions." The beauty of Christian simplicity should be cultivated also here, rather than attractions and appendages borrowed from the world. The Word of God should occupy the all important place in these special services.

4. Who are entitled to ecclesiastical solemnization of marriage?

All members of our Churches whose contemplated marriages are not anti-Biblical and whose confession and conduct does not mark them as unbelievers. This includes not only members-in-full, but also those who have not yet made profession of their faith, though they were baptized in infancy. Even one who is not baptized, but who manifests interest in God and things spiritual, and promises to use the means of grace available to him, might be united in marriage before the Church. However, it should be definitely understood that he (or she) will fully cooperate in permitting the Baptism and Christian instruction of the children which may be born out of the marriage contemplated. If one of the parties be an unbeliever, by profession or conduct or both, their marriage may not be solemnized before the Church. Neither will any Christian Minister desire to unite a believer to an unbeliever in private, as is to be understood.

One belonging to another evangelical Church may be united in marriage to a member of one of our Churches if the "outsider" agrees that the children shall be baptized in one of our Churches and reared in the Reformed faith, just as in the case of an individual as yet belonging to no Church at all. Needless to say, there is no ruling in the Church Order regarding this and kindred questions. We merely give our personal convictions regarding these questions.

Of course, our parents and Ministers should constantly warn our children and young people against the danger of mixed marriages. Marriages with those who belong to one of our own Churches should remain to be the ideal.

5. What should be noted regarding our new Form?

The Form for the Solemnization of Marriage was adopted by our Synod of 1934. It superceded a Form which had been used since Reformation times. The new Form is somewhat shorter and optimistic in tone, whereas the old Form struck a grave and heavy tone, reminding the couple to be married forthwith that married folks must look for many hardships.

The introductory statement, not part of the Form proper, reads: "Where the wedding takes place before the congregation (cf. Art. 70 of the Church Order), the following announcement is to be made on the previous Sunday: . . ." This wording is bound to give the reader the impression that the Form can be used equally well for marriages performed privately. This, however, is not entirely correct. The Form is definitely written for regular Church weddings and can only be used consistently with alterations. For instance, the words: "Beloved in the Lord, we are assembled here in the presence of God . . ." clearly refer to a gathering of the congregation. And the statement, "Since we have received no lawful objections to their proposed union, . . ." are really out of place when the marriage is performed privately, inasmuch as neither the Church, nor anyone else has been given opportunity to object.

Furthermore the declaration, "According to the laws of the State and the ordinances of the Church of Christ, I now pronounce you, . . . , husband and wife, . . ." can hardly be used for private weddings since the Minister in the case of private marriages acts as an agent of the State, but not upon authority of the Church. The only ordinances which the Church has made regarding weddings are contained in Article 70 of the Church Order, and this article provides for weddings before the Church and in no way regulates or authorizes private weddings.

The giving away of the bride to the bridegroom, which the new Form allows, has been borrowed from other old Forms as the very choice of words in "Who gives this woman to this man?" also indicates. Perhaps it would have been better if this optional element had been omitted and left to the betrothal or engagement.

The Roman Church considers holy matrimony to be a Sacrament. We do not. In view of our Reformed conception it is doubtful whether it is wise for the Ministers to declare the bridegroom and bride husband and wife, "in the name of the Father and of the Son and of the Holy Spirit." It is doubtlessly borrowed from the baptismal formula.

6. The engagement.

In the land of our forefathers marriages among Reformed people are consummated in three stages. First comes the engagement. Then follows the solemnization by the civil authorities. And finally the confirmation by the Church takes place. No Reformed man or woman would think of omitting the last step. That would be a disgrace, and would stigmatize the couple instantly.

A word regarding the first step mentioned, the engagement, will not be out of place. For generations back this first step has always been held in honor among Reformed people. Today among us, in very many instances, the engagement is merely a personal agreement between the young man and young woman, often made in secret and kept in secret. The parents are hardly consulted. This is not as it should be. Marriage is a very important institution, and many young people are apt to act rashly and inconsiderately, not realizing their own best interests and the great significance, for good or evil, involved in marriage. Moreover, marriage is not merely the concern of the couple promising marriage. It is to a certain limited extent also the affair of the families involved. Marriage brings families together and consequently the relatives of both sides have an interest. Parents moreover have responsibilities toward their children and their spiritual welfare, also for their future regarding things temporal. Because of these parental responsibilities before God and parental rights towards their children no engagements should take place without the knowledge and approval of the parents or guardians involved. And this is likewise to the best interest of our young people, generally speaking. The old custom which prescribed that the young man asked for the hand of the girl of his choice from the father is wholly commendatory. And engagements should take place with the consent of the parents of both the young man and the young woman. It would be well if more were made in our circles of engagements or betrothals, especially since there is so much looseness and godlessness in regard to marriage.

All hasty marriages, perhaps secretly consummated and announced as a surprise to relatives and friends should be frowned upon and condemned. And no marriages should be consummated by any of our Ministers, either privately or before the Church, unless it is an established fact that parental approval, preferably at the time of the engagement, was obtained. Just because the State does not require parental consent of young people who are of age is no reason why the Church should not require this consent.

As stands to reason, elopements are to be condemned. Neither should marriages be kept secret for weeks and months. All this is of the world and does not fit in with biblical, Reformed conceptions.

It is said that before a Roman priest unites a couple in marriage he confers with them regarding obligations and duties related to marriage. He is said to warn them against worldly standards and morals. Who of us, knowing the ways of the world of today somewhat, would care to say that counsel by a trusted spiritual leader to those about to enter the marriage state, is wholly unnecessary?

7. The duties of Consistories.

The present article states that "the Consistories shall attend to it." Consistories should therefore encourage weddings before the Church of Christ. The matter should be mentioned to young people's classes, in sermons, at the time of family visitations, etc. Church Visitors would do well to inquire whether the Consistories are faithful in this respect. Very often much is made of funerals. A "service" in the Church is insisted upon. But the confirmation of marriages before the Church of Christ is considered as unnecessary. This is not as it should be. Let Consistories enlighten their people regarding these matters.

CONCERNING CENSURE AND ADMONITION

ARTICLE 71

As Christian Discipline is of a spiritual nature, and exempts no one from Civil trial or punishment by the Authorities, so also besides Civil punishment there is need of Ecclesiastical Censures, to reconcile the sinner with the Church and his neighbor and to remove the offense out of the Church of Christ.

ECCLESIASTICAL CENSURE

The fourth main division of our Church Order concerns itself with censure and ecclesiastical admonition. Articles 71 to 81 cover this subject as follows:

Article 71, the character, necessity, objects, and purpose of ecclesiastical discipline.

Articles 72 and 73, mutual discipline according to Christ's rule in Matt. 18.

Articles 74-78, consistorial discipline regarding members in general.

Articles 79 and 80, consistorial discipline regarding office-bearers as such.

Article 81, mutual censure by office-bearers.

Article 82-86, regulate various matters not directly belonging to the department of discipline.

1. The character of ecclesiastical discipline.

Article 71 very definitely stresses the fact that ecclesiastical discipline is spiritual in nature, and that it "exempts no one from Civil trial or punishment by the Authorities." The article clearly distinguishes between ecclesiastical authority and civil authority, between the domain of the Church and the domain of the State. The Church and the State each occupy their own sphere. When a church member commits a crime punishable by law, he is in no wise exempted from punishment by confessing his crime to the Church. For instance, if some church member should commit murder he would naturally be disciplined. In case he should manifest sincere repentance the Church would lift the censure and the sinner in question would be restored eventually to all privileges of full membership. But the reconciliation of this criminal with the Church would in no wise exempt him from trial and punishment by law. The State would be compelled to sentence and punish such a criminal even to the extent of capital punishment, if necessary. As a murderer he may have to die in the electric chair though the Church has readmitted him to the Lord's Supper as one whose sins are forgiven for Christ's sake.

The opening words of Article 71 therefore specify a principle which the Reformed Churches were eager to maintain. They did not believe that the Church should dominate the State (Rome), nor that the State should rule the Church (Erastian, original Lutheran conception). Calvin very vigorously contended for the independence of the Church versus the State in Geneva and also for years contended to keep the articles of Church Discipline in the Church Order of Geneva, while the Civil Authorities desired the cancellation of these articles. Not until 1555 was the Church's biblical right and duty on this score fully established at Geneva. Calvin, it may be said, stressed the need of Church discipline. The same is true for the Reformed Churches of France and Scotland.* And the Churches of the Netherlands also stressed the necessity of Church discipline. The Convention at Wezel, the first general ecclesiastical gathering of the Reformation Churches in Holland, 1568, adopted 21 articles relative to Church Discipline.

But the Reformed Churches never meant to rob the State of its right and duty to punish those guilty of civil transgressions. The Reformed Churches held and still hold that both Church and State have their own spheres of authority from God and their responsibility before Him. Christian discipline is of a spiritual nature and exempts no one from civil trial or punishment. No doubt our fathers also enunciated this principle so clearly to avoid all misunderstanding and to gain the civil approval of the Church Order, which approval was much coveted in those days.

Ecclesiastical "punishment" then bears a spiritual character. It is Christian discipline. Christ gave His Church a spiritual authority which is administered by the officers which He gives to the Church. (Eph. 4:11-16; I Cor. 12:28; Heb. 5:4.) In the exercise of this spiritual "punishment," spiritual means and weapons are used, i.e., admonition, warning, censure, conviction, and excommunication. "For the weapons of our warfare are not of the flesh, but mighty before God to the casting down of strongholds." (II Cor. 10:4.)

It should also be noted in this connection that our Church Order merely indicates certain principles to be followed in the exercise of ecclesiastical discipline. The Church Order does not specify in detail how investigations are to be conducted; how long one should be disciplined before the final step of excommunication is taken; which specific sins are worthy of discipline, etc., etc. The civil authorities have a penal code by which they are guided. The Church has no penal code, for the Church does not seek to administer external punishment, but the Church seeks to save the sinner and to promote the glory of God. To attain these ends each case must be dealt with according to its own peculiar circumstances, and as soon as the end in view has been gained ecclesiastical discipline ceases. On this point Dr. F. L. Rutgers aptly remarked: "No penal code can be constructed for ecclesiastical discipline. The purpose of discipline demands a maximum of variability in its application, not a set of rules for constant application. Just so the principles are established, and just so these are applied in every particular case, for only then will ecclesiastical discipline function correctly."**

Discipline according to the Reformed conception is not the same as punishment. The State punishes to right a wrong committed and to vindicate justice. This principle is primary in the application of civil punishment. In the ecclesiastical sphere, however, the principle of correction is primary. For this reason ecclesiastical discipline is chastisement, rather than punishment, just as in Dutch we distinguish between "tucht" and "straf." In keeping with all this the opening words of Article 71, "Christian Discipline is of a spiritual nature . . ." should receive full emphasis.

---

* **College-Voordrachten,** Dr. F. L. Rutgers over Gereformeerd Kerkrecht, bewerkt door, Dr. J. De Jong, 1918, p. 10.

** Idem, p. 11.

2. The necessity of ecclesiastical discipline.

Dr. F. L. Rutgers is reported to have given four grounds upon which the Reformed have based the Church's right and duty to exercise discipline, namely:

A. Scripture passages which directly or indirectly enjoin discipline: *

1. Matt. 18:15-18. These words clearly indicate that the Church has a right and duty to censure, even to excommunication, although they also teach us that personal wrongs, known to the transgressor and the party wronged only, or to a very limited number, should be settled privately if at all possible.

2. Matt. 16:16-19. In these passages Christ gives to Peter the power to bind and loose. Doubtless Christ here speaks to Peter as representative of all the Apostles, for in John 20:23 the self-same power is attributed to all the Apostles. But the Apostles are but the representatives of the New Testament Church, and so we may conclude that in Matt. 16:16-19 and John 20:23 Christ charges the Church to exercise discipline. The wording of Matt. 18:17, "And if he refuse to hear them, **tell it to the Church**: and, if he refuse to hear the Church also, let him be unto thee as the Gentile and the publican", also pleads for this contention.

3. I Cor. 5. In this passage Paul prescribes excommunication regarding the grievous sinner in the Corinthian Church, and in II Cor. 2:7 he directs his readmission.

4. In numerous passages God's Word tells us not to fellowship with heretics and such as had forsaken the Lord. (Cf. Rev. 2:14-16; Titus 3:10-11; II John 10.)

5. Passages which condemn intermingling of believers and unbelievers, the holy and the unholy. (Cf. II Cor. 6:14.)

B. Old Testament injunctions regarding the removal of sinners out of the congregation of God. (Cf. Ex. 22:20; Lev. 24:11-16.)

C. The fact that from Apostolic days on the early Church exercised discipline, as Cyprian, Tertullian, and other Church Fathers tell us.

D. The general testimony of various ancient Church Councils agrees that the Church cannot continue to exist in its purity unless it exercises discipline.

As will be understood the necessity for ecclesiastical discipline is found particularly in the New Testament injunctions which demand its exercise. In other words, discipline must be maintained in the Church because God commanded it. Besides the passages indicated the following may be cited: Rom. 16:17; I Thess. 5:14; II Thess. 3:6, 14; I Tim. 5:1, 2.

3. The objects of ecclesiastical discipline.

The Roman Church applied censure also to buildings, lands, books, etc. The Reformation Churches would have none of this, inasmuch as they found no Scriptural warrant for the practice. Church discipline should be limited to persons and cannot be applied to lifeless objects. Neither can it apply to persons already dead, (heretics, false teachers, etc.) as Rome sought to do.

According to Article 71 the object of church discipline is the sinner, for we read: ". . . to reconcile the sinner with the Church . . ." Church discipline, therefore, applies to men or women, members of the Church, who have committed censurable sin. It does not apply to those who

* Cf. **College-Voordrachten**, etc., 1918, pp. 14-15.

are outside of the Church (versus Rome), nor to those of the Church who persist in resigning their membership in spite of numerous and urgent and long continued admonitions. Membership in the organized, instituted Church is in the last analysis a matter of personal choice and responsibility before God, and no Church has the right to compel one to be a member of a certain Church against his own conscience or will. Let it be well understood: We regard the resigning of one's membership as a very serious step. As a rule it is a very serious sin, **for very often it is resorted to in order to escape the full force of discipline.** In such cases the Consistory should not yield lightly and should refuse to acquiesce or accept a resignation unless the party concerned insists on resigning. The promises made and the obligations assumed at the time of confession of faith give a Consistory the right to apply censure even to excommunication, and unless the sinner in question persists in severing his relationship with the Church, the Consistory ought to perform its full duty. No easy-going, weak sentimentality should cause a Consistory to be remiss in its duty on this score. The sinner concerned and the Church involved are both entitled to full exercise of discipline. This is in complete harmony with what the Synod of 1918 decided. (Art. 53, p. 66.)

It stands to reason that the Churches should be much more considerate of those members who wish to leave one of our Churches because they no longer agree with our confessional standards and doctrinal position. If such members insist on leaving, because they feel compelled in conscience before God, after the Consistory has endeavored to show them their error, then the Consistory may acquiesce in their action leaving, however, the full responsibility for their departure with them, which fact should also be clearly stated to the congregation.

Those who remove from the Church and fail to affiliate with one of our other Churches by means of an attestation of membership, by their very removal and neglect place themselves outside of the Church and its government. This is a very serious sin, but such people are no longer subject to Church discipline in the full sense, although the nearest Church, if possible, should admonish them persistently. If distance does not prohibit, the Church which they have left should work with them diligently also.

Sometimes members of the Church withdraw themselves from the meetings of public worship and seek edification elsewhere. They do not seek to resign but simply neglect their duty toward their own Church. The Christian conduct of these members may be unobjectionable except for this one irregularity. The Synod of 's Gravenhage, Reformed Churches of Holland, decided in 1914 that Consistories should continue to admonish such irregular members and if need be they should refuse to give them the Sacraments, but that they should not excommunicate them.

It need hardly be mentioned that discipline should always be individual. The Roman Church would interdict whole communities. That is, by order of the Pope the clergy were forbidden to perform religious services or to administer the Sacraments. Whole regions were placed under the papal ban. Thus the innocent and the guilty suffered alike. Our Church discipline is always individual. No two members, though they should be husband and wife and though their sins are identical, are ever disciplined as a group, but always individually.

Only those can be objects of ecclesiastical discipline who are fully responsible. Those who are insane or mentally irresponsible are admonished inasfar as they are susceptible to admonition, but regular Church discipline is not applied to them.

All men, rich and poor alike, are subject to discipline. The Roman Church exempted the Pope, and the Episcopalian and Lutheran Churches exempted civil rulers, but the Reformed Churches placed one and all under the jurisdiction and grace of Christ, no matter what his station in life might be.

Children may also become objects of discipline. But since they are incomplete members, discipline in their case will also be incomplete. They are members who have not yet come to full responsibility and understanding. Consequently they are censured, if need be, through admonitions given, but they are not excommunicated and placed outside of the Church. As a rule Consistories will have to talk to the parents of unruly or worldly children first of all, inasmuch as the parents may be to blame more than the children. But children must also be admonished directly. See Eph. 6:1; Col. 3:20.

Baptized members who have reached years of discretion and who willfully neglect to make profession of their faith also become objects of discipline. They must be instructed and admonished prayerfully. If they continue to be indifferent and unbelieving the Church finally declares that their relationship to the Church has been severed. Their names are stricken from the rolls of the Church. The procedure to be followed in such cases has been indicated by Synod of 1918. (Cf. Art. 52.)

Consistories should not hesitate to do their full duty regarding men or women who have come to years of understanding and manifest no sense of sin and of faith in Jesus Christ. If their words and conduct are anti-Christian action should be all the more drastic. But even those who have a historical faith and still come to divine worship, if there is no real interest and prayerful seeking on their part, although their general conduct may not be altogether godless and wicked, their names should not be carried on the membership books indefinitely. The Church of Christ, strictly speaking, is composed of living members only, though some of these, inasmuch as they are children, are incomplete. The organized or instituted Church should reflect in its membership as much as possible the membership of the Church of Christ, the spiritual body of our Lord. The Churches should therefore only carry complete and incomplete (minor) members. Ideally there is no room for a third class, so called "members-by-baptism." These unfaithful children of the Church, having reached years of understanding, should be labored with persistently, and if they refuse to repent and believe, their names should be removed from the membership book. They should never be accorded a semi-official standing in the Church so that they feel that their position is after all quite normal and unobjectionable.

It is the stand of our Churches, by Synodical conclusion, that if it becomes manifest that a member belongs to a secret, oathbound organization, he shall be disciplined. (Cf. General Rules, Art. 55, 1881.) In harmony with this decision it is the duty of Consistories "to put the question to those who desire to be received as members and admitted to the Lord's Supper whether they belong to any society bound by oath or solemn vow." (Cf. Acts 1867, Art. 15.) The implication is, of course, that those who do belong to a lodge are not to be admitted to the Lord's Table. Their profession of faith is unacceptable.

Why do the Christian Reformed Churches hold to this position regarding lodge-membership? Strictly speaking, because these organizations are essentially anti-Christian in character. The teachings of the lodge imply that if one lives up to the ideals and standards of the lodge, all is well. He who dies as a good lodge member is considered to be saved, even though he did not believe in Christ as Son of God and only Saviour. Thus the lodge is essentially anti-Christian. It is indeed religious, but its religion is not Biblical Christianity. It is far rather a modernistic, paganistic corruption of Christianity. By joining the lodge one expresses agreement with its doctrines. Which means that when one joins the lodge he denies Christ as Saviour and he denies Biblical Christianity. All this takes place upon fearful oaths. We object to the uncalled for secrecy of the lodge and to the fact that members are asked to swear to matters which are only revealed to them after they have sworn to them; we object to the worldly atmosphere which the lodge fosters, etc. But our essential objection to the lodge is its false, anti-Christian teachings. If the lodge is right, Christianity is false. No man can consistently be a member of the lodge and also of the Church of Christ.

It is interesting to note that the Synod of the Reformed Churches of Holland, Utrecht, 1923, Art. 143, came to the following conclusions regarding the Independent Order of Odd-Fellows:

a. That Consistories must continue to admonish members in full, and members by Baptism, to sever their connections with this Order.

b. That Consistories must discipline those who continue in this evil.

It should be clear that the issue is not at all whether the Churches can censure societies or groups of members. To do so would be un-Reformed. To this all agree. But this is the issue: Does lodge-membership involve, expressed or unexpressed, a denial of fundamental Christian doctrines or not? Our Churches have answered this question in the affirmative. We are fully persuaded on this point, and consequently anyone who joins a lodge and refuses to break with it is censured for his anti-Christian profession and conduct.* It may safely be said that he who joins the lodge sins against the First Commandment, for the God of Unitarianism, Modernism, and Lodgism is not the God of the Bible and of the Ten Commandments.

Regarding Church membership and membership in our so-called neutral labor unions various Synods have made pronouncements. Particularly the Synods of 1904 and 1916 dealt with this matter. The latter Synod was somewhat more tolerant in its conclusions than the Synod of 1904 had been. However, the conclusions of 1916 did not settle the issue. To the mind of many these conclusions were taken prematurely and without sufficient warrant. The matter continued to be a subject of debate and study. Synod of 1928 accepted a number

---

* The instruction books written by high officers in various lodges, and for the instruction of lodge members, reveal that the lodge is anti-Christian in character. To this judgment many believers, who have themselves been lodge members, agree. For example, W. P. Loveless, an ex-chaplain of the Masonic Lodge of Wheaton, Ill., testifies: "The whole structure of lodge procedure is built upon the erroneous teachings of the 'universal fatherhood of God' and 'the universal brotherhood of man.' (Jno. 8:44); and the necessity for salvation alone by grace through faith in the Lord Jesus Christ (Eph. 2:8, 9) is entirely ignored." And again: "They (Christianity and lodgism) are two opposite beliefs. I cannot believe that I am saved only by grace through faith in the Lord Jesus Christ, and still believe in the religion of the lodge which teaches that we are saved by character and good works." (Cf. Loveless, **The Christian and Secret Societies**, National Chr. Assn., p. 10.) E. A. Coyle, a Unitarian Minister and at one time also Worshipful Master of the Masonic lodge, Marietta, Ohio, says: "Nearly all of those monitors (books of instructions of fraternal orders) have, as their very heart, the 'fatherhood of God', the 'brotherhood of man,' immortality, and salvation by character." (Quoted by Loveless, p. 13.)

of clear-cut resolutions regarding this question. (Cf. Acts of Synod, 1928, pp. 91-96 or J. L. Schaver, **Christian Reformed Church Order**, pp. 116, 117.)

Synod of 1928 also appointed a committee charged to serve Synod 1930 with advice regarding the question what might be done to revive Christian organizations in the social sphere. (The Christian Labor Union, headquarters in Grand Rapids, had disappeared from the scene due in part to the compromising position which the Synod of 1916 had taken regarding labor unions.)

In response to a report of this committee of which Prof. L. Berkhof served as president and Prof. C. Bouma as secretary, Synod of 1930 adopted a number of important conclusions which may be found on pages 74-76 of the Acts of Synod, 1930.

More than one Synod, the one of 1936 lastly, has recommended the Christian Labor Alliance, headquarters in Grand Rapids, Mich., to our leaders and our people for their moral support and cooperation. (Cf. Acts, 1936, Art. 50.) (Also see Appendix 10, page 370.)

Regarding decisions pertaining to anti-Christian labor unions, it should be remembered that our Churches do not discipline societies or groups of persons, but only individuals who make themselves guilty in doctrine or life regarding censurable sins; who believe and do things which are clearly transgressions of God's Commandments. Our ecclesiastical decisions concerning anti-Christian lodges, unions, etc., are as such not disciplinary decisions against these organizations, but ecclesiastical conclusions mutually arrived at by all the Churches concerned, according to which Consistories are to admonish and discipline Church members if need be.

Synod of 1928 adopted a number of resolutions regarding worldliness, which also concern the matter of discipline. These resolutions read as follows:

> I. Synod reminds our people of the doctrinal and ethical principles which should guide the Christian in his relation to the world in general and in the matter of amusements in particular, and urges all our professors, ministers, elders, and Bible teachers to emphasize these principles in this age of prevailing worldliness.
>
> Some of the most important of these principles follow:
>
> 1. **The honor of God** requires:
>   a. That the Christian's amusements should at the very least not conflict with the honor of God.
>   b. That we and our children should be keenly aware, also in our amusements, of our covenant relation to God as His peculiar people.
>   c. That the Christian shall deem it a matter of loyalty to God not to further the interests of an institution which is manifestly an instrument of Satan for attack on the Kingdom of God.
> 2. From the consideration of the **welfare of man** we conclude:
>   a. That there is a legitimate place in life for such amusements as are recreative for body and mind;
>   b. That no physical recreation or mental diversion should be tolerated which is in any way or in any degree subversive of our spiritual and moral well-being;
>   c. That, even when our amusements are not spiritually or morally harmful, they should not be allowed to occupy more than a secondary, subordinate, place in life.
> 3. The principle of **spiritual separation from the world:**
>   a. Does not imply that Christians should form separate communities or should shun all association with ungodly men (I Cor. 5:99 ff.);
>   b. Forbids friendship, in distinction from fellowship, with evil men (James 4:4);
>   c. Requires that we shun all evil in the world;
>   d. Demands a weaning away of the heart from the transient things of this present earthly sphere (Colossians 3:1, 2).

4. **Christian Liberty:**

a. Consists in freedom from the power of sin; in freedom from the law: its curse, its demands as a condition for earning eternal life, its oppressive yoke; and in liberty of conscience with reference to human ordinances and things neither prescribed nor condemned, either directly or indirectly, in the Word of God;

b. Is limited in its exercise by the law of love (I Cor. 8:9, 13), the law of self-preservation (Matt. 18:8, 9), and the law of self-denial, which often requires the renunciation of things in themselves lawful (Matt. 16:24).

II. While **several** practices are found in our circles which cannot pass the muster of these principles, and while **all** our amusements, not only theatre-attendance, dancing, and card-playing, should be judged in the light of these principles, yet Synod feels constrained, in pursuance of the decisions of the Synod of 1926 in the matter of amusements, to call particular attention to this familiar trio. It greatly deplores the increasing prevalence among us of these forms of amusement, urgently warns our members against them, and further refers our people to the material on the subject given in the report of the Committee on Worldly Amusements, (Agendum, Part I, pp. 31-47).

III. Synod urges all our leaders and all our people to pray and labor for the awakening and deepening of spiritual life in general, and to be keenly aware of the absolute indispensability of keeping our religious life vital and powerful, through daily prayer, the earnest searching of the Scriptures, and through engaging in practical Christian works, which are the best antidote against worldliness.

IV. Synod exhorts all our leaders to warn unceasingly against the prevailing spirit and forms of worldliness in order that our Reformed principles in these matters may be re-emphasized; insists that these warnings shall be given not only in the preaching, but also in our Catechism and Sunday School classes, in family-visitation, and in personal contact whenever occasion presents itself; and urges that these warnings shall be given also in our school-rooms.

V. Synod reminds Consistories that in nominations for or appointments to positions of responsibility in our churches, careful attention should be paid to conduct in the matter of amusements; and suggests that also other bodies, such as Boards of Christian Schools, City Missions, etc., heed this same matter in their appointments.

VI. Synod urge Consistories to deal in the spirit of love, yet also in view of the strong tide of worldliness which is threatening our churches, very firmly with all cases of misdemeanor and offensive conduct in the matter of amusements; and, where repeated admonitions by the Consistory are left unheeded, to apply discipline as a last resort.

VII. Synod instructs Consistories to inquire of those who ask to be examined previous to making public profession of their faith and partaking of the Lord's Supper as to their stand and conduct in the matter of worldly amusements, and, if it appears that they are not minded to lead the life of Christian separation and consecration, not to permit their public profession. (Cf. Acts of Synod, 1928, pp. 86-89.)

We have somewhat considered the nature of these resolutions in our explanation of Art. 61, and shall not repeat here. We merely stress the fact that these resolutions of 1928 should not be interpreted legalistically. The Synod clearly placed the emphasis where it belongs, namely on spiritual, consecrated Christian living. Certain forms of worldly amusements are mentioned, it is true, but only by way of example and because these were being adopted by many of our people, whereas Synod was persuaded that these and like amusements were either wrong in themselves or laden with grave dangers to spiritual life.

It certainly would be unwise and unbiblical for our Churches and Consistories to single out certain sins of worldliness and apply discipline regarding these, while passing by other evils, greater perhaps in some instances than those singled out. No Consistory should raise the familiar trio of theatre-attendance, dancing, and card-playing to shibboleths for membership in good and regular standing in its Church, while passing by many other forms of sin, such as dishonesty; road-house or night-club attendance; Sabbath desecration; the reading of harmful, impure, lustful literature; drunkenness; profanity; the practice of unbiblical birth-control; etc., etc.

It should also be noted that Synod of 1928 declared that discipline should be applied as a last resort, not merely for those who are persistently guilty of worldly living in certain specific forms but with worldliness **in whatsoever form it may manifest itself.** This harmonizes with the fact that the resolutions do not require Consistories simply to ask of those that desire to make profession of faith whether they indulge in theatre-attendance, dancing and card-playing. No, Consistories are to ask applicants regarding "**their stand and conduct in the matter of worldly amusements,** and if it appears that they are not minded to lead the life of Christian separation and consecration, not to permit their public professions." This, as we note, covers the whole field of worldly amusements.

Consistories will do wise to inquire regarding whichever definite forms of worldly amusements may be popular and enticing for the day and circumstances and locality in which a Church finds itself. But whether the familiar trio should be mentioned, or whether other evils deserve special inquiry, or whether an inquiry in general terms is sufficient, will depend on many ever-changing circumstances, and on the parties making profession of faith. Let us be thorough and unafraid, but let us also avoid legalistic externalism. And as to discipline, let us not hesitate to do our full duty, but neither let us set up legalistic, partial standards.

Let the rule of Art. 72, Church Order, which indicates that one must be disciplined if he "errs in doctrine or offends in conduct..." continue to guide us. This rule covers every transgression of God's law and all unchristian conduct.

Synod of 1888 ruled that in case parents refuse to send their children to the catechism classes they shall be admonished, and if need be, disciplined to excommunication. There are good reasons for this ruling. Anyone who fails to instruct his children in God's Word or refuses to have them instructed through the appointed channels of the Church thereby repudiates his profession of Christianity and is guilty of ungodly conduct. Such should be admonished and disciplined.

4. The purpose of ecclesiastical discipline.

The purpose of discipline according to Article 71 is two-fold:

"To reconcile the sinner with the Church and his neighbors and to remove the offense out of the Church of Christ." By "offense" the article means not merely what may hurt the feelings of others, but that which may cause others to sin, that over which others may stumble and fall, as the word used by Christ definitely signifies in the Greek language.

This purpose for Church discipline as indicated in Article 71 accords fully with the Bible. (Cf. I Cor. 5; II Cor. 2:7; II Thess. 3:14.)

Calvin mentions a three-fold purpose for Church discipline: 1) That the name of God may not be blasphemed by the world. 2) To safeguard the loyal members of the Church against the bad influence of the unfaithful. 3) To move the sinner to shame and repentance.

á Lasco, Voetius, and Rutgers all agree essentially with the purpose of discipline as stated by Calvin, though á Lasco mentions but two aims, just as our Church Order does, and though Voetius speaks of a sevenfold purpose, while Dr. Rutgers mentions the three which

Calvin already set forth, although Rutgers gives these three purposes in the reverse order from Calvin. Calvin's order is certainly the logical one, whereas Rutger's order is more the psychological and practical one.

(Also see Appendix 10, page 370, and Appendix 11, 372.)

ARTICLE 72

In case any one errs in doctrine or offends in conduct as long as the sin is of a private character, not giving public offense, the rule clearly prescribed by Christ in Matt. 18 shall be followed.

CAUSES FOR DISCIPLINE AND THE RULE FOR PRIVATE OFFENSES

The two matters covered by Article 72 are indicated above. We first speak of the causes for discipline which Article 72 recognizes and shall then consider the rule which is to be followed regarding private sins.

1. Causes for discipline:

Causes for discipline are two-fold in character according to the conviction of our Churches expressed in Article 72. We read: "In case any one errs in doctrine or offends in conduct..." Errors in doctrine or life shall constitute cause for discipline, so our Churches have agreed by accepting the present article. Offenses in doctrine and life have been considered Biblical causes for discipline by the Reformed Churches since the days of the Reformation. This appears not only from the various synodical decisions regarding discipline, but also from the answer to the 85th question of the Heidelberg Catechism which states that Christian discipline is to be applied to those who "maintain doctrines or practices" inconsistent with Christianity. This same reply also speaks of those who refuse to "renounce their errors and wicked course of life."

As to early conclusion regarding just grounds for discipline the Wezelian Convention of Reformed Churches, 1568, decided that one who advocated strange teachings and heresies, secretly or publicly, should be disciplined, (Chap. VIII, 7) and also that one who led an evil life should be censured. (Chap. VIII, 9.) The first regular Synod, Emden, 1571, maintained these two causes for discipline (Art. 26). Following Synods have maintained in substance what this first Synod adopted. We still find these selfsame grounds in Article 72 of the Church Order.

This position of our Church Order is certainly in keeping with Holy Writ. Doctrinal errors, worthy of discipline do not include, according to the Bible, such matters as the abstention from certain foods or the keeping of certain special days. (Rom. 14.) But it does include false prophesyings or teachings (Matt. 7:15, 2-23; Acts 20: 28-30; Gal. 1: 8, 9); the raising up of discord and occasion for sin (Rom. 16:17, 18); the denial of the resurrection from the dead (I Cor. 15:12-17; II Tim. 2:16-18 and I Tim. 1:18-20); denial of Christ's Sonship and His incarnation (I John 2:22; 4:2, 3; II John 7-11).

But Scripture also condemns ungodly conduct, excluding those who persist in such sins from heaven and enjoining the Churches to discipline them. For example: the lying of Ananias and Sapphira (Acts 5:1-11); the simony of Simon the sorcerer (Acts 8:18-24); the sin of incest in Corinth's Church (I Cor. 5:1-5, 13); and furthermore all kinds of extreme sins and immorality as adultery, theft, covetousness, drunkenness, false testimony, etc. (I Cor. 6:9, 10; Gal. 5:19-21; Eph. 5:3-5; Heb. 13:4; Rev. 21:8).

When does error in doctrine or life merit discipline? When the sin of the transgressor gives offense, i.e., when a sin tends to lead others into sin, and when the guilty party rejects the admonition offered and persists in his sin. Not every sin and error in doctrine and life calls for discipline in the formal sense of that word. We are all imperfect. We all sin with word and deed, in doctrine and life. These sins should be exposed and condemned in the preaching of God's Word and we should all be admonished by each other as believers, and particularly by the office-bearers as overseers at the time of home-visitation or at special occasions. But discipline in the formal sense is not initiated unless the matter is serious and offensive, and unless the sinner refuses to repent and change, as we have indicated.

2. When does the rule of Matt. 18 apply?

The Reformed Churches answer (cf. the present article) ". . . as long as the sin is of a private character, not giving public offense, the rule clearly prescribed by Christ in Matt. 18 shall be followed."

This provision has been incorporated in the Church Order from the very outset. True, the Wezelian Convention applied this rule only to **errors in life**, and not to **errors in doctrine**. If one became erroneous in doctrine his sin had to be reported to the Church forthwith. But the Synod of Emden, 1571, only three years later, made the rule of Matt. 18 applicable to transgressors regarding the doctrines of Holy Writ, as well as to transgressors regarding Christian life.

The Churches at that time held that in Matt. 18 Christ was referring to errors in doctrine as well as to personal offenses or unchristian conduct. Present day reliable commentators agree that Christ referred only to unchristian conduct of one toward another. But the example and instruction which Christ gives us in Matt. 18 regarding personal offenses which are not generally known, and as such may be termed secret sins, that example and instruction may certainly be applied to all kinds of private sins, including those that are doctrinal in character. Sins that are not generally known should not be revealed unless the nature of the transgression should require such, (for example: theft, murder, etc., being crimes against the civil institutions) or that the impenitence of the transgressor should require such. "Love beareth (covereth) all things. (I Cor. 13:7, cf. margin, A.R.V.) "Love covereth a multitude of sins." (I Peter 4:8.) It is our duty and privilege to seek the erring brother's conversion from his sin. For "he who converteth a sinner from the error of his way shall save a soul from death, and shall cover a multitude of sins." (James 5:19, 20.)

Even though one therefore should hold that Matt. 18 speaks only of personal offenses, yet it should be evident that we must distinguish between secret and public sins. Secret sins then are sins known only to one or to a few persons, to a limited number, and which sins have consequently not given general offense.

Matt. 18 states very plainly how one is to deal with a brother who has committed a sin which is still secret. The brother against whom the sin has been committed is to go to the transgressor and show him his fault privately. This injunction of our Lord in no wise relieves the guilty party from going to the offended brother in order to confess his wrong. Not at all (cf. Matt. 5:23, 24). The transgressor should do so. But the offended brother should not wait until the offender calls on him, but he must go to the transgressor and endeavor to convince him of his wrong in order to save him from his sin and ruin. For: "if he hear thee, thou hast gained thy brother," i.e., for the kingdom of heaven. If that end be reached, the whole matter is thereby concluded.

If the guilty party refuses to admit his guilt and to make amends if necessary and possible, then the rule of Matt. 18 requires that the offended brother repeat his visit taking one or two witnesses with him. These witnesses should be reliable Christians, themselves of good repute. As a rule it will be advisable to choose the witnesses from the same Church to which the erring brother belongs. One or two witnesses are to be present so that "at the mouth of two witnesses or three every word be established." Statements made by the erring brother may have to be verified before the Consistory.

If the sinner does not yet repent and consequently a third admonition becomes necessary, then, "it must be told unto the church." Jesus is here seemingly thinking of the little group of followers who believed on Him and who would eventually form the nucleus of the New Testament Church. If a sinner will not repent, the aggrieved party will report the error and plight of the transgressor to the Church so that the whole Church, particularly through its officebearers as representative of Christ Himself, may labor with the erring one for his return.

(It may be noted that Christ here assigns the work of discipline to the particular Church. There is where ecclesiastical discipline consequently belongs essentially.)

After all admonitions prove to be futile the sinner should be regarded by the Church as "a Gentile and a publican." That is to say: one that is outside of the Church of Christ and the kingdom of God.

ARTICLE 73

Secret sins of which the sinner repents, after being admonished by one person in private or in the presence of two or three witnesses, shall not be laid before the Consistory.

SECRET SINS REPENTED

This 73rd article of our Church Order was originally adopted by the first Synod of the Reformed Churches of Holland, that of Emden, 1571. In Article 27 of the Church Order of this Synod we find literally the provision of our present Article 73. But in addition the Synod of Emden also ruled that secret sins, though repented of, which constitute great danger to State or Church such as treason, or the misleading of souls, (als daar zyn Verraderije, ofte verleydinge der zielen) should be reported to the Minister of the Church, so that, his advice having been gained, one might know what to do.

Seven years later the Synod of Dort, 1578, dropped this second provision of the present article and maintained only the first provision. Thus the article reads today. Common sense, however, still tells us that in case a brother or sister has committed a very grievous and dangerous sin, that then it may be to his own best interest and the safety of others, that at least his Minister be informed. In such extreme cases the matter should be reported confidentially, and in some cases if possible with the transgressor's consent.

1. The duty of individual Christians regarding discipline.

Article 73 is a direct continuation of Article 72 which article prescribed that the rule of Matt. 18 should be put into practice when private or secret sins were committed. We need not repeat what has already been said as we considered Article 72.

But it is well to note why the Church Order demands, also in this article, that discipline should begin with the believers as individuals and not with the Consistory. In the first place, this is the rule because Christ so ordained in unmistakable words in Matt. 18 as we have seen. Secondly, many passages in the Bible prescribe mutual discipline. I Thess. 5:11: "Wherefore exhort one another, and build each other up, even as also ye do." Heb. 3:12, 13: "Take heed, brethren, lest haply there shall be in any one of you an evil heart of unbelief, in falling away from the living God: but exhort one another day by day, so long as it is called To-day . . ." Rom. 15:14: "And I myself also am persuaded of you, my brethren, that ye yourselves are full of goodness, filled with all knowledge, able also to admonish one another." This mutual exhortation, urged upon us by Holy Writ, becomes mutual discipline when there is a specific transgression. Gal. 6:1, "Brethren, even if a man be overtaken in any trespass, ye who are spiritual, restore such a one in a spirit of gentleness, looking to thyself, lest thou also be tempted." James 5:19, 20, "My brethren, if any among you err from the truth and one convert him, let him know, that he who converteth a sinner from the error of his way shall save a soul from death, and shall cover a multitude of sins."

Furthermore it may be remarked that Scripture enjoins mutual discipline since all believers are anointed with the Holy Spirit, sharing the anointing of Christ, to be prophets, priests, and kings under Him. (Cf. I Peter 2:9 and also Heidelberg Catechism, Q. 32.) We rightly speak of all believers as office-bearers, as our fathers spoke of "het ambt aller geloovigen."

New Testament believers particularly should not be treated as minors which have no voice in matters (Roman Catholicism), but as having come to years of majority, having definite rights and duties. Official, ecclesiastical admonition and discipline is but the continuation of mutual, believer's discipline. When the latter fails the former begins to function. And again, when believer's discipline cannot act with a view to the best interests of the individual involved and the Church concerned (as in the case of public sins) the special offices begin to act forthwith and initiate disciplinary action. And when Church members refuse to do their Christian duty toward each other and no longer admonish each other, but desire to leave it all to the Consistory, then the backbone of Church discipline is severely injured. Much to the detriment of the Churches concerned, of course. Says Dr. F. L. Rutgers: "The decay of discipline, which began already in the beginning of the 17th century, should certainly be attributed to a large extent to the fact that in the convictions of the church members this principle of our Church Order had been weakened."*

Through the preaching of the Word and through personal admonition the believers should be urged to maintain this Biblical principle.

---

* **College-Voordrachten**, etc., 1918, p. 37.

It may seem much easier merely to report a matter to the Consistory, but personal admonition according to the rule of Matt. 18 should precede. Anyone who refuses to do his duty on this score, anyone who would refuse persistently to act according to the rule of Matt. 18 would make himself worthy of discipline.

2. Can secret and public sins be differentiated?

It is impossible to differentiate strictly between secret and public sins. In general it may be said that sins may be regarded as being secret when they have been committed secretly and when subsequently the transgression has not become known. A sin committed in secret, but not kept secret, is not to be regarded as a secret sin but as a public sin.

Furthermore, in a large Church a sin known to five or six might be considered to be secret, whereas in a very small Church this sin might be regarded as no longer secret. Circumstances alter cases, also regarding this question. As long as a sin is known only to a very limited number, the sinner should be labored with accordingly, particularly if the matter can be kept secret. If a matter is bound to become an "open secret," that fact may lead a believer and a Consistory to regard the matter as a public sin, though as yet the matter is known to only some. Those who help spread a matter are certainly guilty of a great sin, and should be admonished accordingly.

A public sin is one which from its very nature is generally known, or which had to be made known to the Consistory because the sinner refused to repent. Sins committed in public, or in the presence of many, or reported in the newspapers, are public and these should be reported to the Consistory, or the Consistory should take action even though no one comes to report, either from neglect or because it is well-known that the Consistory members bear knowledge of the case.

Jansen reports that the Synod of 1586, 's Gravenhage, was asked to give a distinctive description of secret and public sins. The Synod refused to do so. No Synod and no individual can do so, for reasons stated above, and because every case has its own peculiar setting. Never should we attempt to catalog sins as either secret or public. Reformed Church government does not lay down hard and fast rules going into great detail, but merely establishes certain leading clearly enunciated Biblical principles. This is enough and works for the safety of individual believers and their Churches, also in matters of discipline.

3. Secret sins, duly repented of, are not to be brought before the Consistory.

Article 73 specifies very definitely that secret sins which have been dealt with according to Christ's rule of Matt. 18 and of which the transgressors have repented, shall not be reported to the Consistory. This is as it should be. When discipline has reached the end sought, discipline ends. Matt. 18 says very plainly: "If he hear thee, thou hast gained thy brother." Only in case the guilty one refuses to repent does Christ prescribe further action. Secret sin should be kept secret unless the obstinacy, the unwillingness of the sinner to admit and repent, makes a revelation of the sin committed necessary.

And he who admonishes a guilty brother should always be anxious for a confession, so that the matter may not become public. Never should one go through the prescribed course of Matt. 18 and our Church Order just to be able to report the matter to the Consistory. Good-will, eagerness, and Christian charity should be prominent as we seek to correct and persuade each other. A haughty, superior attitude embitters and divides, and often hardens a sinner in his sin. Let those who in the way of God's providence are called upon to admonish others do so humbly and by all means prayerfully.

ARTICLE 74

If any one, having been admonished in love concerning a secret sin by two or three persons, does not give heed, or otherwise has committed a public sin, the matter shall be reported to the Consistory.

SINS TO BE REPORTED TO CONSISTORY

1. When sins must be reported to the Consistory.

The first major gatherings of the Reformed Churches of Holland, the Wezelian Convention, concluded that if one stubbornly and repeatedly rejected the brotherly admonitions, his sin should be reported to the Consistory. Furthermore, sins committed publicly and with public offense should be reported to the Consistories. (Cf. Acts of Wezel, Chap. 8, Art. 9, 10.) The first Synod, Emden, 1571, unified these two articles of Wezel into one (Emden, Art. 38) and wrote Article 74 (38) into the Church Order as it now reads, except that the Synod of 's Gravenhage, 1587, inserted the words "in love." (Art. 67, 1586.) Some believers would comply with the letter of Christ's rule of Matt. 18, but not with the spirit. Therefore this last mentioned Synod caused the article to read: "If anyone, having been admonished in love concerning a secret sin . . ." Article 74 therefore stipulates that a secret sin of which the guilty party will not repent after having been admonished according to the rule of Matt. 18, must be reported to the Consistory. Likewise that public sins must be reported to the Consistory.

Discipline must be exercised—as noted in our consideration of Article 71—that the name of God may not be blasphemed by the world; to safeguard the loyal members of the Church; and to move the sinner to shame and repentance. If this three-fold aim has not been attained through private admonitions and the labors of believers performed according to Matt. 18, then the office-bearers, the overseers of God's Church, should be notified that they may endeavor to accomplish as special servants of Christ what mutual discipline failed to accomplish. When labors of love performed by dint of the general office of all believers are fruitless, the whole Church through its Christ appointed officers must endeavor to correct and save the erring one.

Public sins are to be reported to the Consistory forthwith, not because the general office of all believers has no duties to perform in such cases, but because of the public offense given, which offense must be removed as soon as possible and because the sin is already known to many and therefore its immediate revelation to the Consistory cannot be termed uncharitable. Fellow believers must certainly show concern when one of their number errs. They should admonish the erring also in case the sin committed is public. But the public offense, the blot upon God's Church and His sacred name must be removed as soon as possible, and that can only be done publicly.

Consequently public sins are to be reported to the Consistory forthwith.

Why are these sins—secret sins not repented of and public sins—to be reported to the Consistory? Does not Matt. 18:17 say: "tell it unto the church" (margin: Congregation)? Indeed. However, there is no conflict between the words of Christ and the words of our Church Order. The Church or congregation at the time when Christ spoke the words of Matt. 18, was not yet organized. At a later day, through the Apostles, Christ ordained Elders in every Church in order that these should oversee and govern the Churches. Consequently Article 74 specifies that report must be made to the Consistory. The Elders represent both Christ and His Church, for Christ functions through the Church. It certainly would not do, after Christ has appointed rulers in His Churches, to ignore these Christ-appointed leaders and go to the body of believers directly. Moreover the best interest of all concerned demands that the office-bearers be informed and that they take all necessary action for the whole congregation. If need be, if irrepentance so require, the whole congregation will be informed, step by step, so that the whole Church may do its duty toward the erring one, praying for him, admonishing him, by giving active or passive approval of what the Consistory is doing, etc. And thus the whole Church will take action. The office-bearers are the organs through which the congregation functions and under whose leadership the believers act.

2. How reports are to be made to Consistories.

A Consistory need not always wait until a transgression is reported to it before taking action. A sin may be so commonly known that virtually the whole Consistory bears knowledge of the facts. In such a case no one will deem it necessary to make a report to the Consistory. The Elders can take action upon their own knowledge of facts.

Furthermore, in case a grievous sin has been committed a sinner may come to the Consistory of his own accord to confess, knowing perhaps that sooner or later the sin will become public. In such a case the Consistory may and must take action, though that action may merely be an announcement to the Church that the party in question has confessed a certain sin before God and the Consistory.

Young people, for instance, who transgress the Seventh Commandment with a resultant early marriage and parenthood may and should confess their sin before the Consistory of their own accord as soon as possible. Their secret sin will soon be generally known, and for all concerned an early announcement regarding penitence is desirable. Thus there may be other instances in which a sinner desires to confess his sin unknown to others, before the Consistory.

He who has labored with an erring brother according to Matt. 18, but without success, should go to the Consistory meeting to report the case. It is better that the reporter go to the Consistory meeting than that he merely gives a message to one or two Consistory members. The whole Consistory should hear the facts first hand.

May one who is not a member of the Church to which one accused belongs come with grievances? Most assuredly. We have a duty toward all our fellow-believers whether they belong to the same local Church or not.

May a Consistory receive a charge against one of its members from one who is not Christian Reformed? Certainly, as long as the witness is known to be trustworthy, and if he is able and willing to give definite information, as to the nature of the sin committed, time, place, etc. Should the charge concern a secret sin and the reporter be a professing Christian, then of course, the Consistory must make sure that the rule of Matt. 18 has been observed.

Consistories should be very careful not to begin an investigation upon the report of an unbeliever who might come with charges against a believer. On the other hand, if the unbeliever is known to be reliable in his testimony, no liar, then a charge made even by an unbeliever should be investigated, provided, of course, that the accuser is willing and able to give details as to time, place, etc. Guesses and suspicions should receive no consideration on the part of the Elders, no matter who pleases to present them.

As a rule unsigned letters containing charges against a member should be laid aside and should not even be received for information. Nevertheless, though no one has a right to make unsigned charges, if the Consistory fears that charges contained in such a letter are well-founded and if the matter be serious, then a quiet investigation is advisable. Persistent and general rumors may also require quiet action on the part of a Consistory in order that the good name of an innocent brother be cleared, if he is innocent, or else, that the offense be removed and the sinner may be corrected. Those who spread false rumors, if they can be located, should be admonished. And those who spread rumors founded on fact without following the rule of Matt. 18 should likewise be admonished and if need be disciplined.

3. Regarding investigations by Consistories.

When a Consistory finds that a certain charge or report requires investigation it should do its utmost to carry on the investigation impartially. He who is accused must receive ample opportunity to defend himself if he denies guilt. He may defend himself in person, orally, or by written statement. During the 16th and 17th centuries those under suspicion and under charge were even permitted to bring someone to talk for them, someone to be his advocate. There can be no objections against this practice. There is much in its favor. Sometimes the accused party has but little ability to state his own case clearly. Sometimes those under accusation are too nervous or agitated to present their cases in a desirable fashion. Therefore as long as the representatives of those accused are reliable and sincere Christians who aim to give a fair presentation of the facts and who agree to abide by the rules of the assembly—Consistory, Classis, or Synod, whichever the case may be—then there is no objection.

As stands to reason the Consistory should hear only trustworthy witnesses, being either members in good standing, not under censure for dishonesty, or some other trustworthy persons, not belonging to the Church. The Consistory should carefully weigh the evidence presented and should not reach a hasty conclusion.

Very seldom should Consistories place people under oath. Our yea, should be yea, and our nay, nay. But if urgency require, an oath may be taken. The trial should be dignified, conducted prayerfully, and absolutely impartial. The procedure should not become overly technical. Consistories do not conduct court trials in the civil sense of the word. Each case should be investigated not according to certain set and highly technical rules, but rather freely, as fairness and sanctified common sense may indicate for every specific case. The only purpose of an ecclesiastical investigation is to determine whether or not the accused party is guilty of a censurable sin. If an accusation proves to be unfounded, the accuser must retract his charge. If he persistently refuses to do so, he himself would ultimately become an object of discipline.

If in any case the Consistory cannot come to a definite conclusion, the Consistory should refrain from taking any action. If the parties involved in a charge in which the Consistory cannot reach a conclusion flatly contradict each other so that evidently one or the other must be lying, then both parties should be admonished very seriously, so that he who wilfully and consciously lies may not continue in his terrible sin and become hardened in his transgression, but may rather confess his fearful sin.

If guilt cannot be established in a given case, but the evidence points in the direction of guilt, then the party should be urged to consider matters very prayerfully, telling him also that if at any future time his Christian conscience should smite him and accuse him of guilt, to come to the Consistory to confess without hesitation and without delay. For the rest, Consistories can only place cases that cannot be established for or against an accused brother into the hands of Him who tries the heart and reigns omnisciently and who will reward both the innocent and the guilty righteously.

If the guilt of one accused is established beyond a just doubt, either through a confession on the part of one guilty or upon due investigation, the Consistory proceeds to admonish such a one.

If repentence follows, then complete reconciliation with the aggrieved parties, and in case of public sins with the whole Church, can follow. If, however, the party concerned has sinned repeatedly, or if the offense is very grievous, it may be well for both the transgressor and the Church that he be ordered to abstain from using the Sacraments for the time being. If the guilty party, having confessed his guilt and professed repentence, gives proof of his sincerity by a Godly walk, he should be fully reinstated in all his rights. If a Consistory deems it advisable to put a repentant sinner on probation, this need not be announced to the Church. His declaration of repentance may be announced without delay. But the fact that he is not as yet to partake of the Sacraments is a matter between the party concerned and the Consistory. Only in extreme cases should the matter of probation be announced to the congregation. Probation period should not last longer than necessary. As soon as one has manifested his sincerity by a Godly walk he should be re-admitted to all the privileges of the Church. Probation periods were perhaps more common in former years than they are now. They should not occur often. As a rule the repentant sinner should be received upon his testimony in the spirit of Christian love which gladly forgives and is eager to believe. Probation periods may range from three or six months to two years. We would not advise ever to extend the period beyond a two year term.

If one refuses to repent, censure follows as indicated in succeeding articles of the Church Order.

ARTICLE 75

The reconciliation of all such sins as are of their nature of a public character, or have become public because the admonition of the Church was despised, shall take place (upon sufficient evidence of repentance) in such a manner as the Consistory shall deem conducive to the edification of each Church. Whether in particular cases this shall take place in public, shall, when there is a difference of opinion about it in the Consistory, be considered with the advice of two neighboring Churches or of the Classis.

RECONCILIATION WITH THE CHURCH

Article 75 as it reads in our Church Order can be traced back to Article 29 of the Church Order of the Synod of Emden, 1571. This article provided in substance that reconciliation should not take place publicly in the presence of the Church unless the whole Consistory agreed that it was advisable. The Synod of 1586 provided that in Churches served by only one Minister, no public reconciliation should take place, except with the advice of two neighboring Churches (1586, Art. 68). The Synod of Dort, 1618-19, left the article as revised in 1586. Only it now became Article 75, as it is still today. The Synod of the Reformed Churches of the Netherlands, 1905, adopted the reading which we now have, our Synod of 1914 following the lead of the Holland Churches, with only this difference: For the Churches in Holland the article merely provides that the advice of two neighboring Churches shall be gained before a Consistory with only one Minister is to decide that a certain reconciliation shall take place before the Church, whereas our Article 75 reads: ". . . with the advice of two neighboring Churches or of the Classis."

1. Which cases demand reconciliation with the Church?

Only those cases in which the sin is public, either from the very nature of the transgression, or because the sinner refused to heed the admonition of the Consistory so that the Congregation had to be informed of the transgressor's sin and failure to repent.

Sins which are private and which are repented of should not be published. The rule of Matt. 18 is very clear on this point. It is also possible that a sinner does not repent when he is admonished by one or two or more individuals, but that he does repent when the Consistory begins to labor with him. In such a case reconciliation takes place privately, either before the whole Consistory or before a committee of the Consistory, depending on the nature of the sin and other circumstances. The believers who admonished him according to the Saviour's rule of Matt. 18 should be present at this reconciliation or they should be notified that reconciliation has taken place. Here also the sin and the circumstances involved should determine the procedure to be followed. But under no circumstance should a Consistory begin to reveal faults and transgressions of which the Congregation is not aware, if the party concerned gives clear proof of repentance.

But if the sin is known to the Church, because of its very nature, or because the Consistory had to announce the transgressor's sin to the Church in the process of discipline, because the guilty party would not repent, then, upon repentance the question arises: How must reconciliation with the Church take place? And to this question Article 75 supplies the answer.

2. Conditions for reconciliation.

Reconciliation of repentant sinners shall take place "upon sufficient evidence of repentance," Article 75 stipulates. Experience has taught the Churches that some people make a confession readily, because it is not heartfelt and is made merely to settle a matter externally. Often these transgressors fall back into the same sins repeatedly. Thus the name of God and His Church is defamed and the offense becomes great. Confessions frequently and easily violated undermine Church discipline, especially in the mind of the youthful and weak. For these reasons, and for the sake of the sinning party Synod of 1581 added the condition under consideration. This condition requires that Consistories do not accept a confession at face value, unless it has reasons to believe that the confessor is sincere. In some cases the Consistory will have to judge regarding the sincerity of a confession not so much by the word uttered or even emotionalism displayed, but rather by the walk of life manifested after the transgression occurs or after repentance was professed. As stands to reason, no Consistory should doubt a confessor's sincerity unless he has given occasion for such doubt by past experience, or by his present doubtful attitude.

In case of extreme sins a Consistory may feel itself bound to withhold the privileges of membership for the time being, especially that of partaking of the sacraments, Synod of 1578, Dort, even made a provision for this step in the Church Order (see Art. 98, Dort, 1578). This article provides that those who have committed grievous sins, disgraceful to the Church or also punishable by the State, even though they manifest repentance, shall nevertheless be excluded from the Lord's Supper to remove the offense, and to test the genuineness of their repentance. This article was left out of the Church Order by the next Synod, 1581. Nevertheless, all authorities agree that a Consistory has the right and duty to exclude a repentant sinner from the Sacraments for the time being. This right is also expressed by implication in the present article and its provision that reconciliation shall take place "upon sufficient evidence of repentance." See our concluding remarks regarding this same matter under Article 74.

3. Should reconciliation take place before the Consistory only, or also in the presence of the congregation?

This question is to be answered by each Consistory for each individual case. But if there is a difference of opinion in the Consistory as a case comes up for consideration, so that the Consistory cannot reach a unanimous decision, then, so Article 75 stipulates, the matter should not be decided by a majority vote, but then the Consistory must first gain the advice of two neighboring Churches or of Classis. This prescribed advice, as Jansen points out, does not imply that two other Consistories or that Classis decides the matter, nor that the Consistory concerned merely gains the advice and then decides as it sees fit regardless of the advice given. But it means that the responsible Consistory will take a decision in conformity with the advice received. If a Classis meeting is near at hand, the matter can be conveniently submitted to Classis. Otherwise two neighboring Consistories are asked to meet with the Consistory seeking advice, and then the three Consistories consider the matter together as one body, and seek to arrive at a united stand. However, each Consistory should take a separate vote. If the Consistory which seeks the advice of two neighboring Consistories can not agree with the choice of these Consistories, the matter is presented to Classis for disposition.

In the Reformed Churches of Holland Consistories which have more than one Minister (some have several) decide this matter by majority vote. The smaller Churches having only one Minister call for the advice of two neighboring Churches. The advice of Classis is not mentioned in the present redaction of Article 75 of the Reformed Churches of Holland. It may be noted, however, that the Synod of Middelburg, 1581, stipulated that public reconciliations should take place with the advice of Classis. (Art. 63, 1581.)

Article 75 does not specify when reconciliation shall be before the Consistory and when before the Church also. Instances and examples are not given either. Every case must be judged in its own setting and upon its own merits or demerits. In general Consistories should be guided by considerations as these: Which form of reconciliation (public or private) will glorify God most? Which is best for the Church? Which form is best for the repentant sinner? Consistories should not give needless publicity to sins committed through confessions or reconciliations before the whole Church in public meeting. Neither should the Consistory permit the name of a repentant sinner to be dishonored before men, if this can be avoided. On the other hand, offensive sins greatly dishonoring God's name and the Church of Christ should be confessed openly and personally so that all may see and know that repentance has taken place and so that the offense may be removed the more effectively. A public reconciliation is very often the best also for the sinner concerned. It tends to remove barriers which otherwise may linger.

There is no special Form for the reconciliation of which Article 75 speaks, neither for a reconciliation before the Consistory, nor for a reconciliation before the whole Church. The manner of reconciliation is left entirely to the Consistory. It must consider, also regarding this matter, the welfare of all concerned. If reconciliation is made before the Consistory certain definite questions should be answered, and the content of these should be included in the announcement to the Church. Matters of discipline should, as stands to reason, not be printed on bulletins, but announced verbally from the pulpit. Announcement to the congregation takes place to remove the offense given, and to reconcile the sinner with all his fellow believers.

When reconciliation is to take place in the midst of the congregation, the Consistory should draft a brief statement in which the character of the sin committed is mentioned, and in which emphasis is placed on the fact of repentance and consequent reconciliation. The purpose of this public confession of guilt and profession of repentance is reconciliation and reinstatement. Its purpose is not the administration of a final word of rebuke, publicly administered for emphasis' sake.

Synods of 1908 and 1930 ruled that: "In case of transgression of the Seventh Commandment before marriage, the form of confession is left to the Consistory, provided the confession is made (at least) before the whole Consistory. The advisability of announcement of the names to the congregation shall be determined by the Consistory in each case." (Cf. Stuart and Hoeksema's Church Order edition, under Art. 75.)

It may be questioned whether it is wise to single out a special sin, as the one referred to, and to make a special rule for it. It is apt to create the impression that this is the sin **par excellence.** The only justification for special rules of this kind can be that the sins in question are very prevalent and on the increase. Reconciliation in public or by a special announcement will emphasize the gravity of the sin and will help to put others on their guard. But why not use, in decisions of this kind, the term of the Church Order, i.e., "reconciliation" which expresses the essence of that which has or is taking place both carefully and beautifully?

Supposing one who is being admonished and censured moves and becomes a member of another of our Churches, which Consistory should then complete the reconciliation, revoking the suspension, etc.? The Consistory of his new Church. By this Church he has been received as a censured and erring member and the new Consistory always continues the process of censure where the former Consistory left off. But our confederation, our bonds of Church unity, would require that the former Consistory, which initiated censure be recognized and be asked for their approval, for they may know the case far better than the new Consistory. In case of extreme sins generally known it is advisable, both for the Church and for the sinner, that announcement of the transgressor's repentance be made to the former Church also. When serious differences of opinion arise between two Consistories in cases as suggested, the advice of Classis should be sought.

ARTICLE 76

Such as obstinately reject the admonition of the Consistory, and likewise those who have committed a public or otherwise gross sin, shall be suspended from the Lord's Supper. And if he, having been suspended, after repeated admonitions, shows no signs of repentance, the Consistory shall at last proceed to the extreme remedy, namely excommunication, agreeably to the form adopted for that purpose according to the Word of God. But no one shall be excommunicated except with consent of Classis.

SUSPENSION FROM THE LORD'S SUPPER

This article concerns temporary suspension or debarment from the Lord's Supper. Suspension from the Lord's Table as a disciplinary measure has been practiced by the Reformed Churches from the very beginning. In Geneva, under Calvin's leadership it was in force. The Reformed Churches of France, of Germany, Scotland, and the Netherlands all adopted temporary suspensions as provided for in Calvin's Church Order.*

The essence of our present Article 76 may be found in the Church Order of Emden, 1571. Later Synods made additions, but no essential changes.

1. Cases which require suspension from the Lord's Table.

The Synod of Emden, 1571, merely mentioned, "Such as obstinately reject the admonition of the Consistory." (Emden, Art. 30.) The Synod of Middelburg, 1581, added, "and likewise those who have committed a public or otherwise gross sin." (Middelburg, Art. 62.)

The first instance refers to such as have rejected the admonition of mutual or believers discipline according to Matt. 18. When these private admonitions remain fruitless the Consistory is notified. (Cf.

* Dr. F. L. Rutgers, **College-Voordrachten**, 1918, p. 52.

our discussion of Art. 74.) The Consistory first of all investigates to see if the claims lodged against a brother or sister are well-founded. If the Consistory finds guilt, it proceeds to admonish the transgressor repeatedly. If the sinner takes the admonition of the Consistory to heart and repents, ecclesiastical discipline in the stricter, technical sense of the word is not necessary. Reconciliation with the aggrieved parties takes place, and the matter is ended. But if, at the other hand the transgressor obstinately rejects the admonition of the Consistory, then he is to be suspended from the Lord's Supper. Let it be clear therefore that only after persistent refusal to heed the admonition of the Consistory, discipline technically begins. Obstinate rejection of the Consistory's admonition is not always outspoken and blunt. Sometimes the transgressor shows only by his conduct that he refuses to heed the admonition given. But anyone who fails to admit his fault and he who fails to mend his ways is guilty of obstinate rejection of admonition. Now then, if the transgressor clearly manifests this refusal to repent he is to be suspended from the Lord's Table. It is definitely irrepentance which brings forth suspension, not the sin committed. There is forgiveness for every sin, if only that sin is sincerely repented of with Godly sorrow. Even a murderer ready to die in the electric chair can be admitted to the Lord's Table if he be repentant.

The second class which calls for suspension according to the present article comprises those that "have committed a public or otherwise gross sin." If a Consistory discovers that one of the members is guilty of a serious sin, generally known, or a sin definitely offensive and scandalous, it decides forthwith that the transgressor shall not partake of the Lord's Supper until confession has been made, or until the Consistory grants him permission to do so after confession has been made.

Sometimes Consistories find it advisable to postpone the celebration of the Lord's Supper because of disturbed relationship in the Congregation. Trouble may arise which involves several members in transgressions. No Consistory should determine to postpone the celebration of the Lord's Supper except for weighty reasons. But if conditions are much disturbed it is permissible and wise to do so. Such a postponement is not a disciplinary measure but simply a means to prevent desecration of the Lord's Supper and the slandering of God's name.

2. The character of suspension according to Art. 76.

Reformed Church government distinguishes between **discipline in the sense of admonition,** directed to transgressors by fellow believers and as individual believers according to Christ's rule of Matt. 18, or by the Consistory in its representative and official capacity, and **discipline in the sense of admonition by the Consistory plus suspension of membership rights.**

Discipline in this second sense of the word, discipline in the stricter, more technical sense of the word, has two stages according to the accepted rules of our Church Order. During the first stage the Consistory labors with the transgressors and bars him from the Lord's Supper and all membership privileges—but no announcement is made to the Congregation; censure is as yet "silent" or secret. (We speak of silent censure from the Dutch, **stille censure.**) This first stage of discipline is regulated and indicated in Article 76 now under consideration. The second stage of discipline is characterized by three distinct announcements to the congregation, sometimes called first, second, and third steps of censure, from the Dutch "eerste, tweede, en derde trap van censure." This second stage of discipline is indicated and regulated in Article 77, the article which we shall consider next.

The first stage of ecclesiastical discipline (Art. 76), silent censure, is a **temporary suspension** from the Lord's Table. The second stage of ecclesiastical discipline is, as to its character, a **definite suspension** from the Lord's Table. As will be understood, the process may be halted at any time by sincere repentance on the part of the transgressor. In such a case excommunication does not take place. The stage of discipline provided for in Article 76 has also been called minor excommunication from the Latin **excommunicatio minor.** This excommunication is minor inasmuch as it deprives one temporarily of the exercise of his membership rights, not of the rights as such. The second stage of discipline, regulated in Article 77 is then designated as major excommunication, from the Latin **excommunicatio major.** This excommunication is major inasmuch as it deprives one of his membership rights and that definitely.

The suspension from the Lord's Supper provided for in Article 76 is therefore disciplinary in character. Sometimes members are kept from the Lord's Table although they are not (as yet) objects of Church discipline in the stricter sense of the word. For example, a member may have made himself guilty of a grievous sin, known to many, concerning which he repents just before the Lord's Supper. Then to avoid offense, the Consistory may bar the brother concerned from the Lord's Table for that celebration.

So also an involved and serious case of discipline may come to a favorable conclusion through repentance by the guilty one, just before the Lord's Supper is to be celebrated. Either because the offense cannot be removed instantly, in a short space of time, or because some details must still be worked out, the Consistory may see fit to tell the party concerned not to come to the Lord's Supper about to be celebrated. Or again, a case of discipline may present itself just previous to the celebration of the Lord's Supper. The Consistory cannot fully investigate the case before the time of celebration but evidence points definitely to guilt. In such a case the Consistory may tell the party in question to refrain from coming to the Lord's Table at the communion service nigh at hand. In Dutch this suspension has been termed "eenvoudige afhouding" or "voorloopige afhouding." We would use the term "simple suspension" or "simple debarment." The latter term has this in its favor that it is less likely to be confused with regular, disciplinary suspension.

Sometimes a Consistory merely advises a member to refrain from going to the Lord's Table for a particular celebration nigh at hand. This is sometimes done if one is at least to some extent guilty of a minor transgression. The matter does not seem to warrant suspension but partaking of the Lord's Supper may offend some. Or, a slight misunderstanding may arise between two communicants so that fraternal relationships are disrupted somewhat. Accusations are made but the whole thing is vague so that the Consistory does not know where the guilt lies inasfar as there is guilt. If then the celebration of the Lord's Supper be nigh at hand, the Consistory may advise both parties to refrain from going to the Lord's Table. Let it be well understood, in these latter cases the Consistory merely advises. The parties concerned may celebrate the Supper if they so desire.

Voluntary refrainment is also possible. A member may refrain from coming to the Lord's Table entirely of his own accord for reasons of his own. He may have committed a sin known to him and a small number of others. He may have repented but he may not have had time to rectify matters inasfar as such is possible. In such a case he may withhold himself from partaking, although no one has urged him to do so. Two or more members between whom an un-Christian spirit has arisen may also agree mutually to refrain from going to the Lord's Table until matters have been set right.

3. Course to be followed when suspension and admonitions fail to bring repentance.

If suspension from the Lord's Supper and the admonitions of the Consistory are heeded so that repentance follows, discipline ceases and reconciliation takes place. But Article 76 tells us what should be done if the sinner persists in his obstinate rejection of all admonition, even after membership rights have been suspended. If one refuses to repent even after he has been barred from the Lord's Table, etc., then the Consistory continues to admonish him. How often should the Consistory admonish? No figures are given. Each case should be dealt with according to its own requirements. The Church Order does prescribe "repeated admonitions." This is as it should be. The transgressor must be warned until the very last. But if all admonitions, those directed before suspension, during or with the suspension, and those addressed to the erring one after suspension do not avail, then the Consistory shall at last proceed to the "extreme remedy." This extreme remedy is definite suspension of all membership rights, or final and complete excommunication. This excommunication is the "extreme remedy." Even by this extreme act the Church hopes to bring about repentance. It desires to save the sinner throughout.

For this excommunication the Churches are to use the "Form adopted for that purpose." This Form may be found in our Psalter Hymnals, appended pages 95, 96. This Form was adopted for the first time by the Synod of 's Gravenhage, 1586.

Excommunication by this Form does not occur very often in our Churches. Why not? Are there no deflections? Are there no members who by their sins and their refusal to repent make themselves worthy of excommunication? The Form is seldom used because members under discipline who obstinately refuse to repent as a rule break with the Church and thus avoid excommunication. But a word of warning should be spoken in this connection. Synod of 1918, Article 53, decided as follows:

"Synod, considering that the withdrawal from discipline, to which one has freely subjected himself, and the breaking off of the fellowship with the Church to which one belongs, for reasons which cannot stand the test of God's Word, is a sin which should not be esteemed lightly, and that those who do so should be supplicated continuously and earnestly that they return from their erroneous way, and that these should not be released hastily; but (considering) also that one's affiliation with the Church as an organization as well as one's continuation in the organized Church, should remain to be, according to Church governmental principles, an act of each one's own personal choice, (therefore Synod) judges that no one can continue to be an object of Church discipline if he persists in resigning his membership." (Translated.)

We have no fault to find with this stand of Synod as to its essential principles. But we do believe that many Consistories accepted "resignation" too easily. We are therefore happy that the Synod of 1936 expressed itself on this matter as it did and adopted the following:

"In such announcements (announcements regarding those that have broken with the Church) it should be plainly stated that the person who resigned his membership in the manner indicated in the decision of 1918, by that very act has committed a grievous sin and that he obstinately refuses to listen to the admonition of the Consistory, though admonished repeatedly and seriously not to commit this sin. It stands to reason that expressions like 'accepting the resignation' should not be used in the announcement, because the full responsibility for his sinful act must remain with the person who withdraws himself from the Church." (Acts of Synod, 1936, p. 121.)

It is true that membership in the organized Church can never be forced and should remain to be the result of voluntary acts on the part of all its members. But it is also true that the members at the time of their confession of faith solemnly promised to be true to the Church and to submit themselves to church discipline if discipline should become necessary. Resigning one's membership is a very grievous sin, and a Consistory should proceed with censuring such a one unless he determinately persists in breaking his relationship with the Church. Very often we fear Consistories have accepted resignations rather quickly in order to be free from the sad duty of excommunicating the party in question. This should never be done. Discipline must ever run its full course unless the object of discipline makes it impossible. Then the full responsibility will also rest on his shoulders. And, Consistories should so labor with resigning members that they can truthfully announce to the Churches that the utmost has been done to restrain the member in question from taking this step and that the responsibility is his.

Article 76 also provides that "no one shall be excommunicated except with consent of the Classis." Article 77 tells us just how and when this advice of Classis is to be sought.

Every Church and Consistory has a right to exercise discipline. There are no office-bearers possessing a higher degree of authority than those of every particular Church. Intrinsically, essentially every Church has a right to govern itself. But the Churches have agreed as a matter of wisdom and safety that no Church should act in certain matters without and against the advice of the other Churches, especially in matters of discipline, partiality and ill-will may assert itself. Besides, many cases are involved and difficult. Consequently the advice of neighboring Churches through Classis is highly desirable. No one can be excommunicated except with the advice, i.e., in harmony with the advice of Classis. Only if a Consistory is fully persuaded that the advice of Classis is contrary to the Word of God or our Church Order, (our basis of co-operation and union) may it refrain from deciding in harmony with the advice of Classis. Then the Consistory, of course, submits the case to Synod.

This request for advice is therefore not an appeal. Classis does not sit as a court of appeal which tries the case for itself. It only checks upon the work and decisions of the Consistory and advises it according to its judgment.

In case the censured party should appeal to Classis, declaring that the Consistory and Classis are mistaken, then the Classis investigates as far as is necessary to arrive at a fair conclusion. In such a case Classis is not bound by its own previous advice.

ARTICLE 77

After the suspension from the Lord's Table, and subsequent admonitions, and before proceeding to excommunication, the obstinacy of the sinner shall be publicly made known to the congregation, the offense explained, together with the care bestowed upon him, in reproof, suspension from the Lord's Supper, and repeated admonition, and the congregation shall be exhorted to speak to him and to pray for him. There shall be three such admonitions. In the first the name of the sinner shall not be mentioned that he be somewhat spared. In the second, with the consent of the Classis, his name shall be mentioned. In the third the congregation shall be informed that (unless he repent) he will be excluded from the fellowship of the Church, so that his excommunication, in case he remains obstinate, may take place with the tacit approbation of the Church. The interval between the admonitions shall be left to the discretion of the Consistory.

THE EXCOMMUNICATION

As noted above, Article 76 concerns the first stage of ecclesiastical discipline. Article 77 concerns the second stage, i.e., the final and definite suspension of all membership rights, also called excommunication. Article 77 has often been misinterpreted. Many have thought that the first step of excommunication according to Article 77 was identical with the disciplinary provisions of Article 76. These thought that the first step of public censure was really the same as the silent censure of Article 76. This, however, is not the case. The suspension from the Lord's Table mentioned in Article 76 is not to be confused with the first admonition or first step of Article 77. Article 76 tells us that when a sinner refuse to repent, "the Consistory shall at last proceed to the extreme remedy, namely, excommunication." Now Article 77 tells us how the Consistory must proceed in applying this extreme remedy.

To prevent confusion the Holland Synod of 1905, and our own Synod of 1914, changed the reading of Article 77 somewhat. The article used to begin as follows: "Before proceeding to excommunication. . ." Now we read: "After the suspension from the Lord's Table, and subsequent admonitions, and before proceeding to excommunication. . ." The added words refer to the provisions of Article 76.

1. The course of discipline from the point of silent censure to excommunication.

Article 77 provides **first of all that a brief account of the case at hand shall be given to the congregation** whenever a Consistory feels that it must proceed with discipline. This brief account must include **a statement of the offense committed.** This statement should be couched in general terms, and should not go into details. If possible the offense should be announced as a sin against one of the Ten Commandments. Thus one guilty of appropriating money unto himself through falsification of books would be said to be guilty of a sin against the Eighth Commandment. The announcement must also include mention of the "care bestowed upon him, in reproof, suspension from the Lord's Supper, and repeated admonition." The Consistory should therefore point out that reproof was given before suspension from the Lord's Supper was resorted to; that subsequently the transgressor was suspended from the Lord's Table; and that afterwards the Consistory had still admonished him several times. From all this "the obstinacy of the sinner" must be clear to the Church. Obstinacy, refusal to convert himself and to repent, calls for discipline, not the sin as such. Finally, the congregation is to be exhorted "to speak to the guilty one, and to pray for him."

The congregation cannot be urged to speak to the transgressor until his name is announced to the Church. This takes place if, after the first step of censure, the sinner persists in his sin. But the congregation can pray for an erring and unrepentant member even though his name is not known. The reference here is not to congregational prayers which are part of our Sunday services but to our personal prayers. These prayers are often neglected. This is a grievous sin. The congregation should be much concerned when one errs in doctrine or life. When one member suffers, all should suffer. And the congregation should feel that the matter of discipline is its concern, and not that of the Consistory merely.

The first section of Article 77 provides for exhortations to the congregation regarding one worthy of discipline. Next, Article 77 tells us how many of such exhortations or admonitions there should be. We read: "There shall be **three such admonitions.**" These three admonitions, as noted above, are often called three steps. It may be noted here that these three admonitions are not addressed to the transgressor but to the Church. The transgressor is admonished much oftener than three times. He is urged to repent repeatedly. But the Church should be urged to labor with and for the erring one at least three distinct times. Concerning the first admonition or step we read: "In the first the name of the sinner shall not be mentioned that he be somewhat spared." The congregation is informed regarding the sin committed and the labors bestowed on the erring one, etc., as we have just seen. But, at the first occasion of announcement and admonition, the name of the transgressor is not mentioned. The congregation is only admonished in this first announcement to pray for the erring one. This admonition should be written out, approved by the Consistory and thus read to the Church. Extemporaneous announcements may involve a Church in difficulties. The party concerned may appeal his case to Classis or Synod, and then all parties involved should know exactly what has been said. Moreover, the admonition must be the conviction not merely of the Minister making the announcement, but the conviction of the Consistory. The statement must be strictly accurate and objective. As the first section of Article 77 demands, this announcement should indicate (a) the nature of the sin committed, (b) the obstinacy of the sinner, (c) the diligence of the Consistory in admonishing the party concerned and in suspending him from the Lord's Supper and in admonishing him still further, (d) and finally the admonition to the Church to pray for the transgressor.

Concerning the second admonition to the Church we read: "In the second, with consent of the Classis, his name shall be mentioned." The second admonition is a repetition of the first with this difference, that in the second admonition the name of the sinner is mentioned and the announcement is made with the advice of Classis. In the first admonition the name of the transgressor was not mentioned in order that he be somewhat spared. In the second his name is mentioned so that the congregation may speak to him, and in the hope that this fact may help him to see the urgency of his situation. A member's good name and reputation must be protected, but not at the expense of his own true welfare. The advice of Classis is required as a safeguard against partiality, and in the interest of strict righteousness. Moreover, classical advice is invaluable for Consistories not so well acquainted with the proper procedure in Church discipline. Concerning the phrase "with the consent of the Classis," it should be remarked that our Synod of 1920 would have done better to translate "with the advice of the Classis." Throughout, the Church Order speaks of "advice," and the official Dutch text from which we derived our translation does not read "met toestemming der Classe," but, "met advies der Classe." Our present translation is clearly a mistake, which was overlooked by the Synod of 1920.

"With the advice of Classis (Latin **ex classis judicio**, i.e., according to the judgment of Classis) so Jansen emphasizes correctly,* does not mean: with the permission of Classis, for that would conflict with the fact that each Church is essentially a self-governing body under Christ, and that there is no superior authority which can dictate to the particular Church above the Consistory in the strict sense of the word. Neither does the expression: with the advice of Classis mean: after Classis has been consulted. In that case the Consistory could ask for advice formally and then do as it saw fit. The expression means: according, or in harmony with, the advice of Classis. This is one of the matters in which the individual Churches have agreed not to follow their own judgment independently of the other Churches, but to follow the judgment of all the other Churches meeting as Classis for mutual deliberation and counsel.** The particular Churches, united in federative bonds according to their intrinsic unity in Christ and the injunctions and examples of Holy Writ, have agreed to abide by the opinion of the majority unless to the mind of the Church or Consistory concerned the opinion of the majority is clearly a violation of God's Word and our basis of union. In that case the way of protest and appeal is open, and ultimately, if need be, acquiesence under protest, or if the voice of conscience will not permit this, separation.

Before a Classis can express its opinion in a given case, it must ascertain: (a) whether the sin is censurable, (b) whether the admonitions and the suspension from the Lord's Table according to Article 76 have taken place; (c) whether the first admonition to the Church has been properly made; (d) whether the Consistory has labored sufficiently with the erring member after the first announcement to the Church; (e) whether it is clear that the transgressor is and remains obstinate in his rejection of all admonitions.

If the Classis advises to proceed and to make the second admonition to the Church, then the Consistory should approve of the announcement to be made to the congregation. This second admonition, briefly stated should mention (a) **the character of the sin committed and the name of the sinner;** (b) **the obstinacy of the transgressor also after the first admonition to the Church;** (c) **an exhortation to the Church to speak to the erring one, and to pray for him.**

As to the third admonition to the Church we read: **"In the third the congregation shall be informed that (unless he repent) he will be excluded from the fellowship of the Church."** This admonition is the last public announcement. In it the Church is informed that the transgressor in question has remained obstinate and that he will be excommunicated in the near future (the exact date should be mentioned), unless repentance takes place before that time. This last an-

* Cf. Jansen: **Korte Verklaring**, etc., 1923, p. 336.

** Cf. Bouwman: **Gereformeerd Kerkrecht**, II, 1934, p. 637.

nouncement is also called an admonition. The Church is once more admonished to labor with the transgressor and to pray for him. At least three or four weeks should elapse between the last admonition and the actual excommunication in order that the transgressor may have ample time for prayer and reflection before he is actually excommunicated and in order that he may have opportunity to appeal his case if he so desire.

Should Classis be asked for advice once more before this third admonition, before this third step is taken and excommunication takes place? Usually this is not done. Jansen favors it, inasmuch as Article 76 says: "But no one shall be excommunicated except with consent of the Classis." However, it may be maintained successfully, we believe, that this provision is fully met by the advice secured from Classis before the second admonition to the Church is made. If a certain Consistory desires the advice of Classis once more, before it proceeds to excommunicate, there can be nothing against this. When such advice is sought, it should be given but it cannot be said that the Church Order requires Consistories to seek it.

2. The excommunication proper.

The excommunication takes place "with the tacit approbation of the Church." That is to say, the third announcement is made to the Church also for this reason, that the congregation may give its silent approval. The Latin phrase used in the Church Order was "tacitis ecclesiae suffragiis", i.e., with the silent vote of the Church. The Church must therefore take an active part in the excommunication as in all other matters. The Church must approve or disapprove. If any member is convinced for sufficient reasons that the Consistory is in error or that the Consistory is too hasty, such a member should make his objection known to the Consistory. The Consistory should carefully weigh the evidence presented and rectify any mistakes that may have been made, or postpone the excommunication. If the Consistory feels that the complaining member has no just grounds for his objections then the complainer should receive opportunity to appeal the matter to Classis. That is to say, if the complainer desires to bring the matter to Classis, the Consistory must not proceed to excommunicate but await the opinion of Classis. If nothing is said regarding an appeal to Classis, and if the Consistory is fully persuaded that excommunication should take place at the time announced, then the Consistory may proceed.

The purpose of excommunication is stated in the following words in our Form of Excommunication: ". . . to the end that he may hereby be made (if possible) ashamed of his sins, and likewise that we may not by this rotten and as yet incurable member, put the whole body of the Church in danger, and that God's name may not be blasphemed."

The implications and the significance of excommunication are stated thus: ". . . for the aforesaid reasons we have excommunicated, and by these, do excommunicate N. from the Church of God, and from fellowship with Christ, and the holy sacraments, and from all the spiritual blessings and benefits which God promiseth to and bestows upon his Church, so long as he obstinately and impenitently persists in his sins, . . ."

Article 77 finally provides that "The interval between the admonitions shall be left to the discretion of the Consistory." This is a very wise ruling. There are no two cases exactly alike, and therefore each Consistory must decide the question of time, as each case may require. As a rule Consistories should move very carefully and slowly. Usually a number of months will elapse between the various admonitions or steps. Some extreme cases may require speedier action but often cases will consume not merely months but years before the final excommunication takes place. Not until the Church has put forth every means and every effort should the meaningful ban of excommunication be applied.

ARTICLE 78

Whenever anyone who has been excommunicated desires to become reconciled to the Church in the way of penitence, it shall be announced to the Congregation, either before the celebration of the Lord's Supper, or at some other opportune time, in order that (inasfar as no one can mention anything against him to the contrary) he may with profession of his conversion be publicly reinstated, according to the Form for that purpose.

RECONCILIATION OF EXCOMMUNICATED

The Form of Excommunication calls excommunication "the last remedy." One of the reasons for which we apply the ban of excommunication is to save the sinner concerned. After all other means have failed the Church hopes and prays that it may please God to use this radical and final step in the process of discipline to bring the transgressor to heartfelt repentance before God. For this reason the Church Order also speaks of excommunication as "the extreme remedy." (Article 76.)

Consequently the Churches ever welcomed repentant sinners, even though such sinners may have been excommunicated. At first Consistories and Classes regulated the reinstatement of banned members without a regulating rule in the Church Order and without a Form for readmitting excommunicated persons. It was soon found, however, that some rule and uniformity was desirable. Synod of 's Gravenhage, 1586, (Article 71) wrote Article 78 as it reads today into our Church Order.

1. Conditions for reconciliation of the Excommunicated.

Article 78 mentions two conditions which must be satisfied before one banned from the fellowship of the Church and all its privileges can be reinstated. First of all, the one excommunicated must desire reconciliation. It must not be someone else's desire to which the excommunicated merely assents, but it must be his own request and heartfelt desire. Secondly, he must desire reconciliation "in the way of penitence." The sincerity of the desire for reconciliation must be proven by penitence. If the banned person does not give a clear testimony of penitence, or if his conduct gives just reasons for doubting the sincerity of his confession, then the reconciliation should not take place until all doubts on this score have been removed. This does not mean that the Church must give the applicant for readmission the cold shoulder. Not at all. It must labor with him and encourage him. And as soon as he can be readmitted without hesitation he must receive a hearty welcome.

It may be said here that if one has broken his relationship with the Church by "resigning," in spite of all the admonitions of the Church, and subsequently desires to be reinstated, that such a one should not be readmitted without the same personal desire and sincere penitence. In many instances such persons should also be readmitted publicly with confession of their guilt.

2. Due acknowledgement of the congregation.

The article provides that the desire on the part of one excommunicated to be readmitted, "shall be announced to the Congregation." Why should the congregation be informed? Article 78 itself gives the answer to this question. "In order that (inasfar as no one can mention anything against him to the contrary) he may with profession of his conversion be publicly reinstated." The Consistory therefore makes this announcement to the Church, not merely as a matter of information, but very definitely to gain its approval. It may be said once more that Reformed Church government would regard the Church as having certain God-given rights. The believers are not minors. They have the anointing of the Holy One, and should be acknowledged. The offices function for the Church, although upon the authority which is Christ-given.

The announcement is made in order that he who may know of reasons why the reconciliation should not take place may report the same to the Consistory. Anyone knowing of such reasons must report them. This is his Christian duty. If no one raises well-founded objections against the contemplated readmittance, then the reconciliation takes place with the approval of the whole Church.

The form for readmission contains an announcement which is to be read to the Church some time previous to the date tentatively set for the readmission, in which notice is given concerning the excommunicated person's request and confession of penitence, and in which the believers are charged to notify the Consistory in due time if they have anything against the proposed readmission. The time for the act of readmission in this first section of the Form is designated as "the next time when by the Grace of God we celebrate the Supper of the Lord."

Supposing the banned person has moved to another locality, then can he be readmitted in the Church of his new location? Indeed he can. But the rules mutually agreed upon and entered into the Church Order should be observed. That is to say, he can only be readmitted by means of the Form for readmission. And his former Church in which the excommunication took place should be acknowledged. This former Church should give its approval. The fact of readmission should, as a rule, be announced to the former Church. If the excommunicated person lives in the same city or environment in which the Church is located which excommunicated him, he should preferably be readmitted by this same Church. The Consistory of the former Church will, as a rule, know the facts in the case far better than the Consistory of the new Church. After his readmission he can then remove to the Church of his new residence. If our Churches maintained definite boundary lines, penitents should be readmitted by and in the Church of their residence. But since boundaries are ignored and forgotten, readmission in and by the Church in which the transgression occurred is proper, though not always necessary. If the former Church objects to the readmission of an excommunicated member by another Church it should definitely state its reasons. If no agreement can be reached between the two Consistories, the Consistory of the former Church should take the matter to Classis, namely the Classis of the Church which desires to readmit the excommunicated party. The readmission will, of course, not take place while the appeal is pending.

3. The manner of reconciliation of those excommunicated.

In the consideration of this point we would first of all call attention to what appears to be a very faulty translation. Our official Dutch text of Article 78 reads, in harmony with the historic reading of this article, ". . . in order that (inasfar as no one can mention anything against him to the contrary) he may with profession of his conversion be publicly reinstated, **at the next celebration of the Lord's Supper** . . ." (". . . teneinde hij ten naastkomende Avondmale . . . openbaarlyk met professie zyner bekeering weder opgenomen worde. . .") The words "at the next celebration of the Lord's Supper" have been omitted from the text, as will be noted.

Perhaps this omission was occasioned by the fact that the first section of Article 78 states, that the announcement regarding the proposed readmittance may be made "either before the celebration of the Lord's Supper, **or at some other opportune time.**" However, this clause merely allows for necessary exceptions to the rule. Which rule? That readmittance of excommunicated persons should take place just before the Church celebrates the Lord's Supper. This is indeed a very appropriate time for readmitting excommunicated persons. At the Lord's Table the Church enjoys one of its most blessed privileges here on earth. At the Lord's Table, moreover, the unity of the saints finds beautiful expression. Furthermore, excommunication implies an excommunication from all the privileges and blessings of the Church of Christ. Foremost of these is admittance to the Lord's Table. Consequently we conclude that this time for reconciling and readmitting the excommunicated was well chosen by the men and Churches of Reformation days: The words **"at the next celebration of the Lord's Supper"** should therefore be restored to the article. Only urgent reasons should cause us to depart from the historic rule. For example, an early removal to a distant locality, the awaiting Baptism of a child of the repentant, etc.

Readmission, according to Article 78, shall take place "according to the Form for that purpose." The reference here is to the **Form for Readmission** (cf. Psalter Hymnal, appended pages 97, 98). This Form as well as that for excommunication is simple but rich in content. These Forms should be studied for their simplicity and beauty, their deep spiritual thought and their significant terminology. Seldom are these Forms used. This is in part due to the fact that we are beginning to weaken in our application of discipline. This is indeed a great danger. Many denominations have undergone fearful corruption in the space of one or two generations because they weakened in their application of discipline. Let us be on the look-out for this evil. Let Church Visitors faithfully admonish negligent Consistories, and not fail to report obvious neglect to the Classes which they represent.

ARTICLE 79

When Ministers of the Divine Word, Elders or Deacons, have committed any public, gross sin, which is a disgrace to the Church, or worthy of punishment by the Authorities, the Elders and Deacons shall immediately by preceding sentence of the Consistory thereof and of the nearest Church, be suspended or expelled from their office, but the Ministers shall only be suspended. Whether these shall be entirely deposed from office, shall be subject to the judgment of the Classis, with the advice of the Delegates of the (Particular) Synod mentioned in Article 11.

CONCERNING CENSURE OF OFFICE-BEARERS

1. Necessity for censure of office-bearers.

If an office-bearer makes himself guilty of a public, gross sin, he makes himself worthy of discipline not only as an individual member of the Church, but also as an office-bearer. If a Consistory finds it necessary to censure an office-bearer as an individual member according to the provisions of Articles 76 he should also be censured as an office-bearer. The former does not make the latter unnecessary, but rather calls for it. No one who has committed a public and gross sin should be permitted to go to the Lord's Table, but neither can such a one function as office-bearer until full satisfaction has been given.

I Tim. 5:19 bids us not to receive an accusation against an Elder except at the mouth of two or three witnesses. We should therefore be very cautious when Elders (and other office-bearers) are accused. But this passage does teach by implication that discipline regarding office-bearers has a rightful place in the Church.

An office-bearer who has made himself guilty of gross public sins has wrought disgrace upon the Church and to some extent has forfeited his influence. He cannot continue to perform the duties of his office uninterruptedly. If the sin is very grievous and offensive he should be deposed. If less serious, he must make a hearty confession of his sin before he can continue his work and his repentance should be announced to the Church.

Personal discipline as stated does not exempt from discipline as an office-bearer. If the former is necessary, the latter is also. But the reverse is not always true. Sometimes it may be necessary to suspend or even depose one from office by reason of a sin committed, but that it is not necessary to apply discipline to him as an individual member. If an office-bearer has made himself guilty of a gross public sin, but clearly manifests sincere repentance, he need not be disciplined as an individual member. Discipline aims at repentance before God and reconciliation with God and His Church. If by God's grace these ends have already been attained why should he still be censured as a member? But his sin may be of such a nature that great offense has been given, so that for some time to come at least, he can no longer function fruitfully as office-bearer. In that case he should be deposed from office, although discipline according to Article 76 would be unnecessary and out of place. Deposition under these circumstances would also be necessary to remove as much as possible the measure of disgrace which the sinning office-bearer has brought upon God's name and His Church.

2. Which sins require discipline regarding office-bearers?

Article 79 answers, "Any public, gross sin, which is a disgrace to the Church, or worthy of punishment by the Authorities." It may be necessary to admonish office-bearers because of minor offenses committed. But these in and by themselves do not call for suspension and deposition. For this reason Article 79 speaks of gross sins. Neither is it always necessary to suspend or depose an office-bearer for a more serious offense committed if the sin is not generally known. If an office-bearer repents sincerely concerning a more serious, secret sin, he need not be suspended or deposed. No public, open offense has been caused and repentance is present. Therefore this article speaks of "any public, gross sin." In this connection it should be remembered that certain sins which are at first secret, sometimes become public because of the sinner's obstinacy and refusal to repent.

The precise meaning and implication of the term "gross sins" is given in Article 80. Here the qualifying statement, "which is a disgrace to the Churches, or worthy of punishment by the Authorities," is added. Not all offenses bring disgrace upon the Church. However, when this is the case suspension from office is in order, and deposition may be necessary. The term "Authorities" here refers to the government. If one commits a sin for which he is liable to arrest and punishment by the civil authorities, then he has made himself worthy of suspension or deposition as office-bearer.

3. How discipline regarding office-bearers should proceed.

The Elders and Deacons, so the article specifies, when they have committed any public, gross sin, shall "immediately . . . be suspended or expelled from their office." The Church Order does not mean to say, "forthwith, without a fair investigation and unbiased hearing," but without first going to Classis. The word "immediately" regarding Elders and Deacons is contrasted in this article with the more involved procedure prescribed regarding the discipline of Ministers.

But no Consistory has the right to suspend or depose one of its Elders or Deacons by itself. Inherently each Consistory does have this right. For this reason we should not be surprised that the very first redaction of the Church Order prescribed that Consistories could and should suspend and depose office-bearers when necessary. The Wezelian Convention, 1586, ruled that Ministers and Elders guilty of grievous public sins (openbare schelmstukken en booze daden) should be deposed by the Consistory without awaiting the advice of Classis. (Chapter 8, Art. 12). The Synod of Emden, 1571, Church Order Article 33, ruled that Elders and Deacons who had made themselves guilty of public sins, bringing disgrace and slander upon the Church or punishable by the civil authorities, should be deposed from office forthwith by the Consistory. The Church Order of Dort, 1578, maintained this position (Article 99). However, the Synod of Middelburg, 1581, Article 64, provided that Elders and Deacons should be deposed only when their own Consistory **and the Consistory of the nearest Church** judged this to be right. This provision gave the Churches an additional safeguard against abuse and partiality. The Churches, in the interest of fairness and good government, agreed to limit themselves in the execution of their inherent right. Henceforth no Elder or Deacon would be deposed except the Consistory of the nearest Church, as well as the Consistory to which the office-bearer in question belonged, felt that deposition was in order.

Ministers, so the Wezelian Convention ruled, could also be deposed by their Consistories alone. (See reference above). But the first Synod, Emden, 1571, ruled that the Consistory should do no more than suspend from office. The deposition of Ministers was referred to the Classis. The Synod of Middelburg, 1581, ruled that Ministers should be suspended only with the concurrent opinion of a neighboring Consistory. Their deposition was left to Classis. Thus matters stand today.

The Church Order in the present article gives rules for four distinct situations, namely, the suspension of Elders and Deacons; the deposition of Elders and Deacons; the suspension of Ministers; the deposition of Ministers.

The suspension of Elders and Deacons. When a Consistory finds that one of its number is guilty of a gross, public sin, it should meet immediately to consider the case. If it is judged that suspension or deposition is in order, it ought to notify the nearest Consistory that its judgment is needed. The two Consistories should meet simultaneously and together to consider the case. Then each Consistory should vote separately. If the judgment of both Consistories concur, if both Consistories vote in favor of suspension, the decision stands and the party concerned is notified to this effect. Almost needless to say, the brother in question should be notified concerning the double Consistory meeting to be held regarding his person, and he should have a full right to speak for himself before both Consistories.

Ordinarily a period of suspension will be from three to six months. In the meantime the suspended brother may not function as office-bearer though he is still in office. The decree of suspension with reasons should be given to the suspended office-bearer in writing and should be read to the Church.

Deposition of Elders and Deacons. If the two Consistories sitting in judgment regarding a certain office-bearer find that a certain offense is so grievous that the brother in question cannot serve the Church with edification even after a period of suspension of several months, these Consistories may decide that immediate deposition is in order. Consistories have the right to depose forthwith, for Article 79 rules that guilty office-bearers shall be "suspended or expelled from their office."

One who is suspended may not exercise the duties of his office while the suspension is in force. One who is deposed or expelled from his office has lost the office itself. Decisions for expulsion from office should be announced to the Church.

Suspension of Ministers. The suspension of Ministers is required when these make themselves guilty of the sins considered above. Ministers, according to the agreement of the Churches contained in Article 79, shall be suspended upon the concurring decision of the two Consistories specified in the article. But, whereas the two Consistories can decide that deposition of Elders and Deacons is in order, these bodies can go no further than suspension regarding Ministers. The deposition of Ministers is subject to the judgment of Classis. This difference is not found in Article 79 because Ministers are better than others, but because they have given themselves to the work of the ministry for life and they have been ordained for life. A premature or mistaken decision to depose would therefore be a more serious matter regarding a Minister, for himself and for the Churches, than regarding an Elder or Deacon. Moreover, Ministers have received certain rights for and by all the Churches. They are allowed to administer the Word and the Sacrament in all the Churches upon request. They have been admitted to the ministry upon the advice of all the

Churches through their representatives. Consequently it is well that all the Churches are consulted before they are suspended or deposed from office.

Suspension of Ministers will as a rule also require a period of three to six months. At the end of the period of suspension the two Consistories can lift the suspension and reinstate the Minister, or they can extend the period of suspension, or they may find that the Minister in question should be deposed, in which case the matter goes to Classis.

Deposition of Ministers. If the case is referred to Classis because deposition from the ministry is deemed necessary, the Synodical Delegates according to Article 11 must be requested to be present in order that they may render their advice to Classis. If the Classis and Synodical Delegates cannot come to agreement the matter goes to Synod for disposition. While a case concerning a deposition is pending because a Classis and the Synodical Delegates according to Article 11 cannot agree, the Minister's suspension from office continues. If a Classis decides to depose and the Synodical Delegates concur, but the Minister involved appeals to Synod, his case should remain in **status quo**; that is, his suspension should be prolonged until Synod has ruled. A Classis would have the right to proceed to deposition under such circumstances, but unless the matter is urgent it is better to wait.

4. May a Classis depose Elders and Deacons?

Some have contended that a Classis may depose Consistories. The present authors feel that no major assembly, according to Reformed Church polity and the Church Order, has the right to depose a minor assembly. The deposition of a Consistory, for example, by a Classis or Synod would seem to be a violation of the integrity and of the rights of the particular Church concerned, whereas the Church Order in more than one article seeks to safeguard this integrity and these rights. (Cf. Article 30, 84.) Moreover, Reformed Church government does not tolerate group-disciplining. Discipline, according to our Reformed conception, is always individual and never communal.

Is it then permissible for a Classis or Synod to depose individual office-bearers? Regarding Ministers Article 79 clearly stipulates that a dual Consistory meeting may suspend a Minister. Furthermore, the article reads, "Whether these shall be entirely deposed from office shall be subject to the judgment of the Classis, with the advice of the Delegates of the (Particular) Synod mentioned in Article 11." This provision is clear. No Minister shall be deposed unless the Classis concerned judges that deposition is in order. Deposition of Ministers "shall be subject to the judgment of the Classis." And Classis shall be guided in rendering its opinion by the advice of the Synodical delegates according to Article 11. Without the concurring advice of these delegates, no Classis may decide that a certain Minister should be deposed. This last provision was added to Article 79 as an additional safeguard by the Holland Churches in 1905, and by our Churches in 1914.

Regarding Elders and Deacons Article 79 specifies that these shall be suspended or expelled from their office by sentence of their Consistory and that of the nearest Consistory.

If any case is so involved and so complicated that the two Consistories concerned judge that the judgment of all the Churches of the Classis is needed, then the matter should be brought to Classis. In such a case the Consistory is expected to abide by the decision of Classis. The Consistory follows the advice of Classis. The Classis in such a case has a full right to appoint certain delegates who are to serve the Consistory with advice and who are to help the Consistory to carry out the conclusions of the Classis.

If the case of an Elder or Deacon is brought to Classis by way of appeal on the part of individual members of the Church, or on the part of one or more consistory members, the appellants feeling and claiming that the Consistory as a whole is negligent or in error, then what is the correct procedure? Then Classis deliberates and draws its conclusions. If the decision is to the effect that the Elder (s) or Deacon (s) should be suspended or deposed, the Consistory concerned is informed regarding this decision and proceeds to execute the judgment rendered. Again, the Classis has a full right to appoint a committee to help the Consistory in the execution of its task. If a Consistory feels that it cannot in good conscience accept the advice, it may appeal to Synod. If Synod sustains the Classis the Consistory should give immediate execution to the judgment of Classis. That is to say, the Consistory should suspend or depose the office-bearer in question. Failure to do so would bear dire consequences. For in such a case those Consistory members and individual members of the Church concerned who desire to adhere to the decisions of Classis and Synod should meet and declare the deflecting or recalcitrant Consistory members to be out of office, and new Elders and Deacons should be elected in their place forthwith. An extraordinary congregational meeting of this kind should be called under the guidance of classical delegates, or of a neighboring Consistory, preferably the former, to give assurance that all things will be done in good order.

If any Consistory member thus deposed refuses to acknowledge his deposition and seeks to exercise his former rights, he makes himself liable to discipline as an individual member.

If one or more deposed Consistory members, together with certain adherents belonging to the Church concerned, refuse to honor the acts of deposition and the election of new office-bearers, and when these moreover begin to hold separate meetings for worship, Classis should declare these members to be a schismatic group, outside of the Christian Reformed denomination and having forfeited all rights and privileges.

It is true that Article 30 specifies that matters which cannot be finished by minor assemblies, though rightfully belonging to their domain, become the business of the major assemblies. But in view of the fact that the disciplinary articles of the Church Order clearly specify how discipline regarding office-bearers is to be exercised and in no way intimate that Elders and Deacons can be suspended or deposed by the major assemblies, we do not believe that the appeal to Article 30 is justified. We believe that it is reasonable to assume that the early Synods at which our Church Order originated purposefully refrained from incorporating a provision in the Church Order which would allow our major assemblies to suspend and depose Elders and Deacons. As has been pointed out before, the early Reformed Churches were eager to safeguard the integrity and the rights of the particular Churches. The significant 84th article of our Church Order used to be Article 1! Let us also recall that it was not until 1581 that the Churches decided that henceforth no Consistory would suspend or depose an Elder or Deacon without the concurrent judgment of its nearest neighbor Consistory. Furthermore, it cannot be denied that the question of deposition of Elders and Deacons is an important one. It is not unreasonable to assume that a provision permitting major assemblies to depose Elders and Deacons was left out of Article

79 purposefully. For notwithstanding the fact that Article 79 tells us how Elders and Deacons shall be deposed it does not provide for the deposition of Elders and Deacons by Classes or Synods. And yet the same Article does specify that Ministers shall be deposed by the judgment of the Classis.

We believe, moreover, that it can be contended successfully that the deposition of minor assemblies by major assemblies constitutes a negation of the general office of all believers, which should begin to function when certain abnormal situations arise, and that it likewise involves an infringement upon the right of reformation which should ever be held inviolate by the Church of God.

We realize that both during the formative period of the Reformed Churches and during their more advanced history, Classes and Synods have sometimes deposed Elders and Deacons and even Consistories. But no one would dare to claim that the Reformed Churches have always been true to themselves in matters of church government and that they have always interpreted their own Church Order correctly. Precedents do not decide this issue either one way or the other. We should seek to determine the basic principles fundamental to Reformed denominationalism, and we should seek the correct historical and exegetical interpretation of the various articles of the Church Order which concern this question. Then we should draw our conclusions as to what is proper and improper.

5. **Sundry matters.**

The lifting of suspension should be done by the same bodies which imposed suspension, namely, the combined Consistories.

Can those who have once been deposed from office be re-instated? Deposed Elders and Deacons may be nominated and elected if sufficient time has elapsed, if the brother in question has acknowledged his wrong and has given sufficient evidence of his repentance, and if the sin committed was not of such a nature that it will constantly hinder him in his work and undermine his influence. Of these matters the Consistory must judge. Re-instatement of Elders and Deacons cannot occur in the sense that the act of deposition is revoked and the brother concerned permitted to resume his place in the Consistory to serve the balance of his unexpired term. This cannot be done, no matter how penitent the brother may be.

No Consistory should nominate deposed office-bearers quickly and lightly.

Regarding deposed Ministers Synod of 1918, Article 52 decided that re-instatement must be effected by the Classis which acted in the deposition. The Holland Synod of Gronigen, 1927, decided that a deposed Minister is not to be re-instated by Classis without the knowledge and approval of the Particular Synod. It might be well if our decision of 1918 (see above) were amended so that no deposed Minister can be re-instated without the approval of the synodical delegates according to Article 11.

The Holland Synod of 1927 also decided that it would not be advisable to make general stipulations as to when a deposed Minister should be re-instated. Each case should be judged on its own merits. Classis should consider the question why the deposition took place, whether true penitence be evident, whether reconciliation was made and whether the deposed brother will be able to labor to the edification of the Church of God and without detriment to the holy character of the Church and the glory of God. No doubt this is wise counsel.

What we term re-instatement the Holland Synods call "beroepbaar verklaren," to declare eligible for a call. This indicates what the manner of procedure should be.

He who erred in doctrine must be carefully examined before he is declared eligible for a call. If there is a difference of opinion Synod should judge.

It is necessary that the Churches act with great prudence, especially when sins have been committed which indicate a weakness of will-power, steadfastness of character, and complete consecration, such as adultery and drunkenness.

Emeritus Ministers are also subject to suspension and deposition. The Church which they last served and its Classis are responsible for an emeritus Minister that needs to be censured, since our emeritus Ministers continue to be Ministers of the Church which they served last, though they have been excused of some or all ministerial duties.

During the period of suspension a Minister is entitled to his salary, but after his deposition, if that should follow, the Church has no financial obligations anymore.

ARTICLE 80

Furthermore among the gross sins, which are worthy of being punished with suspension or deposition from office, these are the principal ones; false doctrine or heresy, public schism, public blasphemy, simony, faithless desertion of office or intrusion upon that of another, perjury, adultery, fornication, theft, acts of violence, habitual drunkenness, brawling, filthy lucre; in short, all sins and gross offenses, as render the perpetrators infamous before the world, and which in any private member of the Church would be considered worthy of excommunication.

SINS REQUIRING SUSPENSION OR DEPOSITION OF OFFICE-BEARERS

1. The purpose of Article 80.

It is not the purpose of Article 80 to give us a complete registry of sins worthy of censure in office-bearers. Article 80 merely enumerates a number of sins so that the Churches may know which type of sins may not be tolerated in office-bearers. Doubtless the list is as long as it is because these things mentioned are indeed gross public sins which merit censure. But the Church Order has in no way endeavored to be exhaustive here. For this reason the article also concludes with the statement that "all sins and gross offenses as render the perpetrators infamous before the world, and which in any private member of the Church would be considered worthy of excommunication," are worthy of suspension or deposition in office-bearers. The enumeration is therefore given by way of example, although it should not be forgotten that the sins enumerated are listed as being "the principle ones" which call for censure in office-bearers.

2. The specific sins mentioned.

False doctrine or heresy. When one deviates from one or more of the fundamental teachings of Holy Writ, as expressed in the confessional standards of the Churches, and that consciously and purposefully, he is guilty of false doctrine and heresy. The Church Order does not refer to variations from generally accepted teachings but which are not definitely expressed in our confessional writings. Neither does Article 80 refer to slight variations regarding subordinate truths. Nor is it the implication that one who unintentionally, through the use of a wrong term or otherwise, states a matter erroneously, thereby makes himself worthy of discipline. The deviation must be conscious and deliberate. However, though one has not taught or spoken false doctrine deliberately and consciously, yet if he should maintain the false views in question and refuse to acknowledge their heretical and erroneous character, the error becomes conscious and wilful, and worthy of discipline.

Public schism. This term concerns those, to use the words of our **Form for the Administration of the Lord's Supper,** who raise "discord, sects, and mutiny in the Church." Those who are guilty of public schism virtually sever their connections with the Church and that because of minor differences in doctrine or church government, or merely because they are seeking self-advancement and vain glory.

Public blasphemy. He who speaks openly in an impious or irreverent manner of God or things sacred is guilty of this sin.

Simony may be defined as the purchase or sale of ecclesiastical preferment. The word is derived from the account of Simon the Sorcerer, to be found in Acts 8:18-24.

Faithless desertion of office or intrusion upon that of another indicates the sin of one who refuses to perform the duties of his office, and particularly does this offense pertain to Ministers who forsake their Church without proper release by Consistory and Classis, and who without a proper call begin to labor in a Church or field belonging to another.

Perjury is the assertion of a falsity under oath. He is guilty of perjury who before God declares that a certain claim or statement is true, while he knows that it is false.

Adultery is the violation of the marriage vow. The Dutch word is **echtbreuk,** that is, the breaking of marriage. Technically adultery may be defined as the sexual relationship of two persons, either of whom is married to a third person.

Fornication is incontinence outside of holy wedlock, or illicit sexual intercourse.

Theft refers to the sin of stealing, forbidden in the 8th Commandment.

Acts of violence refers to all disgraceful and sinful use of brute force.

Habitual drunkenness. One who repeatedly drinks in excess is guilty of this sin. No one who is a slave to strong drink can serve acceptably in the Consistory, even though he should never drink himself drunk.

Brawling. This refers to engagements in uncalled-for fist fights and all noisy, needless quarreling.

Filthy lucre refers to all dishonest gain.

I Tim. 3:3, Titus 1:7, and 2:3 and other passages condemn these and other sins as intolerable in office-bearers.

All sins which cause one to lose his good name before the world at large render an office-bearer worthy of suspension or deposition, so Article 80 states. And again, any sins which would be considered worthy of censure in any private member of the Church renders an office-bearer worthy of suspension or deposition from office, so the article concludes.

ARTICLE 81

The Ministers of the Word, Elders and Deacons, shall before the celebration of the Lord's Supper exercise Christian censure among themselves and in a friendly spirit admonish one another with regard to the discharge of their office.

MUTUAL CENSURE

1. The significance of this ruling.

In Churches holding the hierarchical or episcopal system one office-bearer has greater authority than another. Consequently the higher office-bearers exercise supervision and jurisdiction over those that occupy lower offices. The archbishop supervises the bishop; the bishop supervises the priest, etc. But the Reformed Churches are Presbyterian also in the matter of supervision. The office-bearers are equal in authority, each in his own sphere, and supervision is mutual. They supervise each other, just as the Churches supervise each other (Article 44). Now Article 81 provides for this mutual supervision of office-bearers.

The common term by which this mutual supervision has been known for years back is **censura morum**, which Latin term signifies a censorship or examination of conduct.

This mutual censure, according to Article 81, shall concern the office-bearer's discharge of his office. If an office-bearer is chargeable with neglect of duty or with a wrong approach to his task, the matter should be brought to his attention at the time of mutual censure. Mutual censure concerns itself with the question: Do the Ministers, Elders and Deacons perform their work as it ought to be done?

The matter of this article was first incorporated into the Church Order by the Synod of Dort, 1578, Article 66. This article provided that the investigation should concern "doctrine as well as life." Nothing was said about the execution of the office held. But Synod of 's Gravenhage, 1586, Art. 74, altered the reading of the article. It deleted the provision that the investigation should concern "doctrine as well as life," and provided that the investigation should concern "the discharge of their office." Thus Article 81 reads today. This does not mean that the doctrinal position and general conduct of the office-bearers should be forgotten and silenced at the time of mutual censure. But the Synod of 1586 doubtlessly altered the Article as it did because it wanted the office-bearers to remember that mutual censure concerns the fulfilment of one's duty as office-bearer first of all. However, one's belief and general behavior stands closely related to one's execution of his office, and the matter of doctrine and life cannot be ignored. Nevertheless, the question which presents itself at the time of mutual censure is this: Does any one of the office-bearers desire to criticize one or more of his fellow office-bearers regarding their work as office-bearers?

From the foregoing it will be clear that essentially mutual censure has nothing to do with the celebration of the Lord's Supper. The question is not whether any of the office-bearers have any grievances against one or more of their fellow consistory members, grievances namely which would hinder them in celebrating the Lord's Supper properly. Naturally, brethren in service should never go to the Lord's Table unless the right brotherly relation exists between them. But this is true for all the believers, and should not require a special investigation. Nevertheless, the mistaken conception just noted is quite general. Doubtless this is due to the fact that Article 81 specifies that this investigation shall take place "before the celebration of the Lord's Supper." This provision is not found in the Church Order from the year 1586 on. It is not found therefore in the Church Order redaction of Dort, 1618-19. Neither do the Churches of Holland have it in their 81st article today. We went back to the redaction of 1578 and 1581 in 1914 and re-incorporated this phrase. Why this was done we cannot say. Perhaps it was to give the Churches assurance that mutual censure will be exercised in all Consistories at least four times a year. If the original reading of Article 81 (1578) contained this provision because the Churches at that time deemed it necessary that Consistories exercise mutual censure with a view to the Lord's Supper, an opinion which no authority seems to hold but which is not entirely impossible, then yet it is certain that our Synod of 1914 did not re-incorporate the phrase for this reason.

2. How mutual censure should be exercised.

The manner in which the Consistories were to exercise mutual censure has always been left to the judgment of each Consistory. Years ago consistory members would absent themselves from the meeting, one by one, in order that the others might freely express themselves regarding the absentee. But this procedure should not be necessary. The brethren should be willing to mention the matters that require mention in the presence of the party concerned. This important institution should stand on such a high plane that all office-bearers will accept with Christian grace and forbearance any corrections or improvements which his fellow office-bearers may be able to offer.

In some Consistories the president mentions the names of the office-bearers, one by one, and asks each one of the other Consistory members whether they have any criticism to offer. As a rule, however, the president asks in general whether any of the office-bearers have any criticism to offer to any of his fellow office-bearers regarding the discharge of his office, a reply to this general question being asked of each member individually.

Needless to say, mutual censure must never be turned into fault finding. The purpose should be to assist each other for the benefit of the Church and for the glory of God. And only then has one the right to correct his fellow office-bearers if he can do it in love and fairness, and if he is willing to receive reproof himself if necessary.

In some instances a private heart to heart talk may be preferable to a discussion of the matter in Consistory. But any consistory member has the full right to broach a matter at the time of mutual censure.

ARTICLE 82

To those who remove from the Congregation a letter or testimony concerning their profession and conduct shall be given by the Consistory, signed by two.

CONCERNING MEMBERSHIP CERTIFICATES

The matter of certificates is also mentioned in Article 61, which article provides that none "who come from other (Christian Reformed) Churches" shall be admitted to the Lord's Supper except they have made a confession of the Reformed Religion, besides being reputed to be of a godly walk. This rule requires that members leaving one of our Churches and seeking to join another shall not be accepted without a testimony from the Church which they are leaving, declaring that they are Reformed in doctrine and godly as to conduct. Article 61 therefore concerns certificates from the point of view of the receiving Church.

Article 82 concerns certification from the point of view of the Church to which the departing member belongs.

1. To whom certificates should be given.

Article 82 declares: "To those who remove from the congregation a letter or testimony . . . shall be given." This provision applies first of all to those who are members-in-full, to those who have made profession of their faith. Strictly interpreted the article refers to these only. The specific reference is to those who have come to maturity and have confessed their faith and have received access to the Sacraments and all the privileges of the Church. Members-by-Baptism only are incomplete, immature members who thus far have failed to make a profession or confession and concerning whose profession nothing can therefore be said. But Article 82 speaks specifically of "their profession" concerning which testimony must be given: For this reason we say that strictly interpreted Article 82 refers to members-in-full only. Nevertheless Article 82 does not exclude those who by virtue of their birth and Baptism stand related to the Church and under its care. By implication also the immature, incomplete members are covered by Article 82. Only the statement which Consistories will make concerning those who have not yet professed their faith will differ from the statement issued concerning members-in-full. Concerning members-by-Baptism Consistories can only certify that they have been baptized and what their general, external behavior has been. Such matters as Church attendance and catechism attendance should be included in the testimony.

The question has often been asked: Should Consistories deliver membership certificates to the Consistories to whom application for membership is being made, or should the certificate be given to the party whose membership is being certified so that he may deliver it himself? Article 82 leaves no room for doubt here. We read: "To those who remove from the congregation a letter or testimony . . . shall be given . . ." The opening words: "To those who remove" have sometimes been read to mean: "Concerning those who remove." This, however, is not the significance of the words. Church Order authorities such as Rutgers, Bouwman, and Jansen are all agreed on this. Our Synod of 1914 (Article 63) also came to the conclusion that Article 82 provides that the departing parties shall themselves receive their membership certificates to be given to the Consistory of the Church to which they are going. The fact that this is the provision of Article 82 becomes especially plain from our official and historic Dutch text. We read: "Dengenen, die uit de Gemeente vertrekken, zal eene attestatie of getuigenis . . . **medegegeven worden** . . ." which literally translated would read: "An attestation or testimony shall be **given along with** those who remove from the congregation. . ." Reformed Church government regards believers not as minors but as those who have come to years of majority. It recognizes the rights of believers and encourages the exercise of these rights and responsibilities. Our members should be active and aggressive and not passive. Let those who remove request a certificate and let them deliver this certification of their membership in person as they apply for membership in the Church of their new environment. Only those who would be inclined to hold that our particular Churches are but local divisions of the one super Church, the denomination, can favor the procedure of mailing certificates from one Consistory to another by preference. For in this conception certification of membership is really a transfer of membership from one division to another.

By this we do not mean to say that a Consistory should refuse to mail a certificate directly to the Consistory of the Church a member seeks to join. Not at all. If a member specifically prefers to have his certificate sent to the Consistory of the Church of his new location, there are no reasons why it should refuse to do so. For some members this may be a very good procedure. But, this is the point, the Church Order gives our members a right to personal delivery of their attestations, and in the interest of self-assertion it is well to encourage them in doing so.

If a member moves to another Church community and yet fails to request a certificate, his attention should be called to his neglect. The Consistory has no right to send a certificate to the Church with which he should affiliate without the member's specific request or consent.

In case a member moves to distant parts and fails to request certification the Consistory should write to him, if need be, often. If one of our Churches is found in the place of his new residence, the Consistory of that Church should be informed and asked to call on the negligent member, urging him to request certification, etc. If nothing avails, then the membership of such a one would ultimately lapse. A Consistory would be compelled at long last to announce to the Church that the party or parties in question had by their indifference and negligence, notwithstanding frequent admonitions, nullified their membership, and that consequently the Consistory had declared their rights and privileges void and their names removed from the roll. Such a procedure would not imply nullification on the Consistory's part of their Baptism and confession. God ever holds them responsible for their privileges and promises. But it does mean that all their rights as Church members have been revoked.

In case one moves from the Church, leaving no word or address behind so that he cannot even be contacted by mail, then the Consistory should endeavor, through relatives, friends, etc., to establish contact with him. If all such attempts fail, at long last the Consistory will cancel his membership rights, upon the basis of his neglect and withdrawal, as indicated above.

Synod of 1910, Article 67, ruled that members (in full or only by virtue of their Baptism) moving to localities where no Christian Reformed Church is found, may retain their membership in the Church which they leave, if they notify the Consistory to this effect. If they neglect to do this their membership lapses in one year and six weeks. The membership of such members as are located where no Christian Reformed Church is found must be transferred to the nearest Church. If this is omitted their membership lapses after one year and six weeks. Concerning these decisions of 1910 we would remark that it is well that our members who must sometimes live at great distances from our Churches can retain their membership with us. But we should also urge our membership not to make such moves unless they can give account of themselves before God, unless the circumstances are urgent. Too many of our members have moved to distant localities very unfavorable to their spiritual life and that of their children without a real necessity. Furthermore, for such members to affiliate with the nearest Christian Reformed Church is certainly advisable, provided that that nearest Christian Reformed Church is near enough to permit such members to worship with this Church occasionally, and near enough for the Consistory of this Church to exercise some pastoral care, through home visitation, etc. If the nearest Christian Reformed Church is too far removed to permit this, the party in question can much better retain his membership with the Church which knows him and his situation somewhat. He who desires to retain his membership with one of our Churches at a great distance should write to the Consistory at certain intervals, say at least once a year, informing the Consistory of his state and of his desires for the future. He should also gladly help to contribute to the Lord's cause through the Church in which he retains his membership. Regarding the rule of one year and six weeks, we would remark that these are very arbitrary figures. There are no two cases alike. We believe that it is far better to judge every case upon its own merits. If this is done Consistories may feel that they must bear with certain parties far beyond this term of one year and six weeks.

When one requests a certificate for another Church and also receives said certificate, does his membership in the certifying Church then cease instantly? No, it does not. It has happened in the past that a member received a certificate with the purpose of joining another Church, but that the Church which he desired to join refused to receive him, and that the Church which gave him a certificate refused to recognize him as still a member. Thus members in good and regular standing were suddenly rendered Churchless, and children of God in Christ lost their access to the Sacraments, etc. This situation rested largely on a misconception. It was assumed that if one requested a membership certificate he was by that act severing his relationship with the particular Church in question. Yet the certificate always employed the present tense. Thus for example: "The Consistory of the ——— Christian Reformed Church hereby testifies that ——— is a member of this congregation . . ." He who requests a certificate merely requests to have proof of the fact that he is a member of such-and-such a Christian Reformed Church in order that with this testimony he may join the Church of his new residence. As soon as he has been received as member by the new Church his membership in his former Church ceases, but not before.

The Synod of 1937 appointed a committee to look into this very question and the matter of attestations in general. This committee rendered a well-founded report to the Synod of 1939. We believe that the form for certification of membership approved by the Synod of 1939 does justice to the various requirements of the Church Order and sound Church polity. Let all the Churches use only this form, or let them bear the distinctive features of this form in mind, whenever they certify the membership of any of their members.

2. By whom certificates are to be issued.

Article 82 provides that certificates shall be given "by the Consistory." Requests for attestation or certification must therefore be considered and acted upon by the whole Consistory. Neither the Minister, the clerk, nor the two together have the right to issue certificates of membership. The testimony to be given must be that of the Church's ruling body, not that of one or two office-bearers.

Requests for certification by those who move should be placed as soon as possible. Often members wait until after they have moved.

Then perhaps a Consistory meeting has just been held when the request arrives. Thus there is often needless delay. In larger Churches in which the Consistory does not know all the members sufficiently to write a trustworthy certificate, the request for certification should be announced to the Church, so that those of the congregation who may know of reasons why the applicant should not receive a clear testimony may inform the Consistory. If irregularities are discovered these should be removed before a certificate is given, if this is at all possible. If this is not possible, these irregularities should be noted in the certificate so that the Consistory of the Church which the removing member is joining may see to it that such irregularities are cleared away. The Church should receive three or four days in which to report objections against such as desire to leave the Church with the clerk of the Consistory or a committee on certificates appointed for this purpose.

3. That which a certificate should include.

The Church Order of 1578 specified (see Synod, Dort, 1578, Art. 25 or 10) that the pious and God-fearing should be recommended with these words: that they shall have conducted themselves in the Church of God in a Christian way, without giving occasion for complaint and offense (datse in de Kerke Gods Christelyk [sonder opsprake en ergenis] gewandelt hebben.) The Synod of Dort, 1618-19, Article 82, speaks only of "een Attestatie ofte getuygenisse hares wandels" (an attestation or testimony regarding their conduct.) However, conduct is controlled by convictions. Doubtlessly the early Synods included under "wandel" conduct, doctrine, or confession. This is also the opinion of Jansen. * The Synod of the Reformed Churches of the Netherlands, in their Church Order redaction of the 1905 revised Article 82 to read: "concerning their profession and conduct." We accepted this reading in 1914.

All members who by their profession and conduct have not given occasion for well-founded complaints and who have not given offense are entitled to receive a favorable recommendation, a "clean" attestation. All others, unless the matter can be cleared away satisfactorily, receive a certificate which states facts as they are, so that the new Consistory may do what is necessary.

Denominational unity, federative co-operation according to the unity in Christ and the Word of God requires that the Churches honor and accept each other's certificates. Every certificate issued upon the request of the member concerned because he now lives within the bounds of the Church which he seeks to join, must be accepted, even though the member concerned is being disciplined, or may be known to be rather critical and unreasonable in his attitudes. The sheep of Christ's pasture are not all equally loveable, but all of Christ's sheep must be guided and nourished. Christ loves all of His sheep. We may not cast out any. But this same principle also demands that no Consistory may manipulate certain members into the fold of a neighboring Church just because these members are hard to satisfy etc. Leaving one Church and affiliating with another must always take place upon sufficient reasons. When these sufficient reasons are present application for membership must be accepted.

It should not escape our attention that Article 82 provides that to those "who remove from the Congregation" certificates shall be given. All authorities are agreed that this provision refers to those who

* Jansen, **Korte Verklaring**, etc., 1923, p. 354.

actually remove out of the territory of one particular Church into that of another. Strictly speaking, those who do not change their place of residence, but merely desire to affiliate with another congregation, have no right to a certificate. However, we have almost entirely erased all boundary lines between our particular Churches—a fact much to be regretted for more than one reason—and therefore as a rule issue certificates also to those that do not remove. *

4. How certificates should be authenticated.

Synod of 's Gravenhage, 1586, ordained that certificates should be issued "under the seal of the Church, or, where no seal is, signed by two." Thus the matter of authentication remained until the Holland Churches in the year 1905 caused the article to read "signed by two; or in the case of letters, which are given under the seal of the Church, signed by one." Our Churches adopted this reading in 1914. However, the Synod of 1939 changed the article so that it now simply provides that membership certificates shall be signed by two.

ARTICLE 83

Furthermore, to the poor, removing for sufficient reasons, so much money for traveling shall be given by the Deacons, as they deem adequate. The Consistory and the Deacons shall, however, see to it that they be not too much inclined to relieve their Churches of the poor, with whom they would without necessity burden other Churches.

ASSISTANCE TO DEPARTING POOR

1. Origin of Article 83.

Pressure of circumstances gave birth to the provisions of Article 83. During the early days of the Reformed Churches of Holland the Deacons were often called upon to help, besides their own needy poor, those who passed through, traveling to some city or town in search of work or to escape persecution, but lacking money for food and shelter and for the continuance of their journey. Moreover, a large number of transients called upon the Diaconates of the Reformed Churches for help who were not of the faith but who claimed to be fleeing for their lives and safety. Hundreds, it should be remembered, were driven from their homes by the persecutions. These, in many cases, had to leave all their possessions behind and were completely destitute and certainly in need of help. And, as a rule, this help was gladly given by the faithful to these refugees as they traveled on. Now of this Christian helpfulness the tramps and transients to whom we referred sought to profit. They feigned to be persecuted believers.

* Some of the considerations which lead us to say that our failure to maintain boundary lines between our Churches is to be regretted are the following: 1. Believers should manifest the body of Christ in the place of their providentially determined residence. 2. It is against the intent of Article 82. 3. It fosters the overgrowth of some Churches and the undergrowth of others. 4. It promotes "floating". 5. It promotes a one-sided development. (Birds of a feather flock together.) 6. It stimulates unholy competition. 7. It promotes slothfulness in catechism attendance. 8. It promotes needless Sunday travel. 9. It constitutes a practical denial of the communion of saints.

These impostors took much money intended for needy poor and refugees.

Now in order to counteract these evils the first Synod, Emden, 1571, decided that all who moved from one place to another should carry with them an attestation or certificate. Those who failed to show a good attestation should from henceforth not expect help from the Diaconates of the various Churches. If anyone without an attestation claimed that the persecution prevented him from even securing the necessary document, then the Churches should examine them very carefully regarding their faith, etc., before accepting their testimony.

If it appeared that an applicant for an attestation was moving needlessly, and that his change of residence would most likely reduce him to poverty so that he would become dependent on the Deacons, then no attestation was to be given. He was urged not to move.

Attestations, so the Synod decided, should indicate the full name of the holder, his native country, trade, reason for moving, time spent in the Church giving the attestation, conduct, date of departure, destination, etc. It was furthermore provided that those who moved should receive money sufficient to bring them to the next Reformed Church through which their journey would lead them. Each Church should write on the attestation how much money had been given them, by whom, when, etc. At the end of their journey the Reformed Church there would help them, and also destroy the attestation. *

All these provisions were ultimately reduced to one brief article, our present 83rd Article.

We may conclude therefore that Article 83 owes its origin in the first place to the large numbers of impostors who sought and gained relief under pretense of being Reformed refugees or poverty stricken fellow-believers. In the second place, due to want and poverty and to the economic upheaval caused by wars and persecutions, large numbers sought for work and improvement elsewhere. But for many of these, search for economic betterment ended in complete destitution, with the result that the Churches were thus burdened unnecessarily.

These circumstances occasioned the adoption of the rules noted above, of which Article 83 is a remnant and summary. After the year 1572, when the persecution ceased, elaborate stipulations were less necessary.

2. Significance of Article 83.

Article 83 now pertains to our ordinary needy ones. If any of our poor desire to move and if the Deacons feel persuaded that there are sufficient reasons for their departure, then these poor are entitled to as much help as the Deacons shall deem adequate. Until 1905 for the Churches in Holland, and until 1914 for our Churches, Article 83 stipulated that the amount given to departing poor should be noted on the reverse side of their attestation or certificate. Now, however, this is no longer required. Those who stand in need of traveling expenses are not so numerous, and the Deacons should exercise good will and confidence toward those who are worthy of the Church's help.

3. The warning included.

The conclusion of Article 83 is an addition of the years 1905 and 1914. "The Consistories and the Deacons shall, however, see to it that they be not too much inclined to relieve their Churches of the poor, with whom they would without necessity burden other Churches."

---

* Church Order, Synod of Emden, 1571, Art. 44-47.

It is a privilege for any Church to help in the relief of distress and poverty. This is a beautiful task which we may perform for Christ, the merciful High Priest. But there is a human side to this work of mercy. Sometimes the work of the Deacons becomes very heavy. Then the Consistory or the Deacons might lose sight of the glory of the task of supplying Christ's needy ones with their necessities, and they might encourage the poor to move elsewhere when there is no security that such needy ones will be able to support themselves in the location suggested. Against this practice Article 83 warns. Each Church must support its own poor, if need be through the assistance of neighboring Churches. And only if there is a reasonable expectation that the family or individual in question really will be much better off in the new location should the Consistory and Deacons encourage the move. Almost needless to say, no Church will ever encourage any of its poor to move to a new location because economic betterment may be expected if the financial opportunity would involve at the same time a spiritual loss. It is better to be out of work but with God's people than to be regularly employed but in the midst of the world and far removed from God's people.

Each Church must support its own poor as noted above, but there are partial exceptions to this rule. For instance, when one in need of help moves to an institution of mercy such as Bethesda at Denver, then he should affiliate with one of our Denver Churches, but the Church from which he comes should remain responsible for his support.

When one in need leaves his home Church under extraordinary circumstances and for a Church which is already heavily burdened with needy ones from many places, then the Diaconate of the Churches from which such needy ones hail should correspond with the Diaconate of the Church of which the party concerned becomes a member, and agree to forward the necessary amount weekly or monthly so that the Deacons of the Church to which the needy brother or sister now belongs may supply his need adequately.

ARTICLE 84

No Church shall in any way lord it over other Churches, no Minister over other Ministers, no Elder or Deacon over other Elders or Deacons.

EQUALITY OF CHURCHES AND OFFICE-BEARERS

In Article 17 the Church Order stipulates, regarding Ministers, Elders, and Deacons, that equality "shall be maintained with respect to the duties of their office and also in other matters as far as possible . . ." Article 84 goes beyond Article 17 in that it rules out all hierarchical practices both as to Churches and as to Office-bearers. Article 84 stipulates that there shall be no lording, no domination, no assumption of authority of one Church over another and of one office-bearer over another. First let us consider the origin of this article and then its significance.

1. The origin of this ruling.

The provision of Article 84 is all important and goes back to the very origin of the Reformed Churches. Dr. F. L. Rutgers very correctly calls careful attention to utterance and decision taken at the Wezelian Convention, 1568, the first gathering of Church leaders belonging to the Reformed Church of Holland and nearby territories. Chapter IV, Article 7 of the conclusion of Wezel provides, among other things, that elected Elders shall promise "not to employ domination, neither regarding the Ministers nor regarding the congregation . . ." (Cf. also Chapter IV, Art. 9.)

In Chapter V, Article 19 this same Convention definitely limits the authority of Classes and safeguards the rights of the individual Church. We read: "Nevertheless we do not here acknowledge the classical gatherings to have jurisdiction (recht) over any Church or its offices, except these shall permit it of their own accord, in order that the Churches may not be robbed against their will of their jurisdiction (recht) and authority (gezag).

And once more the gathering at Wezel, doing preliminary and preparatory work with a view to definite ecclesiastical confederation and co-operation, decided that "evident attempts at tyranny over the Church" were not to be tolerated in any Ministers. (Chapter VIII, Article 14.) It was also decided that the Classical gatherings to be held should preferably meet in different Churches and not always in the same Church, "partly to avoid domination of one Church over the other . . ." (Chapter VIII, Art. 20.)

From all these early expressions it is plain that the Churches set themselves to safeguard the rights and individuality of the particular Churches. They made it very clear that they were aiming at denominational co-operation, not a unification of many particular Churches into one super-Church, vested with supreme jurisdiction over its various subdivisions.

The maintenance of the jurisdiction and the individuality of each Church was seemingly so much the concern of these early Reformed Churches that they sought to safeguard these rights **in the very first article** of the Church Order adopted by the first regular Synod (Emden, 1571). This article reads: "Geen Kerke sal over een ander Kerke, geen Dienaar des Woorts, geen Ouderling, noch Diaken, sal d'een over d'ander heerschappije voeren, maar een yegelyk zal hen voor alle suspicien, en aanlokkinge, om te heerschappen wagten." (No Church shall dominate over other Churches, no Minister of the Word, Elder or Deacon shall dominate the one over the other, but every one shall guard himself against all suspicions and enticements to dominate.)

Occasion for placing this all important article upon the foreground may have been the fact that many of the Churches had fears and scruples against the holding of Synods. The Churches of the province of Holland especially hesitated to co-operate. They feared that the particular Churches would lose their independence. Dr. F. L. Rutgers mentions that it required much effort to get the Churches, both those "under the cross" of persecution and those driven to neighboring lands by the persecution, to co-operate in holding a Synod. * Article 1 of the Church Order of Emden (1571) now gave the Churches the assurance that denominational affiliation and co-operation did not at all aim at domination, and that all domination, the lording of one Church over the other, or of one office-bearer over another, stood condemned in the very opening article of the Church Order. This article retained its place in the Church Order, although perhaps for reasons of logical sequence it was soon given a place in the department of Discipline, as Article 84.

---

* Cf. Rutgers, **College Voordrachten,** 1918, p. 153.

At the same time we may believe that the Churches of 1571 formulated the article quoted above because they desired to take a definite stand against Rome with its hierarchical system. Just because one Church was permitted to rule over another, and one office-bearer was permitted to rule over another office-bearer, the hierarchical system of Rome had become possible. Thus corruption had received a mighty, tyrannic weapon. Because the early Christian Churches had yielded their God-given authority and individuality and had been transformed into local subordinate sub-divisions of a great super-Church, general corruption and domination had become possible. The Reformation Churches desired no duplication of this error. Neither did they favor the appointment of Superintendents. Certain English and German Churches (Episcopalian and Lutheran) had appointed Superintendents. The Reformed Churches of these countries were urged by their governments to accept some system of superintendency. And these Reformed Churches in England and Germany had yielded to some extent. The Reformed Churches in Holland disapproved of this. They desired that every Church should retain its individuality and that no Church should be elevated as to authority above the other Churches. And so also the Reformed Churches in Holland insisted that no office-bearer should rule over another office-bearer. Biblical equality was to be maintained. Every tendency to hierarchism was to be avoided.

Let us add right here that we agree heartily with Dr. F. L. Rutgers when he says that although Article 84 gives expression to one of the fundamental principles of Reformed Church government, it is not the only church governmental principle which governs our denominational co-operation. In and by itself Article 84 might be used to plead the cause of Independentism. But Article 84 may not be isolated from other articles of our Church Order regarding our major assemblies, discipline, etc. * Such an erroneous isolation of Article 84 might easily lead one to conclude that in the Reformed system Classes and Synod can only advise and that these bodies cannot take authoritative decisions. Nothing could, however, be further from the truth. (Cf. Art. 36, etc.)

2. The significance of the ruling.

By indicating the origin of Article 84 we have also indicated its purpose and significance somewhat. Briefly stated it may be said that in Article 84 the Reformed Church declared that each particular Church is an individual and complete manifestation of the body of Christ. The essence of the Church of Christ is found in every particular Church. Consequently all Churches are essentially on par, and lording on the part of one Church over another cannot be tolerated. The same holds for all office-bearers. All Churches and all office-bearers are co-ordinate as to their authority, and all Churches and office-bearers are equally subordinate under Christ.

Moreover, Article 84 tells us specifically and emphatically that denominational union does not cancel the individuality of the particular Churches. Reformed Church polity does not dissolve the various local Churches into one authoritative super-Church. The particular Churches have voluntarily confederated themselves in order that they might work together in Classes and Synods. For which purpose? To assist each other and to co-operate regarding two things: Matters which the particular Churches cannot finish by themselves, and matters which concern the particular Churches in common.

---

* Cf. Rutgers: **College Voordrachten,** 1918, p. 156.

It should be well understood that each local Church affiliating itself with the confederacy or denomination by that very act agrees to acknowledge the authority of the united Churches as functioning through Classes or Synods. In so far as the particular Churches have subordinated their own inherent authority to the authority of all the Churches functioning through major assemblies. The particular Churches have agreed beforehand to submit themselves to the opinion of the majority, except when they are convinced before God that the conclusion of the majority is contrary to the Scriptures, or contrary to the rules of government agreed upon (Church Order). Except for this voluntary, self-imposed limitation, denominational unity and co-operation does not infringe upon the freedom and individuality of the local Churches. And only inasfar as the Church Order agreed upon limits the local Churches in the exercise of their native rights are the local Churches limited in this respect. Their individuality in no wise and in no sense of the word is cancelled. *

It should also be very clear from this article that according to the Reformed conception, one office is not to be regarded higher than another. The ministry of the Word, the office of the eldership and the office of the Deacons all stand on par. Only the work assigned to each differs. But a Minister is not a bishop over the Elders. Neither do the Elders function as bishops over the Deacons.

ARTICLE 85

Churches whose usages differ from ours merely in non-essentials shall not be rejected.

ACKNOWLEDGMENT OF KINDRED CHURCHES

1. History of this article.

Jansen is of the opinion that historically Article 85 goes back to the Wezelian Convention, 1586, Chap. I, Art. 9-11; and Synod of Emden, 1571, Art. 21. However, these articles refer only to non-essentials, or indifferent usages practiced by the various particular Churches within the group then meeting in Convention and Synod. The assemblies at Wezel and Emden said nothing concerning other denominations or groups of Reformed Churches, whereas Article 85 does exactly that. Article 85 says nothing concerning the toleration which Churches within our denomination have agreed to observe toward each other in matters that are non-essential, but it stipulates that Churches not belonging to our denomination shall not be "rejected" because of things that are non-essential.

Article 85 was adopted, so we may conclude, because the Reformed Churches of Holland desired to acknowledge the Reformed Churches of other lands as sister Churches. Article 72 (or 20) of the Synod of Dort, 1578, is the first reading of our present Article 85. This 72nd article speaks only of other Churches in general. But the Synod of Middelburg, 1581, (Art. 46) caused the expression "other Churches" to read, "foreign Churches." This reading of 1581 was accepted by the Synod of Dort, 1618-19, and this redaction is still in force today in the Holland Churches. It reads: "In non-essential things, the for-

* Cf. Jansen, **Korte Verklaring**, 1923, p. 359, 360.

eign Churches, which maintain other usages than we do, shall not be rejected." In our revision of 1914 we left out the adjective "foreign" inasmuch as we wanted the article to apply to Reformed denominations right in our own country, as well as to Reformed Churches of other countries.

2. Which non-essentials Article 85 refers to.

The non-essentials of Article 85 refer to ecclesiastical usages. It does not refer to doctrinal or ethical non-essentials, for no doctrine and no ethical, moral, precept is non-essential. The expression "foreign Churches" (de Buytenlandtsche Kerken) during the post-Reformation era always referred to Churches holding the Reformed faith. It referred to the Reformed Churches of France, Switzerland, Germany, and England. Doctrinally these Churches were one. They were all the fruit of the Calvinistic reformatory movement, the natural leaders of which were John Calvin and his Genevan school. Moreover, the word "usages" or Article 85 used to read "ritibus," in the original Latin text. This Latin word refers definitely to rites, that is, ecclesiastical costumes or usages. So, for example, some Ministers at Baptism would sprinkle the person baptized three times; others only once. In some Reformed Churches the communicants stood as they partook of the Lord's Supper; in others the communicants sat. Some desired that a Scripture passage should be read during communion; others favored the singing of psalms. Now, regarding all such and like questions, no Churches of other lands should stand condemned (Latin, **damnandae non erunt . . .**) by the Reformed Churches of Holland. They were to be regarded as Reformed Churches, for these ritualistic differences were non-essential. Article 85, therefore, refers to ecclesiastical usages which are of minor importance. It does not refer to doctrinal matters or matters of Church polity. It refers to matters which the Word of God and apostolic example have left to the various Churches to decide. Things which the Word of God prescribed, or which are clearly indicated by apostolic example, or which are logically deduced from the teachings of the Bible, are never indifferent, non-essential.

This acknowledgment of other Churches was more than theory to these early Reformed Churches of Holland. Witness the fact that the foreign Churches were all invited to co-labor with the Synod of Dort, 1618-19, in regard to the Arminian disputes. Various foreign Churches sent able delegations which took an active part in this all important international Synod.

It may be remarked here that no things are "adiophora" strictly speaking. Essentially many things are indifferent. But practically very few ecclesiastic matters are indifferent. Generally speaking, for example, whether the second service is held on Sunday afternoon or on Sunday evening is a matter of indifference. But for a local Church it is not indifferent, for services should be held at hours which enable the largest number of members to attend regularly.

By implication our Churches in Article 85 do reject or condemn those Churches which differ from us in essential matters. We reject, for example, Baptist, Methodist, and Lutheran Churches. We heartily acknowledge them as Churches of Jesus Christ as long as they confess Christ as their only Saviour according to the Scriptures and accept God's Word as their infallible standard for doctrine and life. But we do not acknowledge them as Reformed Churches, and consequently we do not give them a voice and vote at our assemblies, and we do not accept members from these Churches upon their testimony, etc.

Under present day circumstances full-fledged acknowledgment is not even accorded to all Reformed and Presbyterian Churches inasmuch as some of these bodies have neglected the exercise of discipline and have tolerated false doctrine. In theory, according to their official standards and creeds they are Reformed, but in practice they are not. The only Churches with which we maintain full and unconditional correspondence are the Reformed Churches of the Netherlands and the Reformed Churches of South Africa.

ARTICLE 86

These Articles, relating to the lawful order of the Church, have been so drafted and adopted by common consent, that they (if the profit of the Church demand otherwise) may and ought to be altered, augmented or diminished. However, no particular Congregation, Classis, (or Synod) shall be at liberty to do so, but they shall show all diligence in observing them, until it be otherwise ordained by the General Synod.

REVISION AND OBSERVANCE OF THE CHURCH ORDER

This final article was added to the Church Order by the Synod of Middelburg, 1581, and has been maintained unchanged by the Churches of Holland. Our Churches have also maintained this article, the Synod of 1914 merely placing the words "or Synod," between parenthesis since this expression refers to Particular Synods, which we do not yet have, and eliminating the word "National" from the expression "by the General or National Synod."

The article as it now reads was drafted by the Synod of 1581, but the Wezelian Convention already adopted a concluding article giving expression to the same thoughts in many more words. Reformed Churches were committed to the principles of Article 86 from their very origin.

1. The nature and purpose of the Church Order indicated.

Article 86 first of all informs us that the foregoing 85 articles relate or concern **the lawful order of the Church.** The Church Order seeks to regulate the affairs of the Church, not those of the state or of community affairs. The articles of the Church Order are ecclesiastical rules of order. And the purpose of these articles is the establishment and maintenance of good order in the Church of Christ. (Cf. also Art. 1.) The Church Order aims at the lawful, regular, well-ordered, Biblical organization of the Church of Christ. The word "Church" in the expression: "relating to the lawful order of the Church," does not refer to a local or particular Church, nor to the confederacy or denomination of Churches but to the Church of Christ, the sum total of the believers adhering to the Reformed faith and living within the domains reached by the Churches adopting these articles. The word "Church" cannot apply to a local Church, as all agree. Neither does the word refer to the denomination, for in that case a plural form would have been used. However, the original Latin, Dutch, and French texts all use the singular, as Rutgers points out* (ecclesiae ordinem;

* Dr. F. L. Rutgers: **College-Voordrachten,** 1918, p. 178.

ordeninge der Kerken [genitive singular]; l'ordre legitime de l'Eglise). The Church of Christ, the believers, must be organized into various particular Churches living in close and Biblical co-operation with each other. The offices must be instituted and the Word and Sacraments must be administered wherever God in His grace calls men and women unto Him. And these various particular Churches must live and work together in close harmony advising and assisting each other and recognizing the authority invested in each by God and the leadership of the Spirit promised to each; acknowledging particularly this authority and leadership as exercised and enjoyed by the major assemblies, Classes and Synods. All things must be done decently and in good order. In all things the precepts and examples of God's Word must be respected. For these purposes the foregoing 85 articles have been adopted.

2. Adopted by common consent.

In the second place Article 86 tells us that the articles of the Church Order were adopted by common consent. (Latin, **mutus consensu;** Dutch, **gemeen accoort.**) This does not mean that every one of the delegates to the assembly adopting the Church Order favored the adoption of every article and every stipulation. But it does mean that all the delegates agreed to abide by the decision of the majority. For a time the assemblies would vote twice regarding all issues. The first vote merely established the opinion of the majority. The second vote made the adoption of the matter at hand unanimous, the minority conforming itself to the majority. Thus the Church Order articles were adopted by mutual consent, with common accord. In principle this is still our method of procedure at our assemblies. Confer our remarks regarding this matter on page 144 and 145.

3. Alterations possible and sometimes proper.

In the third place Article 86 tells us that the articles of the Church Order may and sometimes ought to be altered, augmented, or diminished. The articles have been "so drafted and adopted by common consent" that changes are possible. In other words, it was clearly understood when the Church Order was written and adopted that changes could be made and would have to be made at times. The articles of the Church Order are no hard and fast rules which cannot be changed. They are no laws of Medes and Persians. They are rules to maintain good order and to promote the spiritual welfare of God's people. If good order and the welfare of God's people require a change, a change should be made. This was understood from the very start and with this proviso in mind the Churches adopted the rules.

This is the significance of the clause, "if the profit of the Church demand otherwise." If at any time, through change of circumstances, the rules of the Church Order hinder the Churches, and are no longer to their true profit, then a change may and must be made.

As stands to reason, that which is based on unchangable precepts of God's own Word will always be to the profit of the Churches, and should never be changed, though some men may at times call for a change because seemingly the "profit of the Churches" demands a change. But all articles which are merely rules regulating matters not expressly mentioned in the Bible, or for which there are no definite Biblical examples, are changeable.

Changes should not be introduced without due consideration. Frequent and hasty changes in the Church Order make for instability. It tends to undermine the authority of the Church Order. But neither should we hesitate to make changes obviously necessary. Let there be a free discussion and thorough consideration of changes that may appear to be necessary. Then if the Churches are convinced that a change is needed, let no false conservatism hold us back. But again, frequent changes are disturbing. And let us watch our step, Alle verandering is geen verbetering!, as the Dutch say. (Not every change is an improvement!)

Our English redaction of 1920 here reads: "If the profit **of the Church** demand otherwise." Our official Dutch redaction of 1914 is true to the original. It reads: "If the profit **of the Churches** demand otherwise." The English translation in this instance is clearly a mistake. If ever a new redaction of our English translation should be adopted this mistake should be corrected.

4. How only may alteration be made?

No particular Church or Classis has the right to make changes in the Church Order. Only Synod, representing **all the Churches** which drafted and adopted the Church Order shall have the right to make changes. This is reasonable. Disorder would result if the minor assemblies would begin to revise the Church Order. Consequently the Churches agreed in Article 86 to introduce no changes, except through the general Synod.

We should also be careful not to make decisions which virtually set provisions of the Church Order aside, for such decisions are actually changes in the Church Order, although the Church Order is left intact formally.

When a change in the Church Order is deemed necessary the matter ought to be discussed in our Church papers, and at Elders' conferences, Men's Societies, etc. Then the matter should be brought to Classis. If the Classis agrees that the matter is worthy of Synod's consideration the Classis should overture Synod. Matters may of course be brought to Classis forthwith. But we deem a discussion and a careful consideration of the issues involved to be desirable in most cases. Matters concerning changes in the Church Order may also be brought directly to Synod by individual Consistories. (Cf. Art. 30.) But as a rule it is better to bring the matter to Classis first.

5. Observance required.

In the fifth place, this final article of the Church Order requires that the Churches and Classis "shall show all diligence in observing them," i.e., the 85 foregoing articles. The Churches and Classes are therefore in duty bound to observe the rulings of the Church Order. The Church Order is not a book of iron-clad laws, it is not a set of legal laws which must be applied no matter what the result might be. These rules have been adopted to build the Churches, not to break them. Discretion and consideration must always be used. But the Church Order does consist of rules of good order to which all have agreed and which all must keep, "until it be otherwise ordained by the General Synod." If in any particular situation the observance of the Church Order is a physical impossibility or would clearly create harm and disorder, a Consistory or Classis is free to suspend the rule for that instant, if at least the article in question does not concern a definite principle of Holy Writ. But even so it would be well in most instances to gain classical or synodical approval for such exceptional procedure.

It sometimes happens that individuals and Churches make a great deal of the expression "the profit of the Churches." Now surely the adopted rules exist for the sake of the Churches, and not the Churches for the rules. And "the profit of the Churches" should guide us in our deliberations and conclusions. But this phrase should not be used to set aside clearly expressed rules of the Church Order. If alterations are needed, Synod should so decide. For the rest, let us show all diligence in observing the brief, simple, time-tested rules of our honored Church Order. This we have agreed to do, and this will be to the best interest of the Churches.

INDEX

APPENDIX 1

(Pertaining to Article 5, Church Order)

Recent Synods have dealt with matters which concern the calling of Ministers from other denominations.

The Synod of 1943 adopted the following clarification and amplification:

"1. While maintaining the decisions of 1930 and 1934, Synod declare that neither the Consistories nor the Synodical Examiners have a purely discretionary power in the matter.

"2. Synod rule that no Consistory shall nominate a Minister from another denomination without furnishing reasons for so doing to the Synodical Examiners.

"3. Synod rule that no Committee of Synodical Examiners shall disapprove of such nomination without furnishing reasons for its action to the Consistory.

"4. Synod declare that the standard of approval or disapproval to be applied by the Synodical Examiners be:

"a. Soundness of doctrine.
"b. Sanctity of life.
"c. Knowledge and appreciation of Christian Reformed practices and usages.
"d. The need of calling others than those who are of the Christian Reformed Church."

However, these expressions seemingly did not solve all problems and answer all questions, for we find that the Synod of 1945 interpreted a decision of the Synod of 1934 (Acts, p. 133) which reiterated what had been decided in 1928, namely, that a nomination made by a Consistory to fill a ministerial vacancy, and containing the name of a Minister serving a Church other than a Christian Reformed Church, must bear the approval of the Classis or of the counselor representing the Classis, and of "the neighboring Synodical Delegates" (cf. Church Order Articles 4 and 5). The question arose: Which Synodical Delegates? In all cases those who are nearest?

In answer to this question the Synod of 1945 answered "that 'neighboring Delegates' means the Delegates of Classes that are near by."

Synod of 1945 therefore felt that under certain circumstances a calling Church must be accorded the right of calling in one or more Synodical Delegates who live at a greater distance from the calling Church than a Delegate or Delegates who are not called in. It stands to reason that as a rule the calling Church is bound to invite the delegates of those Classes which are nearest. But it would not be wise to make this an inflexible rule. For it may happen that a Delegate living nearer is sick or absent from home. In such cases the calling Church should not be compelled to wait, but it should have the privilege of calling in a Delegate living a bit farther off. But no Consistory may, for arbitrary reasons, pass by a certain near-by Delegate. Nor may it call in a more distant Delegate in preference to a near-by Delegate because it fears a negative vote from the latter, and feels confident of an affirmative vote from the former. All such speculation and manipulation should be out. Under normal circumstances the nearest Delegates must be called in.

The Synod of 1945 also approved certain guiding principles for Synodical Delegates who are asked to approve the nomination of a Minister not of the Christian Reformed denomination. These principles read as follows:

"a. All our Churches should refrain from calling Ministers from other denominations, **except in very exceptional circumstances.** Only by such an attitude are they manifesting the proper spirit of denominational loyalty.

"b. No one, and certainly no Synodical Delegate for examination, may arbitrarily condemn in any and all cases the proposal to call a Minister from another denomination. Such an attitude would not be in conformity with the Synodical decision of 1934, which lays down rules for such calling, and therefore plainly implies that it may, in exceptional circumstances, deserve approbation.

"c. The Synodical Delegates called in must be given the opportunity, and must insist on that opportunity, to give their advice in the same manner as in their more customary labors, namely, in the examination of Candidates, or in the proposed deposition of a minister of the Word. As they, in such cases, sit in with the Classes, and hear all the evidence and are presented with all the data, and give their advice before Classis acts, so also the Consistories, when they seriously consider nominating an outsider (as, for instance, when his name remains on the list from which the Consistory is to choose its nominees), must not proceed to balloting before it calls in the Synodical Delegates, gives the reasons why the name of such an outsider is given serious consideration and then hears and gives serious consideration to the advice of the Synodical Delegates."

To these principles the Synod added the following provision: "When distances are great, Consistories may confer with the Synodical Delegates by mail, and said Delegates shall render their common recommendation by mail." (Cf. Acts, 1945, p. 85).

Concerning the need of calling Ministers not serving in the Christian Reformed denomination, the Synod of 1945 adopted the following interpretation:

1. This question of need must be considered, by Consistory and Delegates, both from a general denominational and from the more specific congregational viewpoint.

2. Upon the Consistory rests the burden of attempting to show that the needs of the local Church justify the nomination of the "outside" Minister or Ministers under consideration. And the Synodical Delegates must give earnest consideration to such consistorial allegations and persuasions, always remembering that the peculiar needs of a local Church are usually understood best by its own people.

3. The phrase "the need of calling others than those who are of the Christian Reformed Church" lays upon both Consistory and Synodical Delegates the solemn responsibility not to nominate or approve the nomination of Ministers outside of our Church, unless there are very special reasons and needs, and to remember that **usually** there is not only no need of calling outsiders, but rather that there is need, with

a view to our distinctiveness and loyalty to our Seminary and our Ministers of limiting nominations to those whom the Church has itself trained. (Acts, 1945, pp. 86, 87).

APPENDIX 2

(Pertaining to Article 8, Church Order)

A four-fold, elucidating statement regarding the admittance of men to the Ministry according to Article 8 was adopted by the Synod of 1947. This statement reads as follows:

1. Synod reminds the Churches that Article 8 of our Church Order was adopted in a time when there was a dire need for Ministers of the Word. This article should function only in case of great need.

2. The "gifts" mentioned in Article 8 should be possessed by a Candidate in a very exceptional measure. No one should be considered unless he has extraordinary qualities.

3. Not only the qualifications mentioned in Article 8 should be considered, but such a Candidate should also possess exceptional knowledge of the Word, knowledge of spiritual needs, and native ability to apply the Word.

4. This article should never be used as a means to ordain all lay-workers who may desire such, and whose prestige would be increased by such action. The Churches are reminded that the regular door to the Ministry is a thorough academic training. This must be maintained in theory and practice.

APPENDIX 3

(Pertaining to Article 12, Church Order)

Relative to our Ministers serving our country as Army or Navy Chaplains, the Synod of 1941 ruled "that a Minister who enters the service of the government as a Chaplain retains his ministerial status as long as he serves in that capacity" (Acts, 1941, page 22).

APPENDIX 4

(Pertaining to Article 13, Church Order)

The Synod of 1940 adopted certain rulings which pertain to Pension and Relief. These rulings read as follows:

(1) Ministers in active service who have not united with the Pension Plan shall not be eligible for a pension.

(2) Ministers who have not united with the Pension Plan shall be eligible for aid from the Relief Fund. This (so it was declared) is in accordance with Article 13 of the Church Order, and the decisions of Synod, Acts, 1932, p. 49.

The decision of 1932 referred to reads: "The position is taken that the support of the Emeriti . . . is the right of the parties and the duty of the Church as a whole."

APPENDIX 5

(Pertaining to Article 29, Church Order)

On the matter of ecumenicity and interchurch correspondence the committee regarding these matters presented a valuable report to the

Synod of 1944. See Acts, 1944, pp. 330-367, or the Agenda, pp. 68-105.

The Synod of 1947 decided to invite the following denominations to establish fraternal relations with our denomination: the Reformed Church of America; the Synod of the Reformed Presbyterian Church, N. A.; the Reformed Presbyterian Church, General Synod; the Associate Presbyterian Church; the Free Magyar Reformed Church in America; the Christian Reformed Church in the Netherlands; Die Nederduits Gereformeerde Kerk of South Africa; the Christian Reformed Church of Japan; the Free Presbyterian Church of Australia.

The significance of this interchurch correspondence, as our Synod conceived of it, the Synod summarized in six points contained in a letter approved by Synod. These six points read as follows:

1. Appointing delegates to each other's supreme judicatories as a token of mutual friendship and interest in the Lord.
2. Keeping each other duly informed of our **gesta ecclesiastica**, notably through the exchange of the Acts of our General Synods (or Assemblies).
3. Bringing to each other's attention our spiritual and ecclesiastical problems together with our attempts at their Scriptural solution; and offering each other help upon request therefore.
4. Warning each other in respect of spiritual dangers that arise and spread and imperil the Church of Christ.
5. Correcting each other in love in the event of unfaithfulness whether by commission or remission on the score of profession and/or practice of the faith once delivered to the saints.
6. Consulting each other regarding the eventual revision of our respective ecclesiastical standards. (Acts, 1947, p. 215).

APPENDIX 6

(Pertaining to Article 39, Church Order)

The Synod of 1947 made a pronouncement regarding the membership and Church attendance of those who are converts of our mission stations or Gospel Chapels. Two Classes requested the Synod to appoint a committee to study this matter and to come with recommendations to a subsequent Synod. However, the Synod wisely refrained from doing so, and immediately adopted the advice of its Advisory Committee. This advice reads:

"Your committee believes that there is no need of a new set of rules to govern the Churches in this matter as we have methods of dealing with this situation in full harmony with Reformed church polity.

"Your committee recommends that Synod remind the Churches and committees that in cases where it is not feasible to have the converts leave the mission and attend the nearest Church, the advisability of establishing a branch Church at such mission stations be considered in order that converts continue to attend the mission where they were converted and the Sacraments may be administered there.

"**Grounds:**

"1. This is the practice in some mission stations and works out well.

"2. This keeps the converts in their own environment, causes them to feel more at home, and gives the more active among them a field of usefulness—their talents can be used for the further extension of God's Kingdom."

APPENDIX 7

(Pertaining to Article 44, Church Order)

(We here reproduce the **Rules for Church Visitation**, as these were approved by the Synod of 1922, and slightly amended by subsequent Synods, the latest alterations having been made by the Synod of 1947.)

The Visitation which, according to Article 44 of the Church Order, must take place in the Churches, in order to proceed properly, calls for the observance of the following particulars:

(1) Every Classis appoints from its midst at least two ministers as visitors, and an equal number of alternates.

(2) At least one week prior to their coming the visitors notify the Consistory of the day and the hour of their visit. The visitors shall so arrange their schedule of work that they allow ample time for each visit.

(3) On the intervening Sunday an approaching visitation is publicly announced to the congregation.

(4) All members of the Consistory give diligence to be present at the meeting arranged for the visitation. Every member that remains absent is to acquaint the meeting with the reasons for his absence. If one-half of the members are absent, the visitation cannot take place.

(5) The Consistory sees to it that all the books of the Church are brought to the meeting for inspection by the visitors.

(6) At the meeting one of the visitors functions as president, and the other as clerk. The visitors record their findings and doings in a book for reference at future visitations, to be retained in the archives of Classis.

(7) If abnormal conditions in a church make it desirable, the visitors shall repeat their call as soon and as often as necessary.

(8) After all the churches have been visited, the visitors shall, with all necessary discretion, prepare a report of their findings and doings, and present the same to the next Classis.

* * * * * * * * * * *

GUIDE FOR THE EXAMINATION

* * * * * * * * * * *

Questions to the Whole Consistory

(1) Do you have preaching services at least twice on each Lord's Day, once from a text the choice of which is left free, and once after the order of the Heidelberg Catechism, so that no Lord's Day is omitted?

(2) Does the Consistory determine what shall be read at reading services?

(3) Is the Lord's Supper celebrated at least four times a year, and is it preceded by a preparatory sermon and followed by an applicatory sermon?

(4) Does the Consistory see to the regular holding of catechetical classes, and to their faithful attendance?

(5) Are the members of the Consistory elected in accordance with Articles 22 and 24 of our Church Order?

(6) Are the Forms of Unity signed by all the members of the Consistory, Minister, Elders, and Deacons?

(7) Does the Consistory meet at stated times according to the needs of the church?

(8) Are all matters calling for the attention of the Consistory dealt with according to our Church Order, and are the acts of the Consistory properly recorded and kept?

(9) Do the members of the Consistory, before each celebration of the Lord's Supper, exercise Christian censure among themselves?

(10) Is Church Discipline administered faithfully in accordance with the Word of God and the Church Order?

(11) Is the Consistory aware of the presence in the congregation of members of secret societies, and if there are such, are they dealt with according to Church Discipline?

(12) Do the members of the Consistory, as their office demands, regularly visit the families, the sick, and the poor?

(13) What is the spiritual condition of the Church? Do unity, peace, and love prevail?

(14) Do the youth of the Church, coming to years of discretion, seek admission to the Lord's Table?

(15) Is the Church to the extent of its ability diligent toward the extension of God's Kingdom?

(16) Are the collections, prescribed by Classis and Synod, taken according to the respective regulations?

(17) Are all the funds and legal papers, both of the Church and of the poor, kept in a safe place, in such a way that there can arise no occasion for distrust, and that a change in office, through death or otherwise, can occasion no difficulties; and is the Church properly incorporated? Are the archives in good order?

(18) Do the parents as far as possible send their children to the Christian schools?

* * * * * * * * * * *

Questions to the Elders and Deacons

(1) Does the Minister faithfully exercise his office in preaching and administering the Sacraments, in adherence to God's Word, the Forms of Unity, and the Church Order?

(2) Does he in the discharge of his ministry use the Forms of the Church, and does he conduct public worship in an edifying manner?

(3) Does he catechize regularly, is he faithful in visiting the sick, and does he take part in the visitation of the families?

(4) How does he manifest himself in his domestic and public life?

(5) Does his work as a teacher and preacher give evidence of diligent study, particularly his preaching of the Catechism?

(6) Does he devote himself as exclusively as possible to the discharge of his official duties?

(7) Does he receive a sufficient income proportionate to the needs of a well-ordered family?

* * * * * * * * * * *

Questions to the Minister or Ministers

(1) Are the Elders regular in their attendance at the meetings of the Church and of the Consistory?

(2) Do they from time to time visit the catechetical classes for the purpose of observing how they are conducted and attended, and do they upon request assist the Minister in catechizing?

(3) Are they doing their part in administering Christian discipline and in maintaining decency and order in all matters?

(4) Do they, according to their ability, visit, comfort, and instruct the members of the Church, and do they try to prevent or remove all offense?

(5) Do they, both at home and in public, lead a life exemplary for the congregation?

* * * * * * * * * * *

Questions to the Minister or Ministers and Elders

(1) Are the Deacons regular in their attendance at the meetings of the Church and of the Consistory, and also, if such are held, of the Deacons?

(2) Are they diligent in collecting alms, and do they faithfully discharge their duties in caring for the poor and the distressed, and in comforting them?

(3) Are the collections counted by the Deacons jointly, or where there are very few Deacons, in the presence of the Pastor or one or more of the Elders?

(4) Do they wisely administer the funds in consultation with the Minister and Elders; do they keep a double record of receipts and disembursements, and do they at stated times render an account thereof?

(5) Do they in their life at home and in public manifest themselves as exemplary Christians?

APPENDIX 8

(Pertaining to Article 61, Church Order)

Classis Grand Rapids East requested the Synod of 1943 "to consider and pass on the nature and ecclesiastical effect of Profession of Faith to our Service Pastors or Chaplains and before Service Groups."

Synod declared "that there is no objection to permit a member of the Armed Forces to make confession of faith before a Christian Reformed Service Pastor (or Christian Reformed Chaplain) in the presence of other believers when the exigencies of military service make it impossible for this person to be examined by the Consistory of the Church of which he is a member, and to make public confession in the home Church, or in a near-by Christian Reformed Church" (Acts, 1943, p. 143).

We would add the following comment: Circumstances of war are extraordinary, and that which is extraordinary justifies unusual procedures, as long as these procedures do not run counter to God's Word and the fundamental principles of our Church Order. None of us would contend that our young men who had an earnest desire to confess Christ openly and publicly before going to the battle front should be withheld this opportunity in the manner indicated in the Synodical commitment cited. But it should also be clear that the matter of confession of faith and admission to the Lord's Table always is and remains a matter pertaining to the local Church. Consequently each Church and its Consistory has the final word in these extraordinary war-time confessions. A Church may validate such a confession without any further examinations and public professions, if it decides to do so. But it may also regard such an army or navy confession as a preliminary step toward the actual and eventual confession in the midst of the home Church. The parties concerned should be altogether ready to repeat their confession, after a brief conference with the Consistory, in the midst of brethren and friends back home.

We believe that this latter approach has much in its favor.

APPENDIX 9

(Pertaining to Article 67, Church Order)

The Synod of 1940 made a commitment in regard to Sunday labor which neither the service of God, necessity, or mercy required. Such labors had been strongly disapproved of by previous Synods.

The Synod of 1940 now went on record as follows: "And if somehow the performance of such labors is tolerated in the case of members in general, this is not to be tolerated in the case of elders and deacons excepting in extraordinary conditions, the presence of which shall be determined by the Consistory concerned" (Acts, 1940, p. 103).

APPENDIX 10

(Pertaining to Article 71, Church Order)

As to Labor Unions the Synod of 1943 reasserted the positions taken in 1916 and 1928, and the conclusions of the report "Christian Social and Industrial Organizations" as adopted by the Synod of 1930.

The Synod of 1943 really adopted a complete revision of all previous decisions, and summarized these decisions in a number of concise principles. We quote these principles:

1. Church membership and membership in a so-called neutral labor union are compatible as long as such union gives no constitutional warrant to sins, nor shows in its regular activities that it champions sin.
2. The Biblical doctrine of corporate responsibility and the Biblical teaching of the Christian's separation from the world make it imperative for members of neutral labor organizations to discontinue membership in any such unions whose common practices are clearly in conflict with the principles of the Word of God.
3. Christian conscience cannot condone membership in a neutral organization if it continues and approves its sinful practices in spite of protests against them.
4. The doctrine of corporate responsibility does not imply that membership in unions which have engaged in sinful practices of itself makes one liable to ecclesiastical censure; however, when

members of the Church render themselves guilty of acts which are contrary to the Word of God there shall be the usual application of the rules for discipline. Corporate responsibility may render one worthy of ecclesiastical discipline, but the degree of guilt must be determined by the local consistories.

5. Consistories and Classes should take careful note of the practices of all labor organizations existent in their respective communities to determine whether membership in our Church and membership in such organizations are compatible.

Besides these principles this Synod also adopted the following resolution:

Synod exhort the ministers of the Church to emphasize the Scriptural principles of the Christian's separation from the world, and the sinful consequences of putting on an unequal yoke with unbelievers to obtain right and justice through means condemned by the Word of God. Further, Synod admonish the membership of the Church to break with all organizations which by common practice reveal an anti-Christian spirit. In short, Synod urge upon ministers and elders by vigorous use of the keys intrusted to them to declare the principles of the Word of God which must guide the members of the Church in their relation to the world and the organizations of the world. (See Acts, 1943, pp. 102-103, and Agenda I, pp. 1-25, 1943.)

It will be noted that the principles of 1943 mention the matter of corporate responsibility. There was a specific request at the Synod of 1943 for greater clarification regarding the expression and principle of corporate responsibility. Classis California requested a study and clarification of this principle. Synod appointed the following committee regarding this matter: Prof. L. Berkhof, Prof. Dr. C. Bouma, Dr. R. Danhof, Prof. Dr. Wm. Hendriksen, and the Rev. C. Huissen.

This committee presented its study and advice to the Synod of 1945. Synod in turn adopted the following five points on corporate responsibility:

1. Active participation in the sinful practices of an organization to which one belongs not only renders one guilty before God but may even make one an object of ecclesiastical discipline.
2. In order to be responsible for the sinful deeds of the organization or the group with which one is associated it is not necessary to be an active participant, in the usual sense of that term. By requesting, promoting, encouraging, or in any manner abetting the wrongdoing, one is rendered responsible, even if the support which one gives amounts to no more than consent or approval. In connection with all this the discipline of the Word should be vigilantly exercised.
3. In order to be responsible for the sins of the group one need not even be an abetter; mere passivity or silence also renders one guilty; failure to reprove makes one accountable before God.
4. It is possible, moreover, that one neither engages actively in the sinful acts of his associates (1), nor promotes them or consents to them in any manner (2), nor even fails to reprove them (3), and yet involves himself in co-responsibility for these evil practices; namely, if one remains a member of such organizations which refuse to mend their evil ways when the latter have been exposed and reproved.

(5) Finally, it is even possible that although a person does not become guilty of any of the sins described in the preceding four points, he, nevertheless, becomes responsible, in a measure, for the evil decisions and practices of the group; namely, by becoming a member of the organization whose aims or practices are known to be evil.

In connection with these principles the Synod of 1945 also adopted the following significant recommendations:

Your committee further recommends that Synod call the attention of our people to the fact that these principles are intended to be applied not only to labor unions, but also to all industrial, business, and professional organizations, as well as to any other types of group activity.

Your committee suggests further that the following recommendation of the committee on Corporate Responsibility be adopted by Synod, "They (that is, these principles) should be faithfully expounded from the pulpit, in personal visits, and family-visits, and in the religious press. The question of their application to concretely existing local, state, or national conditions is a matter for the individual Consistory and Classis, and especially for the conscience of each person who becomes involved in it (Agenda, p. 37).

Your committee also recommends that, in view of the moral and spiritual dangers of membership in non-Christian organizations, Synod urge all our people, wherever possible, to establish and promote definitely Christian organizations in the social sphere.

Once again the matter of Labor Unions received consideration at the Synod of 1946. The previous Synod had decided, upon a specific overture and request, to "appoint a committee to formulate the grounds for the position taken by the Synod of 1943 regarding the compatibility of church membership and membership in the so-called neutral labor union." The following brethren served on this committee: Prof. Dr. C. Bouma, Prof. Dr. Wm. Hendriksen, Prof. L. Berkhof, Dr. R. J. Danhof, Mr. Joseph Gritter, Rev. C. Huissen, Prof. Dr. H. J. Ryskamp, Prof. Dr. S. Volbeda.

In harmony with the advice of this committee the Synod of 1946 declared That the position adopted by the Synod of 1943 and by previous Synods; namely, that "church membership and membership in so-called neutral labor unions are compatible," is based upon the following grounds:

1. Becoming a member of such a so-called neutral labor union does not as such constitute a sinful act, inasmuch as according to Synod's circumscription such unions as here meant give no constitutional warrant to sin, and do not show in their regular activities that they champion sin or that they are in conflict with the universal principles of justice contained in the Word of God.
2. It follows that becoming a member of a so-called neutral labor union, as thus described, does not constitute a censurable act.
3. To adopt the principle, making it applicable to every case, that church membership is incompatible with membership in labor unions which give no constitutional warrant to sin and which do not show in their regular activities that they champion sin or that they are in conflict with the universal principles of justice contained in the Word of God would amount to dangerous sepa-

ratism, which is condemned by Scripture, John 17:15, I Cor. 5:9-11. See explanation of these passages in the Agenda of 1926, pp. 116-117.

The Synod of 1946, furthermore, adopted the following declarations:

With respect to membership in organizations (in any sphere, including labor) which **do** give constitutional warrant to sin and/or show in their regular activities that they **do** champion sin, Synod call the attention of the church to the Report on Corporate Responsibility, whose conclusions were adopted by the Synod of 1945, and which gives adequate advice to consistories and classes with respect to the matter. See Acts of the Synod of 1945, Article 100. Note also the detailed exegesis of the Scripture-passages upon which these conclusions are based, Agenda, 1945, pp. 28-37.

Whereas it is undeniable that many organizations in whatever sphere (whether labor, business, or professional) have assumed or tend to assume a character which excludes them from the class of so-called neutral unions, as circumscribed by the Synod of 1943, and places them in a class of organizations against which the Synod of 1945 has issued a warning, and whereas membership in such worldly unions or organizations entails moral and spiritual danger, Synod repeat the exhortation given in the Conclusion of the Report on Corporate Responsibility and adopted by the Synod of 1945, namely, that wherever feasible our people "establish and promote definitely Christian organizations in the social sphere."

And finally the Synod of 1947 was requested to rule "that membership in the A.F. of L. or the C.I.O. shall be incompatible with membership in the Consistories of the Christian Reformed Church."

In answer to this overture Synod decided "not to accede to this request." Synod based this decision on the following two grounds:

1. Synod has laid down principles for Consistories and Classes to deal adequately with matters of this nature, in the decisions on corporate responsibility adopted in 1945. Cf. especially points 3, 4, and 5 as adopted in 1945 (Acts, p. 103).
2. The rule that they (the petitioners) request, would be in violation of the synodical decision, that membership in a neutral organization is not per se actionable.

APPENDIX 11

(Pertaining to Article 71, Church Order.)

The Synod of 1951 adopted a number of valuable clarifying statements regarding the 1928 resolutions pertaining to worldly amusements. For the statements see Acts 1951, pages 65 and 66.

CHURCH ORDER

of the

CHRISTIAN REFORMED CHURCH

Being the Original Church Order of Dort, 1618-19

Revised by the Christian Reformed Synod of 1914 and Amended by Subsequent Synods

Article 1.

For the maintenance of good order in the Church of Christ it is necessary that there should be: offices, assemblies, supervision of doctrine, sacraments and ceremonies, and Christian discipline; of which matters the following articles treat in due order.

OF THE OFFICES

Article 2.

The offices are of four kinds: of the Ministers of the Word, of the Professors of Theology, of the Elders, and of the Deacons.

Article 3.

No one, though he be a Professor of Theology, Elder or Deacon, shall be permitted to enter upon the Ministry of the Word and the Sacraments without having been lawfully called thereunto. And when any one acts contrary thereto, and after being frequently admonished does not desist, the Classis shall judge whether he is to be declared a schismatic or is to be punished in some other way.

Article 4.

The lawful calling of those who have not been previously in office, consists:

First, in the ELECTION by the Consistory and the Deacons, after preceding prayers, with due observance of the regulations established by the consistory for this purpose, and of the ecclesiastical ordinance, that only those can for the first time be called to the Ministry of the Word who have been declared eligible by the churches, according to the rule in this matter; and furthermore with the advice of Classis or of the counselor appointed for this purpose by the Classis;

Secondly, in the EXAMINATION both of doctrine and life which shall be conducted by the Classis, to which the call must be submitted for approval, and which shall take place in the presence of three Delegates of Synod from the nearest Classes;

Thirdly, in the APPROBATION by the members of the calling church, when, the name of the minister having been announced for two successive Sundays, no lawful objection arises; which approbation, however, is not required in case the election takes place with the co-operation of the congregation by choosing out of a nomination previously made.

Finally, in the public ORDINATION in the presence of the congregation, which shall take place with appropriate stipulations and interrogations, admonitions and prayers and imposition of hands by the officiating minister (and by other ministers who are present) agreeably to the Form for that purpose.

Article 5.

Ministers already in the Ministry of the Word, who are called to another congregation, shall likewise be called in the aforesaid manner by the Consistory and the Deacons, with observance of the regulations made for the purpose by the Consistory and of the general ecclesiastical ordinances for the eligibility of those who have served outside of the Christian Reformed Church and for the repeated calling of the same Minister during the same vacancy; further, with the advice of the Classis or of the counselor, appointed by the Classis, and with the approval of the Classis or of the Delegates appointed by the Classis, to whom the ministers called show good ecclesiastical testimonials of doctrine and life, with the approval of the members of the calling congregation, as stated in Article 4; whereupon the minister called shall be installed with appropriate stipulations and prayers agreeably to the Form for this purpose.

Article 6.

No Minister shall be at liberty to serve in institutions of mercy or otherwise, unless he be previously admitted in accordance with the preceding articles, and he shall, no less than others, be subject to the Church Order.

Article 7.

No one shall be called to the Ministry of the Word, without his being stationed in a particular place, except he be sent to do church extension work.

Article 8.

Persons who have not pursued the regular course of study in preparation for the Ministry of the Word, and have therefore not been declared eligible according to Article 4, shall not be admitted to the Ministry unless there is assurance of their exceptional gifts, godliness, humility, modesty, common sense and discretion, as also gifts of public address. When such persons present themselves for the Ministry, the Classis (if the [particular] Synod approve) shall first examine them, and further deal with them as it shall deem edifying, according to the general regulations of the churches.

Article 9.

Preachers without fixed charge, or others who have left some sect, shall not be admitted to the Ministry in the Church until they have been declared eligible, after careful examination, by the Classis, with the approval of Synod.

Article 10.

A Minister, once lawfully called, may not leave the congregation with which he is connected, to accept a call elsewhere, without the consent of the Consistory, together with the Deacons, and knowledge on the part of the Classis; likewise no other church may receive him until he has presented a proper certificate of dismission from the church and the Classis where he served.

Article 11.

On the other hand, the Consistory, as representing the congregation, shall also be bound to provide for the proper support of its Ministers, and shall not dismiss them from service without the knowledge and approbation of the Classis and of the Delegates of the (particular) Synod.

Article 12.

Inasmuch as a Minister of the Word, once lawfully called as described above, is bound to the service of the Church for life, he is not allowed to enter upon a secular vocation except for such weighty reasons as shall receive the approval of the Classis.

Article 13.

Ministers, who by reason of age, sickness, or otherwise, are rendered incapable of performing the duties of their Office, shall nevertheless retain the honor and title of a Minister, and the Church which they have served shall provide honorably for them (likewise for the orphans and widows of Ministers) out of the common fund of the Churches, according to the general ecclesiastical ordinances in this matter.

Article 14.

If any Minister, for the aforesaid or any other reason, is compelled to discontinue his service for a time, which shall not take place without the advice of the Consistory, he shall nevertheless at all times be and remain subject to the call of the congregation.

Article 15.

No one shall be permitted, neglecting the Ministry of his Church or being without a fixed charge, to preach indiscriminately without the consent and authority of Synod or Classis. Likewise, no one shall be permitted to preach or administer the Sacraments in another Church without the consent of the Consistory of that Church.

Article 16.

The office of the Minister is to continue in prayer and in the ministry of the Word, to dispense the Sacraments, to watch over his brethren, the Elders and Deacons, as well as the Congregation, and finally, with the Elders, to exercise church discipline and to see to it that everything is done decently and in good order.

Article 17.

Among the Ministers of the Word equality shall be maintained with respect to the duties of their office and also in other matters as far as possible according to the judgment of the Consistory, and if necessary, of the Classis; which equality shall also be maintained in the case of the Elders and the Deacons.

Article 18.

The office of the Professors of Theology is to expound the Holy Scripture and to vindicate sound doctrine against heresies and errors.

Article 19.

The Churches shall exert themselves, as far as necessary, that there may be students supported by them to be trained for the Ministry of the Word.

Article 20.

Students who have received permission according to the rule in this matter, and persons who have according to Article 8 been judged competent to be prepared for the Ministry of the Word, shall, for their own training, and for the sake of becoming known to the Congregations, be allowed to speak a word of edification in the meetings for public worship.

Article 21.

The Consistories shall see to it that there are good Christian Schools in which the parents have their children instructed according to the demands of the covenant.

Article 22.

The Elders shall be chosen by the judgment of the Consistory and the Deacons according to the regulations for that purpose established by the Consistory. In pursuance of these regulations, every church shall be at liberty, according to its circumstances, to give the members an opportunity to direct attention to suitable persons, in order that the Consistory may thereupon either present to the congregation for election as many elders as are needed, that they may, after they are approved by it, unless any obstacle arise, be installed with public prayers and stipulations; or present a double number to the congregation and thereupon install the one-half chosen by it, in the aforesaid manner, agreeably to the Form for this purpose.

Article 23.

The office of the Elders, in addition to what was said in Article 16 to be their duty in common with the Minister of the Word, is to take heed that the Ministers, together with their fellow-Elders and the Deacons, faithfully discharge their office, and both before and after the Lord's Supper, as time and circumstances may demand, for the edification of the churches to visit the families of the Congregation, in order particularly to comfort and instruct the members, and also to exhort others in respect to the Christian Religion.

Article 24.

The Deacons shall be chosen, approved and installed in the same manner as was stated concerning the Elders.

Article 25.

The office peculiar to the Deacons is diligently to collect alms and other contributions of charity, and after mutual counsel, faithfully and diligently to distribute the same to the poor as their needs may require it; to visit and comfort the distressed and to exercise care that the alms are not misused; of which they shall render an account in Consistory, and also (if anyone desires to be present) to the Congregation, at such a time as the Consistory may see fit.

Article 26.

In places where others are devoting themselves to the care of the poor, the Deacons shall seek a mutual understanding with them to the end that the alms may all the better be distributed among those who have greatest need. Moreover, they shall make it possible for the poor to make use of institutions of mercy, and to that end they shall request the Board of Directors of such institutions to keep in close touch with them. It is also desirable that the Deaconates assist and consult one another, especially in caring for the poor in such institutions.

Article 27.

The Elders and Deacons shall serve two or more years according to local regulations, and a proportionate number shall retire each year. The retiring officers shall be succeeded by others unless the circumstances and the profit of any church, in the execution of Articles 22 and 24, render a re-election advisable.

Article 28.

The Consistory shall take care, that the churches for the possession of their property, and the peace and order of their meetings can claim the protection of the Authorities; it should be well understood, however, that for the sake of peace and material possession they may never suffer the royal government of Christ over His Church to be in the least infringed upon.

OF THE ECCLESIASTICAL ASSEMBLIES

Article 29.

Four kinds of ecclesiastical assemblies shall be maintained: the Consistory, the Classis (the Particular Synod), and the General Synod.

Article 30.

In these assemblies ecclesiastical matters only shall be transacted and that in an ecclesiastical manner. In major assemblies only such matters shall be dealt with as could not be finished in minor assemblies, or such as pertain to the Churches of the major assembly in common.

Article 31.

If any one complains that he has been wronged by the decision of a minor assembly, he shall have the right to appeal to a major ecclesiastical assembly, and whatever may be agreed upon by a majority vote shall be considered settled and binding, unless it be proved to conflict with the Word of God or with the Articles of the Church Order, as long as they are not changed by a General Synod.

Article 32.

The proceedings of all assemblies shall begin by calling upon the Name of God and be closed with thanksgiving.

Article 33.

Those who are delegated to the assemblies shall bring with them their credentials and instructions, signed by those sending them, and they shall have a vote in all matters, except such as particularly concern their persons or Churches.

Article 34.

In all assemblies there shall be not only a president, but also a clerk to keep a faithful record of all important matters.

Article 35.

The office of the president is to state and explain the business to be transacted, to see to it that everyone observe due order in speaking, to silence the captious and those who are vehement in speaking; and to properly discipline them if they refuse to listen. Furthermore his office shall cease when the assembly arises.

Article 36.

The Classis has the same jurisdiction over the Consistory as the Particular Synod has over the Classis and the General Synod over the Particular.

Article 37.

In all Churches there shall be a Consistory composed of the Ministers of the Word and the Elders, who at least in larger congregations, shall, as a rule, meet once a week. The Minister of the Word (or the Ministers, if there be more than one, in turn) shall preside and regulate the proceedings. Wherever the number of Elders is small the Deacons may be added to the consistory by local regulation; this shall invariably be the rule where the number is less than three.

Article 38.

In places where the Consistory is to be constituted for the first time or anew, this shall not take place except with the advice of the Classis.

Article 39.

Places where as yet no Consistory can be constituted shall be placed under the care of a neighboring Consistory.

Article 40.

The Deacons shall meet, wherever necessary, every week to transact the business pertaining to their office, calling upon the Name of God; whereunto the Ministers shall take good heed and if necessary they shall be present.

Article 41.

The classical meetings shall consist of neighboring Churches that respectively delegate, with proper credentials, a Minister and an Elder to meet at such time and place as was determined by the previous classical meeting. Such meetings shall be held at least once in three months, unless great distances render this inadvisable. In these meetings the Ministers shall preside in rotation, or one shall be chosen to preside; however, the same Minister shall not be chosen twice in succession.

Furthermore, at the beginning of the meeting, the president shall, among other things, present the following questions to the delegates of each Church:

(1) Are the consistory meetings regularly held in your Church; and are they held according to the needs of the congregation?
(2) Is church discipline faithfully exercised?
(3) Are the poor adequately cared for?
(4) Does the consistory diligently promote the cause of Christian day schools?
(5) Have you submitted to the stated clerk of Classis the names and addresses of all baptized and communicant members who have, since the last meeting of Classis, moved to where no Christian Reformed Churches are found?

And finally, at one but the last meeting and, if necessary, at the last meeting before the (Particular) Synod, delegates shall be chosen to attend said Synod.

Article 42.

Where in a Church there are more Ministers than one, also those not delegated according to the foregoing article shall have the right to attend Classis with advisory vote.

Article 43.

At the close of the Classical and other major assemblies, censure shall be exercised over those, who in the meeting have done something worthy of punishment, or who have scorned the admonition of the minor assemblies.

Article 44.

The Classis shall authorize at least two of her oldest, most experienced and competent Ministers to visit all the Churches once a year and to take heed whether the Minister and the Consistory faithfully perform the duties of their office, adhere to sound doctrine, observe in all things the adopted order, and properly promote as much as lies in them, through word and deed, the upbuilding of the congregation, in particular of the youth, to the end that they may in time fraternally admonish those who have in anything been negligent, and may by their advice and assistance help direct all things unto the peace, upbuilding, and greatest profit of the Churches. And each Classis may continue these visitors in service as long as it sees fit, except when the visitors themselves request to be released for reasons of which the Classis shall judge.

Article 45.

It shall be the duty of the Church in which the Classis and likewise the (Particular) or General Synod meets to furnish the following meeting with the minutes of the preceding.

Article 46.

Instructions concerning matters to be considered in major assemblies shall not be written until the decision of previous Synods touching these matters have been read, in order that what was once decided be not again proposed, unless a revision be deemed necessary.

Article 47.

(Every year [or if need be oftener] four or five or more neighboring Classes shall meet as a Particular Synod, to which each Classis shall delegate two Ministers and two Elders. At the close of both the Particular and the General Synod, some church shall be empowered to determine with advice of Classis, the time and place of the next Synod.)

Article 48.

(Each Synod shall be at liberty to solicit and hold correspondence with its neighboring Synod or Synods in such manner as they shall judge most conducive to general edification.)

Article 49.

(Each Synod shall delegate some to execute everything ordained by Synod both as to what pertains to the Government and to the respective Classes, resorting under it, and likewise to supervise together or in smaller number all examinations of future Ministers. And, moreover, in all other eventual difficulties they shall extend help to the Classes in order that proper unity, order and soundness of doctrine may be maintained and established. Also they shall keep proper record of all their actions to report thereof to Synod, and if it be demanded, give reasons. They shall also not be discharged from their service before and until Synod itself discharges them.)

Article 50.

The General Synod shall ordinarily meet annually. Each Classis shall delegate two Ministers and two Elders to this Synod. If at least a majority of the Classes deem it necessary that the Synod meet either earlier or later than the regular time, the local Church charged with convening the Synod shall in due season determine when and where it is to meet.

Article 51.

The Missionary Work of the Church is regulated by the General Synod in a Mission Order.

Article 52.

Inasmuch as different languages are spoken in the Churches, the necessary translations shall be made in the ecclesiastical assemblies, and in the publication of recommendations, instructions and decisions.

OF DOCTRINES, SACRAMENTS AND OTHER CEREMONIES

Article 53.

The Ministers of the Word of God and likewise the Professors of Theology (which also behooves the other Professors and School Teachers) shall subscribe to the Three Formulas of Unity, namely, the Belgic Confession of Faith, the Heidelberg Catechism, and the Canons of Dordrecht, 1618-'19, and the Ministers of the Word who refuse to do so shall de facto be suspended from their office by the Consistory or Classis until they shall have given a full statement, and if they obstinately persist in refusing, they shall be deposed from their office.

Article 54.

Likewise the Elders and Deacons shall subscribe to the aforesaid Formulas of Unity.

Article 55.

To ward off false doctrines and errors that multiply exceedingly through heretical writings, the Ministers and Elders shall use the means of teaching, of refutation, or warning, and of admonition, as well in the Ministry of the Word as in Christian teaching and family-visiting.

Article 56.

The Covenant of God shall be sealed unto the children of Christians by Baptism, as soon as the administration thereof if feasible, in the public assembly when the Word of God is preached.

Article 57.

The Ministers shall do their utmost to the end that the father present his child for Baptism.

Article 58.

In the ceremony of Baptism, both of children and of adults, the Minister shall use the respective forms drawn up for the administration of this Sacrament.

Article 59.

Adults are through Baptism incorporated into the Christian Church, and are accepted as members of the Church, and are therefore obliged also to partake of the Lord's Supper, which they shall promise to do at their Baptism.

Article 60.

The names of those baptized, together with those of the parents, and likewise the date of birth and baptism, shall be recorded.

Article 61.

None shall be admitted to the Lord's Supper except those who according to the usage of the Church with which they unite themselves have made a confession of the Reformed Religion, besides being reputed to be of a godly walk, without which those who come from other Churches shall not be admitted.

Article 62.

Every Church shall administer the Lord's Supper in such a manner as it shall judge most conducive to edification; provided, however, that the outward ceremonies as prescribed in God's Word be not changed and all superstition avoided, and that at the conclusion of the sermon and the usual prayers, the Form for the Administration of the Lord's Supper, together with the prayer for that purpose, shall be read.

Article 63.

The Lord's Supper shall be administered at least every two or three months.

Article 64.

The administration of the Lord's Supper shall take place only there where there is supervision of Elders, according to the ecclesiastical order and in a public gathering of the Congregation.

Article 65.

Funerals are not ecclesiastical, but family affairs, and should be conducted accordingly.

Article 66.

In time of war, pestilence, national calamities, and other great afflictions, the pressure of which is felt throughout the Churches, it is fitting that the Classes proclaim a Day of Prayer.

Article 67.

The Churches shall observe, in addition to the Sunday, also Christmas, Good Friday, Easter, Ascension Day, Pentecost, the Day of Prayer, the National Thanksgiving Day, and Old and New Year's Day.

Article 68.

The Ministers shall on Sunday explain briefly the sum of Christian Doctrine comprehended in the Heidelberg Catechism so that as much as possible the explanation shall be annually completed, according to the division of the Catechism itself, for that purpose.

Article 69.

In the Churches only the 150 Psalms of David and the collection of hymns for Church use, approved and adopted by Synod, shall be sung. However, while the singing of the Psalms in divine worship is a requirement, the use of the approved hymns is left to the freedom of the Churches.

Article 70.

Since it is proper that the matrimonial state be confirmed in the presence of Christ's Church, according to the Form for that purpose, the Consistories shall attend to it.

OF CENSURE AND ECCLESIASTICAL ADMONITION

Article 71.

As Christian Discipline is of a spiritual nature, and exempts no one from Civil trial or punishment by the Authorities, so also besides Civil punishment there is need of Ecclesiastical Censures, to reconcile the sinner with the Church and his neighbor and to remove the offense out of the Church of Christ.

Article 72.

In case any one errs in doctrine or offends in conduct as long as the sin is of a private character, not giving public offense, the rule clearly prescribed by Christ in Matth. 18 shall be followed.

Article 73.

Secret sins of which the sinner repents, after being admonished by one person in private or in the presence of two or three witnesses, shall not be laid before the Consistory.

Article 74.

If any one, having been admonished in love concerning a secret sin by two or three persons, does not give heed, or otherwise has committed a public sin, the matter shall be reported to the Consistory.

Article 75.

The reconciliation of all such sins as are of their nature of a public character, or have become public because the admonition of the Church was despised, shall take place (upon sufficient evidence of repentance) in such a manner as the Consistory shall deem conducive to the edification of each Church. Whether in particular cases this shall take place in public, shall, when there is a difference of opinion about it in the Consistory, be considered with the advice of two neighboring Churches or of the Classis.

Article 76.

Such as obstinately reject the admonition of the Consistory, and likewise those who have committed a public or otherwise gross sin, shall be suspended from the Lord's Supper. And if he, having been suspended, after repeated admonitions, shows no signs of repentance, the Consistory shall at last proceed to the extreme remedy, namely, excommunication, agreeably to the form adopted for that purpose according to the Word of God. But no one shall be excommunicated except with consent of the Classis.

Article 77.

After the suspension from the Lord's Table, and subsequent admonitions, and before proceeding to excommunication, the obstinacy of the sinner shall be publicly made known to the congregation, the offense explained, together with the care bestowed upon him, in reproof, suspension from the Lord's Supper, and repeated admonition, and the congregation shall be exhorted to speak to him and to pray for him. There shall be three such admonitions. In the first the name of the sinner shall not be mentioned that he be somewhat spared. In the second, with the consent of the Classis, his name shall be mentioned. In the third the congregation shall be informed that (unless he repent) he will be excluded from the fellowship of the Church, so that his excommunication, in case he remains obstinate, may take place with the tacit approbation of the Church. The interval between the admonitions shall be left to the discretion of the Consistory.

Article 78.

Whenever anyone who has been excommunicated desires to become reconciled to the Church in the way of penitence, it shall be announced to the Congregation, either before the celebration of the Lord's Supper, or at some other opportune time, in order that (in as far as no one can mention anything against him to the contrary) he may with profession of his conversion be publicly reinstated, according to the Form for that purpose.

Article 79.

When Ministers of the Divine Word, Elders or Deacons, have committed any public, gross sin, which is a disgrace to the Church, or worthy of punishment by the Authorities, the Elders and Deacons shall immediately by preceding sentence of the Consistory thereof and of the nearest Church, be suspended or expelled from their office, but the Ministers shall only be suspended. Whether these shall be entirely deposed from office, shall be subject to the judgment of the Classis, with the advice of the Delegates of the (Particular) Synod mentioned in Article 11.

Article 80.

Furthermore among the gross sins, which are worthy of being punished with suspension or deposition from office, these are the principal ones; false doctrine or heresy, public schism, public blasphemy, simony, faithless desertion of office or intrusion upon that of another, perjury, adultery, fornication, theft, acts of violence, habitual drunkenness, brawling, filthy lucre; in short, all sins and gross offenses, as render the perpetrators infamous before the world, and which in any private member of the Church would be considered worthy of excommunication.

Article 81.

The Ministers of the Word, Elders and Deacons, shall before the celebration of the Lord's Supper exercise Christian censure among themselves and in a friendly spirit admonish one another with regard to the discharge of their office.

Article 82.

To those who remove from the Congregation a letter or testimony concerning their profession and conduct shall be given by the Consistory, signed by two.

Article 83.

Furthermore, to the poor, removing for sufficient reasons, so much money for traveling shall be given by the Deacons, as they deem adequate. The Consistory and the Deacons shall, however, see to it that

they be not too much inclined to relieve their Churches of the poor, with whom they would without necessity burden other Churches.

Article 84.

No Church shall in any way lord it over other Churches, no Minister over other Ministers, no Elder or Deacon over other Elders or Deacons.

Article 85.

Churches whose usages differ from ours merely in non-essentials shall not be rejected.

Article 86.

These Articles, relating to the lawful order of the Church, have been so drafted and adopted by common consent, that they (if the profit of the Church demand otherwise) may and ought to be altered, augmented or diminished. However, no particular Congregation, Classis, (or Synod) shall be at liberty to do so, but they shall show all diligence in observing them, until it be otherwise ordained by the General Synod.